THE MEN WHO MADE
SCOTLAND

THE MEN WHO MADE
SCOTLAND

The definitive Who's Who of
Scottish Football Internationalists
1872-1939

Andy Mitchell

The Men Who Made Scotland:
The definitive Who's Who of Scottish Football Internationalists 1872-1939

First published 2021 by Andy Mitchell Media, Dunblane, Scotland.
Contact: *andymitchellmedia@gmail.com*
Website: *www.scottishsporthistory.com*

ISBN: 979-8513846642
Copyright © Andy Mitchell
All rights reserved. No part of this publication may be reproduced, stored in a retrieval system, or transmitted in any form by any means electronic, mechanical, photocopying, recording or otherwise, without the prior written permission of the copyright owners.

Andy Mitchell is a leading writer and researcher on football history. He runs a sports history website and has written several books including a biography of Arthur Kinnaird and the story of the world's first football club. Brought up in Edinburgh, he went to his first football match in 1970 and was immediately hooked on the game. After graduating from university he embarked on a media career and is fortunate enough to have worked in football since 1997, as head of communications at the Scottish Football Association and currently as a freelance media officer for UEFA. He lives in Dunblane.

Previous publications
Arthur Kinnaird, First Lord of Football
First Elevens: The Birth of International Football
Come Awa' the Heather! The story of Dunblane FC
1824: the World's First Foot-Ball Club (with John Hutchinson)
The Scotland International Programme Guide
A short history of St Bernard's Football Club

Front cover: a Scotland shirt badge which was originally worn by Jimmy McCall of Renton in his appearances against England between 1887 and 1890 (from author's collection).

Cover designed by **Maureen Mitchell.**

Title page: Robert Gardner, Scotland's captain, guarding his goal at the first international match, Scotland v England at the West of Scotland Cricket Ground on 30 November 1872. It was one of a series of images drawn by William Ralston and published in *The Graphic* two weeks later.

INTRODUCTION

PLAYING FOR SCOTLAND! It is an achievement that should live for ever. Every young Scottish footballer dreams of pulling on the dark blue jersey and you might think that every hero who has been capped will be revered in the annals of the game.

Sadly, it isn't true. For every Andrew Watson, Alec James and Hughie Gallacher there are internationalists who have been lost to the winds, whose stories are forgotten, whose very identities are barely known.

Now, for the first time, that has been put right.

This book contains comprehensive biographies of every one of the 615 internationalists who represented Scotland between 1872 and 1939. It was a pioneering age, starting with a historic clash against England, a rivalry which became the pinnacle of British sport, progressing through the formation of the British Championship, the spread of professionalism, record-breaking crowds and the first foreign matches.

The players who took part in these contests are key to our football history. This book is my tribute to their achievements: the men who made Scotland.

Why is this book necessary?

My initial interest was sparked way back in 1981, when a football historian called Doug Lamming wrote to me and asked for help in finding the dates of birth and death of Scotland players. I had time on my hands, and made a number of visits to Register House in Edinburgh to look them up for him.

In those days conducting research was tortuously slow: once you identified a name in a yearly index, an assistant would accompany you up a spiral staircase to the relevant leather-bound volume of birth or death registrations, take it off the shelf, and lay it in front of you at the correct page. You could then take notes of the entry in pencil and he would return the volume to the shelf, before accompanying you back to the front desk. Each visit to Register House cost £4, and a good day would uncover about 20 or 30 dates.

By supplying these nuggets of information I made a contribution to Lamming's ground-breaking *Who's Who of Scotland Internationalists,* published in 1987. It remains the starting point for researchers but it was compiled in a pre-internet age and inevitably there were many gaps. As time went on, more and more errors were identified.

Since then, facilities for researchers have changed beyond recognition. The internet has brought digitised newspapers, online archives, genealogical records and much more, a treasure trove of information which is all searchable from a computer desk. Although a few other historians attempted an updated Scotland Who's Who, they included little new research and concentrated mainly on players of the modern era, so I always had it in the back of my mind that the job needed to be done properly.

The catalyst for me embarking on this Who's Who was a bizarre case of mistaken identity which I helped to clear up. I used to work at the Scottish FA, and one day took a call from a man who explained he was a friend of Charlie Cox, a name which was familiar as I knew Cox had won a cap in 1948. To my astonishment, he told me this was not true, and in fact Charlie was so exasperated at being hailed as a Scotland international that he asked his friend to call the SFA and put things right.

This was extraordinary – how could someone mistakenly be credited with a cap? This is how it happened: Scotland played in Paris in May 1948 and a late change to the team saw a reserve called Cox drafted in. There were no Scottish journalists in France and some papers assumed that Charlie Cox of Hearts had been honoured. Subsequently, that's what the record books went with.

Actually, it was Sammy Cox of Rangers who made his debut that day. I managed to track him down and phoned him at his home in Canada to get to the bottom of it. He explained that he was a travelling reserve, not expecting to play, when Billy Campbell of Morton split a boot in the warm-up. He had no spare footwear so Sammy was hastily summoned to the dressing room and told to strip. He had just eaten a rather large lunch, and spent the first half of his Scotland debut trying not to be sick.

I was fascinated by the story, yet also aghast. The Cox statistics could be changed retrospectively, but what else was wrong with our national team records? Quite a lot, as it turned out.

The deeper I dug into them, the more I discovered. It was clear that the standard of record-keeping in our national game has been little short of shambolic at times, with mistaken identities and unknown players. I decided to tackle this monumental project afresh and this is the end result.

After all that, Sammy Cox does not feature in this book as I took a practical decision to focus on the 1872-1939 era, in which time Scotland played 188 matches. Bringing this record up to the present day would have resulted in a book more than four times this size, as at the time of going to print Scotland had completed nearly 800 matches, and in any case, most players after the Second World War are better known.

How accurate is it?

I have gone to great lengths to confirm the identities of the players. Historians will soon notice that many details differ to those previously published, and that is because I have taken nothing for granted and have consulted original records wherever possible. As a result, I believe the wealth of detail I have uncovered is as complete and as accurate as it is possible to be. However, I am human and I apologise if I have made any mistakes.

While mass digitisation has transformed research, there is no getting round the fact that many records still exist only in paper form. For example, an essential component of my research was the leather-bound Scottish FA player registers, which sit in the Scottish Football Museum. They record the home address of every player from 1888 onwards who took part in a Scottish Cup tie, and if that crucial detail could then be found in a census return, it was usually possible to establish an identity.

I cross-checked birth, marriage and death certificates to ensure they matched, and have included precise locations such as street names rather than simply a town or city. Confirming all these details was a time-consuming process, and was not always straightforward as players changed their names for a variety of reasons: Donald Colman, Tom Hyslop, Ronnie Orr and Jimmy Campbell all played under false names throughout their playing careers, while others amended their spelling so that Donaghy became Donnachie, McMenamin became McMenemy, Lynden became Lundie, and so on. Some were born illegitimate and took their father's surname when their mother subsequently married; some parents were illiterate and could not write down their name so their surnames were recorded phonetically, such as Bracelan instead of Breslin. A few concealed their true age, most spectacularly Jimmy Lawrence who made himself six years younger than he really was.

There have been several major revelations along the way. For example, there was the case of John Lambie, who famously played for Scotland aged just 17. Except he didn't, as he called off late and his place was taken by another player. Curiously, however, he still holds the record as our youngest internationalist as he did make his Scotland debut the following year.

I found that Hugh Wilson of Dumbarton was capped in 1885 but is missing from every modern publication; like Sammy Cox, he was a late call-up to the team and was then forgotten about. And I established that the records of two players called James Gourlay, who both played for Cambuslang in the 1880s, had mistakenly been merged.

To compound it all, not all Scotland internationalists were Scottish. Did you hear the one about the Englishman and Irishman who played for Scotland against Wales? It happened in 1898 when goalkeeper Willie Watson, born in Northumberland, and Jimmy McKee, born in County Down, were both selected for the Scotland team that beat Wales 5-2. Nobody realised at the time that 'our' two players were not born in Scotland, as the rules required.

One by one, I tracked them all down, dug into their lives and I feel like I got to know some of them rather well. I published several articles about them on my website, and from time to time a descendant of one of the players would read my work and get in touch, which was gratifying. Occasionally, they even had photos and memorabilia which added to the stories.

By the time I went to print there were just three players whose fate remains unknown. Despite exhaustive searches, I have found no trace yet of the deaths of Willie Anderson, John D Macpherson and William Thomson. There are also nine players whose precise date of birth is unknown as their births were not registered, although I have worked out roughly where and when they were born. Apart from that, I believe the records are complete.

Establishing the correct dates and statistics of everyone who played for Scotland was just the start, as there are 615 life stories and what I found gripping was that they all had a tale to tell beyond their sporting achievements. Once you scratch the surface, there are criminals, drunks and wife-beaters among our international heroes. There are the desperately sad fates of those who died too soon, from the scourges of tuberculosis, alcoholism and mental illness, or from injuries while playing the game.

On the other hand there are heart-warming success stories, players who used football to raise themselves out of poverty and create a better life. There are successful businessmen, war heroes, devoted family men and fine upstanding citizens.

They all had one thing in common, the honour of playing for Scotland, and I dedicate this book to their memory.

Acknowledgements

There are many people who have contributed to this book in some way, great or small. I am indebted to an army of football historians and family genealogists who have made my research easier by uncovering dates, statistics and stories that I might have struggled to establish by myself, whether in books, on websites or via personal correspondence. Please forgive me for not mentioning every one individually as there are so many.

I would like to highlight several football historians who have gone out of their way to offer assistance, notably in checking and advising on my draft entries. They include Paul Joannou, Cris Freddi, David Speed, Douglas Gorman, Gabriele Tossani and George Park.

Among institutional resources I made extensive use of National Records of Scotland through their ScotlandsPeople centres, the British Newspaper Archive and the Scottish Football Museum. On the other hand, I tried to avoid Wikipedia, which has its uses but is rarely a source of reliable information.

I must also pay tribute to my wife Maureen who not only tolerated my obsessive research for many years, but designed the attractive cover of this book.

Andy Mitchell

Key to the player biographies

The heading, in capital letters, is the name by which the player was most commonly known, together with their Scotland caps total and goals total.

The second line is the player's full formal name. In a few cases his name or the spelling changed during his lifetime and this is mentioned in the text. Where there is uncertainty over spelling (in particular for Mac or Mc) I have tried to verify it with a personal signature.

Birth and death places and dates are taken from original certificates wherever possible. Occasionally these details are contradicted by other records and I have done my best to resolve any inconsistencies, with an explanation in the text in some cases.

Each player's Scotland career lists the opponents they faced and the calendar year of each match. The number of goals in a match is indicated in brackets, although it should be borne in mind that contemporary reports often disagreed on who scored and there is no way of knowing definitively if the goalscoring records are correct. If a player captained Scotland, this is indicated with a 'c'. In the few instances Scotland when played the same country twice in one calendar year (Wales Feb & Oct 1925, Ireland Feb & Sept 1931 and Czechoslovakia May & Dec 1937) I have added the month to indicate which match is referred to. For simplicity, I have continued to refer to Ireland (rather than Northern Ireland) after partition, and indeed this is how the Irish FA referred to their own internationals before WW2.

Each player's club career is a chronological listing, including major honours won with each club. If a player changed club in the close season only the year is given, but if they transferred during the season I have indicated the month as well. Guest and trial appearances are noted in square brackets but some players in the amateur era and in wartime made large numbers of guest appearances and these records may not be complete. Service with junior and juvenile clubs is often sketchy.

The text section of the player biographies is an overview of the key events and achievements in their playing career and life, together with any interesting anecdotes. Inevitably, some are considerably longer than others and it is clear that many players would be worthy of a full biography.

Illustrations are included if they are available in sufficiently high resolution for printing, and most of them come from my personal collection of photographs and cigarette cards. I am well aware of images of many other players which would not be suitable for reproduction here.

If you think you can add substance to the biographies in this book, want to query a detail or suggest a correction, please don't hesitate to let me know.

SCOTLAND'S INTERNATIONALISTS

A

Jimmy ADAMS (3/0, 1889-93)
James Adams
Born 17 August 1864 Home Street, Tollcross, Edinburgh
Died 21 April 1943 Devon Street, Kearny, New Jersey, USA
Scotland v Ireland 1889, 1893; Wales 1892.
Norton Park; Heart of Midlothian 1885-94 (Scottish Cup 1891); Everton 1894-96; Heart of Midlothian 1896-97; St Bernard's 1897-98.
A right back renowned for his fitness, Adams enjoyed over a decade at the top level and was described as 'a tackler of the old severe school, a very fast man and a rousing captain'. He was said to be indirectly responsible for the introduction of the penalty kick, preventing a certain goal by handling the ball in a Scottish Cup quarter final against East Stirlingshire in December 1890. A protest by the losing side was dismissed by the Scottish FA, but the incident galvanised support for the introduction of the new rule the following summer. His offence was worth it as Hearts went on to win the Scottish Cup, the club's first national trophy, and Adams started the move which led to the only goal of the final against Dumbarton. His international career was fleeting, with just three Scotland caps although he also played twice for the Scottish League against the English, captaining the team in 1893. When he turned professional with Everton in 1894 he left Hearts under a cloud, so much so that the club took him to court for the return of a silver athletics trophy he had won at their annual sports. He had two fine seasons on Merseyside but two years later, to general surprise, the Edinburgh club paid a 'hefty' fee to bring him back to Tynecastle. It proved to be a short-lived reunion, and he wound down his playing career across the city at St Bernard's. He took up refereeing before emigrating with his wife Fanny and their children to the USA in 1901. They settled in Kearny, New Jersey where he used his skills as a stonemason and monumental sculptor, despite losing several fingers in an accident at work. Later in life he was janitor of Kearny High School.

Bill AGNEW (3/0, 1907-08)
William Barbour Agnew
Born 30 December 1880 Kiln Row, by Gatehead, Ayrshire
Died 19 August 1936 Beechgrove Bowling Green, Moffat, Dumfriesshire
Scotland v Ireland 1907, 1908; Wales 1908.
Afton Lads; Kilmarnock 1900-1902; Newcastle United 1902-04; Middlesbrough 1904-06; Kilmarnock 1906-08 [guest for Ayr Parkhouse May 1907]; Sunderland 1908-10; Falkirk 1910-12; Scottish Amateurs Aug 1913; East Stirlingshire Sep 1913-14.
A powerful full-back who could play on either side of defence, Agnew's career took him to all three major north-east of England clubs, but his biggest impact was during his second spell at Kilmarnock, where he won all three of his caps as well as making two appearances for the Scottish League. The son of a coal miner, he moved to New Cumnock as a boy and although he followed his father down the pit, he started out in football with local junior side Afton Lads, stepping up to Kilmarnock in the summer of 1900. His league debut was hardly auspicious, a 7-0 defeat to Hearts, but he kept his place and a transfer to Newcastle in 1902 gave him the opportunity to become a full-time professional. He was an ever-present in his first season on Tyneside then fell out of the picture and moved on to Middlesbrough, where a narrow escape from relegation prompted a return to Rugby Park. Here, he not only marshalled the defence, he scored goals and was joint top scorer in 1906-07 (with five), also picking up a medal with a guest appearance for Ayr Parkhouse in the Ayr Charity Cup final. In January 1908 he was one of four Kilmarnock players who missed an away fixture at Port Glasgow due to fog, leaving the team to play the match with just seven men. His fine form brought him international recognition and he won his first Scotland cap in 1907 against Ireland and two more in 1908 against Ireland and Wales. In turn, this attracted top English sides and he returned to the north-east that summer with Sunderland but it was not a great success and two years later he was back in Scotland with Falkirk. In 1912 he had to stop playing due to a recurrent knee injury and took over a newsagent's shop in Falkirk, but after a season out he decided to make a comeback and was reinstated as an amateur. He played briefly for Scottish Amateurs and then concluded his career with East Stirlingshire, winning the Stirlingshire Cup in 1914. He later worked in insurance, living in Glasgow and then Elderslie. An enthusiastic bowler, he won the Scottish Rink Championship with Wellcroft BC in 1926 and bowled for Scotland in 1928, but died after collapsing on the green while taking part in the annual Moffat open tournament, which he had won in 1923 and 1926. NB his parents had another son of the same name on 16 December 1879, who died aged six weeks, which has led to some confusion.

Andy AITKEN (14/0, 1901-11)
Andrew Aitken
Born 25 July 1875 Hall's Vennel, Ayr
Died 15 February 1955 Ponteland Hospital, Northumberland
Scotland v England 1901, 1902c, 1903, 1904, 1905, 1906, 1907, 1908, 1910, 1911; Wales 1903, 1905, 1907; Ireland 1911c.
Elmbank; Ayr Thistle; Ayr Parkhouse 1894-95; Newcastle United 1895-1906 (Football League 1905) [loan to Kilmarnock Feb-Mar 1899]; Middlesbrough 1906-09 player-manager; Leicester Fosse 1909-11 player-manager; Dundee 1911-12; Kilmarnock 1912-13.

Aitken's relentless energy from the half-back line helped to establish Newcastle United as a national powerhouse. Known from an early age as 'Daddler', an obscure nickname which appears to come from the slang term for a farthing coin, he was equally adept in attack and defence, could tackle fiercely, win the ball and pass it well. His first success came with Elmbank who won the Ayr Junior Cup in 1892, and by the time he joined Newcastle United in 1895 he had senior experience with Ayr Parkhouse. In a decade with the north-east club he made well over 300 league appearances, gaining promotion to Division One in 1898 and reaching a high spot in 1904-05 when Newcastle came desperately close to the double, winning the league title but falling to Aston Villa in the FA Cup final. They also contested the following year's final, this time losing to Everton. Aitken made his Scotland debut in 1901 when Neilly Gibson had to call off, and was such a success that he was first choice for a decade, making ten appearances against England, one short of Bobby Walker's record. When he left Newcastle in 1906, unusually he combined playing with management at Middlesbrough and Leicester, and even more unusually he played for Scotland as a club manager. He wound up his career with a season each at Dundee and Kilmarnock until injury forced his retirement in 1913. He then managed Gateshead for six months and ran a pub in Newcastle, also reporting on football with a column in the *Sunday Post* and *Topical Times*. In 1921 he took over the Railway Hotel in Galashiels and was appointed an honorary President of Gala Fairydean, but a promise to resume playing for them at the age of 46 appears to have come to nothing. When he moved to Manchester on business in the 1930s he was briefly the trainer of Manchester United and Arsenal's scout in the city, then he returned to the north-east as proprietor of the Black Bull Hotel in Wallsend and lived in the area until his death in 1955.

Ralph AITKEN (2/1, 1886-88)
Ralph Allan Aitken
Born 16 February 1863 Shuttle Street, Kilbarchan, Renfrewshire
Died 10 January 1928 Glasgow Road, Dumbarton
Scotland v England 1886; Ireland 1888 (1).
Dumbarton 1883-86; Newcastle West End 1886-87; Dumbarton Jan 1887-89; Alloa Athletic Oct 1889-90; Our Boys Aug 1890; Southampton Naval Works 1890-91.
A left winger, renowned for his charging, tenacity and most of all speed, Aitken spent a couple of years in the reserves before he came to prominence with Dumbarton, and was selected to face England in 1886 just a year after making his first team debut. He was familiar with the north-east of England having spent part of his childhood in Hartlepool where his father was working as a ship plater, and followed his father into the same trade. This meant he moved where the work was, and he had six months with Newcastle West End before returning to Dumbarton, where he scored the opening goal in the 1887 Scottish Cup final although ending up on the losing side. Later he had a season with Alloa before joining Dundee side Our Boys, but after just two appearances he left for a job in a Southampton shipyard, where he played for the works team. He returned to Dumbarton after a couple of years and spent the rest of his life working as a plater in the shipyards on the River Leven. His son William also played for Dumbarton and was a club director.

Wattie AITKENHEAD (1/2, 1912)
Walter Allison Campbell Aitkenhead
Born 21 May 1887 Balmore Street, Possilpark, Glasgow
Died 19 July 1966 Royal Hospital, Cheadle, Cheshire
Scotland v Ireland 1912 (2).
Maryhill Juniors; Partick Thistle Aug-Sep 1906; Blackburn Rovers Oct 1906-16 (Football League 1912, 1914) [guest for Preston North End Apr 1916].
Generally an inside left, Aitkenhead was versatile enough to play in other forward positions and even at half-back. He played only four games for Partick Thistle before being snapped up by Blackburn Rovers in 1906, aged 19, and he spent the rest of his playing career at Ewood Park. Although it took him a good three seasons to establish himself as a first-team regular, he was top scorer when Blackburn won the league title in 1912, outstanding form which attracted the international selectors. His Scotland debut could hardly have started better, with two first-half goals setting up a comprehensive victory over Ireland, but he was never selected again. He won a second Football League medal in 1914 as his influence started to fade and there was, in any case, little opportunity to play after 1915 when Rovers closed down for a season. He joined the Royal Field Artillery as a reservist, which allowed him to feature in sporadic matches for Rovers when they restarted in 1916, as well as making a guest appearance for Preston NE. He was called up for active service as a gunner in the final year of the War and emerged from the conflict suffering from a neurological disorder. However, he had a bright future outside the game, as when he originally joined Blackburn Rovers, he did so on condition that a job was found for him. He was employed as a cloth salesman for the Fernhurst Mill, which was across the road from Ewood

Park and owned by the club chairman and town's mayor, Alderman Lawrence Cotton. In 1915 he married the mayor's daughter, Ethel, and was made manager of the mill, taking over as managing director on his father-in-law's death (which brought him and his wife a substantial legacy). He took up golf and was elected captain of Pleasington Golf Club in 1931, and his home was still in Pleasington at the time of his death in 1966, leaving an estate valued at £55,000.

Davie ALEXANDER (2/0, 1894)
David Alexander
Born 22 April 1869 Stane, Shotts, Lanarkshire
Died 14 January 1941 Bedlay Street, Springburn, Glasgow
Scotland v Wales 1894; Ireland 1894.
East Stirlingshire 1890-91; Darwen 1891-92; Accrington 1892-93; East Stirlingshire 1893-1900 [trial for Heart of Midlothian Sep 1896].
A prolific centre forward, Alexander initially came to East Stirlingshire, at that time in the Midland League from his home town of Shotts, where he probably learned to play football. After a successful year, in 1891 he tried his hand in England as a professional but a season each with Darwen and Accrington was enough. He returned to the Merchiston Park club and his continuing good form ensured he was selected for both the 'lesser' internationals of 1894, a 5-2 win over Wales and retaining his place for the following week's match in Belfast. Although Hearts gave him a trial in a league match against Celtic in 1896, he played for Shire until the end of the decade, scoring twice when they won the Scottish Qualifying Cup in 1898. His career came to an abrupt end with a badly broken leg in a league match against Abercorn in September 1900. After hanging up his boots he remained as a club official and referee, and was an iron moulder to trade.

Davie ALLAN (3/3, 1885-86)
David Steele Allan
Born 30 April 1863 Railway Station, Dundonald, Ayrshire
Died 26 June 1930 St Andrews Drive, Pollokshields, Glasgow
Scotland v England 1885; Wales 1885 (1), 1886 (2).
Queen's Park 1880-91 (Scottish Cup 1881, 1884, 1886, 1890) [guest for Corinthian Apr 1885].
The son of a station master, Allan was educated and learned football at Ayr Academy, which had already produced a number of prominent players including John Smith and WW Beveridge. Although he was a keen cyclist, when he came to Glasgow as a young man to embark on a career in stockbroking, he joined Queen's Park and soon excelled at football. He made his competitive debut just before his 18th birthday in the replayed Scottish Cup final of 1881, taking the place of the injured Harry McNeil, and duly established himself at inside left for a decade. By the middle of the decade he was in the Scotland team, making his debut against England in 1885 and going on to score three times in two appearances against Wales. Among his honours he won four Scottish Cup medals as well as a number of other trophies, including the Glasgow Merchants' Charity Cup four times and the Glasgow Cup twice. He played in both of Queen's Park's FA Cup finals of 1884 and 1885, and was subsequently invited to join the Corinthians, scoring the only goal of a game against Preston in 1885. He retired from the game in 1891, married Margaret, a sister of fellow internationalist Tom Waddell, and continued to work in Glasgow as a stockbroker until his death. He is buried in Cathcart Cemetery.

'Dod' ALLAN (1/0, 1897)
George Horsburgh Allan
Born 23 August 1875 Linlithgow Bridge, West Lothian
Died 17 October 1899 St Ford Cottage, Earlsferry, Fife
Scotland v England 1897.
Broxburn Shamrock 1893-94; Bo'ness 1894-95; Leith Athletic Mar-Jun 1895; Burnley Jun 1895 (registration only); Liverpool 1895-97 (Second Division 1896); St Bernard's 1897 (registration only); Celtic 1897-98 (Scottish League 1898); Liverpool 1898-99.
Allan was a fine centre forward who packed a great deal into his short career, which was cut short by the illness which killed him aged just 24. His powerful physique made him a fearsome opponent, added to which he was very fast and could run with the ball at his feet. He played for local teams Broxburn Shamrock and Bo'ness, winning the East of Scotland Shield with the latter in March 1895. The following week he joined Leith Athletic and made his Scottish League debut, but it was a brief association with the club and he played his last game at the end of May in the Rosebery Charity Cup final. That summer he signed for Burnley but before he even played a game they changed their minds and sold him for just £5 to Liverpool, who made the most of his abilities. He led the line as they clinched the Second Division championship in 1896, and the following season finished runners-up in the First Division. Although Anfield was packed with Scots talent, in 1897 Allan was the first of the club's players to win a cap for Scotland, and what is more, it was against England. Later that year, via another 'ghost registration' for St Bernard's he returned to Scotland and was welcomed with open arms at Celtic Park. He duly scored almost a goal a game for the team on their way to the Scottish League title in 1898 but was again tempted to go south, attracted back to Merseyside by a club record wage of £8 per week. He appeared to have a great career ahead of him and in April 1899 was appointed captain of Liverpool, then his tragic illness intervened. In August it was reported that he had gone to the Fife seaside resort of Elie to try and restore his failing health. Tuberculosis had no cure, however, and his death followed two months later. It was a great shock, especially for Liverpool manager Tom Watson who received a letter from Allan expressing his regret that he could not be with his colleagues, then an hour later had a cable announcing his death. He was buried at Linlithgow Cemetery with wreaths and mourners from his former clubs.

Harry ALLAN (1/0, 1902)
Henry Hogg Allan
Born 8 October 1872 Kingseat, Fife
Died 10 April 1965 West 41st Avenue, Vancouver, Canada
Scotland v Wales 1902.
Lassodie 1890-92; Dunfermline Athletic 1893-95; Cowdenbeath 1895-96; Heart of Midlothian Jan 1896-1903 (Scottish Cup 1901); East Fife 1903-04.

A strong-tackling right back, Allan was a key figure in the Hearts side which lifted the Scottish Cup in 1901 and the following season was called up to replace the injured Nicol Smith for his single Scotland appearance, a convincing victory over Wales at Cappielow. His football career had got off to a low-key start as he combined playing with his work as a coal miner in his home village of Kingseat, near Dunfermline. He started out with local team Lassodie and when a move to Dunfermline initially proved unsuccessful he applied to be reinstated as an amateur but was turned down by the SFA. He had a brief spell at Cowdenbeath then stepped up to Hearts, who were at the top of the Scottish game, and from 1897 he established himself in the first team for six eventful seasons. In 1903 he was one of the first players to sign for newly-founded East Fife, captaining the team in their opening match which happened to be against Hearts. However, he was forced to give up the game halfway through the season when his old injuries caught up with him. He emigrated to Canada in 1905 and settled in Vancouver, where he died 60 years later at the grand old age of 92.

Johnnie ALLAN (2/2, 1887)
John Allan
Born 17 June 1866 Bridgend, Kilwinning, Ayrshire
Died 4 November 1945 Main Street, Kilwinning, Ayrshire
Scotland v England 1887 (1); Wales 1887 (1).
Monkcastle 1884-86 [guest for Rangers Mar & Aug 1885]; Queen's Park 1886-87; Monkcastle 1887-89 [guest for Kilbirnie 1887, 1888; for Rangers Apr-May 1888]; Rangers 1889-90; Monkcastle 1890-92 [guest for Rangers May 1892].

Allan crammed almost all his football highlights into just one season with Queen's Park, yet a family story goes that his parents did not even know he was starring for the Glasgow club until a telegram came one day, asking why he had not turned up the previous Saturday – he had flu. Brought up in Kilwinning, he spent most of his playing career with his home town team, Monkcastle, and had already won county honours for Ayrshire when he came to Glasgow aged 20 and joined Queen's Park. He made the most of the 1886-87 season at Hampden by scoring plenty of goals and duly earned the attention of the selectors. He was picked for Glasgow against Edinburgh and Sheffield and then came into the full Scotland team in the spring of 1887 against England and Wales. Unusually, Scotland played an unchanged side for the two away games in Blackburn and Wrexham, and Allan scored in both of them, giving him a record of two caps, two victories and two goals, including the winner in a 3-2 defeat of England on his debut. The next season he was back with Monkcastle, where he was also match secretary, but opportunities in Ayrshire football were limited so he made regular excursions to Glasgow. He became a member of Rangers and played for them throughout the 1889-90 season and on several other occasions, including three league matches in May 1892. An all-round sportsman, he was a prominent tradesman in Kilwinning, as a shopkeeper and then licensee of the Crown Inn in Main Street. NB he has been confused with James Allan, no relation, who was secretary of Queen's Park in the 1890s and President of the Scottish Amateur Athletic Association in 1911.

Bobby ANCELL (2/0, 1936)
Robert Francis Dudgeon Ancell
Born 16 June 1911 Nunholm Villas, Dumfries
Died 5 July 1987 Stewart Terrace, Monifieth, Angus
Scotland v Ireland 1936; Wales 1936.
Mid Annandale; St Mirren Feb 1930-36; Newcastle United 1936-44 [guest during WW2 for Carlisle United 1939-40, Blackpool 41-42, Rochdale 41-42, Blackburn Rovers 41-43, Aberdeen 41-44, Derby County 43-44]; Dundee 1944-49 [guest for Burnley Sep 1945]; Aberdeen Jan-May 1949; Dundee 1949-50; Berwick Rangers 1950-52 player-manager.

As a Dumfries schoolboy, Ancell gave a clear indication of his considerable sporting talent at cricket, rugby and golf, but it was football which defined him. He started playing for Mid Annandale of Lockerbie, and although they had no regular league at the time they did qualify for the Scottish Cup in 1930. This brought him to the attention of St Mirren, whom he joined in February that year, and he soon established himself at full back while continuing to live in Dumfries where he worked as a linotype operator. In the summer he played for Dumfries Cricket Club. Saints reached the Scottish Cup final in 1934 which ended in heavy defeat to Rangers, and worse was to follow the next season when they were relegated. Speculation was rife that he was about to move to England, but it took another year, in which he helped Saints to win promotion, before Newcastle came in with a successful bid of £2,500 in the summer of 1936. He actually signed for Newcastle in the buffet of Dumfries Railway Station, near his home. Going straight into the team and performing to a high standard, he won his two caps that autumn at left back, but he was injured early in the defeat to Wales and was not selected again, although he made one wartime appearance against England in December 1939. Like so many players, the Second World War disrupted his career and when he joined the RAF in 1941 as a PT Instructor it effectively ended his association with Newcastle. When duties permitted he turned out for various teams, most notably Aberdeen for three seasons, and played several representative matches for services sides. In the summer of 1944 he signed for Dundee but illness and his continued RAF service, which saw him stationed in Dumfries and near Manchester, limited his appearances until he was demobbed in March 1946. He remained at Dens Park until 1950, apart from a few months at Aberdeen, and when his playing days wound down he embarked on a highly successful coaching and managerial career. He took Berwick Rangers from the East of Scotland League to the Scottish League, moved on to Dunfermline Athletic from 1952-55, and really made an impact at Motherwell over a decade from 1955. His young side was known as the Ancell Babes, and he ended his spell at Fir Park with victory in the Summer Cup. His final managerial position was at Dundee 1965-68, taking them to the semi-final of the Fairs Cup and the final of the Scottish League Cup. After that he restricted his football involvement to some scouting and focussed on his golf, playing off scratch.

Andy ANDERSON (23/0, 1933-38)
Andrew Smellie Anderson
Born 21 February 1909 Pearl Cottage, Academy Street, Airdrie, Lanarkshire
Died 18 August 1991 Monklands Hospital, Airdrie, Lanarkshire
Scotland v England 1933, 1934, 1935, 1936, 1937, 1938; Ireland 1933, 1934, 1935, 1936, 1937; Wales 1933c, 1934, 1935, 1936, 1937, 1938c; Austria 1933, 1937; Germany 1936; Netherlands 1938; Czechoslovakia Dec 1937c; Hungary 1938c.
Baillieston Juniors 1926-29; Heart of Midlothian 1929-41.

At top junior club Baillieston, Anderson won his first honours in a team which won the inaugural Intermediate League in 1928, during a time of dispute within the junior game in Scotland that probably delayed him turning senior. Having joined Hearts in the summer of 1929 he had to wait several months before making his first team debut, but once in the side he was a mainstay at full back for a decade. In all, 'Tiger' played over 400 games for Hearts. He became a fixture in the Scotland team, playing 16 consecutive internationals from his debut in 1933 before he missed one, and going on to win 23 caps. He was appointed Scotland captain in only his third match, and was subsequently given the honour three more times. He also made four appearances for the Scottish League and went on the SFA transatlantic tour of 1935. A joiner to trade, he continued to live in Lanarkshire and wanted to retire shortly after the outbreak of war, but was persuaded to carry on at Hearts until 1941. After the conflict he worked as a lorry driver for a Lanarkshire quarry company.

Fred ANDERSON (1/1, 1874)
Frederick Anderson
Born 17 November 1855 Queen's Terrace, Strathbungo, Glasgow
Died 5 January 1940 Standen Manor, Hungerford, Berkshire
Scotland v England 1874 (1).
Clydesdale 1872-74.
Anderson was born into a wealthy family and attended Glasgow Academy as a boy but when he was 12 his father, a cotton merchant, moved to Wilmslow in Cheshire and Fred continued his schooling at Hawthorn Hall. However, he returned to Glasgow early in the 1870s and played football for Clydesdale which was primarily a cricket club but had an active football section. He won his sole cap for Scotland in March 1874 aged just 18 and he rewarded the faith put in him by scoring the opening goal. He remains Scotland's youngest-ever scorer to this day. The following week he was selected for Glasgow to face Sheffield, and the week after that he played in the first ever Scottish Cup final as Clydesdale went down to Queen's Park. That summer he returned south to embark on a business career which took him all the way to China. After arriving in Shanghai around 1881 he continued playing football, mainly under rugby rules, although his main sporting activity appears to have been cricket and he was appointed secretary of Shanghai Cricket Club, and later its President. Anderson's career prospered as he became chairman of Shanghai Municipal Council and was a director of rubber exporting companies in Malaysia. After his retirement in 1909 he became a governor of the School of Oriental and African Studies in London, ultimately donating his library to the institution. He died in 1940 at his home near Hungerford, leaving a fortune worth £261,000.

George ANDERSON (1/0, 1901)
George Anderson
Born 29 September 1878 Greenwood, Dreghorn, Ayrshire
Died 20 May 1930 Market Lane, Kilmarnock, Ayrshire
Scotland v Ireland 1901.
Rugby XI; Kilmarnock 1897-1905 (Second Division 1898, 1899); Luton Town 1905-06; Kilmarnock 1906-09 [guest for Hurlford 1906, Ayr Parkhouse 1907].
Powerfully built and with a fine football brain, Anderson could control the game at centre half with his intelligent passing. He was described as the 'here, there and everywhere' type, but was also criticised for being 'a little rough' and he was no stranger to the SFA disciplinarians. Having stepped up from local junior side Rugby XI, he immediately made an impact as Kilmarnock won two successive Second Division titles and were duly elected to the First, and reached the Scottish Cup final of 1898 which was lost to Rangers. His only international appearance was an 11-0 rout of Ireland, but he performed poorly in the game and was not selected again although he played twice for the Scottish League. He had a season with Luton Town in the Southern League then returned to Kilmarnock in 1906. The club granted him a testimonial in August 1908 but only fielded a reserve team against St Mirren, losing 6-0 at home, which must have hurt and certainly was not a money-spinner. A coal miner, he suffered from ill health and died at home in Kilmarnock of alcohol poisoning, aged 51.

Harry ANDERSON (1/0, 1914)
Henry Alexander Anderson
Born 17 July 1888 Blenheim Street, Dennistoun, Glasgow
Died 8 November 1939 Belvidere Hospital, Glasgow
Scotland v Wales 1914.
Vale of Clyde; Third Lanark 1909-10; Hibernian 1910-12; Raith Rovers 1912-15; Third Lanark 1915-16; Raith Rovers 1919-20 [loan to St Mirren Mar-Jun 1919 (Victory Cup)]; St Mirren 1920-21; Clydebank 1921-22.

After stepping up from the juniors, a season at Third Lanark only brought reserve team football for Anderson, before a move to Hibs gave him his chance to prove himself. His versatility at half-back, which included a goal-scoring threat, made him a target for Raith Rovers, who snapped him up in 1912. In his first season he helped the Kirkcaldy side to the

Scottish Cup final, which they lost 2-0 to Falkirk, and the following year his continuing good form earned him a Scotland cap against Wales. With the outbreak of war he returned to Glasgow with Third Lanark, an opportunity which was curtailed when he was called up to the Royal Field Artillery in March 1916 and posted to England. He played no more senior football for three years as he saw active service until he was demobbed in March 1919 with the rank of Corporal. He was signed by St Mirren, notionally on loan from Raith Rovers, and played a major role in their successful Victory Cup campaign before resuming in Kirkcaldy for a year. He then returned to Paisley but it was a disastrous season as Saints finished bottom of the league, and the following year he wound down his career at Clydebank, who also finished last. After hanging up his boots he remained in Glasgow and was working as a house factor's clerk when he died of a heart attack aged just 51. His elder brother David was a professional footballer before WW1 with Airdrieonians, Dumbarton, Hibernian and Third Lanark.

Kenny ANDERSON (3/0, 1896-98)
Kenneth Anderson
Born 23 July 1875 Abbotsford Place, Gorbals, Glasgow
Died 29 August 1900 Balmoral Crescent, Queen's Park, Glasgow
Scotland v Ireland 1896, 1898; England 1898.
Third Lanark 1893-94; Queen's Park 1894-98.
Anderson started out at Third Lanark as an 18-year-old, and after one season at Cathkin he moved to Queen's Park. Although the club was still holding back from Scottish League membership and only took part in cup competitions and friendlies, he made his mark and was clearly an outstanding goalkeeper. This was recognised with his selection for the national team in 1896, but he conceded three on his debut in Belfast, including the first penalty kick awarded in international football. Two years later he was selected twice more, culminating in the accolade of a cap against England. He won the only medal of his career in the Glasgow Cup final victory of November 1898 against Rangers, which proved to be his final competitive match as his health started to deteriorate soon afterwards. He went abroad in search of a cure to no avail and he died of tuberculosis aged just 25. Always an amateur, he worked as a letterpress printer in Glasgow, following the trade of his father, and the family was clearly well-off as there were several servants in the household. He is buried in Cathcart Cemetery.

Willie ANDERSON (6/4, 1882-85)
William Anderson
Born 25 April 1862 Glasgow Street, Ardrossan, Ayrshire
Died after 1911
Scotland v England 1882, 1883, 1884, 1885; Wales 1883 (1), 1885 (3).
Abington; Shawlands Athletic; Queen's Park 1879-86 (Scottish Cup 1881, 1882, 1884); Chicago Thistles 1890.
Anderson was such an exciting man to watch that he was dubbed 'The Demon Dodger' in recognition of his exploits on the right wing. Born in Ardrossan and brought up on the south side of Glasgow in a middle class family, he followed his father into the insurance business and was therefore an ideal candidate for the 'gentlemen' of Queen's Park whom he joined in 1879 after a grounding in local juvenile football. It was a time of considerable success for the club, with whom he won the Scottish Cup three times and the Glasgow Charity Cup four times, as well as playing in the FA Cup finals of 1884 and 1885. He made his Scotland debut aged 19 in the 5-1 win over England in 1882 and never suffered defeat in any of his six caps, scoring a hat-trick against Wales on his final appearance. In the summer of 1886 he crossed the Atlantic, initially to Montreal but then settled in Chicago where he played for the Thistles team. He also got married there to Grace Kemp, originally from Kent, whose father George had recently absconded to America with the funds of the Whitstable Oyster Company. Anderson and his wife returned to Glasgow in 1893 and he took up cricket, playing for Poloc, while his career in insurance prospered. He was appointed local manager for the Paisley Refuge Assurance Society before moving to the West Midlands where he was listed in the 1911 census as an insurance company district secretary. What happened to him after that is not yet known, although his wife was described as a widow in 1939.

Peter ANDREWS (1/1, 1875)
Peter Andrews
Born 10 November 1845 Kilwinning, Ayrshire
Died 24 July 1916 Royal Alexandra Infirmary, Paisley, Renfrewshire
Scotland v England 1875 (1).
Callander Nov 1873; Eastern 1873-76 [guest for Partick Jan 1876]; Clydesdale Apr 1876; Leeds Athletic Oct-Nov 1876; Heeley Nov 1876-80; Wednesday Mar-Oct 1881; Surrey Oct 1880-82.
Andrews had a challenging childhood as his father died when he was young and his mother worked as a washerwoman. He served an apprenticeship in Ayrshire as a baker before coming to Glasgow where he took up football and came to the fore as a goal-scoring forward with Eastern, who he captained. In February 1875 he represented Glasgow against Sheffield, then the following month travelled to London where he won his only international cap, scoring a late equaliser for Scotland. His life changed in 1876 shortly after another appearance for Glasgow, when he moved to England and was one of first Scots to play south of the border. He was already familiar to the small football community in the north of England having played for Partick in Darwen, and for Glasgow and Clydesdale in Sheffield. He went initially to Leeds, where there were few sporting opportunities at the time, but when his work then took him to Sheffield, he joined Heeley and started to play for them in November 1876. This was a few weeks before JJ Lang arrived in the city to play for Wednesday. Already a veteran in his 30s, Andrews became an influential player in the city and played numerous times for the Sheffield select, including against his home town of Glasgow. He remained active in the game throughout his time in Sheffield, moving on from Heeley to play for Wednesday and Surrey. In the early 1880s he returned to Scotland and according to one memoir he played for Clyde, which had been born out of the ashes of his old club Eastern, but this seems unlikely. He settled in Paisley where he was foreman in a cotton mill and a director of the Paisley and District Ayrshire Association until his death in 1916.

Sandy ARCHIBALD (8/1, 1921-32)
Alexander Archibald
Born 23 November 1896 Back Street, Crossgates, Fife
Died 29 November 1946 Droverhall Place, Crossgates, Fife
Scotland v Wales 1921, 1922 (1), 1924; England 1922, 1924, 1931, 1932; Ireland 1923.
Crossgates Mayflower; Dunfermline Juniors; Raith Rovers Mar 1916-17; Rangers 1917-34 (Scottish League 1918, 1920, 1921, 1923, 1924, 1925, 1927, 1928, 1929, 1930, 1931, 1933, 1934; Scottish Cup 1928, 1930, 1932); Raith Rovers Nov 1934-35 player-manager.

Archibald was one of the most successful players of the inter-war era, winning 13 league titles and three Scottish Cups, not to mention eight Glasgow Cups and ten Glasgow Charity Cup victories. He had started out at Dunfermline Juniors before making his debut for Raith Rovers in March 1916. A year later, when Rovers were obliged to leave the Scottish League in the summer of 1917, he moved to Rangers and was just in time for their last match of the 1916/17 season, a Charity Cup tie against Celtic. In the following 17 years playing on the right wing at Ibrox, he not only made goals for his fellow forwards, he had a powerful shot which enabled him to score well over a hundred himself. Yet his international career was sparse by comparison, and there was a long gap of seven years between his sixth and seventh Scotland caps. He also made 12 appearances for the Scottish League. He returned to Raith in November 1934 and was appointed secretary/manager, making just five more appearances before he hung up his boots to focus on management. On the outbreak of war he took up a similar post with Dunfermline Athletic which he held from October 1939 while engaged in wartime work at Rosyth Dockyard. The stress of combining the two jobs was said to have contributed to his death at home, just a few days after his 50th birthday.

Matt ARMSTRONG (3/0, 1935-36)
Matthew Armstrong
Born 13 November 1911 Police Station, Newton Stewart, Wigtownshire
Died 4 October 1995 Woodend Hospital, Aberdeen
Scotland v Wales 1935; Ireland 1935; Germany 1936.
Port Glasgow Juniors; Aberdeen 1931-46 [guest for Chelsea Dec 1939; Birmingham Feb 1940; Nottingham Forest Apr-May 1940; Clapton Orient Nov 1940 & 1941-43; Brentford Oct & Dec 1942, Feb 1943; West Bromwich Albion Aug-Dec 1943; Wrexham Mar 1944 & Apr-Oct 1945; Walsall Oct-Dec 1944; Chester Dec 1944-Feb 1945]; Queen of the South Mar 1946-47; Elgin City 1947-50 player-coach; Peterhead 1950-51.

The son of a policeman, Armstrong had played for the Scottish Junior League while with Port Glasgow and was signed for Aberdeen in 1931 by Pat Travers. He made just sporadic appearances for the first eleven until 1934 but then became first choice at centre forward for the rest of the decade, ending up as top scorer four times. The highlight was reaching the Scottish Cup final of 1937 in which he scored an equaliser before Aberdeen eventually lost 2-1 to Celtic. His form was rewarded with three Scotland caps but unfortunately he failed to find the net in any of them, and scored just once in three appearances for the Scottish League. Shortly after the outbreak of war in 1939 he joined the Royal Army Service Corps and was only able to play occasionally for Aberdeen until he was demobbed in 1945. Meanwhile he turned out as a guest for a number of English clubs, notably Clapton Orient while stationed in London. He left Pittodrie for good in the spring of 1946 and had a season with Queen of the South before returning to the north east as player-coach of Elgin City. Right to the end of his career he could be relied upon to score goals, and was top scorer in the Highland League in his first season at Borough Briggs and remained his club's leading scorer for the two succeeding years. His final club was Peterhead, then after retiring he was a scout for Falkirk and continued to live in Aberdeen until his death in 1995.

Wattie ARNOTT (14/0, 1883-93)
Walter Arnott
Born 12 May 1861 Linden Terrace, Pollokshields, Glasgow
Died 18 May 1931 Carolside Avenue, Clarkston, Glasgow
Scotland v Wales 1883, 1885, 1887; Ireland 1884c; England 1884, 1885, 1886c, 1887, 1888, 1889, 1890, 1891c, 1892, 1893.
Matilda; Pollokshields Athletic 1880-82; Queen's Park 1882-84 (Scottish Cup 1884); Pollokshields Athletic 1884-85; Queen's Park Jan 1885-93 (Scottish Cup 1886, 1890) [guest for Blackburn Rovers Apr 1886, Newcastle West

End Dec 1887, Corinthian Feb 1888, London Caledonians Apr 1891, Third Lanark Oct 1892]; St Bernard's Mar 1893-94; Notts County Feb 1895; Celtic Feb 1895; Mossknow Rovers 1896-98.

Arguably the greatest Scottish footballer of the amateur age, Arnott was hailed by William Pickford as 'a giant among giants' and said 'Not only was he the best defender, but he was also the most artistic back I have ever seen'. He had speed, strength, and could tackle and pass the ball with precision. Arnott was an engaging character who had a life-long love affair with the game, and told a romantic tale that he was inspired to take up football as a boy when he saw the first international at Hamilton Crescent in 1872, looking over the wall while standing on the roof of a hansom cab. Growing up on the southside of Glasgow, he developed his style at Pollokshields Athletic, where he was first selected to represent the city against Sheffield in 1881. Then the following year he made the natural progression to Queen's Park, who needed a new right back after Andy Watson's departure for London. He won his first cap against Wales in 1883, then his second season was a triumph, with Queen's Park victories in the Scottish Cup and the Merchants' Charity Cup and an appearance in the FA Cup final. He also made the first of ten consecutive appearances for Scotland against England and was carried off the field in triumph. The *Athletic News* positively gushed about his performance: 'What will live in history as the most wonderful feature of Saturday's game is the back play of Walter Arnott. I never in all my life saw anything like it.' In 1884 he returned to Pollokshields as club captain, then a few months later was persuaded to rejoin Queen's Park for their second heroic tilt at the FA Cup. Over succeeding years he was easily the best-known player in the country, and although he was notionally a Queen's Park man he was keenly sought for guest appearances by Corinthians and a host of other clubs, regularly going where the whim (and perhaps the money) took him. In the summer of 1888 he announced he was retiring, and a testimonial match was played for his benefit between Renton and Preston NE. He missed half a season before the Queen's Park committee implored him to come back, and he duly helped the club to win the Scottish Cup again in 1890. Early in 1891 he got a job in Belfast but contrary to some reports, he did not play for Linfield (his younger brother Willie did, winning the 1892 Irish Cup at left back). Arnott returned to Glasgow to play for Queen's Park whenever possible, and his international career persisted. Although he was not originally selected for the England match in 1892, he was called in at the last minute due to Smellie's illness. With his powers on the wane, he made his last appearance for Queen's Park early in 1893 and was left out of their Scottish Cup final team, yet was still selected to face England for the tenth and last time the following month. Upset at his treatment by the club, he severed his connections and joined St Bernard's, where he regained his form and could even have made a final appearance for Scotland in 1894 against Ireland, but was prevented by business commitments. He played briefly for Notts County and Celtic before retiring from top level football in 1895, although he continued to turn out for a junior side in the Dumfriesshire village of Kirkpatrick Fleming, where he was working at a quarry. He returned to Glasgow in 1904 and maintained a close connection with the game as a writer and an after-dinner speaker, and indulged in other sports such as tennis (club champion at Pollok), curling (secretary of Crossmyloof Curling Club) and yachting (winning over 200 races from his holiday home in Millport). Arnott's boots, together with his heavily embroidered Scotland cap, are in the Scottish Football Museum.

Johnnie AULD (3/0, 1887-89)
John Robertson Auld
Born 7 January 1862 Boyd Street, Kilmarnock, Ayrshire
Died 29 April 1932 Roker Park Road, Sunderland, County Durham
Scotland v England 1887; Wales 1887, 1889.
Lugar Boswell; Third Lanark 1883-87; Queen's Park 1887-88; Third Lanark 1888-89 (Scottish Cup 1889); Sunderland 1889-96 (Football League 1892, 1893, 1895); Newcastle United Oct 1896-97.

Auld cut his footballing teeth as an outside left with Lugar Boswell, where he won the Ayrshire Cup in 1881 and played for his county, then moved to Glasgow in 1883 to work as manager of an outfitter's shop. There, he joined Third Lanark and not only transformed himself into a defender, he pioneered the role of centre half. The third half-back was a tactical innovation and after Auld successfully demonstrated its efficacy the Scotland selectors chose three half-backs for the first time in 1887 for the games against England and Wales. The tactic succeeded as Scotland won them both, and Auld can therefore claim to be the national team's first-ever centre half. He had six years at Cathkin, punctuated by a season with Queen's Park where he didn't really fit in, and made a name for himself as a dominant figure who was not afraid to get into a scrape. The story goes that in a friendly for Third Lanark at Bolton his nose was broken, and the following day at West Bromwich he dislocated his right shoulder, but he managed to finish both matches. Later in his career, he broke his collar bone and ribs but always bounced back. His reputation was enhanced by a Scottish

Cup win for Thirds and he won his third cap in 1889, not to mention a selection against Canada in 1888 and seven appearances for Glasgow. Aged 27 he was recruited by Sunderland, where he became their playmaker and was appointed captain as they entered the Football League. He played a key role in the creation of the 'team of all the talents' that won the league three times in four years. In the third of those, he only made four appearances for Sunderland and appeared to be in the twilight of his career, so chose to move on to Newcastle. This provoked something of a falling-out as he was reinstated as an amateur, which meant Sunderland were not due a fee, but he only played a handful of games. The following summer, on retiring from playing, he was appointed a director of Newcastle United and became part of their three-man talent identification sub-committee whose job was to find players. They made such a good job of it that the greatest side of the Edwardian era took shape. Auld remained on the Newcastle board until 1906 before stepping down to focus on his business: a shoemaker (like his father), he had ensured that his transfer to Sunderland was financially rewarding with a healthy wage packet and signing on fee, which was further sweetened with him being set up with his own shop. He lived for the rest of his life in the shadow of Roker Park while running his boot and shoe store, and was prominent in local affairs, serving as president of Sunderland Chamber of Commerce, elder of Roker Church and president of Brampton Bowling Club. His death in 1932 followed a heart attack, caused by a fall from a tramcar.

B

Andrew BAIRD (2/0, 1892-94)
Andrew Baird
Born 11 June 1866 Annick Lodge Colliery, Irvine, Ayrshire
Died 28 August 1936 Clarkston Road, Muirend, Glasgow
Scotland v Ireland 1892; Wales 1894.
Irvine Academicals 1881-87; Irvine 1887-90 [guest for Kilbirnie Jun 1888, Mar 1890]; Queen's Park 1890-94 (Scottish Cup 1893).
The son of a colliery manager, Baird was educated at Irvine Royal Academy where he was a keen young footballer, soon proving himself to be a talented goalkeeper with his old school side, the Academicals, which later shortened its name simply to Irvine. He was selected for Ayrshire several times from 1888, including at least once as captain, until he resigned in 1890 to move to Glasgow. He joined Queen's Park and made an impressive start by keeping a clean sheet on his debut against Corinthians in February 1891. This led to a Scotland trial in 1891 and he won his first cap the following year against Ireland. The highlight of his time at Queen's Park was winning the Scottish Cup in 1893 and he went on to win another cap, but appears to have given up the game after the humiliation of letting in eight goals to Sunderland in a friendly in October 1894. He had other sporting talents to keep him occupied, however, and was a scratch golfer at Irvine GC. Having trained as a legal clerk in Irvine, he worked for many years for Glasgow Corporation as a bookkeeper in the City Chamberlain's office.

Davie BAIRD (3/1, 1890-92)
David Baird
Born 4 March 1869 Silvermills, Edinburgh
Died 19 March 1946 Pentland Street, Loanhead, Midlothian
Scotland v Ireland 1890; England 1891; Wales 1893 (1).
Dalry Primrose; Heart of Midlothian 1888-1903 (Scottish Cup 1891, 1896, 1901; Scottish League 1895, 1897) [guest for St Bernard's Apr 1890, May 1892]; Motherwell 1903-04.
Baird's career with Hearts spanned an impressive 15 years, during which he became the only man to win three Scottish Cups with the club. The sweetest of those was probably the first all-Edinburgh cup final in 1896, in which he scored the opening goal from the penalty spot as Hearts defeated Hibernian 3-1 at Logie Green. He almost made it four cups, but in his last season Hearts lost the 1903 final to Rangers after two replays. He played a major role as Hearts won two league titles in 1895 and 1897. Unusually for the time, he could play almost anywhere and his cup medals were won at left back, inside right, outside left respectively. For the national team, he was recognised with three Scotland caps, which would have been four but he was unable to play against Ireland in 1892. There were also two appearances for the Scottish League, and eight games for the Edinburgh select – a fine haul for a man who was not a specialist. He joined Motherwell in 1903 in the twilight of his career and made just one appearance for them before retiring. He retained close connections with Hearts and was a club director for ten years from 1926. Meanwhile, he worked as a letterpress printer in Edinburgh until he retired to Loanhead, where he died in 1946.

Jack BAIRD (3/2, 1876-80)
John Campbell Baird
Born 27 July 1856 Bonhill, Dunbartonshire
Died 4 March 1902 Craigandro, Renton, Dunbartonshire
Scotland v England 1876, 1880 (1); Wales 1878 (1)
Vale of Leven 1872-81 (Scottish Cup 1877, 1878, 1879).
A founder member of Vale of Leven, along with his brother James (1855-1928), Baird partnered John McDougall on the left wing in the triumphant Vale team that won the Scottish Cup three times in succession. He won his first Scotland cap against England aged just 19, and later scored in both his other two internationals. For a while, Vale of Leven took over the mantle of Queen's Park, who they defeated in the Scottish Cup in December 1876, the first time QP had lost to any Scottish club. This opened the door to the final against Rangers, which went to two replays, with Baird scoring one of the

goals in the decisive third match. In 1878, having retained the trophy by beating Third Lanark in the final, Vale went to London to play the FA Cup winners Wanderers and had a comfortable 3-1 victory. Their third final in 1879 against Rangers was drawn 1-1, and when their opponents refused to replay the SFA awarded the cup to Vale. In commemoration of their feat, a loving cup was commissioned and now sits in the Scottish Football Museum. Baird eventually gave up playing in 1881 but remained closely involved with the club and was an enthusiastic participant when the Vale former players held their annual gatherings on Loch Lomond from the 1890s. A yarn buyer for the United Turkey Red dye works, he died of pneumonia in 1902, aged 45, and the streets of Alexandria were packed for his funeral procession, with the coffin carried by six of his old team mates.

Willie BAIRD (1/0, 1897)
William Urquhart Baird
Born 1 October 1874 Meadowbank, Edinburgh
Died 21 February 1943 Mount Vernon Hospital, New York, USA
Scotland v Ireland 1897.
St Bernard's 1891-99; Rangers Feb-Mar 1899; Dundee 1899-1901; St Bernard's Aug-Oct 1901.
Brought up in Edinburgh, Baird broke into the St Bernard's first eleven towards the end of 1891 as a 17-year-old and soon became an integral part of the team at centre half. He was with Saints as they entered the Scottish League in 1893 and was still only 20 when appointed club captain the following summer. However, he was unlucky enough to miss Saints' famous Scottish Cup victory in 1895 through injury but still appeared in the traditional winners' team photo wearing a suit. He was dropped from the side in 1898, the year he was a founder of the Scottish branch of the Players' Union, and early the following year he had a short-term transfer to Rangers. Next, he made a permanent move to Dundee, where he switched to right back. After two seasons he made a brief return to Saints in the autumn of 1901 before retiring from the game. A plumber and gasfitter in Edinburgh, he then emigrated to the USA and spent the rest of his life in Yonkers, in New York State, where he worked as a delivery driver and an accountant, and kept up his involvement in football as President of Yonkers FC.

Alick BARBOUR (1/1, 1885)
Alexander Barbour
Born 7 June 1862 William Street, Dennystown, Dumbarton
Died 29 December 1930 Main Street, Bonhill, Dunbartonshire
Scotland v Ireland 1885 (1).
Renton 1883-85 (Scottish Cup 1885); Our Boys (Dundee) Jan-May 1885; Renton 1885-87; Our Boys (Dundee) 1887-88; Bolton Wanderers 1888-1889; Nelson Dec 1889-90; Bolton Wanderers 1890-91; Glossop North End 1891-92; Nottingham Forest 1892-93; Renton 1893-94.
A speedy inside right who could also play on the left, Barbour combined his knowledge of the game as a pioneering trainer and tactician. Having grown up in the football hotbed of Renton, he played for the local club and was in the team which won the Scottish Cup in 1885. Oddly enough at this stage he was working in Dundee and playing for Our Boys, but agreed to return to Renton for cup ties, including the final. Back home that summer he was appointed club captain, as Renton reached another Scottish Cup final and won the prestigious Glasgow Charity Cup in 1886 and 1887. During this time Renton were heavily defeated by Preston North End, which prompted Barbour to approach Preston captain Jimmy Ross to ask him to explain in detail their system of play. Armed with this knowledge, Barbour is said to have introduced a new tactical approach to Scotland which he first put into practice in Dundee, where he spent a year as player/trainer of Our Boys. He then went south in 1888 to Bolton as a professional, but in December 1889 he was reported to have left Bolton Wanderers to join Nelson, on the grounds that he felt he was not good enough to play league football week after week. His fellow Bolton players presented him with a gold horseshoe pin as a farewell thank-you, but it was only a brief parting as he returned to the club the following summer as coach and trainer. He had such a fine reputation as a fair and honest player, that when he was sent off while playing for Bolton against Accrington in an FA Cup tie, the FA accepted his plea of innocence and took no further action. He had a season each at Glossop and Nottingham Forest before coming home to Renton in 1893, and even after he retired he continued his connection as a referee. Throughout his playing career he worked in cloth dye works, and returned to his trade full time when his football days were over.

John BARKER (2/5, 1893-94)
John Bell Barker
Born 28 June 1869 Govan Road, Govan, Glasgow
Died 29 June 1941 Nimmo Drive, Govan, Glasgow
Scotland v Wales 1893 (3), 1894 (2).
Linthouse 1888-92; Rangers Feb 1892-96 (Scottish Cup 1894); Linthouse 1896-1900.
A reliable scorer from the left wing, Barker won the Scottish Alliance title with Linthouse in 1891/92 and was selected to represent Glasgow. He was clearly capable of better things so when the small Govan club failed in its application to join the Scottish League, he moved over to near-neighbours Rangers. At Ibrox, he fitted in well and helped Rangers to win the Scottish Cup for the first time in 1894, scoring the second goal in their 3-1 win over Celtic. He also won the Glasgow Cup in each of his first two seasons at Ibrox. He was capped twice for Scotland, scoring a hat-trick on his debut against Wales in 1893, and two more against the same opponents the following year, but despite that remarkable record was not chosen again. However, he did make two appearances for the Scottish League, against the English in 1894 and the Irish the following year. After four years at Rangers, his old clubmates persuaded him to return to Linthouse, which by now had achieved its aim of a Scottish League place, but had just finished in bottom position. He was clearly still in good form as he was selected once more for Glasgow late in 1897. He retired in 1899 and remained on the Linthouse committee, even playing a couple of times in an emergency, before the struggling club disbanded a year later. A draughtsman, he worked in the Govan shipyards for many years.

Frank BARRETT (2/0, 1894-95)
Francis Barrett
Born 2 August 1872 Nelson Street, Dundee
Died 17 August 1907 Jamaica Street, Dundee
Scotland v Ireland 1894; Wales 1895.
Johnstone Athletic 1888-89; Dundee Harp 1889-93; Dundee Dec 1893-96; Newton Heath 1896-1900; New Brighton Tower 1900-01; Arbroath Aug-Sep 1901; Manchester City Sep 1901-02; Dundee Wanderers Oct-Nov 1902; Dundee Nov 1902-03; Aberdeen 1903-05.

Goalkeeper of many clubs, Barrett spent the early part of his career in his native Dundee, winning two Scotland caps and featuring in the Dundee team which reached the Scottish Cup semi-final for the first time in 1895. The following season he moved south and played over 100 second division matches for Newton Heath in his four seasons there, helping the club to a top four finish each year. Nearby rivals New Brighton Tower signed him in 1900 but despite finishing high in the second division the club went out of business in the summer of 1901. Without a club, he came home to Scotland where a brief spell at Arbroath put him in the shop window and before long Manchester City signed him as a back-up for the season. Finally he had the opportunity to play in the First Division, but he only appeared five times as City were relegated and he was released. Back in Scotland, he had short associations with two Dundee clubs before he moved north and played in Aberdeen's first match in 1903. Sadly, the following year his health declined and he was forced to give up the game. Aberdeen played a benefit match for him in 1906 but the following summer he died at home in Dundee, aged just 35. Manchester United did not forget his contribution and sent a cheque to his widow.

Barney BATTLES (3/0, 1901)
Bernard Battles
Born 13 January 1875 Centre Street, Springburn, Glasgow
Died 9 February 1905 London Road, Gallowgate, Glasgow
Scotland v Ireland 1901; Wales 1901; England 1901.
Linlithgow Juniors; Bathgate Rovers; Bathgate Shamrock; Bathgate 1893-94; Heart of Midlothian 1894-95 (Scottish League 1895); Celtic 1895-97 (Scottish League 1896) [loan to Liverpool Mar 1896]; Dundee 1897-98; Liverpool Mar-Oct 1898; Celtic Oct 1898-1904 (Scottish Cup 1899, 1900); Kilmarnock 1904-05.

Born in Springburn, Battles lived in Durham and Ayrshire as a boy depending on where his miner father was working, before settling in Bathgate. He spent several years down the pit himself, before his football skills gave him an escape route. His muscular build combined with athleticism and commitment made him a fearsome defender, and he starred for a variety of local sides before he made the step up to Hearts in 1894. His first season as a professional earned a Scottish League title, and he was persuaded to join Celtic where he promptly repeated that success. However, while he was a hero to the fans, his personality put him at odds with the club. Loaned to Liverpool for a match in March 1896 after the league was won, he fell out with Celtic in October that year after refusing to play (along with two others), was suspended, and ended up being transferred to Dundee. He had a longer spell at Liverpool in 1898 but Celtic realised they needed him back after a disastrous start to their season and he reappeared at Celtic Park in October 1898. His presence galvanised the team which went on a lengthy winning run, and although this was too late for the league race, they nevertheless won the Scottish Cup and retained it in 1900. Belated international recognition came the following year, when he was chosen for all three Scotland matches and he played one of his greatest games in the 2-2 draw with England at Crystal Palace. His form was intermittent, however, and having fallen out of the picture at Celtic in 1904 he moved on to Kilmarnock. Despite apparently having several years ahead of him, he went down with flu after playing at Ibrox, which then developed into a fatal bout of pneumonia, and he died just after his 30th birthday. His funeral attracted huge crowds, and Battles was held in such high regard by Celtic that when Scotland played Ireland at Celtic Park in March 1905, they donated their share of the gate receipts to his pregnant widow. His son was born eight months later, named in his honour, and also went on to play for Scotland.

Barney BATTLES junior (1/1, 1930)
Bernard Joseph Battles
Born 12 October 1905 North High Street, Musselburgh, Midlothian
Died 15 November 1979 Belmont Road, Juniper Green, Edinburgh
Scotland v Wales 1930 (1).
Boston Celtics 1924; Boston Soccer Club 1925-28; Heart of Midlothian 1928-34 and 1935-36.

Battles is one of only four men to have been capped by another country as well as Scotland, thanks to an unusual pedigree and upbringing. He inherited his skill and his name from a father he never knew, the Celtic and Scotland defender who died eight months before the youngster was born. Although schooled in Edinburgh, as a teenager he emigrated with his mother to the USA and started his adult life there. After catching the eye with a local side, in 1925 he signed for Boston in the American Soccer League, a team known as the 'wonder workers', managed by the former Rangers player Tommy Muirhead. Battles soon made his mark as a precocious goalscoring talent and aged only 19 was selected at outside right for the USA against Canada in Montreal, a 1-0 defeat. When the fledgling game in America hit financial problems in 1928, Battles returned to Scotland to sign for Hearts, where he was an instant success. He not only set a new club scoring record in his first season, he made himself particularly popular at Tynecastle for his knack of scoring against Hibs: in one memorable month, a series of local cup matches saw him hit no fewer than 11 against their Edinburgh rivals. He set a new mark as Scotland's top scorer in 1930-31 with 44 league goals, still the Hearts record, yet he was given few opportunities to shine on the international stage at a time when Scotland could choose from great strikers such as Hughie Gallacher and Jimmy McGrory. Battles won just one full cap for Scotland in 1930, scoring the equaliser against Wales in a 1-1 draw, but was more successful for the Scottish League, with 13 goals in five appearances. His career was curtailed by a loss of form brought about by a persistent knee injury which forced him to give up the game for a season, and then definitively in 1936. He trained as a masseur, with an extensive practice in Edinburgh, then after the War he worked as a sports journalist for the *Sunday Chronicle* and *Evening Dispatch*, and ran the Boatie Row Tavern in his native Newhaven.

Bobby BAXTER (3/0, 1938-39)
Robert Denholm Baxter
Born 23 January 1911 Ravenscroft Place, Gilmerton, Edinburgh
Died 5 April 1991 Pine Lodge, Middleton St George, County Durham
Scotland v Wales 1938; Hungary 1938; England 1939c.
Musselburgh Bruntonians; Middlesbrough 1931-45 [loan to Heart of Midlothian 1939-40; Hibernian 1940-45]; Heart of Midlothian 1945-47.

In 1931, Baxter went straight from junior football to Middlesbrough, where he became known as a cool and calculating player who would always try to distribute the ball with intelligence. Although his main position was centre half, he could play almost anywhere. Middlesbrough improved as the 1930s progressed and by 1938-39 they finished fourth. Baxter had been knocking on the door of the Scotland team for some time and that season he eventually won three caps, being appointed captain against England in the last of them. Sadly, the War interrupted his career and he returned home to Edinburgh to work as a miner. Not surprisingly, the city clubs wanted him and he was snapped up by Hearts in October 1939 but after a season was persuaded to join rivals Hibs, where he spent five years, notably scoring the winning goal in the Summer Cup final in 1941. In wartime he was selected four times for Scotland, the last against England in 1944. Middlesbrough recalled him in 194, only to sell him back to Hearts, who appointed him captain. He started coaching the Hearts reserve side in 1947, assisting David McLean with the administration of the business, and gave up playing in 1948 to become manager of Leith Athletic. Unusually, his role covered not just the football team at Old Meadowbank but also the speedway outfit which was based there. He resigned in 1950 and after a year out of the game was appointed manager of Cowdenbeath. The first couple of seasons were reasonably promising, then Cowdenbeath came close to dropping into the obscurity of Division C and he resigned in February 1955. He fell back on the newsagent and tobacconist shop in Edinburgh which he had bought in 1945, and was an accomplished golfer and a breeder of spaniels. His son Bobby played for Darlington, Brighton and Torquay.

Andy BEATTIE (7/0, 1937-38)
Andrew Beattie
Born 11 August 1913 Park Street, Woodside, Aberdeen
Died 20 September 1983 West Bridgford, Nottinghamshire
Scotland v England 1937, 1938; Austria 1937; Czechoslovakia May 1937; Ireland 1938; Wales 1938; Hungary 1938.
Inverurie Locos; Preston North End Mar 1935-47 (FA Cup 1938) [guest for Aldershot 1939-41, Derby County 1939-40 and 42-43, Notts County 1939-41, Northampton Town Mar 1941; Aberdeen Jan 1942, May 1942, Apr 1943].

A stylish left back, noted for astute tackling and a cool head, Beattie spent his entire playing career with Preston North End, yet he was associated with a large number of clubs during his long life in football. He was a late starter in the professional game, having moved from Aberdeenshire junior football to Preston when he was already 22. Making up for lost time, within a couple of years he made his Scotland debut against England in 1937, and by the end of 1938 he had amassed seven caps and won the FA Cup. He was at his peak when war intervened and although he played for Preston when he could get away, winning the Football League War Cup in 1941, he turned out on loan for a variety of clubs around the country including Aberdeen when home on leave. He won five wartime caps for Scotland, including two rare victories over England. Army service took him to North Africa, where he was a Company Sergeant Major with the Physical Training Corps, in charge of a remedial exercise unit, and he captained the 8th Army football team. He gave up playing in 1947 to embark on a long and distinguished career in management, starting with Barrow. He then he managed Stockport County 1949-52, Huddersfield Town 1952-56 (where his assistant was Bill Shankly), Carlisle United 1958-60 (simultaneously running a post office in Preston), Nottingham Forest 1960-63, Plymouth Argyle 1963-64, Wolverhampton Wanderers 1964-65 and Notts County 1965-67. He was briefly manager of the Scotland team in 1954 and took them to the World Cup finals in Switzerland but resigned during the tournament in frustration at the lack of SFA support. Somewhat surprisingly, he was appointed again to the Scotland job in March 1959 on a part-time basis until October 1960 when he was appointed at Nottingham Forest. As well as his managerial success, he could spot talent and among his great discoveries was Denis Law for Huddersfield, while later he put Liverpool on the trail of Kevin Keegan. He also scouted for Brentford, Wolves, Walsall and his last job was chief scout at Notts County, near his home in West Bridgford. He died there in 1983.

Bobby BEATTIE (1/0, 1938)
Robert Beattie
Born 24 January 1916 Limekiln Road, Stevenston, Ayrshire
Died 21 September 2002 Crosshouse Hospital, Kilmarnock, Ayrshire
Scotland v Wales 1938.
Kilwinning Rangers; Kilmarnock 1933-37; Preston North End Oct 1937-55 (FA Cup 1938, Second Division 1951) [guest for Northampton Town 1940-42, Everton Apr 1943, Blackpool 1942-44, Liverpool 1943-44]; Wigan Athletic 1955-56.

Beattie won two Scotland junior caps with Kilwinning in 1933, after which he was immediately signed by Kilmarnock who gave him his first team debut aged 17. A clever inside forward, he was watched by several English clubs before Preston took him south and he joined his namesake, Andy Beattie. Although not related, the Beatties made a fine combination and not only won the FA Cup in 1938, they both played against Wales that autumn, when Bobby was one of four debutants. Perhaps one of the finest technical players of his generation, the War intervened before his cap tally could increase. During his service for the RAF, he bounced around a number of clubs, playing for Preston when he could, notably when he scored the goals that won the League War Cup final for them in 1942, although later he was based in Germany. He returned to action with the club early in 1946, and while many thought his career would be finished when Preston were relegated in 1949, they valued his masterly ball control and he made a major contribution to their Second Division title win two years later. He was finally released in 1955 and spent a season playing for Wigan Athletic, also coaching their reserves, before he retired aged 40. He later returned to Ayrshire where he coached junior side Ardeer Recreation, and lived in Stevenston until his death in 2002.

Isaac BEGBIE (4/0, 1890-94)
Isaac Begbie
Born 4 June 1868 Tynecastle Road, Gorgie, Edinburgh
Died 30 September 1958 City Hospital, Greenbank Drive, Edinburgh
Scotland v Ireland 1890; England 1891, 1894; Wales 1892.
Pentland; Western; Dalry Albert; Heart of Midlothian 1888-1900 (Scottish League 1895, 1897; Scottish Cup 1891, 1896) [guest for St Bernard's Aug 1892]; Leith Athletic 1900-01; Bathgate Jan-May 1902; Falkirk Nov 1902-03.

Born within a free-kick of Tynecastle Park, the son of a pig dealer, there was little surprise that Begbie should make his name with Hearts having shown promise as a right half with local juvenile teams. He joined the club in 1888 and was elected captain in 1892 (in a competitive vote), going on to be a mainstay of the superb team that won the Scottish Cup and League twice each in the 1890s. However, his national team appearances were limited to just four caps, two of them against England; he was also selected v Ireland in 1895 but had to withdraw through illness. He played once for the Scottish League in 1893. Off the field he had a calm personality and a reputation as happy-go-lucky, but on the pitch he was totally committed and one newspaper remarked 'he is so intent on play that he has never been known to smile during its progress', adding that 'he knocks people down like an auctioneer'. Sometimes he went in too hard, and was suspended for two months in January 1899 for rough play against Rangers. His career was interrupted for several months in September 1896 when he was badly injured after being hit by a cyclist on the running track inside Tynecastle. At the end of his career he had a season at Leith Athletic and brief spells at Bathgate and Falkirk before hanging up his boots. For many years he ran a dairy shop in Gorgie, not far from the Hearts ground in Edinburgh, and had just turned 90 when he died in 1958.

Alex BELL (1/0, 1912)
Alexander Bell
Born 20 October 1882 Cape Town, South Africa
Died 30 November 1934 Brundretts Road, Chorlton-cum-Hardy, Manchester
Scotland v Ireland 1912.
Westerlea; Ayr Parkhouse 1900-03; Manchester United Jan 1903-13 (Football League 1908, 1911, FA Cup 1909); Blackburn Rovers 1913-15.

Born in Cape Town to Scottish parents, Bell's family returned to Ayr when he was a small boy and he grew up in the town. While training as a joiner he played football for local sides and then at centre half for Ayr Parkhouse, with whom he won the Ayrshire Cup in 1902. During the following season, after a few games at centre forward, he was signed by Manchester United, who paid him a £10 fee plus £4 a week. At Old Trafford he became part of one of the club's finest half-back lines, Duckworth Roberts and Bell (Charlie Roberts later named a range of cigars 'Ducrobel' in the trio's honour). His successes there included two league titles in 1908 and 1911, with the FA Cup in 1909, and although he was mooted for a cap for several years his colonial birthplace told against him until the Scottish FA finally selected him in 1912. He left United the following year after a disagreement about a second benefit and signed for Blackburn Rovers, reportedly for a £700 fee, but failed to win a regular first team spot there. He resumed his trade as a joiner and retired from football on the outbreak of war, serving in Salonika with the Royal Army Ordnance Corps during the conflict. Although he was reported to have signed for Ayr United on a free transfer as late as 1920 there is no record of him playing for the team. He was appointed trainer of Coventry City in 1922, then of Manchester City from 1925 until his death aged 52. His son William played for Coventry City and Chester.

Jack BELL (10/5, 1890-1900)
John Watson Bell
Born 6 October 1868 Ewing's Land, Church Street, Dumbarton
Died 12 April 1956 Birket Square, Leasowe, Cheshire
Scotland v Ireland 1890, 1899 (1); England 1892 (1), 1896 (1), 1897, 1898, 1899, 1900 (1); Wales 1899, 1900 (1).

Dumbarton Union; Dumbarton 1887-93 (Scottish League 1891, 1892); Everton Mar 1893-98; Celtic 1898-1900 (Scottish Cup 1899, 1900); New Brighton Tower Nov 1900-01; Everton 1901-03; Preston North End 1903-08 (Second Division 1904).

Bell established a fine reputation at Dumbarton as a flying winger and won the first two of his ten Scotland caps, as well as two Scottish League titles. He was nearly lost to the game in 1893 when he finished his engineering apprenticeship with Denny & Co and was offered the chance to work in Rangoon, Burma. However, he changed his mind when Everton offered a substantial inducement to turn professional and he moved to Merseyside instead. His five years at Everton confirmed his talent, but the closest he came to honours was the FA Cup final of 1897, which was lost to Aston Villa despite his fine personal performance. Meanwhile, he helped to establish the Players' Union and was elected chairman. He resumed his international career in 1896 when Scotland began picking players with English clubs, scoring what turned out to be the winning goal against England. He continued to be named in the team to face England each year up to 1900, and meanwhile returned to Scottish football with Celtic in 1898. At the peak of his form, he barely missed a match over two seasons at Parkhead, which reaped two Scottish Cup final victories over Rangers and Queen's Park. In the summer of 1900, shortly after scoring once more against England in the 'Rosebery International', he went back to Liverpool to open a cycle dealership in the appropriately named Scotland Road. It took a few months to negotiate his release from Celtic and in the meantime he turned out for New Brighton Tower until he could sign at Everton. Now in his thirties, he still had several years left in him and after two seasons at Goodison Park he helped Preston win the Second Division title and remained with them in the top division for four more years. He was nearly 40 when he retired in 1908, and Preston gave him a benefit match against Blackburn Rovers. He emigrated to Canada in 1911 but returned in the summer of 1914 and was immediately appointed coach of Preston North End. After an interruption for the War, he resumed the role in 1919 then left to focus on his cycle business, remaining on Merseyside for the rest of his life.

Mark BELL (1/0, 1901)
Mark Dickson Bell
Born 8 February 1881 Leslie Place, Stockbridge, Edinburgh
Died 22 October 1961 Greenbank Drive, Morningside, Edinburgh
Scotland v Wales 1901.
Rosebery; St Bernard's 1898-1900; Heart of Midlothian Nov 1900-02 (Scottish Cup 1901); Southampton 1902-03 (Southern League 1903); Heart of Midlothian 1903-04; Fulham 1904-07 (Southern League 1906); Clapton Orient 1907-10; Leyton 1910-12; Gillingham 1912-13; Fulham 1914-16.

A man of many clubs, Bell started out as a forward, but half-way through his career he was asked to play centre-half at Fulham, and was transformed into a half-back for the rest of his playing days. From Edinburgh juvenile club Rosebery he made his bow in senior football with St Bernard's and after a couple of years he joined Hearts in November 1900. Within a few months he was capped for Scotland against Wales, and then he set up the winner in a thrilling Scottish Cup final as Hearts beat Celtic 4-3 to take his first major club honour. A year later he was part of an exodus to Southampton, winning the Southern League title in his only season there, then came home for another year at Tynecastle. Next time he moved south, in 1904, it was permanent and he spent the rest of his playing career in the south east. At Fulham he won a second Southern League title, and subsequently he played with Clapton Orient, Leyton and finally Gillingham. In January 1909 he travelled home to Edinburgh on hearing his father had died, only to find on arrival that his mother had died the same day from shock. He emigrated to Australia in September 1913 with his family but returned on the outbreak of war to join the Royal Army Medical Corps, and while he was in London resumed playing for Fulham. After the conflict he settled back in Edinburgh and worked on the railways as a porter.

Alec BENNETT (11/2, 1904-13)
Alexander Bennett
Born 20 September 1881 Lizzieville Place, Rutherglen, Lanarkshire
Died 9 January 1940 Victoria Infirmary, Glasgow
Scotland v Wales 1904, 1908 (1), 1909, 1910, 1911; Ireland 1907, 1909, 1913 (1); England 1909, 1910, 1911.
Rutherglen Woodburn; Rutherglen Glencairn [trial for Heart of Midlothian Apr 1903]; Celtic Apr 1903-08 (Scottish League 1905, 1906, 1907, 1908; Scottish Cup 1907, 1908); Rangers 1908-19 (Scottish League 1911, 1912, 1913) [loan to Ayr United Dec 1917]; Dumbarton Mar 1919-20; Albion Rovers 1920-21.

Brought up in Rutherglen, Bennett progressed through local football with such success that he had won the Scottish Junior Cup and four Scotland caps at Glencairn before senior sides cottoned on to his abilities. He signed for Celtic in 1903, having impressed against them in a trial for Hearts, and was soon in the first team, where he enjoyed five glorious years at outside right. There were four consecutive league titles, the latter two coinciding with Scottish Cup victories, and he won his first three Scotland caps. As a confirmed favourite with Celtic, it was a major shock when he made the highly unusual move to Rangers in 1908 and he spent a decade with the Ibrox side, winning a further eight caps and three more league championships. He was still a regular player during the War when he signed up in 1916 and saw active service in France with the Highland Light Infantry, reaching the rank of Second Lieutenant. When he returned he was allowed to leave Rangers and spent a year each at Dumbarton and Albion Rovers before retiring just before he turned 40. He was appointed manager of Third Lanark in 1921 but left after three years of low table finishes, then had some success with Clydebank by taking them to promotion in 1925. He left them the following year and afterwards worked as a journalist. He lived in Glasgow's Pollokshaws Road and died relatively young aged 58 of lung cancer.

Bob BENNIE (3/0, 1925-26)
Robert Hunter Brown Bennie
Born 26 March 1900 Limerigg, Stirlingshire
Died 27 July 1972 Law Hospital, Carluke, Lanarkshire
Scotland v Wales Feb 1925; Ireland 1925, 1926.
Parkhead Juniors; Third Lanark 1917-20; Airdrieonians Dec 1920-28 (Scottish Cup 1924); Heart of Midlothian 1928-33; Raith Rovers Oct 1933-34.
Right or left half, creative and intelligent, Bennie came from a football family, with several uncles playing professionally. He was born in Limerigg where his father was a miner, and spent almost all his life in nearby Airdrie, where he soon showed he had inherited the football genes. After winning the Airdrie Schools Cup four times with Albert School by the age of 14, he moved on to Airdrie Academy. Then, when he left school in 1916 he had a season with Parkhead before signing for Third Lanark. Despite his youth he slotted straight into the first team, initially as an inside forward before finding his best position at half-back. His home town club came calling and he duly arrived at Broomfield in December 1920 in an exchange deal for Alex Reid. It was to prove an inspired signing for Airdrie as in his time there the club won its only major honour, the Scottish Cup of 1924, and were consistently good enough to be runners-up in the Scottish League for four consecutive seasons. He was rewarded with international recognition, appearing twice for Scotland in 1925, and was much sought after by English clubs but Airdrie resisted the temptation to sell. By the time he was allowed to leave in 1928 Bennie had played over 300 matches and was club captain for his last three years. He was transferred to Hearts and was clearly still at the top of his game, selected for the Scottish League against the English that autumn. Then as age caught up with him he retired from playing in the summer of 1933 and was appointed manager of Raith Rovers in October, but found the team so short of quality players that he had to register himself and played one more match. His management was not a success and he resigned after just a year in charge, to be succeeded by another internationalist, Sandy Alexander. He returned to live Airdrie and was a faithful member of Airdrie Bowling Club.

'Dyke' BERRY (3/2, 1894-99)
Davidson Berry
Born 27 May 1875 Grange Terrace, Cathcart, Glasgow
Died 26 November 1952 Trefoil Avenue, Shawlands, Glasgow
Scotland v Wales 1894 (1), 1899; Ireland 1899 (1).
Queen's Park 1892-99; Scottish Amateurs 1897-1900.
Born a stone's throw from Hampden Park, Berry was a stylish and graceful inside forward who followed his elder brother Willie (below) to Queen's Park. He soon had an opportunity to demonstrate his promise as he made his competitive debut in the Scottish Cup semi-final of 1893, aged 17, but although he scored twice against Broxburn Shamrock, he lost his place to William Sellar for the final. There was no denying his precocious talent, however, and he was still only 18 when he made a scoring international debut for Scotland against Wales the following year. Further honours had to wait until 1899, when he played against both Wales and Ireland as well as winning that season's Glasgow Cup. That summer he decided to step back from regular action, probably the consequence of a leg injury, and offered to play for QP only in an emergency. He was lost to the game too soon although he continued to make occasional appearances for the Scottish Amateurs club. Meanwhile he focussed on golf and had a single figure handicap, featuring in tournaments around the country for many years as a member of Pollok GC, where he was elected Captain in 1927. He worked for Glasgow Corporation in the Electricity Department.

Willie BERRY (4/0, 1888-91)
William Hall Berry
Born 20 August 1867 Great Hamilton Street, Calton, Glasgow
Died 5 February 1919 Queensborough Gardens, Hyndland, Glasgow
Scotland v England 1888, 1889, 1890, 1891.
Rawcliffe; Queen's Park 1886-99 (Scottish Cup 1890); Scottish Amateurs 1897-1900.
Lightly built with 'twinkling feet', Berry was an effective centre forward who preferred accuracy to brute force and scored many goals by placing the ball out of reach of the goalkeeper. The elder brother of Dyke (above), his international debut was a disaster, losing 5-0 to England, yet he retained his place for the following year's encounter which Scotland won 3-2, and for the following two years. He also played in the unofficial match against Canada in 1891. Meanwhile he won the Scottish Cup with Queen's

Park in 1890, and the Glasgow Cup twice, in 1889 and 1890. He stopped appearing regularly for the first team in 1893, preferring instead to play occasionally for the QP Strollers and then after 1897 for the Scottish Amateurs touring side, but was called back for a couple of games in 1898 in a time of need. He was a member of the Queen's Park committee. He worked in Glasgow for the business set up by his father, Thomas Berry & Co, wholesale umbrella, bag and portmanteau manufacturers and was only 51 when he died after a short illness.

Willie BEVERIDGE (3/1, 1879-80)
Rev. William Wightman Beveridge TD
Born 27 November 1858 Barrhill, Cumnock, Ayrshire
Died 26 January 1941 Sir Michael Street Church, Greenock, Renfrewshire
Scotland v England 1879; Wales 1879, 1880 (1).
Ayr Academy; Glasgow University 1875-79; Edinburgh University 1879-81.

The son of a solicitor, Beveridge was educated in that hotbed of football talent, Ayr Academy. A hugely talented all-round athlete, he developed his sporting abilities at Glasgow University while studying for the ministry and in addition to winning his three caps for Scotland, he was Scottish sprint champion for three years in succession. Indeed he dominated athletic events around the country and from 1879-81 he won the national titles at 100 yards and the quarter mile, winning outright the Athole Challenge Cup sprint trophy. In 1879 he had moved to Edinburgh to study at the United Presbyterian Theological College, and played football for the university there as well as for Scotch Counties before scoring a goal on his final Scotland appearance. However, on qualifying for the ministry in 1881 he promptly gave up all competitive sport and focused on his vocation. He was a great loss to Scottish sport, but at least he wrote a fascinating chapter about the early days of Scottish football in NL Jackson's book *Association Football* (1900). For over 50 years he was minister of Princes Street Church in Port Glasgow and had a long association with the volunteer movement and the Territorial Army. In 1911 he received the Territorial Decoration and was promoted to the rank of Colonel, in which capacity he saw service during WW1, being sent to the front line in France in 1915 as senior chaplain to the Imperial Forces. He was a strong advocate of temperance and in 1906 published a pamphlet *The Athlete and Alcohol: a Message for Young Men* which was translated into several languages. He collapsed and died suddenly while taking a service at Sir Michael Street Church in Greenock, near his home.

Andy BLACK (3/3, 1937-38)
Andrew Black
Born 23 September 1917 Abbey Road Dairy, Stirling
Died 16 October 1989 Bannockburn Hospital, Stirling
Scotland v Czechoslovakia Dec 1937 (1); Netherlands 1938 (1); Hungary 1938 (1).
Strathallan Hawthorn; Shawfield Juniors; Heart of Midlothian Mar 1934-46 [guest for King's Park Oct 1939-40; Portsmouth 1940-42; Grimsby Town 1942-43; Crewe Alexandra 1943-44; Aldershot 1943-44; Liverpool Jan 1944; Chester Apr 1944-Dec 1945]; Manchester City 1946-50; Stockport County 1950-53.

A prolific scorer from the inside left role, Black achieved some remarkable feats, scoring over a goal a game for Hearts in 1937-38 including five hat-tricks, while at Manchester City he headed a goal from outside the box against Charlton to complete another hat-trick in 1947. However, like so many players, his career was interrupted by wartime and he could have achieved so much more. He grew up in Stirling where he played for Bridge of Allan juvenile side Strathallan Hawthorn, and had less than a season with Shawfield Juniors before Hearts took him to Edinburgh as a 16-year-old in 1934. He did not make his first team debut for over a year, but soon showed what he could offer, sufficient for Portsmouth's offer of £6,000 to be turned down when he was just 19. He came into the international reckoning and scored in the first minute of his Scotland debut, going on to find the net in all three of his caps, all of which came against continental opposition. He also scored three goals in two Scottish League selections. When war broke out he returned to Stirling where he played for local side King's Park until the end of the season, then joined the Army. As a Sergeant Instructor in physical training, he played wherever he was posted, with occasional appearances for Hearts when he came home on leave. While on his travels he had two seasons with Portsmouth, reaching the War Cup final in 1942, and won the Portsmouth United Services Challenge Cup in 1940 with HMS Vernon. Late in 1942 he was posted north and turned out for a variety of sides, including services selects, concluding with a successful spell at Chester. He also made three wartime appearances for Scotland against England, as well as a couple of tour matches in Belgium in 1945. With the conflict over, Hearts sold him to Manchester City in the summer of 1946, and he continued to shine at the top level in England for several seasons. He ended his career at Stockport, where he coached the team, and for a while he ran the Tatton Arms pub in Manchester. He then moved back to his home town of Stirling where he lived in Cowane Street and worked as an ordnance storeman.

Davie BLACK (1/1, 1889)
David Gibson Black
Born 22 January 1870 Riccarton, Ayrshire
Died 14 December 1951 Red Cross Street, Wolverhampton, Staffordshire
Scotland v Ireland 1889 (1).
Hurlford 1887-89; Grimsby Town 1889-91; Middlesbrough 1891-93; Wolverhampton Wanderers 1893-96; Burnley Dec 1896-97; Tottenham Hotspur 1897-98.

A tricky inside left, Black was one of the smallest players ever to represent Scotland, reported to be just 5 feet 4 inches and was accordingly known as 'Wee Davie'. Born into a coal-mining family, his mother died when he was an infant and he was brought up by his grandmother. He escaped a life down the pit through his football talents, and his career got off to a flyer when he was selected for Ayrshire in 1888, then won the Ayrshire Cup with Hurlford in February 1889. A month later he scored for Scotland on his debut against Ireland, just a few weeks after his 19th birthday. That early success was a springboard to a professional contract at Grimsby where there was already a colony of Scots including former internationalist Jimmy Lundie. To supplement his football income he worked as a fish packer. After two years he transferred to Middlesbrough, then in 1893 stepped up to Wolves, the first time he played in the Football League. The highlight was reaching the FA Cup final of 1896, in which he scored Wolves' equaliser but ultimately the game was lost to Sheffield Wednesday. While in Wolverhampton he married a publican's daughter and together they ran the Crown Inn there, but after a court case when they were both accused of being drunk and disorderly, he was sold to Burnley. Six months later he moved to London with Spurs, where despite scoring regularly he decided to retire after a season to come back to Scotland. In the summer of 1898 he was reported to have spent his savings of £3,000 to buy the Bridge Hotel in Irvine, and he also took over the Irvine football club. However, the venture did not work out and within two years he had sold the hotel. He and his wife Lizzie returned to Wolverhampton where he worked for the Corporation Tramways.

John BLACKBURN (1/0, 1873)
Colonel John Edward Blackburn CB
Born 30 April 1851 Great Stuart Street, Edinburgh
Died 29 September 1927 Ashley Gardens, Westminster, London
Scotland v England 1873.
Royal Military Academy 1869-71; Royal Engineers 1871-77.

Blackburn came through the public school system with an education at Edinburgh Academy, Glenalmond, Eton and Wimbledon School, all of which placed a premium on sport although their interpretation of football rules varied considerably. In 1869 he entered the Royal Military Academy at Woolwich, which had a long tradition of football dating back to the 1850s, and he carried on playing the game when he was commissioned in the Royal Engineers in 1871. Generally playing on the right of the forward line, Lieutenant Blackburn's abilities in the RE team earned him a cap on the Scotland team's first visit to London in 1873. He also played in the FA Cup final of 1874 which the Engineers lost to Oxford University and remained a regular in the team until 1877. A career soldier, he served with the Royal Engineers at home and abroad over a long career which included the battle of Tel-el-Kebir in 1882 during the Egyptian campaign. He rose to the rank of Colonel, retired in 1908, and was made a Companion of the Order of the Bath in 1915. He died in London but his body was returned to Edinburgh for burial and his headstone is in the Dean Cemetery.

Danny BLAIR (8/0, 1928-32)
Daniel Blair
Born 2 February 1905 Salamanca Street, Camlachie, Glasgow
Died 5 August 1985 Fluke Hall Lane, Pilling, Lancashire
Scotland v Wales 1928, 1931, 1932; Ireland 1929, Sep 1931; England 1931; Austria 1931c, Italy 1931.
Toronto Scottish; Toronto Willys-Overland; Davonport Albion; Providence Clamdiggers 1924-25; Parkhead Juniors Aug-Nov 1925; Clyde Nov 1925-31; Aston Villa Nov 1931-36; Blackpool 1936-43 [guest for Southport 1941-43].

After leaving school in Glasgow, Blair went to Canada where he enjoyed an early career with various Toronto clubs, then turned professional in the USA with Providence Clamdiggers in Rhode Island. He was still only 20 when he returned to Scotland in 1925. He had a few months with Parkhead, breaking his collar bone early in the season before representing the Glasgow Junior League, then joined Clyde in November. He was quickly recognised as an excellent full back and was invited on the Scottish FA tour of North America in 1927, which clearly impressed the selectors as he went on to win eight Scotland caps over the next four years. The highlight was the 2-0 victory of an all-Tartan eleven over England in 1931, but this was followed by a number of set-backs: he captained the side for a 5-0 defeat to Italy, and his final cap was the humiliating 5-2 home defeat to Wales in 1932. He also earned three selections for the Scottish League, and was due to play against the Football League in November 1931 but was transferred to Aston Villa a couple of days before the match. It was a substantial deal worth a five figure sum, as he signed together with Clyde half back William Simpson, but although Blair was part of the Villa team which was runner-up in the league in 1933, much of his time at Villa Park was not a great success and he regularly spent time in the reserves. He was eventually offloaded when they were relegated in 1936, moving to Blackpool where he was made club captain and helped them to an immediate promotion to Division One. He last played for the club in 1940, although he was a wartime guest for two seasons with Southport before finally retiring in 1943. He continued to live in Blackpool, where he worked for the Post Office and coached the youth team.

Jimmy BLAIR (8/0, 1920-24)
James Blair
Born 11 May 1888 Shankramuir, Cadder, Lanarkshire
Died 28 February 1964 Watersmeet Road, Sheffield, Yorkshire
Scotland v Ireland 1920, 1923c; England 1920, 1921, 1922c, 1923; Wales 1923, 1924c.

Bonnybridge Thistle; Ashfield 1906-08 [trial for Falkirk Jan 1908]; Clyde 1908-14; Sheffield Wednesday 1914-20 [guest for Clydebank 1915-16; Rangers 1916-19 (Scottish League 1918); Alloa Athletic Aug-Oct 1919]; Cardiff City Nov 1920-26; Bournemouth & Boscombe Athletic Dec 1926-28.

An uncompromising left back who was no stranger to the SFA disciplinary code, Blair was in demand at Ashfield after being selected a couple of times for the Glasgow junior select in 1908, and chose to sign for Clyde that summer. He grew in stature in his six years at Shawfield, helping them to reach the Scottish Cup finals of 1910 and 1912, both lost, and showed his speed and versatility by sometimes featuring at centre forward. There were regular rumours of a move down south, before he was finally transferred to Sheffield Wednesday just before the War for a fee reported to be £2,000. He had little opportunity to prove his worth as his debut was delayed due to a motorcycle accident, he missed six weeks through illness and then fractured a cheekbone. In 1915 he came back to Glasgow to work in a munitions factory and played as a guest for Clydebank, winning the Dunbartonshire Cup, and then had three years at Rangers, picking up a league medal in 1918. He returned to Sheffield late in 1919 after a few months at Alloa, but could not settle and went to Cardiff the following year for a fee of £4,250. By then he had finally won his first full cap for Scotland, aged 31, and it had been a long time coming as he had played in several international trials and made three appearances for the Scottish League starting in 1911, not to mention three Victory Internationals. His experience was invaluable to the national team and he captained Scotland three times, including a memorable win against England in 1922. His final cap came in 1924 at the age of 35 against Wales in Cardiff, his club stadium, and ended in defeat. He played for Cardiff in the FA Cup final of 1925 and was released the following summer but had one last club as he moved to Bournemouth and retired in 1928 aged 40. He remained in Cardiff for many years and ran the Ninian Park Hotel, then the Red Dragon Inn in Cowbridge, near the city, until 1949. His son Jimmy played for Blackpool and was capped by Scotland in 1946.

Johnny BLAIR (1/0, 1933)
John Blair
Born 3 September 1911 Harriet Street, Pollokshaws, Renfrewshire
Died 15 August 1976 MacDonald Crescent, Clydebank, Dunbartonshire
Scotland v Wales 1933.
Yoker Athletic; Motherwell 1931-44; Morton 1944-45; Clapton Orient 1945-46.

A centre half with excellent passing skills and a decent turn of speed, Blair joined Motherwell in the summer of 1931 from Yoker Athletic. He only played four games in Motherwell's title-winning season, but went on to become a legendary figure at the club through the rest of the decade, making a total of 275 league and cup appearances, including the Scottish Cup finals of 1933 and 1939, although both were lost. He was capped just once by Scotland in 1933, a defeat to Wales, and played twice for the Scottish League, both against the Irish League. As club captain, he was renowned for his tactical organisation which included a well-regimented offside trap, and he was still considered to be in the mix for international honours when war broke out. He served as special constable in Clydebank during the conflict, which was a harrowing experience during the blitz of 1941. His involvement in football was limited and when he moved to an aircraft factory a couple of years later he announced he was giving up football entirely due to the long hours. However, he was brought back into the game by Morton in the summer of 1944, and wound up his career with a handful of games for Clapton Orient in 1945, where he also coached. His nephew Charlie Cox played for Hearts and Motherwell.

Willie BLAIR (1/0, 1896)
William Blair
Born 6 December 1870 Pottery Lands, Greenock, Renfrewshire
Died 21 November 1947 Divert Road, Gourock, Renfrewshire
Scotland v Wales 1896.
Morton 1889-91; Third Lanark 1891-97; Morton 1897-1901.
Brought up in Greenock, where he played for Morton, Blair was an excellent left half despite lacking in stature. He moved to Third Lanark in 1891 and played the best of his football in Glasgow over six seasons at Cathkin. Described in the *Scottish Referee* as 'one of the steadiest and ablest players that ever donned a Third Lanark jersey' he was regularly touted as a possible internationalist but was only

selected once for Scotland, against Wales in 1896, shortly after turning down a Scottish League cap due to club commitments. He returned to his home town team in 1897, reverting to amateur status for a while before Morton made him a professional again to deter other clubs signing him. He was appointed captain and played his last game in 1901. A fishmonger to trade, he spent the rest of his life on the Clyde coast.

Jimmy BLESSINGTON (4/1, 1894-96)
James Blessington
Born 28 February 1874 High Street, Linlithgow, West Lothian
Died 18 April 1939 Torbay Hospital, Torquay, Devon
Scotland v Ireland 1894, 1896 (1); England 1894, 1896.
Harp Athletic; Hibernian 1890-91; Leith Hibernians Feb-May 1891; Leith Athletic 1891-92; St Bernard's Aug 1892; Celtic 1892-98 (Scottish League 1893, 1894, 1896); Preston North End Feb 1898-99; Derby County Jun-Oct 1899; Bristol City Oct 1899-1900; Luton Town 1900-03; Leicester Fosse 1903-09 player-manager.

An inside right, Blessington had a brief connection with the original Hibs club before it foundered on financial difficulties, then threw in his lot with Leith Athletic. He partnered Bob Clements and Matt McQueen in the team which beat Hearts in the Rosebery Cup final of 1892 but the club lost almost all its players that summer, with Blessington himself moving to Celtic. He was still only 18. He had a highly successful six seasons in Glasgow, winning three league titles for his club and took part in the Scottish Cup final defeats of 1893 and 1894, while winning the Charity Cup twice and the Glasgow Cup once. These contributed to a reputed 42 gold medals won during his career. There were also four Scotland caps, never on the losing side, and he played five times for the Scottish League. Early in 1898 he went on loan to Preston, and was such a hit that he remained in England for the rest of his career. After short spells with Preston, Derby and Bristol he had three fine seasons with Luton Town in the Southern League, and a long swansong with Leicester Fosse, which culminated in his first foray into management. He left the club when they were relegated in 1909 and moved to Belfast, where continued to take up coaching posts, including appointments with Cliftonville and Belfast Celtic; he also coached Louth in the Gaelic football All-Ireland final. He was about to take up a position in Germany when war broke out and during WW1 he served in the mercantile marine on the cargo ship *Cassandra*, carrying supplies across the Atlantic. In 1921 he was appointed manager of Abertillery Town but resigned after four months to run the Victoria Hotel in St Peter Port, Guernsey, where he coached the island side to success in the Muratti Cup. Later he was a licensee for 12 years at the Bradley Hotel in Newton Abbot, and died after a long illness in Torbay Hospital in 1939.

Jimmy BOWIE (2/0, 1920)
James Bowie
Born 9 July 1888 Gardner Street, Partick, Lanarkshire
Died 7 August 1972 Broomhill Drive, Thornwood, Glasgow
Scotland v Ireland 1920; England 1920.
Rockbank; Maryhill Juniors; Queen's Park 1908-10; Rangers Dec 1910-22 (Scottish League 1912, 1913, 1918, 1920, 1921).

Inside right or inside left, occasionally a half-back, Bowie was an influential and creative player who was deceptively slight but could handle himself physically. He was capped for Glasgow Schools and started out with a juvenile side in Partick before playing junior with Maryhill. In 1908 he embarked on two and a half years at Queen's Park, during which time he was selected for Glasgow against Sheffield, and turned professional with Rangers in December 1910. As a key member of the dominant Rangers side which won several league titles, he was selected four times for the Scottish League by 1915, but had to wait until the War was over for more representative honours. He played in three Victory internationals in 1919, then finally at the age of 31 he won two full Scotland caps in 1920, the latter being the mud-spattered 5-4 defeat to England at Sheffield. He later said he regretted never winning the Scottish Cup during the long Rangers 'hoodoo' and recalled being off the field for treatment when Partick Thistle scored the only goal of the 1921 final. After retiring in 1922 he became a director of Rangers from 1924 and later served as chairman until he was deposed in a boardroom split in 1947. He was also a member of the SFA international selection committee and President of the Scottish Football League from 1939 until he left Rangers.

William BOWIE (1/0, 1891)
William Bowie
Born 31 December 1869 Harmony Row, Govan, Glasgow
Died 9 June 1934 Southern General Hospital, Govan, Glasgow
Scotland v Ireland 1891.
Linthouse 1888-91; Clyde 1891-93; Accrington Jan-Apr 1893; Clyde 1893-97; Linthouse Mar 1897-98.

Bowie became Linthouse's only internationalist in 1891 when he was selected at centre forward for Scotland against Ireland. Unfortunately he was injured in the first half which saw him hobbling for the rest of the game, and not surprisingly he did not score in a narrow 2-1 victory. That summer he joined Clyde, which had just entered the Scottish League, and played in their first match at centre half, the position he retained for the rest of his playing career. He went south early in 1893 and experienced the English first division with Accrington, then when they were relegated after losing a test match he came back to Scotland and resumed with Clyde. In 1897 he returned to his first club Linthouse, which had just been elected to the Scottish League, but injuries and illness the next season brought a premature end to his football days. Bowie reportedly stood over six feet tall and although somewhat ponderous in his movements, his size and weight often gave him an advantage over smaller opponents. He spent all his working life in Govan, where he was a ship plater, and died there in 1934. He is buried in Cardonald Cemetery.

Geordie BOWMAN (1/0, 1892)
George Alexander Bowman
Born 27 June 1872 Melville Lane, Montrose, Angus
Died 13 July 1942 Killin Golf Club, Killin, Perthshire
Scotland v Ireland 1892.
Belmont; Montrose 1890-93; Third Lanark 1893-97; Montrose 1897-1900 [loan to Third Lanark Oct 1897, Oct 1898]; Dundee 1900-01; Montrose 1901-05.

A robust right back, Bowman was one of two Montrose players capped in the same match (the other was Sandy Keiller), called up after the Renton contingent of Hannah, McColl, McCall and Lindsay all refused to play. Montrose had a fine team at the time, having just won the Forfarshire Cup, and Bowman had already represented Forfarshire several times, so a solid performance in an international trial was enough to clinch his surprise selection aged 19. A strong tackler and a sound passer of the ball, the following year he turned professional with Third Lanark and had four good years in Glasgow before returning to Montrose in the summer of 1897. He had made occasional appearances in the interim, and by the time he came back for good his stature was such that he was appointed captain not just of the club, but of the county team. He also played sporadic games for Thirds when they needed him. In 1900, he joined Dundee and although he played in the reserves his season was a success as he won the Forfarshire Cup and the Dewar Shield. After a year Montrose came calling yet again and he combined playing with his election as club President, an unusual combination yet a successful one as Montrose won the Northern League in 1903-04. His younger brothers Alex and Charles were also useful players with Montrose around that time. Bowman had served an apprenticeship as a printer with the Montrose Review, and followed his trade when he moved to Glasgow, where his home was in Knightswood. He was on holiday in Killin and playing golf when he collapsed and died on the tenth green.

Jimmy BOYD (1/0, 1933)
James Murray Boyd
Born 29 April 1907 Keppochhill Road, Petershill, Glasgow
Died 23 March 1991 Marlborough Road, Bournemouth, Hampshire
Scotland v Ireland 1933.
Petershill; St Bernard's Oct 1924-25; Newcastle United 1925-35 (FA Cup 1932); Derby County 1935-37; Bury Jan-Sep 1937; Dundee Sep 1937-38; Grimsby Town 1938-44 [guest for St Mirren Nov 1939; Morton Aug 1941; Hamilton Academical Nov-Dec 1941; Clapton Orient Jan-Feb 1944; Brighton and Hove Albion 1944].

Boyd joined Newcastle as a raw 18-year-old from Edinburgh second division side St Bernard's, and took some time to establish himself as a first team regular: in their title-winning season of 1926-27, for example, he only played twice. Once he settled in he was a consistent scorer from outside right and spent a fruitful decade on Tyneside, the highlight being a famous FA Cup win in 1932. Unfortunately his only Scotland cap was a woeful home defeat to Ireland in 1933, and he was not selected again. In 1935 he moved to Derby County, and despite a scoring debut in an all-Scottish forward line, it was not a long association as he embarked on a whirlwind tour of the country with four clubs in four years before war intervened. That effectively ended his senior career and while he did make sporadic appearances for Grimsby Town during the War, and for some Scottish clubs as a guest, opportunities were few and far between and he gave up playing at the end of 1941. However, he made a brief return to action in 1944 with Clapton Orient, alongside his international namesake Billy Boyd, and also at Brighton. He was appointed as a coach at Grimsby in 1946 after being demobbed from the Army, then coached for a couple of years in Sweden before returning to Glasgow to work as a PE instructor for the city council. He kept involved in football as a Scottish scout for Newcastle and later for Middlesbrough. He retired to Bournemouth and left an estate worth £115,000 when he died aged 83.

Bobby BOYD (2/2, 1889-91)
Robert Boyd
Born 2 July 1867 Waddell's Land, Whifflet, Lanarkshire
Died 11 August 1930 Front Street, Mossend, West Lothian
Scotland v Ireland 1889; Wales 1891 (2).
Mossend Swifts 1886-92 [guest for St Bernard's Aug 1887; Heart of Midlothian Mar 1890, Mar 1891]; Third Lanark 1892-93; Mossend Swifts 1893-94; Leith Athletic 1894-96; Mossend Swifts 1896-99.

When Mossend joined the Scottish FA in 1886, Boyd was already part of the team, and he grew in stature as the team prospered and the local shale industry boomed. After representing the East of Scotland, in 1889 he was the first Mossend player to be capped for the full national side, playing on the left wing against Ireland. Two years later, he earned his second Scotland cap, albeit as a late call-up in place of Richardson of Hurlford. This time he partnered Sandy Keiller of Montrose on the left, and scored twice in a 4-3 win, in each case dispossessing Wales goalkeeper Trainer. He played a handful of tour matches for Hearts in England, and in the summer of 1891 he signed for Middlesbrough then had a rapid change of heart and disappeared without playing a game; he later had to return his signing fee of £11 5 shillings. He might have remained with Mossend but when the slump in shale oil came in 1892, the club disbanded and the key players left. Boyd spent a season at Third Lanark, then returned home when his local team started up again. He also had a couple of years at Leith Athletic, who lost their place in the First Division in 1895, and concluded his playing career back in Mossend. He lived in the village all his life while working in the West Lothian shale mines.

Willie BOYD (2/1, 1931)
William Gillespie Boyd
Born 27 November 1906 Sauchiebog, Cambuslang, Lanarkshire
Died 14 December 1967 Royal Infirmary, Bristol, Gloucestershire

Scotland v Italy 1931; Switzerland 1931 (1).
Regent Star; Larkhall Thistle 1927-30; Clyde Dec 1930-33; Sheffield United Dec 1933-35; Manchester United Feb-Sep 1935; Workington Sep-Dec 1935; Luton Town Dec 1935-36; Southampton 1936-37; Weymouth 1937-38; Workington 1938-39; Nuneaton Borough 1939-40; Clapton Orient Jan-Feb 1944.

Boyd made quite an impact as a centre forward with Larkhall Thistle, where he scored over 200 goals in three years. This persuaded Clyde to sign him in December 1930, just after his 24th birthday, and his first few months as a professional were so impressive that he ended the season with a call-up to the national team. On Scotland's continental tour of 1931 he was perhaps fortunate to miss the opening 5-0 thrashing from Austria and he made his two appearances in the remaining matches, which included a goal against Switzerland. That was the end of his international career but he was selected three times for the Scottish League as he continued to score regularly for Clyde, setting a club record of 32 in 1932/33. After much speculation about a move to England, a fine performance for Glasgow in Sheffield sealed a transfer to Sheffield United in December 1933. Despite scoring 15 times for them by the end of the season, including a memorable hat-trick against city rivals Wednesday, he could not save them from relegation and moved on to Manchester United early in 1935. However, he struggled to maintain his form at Old Trafford after scoring four goals in six games and when he was released in the autumn he signed for Workington in the North Eastern League and had a few months at Luton Town. Things really started to unravel after he joined Southampton in the summer of 1936. They terminated his contract midway through the season for taking unsanctioned leave and he was then prosecuted for non-payment of tax. He dropped into non-league football down the coast at Weymouth, but was clearly distracted by a troubled personal life, which hit the newspapers in March 1938 when he was fined for failing to pay maintenance to his wife and family. In court he was disparaged as 'a cause of trouble to the Public Assistance Department for several years' with his downfall due to 'drink and bad company'. He went back to Workington (where his full-back was another Scotland internationalist, Bob MacAulay) and finally to Nuneaton Borough just before War broke out. He served with the Royal Artillery, making a couple of appearances for Clapton Orient while stationed in London, and after the War he settled in Bristol.

Tom BRADSHAW (1/0, 1928)
Thomas Bradshaw
Born 7 February 1904 Hatton, Bishopton, Renfrewshire
Died 22 February 1986 Monklands Hospital, Coatbridge, Lanarkshire
Scotland v England 1928.
Woodside Juveniles; Bury 1922-30; Liverpool Jan 1930-38; South Liverpool Sep 1938; Third Lanark Sep 1938-39; South Liverpool 1939-40.

One cap for Scotland, but what a cap! Centre half of the Wembley Wizards, Bradshaw had all the attributes for a half-back: tall enough to be known as 'Tiny', strong and remarkably agile, described by one observer as having 'the build of Ron Yeats and the touch of Alan Hansen'. He was a thoughtful player who could distribute the ball with accuracy, and would sometimes venture upfield to score some useful goals. There is a story that he was not a regular footballer as a youth and was spotted kicking a ball about on rough ground by Bury manager WS 'Kilty' Cameron. He was so impressed by Bradshaw's size and raw talent that he offered him a contract on the spot, and when the boy reportedly responded 'But I don't know how to play football!' he had to be persuaded to give it a try. In fact, contemporary reports reveal he joined Bury from Woodside, a Coatbridge juvenile side, and had already had a trial with Hamilton Accies. After a year learning his trade in the reserves, his first full season was a success as Bury won promotion to the First Division. He was a fixture in their side for the rest of the decade, notably as Bury had their highest ever league finish, fourth place in 1925-26. Conversely, he missed the first half of 1929 with knee trouble, and without him Bury were relegated. He recovered to play as well as ever and Liverpool paid £8,000 for him in January 1930. He became club captain at Anfield and although a dip in form saw him lose his place in the team, he fought back to become first choice again. When his powers started to decline Liverpool let him go, initially to near neighbours South Liverpool but after one match he left to join Third Lanark. At the end of the season he made the return journey and had just re-signed for South Liverpool, in the Lancashire Combination, when war broke out. He joined the RAF and continued to play occasional services football, then after the War he coached in Holland for a couple of years and was later appointed chief scout for Norwich City. A keen cricketer, he played for Motherwell in his summer holidays. He returned to Scotland and lived in Coatbridge, and was the last surviving member of the Wembley Wizards when he died in 1986, aged 82.

Tom BRANDON (1/0, 1896)
William Thomas Brandon
Born 3 October 1867 Glengarnock, Kilbirnie, Ayrshire
Died 24 November 1941 Keir Street, Edinburgh
Scotland v England 1896.
Clippens; Johnstone 1885-86; Port Glasgow Athletic 1886-87; St Mirren 1887-89; Blackburn Rovers 1889-91 (FA Cup 1891); Sheffield Wednesday 1891-93; Nelson Aug-Dec 1893; Blackburn Rovers Dec 1893-1900; St Mirren Sep 1900-01.

A powerful full back, Brandon was born near Kilbirnie and although registered as William he was known throughout his life as Tom. His family moved when he was very young to Kilbarchan in Renfrewshire, where he started his football career with local clubs Johnstone, Port Glasgow Athletic and St Mirren where he played alongside his elder brothers Robert (1860-1950) and James (1865-1942). They all later played professionally at Sheffield Wednesday, as did their cousin Harry. Tom was recognised as a talent early on and was selected several times for Renfrewshire from 1887, also winning the Renfrewshire Cup with St Mirren in 1888. He was considered the finest full back in Scotland when he was signed by Blackburn Rovers in 1889, who spent freely that summer to attract the best. Their investment paid off as Rovers won the FA Cup in 1890 but Brandon was discovered to be ineligible under the rules of the time, and after playing in every other game that season he had to be dropped for the semi-final and final. However, he did win a medal in 1891 when Rovers retained the cup, beating Notts County in the final, and was selected for the Football League against the Football Alliance. By then, he had signed a controversial pre-contract agreement to move to Sheffield Wednesday, and part of the deal was him taking over the Woodman Inn. He returned to Blackburn in September to get married to Elizabeth Duckworth, whose sister had already married fellow internationalist George Dewar. Appointed club captain, he fulfilled two years with Wednesday then wanted to return to Blackburn in 1893 but his club refused to grant him a transfer, as they were entitled to do under Football League regulations. As a way out of the impasse he signed for Nelson, in the Lancashire League, until Wednesday caved in and took a fee for his transfer to Rovers in December – one of the earliest examples of a transfer fee, with the amount widely quoted (and then denied) as £150. He made his international debut in 1896 when the SFA finally ended its policy of selecting only Scottish-based players, and Brandon was one of several to feature against England. Although he did well, it turned out to be his only cap. That summer he hit the headlines for the wrong reasons, as he was charged with persistent cruelty to his wife, who appeared in the witness box with a black eye and was duly granted a separation order and a weekly maintenance payment. He played his last match for Blackburn in March 1900 and returned to St Mirren that autumn. Within a month he was back in court, charged with arrears on maintenance for his wife and was sent to prison for one month with the option to settle the arrears. He chose the latter, made his last appearance for Saints in January 1901 and left the country. He was soon reported to be living in Rhode Island, USA, but later returned to Scotland to go back to work as a coal miner, and lived in Edinburgh with his new partner and her family until his death in 1941. He is buried in the city's Warriston Cemetery. His son Tommy (William Thomas Brandon 1893-1956) was a footballer for Blackburn Rovers, West Ham, Bristol Rovers, Hull City and Bradford.

Thomas BRECKENRIDGE (1/1, 1888)
Thomas Breckenridge
Born 26 February 1865 Catherine Street, Edinburgh
Died 3 May 1898 Cadzow Place, Edinburgh
Scotland v Ireland 1888 (1).
Heart of Midlothian 1884-88; Leith Athletic 1888-89.
A left winger, Breckenridge joined Hearts as a young man and got into the first team in time to win the Rosebery Charity Cup in June 1886, a rare triumph at a time when Hearts were struggling generally and were overshadowed by their Edinburgh rivals. In his time at the club, he played for Edinburgh several times and won his only cap against Ireland in 1888, scoring one of the goals in a crushing 10-2 victory in Belfast. He was a shining light for Hearts on and off the pitch, and was one of a trio of internationalists at Tynecastle, along with Tom Jenkinson and Jimmy Adams. In 1888 he moved over to Leith Athletic for a brief spell before hanging up his boots to conclude a short career. A bookbinder, he died after a long illness, during which there was a public appeal for funds to help him while he was unable to work. He was only 33, and was buried at Warriston Cemetery. NB throughout his career his surname was consistently mis-spelled Brackenridge or Brackenbridge by the Edinburgh newspapers.

Barney BRESLIN (1/0, 1897)
Bernard Breslin
Born 2 May 1874 Carfin, Lanarkshire
Died 10 November 1913 Main Street, Harthill, Lanarkshire
Scotland v Wales 1897.
Carfin Shamrock; Hibernian 1893-1906 (Second Division 1894, 1895; Scottish Cup 1902; Scottish League 1903) [trial for Celtic Jan 1899].

A gifted right half, Breslin was spotted by Hibs at Carfin Shamrock and moved east in September 1893, remaining loyal to the Edinburgh club throughout his career. Not the quickest of players he had a keen football brain and according to the *Scottish Referee* 'what he lacks in this respect he amply atones for with his energetic tackling and the judgement he displays in placing the ball to his forwards'. His first task was to get Hibs out of the Second Division, and after winning it twice in a row they were granted promotion in 1895. After winning his Scotland cap in 1897, and making the first of four appearances for the Scottish League, he had numerous offers to go elsewhere and was even given a trial at Celtic early in 1899. However, they signed Harry Marshall from Hearts instead, which was a blessing in disguise for Breslin as he went on to captain the Hibs side which won the Scottish Cup and the Glasgow Charity Cup in 1902, then the Scottish League title the following season. In December 1902, with the championship already in the bag, he broke his arm in two places while playing against St Bernard's, which kept him out for nine months. He returned to action and continued to play until retiring in 1906. He was one of five Breslin brothers who all played football, although Barney was the stand-out. Originally from a coal-mining family, in 1899 he invested his money in the Athletic Bar in Fauldhouse and ran it for several years before selling up and moving to Harthill, where he was working as a barman when he died of tuberculosis, aged 39. NB His surname at birth was recorded phonetically as 'Bracelan'.

'Dod' BREWSTER (1/0, 1921)
George Brewster MM
Born 7 October 1891 Auchmacoy, Kirkton of Logie Buchan, Aberdeenshire
Died 23 November 1964 Chorley Street, Ince, Lancashire
Scotland v England 1921.
Mugiemoss; Aberdeen Feb 1913-20; Everton Jan 1920-22; Wolverhampton Wanderers Nov 1922-23; Wallasey United 1923-24; Brooklyn Wanderers Mar-Jun 1924; Inverness Caledonian 1924-31.

A strapping centre half standing over six feet tall, Brewster quickly established himself in the Aberdeen side after joining from local junior team Mugiemoss early in 1913. However, his career was interrupted by the War, and when Aberdeen closed down in 1917 he signed up to fight, seeing active service in France as a Sapper with the Royal Engineers; he was awarded the Military Medal in 1918. When he returned to Aberdeen he had half a season before Everton came up with a club record fee of £2,400 to take him to Goodison Park. In 1921 he won his only international cap in the 3-0 win over England at Hampden, but the following year his form took a dip and Everton narrowly avoided relegation. With no sign of improvement he was sold to Wolves, who were engaged in a fruitless fight against relegation to the Third Division, and he was deemed so ineffective that within four months he was placed on their transfer list. Wolves wanted their money back and demanded a hefty fee which deterred potential purchasers, so Brewster felt he had no option but to drop out of league football altogether. He signed for Wallasey United, who were struggling in the Cheshire County League, so he accepted an offer to cross the Atlantic and spent a few months playing for and training Brooklyn. When his visa expired he was sent home and took up an offer from Inverness Caledonian, who appointed him player-manager and found him a job in a local woollen mill. He remained with the club for six years, did some scouting for Liverpool, and ultimately he and his family came back to Merseyside, where he spent the rest of his life until his death in 1964.

Sandy BROWN (1/0, 1904)
Alexander Brown
Born 21 December 1877 Glenbuck, Ayrshire
Died 6 March 1944 Granity, South Island, New Zealand
Scotland v England 1904.
Glenbuck; Kilsyth Wanderers 1894-95; St Bernard's 1895-96; Preston North End 1896-99; Portsmouth 1899-1900; Tottenham Hotspur 1900-02 (FA Cup 1901); Portsmouth 1902-03; Middlesbrough 1903-05; Luton Town 1905-07.

Born as Alexander White, his mother married William Brown six months later and he took his father's surname. After a few appearances with Glenbuck and Kilsyth Wanderers, he came to Edinburgh as a 17-year-old to join Scottish Cup holders St Bernard's, and scored on his debut in August 1895. A successful season at centre forward brought offers from England and he chose Preston, where he spent three years without really hitting the high spots. When a new professional club was founded in Portsmouth in 1899 he was persuaded to move to the south coast along with a number of seasoned players from around the country and they had an excellent first season as Portsmouth finished runners-up in the Southern League. The title was won by Tottenham, who promptly persuaded Brown to join them and it was an inspired decision as he scored in every round of their triumphant FA Cup campaign in 1901, including two in the drawn final against Sheffield United and another in the replay. One unlikely consequence was that he brought the cup home to Glenbuck where it went on display in a shop window. The following year he was selected for Scotland against England, but his international debut turned out to be the Ibrox Disaster match, subsequently declared unofficial, and as he was injured when the teams met again the following month he missed out on a cap. That summer he went back to Portsmouth for a single season, then returned to the Football League with Middlesbrough for a couple of years, and it was during this period that he was finally capped by Scotland in 1904. His final club was Luton Town, where he also managed the Dewdrop Inn for a while. After retiring from football he returned home to Glenbuck where he worked as a miner and played for the village quoiting team. On the outbreak of WW1 he signed up to the Cameronian Highlanders and was injured on active service in France in 1916, losing the use of his left arm, but he continued in the regiment as a staff sergeant. He emigrated to New Zealand in 1922 and remained there until his death. His younger brother Thomas played for several clubs including Leicester and Portsmouth.

Andy BROWN (2/0, 1890-91)
Andrew Campbell Brown
Born 2 September 1865 Wallace Street, Paisley, Renfrewshire
Died 26 September 1904 Victoria Park, Brookfield, Renfrewshire
Scotland v Wales 1890, 1891.
Westmarch; St Mirren 1883-96.
A versatile player who could feature at centre forward or centre half, Brown was part of a famous St Mirren eleven that included several internationalists: John Patrick, David Crawford, Dick Hunter, Eddie McBain and James Dunlop. Stepping up from St Mirren's reserve team, Westmarch, in

1883 he showed early signs of talent and represented Renfrewshire as an 18-year-old on the left wing. He then moved to centre forward before stepping back to centre half on the introduction of the three half-back system, and that was the position where he was twice capped against Wales, in 1890 and 1891. After his first international he was criticised by *Scottish Referee* as 'dull and dilatory' although the same paper noted in 1894 that he had been 'very shabbily treated by the SFA' by not giving him more honours. He has an unusual claim to fame as one of football's first substitutes, coming on for the injured Wylie in the Scottish League game against the Irish League in 1893. He was made a life member of St Mirren when he retired in 1896, but sadly his life was cut short as he contracted tuberculosis and died aged 39 after a lengthy illness, leaving a wife and young family. He worked as a clerk in a local carpet factory.

George BROWN (19/0, 1930-38)
George Clark Phillips Brown, MA Hons.
Born 7 January 1907 Alexander Street, Partick, Glasgow
Died 3 June 1988 Western Infirmary, Glasgow
Scotland v Wales 1930, 1931, 1934, 1935, 1936, 1937; Ireland Sep 1931, 1936; England 1932, 1933, 1935, 1936, 1937, 1938c; Austria 1933; German 1936; Czechoslovakia May 1937, Dec 1937; Netherlands 1938c.
Strathallan Hawthorn; Glasgow University 1924-26; Ashfield 1926-29; Rangers 1929-42 (Scottish League 1930, 1931, 1933, 1934, 1935, 1937, 1939; Scottish Cup 1932, 1934, 1935, 1936).

Brown played on the left side of a superb half-back line in the Rangers side of the 1930s, which dominated Scottish football by winning numerous league titles and Scottish Cups. However, he had started out at inside right with the Ibrox club when he joined them from Ashfield in 1929 and scored six goals in his first seven games, including a late winner against Celtic as Rangers marched to the title. It was not until the following season that he moved to left half. He won his first cap in the autumn of 1930, going on to play in the majority of Scotland's games over the decade, culminating in him captaining his country to successive victories over England and Netherlands in 1938. He also played five times for the Scottish League and in one wartime international in 1941. When he retired in 1942 he was immediately invited to join the board of directors at Ibrox and remained a director until the 1970s. His late entry to senior football was due to his taking a degree at Glasgow University and he qualified as a teacher, and he went on to become principal teacher of English at Hamilton Crescent School and later headmaster of Bellahouston Academy when it opened in 1963. He was appointed in 1951 by Clement Attlee, the Prime Minister, as a member of the Royal Commission into marriage and divorce law.

Jock BROWN (1/0, 1938)
John Bell Brown
Born 21 February 1915 Templehill, Troon, Ayrshire
Died 30 August 2005 Biggart Hospital, Prestwick, Ayrshire
Scotland v Wales 1938.
Glenburn Rovers; Clyde 1934-42 (Scottish Cup 1939) [loan to Shawfield 1934-35; guest for St Mirren May 1940, Aberdeen Dec 1941, Hamilton Academical Oct 1942]; Hibernian Nov 1942-48 (Scottish League 1948) [guest for Gillingham Sep-Dec 1945, Airdrieonians Apr 1946]; Dundee Jan 1948-49; Kilmarnock 1949-50.

Dominant in the air for crosses and ahead of his time in narrowing the angle against a shot, Brown was a superb goalkeeper whose career spanned the Second World War. His peak came in 1938/39 when he was selected for Scotland and the Scottish League, then helped Clyde to win the Scottish Cup. Although the cup run was remarkable as he only conceded one goal, and that a penalty, he later said that his Scotland cap was the proudest day of his career. He was already a junior internationalist with Glenburn Rovers when he signed for Clyde in 1934, and when they sent him on a season's loan to Shawfield to gain more experience, he promptly won two more junior caps. After Clyde's cup triumph, war intervened and he made one wartime appearance for Scotland before joining the Royal Navy as a Physical Training Instructor, spending some of the War at the naval base in Freetown, Sierra Leone. He moved to Hibs in 1942, having lost his place in the Clyde team, and returned to play for the Edinburgh side whenever he could, also making occasional guest appearances for other teams, the highest profile being a League Cup semi-final for Airdrieonians in 1946. He played 11 times as Hibs won the Scottish League title in 1947/48, although he joined Dundee midway through the season. He was largely a reserve at Dens Park and his final senior appearance was for Kilmarnock in 1949 before he concentrated on his career as a physiotherapist. Initially he worked for the club but as a freelance he later assisted the All Blacks on their 1967 tour and was then appointed to the role with the Scottish Rugby Union. He remained in his home town of Troon, living in Academy Street, until his death aged 90. A scratch golfer, he came from a notable sporting family, as his brothers Tom and Jim were professional footballers, with Jim representing USA in the 1930 World Cup, while his sons Peter and Gordon were both Scotland rugby internationalists.

'Sparrow' BROWN (2/0, 1884)
Robert Brown
Born 1856 Dumbarton
Died 10 January 1904 Knoxland Square, Dumbarton
Scotland v Ireland 1884; Wales 1884.
Dumbarton 1878-85 (Scottish Cup 1883); Dumbarton Athletic 1885-87.

A right wing forward, Brown appeared in Dumbarton line-ups from 1878 but he was probably playing before then. Selected by Scotch Counties for the first time in 1881, he played in the Scottish Cup finals of 1881 and 1882, both lost to Queen's Park, before finally winning the Scottish Cup against Vale of Leven in 1883. He was capped the following year, making his Scotland debut in Ireland, a match played in a fierce storm which continued through the return journey and caused the boat to arrive in Glasgow several hours late. The last bus had gone and Brown had no option but to walk all the way back to Dumbarton together with Johnny Forbes. Thankfully he was selected for another cap a few weeks later against Wales. To distinguish him from his teammate of the same name, he was known as Sparrow as he 'flew' down the wing, or more formally as Brown No 1 or Brown senior. A journeyman engineer, he never married and died in his 40s. His precise age is uncertain as, although records indicate he was born in Dumbarton in 1856, his birth does not appear to have been registered.

'Plumber' BROWN (1/0, 1885)
Robert Brown
Born 11 February 1860 Main Street, Motherwell, Lanarkshire
Died 2 December 1940 Kenilworth Avenue, Dundee
Scotland v Wales 1885.
Dumbarton 1882-87 (Scottish Cup 1883).
A plumber in the shipyards, hence the nickname, he was known as Brown No 2 or Brown junior to avoid confusion with his club namesake. An attacking half back, he sometimes played inside forward in partnership with the other Brown, and both featured in Dumbarton's Scottish Cup winning side of 1883 in his first season with the club. He was selected for Scotch Counties and Dunbartonshire and was then considered for full international honours in 1885 but declined as he was too busy at work, on a secondment to London. However, when William Sellar was injured in the England match on Saturday, Brown responded to an urgent summons and travelled to Wrexham on the Monday to play against Wales, out of position on the right wing. Back home in Dumbarton he featured in another Scottish Cup final, lost to Hibernian in 1887, then gave up football when he married Eliza Brodie that summer. His club gave him a silver biscuit barrel as a wedding present, which was still in daily use 50 years later according to an interview he gave for his golden wedding. He moved to Dundee in 1906 to take up a job at Gourlay's Shipyard, then when it closed down a few months later he became foreman plumber with the Caledon yard and remained there until he retired in 1933. In WW1 his elder son, also Robert, was killed while his younger son Thomas was decorated with the Military Cross while with the Black Watch.

Bob BROWN (1/0, 1890)
Robert Neilson Brown
Born 19 August 1870 Lilybank Road, Tradeston, Glasgow
Died 17 August 1943 Fishpool House Hospital, Farnworth, Lancashire
Scotland v Wales 1890.
Blantyre Thistle; Cambuslang 1888-91; Sheffield Wednesday Nov 1891-94; Third Lanark 1894-95; Bolton Wanderers 1895-1902 [loan to Burnley Mar-Apr 1897].
An attack-minded player who was reputed to have played everywhere except in goal, Brown's favoured position was inside right. From junior football in Blantyre, he soon came to the fore at Cambuslang and won a cap against Wales aged 19. Sometimes known as 'Sparrow' like his internationalist namesake at Dumbarton in the previous decade, the following year he represented Glasgow in Sheffield and later in 1891 he turned professional with Sheffield Wednesday, at that time in the Football Alliance. He spent most of his career in England, with two seasons at Wednesday in the Football League, and was selected for the Midlands against the North in 1892. Described in the local press as 'one of the cleverest forwards Sheffield has ever seen', he returned for a year at Third Lanark before making a permanent move to Bolton in 1895. Having dropped back to centre half, he was loaned to Burnley at the end of 1896/97 for four appearances but could not save them from relegation. Towards the end of his time at Bolton he was used as an emergency stop-gap, for example in November 1901 when the club secretary failed to register a new signing in time, Brown stepped in at outside left. A pattern-maker in the textile industry, he spent the rest of his life in Bolton and was subsequently an insurance agent.

Johnny BROWNING (1/0, 1914)
John Browning
Born 29 November 1888 Doveholm, Bonhill Road, Dumbarton
Died 14 November 1964 Vale of Leven Hospital, Alexandria, Dunbartonshire
Scotland v Wales 1914.
Bonhill Hibernian; Mossfield Amateurs; Dumbarton Harp 1908-09; Vale of Leven Oct 1909-11; Dumbarton Harp 1911-12; Vale of Leven Aug-Oct 1912; Celtic Oct 1912-19 (Scottish Cup 1914, Scottish League 1914, 1915, 1916, 1917, 1919); Chelsea 1919-20; Vale of Leven Jun-Sep 1920; Dumbarton Sep 1920-22; Vale of Leven 1922-24.
A pacey left winger or inside left, Browning had a lengthy apprenticeship with local sides Dumbarton Harp and Vale of Leven, winning the Dunbartonshire Cup with the latter in 1911, before Celtic signed him in the autumn of 1912. He was already 23 when he made his debut for Celtic but soon made up for lost time and was almost ever-present for the next six years. He played a key role in four successive league titles and lifted the Scottish Cup in 1914, scoring twice in the final against Hibs. He was capped against Wales that year, a disappointing 0-0 draw, yet never had the opportunity to play for Scotland again because of the War. However, he did represent the Scottish League twice in the autumn of 1914 and played in various wartime representative matches. He drifted out of the Celtic team in 1918-19 and moved to Chelsea but his time there was curtailed by a serious knee injury which restricted him to just five appearances in a season. Returning to Scotland in 1920, he played out his career in the lower league until it came to a sad end. He was captain of Vale of Leven in 1924 when he was convicted of attempting to fix a match between Bo'ness and Lochgelly United and was duly jailed. On his release, with no future in Scottish football, he applied unsuccessfully to coach in Bavaria 1925 and remained in the Dumbarton area until his death. His son John played for Liverpool in the 1930s.

Jamie BROWNLIE (16/0, 1909-14)
James Brownlie
Born 15 May 1885 Broomhill, Blantyre, Lanarkshire
Died 29 December 1973 King's Cross Hospital, Dundee
Scotland v Ireland 1909, 1910, 1911, 1912, 1913, 1914; England 1909, 1910, 1912, 1913, 1914; Wales 1910, 1911, 1912, 1913, 1914.

Blantyre Victoria [trials for Partick Thistle, Heart of Midlothian, Celtic]; Third Lanark 1906-23 [guest for Morton Oct 1918-19]; Dundee United 1923-24 [emergency in Feb 1926].

One of the greatest goalkeepers of his era, Brownlie was already 21 and had been given trials by several clubs when he was signed by Third Lanark in 1906, shortly after winning a Scotland Junior cap with Blantyre. He became a club legend and remained at Cathkin for almost two decades, and while the team won no national honours he did win a Glasgow Cup medal in 1909 and enjoyed their adventurous tours to Spain in 1914 and North America in 1921. He even scored a couple of goals in league matches, both from the penalty spot and both against Motherwell. With Scotland, he was peerless and after he came into the national team in 1909 he missed just one game in six years before war intervened, also representing the Scottish League 14 times. In 1916 he joined the Army as a gunner in the Royal Field Artillery and saw active service in France during the last year of the War. On his return he played as a guest for Morton for a few months, then came back to the Third Lanark team where he showed he was still in fine form, and was selected for all four of Scotland's Victory internationals. He finally left Third Lanark in 1923 and moved to Dundee United who had just returned to the Second Division from a chastening season in the Scottish Alliance. A year later he hung up his boots in 1924 to focus on managing the team, very successfully too, winning the championship in his first season in charge. However, in 1926 he was forced to take the field one last time aged 40, picking himself as an emergency in a Scottish Cup replay against Hearts, letting in six goals. He had three distinct spells as manager at Tannadice before stepping down for good in 1939, and continued to live in Dundee until his death.

Dan BRUCE (1/0, 1890)
Daniel Rodger Bruce
Born 21 March 1868, Braehead, Bonhill, Dunbartonshire
Died 6 February 1931 Joint Fever Hospital, Dumbarton
Scotland v Wales 1890.
Bonhill; Vale of Leven 1888-92 [guest for St Bernard's Aug 1889]; Rangers Aug-Sep 1892; Notts County Sep 1892-95 (FA Cup 1894); Small Heath Nov 1895-96; Vale of Leven 1896-1902 [trial for St Mirren Nov 1897].
A speedy outside left with excellent ball control, Bruce packed a powerful shot. He grew up in the football hotbed of Bonhill, and when he joined Vale of Leven he formed a fine left wing partnership with James McMillan which reached its peak in 1890. In the Scottish Cup final that year he opened the scoring in the replay which gave great hope to Vale of Leven before Queen's Park came back to win. A month later, having scored a hat-trick in an international trial, he was duly capped against Wales, but despite a 5-0 win and a good performance it turned out to be his only appearance. After a brief spell at Rangers in which he scored five goals in four league matches, he turned professional with Notts County in 1892, where the highlight of three seasons was an FA Cup victory in 1894. He was impressive enough for Small Heath to expend a fee of around £100 for him in the autumn of 1895 but he did not settle in Birmingham and they let him go the following summer. With no offers from other clubs, he went back to Bonhill where Vale of Leven were now a shadow of their former selves, playing sporadic friendlies and cup ties. Having failed to impress in a trial for St Mirren he remained loyal to his old club, and was last reported playing for them in the Dunbartonshire and District League in 1902. He spent the rest of his life in the area and worked in the local cotton mills until his death from pneumonia aged 62. His younger brother Walter played for Vale of Leven, Renton and St Mirren, and was selected for the Scottish League.

Bobby BRUCE (1/0, 1933)
Robert Bruce
Born 20 January 1906 Blackhall Street, Paisley, Renfrewshire
Died 6 April 1978 Main Road, Elderslie, Renfrewshire
Scotland v Austria 1933.
St Anthony's; Aberdeen 1924-28; Middlesbrough Feb 1928-35 (Second Division 1929); Sheffield Wednesday Oct 1935-36; Ipswich Town 1936-38 (Southern League 1937); Mossley 1938-39 player-manager.
Born in Paisley where he started out in Boys Brigade football, Bruce was spotted while playing as a junior with St Anthony's in Govan, and became Pat Travers' first signing for Aberdeen. He made his debut at Pittodrie aged just 18 and although it took a couple of years to establish himself in the team he never looked back. On the small side at 5 feet 6 inches, he was fast and direct, could play at inside left or centre forward, and finished as top scorer in 1926-27. His continued good form induced Middlesbrough to pay £4,500 to take him south in February 1928, hoping that his goals would save them from relegation but they ended two points from safety. However, he soon proved himself on Teesside by helping the team to bounce right back and win the Second Division title in 1929, and maintained his scoring record in over 250 appearances as they retained their top league status. That consistency earned him his sole Scotland cap, a 2-2 draw with Austria in November 1933. He moved on in the autumn of 1935 to Sheffield Wednesday where he failed to make the mark, playing only five games before being released to join Ipswich Town, who had just entered the Southern League. They won it at the first attempt, and in 1938 were successful in winning election to the Football League but Bruce did not continue on their journey. Instead he tried his hand at coaching at Mossley, in the Cheshire League, but could only guide them to a mid-table position and was released in the summer of 1939. When war broke out he joined the RAF and continued to play football in the services, including a cup final in South Africa in 1942. After the conflict, having spent his playing career in far-flung locations, he returned to his home town of Paisley and worked as a labourer.

John BUCHANAN (1/0, 1889)
John Buchanan
Born 28 June 1866 Clyde Iron Works, Coatbridge, Lanarkshire
Died 22 September 1942 Stewarton Drive, Cambuslang, Lanarkshire
Scotland v Ireland 1889.
Cambuslang 1884-92 [guest for St Bernard's 1888-89].
From humble beginnings, the son of a coal miner, Buchanan went on to a career in education and became a head teacher. Born in Coatbridge, he came to Cambuslang as a young man and was the local team's left half when they were a force to be reckoned with, notably playing alongside his elder brother James in the 1888 Scottish Cup final, which Cambuslang lost 6-1. He was capped by Scotland the following year against Ireland, despite spending some of the season as a guest at St Bernard's. When Cambuslang became a founding member of the Scottish League he played regularly in their first two seasons, although in 1890 he was suspended by the SFA for professionalism in connection with his links to St Bernard's. The ban was originally for a year but later reduced to three months on appeal. An all-round sportsman, he won many athletics trophies as a sprinter. He gave up football in 1892 when he got married and focussed instead on his teaching career with his first appointment at Hallside School in 1886. Over the following decade he studied privately for his BA degree, eventually passing his exams in 1899 at the Royal University of Ireland (the Open University of its day). He then moved to Cambuslang Public School and reached the top of his profession in 1916 when he was appointed head teacher of West Coats Higher Grade School, also in Cambuslang. He left over £5,000 when he died in 1942.

Jock BUCHANAN (2/0, 1929-30)
John Buchanan DCM
Born 25 February 1894 Howie Street, Paisley, Renfrewshire
Died 3 October 1947 Newton Terrace, Paisley, Renfrewshire
Scotland v England 1929, 1930.
Johnstone 1913-14; St Mirren 1919-21; Morton 1921-27 (Scottish Cup 1922); Rangers Dec 1927-31 (Scottish League 1928, 1929, 1930, 1931, Scottish Cup 1928); Linfield 1931-32 (Irish League 1932); East Stirlingshire 1932-33.
Buchanan is perhaps best known for being the first man ever sent off in a Scottish Cup final, but there was a great deal more to this fine half-back, both on and off the pitch. He was decorated for gallantry in the First World War, and a decade later became the oldest man to win a first cap for Scotland. Born into a football family – his father George played for Abercorn, his elder brother George was a professional on both sides of the border – he played his first matches with Johnstone in the Second Division before war broke out in 1914. He joined the Seaforth Highlanders and saw active service with them throughout the conflict, being hospitalised in France in April 1915 with a gunshot wound to his arm. After his recovery he was drafted to the Eastern Front and in 1917 Lance Corporal Buchanan was awarded the Distinguished Conduct Medal for his exceptional bravery under heavy fire in Mesopotamia. By the time he returned to Scotland he was already 25 when he restarted his football career with St Mirren in the summer of 1919. He had two years in Paisley then moved to Morton where he played at centre forward in their famous Scottish Cup final win of 1922, in place of the injured George French. He remained at Cappielow but then at the age of 33 his career took a surprising turn in 1927 after Morton were relegated in 1927. He spent the summer on tour with the Scottish FA in Canada in 1927, then when Morton struggled to adjust to the Second Division he asked for a transfer, which materialised in a surprising direction. Rangers took him to Ibrox in December and within a couple of months he had replaced Tommy Muirhead in the team, and by the end of the season he had won the Scottish League, the Scottish Cup and the Charity Cup. His affection for the Scottish Cup must have diminished somewhat when he was sent off in the 1929 final but a week later he won his first Scotland cap. At 35, he was the oldest international debutant until Ronnie Simpson broke the record in 1967, and what is more he was called back to face England the following year when Jimmy Gibson was injured. He missed out on another cup medal in 1930 after he injured his knee in the drawn final against Partick Thistle and was unable to play in the replay. However, by the time he left Rangers in 1931 he had won four league titles. Not content with that, he went over to Belfast for a season with Linfield, where he won the Irish League, and finally wound down his career with East Stirlingshire. He later ran a grocery business in his native Paisley and died relatively young, aged 53, in 1947.

Peter BUCHANAN (1/1, 1937)
Peter Symington Buchanan
Born 13 October 1915 Meadowpark Street, Dennistoun, Glasgow
Died 26 June 1977 Stonehouse Hospital, Lanarkshire
Scotland v Czechoslovakia Dec 1937 (1).
New Stevenston United; Chelsea 1933-34; Wishaw Juniors 1934-35 [trial for Falkirk, Nov 1935]; Chelsea Dec 1935-46 [guest for Aldershot 1939-40 & 1944, Portsmouth 1940 & Jan-Sep 1943, Southampton 1942-44, Millwall 1944-45, Crystal Palace 1944-45, West Ham United 1944-45, Fulham Apr 1945-46]; Fulham Mar 1946-47; Brentford 1947-49; Headington United 1949-50.

Peter Buchanan's star shone brightly but briefly, as after winning his only international cap his career fizzled out. After starting out in juvenile football with New Stevenston, an early move to Chelsea came to nothing due to homesickness and he returned to junior football at Wishaw. Here, he did well enough at outside right to attract interest from several clubs, and even played a couple of league matches as a trialist for Falkirk, scoring in both. However, his uncle Willie was Chelsea's chief scout in Scotland, so it was little surprise that he was persuaded to return to Stamford Bridge in

December 1935, where he was hailed as 'a second Alec Jackson'. It took a while for his talent to catch up with his reputation, and he didn't make his first team debut until the spring of 1937. That autumn, he had an extended run which coincided with Chelsea reaching top spot in the league for the first time in many years. His goals and speed won him his Scotland cap, and he scored against Czechoslovakia, but would gain no further honours. On the contrary, by the end of the 1937/38 season his form and fitness had dipped and he was dropped, not appearing again in Chelsea's first team until March 1939. With the outbreak of war, although most of his appearances were for Chelsea, the vagaries of wartime football meant he guested for Aldershot and a number of London clubs, and had an extended spell on the south coast at Southampton and Portsmouth. He finally moved on in March 1946 to Fulham, where he had played as a guest, and a year later to Brentford where he spent a couple of seasons. Although Buchanan planned to retire in 1949 he was persuaded to sign for Headington United in the Southern League for a season before finally hanging up his boots. He returned to Scotland and ran a pub in Larkhall until his death in 1977.

Bob BUCHANAN (1/1, 1891)
Robert Blackburn Buchanan
Born 4 June 1866 Graham Street, Johnstone, Renfrewshire
Died 21 December 1907 St Mary's Hospital, Paddington, London
Scotland v Wales 1891 (1).
Johnstone 1885-87; Abercorn 1887-91; Sunderland Albion 1891-92; Burnley 1892-94; Woolwich Arsenal Oct 1894-96; Southampton 1896-99 (Southern League 1897, 1898); Sheppey United 1899-1900.

An inside forward, Buchanan started at his local side Johnstone, where he represented Renfrewshire against Stirlingshire in 1887, then moved down the road to Abercorn where he continued to play for the county. However, he became really well known for the wrong reasons in December 1888 after getting into a fight with Alex Lochhead of Third Lanark in a Scottish Cup tie, and both players were prosecuted in the courts. This appears to have had little impact on his football career and he was capped for Scotland in 1891 against Wales, scoring in a 4-3 win in Wrexham. He was persuaded to turn professional with Sunderland Albion later that year, and spent the rest of his career with English clubs. When Albion collapsed in 1892 he joined Burnley, then a couple of years later he moved to Arsenal, where he was selected for Kent, and then to Southampton where he was selected for Hampshire. His goals were crucial as Saints won the Southern League title twice, but there was disappointment in the snowstorm FA Cup semi-final in 1898 when Nottingham Forest were 'blown' into the final at Southampton's expense. A colleague recalled: 'One of the best was Bob, keen as mustard to the last whistle and always anxious to win. I shall always see him in my mind's eye after that fateful semi-final. He simply could not speak for disappointment, and as he looked at the raging snowstorm outside the pavilion the tears stood in his eyes for the very vexation. Buchanan was not a brilliant forward, but he always kept bustling, was most unselfish, and had a cute eye for the main chance when he got near goal.' He only played a couple of times as Southampton won the league for a third time, and retired in 1900 after a season with Sheppey United, also in the Southern League. He died just a few years later aged 41 in a London hospital and is buried in Willesden cemetery. NB as his parents were unmarried he took his mother's surname, but unusually he used his father's surname Blackburn as his middle name.

Albert BUICK (2/2, 1902)
Albert Thoroughgood Buick
Born 17 January 1875 Brechin Road, Arbroath, Angus
Died 25 March 1948 Arbroath Infirmary, Angus
Scotland v Ireland 1902c (1); Wales 1902 (1).
Arbroath 1893-96; Heart of Midlothian 1896-1903 (Scottish Cup 1901); Portsmouth 1903-11.

Buick looked frail for a centre half, but could withstand heavy charges and was a prodigious worker. He grew up in Arbroath and played for the local team as a young man, notably a Scottish Cup tie against cup-holders Queen's Park in 1893. He had captained the side to the Forfarshire Cup by the time he joined Hearts in 1896, the start of a long professional career. Honours followed, he was selected by the Scottish League in 1899, won the Scottish Cup with Hearts in 1901 and a year later was made captain of Scotland on his debut. However, despite scoring in both of his internationals, each of them impressive wins over Ireland and Wales, he was never capped again. In 1903 Hearts reached another Scottish Cup final, drawing twice with Rangers before injury forced Buick to miss the second replay, which they lost. He moved to Portsmouth that summer, was soon appointed club captain, and went on to spend eight years with the club in their Southern League days. He retired in 1911 just as Portsmouth was relegated and returned home to Arbroath where he took over a shop in the town, selling china and glass. He remained in business for many years and was a well-known locally as a pigeon fancier, having taken up the pastime while in Portsmouth, and on occasion he would sweep the board of prizes at Arbroath Racing Pigeon Society.

Matt BUSBY (1/0, 1933)
Sir Matthew Busby CBE, KCSG
Born 26 May 1909 Old Orbiston, Bellshill, Lanarkshire
Died 20 January 1994 Alexandra Hospital, Cheadle, Cheshire
Scotland v Wales 1933.
Alpine Villa; Uddingston Thistle; Denny Hibernian 1927-28; Manchester City Feb 1928-36 (FA Cup 1934); Liverpool Mar 1936-45 [guest for Chelsea 1939-40 (3 apps); Middlesbrough 1940-41; Hibernian 1941-43; Reading 1943-45; Brentford 1944-45 (one app); Bournemouth 1945 (2 apps)].

Busby is regarded as one of the greatest managers of all time, his finest achievement taking Manchester United to the European Cup in 1968, a feat for which he was knighted. Born in a small Lanarkshire mining village, his father was killed in the First World War and his early life was a struggle but he found his vocation in football. His earliest success came in 1926 with the Bellshill juvenile club Alpine Villa who won the Mavor Cup, a national competition run by the Scottish Welfare FA, and it had added significance as at the celebration supper Busby met his future wife Jean. He moved on to Uddingston Thistle, then turned junior with Denny Hibs where in his first season he caught the eye of several professional clubs. He opted to sign for Manchester City, who were alerted to his potential by Jimmy McMullan, who also came from Denny, and initially he struggled at inside left. It was only after he dropped to half back in City's third team that he found his natural position. Then there was no looking back, and his greatest moment with City was winning the FA Cup in 1934, a year after defeat in the final of the same competition. The same season he won his single Scotland cap, a defeat to Wales in October 1933. After an injury caused him to lose his place in the City team, in March 1936 he asked for a transfer. This was a godsend to Liverpool who were battling relegation and they splashed out £8,000 to take Busby to Anfield, a ploy that worked as they avoided the drop by three points. He fitted in well and was almost ever-present in the next three years until, like so many other players, his career was interrupted by the War. His wartime role as a Physical Training Instructor with the Army restricted his appearances for Liverpool, and he guested for a variety of clubs. He played three matches for Chelsea in 39-40, 19 for Middlesbrough the following season, then spent a couple of years in Scotland. When he knew he was going to be based there he offered himself to Celtic but they turned him down, and in the summer of 1941 he joined Hibs. He soon won a medal as the club lifted the Scottish Summer Cup in July 1941 and he remained with them until February 1943. Returning south to the Royal Military College he turned out regularly for Reading until the autumn of 1945, made a single appearance for Brentford, and his final game was the second of two guest matches for Bournemouth, an 8-1 win over Bristol City in September 1945. He made seven wartime appearances for Scotland, captaining them for the last time in April 1945, and played regularly for a variety of Army select elevens. By this time he had signed an agreement to manage Manchester United, but could not join them until October 1945 when he left the Army. It was the start of a wonderful managerial career that would establish United as one of the world's top clubs, leading them through the tragedy of Munich to five league titles, two FA Cups and of course that famous European Cup victory in 1968. Along the way he managed the Great Britain side at the 1948 Olympics, and Scotland in the autumn of 1958. He retired in 1969, becoming a club director, and died of cancer in hospital aged 84. Numerous books have been written about him, the most comprehensive being *Matt Busby: the definitive biography* by Patrick Barclay. NB some sources attribute him with the additional forename of Alexander, but his birth, marriage and death certificates are all plain Matthew Busby.

C

Tommy CAIRNS (8/1, 1920-25)
Thomas Cairns
Born 30 October 1892 Merryton Rows, Hamilton, Lanarkshire
Died 17 December 1967 Hartwood Hospital, Shotts, Lanarkshire
Scotland v Wales 1920 (1), 1923, Feb 1925; England 1922, 1923, 1925; Ireland 1924, 1925.
Larkhall Thistle; Burnbank Athletic; Bristol City 1911-12; Peebles Rovers 1912-13; St Johnstone Aug-Nov 1913; Rangers Nov 1913-27 (Scottish League 1918, 1920, 1921, 1923, 1924, 1925, 1927); Bradford City 1927-32 (Third Division North 1929).
Cairns showed considerable promise as a young man, playing for the Lanarkshire Junior League while at Larkhall, then moved on to Burnbank, and signed for Bristol City aged 18. However, he was stuck in the reserves for a season and was released. Back in Scotland he had a year with Peebles Rovers which was the springboard to St Johnstone, where he made such a strong impression in his first three months that Rangers bought him in the autumn of 1913. Initially he was consigned to the reserves but once he established himself in the first team in 1914, he became an integral part of the Rangers side for over a decade. The medals started to flow in 1917/18 with the first of seven league titles, not to mention the first of several Glasgow Cup wins, although the Scottish Cup eluded him despite establishing a fine partnership with Alan Morton on the right wing. Meanwhile he tried to set up a Scottish footballers' union but there was little support from his fellow players. In 1920 he made his debut for the Scotland team and scored a face-saving goal to rescue a draw against Wales, but did not manage to find the net again in subsequent selections despite never being on a losing side. He also made six appearances for the Scottish League. In

1927, in his mid-thirties, he made a surprise move alongside Willie Summers to Bradford City, and used his experience to lead the side to the Third Division North title in 1929 and carried on playing until he was nearly forty. He returned to Lanarkshire, and from his base in Larkhall was Scottish scout for Arsenal for over two decades.

Davie CALDERHEAD (1/0, 1889)
David Calderhead
Born 19 June 1864 Holmes Colliery, Galston, Ayrshire
Died 9 January 1938 Finlay Street, Fulham, London
Scotland v Ireland 1889.
Wishaw Thistle; Queen of the South Wanderers 1881-89; Notts County 1889-1900 (FA Cup 1894, Division 2 1897); Lincoln City 1900-01.
As a young coal miner, when Calderhead was 17 he went to Dumfries to work and found a place in the local football team. Over the next eight years he developed into a fine centre half with Queen of the South Wanderers, where his form was good enough to earn him a Scotland cap against Ireland in 1889. That led to a transfer to Notts County, one of the top clubs at the time, and in over a decade there he played over 300 matches, including two FA Cup finals, losing the first in 1891 before captaining them to victory at the second attempt in 1894, as Bolton Wanderers were beaten 4-1. He was even selected by the Football League, and for the Rest of the League against champions Aston Villa, but no further international honours came his way. Nonetheless, he was immensely proud of his single Scotland cap, and related how he once came home to find his wife using it as an iron holder. 'She didn't get a second chance of doing it,' he said. In 1900 he went to Lincoln as secretary, and gave up playing after a season to focus on managing the team. Then in 1907, after a shock FA Cup victory over Chelsea, he was offered the job as the London club's manager and spent the rest of his working life there. A quiet man, known as the 'Sphinx of Stamford Bridge' for his intense dislike for publicity, he won no major honours in his time there but his legacy was in embedding the club in the football firmament. In true Chelsea style, he helped establish the fashion of paying big transfer fees for celebrated players, most notably Hughie Gallacher and Alex Jackson. He held the role until his retirement in 1933 and died five years later at home in Fulham. He was buried in Putney Bridge Cemetery. His son, also David, followed him as a player at Lincoln and Chelsea, but was not as successful in management.

Bobby CALDERWOOD (3/2, 1885)
Robert Calderwood
Born 4 October 1862 Russell's Land, Main Street, Busby, Lanarkshire
Died 13 May 1939 Bon Accord Cottages, Busby, Lanarkshire
Scotland v Ireland 1885 (1); England 1885; Wales 1885 (1).
Cartvale 1879-82; Paisley Athletic 1882-83; Cartvale 1883-86; Cowlairs 1886-87; Bootle Aug 1887; Cowlairs 1889-90; Newcastle West End 1890-91; Glasgow Thistle 1891-92; Cartvale 1892-94.
Brought up in Busby, Calderwood was a left winger who learned the game with Cartvale, although his first honour came in a short spell with Paisley Athletic, where he was picked for Renfrewshire. Then when he came back to his home town team Cartvale his form was so impressive that he was picked for all three Scotland matches of 1885, scoring against Ireland and Wales. He moved together with Mick Dunbar from Cartvale to Cowlairs for a season, then in the summer of 1887 signed a professional contract for Bootle, having answered a newspaper advert for players. He quickly changed his mind and returned to Scotland after only three days in Liverpool, but made the mistake of taking money both from Bootle and Cowlairs, which was enough to have him branded a professional. The Scottish FA suspended him for two years in September 1887 and he served the full term before he was able to return to action in 1889 with Cowlairs. In 1890 he had a second attempt at England, this time in Newcastle, and decided to come home after a year. He was reinstated as an amateur in Scotland, played a season with Glasgow Thistle then returned to Busby where he picked up again at Cartvale, and as late as 1894 the *Scottish Referee* thought he might be in with a shout for an international recall: 'Calderwood is in great form, displays great judgement, capital shot at goal and very speedy.' After he retired he was Cartvale's secretary and he lived in Busby for the rest of his life, working as a general labourer.

Paddy CALLAGHAN (1/0, 1900)
Patrick Callaghan
Born 17 May 1877 Hurlford, Ayrshire
Died 26 February 1959 Dalgety Avenue, Edinburgh
Scotland v Ireland 1900.
Blantyre Priory Rovers; Mossend Celtic 1897-98; Jordanhill 1898-99; Hibernian Feb 1899-1914 (Scottish Cup 1902, Scottish League 1903).
Born in Ayrshire, Callaghan was still a baby when the family moved to Blantyre, where he was brought up and followed his father down the pits as a coal miner. Meanwhile, he developed a talent for football in the junior ranks and early in 1899 he joined Hibs from Glasgow side Jordanhill. Despite a gloomy assessment by the *Scottish Referee* that he was 'hardly class for First Division company' he was to prove a magnificent servant for the Edinburgh side, his only senior club, making over 350 competitive appearances. Playing mainly on the left wing, he could also feature on the right and even occasionally in goal, and in his first full season he made such an impact that he was selected for the Scottish League and then won his international cap, both against the Irish. He was perhaps fortunate to be capped as he was a late replacement for the injured Willie Maxwell of Stoke, although the following year he was named in the Scotland team but this time he himself was injured and his replacement, Alex McMahon, scored four. Callaghan played once more for the Scottish League in 1903. More importantly, he helped Hibs to secure two major honours.

In 1902 his corner kick led to the late goal against Celtic that took the Scottish Cup back to Edinburgh, in what would turn out to be Hibs' last success in the competition for over a century. Then the following season, Hibs romped to the Scottish League title by a six-point margin over Dundee. Callaghan resisted any temptation to seek pastures new and played 13 full seasons with Hibs. He was given a benefit match in 1907, and even after he finally drifted out of the first team in 1912 he continued to play mainly in the reserves for another couple of years. He went into the wine and spirits trade in Edinburgh and died in 1959. NB his birth surname was Kallahan but in time the spelling was adapted to Callaghan.

John CAMERON (1/0, 1886)
John Cameron
Born 26 August 1860 Blanefield, Stirlingshire
Died 28 August 1936 Clyde Terrace, Bothwell, Lanarkshire
Scotland v Ireland 1886.
Govan; Renfrew 1880-82; Rangers 1882-87.

A dependable half back who was a mainstay of the Rangers team in the 1880s, Cameron was born in Stirlingshire and came to Govan as a baby when his father found work there. His talent as a footballer was first recognised while he was at Renfrew, where he was selected for Renfrewshire and then in 1882 for Scotch Counties. He clearly had a good turn of speed as he competed as a sprinter in many summer sports meetings, and that may have been a factor in his move to Rangers, which had a vibrant athletics section at the time. At Rangers he developed an excellent half-back partnership with Tuck McIntyre and was selected for Glasgow and Lanarkshire before his one international cap, for Scotland against Ireland in 1886. The following season Cameron played in every match as Rangers reached the FA Cup semi-final, the last season that Scottish clubs were allowed to enter the competition. There were no significant trophies during his time at the club, but Rangers were awarded a silver cup for taking part in the Edinburgh Exhibition tournament in October 1886, and as a mark of esteem it was presented to Cameron. After retiring around 1887 he joined the Rangers committee, serving as the club's vice-president from 1891-94. He was also a referee in the Scottish League through most of the 1890s. In his business life he followed his father into the Govan shipyards, where he worked as a clerk, then lived in Bothwell where he was a timekeeper in a colliery.

John CAMERON (1/0, 1896)
John Cameron
Born 13 April 1872 Contrast Street, Ayr
Died 17 April 1935 Easter Road, Leith, Edinburgh
Scotland v Ireland 1896.
Ayr Grammar School; Ayr Parkhouse 1891-95; Queen's Park Mar 1895-96; Everton Sep 1895-98; Tottenham Hotspur 1898-1904 player/secretary (Southern League 1900; FA Cup 1901).

A centre forward with 'plodding, painstaking power', Cameron was impressive enough with Ayr Parkhouse to receive offers from English clubs but was adamant he needed a job in the right profession to go with it. It was only when he was offered a position with Cunard shipping line in their Liverpool office that he took the opportunity to join Everton. He was still an amateur, which allowed him to gravitate between Queen's Park (still outside the league system) and Everton for over a year before he eventually signed professional forms at Goodison Park in November 1896. During that period, he won his only Scotland cap, as a Queen's Park player, in a 3-3 draw with Ireland. He was appointed secretary of the fledgling Football Players' Union, although he had to give up the post in 1898 when he moved to London to play for Tottenham Hotspur.

In London, his influence blossomed both on and off the pitch as he held a full-time post as secretary of Spurs while playing in their momentous campaigns that saw them capture the Southern League title in 1900 and the FA Cup a year later. He stopped playing in 1904 then remained with Spurs as team manager until March 1907, resigning on a difference of opinion with the directors. In his subsequent 'down time' he worked as a sports journalist and published an influential book, *Association Football and How to Play It* (1908). He kept match fit and even reappeared for Southend United reserves late in 1908. He went to Germany in 1912 for a coaching position with Dresdner SC and was still there on the outbreak of war, which saw him interned for four years in Ruhleben Camp. Along with a number of other famous sportsmen, his influence ensured that football was an essential part of daily life there, vital for morale. After his release in 1918 he returned to Ayr and was appointed manager of Ayr United but only spent a season at Somerset Park before becoming a journalist again. He was a great cricket lover, having learned to play at school and continued as an adult.

Jack CAMERON (2/0, 1904-09)
John Bell Cameron
Born 16 February 1879 Reid's Rows, Baillieston, Lanarkshire
Died 5 July 1950 Hope Street, Blackburn, Lancashire
Scotland v Ireland 1904; England 1909.
Kirkwood Thistle; St Mirren 1900-04; Blackburn Rovers Apr 1904-07; Chelsea Oct 1907-13; Port Vale 1913-19.

Cameron was one of the most sought-after left backs of his generation and started his career with junior side Kirkwood Thistle, near his home on the outskirts of Coatbridge where he worked as a coal miner. He had a tough upbringing, his father died when he was small, and football gave him a means of escape from the mines. After playing for the Lanarkshire junior select, he was courted by several teams and had a trial with Third Lanark before deciding to join St Mirren in the summer of 1900. So impressive was his full back partnership with Tom Jackson that in 1904 they were selected together for Scotland against Ireland in Dublin, and nine days later against the Football League. That was the last of Cameron's three caps for the Scottish League, as the following week he was snapped up by Blackburn Rovers for £475 and went straight into the team, helping them narrowly to escape relegation. He went on to form another partnership with England's Bob Crompton, but although ever-present in his first full season at Ewood Park, he later drifted out of the team and was sold to Chelsea for £900 in the autumn of 1907, part of a spending spree by the Stamford Bridge club. He won a second Scotland cap in 1909 but the match did not go well for him against England's George Wall, who scored twice in the opening ten minutes. Cameron was a success at Chelsea, however, and captained the side. When age started to catch up he was released by Chelsea in 1913 and moved to Port Vale, at that time in the Central League. He remained with them throughout the war years, and spent his final season with the additional responsibility of team manager before he retired in 1919 aged 40. He returned to Blackburn, his wife's home town, where he worked as a general labourer.

Charlie CAMPBELL (13/0, 1874-86)
Charles Campbell
Born 20 January 1854 Balbrogie Farm, Coupar Angus, Perthshire
Died 23 April 1927 Kilkea, Co Kildare, Republic of Ireland
Scotland v England 1874, 1877c, 1878c, 1879c, 1880, 1881, 1882c, 1884c, 1885, 1886; Wales 1876c, 1877c, 1882.
Queen's Park 1873-87 (Scottish Cup 1874, 1875, 1876, 1880, 1881, 1882, 1884, 1886) [guest for Corinthian Apr 1885; I Zingari 1886-87; London Caledonians Apr 1887].

Born on his father's farm near Coupar Angus, Campbell moved to County Kildare aged 7 and reportedly considered himself more Irish than Scottish. However, he was sent to Edinburgh Institution for his schooling and then moved to Glasgow to work. Here, he joined Queen's Park and made his first team debut in 1873, showing such impressive form that he was selected to face England the following spring, just after his 20th birthday. Standing over six feet tall, he was an immense figure in every respect, appointed captain of Scotland from his second cap onwards. He was selected ten times against England and only missed the 1883 game due to a dip in form which saw him have a 'wretched game' in a trial. With Queen's Park, he won the Scottish Cup eight times, the Glasgow Charity Cup six times, and played in the FA Cup finals of 1884 and 1885. Often he used the pseudonym C Elliot, initially in the 1881 Scottish Cup final and regularly thereafter. He tried to retire from the game in 1886 but was brought back into service during the season and played until the following summer, making a guest appearance for London Caledonians and occasionally for an amateur select, the I Zingari, who were chosen as much for their musical ability as their football talent. He was invited to play for Corinthians against Preston North End in 1885, but the Scottish FA refused permission for any further matches. Meanwhile he combined playing with administration and spent 16 years on the Queen's Park committee, was elected President for 1879/80, and held senior office at the Scottish FA, serving as its President in 1889/90. He occasionally refereed matches, including the 1889 Scottish Cup 'snow final'. For many years he was a partner in William Colvin & Co, iron merchants in Glasgow, and represented them at the Glasgow stock exchange. Then in 1907 he went back to Ireland to take over the family farm in County Kildare, about 60 miles south-west of Dublin, and died there in 1927.

Harry CAMPBELL (1/0, 1889)
Henry Campbell
Born 6 June 1867 Main Street, Renton, Dunbartonshire
Died 15 November 1915 New Park Street, Blackburn, Lancashire
Scotland v Wales 1889.
Renton 1886-89 (Scottish Cup 1888); Blackburn Rovers 1889-95 (FA Cup 1890).

The first man to win both the Scottish and FA Cups, Campbell was an industrious right-sided forward who was fortunate enough to be in the great Renton side which dominated domestic football in the late 1880s. He first came to prominence in a famous FA Cup tie against Preston North End in 1887, at a time when Scottish clubs still took part in the English competition. Then in 1888 he helped Renton to win the Scottish Cup with a record-breaking 6-1 defeat of Cambuslang in the final, following which they defeated FA Cup winners West Bromwich Albion to be declared unofficial Champions of the World. In 1889 Renton further demonstrated their strength by winning the Glasgow Charity Cup for the third successive season, while Campbell was capped for Scotland against Wales, but that was the last hurrah as half the team was tempted south as professionals, Campbell among them. Blackburn Rovers had previously tried to persuade him to join them as an amateur before finally he signed in the summer of 1889, along with George Dewar of Dumbarton and Tom Brandon of St Mirren. The move worked out well for Campbell as within a year he was an FA Cup winner, although he missed the following year's cup win through illness. He was an excellent servant to Rovers, who gave him a benefit in October 1893 and he remained with the club until he retired from the game in 1895. He settled in the Lancashire town for good with a job as a steward at the Blackburn Reform Club, quite a change from his original trade as a calico printer in Scotland. He also took a post as football coach to Stonyhurst College. He married in 1910, but sadly died five years later aged just 48, after a long illness.

'Bummer' CAMPBELL (2/0, 1891-92)
James Paterson Campbell
Born 29 March 1869 Braeside, Kilmarnock, Ayrshire
Died 20 April 1938 Kennedy Street, Kilmarnock, Ayrshire
Scotland v Ireland 1891; Wales 1892.
Kilmarnock Thistle; Kilmarnock 1888-1901 (Second Division 1898, 1899) [guest for Leith Athletic Jun 1891, Third Lanark Aug & Oct 1892].

The *Ayrshire Post* described Campbell as 'one of the most accomplished forwards in the country' while still he was with junior side Thistle, and certainly he lived up to expectations. Having joined Kilmarnock in 1888 he spent his entire senior career with the club, although he was happy to guest with other teams, winning the Rosebery Charity Cup with Leith Athletic in 1891 and playing in friendlies for Third Lanark the following year. Kilmarnock used him initially as a centre half, his position in two international appearances early in his career, then he moved upfield to centre forward around 1894. He was not afraid to use his strength, in fact he seemed not to be afraid of anything, and goals were his business: he once scored eight against Saltcoats in the Scottish Cup, and countless others. Famed throughout Scotland, he resisted attempts to sign elsewhere and remained with Kilmarnock when they entered the Scottish League in 1895, then helped them to win two consecutive Second Division championships which ensured their election to the top flight. They reached the 1898 Scottish Cup final, which was lost to Rangers, and there were several other triumphs in the Ayrshire Cup. He was given a benefit match against Celtic in 1900, and retired the following year. Always a part-timer, he worked as a boilermaker and spent his whole life in Kilmarnock. Latterly he was in poor health for many years and another benefit match, this time against Rangers, raised funds for him. He died of heart failure in 1938, three days before Kilmarnock played in another Scottish Cup final.

Jimmy CAMPBELL (1/0, 1913)
James Clark
Born 5 February 1887 Pier Place, Newhaven, Edinburgh
Died 19 May 1925 Craiglockhart Sanatorium, Edinburgh
Scotland v Wales 1913.
Leith Athletic 1908-11 (Second Division 1910); Sheffield Wednesday Feb 1911-20; Huddersfield Town 1920-21; St Bernard's 1921-23.

Campbell's real surname was Clark but he played under an assumed name throughout his career, perhaps to hide his age as he was in his 20s when he first played professionally. A powerfully-built half back who was capable of playing on left or right, he joined the Army after he left school and did not come to Leith Athletic until 1908. He was part of a successful team which won the Scottish Qualifying Cup and the Second Division title in 1909/10, and the following year he joined Sheffield Wednesday together his teammate Marr Paterson. Apparently Paterson was their main target, but the director who was making the signing was so impressed by Campbell that he decided to add him into the deal. Two weeks later Campbell made his Wednesday debut at left half and was such a success that he played in every competitive match for the next three years. He was capped by Scotland against Wales in 1913, a 0-0 draw, but was denied the chance of further honours as, like many footballers, his career was interrupted by war service. As a reservist, he was called up to the Royal Field Artillery as soon as the conflict broke out and was on active service in France by September 1914, as a driver attached to the 45th Brigade. He was invalided home in the summer of 1915 through an attack of pleurisy and after recovering in hospital he was sent back to the front, thankfully surviving the rest of the War without injury. Although he made occasional appearances for Wednesday on leave, he could only resume playing regularly in March 1919 when he was demobilised. However, he never recovered his pre-war form and moved on to Huddersfield Town in 1920, only making a single league appearance before he was freed in March. He came back to Edinburgh with St Bernard's, who immediately appointed him captain for their return to the Scottish League that summer. He gave up the game in 1923 and within two years he died of tuberculosis aged 38. He left a widow and three children, and to help them out his old friends in Sheffield held a benefit concert.

John CAMPBELL (1/1, 1880)
John Campbell
Born 2 June 1856 McNeill Street, Glasgow
Died 29 August 1929 Ruchill Hospital, Glasgow
Scotland v Wales 1880 (1).
South Western 1878-82.

Campbell was a right-sided forward who featured for a few years with the obscure South Western club, whose grounds were at Copeland Park in Govan. He was a late selection for the Glasgow team at Sheffield in February 1880, after George Ker pulled out, and must have made a good impression as the following month he was selected for the national team, scoring one of Scotland's goals in a 5-1 win over Wales. The Scottish Football Annual of 1880 described him succinctly in just four words as a 'fair left wing forward' but he did not build on his reputation and disappears from match reports after 1882. He did not marry and spent all his life in Glasgow, where he lived in Trongate and worked as a bricklayer until his death in 1929. His wider family had a great sporting tradition: he and his elder brother Daniel, who was a defender for South Western, took part in sports meetings around Glasgow, and at the 1880 South Western club sports the prizes were presented by Mrs J Campbell, probably his mother. His father Robert and uncle Colquhoun were both famous rowers, while his nephew Geordie Campbell was a pioneer of football in Toronto, played for Canada, and is in the Canadian Soccer Hall of Fame.

Johnny CAMPBELL (12/4, 1893-1903)
John Campbell
Born 19 August 1872 Middleton Place, Royston, Glasgow
Died 2 December 1947 Monreith Road, Newlands, Glasgow
Scotland v Ireland 1893, 1898, 1900 (2), 1901, 1902; England 1893, 1898, 1900, 1901 (1); Wales 1901, 1902c (1), 1903.
Possil Hawthorn; Benburb; Celtic 1890-95 (Scottish Cup 1892; Scottish League 1893, 1894); Aston Villa 1895-97 (Football League 1896, 1897; FA Cup 1897); Celtic 1897-1903 (Scottish League 1898, Scottish Cup 1899, 1900); Third Lanark 1903-05 (Scottish League 1904).

Campbell had a superb haul of medals from his career, with six league titles and four national cups on both sides of the border. His prime years were spent with Celtic where he was one of their all-time greats, having come to the club from junior football as an 18-year-old. He soon found a permanent place in the forward line, generally on the left but willing and able to play anywhere, and won his first major honour in 1892 when his two goals in the final set Celtic on their way to the club's first Scottish Cup win in 1892. They went on to win the Scottish League title in the next two seasons but, for reasons which are not clear, he was allowed to leave Glasgow in 1894 and was welcomed with open arms at Aston Villa. He continued his winning ways with Villa and won two successive titles, the second of which completed the legendary FA Cup and Football League 'double' in 1897. Tom Maley pleaded with him to come home to Celtic and he responded by winning his third successive league title, followed by two more Scottish Cups in 1899 and 1900. His international career took some time to lift off, as he had to wait five years after winning his first two caps for further honours, thanks to his spell in England. However, he was back in the fold by the turn of the century and made up for lost time with a series of outstanding performances, such as the 4-1 'Rosebery' victory over England in 1900, and scored against them the following year. He was respected enough to be chosen as captain of Scotland against Wales in 1902. Celtic thought he was slowing down and allowed him to leave in 1903 yet he continued to have an impact at Third Lanark, winning another Scottish League title in his first season with them. He began coaching the team and retired from playing in 1905, not taking part in Third Lanark's Scottish Cup victory that year which would have added to his medal collection. Off the field, he had a tangled life which led to him being sued for breach of promise in 1899. He did eventually settle down and raise a family, and his sons William and James played briefly for Third Lanark before becoming lawyers.

Johnny CAMPBELL (4/5, 1899-1901)
John William Campbell
Born 2 October 1877 Springfield Road, Govan, Glasgow
Died 20 January 1919 Knightswood Hospital, Glasgow
Scotland v Wales 1899 (2); Ireland 1899 (1), 1901 (2); England 1899.
Ferntower; Linthouse 1894; Partick Thistle 1894-96; Blackburn Rovers 1896-98; Rangers 1898-1902 (Scottish League 1899, 1900, 1901, 1902); West Ham United 1902-03; Hibernian 1903-05; New Brompton Nov 1905-06; Partick Thistle 1906-07; Bo'ness 1907-09; Dumbarton Harp 1909-10.

From junior football with Govan side Ferntower, Campbell had a fleeting association with Linthouse before he was snapped up by Partick Thistle, and scored on his competitive debut in a Second Division match in August 1894, aged only 16. An outside right who could play equally well on the left, he was small and light but more than made up for that with his nimble dribbling and shooting. Recognised as a great talent after two years with Thistle he transferred to Blackburn Rovers, and played over 50 league matches in two years there before Rangers brought him back to Scotland in 1898. He became an integral member of the side that won every game in 1898-99, and went on to win three further league titles in the rest of his time at Ibrox. Meanwhile, he burst onto the international scene, playing for Scotland on four consecutive Saturdays in March-April 1899, scoring in the first three of them: two on his debut in Wales, then a goal apiece against Ireland and the Football League. He thought he had completed the set against England at Birmingham, but his effort was ruled offside. He only won one more cap, partnering his namesake against the Irish in 1901 in which he scored twice. A transfer to Hearts in February 1900 fell through due to his financial demands, and he left Rangers in 1902 for a season at West Ham in the Southern League. Thereafter he moved around, playing at Hibs, New Brompton (Gillingham), Partick Thistle, Bo'ness and Dumbarton Harp until he retired in 1910. He continued to live in Glasgow and was working as a ship's steward when he died of tuberculosis aged 41.

Kenny CAMPBELL (8/0, 1920-22)
Kenneth Campbell
Born 6 September 1892 Carfin Street, Govanhill, Glasgow
Died 28 April 1977 Chesham Road, Wilmslow, Cheshire
Scotland v Wales 1920, 1921c, 1922; Ireland 1920, 1921, 1922; England 1920, 1922.
Clyde Vale; Rutherglen Glencairn; Cambuslang Rangers 1910-11; Liverpool 1911-20 [guest for Southport Central 1916-17; Partick Thistle Feb 1919]; Partick Thistle Apr 1920-22 (Scottish Cup 1921); New Brighton 1922-23; Stoke Mar 1923-25; Leicester City Nov 1925-29; New Brighton 1929-31.

A terrific goalkeeper, Campbell won two Scotland junior caps among many honours while at Cambuslang and was in such demand that 17 clubs made him an offer to turn professional. He chose to sign for Liverpool for the princely sum of £10 down and £4 a week, and was initially understudy to the great Sam Hardy. A year later Hardy was transferred to Aston Villa and he became a first team regular. Campbell had originally travelled south with Bob Pursell (older brother of Scotland cap Peter), and three years later they both played against Burnley in the 1914 FA Cup final, which was attended by King George V. In the First World War he joined the Royal Garrison Artillery, and was promoted to Corporal in April 1916. Stationed at Crosby, he was not sent on active service due to the peculiarity of having one arm shorter than another. The military authorities decided he needed an operation, and he played for Liverpool with only one fully-functioning arm. After the War, he made his international debut in 1920 in Wales but by the time he won his third cap against England a couple of months later he was a Partick Thistle player, having put in a transfer request. He was first choice in goal for Scotland over the next couple of years, captaining the side once, and helped Partick Thistle to win the Scottish Cup in 1921 for the only time in their history with a clean sheet against Rangers in the final. However, as his wife and family continued to be based in Liverpool he was pleased to return to Merseyside in 1922 with New Brighton in the Lancashire Combination. He was clearly capable of playing at a higher level and joined Stoke the following spring, just before they were relegated, and then late in 1925 moved to Leicester City, where he had a final spell in the First Division. Latterly he was mainly in Leicester reserves and he finished his career with a couple of years back at New Brighton before retiring in 1931. By then he had opened a shop in Wallasey, Kenny Campbell Sports, which was his base for the rest of his life as he did not retire until he was in his eighties. He died in 1977 at his son's home in Wilmslow.

Peter CAMPBELL (1/0, 1898)
Peter Campbell
Born 17 January 1875 Cartsburn Street, Greenock, Renfrewshire
Died 4 May 1948 Mearns Street, Greenock, Renfrewshire
Scotland v Wales 1898.
Greenock Volunteers; Glasgow Perthshire 1894-95 [trial for Morton Nov 1894]; Burton Swifts Jan 1895-96; Morton 1896-98; Burton Swifts 1898-99; Morton 1899-1904.
After developing his skills in the juniors with Greenock Volunteers and Glasgow Perthshire, Campbell became a clever centre half with an unusual career path. Despite overtures from home town side Morton, who gave him a trial, he turned professional in January 1895 with Burton Swifts, at that time in the Football League Second Division. In return, they paid him £2 a week and found him a job locally as a boilermaker. A year and a half later he came home to Greenock and after two excellent seasons with Morton he won his only Scotland cap, a 5-2 win over Wales. He was tempted back to Burton in 1898 for one more campaign, before concluding his career with five years at Cappielow. He continued his trade as a boilermaker in Greenock, and remained in the town for the rest of his life.

Peter CAMPBELL (2/3, 1878-79)
Peter McGregor Campbell
Born 6 March 1857 Craigellan, Garelochhead, Argyllshire
Died February 1883 Bay of Biscay, off France.
Scotland v Wales 1878 (2), 1879 (1).
Rangers 1872-79; Blackburn Rovers 1879-80; Rangers 1880-82.
A key figure in the early history of Rangers, Campbell was a founder of the club in 1872. The son of a harbourmaster, he came from a comfortable background, brought up in a large villa; his uncle was honorary surgeon to Queen Victoria. A talented left-sided forward, he was the first Rangers player to win representative honours when he was selected by Glasgow against Sheffield in 1876, alongside clubmate Moses McNeil. Two years later in 1878 he was the first Rangers player to score a goal for Scotland, with two against Wales in a comprehensive 9-0 victory, and he scored another against the Welsh the following season. He was also in the first Rangers team to win a trophy, the Glasgow Charity Cup in 1879. That summer he was tempted south to join Blackburn Rovers, probably as a veiled professional, returning to Glasgow after a season. He gave up football in 1882 when, following in his father's footsteps, he qualified as a maritime engineer and pursued a seagoing career. Sadly, one of his earliest overseas voyages ended in tragedy. His ship the St Columba sailed from Penarth in South Wales on 28 January 1883 with a load of coal, bound for India, and ran into a storm in the Bay of Biscay; it sank with all hands and his body was never found. A memorial plaque in Penarth's Italian Gardens records his fate.

Jimmy CARABINE (3/0, 1938-39)
James Carabine
Born 23 November 1911 Forrest Street, Blantyre, Lanarkshire
Died 2 December 1987 Victoria Infirmary, Glasgow
Scotland v Netherlands 1938; Ireland 1938c; England 1939.
Larkhall Thistle; Third Lanark 1931-47 (Second Division 1935).

Carabine signed for newly-promoted Third Lanark aged 19 from junior side Larkhall Thistle, and spent the rest of his professional career with the Cathkin side. He was soon first choice at right back and remained in place throughout the 1930s. Although he experienced relegation in 1934, the team bounced right back with promotion as champions, and then reached the Scottish Cup final in 1936, only to lose narrowly to Rangers. Newcastle United tried very hard to take him south, but Thirds knew his worth and insisted he was not for sale, while the player himself was not keen. He came into the national team in 1938, winning three caps including one as captain of Scotland against Ireland which he described as the proudest day of his life. He also played five times for the Scottish League and went on the lengthy SFA tour of North America in the summer of 1939, showing his versatility by playing up front and scoring three in a match New York, and would surely have won more honours had it not been for the Second World War.

During the conflict he served in the Home Guard and then the Royal Corps of Signals, which allowed him to continue playing for Third Lanark when Army commitments allowed, and he made nine wartime appearances for Scotland against England, ending with the humiliating 8-0 defeat in October 1943. In December 1946 he was appointed as manager of Third Lanark, but continued to play until the end of the season before retiring. Three years later he decided he had had enough of management and resigned in March 1950. Subsequently he worked as a sports writer for the *Scottish Daily Express*, and lived in Rutherglen until his death in a Glasgow hospital.

Joe CASSIDY (4/1, 1921-24)
John Joseph Cassidy MM
Born 14 February 1894 John Street, Govan, Glasgow
Died 21 July 1949 Eastern Hospital, Duke Street, Glasgow
Scotland v Wales 1921, 1924; Ireland 1921 (1), 1923.
Vale of Clyde; Celtic Oct 1912-24 (Scottish League 1922; Scottish Cup 1923) [loans to for Vale of Atholl Oct-Dec 1913, Kilmarnock Nov 1913, Abercorn Dec 1913, Ayr United Dec 1913-15, Clydebank Sep 1915; Reading Dec 1915-16]; Bolton Wanderers 1924-25; Cardiff City Oct 1925-26; Dundee 1926-28; Clyde 1928-29; Ballymena Jan 1929-31 (Irish Cup 1929); Dundalk Apr-Aug 1931; Morton Aug 1931; Dundalk Sep 1931-32.

Brought up in Dalbeth, Cassidy was spotted at Vale of Clyde and signed for Celtic after a reserve team trial in 1912. At that time the inside right role was firmly in the grip of Jimmy McMenemy, so although he made his Celtic league debut in March 1913 he only appeared sporadically and was loaned out for experience to a variety of clubs, notably Ayr United. He had joined the Army in November 1915 and in his training period at Aldershot he played for Reading, before travelling to the front the following autumn. His active service as a Trooper with the Black Watch and the Scottish Horse (Lovat's Scouts) earned him the Military Medal in 1918. It was not until after the War that he was able to focus on his career with Celtic, and on his return to Glasgow he became a first team regular in 1919, and his clever footwork impressed the fans. His goals were invaluable and he was top scorer for Celtic in three seasons, including the title win of 1921-22. He headed the only goal of the game when Celtic beat Hibs in the Scottish Cup final of 1923 and in fact he scored 11 out of Celtic's 13 in the competition that season. Bolton Wanderers bought him in the summer of 1924, but his best days were behind him and he was unfortunate to lose weight from a severe illness that affected his stamina. When they let him leave after a year, at the age of 30 he embarked a bewildering tour of clubs in all parts of the British Isles, one consequence of which was that his first four children were born in different countries while he was at Celtic, Bolton, Cardiff and Ballymena, where he won the Irish Cup and played three times for the Irish League. He could not settle anywhere for long, and his career came to an end when he left Dundalk in January 1932, with no other club wanting to take him on. Struggling to cope with life outside football, allied to the tragic accidental death of his eldest son, he had a fall from grace in June 1933 when he was sentenced to four months hard labour for his part in stealing a haul of sovereigns from a house. He lived in Paisley at the time of his death in 1949 from stomach cancer, aged 55.

Willie CHALMERS (1/0, 1885)
William Crawford Chalmers
Born 27 July 1860 Mains Street, Blythswood, Glasgow
Died 13 May 1940 Jedburgh Avenue, Rutherglen, Lanarkshire
Scotland v Ireland 1885.
Rangers 1883-87; Clyde Sep 1887-89; Queen's Park Jan 1890; Birtley Jan-Mar 1890; Middlesbrough Ironopolis Apr 1890-92 (Northern League 1891, 1892); Darwen 1892.
Chalmers was an excellent goalkeeper who was already 23 when he joined Rangers in 1883, possibly from Athole FC, and was first choice for the best part of four years. In his first season with Rangers he was picked for the Glasgow eleven to face Sheffield, the first of many inter-city honours, and was also a reserve for Scotland. He was duly selected for Scotland in 1885 against Ireland, but had little to do in his one international as the forwards knocked in eight then he let in two late goals. The closest he came to honours with Rangers was in their FA Cup run of 1886-87, in which they reached the semi-final. However, Chalmers reportedly let the side down by eating too much at the pre-match meal, and was consequently immobile against Aston Villa, who won 3-1 and lifted the trophy the following month. He left Rangers that autumn and signed for Clyde, where he continued to be selected for Glasgow, until he moved to Sunderland to work as a joiner towards the end of 1889. Temporarily club-less, he answered a call from Queen's Park to return to Glasgow to face Corinthians in their New Year game, and played a few games for village side Birtley in County Durham. Then in April 1890, Middlesbrough Ironopolis signed him and he spent two great years with the club in which they won the Northern League twice. In 1892 he signed for Darwen but unknown to them he was carrying a serious knee injury, which prevented him from playing for the club. After a few months' rest he tried to train but his right knee buckled, confirming that his career was over. He returned to Middlesbrough, and subsequently to Glasgow, where he continued his trade as a joiner.

Stewart CHALMERS (1/0, 1929)
William Stewart Chalmers
Born 5 March 1907 Somerville Drive, Mount Florida, Glasgow
Died 13 November 1989 Crosshouse Hospital, Kilmarnock, Ayrshire
Scotland v Ireland 1929.
Queen's Park 1924-29; Heart of Midlothian 1929-32; Manchester United Sep 1932-34; Dunfermline Athletic Sep 1934-38.
Chalmers grew up in the shadow of Hampden Park and it was a natural choice to join Queen's Park while a student. A skilful inside forward who was equally adept with either foot, he was capped twice for Scotland amateurs, scoring

twice against England on his debut in 1928, and still held amateur status when he appeared for the full Scotland team against Ireland in February 1929 as a late replacement for Jimmy Dunn. His cap came after five years with the club, culminating in a successful season in which they scored 100 goals to finish fifth in the Scottish League, their highest ever placing. That summer he was faced with a choice between working full-time as a chartered accountant, having recently passed his exams, or becoming a professional footballer. He chose the latter having been offered excellent terms by Hearts and spent three seasons at Tynecastle, then moved to Manchester United where, although he made a great start, he never really settled. He came back to Scotland in 1934 and concluded his career with four years at Dunfermline Athletic where he was very much the star forward but he lost his enthusiasm after they were relegated in 1937. He retired from the game a year later and reverted to his profession as a chartered accountant, becoming a director of a soft drinks bottling company in Paisley for many years. He died in hospital in Kilmarnock aged 82.

Thomas CHAMBERS (1/2, 1894)
Thomas Chambers
Born 25 December 1872 Holygate, Broxburn, West Lothian
Died 24 December 1953 93rd Street, Edmonton, Alberta, Canada
Scotland v Wales 1894 (2).
Broxburn; St Bernard's Aug-Sep 1892; Heart of Midlothian Sep 1892; Burnley Sep 1892-93; Heart of Midlothian Oct 1893-96 (Scottish League 1895); Burnley 1896-97; St Bernard's 1897-98; East Stirlingshire Jan-Mar 1899; Broxburn 1902-1906.
An inside right with Broxburn, by the time he was 19 Chambers had plenty of offers and in the summer of 1892 he played the field by turning out for St Bernard's, Hearts and Burnley. After one game as a professional he wanted to return to Edinburgh, but the SFA refused to reinstate him as an amateur, so he simply went back to Burnley and played out the season in England. The following year professionalism was legalised in Scotland, which opened the door to a return and he became a regular in the Hearts team. With them he won the Scottish League title in 1895, but missed their Scottish Cup success the following year. Meanwhile, he was picked for Scotland and scored two second half goals against Wales on his only cap. He went back to Burnley for another season and had a few games with St Bernard's before taking a break from the game. Early in 1899 he had a brief association with East Stirlingshire, then he left the game again for three years before agreeing to assist a new senior club in Broxburn. The rest must have done him good as he served Broxburn for four years while working as a shale miner in West Lothian. However, he was ostracised for taking part in trade union activity and felt he had little choice but to emigrate. He travelled to Canada with his wife and three small children in 1906 and after a few years in British Columbia they settled in Alberta where he spent the rest of his life, and worked for 15 years as postmaster in the hamlet of Robb until he retired to Edmonton in 1949. NB he was born a year after his parents had another son called Thomas, who died in infancy.

George CHAPLIN (1/0, 1908)
George Duncan Chaplin
Born 26 September 1887 Court Street, Dundee
Died 4 May 1963 Warwick Hotel, Leamington Spa, Warwickshire
Scotland v Wales 1908.
Dundee Arnot; Dundee 1906-08; Bradford City Oct 1908-19 [guest for Hull City Jan-Apr 1916 and 1917-18; Chesterfield Apr 1917]; Coventry City 1919-23.
Brought up in Dundee just a few yards from Dens Park, Chaplin developed into a great talent at left back. Tall and powerful, he joined from local junior side Dundee Arnot and was such a hit in his first full season in senior football that he was capped against Wales in March 1908. His shirt from the international is now displayed in the Dens Park boardroom. That autumn, and little over a year after his league debut, Bradford City paid £600 for him in October and curiously his elder brother Jack took over the left back spot he vacated in the Dundee team. Chaplin spent over a decade at Valley Parade, although not without difficulties. After initially doing well he was selected again for Scotland in 1910 but had to withdraw through illness, which turned out to be the first sign of the tuberculosis that struck him down early in 1911. He was forced to miss two seasons, including Bradford's FA Cup victory, but was fortunate enough to recover fully and return to action, and had regained a regular place in the first team by the time war broke out. Because of his illness he was deemed unfit for front line service and worked as a driver during the conflict while continuing to play football. In 1919 he moved to Coventry City, newly elected to Division Two, and they appointed him captain. However, in the final game of the season he was involved in a plot to bribe a couple of Bury players to let Coventry win (which they did, 2-1), saving Coventry's place in the Football League by two points. The incident was not fully investigated for another three years, by which time Chaplin's career was virtually over and, finding him guilty, the FA banned him and nine others from football for life. Initially he denied the offence then in 1938 he made a full confession in a newspaper interview. The ban was lifted in 1946, by which time he was in the hotel business, having managed the Cottage Inn in Earlsdon, outside Coventry, then in the 1930s the Black Horse Inn at Marton, near Rugby, and from 1940 the Warwick Hotel in Leamington Spa, where he died.

Alec CHEYNE (5/4, 1929-30)
Alexander George Cheyne
Born 28 April 1907 Camden Street, Gorbals, Glasgow
Died 5 July 1983 Arbroath Infirmary, Arbroath, Angus
Scotland v England 1929 (1); Norway 1929 (3); Germany 1929; Netherlands 1929; France 1930.
Shettleston Juniors; Aberdeen Nov 1925-30; Chelsea 1930-32; Nimes Olympique 1932-34; Chelsea Mar 1934-37; Colchester United 1937-40 [guest for Chelmsford City 1939-40].
Cheyne is famous as the man who created the Hampden Roar. He scored direct from his trademark in-swinging corner in the last minute against England on his debut in 1929, and the resulting roar from the crowd took Scotland over the line for an unlikely victory. Strangely, Cheyne was only in the team as a late replacement for the injured

Tommy Muirhead. A year later, he went on Scotland's successful tour of Europe that summer, playing in all three matches and scoring a treble against the Norwegians, but he only won one more cap, in Paris the following summer. Cheyne had made his name as an inside right at Aberdeen, after coming north from Shettleston in 1925, although it was a year before he got a run in the team. He delighted the crowds at Pittodrie but was something of a rebel, describing a football career as 'bondage' and was hugely critical of the wage structures and the retain and transfer system. He advocated fixed term contracts for players, decades before Bosman became a reality. When he demanded a pay rise from Aberdeen there was little surprise that Chelsea paid a club record fee of £6,000 in 1930 to take him to London. He found it hard to settle at Stamford Bridge and when Chelsea tried to reduce his wages he left to try his luck at Nimes in France, where professionalism had just been legalised. Although he doubled his wages he found himself isolated, despite the company of fellow Scot Andy Wilson, and after a year and a half he asked for his contract to be cancelled. There were offers from other clubs in France but he returned to Chelsea, which still held his registration. By then he had lost much of his sharpness and played mainly in the reserves, yet when he wanted to leave he was disappointed that Chelsea asked for a transfer fee of £2,000. Rather than wait to see if any offers came along, in 1937 he signed for Colchester United, then a non-league team, and stayed until the outbreak of war. He was player-manager of Chelmsford City for a season then served with the Royal Armoured Corps and the RASC during the conflict. He then returned to Aberdeen where he worked as a bookkeeper at the Labour Exchange and was manager of Arbroath from 1949 to 1955. He also coached Banks o' Dee juniors in Aberdeen.

Alec CHRISTIE (3/1, 1898-99)
Alexander Jack Christie
Born 28 September 1873 Braeport, Dunblane, Perthshire
Died 26 March 1954 McAlpin Nursing Home, Hill Street, Glasgow
Scotland v Wales 1898; Ireland 1899 (1); England 1899.
Dunblane 1892-94; St Bernard's 1894-97; Queen's Park 1897-1901; St Bernard's 1901-02; Queen's Park 1902-04; Dunblane 1904-05.
Younger brother of the more famous Bob (below), Christie was educated at Daniel Stewart's College in Edinburgh where he played rugby, but decided to focus on association football after leaving school. He was fast, versatile and hard-working, playing mainly at centre half but equally at home in the forward line or defence. Having started out with his home town team in Dunblane he then moved around the central belt, playing as an amateur for St Bernard's while he trained and worked in Edinburgh, and then in Glasgow for Queen's Park, where he had his best years. He was capped against Wales in 1898, and against Ireland and England the following year, as well as scoring QP's opening goal in the Scottish Cup final of 1900, which was ultimately lost to Celtic. He also represented Perthshire five times due to his connection to Dunblane, where he finished his career in 1905, and occasionally played rugby for Stewart's College FP. Resolutely amateur, he was a founder of the Scottish Amateur FA in 1909. He had qualified as a lawyer in 1899, and practised as a solicitor in Glasgow in partnership with William Sellar, another Scotland internationalist. He lived in Bothwell until his death in 1954.

Bob CHRISTIE (1/0, 1884)
Robert Main Christie
Born 15 November 1865 Braeport, Dunblane, Perthshire
Died 15 May 1918 Red Cross Hospital, Rouen, France
Scotland v England 1884.
Dunblane 1879-82; Edinburgh University 1882-83; Queen's Park 1883-86 (Scottish Cup 1884, 1886); Dunblane 1886-87 and 1889-92.

By the age of 18, Christie had played for Scotland, won the Scottish Cup and scored in an FA Cup final. He could have become one of the great talents of his era but his top level career was cruelly cut short by injury. The son of a school teacher, he first played football as a youthful founder of Dunblane FC, and was already its star player when he went to Edinburgh University in 1882. In one year as a student he won the East of Scotland Shield and represented Edinburgh twice, then when he moved to Glasgow to train as an architect he was snapped up by Queen's Park. He quickly established himself on the left wing of the country's finest team and his first season, 1883-84, was extraordinary not just for 18-year-old Christie and his new club but for Scottish football in general. He was in the Queen's Park side which won the Scottish Cup for the fourth time in five years, did well enough to be chosen for Glasgow and then came the great honour of cap for Scotland against England. His dashing runs helped to carve out a 1-0 victory and he remains our third youngest internationalist of all time. The icing on the cake would have been an FA Cup triumph, and Queen's Park were the favourites for the showdown in London against Blackburn Rovers. Early in the match the Scots hit the post twice and Christie had a goal disallowed for offside, then Rovers scored two in quick succession. Christie registered a legitimate goal before the break to make it 2-1 but the second half passed without further scoring and the opportunity was lost. The following season, Christie twisted his knee in an FA Cup tie at Notts County, which put him out for the rest of the campaign. He recovered to score one of the goals that won the 1886 Scottish Cup final against Renton, then wrenched his knee in the match, an injury that effectively ended his top level career. He was able to continue playing in the less demanding environment of Dunblane, where he won the Perthshire Cup and was capped by Perthshire, and fully recovered his fitness while working for a couple of years in Paraguay. He played until 1892 and was Dunblane's guiding light as club secretary and rose to the top of the game as an administrator, being elected President of the Scottish FA in 1903. In other sports, he represented Scotland at curling, and was founding secretary of Dunblane's first golf club. A chartered surveyor and architect, he ran a practice in Dunblane, where his projects included the Burgh Chambers and his own house, now the Westlands Hotel. He was a dedicated volunteer and saw active service with the Black Watch in the South African War, and as a Major with the Labour Company in WW1. Sadly, he was killed in action in May 1918, having been gassed in a shell attack.

Jack CLELLAND (1/0, 1891)
John White Clelland
Born 6 January 1863 Woodside, Hamilton, Lanarkshire
Died 7 September 1944 Union Street, Larkhall, Lanarkshire
Scotland v Ireland 1891.
Royal Albert 1883-85; Cowlairs 1885-87; Royal Albert 1887-99 [guest for Battlefield Feb 1892].
Clelland, a centre half or right back, devoted most of his football career to Royal Albert in his home town of Larkhall. He captained the team in several good Scottish Cup runs and won the Lanarkshire Cup four times during his time there. His younger brothers Archibald and Robert also played for the club. He represented Lanarkshire many times as well as captaining Glasgow during a spell with Cowlairs, and finally achieved national recognition when he won his Scotland cap against Ireland in 1891. An all-round sportsman, in his earlier days he was a distance runner and won numerous athletics prizes at club meetings and ran for Clydesdale Harriers. For many years he was a mainstay of Larkhall Bowling Club and in 1911 he travelled to London to represent Scotland at bowls, while he was President of Larkhall Cycling Club and a prize-winning homing pigeon breeder. Outside of sport, he was a prominent figure in Larkhall as a parish councillor and as host of a pub in Raploch Street, close to Royal Albert's ground.

Bob CLEMENTS (1/0, 1891)
Robert Clements
Born 15 May 1866 Giles Street, Leith, Edinburgh
Died 23 May 1947 Anderson Place, Leith, Edinburgh
Scotland v Ireland 1891.
Leith Athletic 1888-92 [guest for St Bernard's Aug 1890].
A right half, then inside forward, Clements had a short career in which he only belonged to one senior team, Leith Athletic. He was clearly a creative player, valued for his cross balls to the forwards as well as pitching in with the occasional goal himself. Selected for East of Scotland in his first season with Leith, he reached his peak in 1891, captaining the East of Scotland team against Renfrewshire and then selected for Scotland against Ireland in March. At the end of the season Leith Athletic won the Rosebery Charity Cup, defeating Hearts in the final. They entered the Scottish League that summer and finished fourth in their first season, but could not maintain that level of form as several players left for England, while Clements himself was injured in the spring of 1892. That probably brought an end to his career as he had disappeared from the team by the autumn. A boilermaker to trade, he remained in Leith for the rest of his life.

Willie CLUNAS (2/1, 1924-25)
William McLean Clunas
Born 28 April 1899 Buchanan Street, Johnstone, Renfrewshire
Died 1 September 1967 Royal Alexandra Hospital, Paisley
Scotland v England 1924; Wales Oct 1925 (1).
Kilbarchan Athletic; St Mirren Mar 1921-23; Sunderland Nov 1923-31; Morton 1931-33; Basel 1933-34; Inverness Thistle 1934-37 player-coach.
Clunas was an imposing right half who displayed a 'blend of artistry and strength' according to one observer. Born in Johnstone, he moved down the road to Kilbarchan where his father was a police inspector, and his early football career was deferred as he served with the Royal Engineers Signals in the last year of the War. When demobbed he had a spell with the local junior side before he was signed by St Mirren in March 1921. In two seasons there he established himself as a fine talent and Sunderland paid a substantial fee to take him to Roker Park in November 1923. He enjoyed the best part of his career with Sunderland, winning two Scotland caps and he even scored a rare goal from long distance in his second match against Wales, although most of his goals came via the penalty spot. As he approached the veteran stage he spent two years at Morton but left when they were relegated in 1933. He coached Basel for a season then took up a position as player-coach at Inverness Thistle, transforming the team into an efficient unit and captained the team up to his retirement in 1937. He then returned to Paisley where he was match secretary of Johnstone Athletic. His elder brother Charles, who was killed in action in 1916, had played for Clyde.

Bill COLLIER (1/0, 1922)
William Collier
Born 11 December 1892 Sinclairstown, Dysart, Fife
Died 17 April 1954 Bridge of Earn Hospital, Perthshire
Scotland v Wales 1922.
Kirkcaldy United 1912-15 [guest for Raith Rovers Mar 1915]; Raith Rovers Feb 1920-24; Sheffield Wednesday 1924-25; Kettering Town 1925-30 player-manager.

Brought up in Kirkcaldy, Collier worked as a miner in the Pannie Pit and played football as an amateur for Kirkcaldy United before the First World War, making a single guest appearance for Raith Rovers. In May 1915 he joined the Fife and Forfar Yeomanry and played regularly for his regimental team, seeing active service in Egypt where he was wounded in November 1917 (the same year his brother Walter was killed in action). His football career really only took off after he left the army. He signed for Raith Rovers in 1920 and was such a success on the left of the famed half-back line of Raeburn, Morris and Collier that he was capped against Wales in 1922, aged 29. There was adventure in 1923 when he went on tour with Raith Rovers to the Canary Islands, but he struggled to return to the heights of performance that won him a cap. Sheffield Wednesday paid over £500 for his signature in the summer of 1924, but he was soon dropped from the first team and moved to non-league Kettering the following summer where he combined playing with management, and did well in the transfer market, particularly with Scottish clubs. In 1930 he was appointed manager at Dartford, where among his discoveries was Eddie Hapgood, who went on to star for Arsenal and England. He resigned in 1937 to return to Dunfermline where he ran the Unicorn Bar, and was still living in the town at the time of his death in hospital. His brother John was with Hull City and York City in the 1920s. Confusingly, he had a cousin also called Bill Collier who played left back before the War with Raith Rovers then emigrated to Canada.

Tom COLLINS (1/0, 1909)
Thomas Collins
Born 16 April 1882 Carlow Place, Leven, Fife
Died 30 July 1929 Church Road, Tottenham, London
Scotland v Wales 1909.
Leven Thistle; Heart of Midlothian 1903-05 [loan to Bathgate Feb 1905]; East Fife 1905-06; Heart of Midlothian 1906-10; Tottenham Hotspur Nov 1910-1915; East Fife Aug-Oct 1915.

Brought up on the Fife coast, Collins was an excellent golfer but made his name in football as a hard-working right back with great positional sense, although sometimes ponderous. He initially went to Hearts in 1903 but had a slow start to his career and was allowed to leave after two years at the club. However, he blossomed with his newly-formed local side East Fife and returned to Tynecastle with an enhanced reputation after a season. He had missed their Scottish Cup victory but did feature in their run to the final of 1907 which was lost to Celtic, becoming the mainstay of the Hearts defence. This led to him being selected in 1909 for the Scottish League against the Football League and, just two days later, for the national team against Wales in Wrexham. Sadly, tragedy struck in the summer of 1910 when his wife Andrina died of tuberculosis and although he remained at Hearts long enough to represent the Scottish League once more, he moved south in November to join Spurs. He made a fresh start in north London, marrying again a couple of years later, and persevered with a struggling Spurs side which narrowly avoided relegation most years. When football was suspended for the War in 1915 he returned home to play as a guest for East Fife and also planned to sign for Dundee Hibernians but the paperwork was never completed as he signed up with the Royal Field Artillery as a gunner. He saw active service in France for two years until he was badly wounded by an exploding shell in December 1917, three weeks after being promoted to Sergeant, losing his left arm and leg and suffering shrapnel wounds to his neck and head. He spent three months in hospital and initially he returned to Leven, where he was presented with a cheque for £250 by well-wishers, before he settled back in Tottenham. Fitted with an artificial leg, he lived a short distance from White Hart Lane and often went to see Spurs in his invalid chair until he died from kidney disease and the long-term effects of his injuries, aged just 47.

Donald COLMAN (4/0, 1911-13)
Donald Cameron Cunningham
Born 14 August 1878 Main Street, Renton, Dunbartonshire
Died 5 October 1942 King Street, Aberdeen
Scotland v Wales 1911; Ireland 1911, 1913c; England 1911.
Glasgow Perthshire; Tontine Athletic; Renton 1896-97; Maryhill Juniors 1897-1905; Motherwell 1905-07; Aberdeen 1907-20 [guest for Renton May 1916; Ayr United Jan-Apr 1918; St Mirren Mar-Apr 1919; Brann Bergen 1919]; Dumbarton 1920-23 player-manager.

His real name was Cunningham but he adopted his grandmother's surname of Colman in a youthful attempt to hide his footballing activities from his parents, and the name stuck. He made his bow in the Scottish League with Renton in 1896 before reverting to a lengthy time in the juniors at Maryhill. He made three junior appearances for Scotland and lifted the Junior Cup with them in 1900, then played in two further finals before he finally stepped back to the senior game with Motherwell at the late age of 27. He had a couple of years at Fir Park then in 1907 joined Aberdeen where his career finally took off. He was virtually ever-present at right back for a decade at Pittodrie, winning his first international cap in 1911 aged 32, also appearing twice for the Scottish League. When Aberdeen were forced to close in 1917 he undertook wartime service with the Royal Engineers and made guest appearances for Ayr United and St Mirren. He returned to Pittodrie for the 1919-20 season after the first of several annual summer coaching stints with Brann Bergen, which he enjoyed so much that he undertook them every year for a decade. Despite his advancing years he still had ability and he wound down his career close to home at Dumbarton, initially as a player and then as manager from 1922. He played his last game in 1923 aged 44 and remained at Boghead until 1931 when he returned to Aberdeen as trainer from 1931-39. He achieved lasting fame by inventing the dug-out, forerunner to today's bench and technical area, as he was convinced that it was the best place to watch players' footwork. Sadly, he died of tuberculosis in 1942.

James CONNOR (1/0, 1886)
James Connor
Born 22 February 1861 North Street, Airdrie, Lanarkshire
Died 29 January 1899 Tuphall Terrace, Hamilton, Lanarkshire
Scotland v Ireland 1886.
Excelsior 1878-81; Airdrieonians 1881-93 [guest for Queen's Park Dec 1885, Jan 1887, Dec 1887; Corinthians Jan 1886].

A founder member of Excelsior in 1878, Connor played originally at half-back before dropping back to goalkeeper after the club changed its name to Airdrieonians in 1881. In this position he was the first man from Airdrie to win a Scotland cap, travelling to Belfast for a convincing 7-2 victory in 1886. This reflected Airdrieonians' local supremacy at the time, as they also won the Lanarkshire Cup that season, with Connor keeping goal. His other claim to fame was that he faced the world's first penalty kick in June 1891, in which he was beaten by James McLuggage's shot from 12 yards in the Airdrie Charity Cup final. He remained loyal to Airdrieonians throughout his career, although he made occasional guest appearances for Queen's Park in friendlies and once for Corinthians. After giving up playing he continued as a committee member and was President of Airdrieonians in 1894/95. He then moved to Hamilton but shortly afterwards he died of pneumonia aged 37, leaving a wife and young family, for whom Celtic played Queen's Park in a benefit match.

Jimmy CONNOR (4/0, 1930-34)
James Connor
Born 1 June 1909 Richard Street, Renfrew, Renfrewshire
Died 8 May 1980 Grange Park Avenue, Sunderland
Scotland v France 1930; Ireland Sep 1931, 1934; England 1934.
Glasgow Perthshire; St Mirren 1926-30; Sunderland 1930-39 (Football League 1936).

An outstanding left winger, Connor could do more with his left than many players could do with both feet. The great Raich Carter rated him better than Stanley Matthews and wrote that Connor was the best outside left he ever saw: 'If Jimmy didn't hypnotise the right backs, he tortured them. I've seen him move in from the corner flag, beat five opponents along the byeline then cut the ball into the goalmouth'. A junior internationalist with Glasgow Perthshire, in 1926 Connor was signed by St Mirren manager Johnny Cochrane, and when Cochrane went to Sunderland he made sure his star winger followed. He arrived at Roker Park in May 1930, just before his first Scotland appearance against France, having already been a reserve for the home internationals, and went on to win three more caps. His talent captivated not just the Sunderland fans, but also the Spanish public on two tours to Spain with Sunderland in 1934 and 1935. He played in all 42 games as Sunderland won the Football League in 1936 but the following February he was seriously injured in a cup tie which meant he missed their FA Cup victory. Although he recovered by the autumn he had lost his place in the team to Eddie Burbanks and decided to retire in 1939. He resumed his trade as a joiner and lived in Sunderland for the rest of his life.

Willie COOK (3/0, 1934)
William Lindsay Cook
Born 11 March 1903 Rosebank Street, Dundee
Died 7 June 1981 Royal Infirmary, Dundee
Scotland v England 1934; Ireland 1934; Wales 1934.
Dundee North End; Forfar Athletic 1924-25; Dundee 1925-28; Bolton Wanderers Dec 1928-36 (FA Cup 1929); Blackpool Apr 1936-37; Reading Apr 1937-38; Dundee Oct 1938-42 [guest for Hibernian 1940-41; Dundee United Nov 1941]; Carnoustie Panmure 1942-43.

A diminutive left winger standing just 5 feet 4 inches tall, Cook was one of the smallest players ever to represent Scotland although he had a long wait for his cap. His club career had started with a season at Forfar Athletic then he had a steady three years at Dundee where he was talented enough to be compared to Alan Morton. He was selected twice for the Scottish League, both against the Irish, and toured North America with the SFA in the summer of 1927, but after that there was a seven year gap before he finally played for the full Scotland team. By then he was 31 years old, having joined Bolton Wanderers in December 1928 for a £4,000 fee. Within a few months of going south he had helped Bolton to win the FA Cup. The team was relegated in 1933, and curiously it was while they were in the Second Division that he won all three Scotland caps. Bolton were promoted in 1935 and Cook moved on the following year to Blackpool but while they, too, won promotion he could not enjoy it as he suffered a broken leg. He signed for Reading in the Third Division South and by 1938, firmly at the veteran stage, he was welcome back home at Dundee. After the outbreak of war he continued to play while serving as a fitness officer in the forces, and finally retired in 1943 after a season with his local junior side. A clerk with a timber firm, later he ran Cook's Bar in Hilltown, Dundee, and indulged his passion for golf near his home in Carnoustie.

Jimmy COWAN (3/0, 1896-98)
James Cowan
Born 17 October 1868 Burn Street, Bonhill, Dunbartonshire
Died 12 December 1918 St Barts Hospital, London
Scotland v England 1896, 1897, 1898c.
Vale Athletic; Vale of Leven 1887-89; Aston Villa 1889-1902 (Football League 1894, 1896, 1897, 1899, 1900; FA Cup 1895, 1897).

Cowan was probably the finest Scottish centre half of his time. A born tackler and excellent passer of the ball, he was renowned for his uncanny judgement and anticipation, and his strong and powerful build meant he was able to charge opponents and take their knocks with impunity. If he had a fault, he was notorious for his poor shooting. After a couple of years at Vale of Leven, where he represented Dunbartonshire several times, he was tempted south in 1889 by Warwick County but he never played for them as he was intercepted by Aston Villa and spent the rest of his career with the club in a period of extraordinary success. He was at the heart of the team which won with five league titles and two FA Cups in seven seasons, including the 'double' in 1897 when he played alongside his brother

John, a left winger. Described in one paper as 'certainly the best half back who ever kicked a ball, a player of great judgement and dash', he was an obvious choice for Scotland in 1896, the first year that English professionals were selected. He remained first choice for the next two years and in 1898 he was honoured with the captaincy of the Scotland side. However, a desperately poor performance against England filled with erratic behaviour led to claims that he was drunk. Although Cowan threatened his accusers with legal action, the mud stuck and he was never capped again. Nonetheless he continued to be the engine room of continued Villa success. On the side, he won the famous Powderhall sprint handicap in Edinburgh at New Year 1896, and took his preparation so seriously that he took leave from Aston Villa, claiming he needed to recover from an injury, only to spend a month at Saltcoats undergoing special training. His winnings more than covered a club fine, but the trick did not work the following year, with Villa refusing him permission to take part. After he retired in 1902 he coached at Villa, then went to London where he transformed the fortunes of Queen's Park Rangers, managing them to two Southern League titles. He left abruptly in the autumn of 1913, apparently on the grounds of ill health, and died five years later in a London hospital.

Willie COWAN (1/1, 1924)
William Duncan Cowan
Born 9 August 1896 Murdoch Terrace, Edinburgh
Died 24 January 1965 Gosforth, Northumberland
Scotland v England 1924 (1).
Dalkeith Thistle; Tranent Juniors; Dundee Jan 1920-23; Newcastle United 1923-26 (FA Cup 1924); Manchester City 1926-27; St Mirren 1927-29; Peebles Rovers Feb-Nov 1929; Northfleet United Nov 1929-Feb 1930; North Shields Feb-Sep 1930; Hartlepools United Sep-Oct 1930; Darlington Oct 1930-31; Bath City 1931-33.

A late starter in senior football, perhaps because of war service, Cowan was already 23 when he joined Dundee from Tranent Juniors early in 1920. Playing at inside right, he was recognised as an elegant and creative player who could make and score goals, but only really became a fixture in the team in his third season at Dens Park. He was selected to face the Football League in 1923 only to withdraw through injury, then just after he returned from Dundee's tour of Spain that summer he was signed by Newcastle United for around £3,000. He had a great start on Tyneside and in his first season he won the FA Cup, and two weeks later he returned to Wembley to play his one match for Scotland, scoring the opening goal in a 1-1 draw. Subsequently, however, a drop in form led to him being barracked by the crowd and he asked for a transfer. He was persuaded to stay and lasted another couple of years, making over 100 appearances for Newcastle before going to Manchester City in 1926. That turned out a failure, as was his next move to St Mirren, and by the end of the decade he was playing in non-league football. He jumped from Peebles Rovers to a selection of clubs around England, never finding his form or settling, although he had a belated swansong with Bath City in the Southern League, captaining the side for over two years. He returned to the north-east where he worked for the Ministry of Fuel and lived in Gosforth's Kenton Road until his death in a nursing home in 1965.

Allan CRAIG (3/0, 1929-32)
Allan Leggat Craig
Born 7 February 1904 Springbank Road, Paisley, Renfrewshire
Died 12 November 1983 Royal Alexandra Infirmary, Paisley, Renfrewshire
Scotland v Norway 1929; Netherlands 1929; England 1932.
Paisley Carlisle; Saltcoats Victoria; Motherwell Dec 1924-33 (Scottish League 1932); Chelsea Jan 1933-39; Dartford Aug-Sep 1939.

An exemplary centre half who was a model of consistency throughout his career, Craig is remembered chiefly for the blunder that cost a cup final. He joined Motherwell in December 1924 after just a few months of junior football and went straight into the first team. It was something of a baptism of fire for the young defender at a difficult time for the club, which only just avoided relegation on goal average at the end of his first season. However, from 1926 until he left the club, they never finished out of the top three and Craig was always in the thick of it, his headers and powerful physique helping to subdue the most potent opposition forwards, although if he had a weakness it was his passing. His abilities were recognised by Scotland when he went on the tour of Europe in 1929, playing in two of the matches, and he was recalled to face England in 1932. He also played once for the Scottish League in 1930. The defining drama of his life came in the Scottish Cup final of 1931, as Motherwell were heading for victory against Celtic until the very last minute when Craig headed an innocuous cross into his own net. They lost the replay and the chance was gone. That tragedy was, thankfully, succeeded by the summit of Motherwell's achievements, winning the Scottish League in 1931-32, the only time in the inter-war years that the title left Glasgow. He was made club captain but just a few months later, in January 1933, he had been displaced from the team by John Blair and was sold to Chelsea. For six years he was a dominant figure with the London club, being appointed captain for a while, but when Chelsea had a clear-out in 1939 he signed for Southern League side Dartford. However, war intervened a few days later and his football career was over. He returned to Paisley where he worked as a lorry driver and labourer, and continued to be a lifelong supporter of his old club Motherwell.

'Tully' CRAIG (8/1, 1927-30)
Thomas Craig
Born 12 October 1897 Black Close, Bainsford, Falkirk
Died 29 January 1963 Railway Hotel, Ovenden, Yorkshire
Scotland v Ireland 1927, 1928, 1930; Norway 1929c (1); Germany 1929c; Netherlands 1929c; Wales 1929; England 1930.
Grange Rovers; Celtic 1919-22; Alloa Athletic 1922-23; Rangers 1923-35 (Scottish League 1924, 1925, 1927, 1928, 1929, 1930, 1931; Scottish Cup 1928, 1930).

Craig's nickname Tully relates to Tullibody where he spent several years as a child, although he spent most of his life in Carronshore, where he was working as a dock labourer when he first started playing senior football in 1919. He had just been demobbed from First World War service with the Argyll and Sutherland Highlanders, and was spotted at inside left playing for Grange Rovers, who reached the Stirlingshire Junior Cup final. Although Everton gave him a trial he signed for Celtic and spent three years there but failed to reach his potential, playing only nine first team games before he was released to join Alloa in part exchange for Willie Crilley. Here he finally started to show his class, and after just one season he was signed by Rangers for £750. It was an inspired move as he had an impressive decade at Ibrox, mainly at left half, winning seven league titles and two Scottish Cups, the first in 1928. He missed a penalty in the 1929 final, then experienced the joy of scoring the winner in the 1930 final replay, his speculative lob landing in the net after Partick goalkeeper John Jackson was blinded by the sun. He first achieved international recognition in 1927 and was appointed captain of the Scotland team that toured Europe in 1929. Used sparingly by Rangers from about 1931 onwards, he stopped playing football in 1935 and was immediately appointed manager of Falkirk, a post he held for 15 years. He took them to the Second Division title in his first season and a fourth-place finish in 1938, a year in which he oversaw Scotland's first all-ticket match, a Scottish Cup tie against Rangers. With the team struggling in the post-war years, he eventually resigned in the summer of 1950. He managed Linfield for a year from February 1951, then left football and spent his final years in Yorkshire where his son ran a hotel near Halifax.

Jimmy CRAPNELL (9/0, 1929-32)
James Scrymagour Crapnell
Born 4 June 1903 Thread Street, Paisley, Renfrewshire
Died 24 December 1991 Dykebar Hospital, Paisley, Renfrewshire
Scotland v England 1929, 1932c; Norway 1929; Germany 1929; France 1930c, 1932; Ireland Feb 1931, 1932c; Switzerland 1931c.
Ardeer Thistle; Cambuslang Rangers; Airdrieonians Nov 1926-33; Motherwell Jan 1933-35.

A tenacious right back with 'dash and power' who gave his all for 90 minutes, Crapnell is the most capped player in Airdrie's history. As well as nine appearances for Scotland, four of them as captain, he played five times for the Scottish League. He started out with Ardeer Thistle, where he won the Ayrshire Junior Cup in 1925 alongside his brother Joe, then briefly at Cambuslang Rangers until Airdrie paid £100 for him in November 1926. Despite a lack of inches at 5 feet 5, he immediately slotted into the Airdrie defence where he was a pillar for several years. The club was no longer the attacking power it was, following the departure of Hughie Gallacher, but the excellent full-back partnership of Crapnell and George McQueen ensured a series of mid-table finishes. He won his first cap in the last-minute 1-0 win over England in 1929 before going on Scotland's continental tour that summer and made his first appearance for the Scottish League in the autumn. A model of consistency who rarely missed an Airdrie match, remarkably he was a part-time player, working as an engineer at the Rolls-Royce factory in Hillingdon. He captained Scotland against France in 1930, and won four more caps over the next couple of years. Eventually, Airdrie's financial problems forced the club to sell him and although there were rumours of interest from English clubs, he joined Motherwell who paid a club record fee in January 1933. A few months later he featured in their Scottish Cup final defeat to Celtic, which turned out to be his final chance of glory as he suffered a series of injuries including a dislocated shoulder on Motherwell's tour of South Africa. He made a reluctant decision to retire in October 1934, although he did return for some reserve matches later in the season. After the Second World War he was appointed manager at Alloa in 1945 to get the club back on its feet, but left after a season as he found the travelling too much. He then managed St Johnstone from 1947 for six years but aside from rare highlights such as the discovery of Paddy Buckley, later sold to Aberdeen, it was mainly a struggle and the side never challenged for promotion in his time there. Eventually he decided that management was too stressful and resigned early in 1953, albeit on good terms. He returned to his trade as an engineer in Paisley, and lived in the town until his death in 1991.

David CRAWFORD (3/0, 1894-1900)
David Crawford
Born 9 March 1873 King Street, Paisley, Renfrewshire
Died 23 August 1937 Crichton Royal Hospital, Dumfries
Scotland v Wales 1894, 1900; Ireland 1894.
Victoria Juniors; St Mirren 1892-94; Rangers 1894-1903 (Scottish League 1899, 1900, 1902) [loan to Raith Rovers Apr 1903]; St Mirren 1903-07.

As a promising right back at St Mirren, Crawford was capped twice by Scotland in the space of a week in March 1894. Anxious to take advantage of his professional status he signed for Rangers that summer, but although he spent nearly a decade at Ibrox, most of the time he was unable to secure a regular first team spot as he was understudy to the great Nicol Smith and Jock Drummond. He did not really establish himself until 1898 when he won a Glasgow Cup medal and then switched to left back to replace the injured Drummond. He grabbed the opportunity and partnered Smith in defence for 1898/99, missing just one game in the memorable season when Rangers famously won every league match. He was back in the understudy role the following season but his reliability was recognised in 1900 with a third and final Scotland cap, and he made sufficient appearances to win a medal in two more title-winning seasons. He returned to St Mirren in 1903 and was clearly still a powerful influence, being selected as late as 1906 by the Scottish League against the Football League. He retired the following year and worked as a mercantile clerk in Paisley. Latterly he lived in Scotstoun, Glasgow, and died of epilepsy in a Dumfries hospital.

Jimmy CRAWFORD (5/0, 1931-33)
James Crawford
Born 21 May 1904 Park Grove Terrace, Tollcross, Glasgow

Died 24 May 1976 Robb Place, Castle Douglas, Kirkcudbrightshire
Scotland v Ireland Sep 1931, 1932; France 1932; Wales 1932; England 1933.
Queen's Park 1922-37 (Second Division 1923).

Crawford was a ferociously fast right winger who could regularly cut inside to score goals. Brought up in Dennistoun where he went to Whitehill School, he had already been capped as a schoolboy when he joined Queen's Park in 1922, and immediately settled into the team as the club won the Second Division title in his debut season. He spent the rest of his career in the First Division, as Queen's reached great heights in the league, finishing fifth in 1929, their highest-ever position, and they were still in the top league when he retired in 1937. However, his career is remarkable for his prominence on the international stage, although he had to forego what should have been his first full cap in 1930 due to appendicitis. In the early 1930s he made a bewildering series of appearances for different Scotland teams and ended up with five full caps, ten amateur caps, and played three times for the Scottish League. In 1933, he faced England twice in consecutive weeks for the amateur team and the full national team, as did Bob Gillespie who captained both sides. Then in 1936 he became the first Scot to play football for Great Britain in the Olympic Games, featuring in both their matches against China and Poland in Berlin. He was also an athletics sprint champion, sufficient for him to win the Scottish 100 yard title three times and the 220 yards once, while he set Scottish record over 75 yards in 1930 running for Shettleston Harriers, and equalled the 100 yard record in 1926 while competing for Scotland at Hampden Park. As an amateur sportsman he needed a flexible career and, unusually, he worked in retail sales for ladies' wear. During the Second World War he served with the RAF as a Flight Sergeant in England.

Willie CRINGAN (5/0, 1920-23)
William Cringan
Born 15 May 1890 Midhouse Row, Muirkirk, Ayrshire
Died 12 May 1958 High Street, Bathgate, West Lothian
Scotland v Wales 1920c, 1923c; Ireland 1922; England 1922, 1923c.
Douglas Water Thistle; Sunderland 1910-17 [guest for Wishaw Thistle Aug-Dec 1915; Ayr United Jan 1916-17; Heart of Midlothian May 1916]; Celtic 1917-23 (Scottish League 1919, 1922; Scottish Cup 1923); Third Lanark Oct 1923-24; Motherwell 1924-25; Inverness Thistle Mar-May 1925 player-coach; Bathgate Nov 1925-27.
A cool centre half with sound positional sense, Cringan was brought up in the Lanarkshire mining community of Ponfeigh, near Douglas Water, where he was a neighbour of Peter Nellies, another Scotland half-back. From his local junior side he joined Sunderland in 1910 and played in their FA Cup final defeat to Aston Villa in 1913. When Sunderland closed down in 1915 he returned to work in the pits at home in Douglas Water, playing as a guest for Wishaw Thistle and Ayr United, and even won a Rosebery Cup winner's medal with Hearts. Eventually in 1917 he was transferred formally to Celtic for a substantial fee and this gave him the stage he needed. He was selected for a Victory international against Ireland and was made Scotland captain on his full debut against Wales in 1920, the first official international after the War. He went on to raise his caps total to five, the last two of them as captain, although he had to retire through injury at half-time against Wales in 1923. Meanwhile he played three times for the Scottish League, won the league twice with Celtic and captained the side to victory in the Scottish Cup final of 1923. Unfortunately he then upset the directors at Celtic by trying to negotiate higher bonuses for the players, and was told to leave. He moved across the city to Third Lanark but had another falling-out with the directors, this time over his best position, and he wound down his career at Motherwell, Inverness and finally Bathgate, then in the Second Division. The West Lothian town appealed to him and he settled down there, running the Star Inn for many years until he retired in 1953. His other sport was quoits and he regularly reached the latter stages of the Lanarkshire championship. His brother Jimmy played for Birmingham.

Jimmy CROAL (3/0, 1913-14)
James Anderson Croal
Born 27 July 1885 Florence Street, Gorbals, Glasgow
Died 16 September 1939 River Parrett, South Petherton, Somerset
Scotland v Ireland 1913; Wales 1914; England 1914.
Falkirk Juniors; Rangers 1905-06; Ayr Parkhouse Apr-May 1906; Stenhousemuir Aug-Oct 1906; Ayr Parkhouse Oct 1906-07; Stenhousemuir Feb-May 1907; Alloa Athletic 1907-10; Dunfermline Athletic Aug-Nov 1910; Falkirk Nov 1910-14 (Scottish Cup 1913); Chelsea Apr 1914-22; Fulham Mar 1922-24.
A teacher by profession, Croal showed his intellectual potential as a 13-year-old when he won a scholarship to Falkirk High School. Playing with Falkirk Juniors, he had captained the Scotland junior side by the time he joined Rangers in 1905, but made little impact at Ibrox and played just three competitive matches. He was allowed to leave at the end of his first season and bumped around the lower leagues for several years while Rangers retained his registration. Three years at Alloa made him a much better player and he really started to attract attention in a short spell with Dunfermline. They wanted to keep him but in November 1910 Falkirk stepped in to pay the £10 which Rangers demanded for his signature. It was an outlay they would recoup many times over as they won the Scottish Cup in 1913 and Croal was honoured with three international caps and a Scottish League appearance, on top of which they sold him to Chelsea for £2,500. Within months of his move to London in 1914 the First World War broke out, and although he played on for a while, reaching the FA Cup final in his first season, in 1916 he signed up to serve with the King's Royal Rifle Corps, rising to the rank of Sergeant Major. He resumed playing at Stamford Bridge after the conflict and in 1922 moved down the road to Fulham for his last two seasons. Throughout his football

career he worked as a school teacher, initially in Falkirk then in Paddington while at Chelsea, and after hanging up his boots he taught at Lambeth and lived at Streatham Common. His story has a sad ending, as shortly after the outbreak of the Second World War in 1939 he went to Somerset with a group of child evacuees, then went missing. His body was found a week later in the River Parrett near Yeovil.

Johnny CROSBIE (2/0, 1920-22)
John Crosbie
Born 9 October 1895 Grasshill Row, Glenbuck, Ayrshire
Died 1 February 1982 Blackfriars Walk, Ayr
Scotland v Wales 1920; England 1922.
Glenbuck Cherrypickers; Muirkirk Athletic; Ayr United Oct 1913-20; Birmingham 1920-32 (Second Division 1921); Chesterfield July-Nov 1932; Stourbridge Nov 1932-33 player-manager.

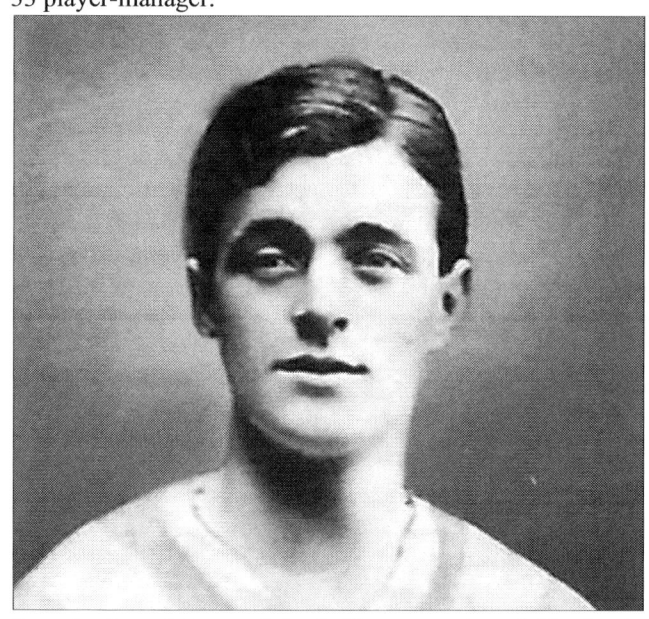

Born in the mining and football community of Glenbuck, Crosbie took his unmarried mother's surname. He started out in football with the famous Cherrypickers then had a brief association with Muirkirk before joining Ayr United aged 18. He made such an impact at inside right that he was even called 'a new Bobby Walker', although any ambitions had to be put on hold. A Territorial, he was called up to fight in the first month of the War and was a Trooper with the Lanarkshire Yeomanry but he appears not to have seen active service, remaining in Scotland until his discharge at the end of 1918. This allowed him to continue to play for Ayr when military duties allowed. His talent was recognised with his selection against Ireland in a Victory International as a replacement for Jimmy Bowie, then he won his first full cap in 1920 in Wales, having formed an excellent right wing partnership at Ayr with his brother William. A couple of months later he signed for Birmingham for a fee of nearly £4,000, of which he received £650, and the English club got great value for money as he was an ever-present in his first season when the team won the Second Division title, and he won his second Scotland cap against England in 1922. He spent the best years of his professional career at Birmingham, making the most of his creativity and ability to dictate a game, and featured in the 1931 FA Cup final which was lost to near rivals West Brom. After he left Birmingham in 1932 he played briefly with Chesterfield and Stourbridge, and had a coaching appointment in Gothenburg before retiring from the game.

Jock CROSS (1/0, 1903)
John Halliday Cross
Born 12 February 1881 Belhaven Road, Wishaw, Lanarkshire
Died 3 May 1955 Belhaven Road, Wishaw, Lanarkshire
Scotland v Ireland 1903.
Wishaw Rovers; Dalziel Rovers; Petershill; Third Lanark Nov 1898-1904 (Scottish League 1904); Queen's Park Rangers 1904-05; Third Lanark 1905-10; Wishaw Thistle 1910-14.

Cross was a talented youngster who had just been selected for the Lanarkshire Junior League aged 17 when he impressed Third Lanark in a trial and was immediately signed up in November 1898. He had an excellent decade with the club, and played in every match of their title-winning season in 1903-04, when they retained the Glasgow Cup into the bargain. By then he had made his Scotland debut against Ireland in 1903, a month after representing the Scottish League. However, although he played for Glasgow there would be no further international honours. He missed Third Lanark's Scottish Cup win of 1905 as he was spending a season in the Southern League with QPR, accompanied by his younger brother William, but soon returned to Cathkin and there was another Scottish Cup final in 1906, which was lost to Hearts. He was mainly a left half, but on occasion Thirds played him at outside left, in which position the great Alex McNair named him as one of the best he had ever played against because of his unpredictability and his directness: 'He nurses the ball well and his centres and shots are always a source of danger.' Shortly after another Glasgow Cup win in 1908 Cross had a bizarre injury, tripping over a small dog at training and suffering badly scraped knees. He played one match in goal for Thirds, against Hearts in April 1910 while Jimmy Brownlie was on Scotland duty, and that summer he left the club to join Wishaw Thistle. He spent four years with his home town club and ended his playing career there, although in 1912 he was suspended by the SFA for six months for playing in a works competition during the close season. When war broke out he joined the Sportsman's Battalion in 1915, serving with the Highland Light Infantry, and was wounded. After the War he returned to Wishaw where he worked in a local factory, coached Overtown Juniors, and was closely involved with the Salvation Army. He remained in the town for the rest of his life, dying in 1955 two weeks after his wife, in the same street as he was born.

Johnny CRUM (2/0, 1936-38)
John Crum
Born 1 January 1912 Main Street, Maryhill, Glasgow
Died 6 July 1969 Dudley Drive, Hyndland, Glasgow
Scotland v England 1936; Ireland 1938.
Kilmun Thistle; Ashfield; Celtic Feb 1932-42 (Scottish League 1936, 1938; Scottish Cup 1937); Morton 1942-46.
A junior internationalist with Ashfield, scoring Scotland's goal in a 1-0 win over England, Crum signed for Celtic

early in 1932 but had to wait for his chance, although he did find the net twice on his first team debut in October that year. Two footed, he generally featured in the centre or at inside left with Celtic when he became a regular, so it was a major surprise when he was selected at outside right to face England in 1936. His first cap might have been even more memorable as he was on the point of scoring late in the game when he was fouled, and Tommy Walker equalised from the resulting penalty while Crum was still receiving treatment. He had a knack of being involved in key goals, scoring the opener of Celtic's Scottish Cup victory against Aberdeen in 1937, and crashing home the winner against Everton in the Exhibition Trophy final of 1938. That turned out to be quite a week as he got married a few days later. Also in 1938 he won his second and final cap, at centre forward against Ireland. When he moved to Morton in 1942, who unusually for wartime paid a transfer fee, Celtic might have thought they were offloading a veteran but he continued to shine and scored regularly until he gave up football in 1946. Originally a railway worker, after retiring he became a sales manager in a sports shop in Glasgow. NB he was born with the surname Crumbe, and changed it to the shortened version before he started playing.

Dave CUMMING (1/0, 1938)
David Scott Cumming
Born 6 May 1910 Woodside, Aberdeen
Died 18 April 1993 Stracathro Hospital, Brechin, Angus
Scotland v England 1938.
Woodside Thistle; Hall Russell's; Aberdeen 1930-34; Arbroath 1934-36; Middlesbrough Oct 1936-48 [guest for Newcastle United 1943-45].
Cumming became a footballer almost by accident when he was asked to fill a gap in a juvenile side, and proved such an adept goalkeeper that two years later he stepped up from junior side Hall Russell's to Aberdeen. It proved something of a false dawn as, after an initial run of six matches in 1930, he only played twice more in four years and was given a free transfer in 1934. However, he was rejuvenated at Arbroath where he helped them to win promotion in his first season, and had already been named as a Scotland reserve when Middlesbrough paid £2,000 for him in October 1936. He was finally given a cap in 1938 and proved his worth with a shutout on his international debut against England, which earned a 1-0 victory at Wembley. This proved to be his only full cap, although he did play there again for Scotland in wartime in October 1944. He continued to play for Middlesbrough until a serious knee injury in 1947 caused the end of his career, as an operation failed to cure it. He had managed a billiard saloon before he went full-time, and after his playing days he returned to the north-east where he worked in a woollen mill. His brother Willie was also a goalkeeper.

George CUMMINGS (9/0, 1935-39)
George Wilfred Cummings
Born 5 June 1913 Thornbridge, Stirlingshire
Died 9 April 1987 Harleston Road, Great Barr, Birmingham
Scotland v England 1935, 1936, 1939; Wales 1935, 1937; Ireland 1935, 1937; Germany 1936; Czechoslovakia Dec 1937.
Thornbridge Welfare; Grange Rovers 1931-32; Partick Thistle 1932-35; Aston Villa Nov 1935-49 (Second Division 1938) [guest for Birmingham City Sep-Dec 1939, Solihull Town Feb-Mar 1940, Nottingham Forest Apr 1940, Northampton Town Aug-Dec 1940, Falkirk Dec 1940].

A full back known as 'Icicle' for his coolness under pressure, Cummings was two-footed, fearless and fast, with superb positional sense and anticipation, reputedly one of the few who could master Stanley Matthews. Born into a football family, with a father who was goalkeeper for Stockport County and three brothers who were professional players, he was soon recognised as a potential star. At Grange Rovers he won a junior cap for Scotland in 1931, and had trials for a number of teams including Falkirk, King's Park and Rangers before choosing Partick Thistle in 1932. He had an extraordinary introduction to the team, which won 12 league matches in a row after his debut. In 1934-35 he not only won the Glasgow Cup and Glasgow Charity Cup with Thistle, he was selected for the first of two Scottish League caps, and then chosen for his first full cap, a 2-0 win against England. He also went on the SFA tour of North America in 1935. That autumn he realised a schoolboy dream of playing for Aston Villa, with Thistle receiving a fee just short of £10,000. However, his dream turned sour as Villa were relegated for the first time ever, then in February 1937 the club announced he would never play for them again after a drink driving conviction. After several months in the cold, they relented and he was reinstated at the start of the following season and was in top form as Villa stormed to the Second Division title. Meanwhile, he continued to be chosen for Scotland on a regular basis up to the outbreak of war. Aston Villa closed down until 1942, and in the meantime he worked as an aluminium moulder at Revo Electric in Birmingham and guested for several sides until he could return to Villa. There was another enforced break when he was suspended *sine die* by the Football Association in January 1943 for an incident in a match against Leicester City on Christmas Day, although the ban was lifted in the summer. He won the League North Cup in 1944, and made one wartime appearance for Scotland in October that year, and continued his fine form for Villa until he retired in 1949. He opened a newsagent shop near Villa Park, while acting as third team coach for a couple of years. Later he managed Hednesford in the Birmingham League for a season, and briefly scouted for Wolves, but did not work in football again, although he played for veteran teams as late as 1969. His life story was serialised in the *Sports Argus* in 1960.

Andy CUNNINGHAM (12/5, 1920-27)
Andrew Cunningham
Born 31 January 1891 Titchfield Street, Galston, Ayrshire
Died 8 May 1973 Victoria Infirmary, Glasgow
Scotland v Ireland 1920 (1), 1922c, 1924 (1), 1926 (1); Wales 1921, 1923, 1926; England 1921 (1), 1923 (1), 1924, 1926, 1927.
Newmilns 1907-09; Kilmarnock 1909-15; Rangers Apr 1915-29 (Scottish League 1920, 1921, 1923, 1924, 1925, 1927, 1928; Scottish Cup 1928); Newcastle United Jan 1929-30 player-manager.

A goalscoring inside forward, Cunningham had a top-level career that spanned over twenty years. He won a Scotland junior cap in 1908 with Newmilns and was already highly regarded when he joined Kilmarnock the following year, repaying their faith as top scorer with 18 goals in his first season, and he hit double figures in almost every campaign over the coming six years. Rangers wanted to buy him but were initially rebuffed and had to make several offers before he finally went to Ibrox in April 1915, in time to play in their last three league matches. However, midway through his first season at Rangers, having averaged a goal a game, he signed up with the Royal Field Artillery and his war service meant there was little opportunity to make an impact over the next three years until the conflict was over. Once he returned to regular action early in 1919 there was no stopping him and in 1919/20 he was top scorer for Rangers when he won the first of seven league titles in nine years. He made a scoring debut for Scotland against Ireland in 1920, going on to be selected 12 times. He also made ten appearances for the Scottish League between 1912 and 1928. The one medal missing was the Scottish Cup, which he finally won aged 37 in the memorable 1928 final, after suffering several cup final defeats. Shortly after completing that league and cup double, he made a surprising move to Newcastle United as player-manager and played his first Football League match three days after his 38th birthday, although he only appeared in a dozen games as he concentrated on management. He guided the team to FA Cup success in 1932 then experienced the low of relegation two years later and resigned in 1935, after which he was appointed manager of Dundee where he remained until 1940. He continued to live in the city while he worked as a sports writer for the *Scottish Daily Express* and it was still his home at the time of his death in a Glasgow hospital in 1973.

D

Davie DAVIDSON (5/1, 1878-81)
David Davidson
Born 31 August 1850 Cathcart, Glasgow
Died 7 March 1919 Lilybank, Garelochhead, Argyllshire
Scotland v Wales 1878, 1879, 1880c (1), 1881; England 1881.
Third Lanark 1873-77; Queen's Park 1877-82 (Scottish Cup 1880, 1881, 1882).

Davidson was known as 'The Iron Horse' as he worked in his father's iron foundry, and his muscular build made him an ideal figure for a central defender. He started playing football in the early 1870s while he was a private in the Third Lanarkshire Rifle Volunteers and was asked to join in a practice match. He was soon featuring regularly for Third Lanark at half back or full back, and by the time he resigned from the regiment in April 1876 he had just been in the side which narrowly lost that year's Scottish Cup final. Although tempted to give up the game at that point, he was destined for greater things and joined Queen's Park in the summer of 1877. He continued to blossom and won five Scotland caps starting in 1878, once as captain, culminating in a memorable double-header of victories over England and Wales in 1881. Renowned for his powerful kicking, he played alongside Charles Campbell at Queen's Park, and won the Scottish Cup in three successive years before he retired in 1882. He later went into business on his own account as a foundry manager.

Stewart DAVIDSON (1/0, 1921)
Stewart Davidson
Born 1 June 1886 St Andrew Street, Aberdeen
Died 26 December 1960 Calverton Road, East Ham, Essex
Scotland v England 1921.
Shamrock; Aberdeen 1905-13; Middlesbrough Apr 1913-23 [guest for Aberdeen Jan-Apr 1917; Chelsea Dec 1918]; Aberdeen 1923-26; Forres Mechanics 1926-27 player-manager.

Davidson embarked on a lifelong career in football when he joined Aberdeen from a local juvenile club in 1905. Starting out on the wing, he later switched to right half and while it took a good six years to establish himself in the first team, he became a formidable player with excellent passing ability. He was sold to Middlesbrough for a substantial fee in April 1913 and spent ten years in the north-east, interrupted by active service with the Machine Gun Corps during WW1. Late in the War he was gassed, leading to a spell in hospital, but thankfully he recovered fairly quickly. His one international honour came late in his career, a memorable 3-0 win for Scotland against England in 1921 at the age of 34. In 1923 he returned to Pittodrie and had three more years with Aberdeen although he only played a handful of games after the first season. He finished his playing career with an eventful season at Forres Mechanics in which he led them to victory in the North of

Scotland Cup, before financial difficulties forced the club to revert to amateur status and he left. He moved to the south of England to coach with the Kent County FA in the 1930s, and was appointed assistant manager of Chelsea just before the Second World War, retaining the post until his retiral in 1957, which of course included the club's league-winning season of 1954-55. Unusually, he was with Aberdeen and Middlesbrough long enough to receive a benefit match from each of them.

'Jerry' DAWSON (14/0, 1934-39)
James Dawson
Born 30 October 1909 Griffiths Street, Falkirk, Stirlingshire
Died 19 January 1977 Falkirk Royal Infirmary, Falkirk, Stirlingshire
Scotland v Ireland 1934, 1936, 1937, 1938; England 1936, 1937, 1939; Germany 1936; Wales 1936, 1937; Austria 1937; Czechoslovakia May 1937; Netherlands 1938; Hungary 1938.
Gairdoch Juveniles; Camelon Juniors; Rangers Nov 1929-46 (Scottish League 1933, 1934, 1935, 1937, 1939; Scottish Cup 1935, 1936); Falkirk 1946-49.

Dawson grew up in Falkirk and was soon recognised as an outstanding goalkeeper in local juvenile and junior football. He signed for Rangers from Camelon late in 1929 and although he had to wait until 1931 for his competitive debut in place of Tom Hamilton, he went on to be undisputed number one for many years at Ibrox. With lightning reflexes, bravery and good humour, he was the back line of the outstanding Rangers side of the 1930s, winning five league titles and two Scottish Cups, not to mention numerous Glasgow honours. On the Scotland front, he made his debut against Ireland in 1934, and from 1936 onwards was first choice for the national team. He was also selected ten times by the Scottish League. The outbreak of war came while he was at the height of his powers and he played in Scotland's first nine wartime internationals. During the Second World War he returned to his original trade as a lathe operator and worked in a munitions factory while continuing to play for Rangers until he broke his leg in the Scottish War Cup final of 1944. He did return to the first team a year later, then chose to move to home town club Falkirk in May 1946, curiously making his debut against his old club, and kept on playing until just before his 40th birthday. When he retired he published a book of reminiscences, *Jerry Dawson's Memoirs*, in 1949, and made a career out of journalism before being appointed East Fife manager in 1953. They won the League Cup soon after he joined the club, but he left in 1958 when they were relegated and reverted to the newspaper business.

Jimmy DELANEY (15/6, 1935-48)
James Delaney
Born 3 September 1914 Omoa Road, Cleland, Lanarkshire
Died 26 September 1989 Fir Place, Cleland, Lanarkshire
Scotland v Wales 1935, 1938, 1947; Ireland 1935, 1937, 1938 (1), 1947; Germany 1936 (2); England 1937, 1947, 1948; Austria 1937; Czechoslovakia May 1937; Belgium 1946 (2); Switzerland 1946 (1).
Cleland St Mary's; Stoneyburn Juniors; Celtic 1934-46 (Scottish League 1936, 1938; Scottish Cup 1937); Manchester United Feb 1946-50 (FA Cup 1948); Aberdeen Nov 1950-51; Falkirk Dec 1951-54; Derry City Jan 1954-55 (Irish Cup 1954); Cork Athletic Dec 1955-56 player-manager [guest for Drumcondra Jan 1956]; Elgin City Sep 1956-57.

Delaney had an extraordinarily long career which brought success and medals in four countries and he was one of the few players whose top-level career spanned the Second World War. He joined Celtic from Stoneyburn Juniors in 1934, just before his 20th birthday and quickly established himself on the right wing. In the course of five seasons Celtic won the league twice and the Scottish Cup once, not to mention the Empire Exhibition Trophy of 1938. Delaney embarked on an impressive career for Scotland in August 1935 with the unofficial King George V Jubilee match at Hampden, when he scored against England, and he won his first full cap a few months later in Wales. He had nine Scotland caps and had made six appearances for the Scottish League when his career came to a shuddering halt in April 1939, shattering his left arm so badly in a match against Arbroath that there were fears it could be lost. It took over two years and several operations before he recovered sufficiently to play again, which not only interrupted his Celtic career, it curtailed his wartime international appearances as the SFA found it difficult to obtain insurance for him. He finally made his Scotland comeback at Hampden in April 1944, in front of the highest wartime attendance of around 133,000, although it turned out to be a sad day as his 18-month-old son Michael died that evening at home. When life started to return to normal, he scored twice in Scotland's first post-war match against Belgium in January 1946, then a month later he asked for a higher wage and Celtic took umbrage. They let him go to Manchester United where Matt Busby was only too happy to pay £4,000. United finished second in the first three post-war seasons and won the FA Cup in 1948 when Delaney faced another veteran right winger called Stanley Matthews, a few months his junior. Two weeks before the final, the two had been in opposition at Hampden in Delaney's last Scotland appearance. When he left Old Trafford late in 1950 he still had plenty of legs left, and spent a year at Aberdeen, then despite his age Falkirk paid £4,000 for his signature in December 1951, and he helped them get promotion and establish themselves in the First Division. Moving on in January 1954 to Derry City for an Irish record fee of £1,500, a few months later he added an Irish Cup victory to his honours as Glentoran were beaten in the twice-replayed final. His next stop was a six-month spell at Cork Athletic when he nearly won another national cup, but his team threw away a two goal lead in the last 15 minutes of the FAI Cup final. His final senior appearances were for Elgin City in the Highland League, travelling north each weekend from his home in Cleland until he retired aged 42. See his biography *The Stuff of Legend* by David Potter. His son Pat played for Motherwell and other clubs in the 1960s, while his grandson John Kennedy was also at Celtic and played for Scotland.

Archie DEVINE (1/1, 1910)
Archibald Forbes Devine
Born 9 April 1886 Lochore Rows, Ballingry, Fife
Died 30 September 1964 Stratheden Hospital, Cupar, Fife
Scotland v Wales 1910 (1).
Lochgelly United 1904-07 [trial for Hearts Mar 1905]; Raith Rovers 1907-08; Heart of Midlothian Aug-Nov 1908; Falkirk Nov 1908-10; Bradford City Apr 1910-13 (FA Cup 1911); Woolwich Arsenal Feb 1913-14; Shelbourne 1914-15 (Gold Cup 1915); Lochgelly United 1915-16; Dunfermline Athletic 1919-20; Lochgelly United 1920-21.

A powerfully-built inside left with a deadly shot, Devine started out in the Northern League with Lochgelly, and it took some time before his career took off. He had a trial with Hearts in a league match in March 1905, spent a season with Raith Rovers, and had another short spell at Hearts where he played in three friendlies but was not offered a contract. It was only after he signed for Falkirk in 1908 that he was able to establish himself, and his excellent form led to a Scotland cap in 1910, a month after he was selected by the Scottish League. He scored the winner on his Scotland debut, a rocket from 30 yards late in the game, and this sparked a momentous period in his career. He joined Bradford City a few weeks later for a substantial fee and played a major part in their successful FA Cup campaign the following season, scoring in the semi-final before Newcastle were defeated in the final. He was transferred to Arsenal early in 1913 but could not prevent them being relegated, although he earned a place in club history by scoring the winner in their first match at Highbury in September. Placed on the transfer list in 1914, he tried his luck in Ireland with Shelbourne and his medal from their Gold Cup win in 1915 is in the National Football Museum. During the First World War, he returned to his original occupation as a miner in Lochgelly, and played for the local side for a season before giving up football for a while, then picked up again in 1919 and had two more seasons before he retired, one each with Dunfermline and Lochgelly in the Central League. He remained in the town for the rest of his life, and died in hospital in Cupar in 1964.

Geordie DEWAR (2/1, 1888-89)
George Dewar
Born 20 July 1867 Church Street, Dumbarton
Died 2 September 1915 Selly Oak Hospital, Birmingham
Scotland v Ireland 1888 (1); England 1889.
Dumbarton Athletic 1884-87; Dumbarton 1887-89 [guest for Leith Athletic Apr 1889]; Blackburn Rovers 1889-97 (FA Cup 1890, 1891); New Brighton Tower 1897-98; Southampton 1898-99.

As a young man in Dumbarton, Dewar served an apprenticeship as a ship upholsterer while developing into a fine centre half. He was soon too good for Dumbarton Athletic, and joined the town's senior side in 1887, going on to win his first cap in 1888 against Ireland, a 10-2 victory in Belfast, in which he is credited with the opening goal. A year later he was selected for the England match, the mark of a major talent, so it was little surprise that he was persuaded to turn professional. One of England's top clubs, Blackburn Rovers, were on a Scottish recruiting spree and Dewar headed south along with Tom Brandon (St Mirren) and Harry Campbell (Renton). It proved a happy decision as within a year he had won the FA Cup as Sheffield Wednesday were thrashed 6-1 in the final, and a year later he won it again, scoring a rare goal in the 3-1 defeat of Notts County. In 1891 he played for the Football League against the Football Alliance, one of six Scots in the team, and meanwhile the club set him up as landlord of the Swan Hotel in Blackburn but it was not a success and he left the hotel business in 1893. While he remained a regular in the Rovers team, clearly things were not going well off the pitch as he was taken to court in 1895 for assaulting his wife, who was granted a judicial separation. In 1897, just turned 30, he signed for New Brighton Tower, who won the Lancashire League in his year with them, then he moved on to Southampton in the Southern League for a final season before retiring. He settled in Birmingham where he reverted to his old trade as an upholsterer in a King's Norton motor works, and died of cancer in hospital aged 48.

Neilly DEWAR (3/4, 1932)
Neil Dewar
Born 11 November 1908 Hogg's Land, Old Kilpatrick, Dunbartonshire
Died 10 January 1982 Jubilee Terrace, Lochgilphead, Argyllshire
Scotland v England 1932; France 1932 (3); Wales 1932 (1)
Lochgilphead United; Third Lanark 1929-33 (Second Division 1931); Manchester United Feb-Dec 1933; Sheffield Wednesday Dec 1933-37; Third Lanark 1937-40; Albion Rovers 1940-41.

When Third Lanark were relegated in 1929 and needed a new centre forward, they found one from the unlikely source of Lochgilphead United of the Mid-Argyll and District FA. The strapping figure of Neilly Dewar, who wanted to escape his work as a trawlerman, had gone to Glasgow to seek trials with several clubs, and Thirds was the only club who recognised his potential. They soon realised they had found a gem, and Dewar was immense as the Cathkin side won the Second Division title in 1931, and continued to bang in the goals, 35 of them, as they surged to fourth place in the top league. Despite the unfortunate nickname of 'the silver sleeve' for his habit of wiping his nose on his shirt, his uncanny nose for goal made him an obvious candidate for international honours. He made his Scotland debut against England in 1932, and two more caps followed the same year, including a memorable first-half hat-trick against France in Paris. Manchester United paid £5,000 to take him south, but the goals soon dried up and with the club at risk of relegation to the Third Division, after less than a year he moved on to Sheffield Wednesday. The transfer provoked an emotional turmoil for the big striker as he was in love with Betty Thomson, daughter of a Manchester United director, and the pair duly eloped. The scandal made front page news and had a happy ending as they were soon married. Dewar missed Wednesday's 1935 FA Cup success but scored the only goal in the Charity Shield at the start of next season. When Wednesday were relegated in 1937, albeit with Dewar as top scorer, he returned to Third Lanark and continued to be their leading scorer in the last two pre-war seasons. He was still potent enough to play in 1940 for a Glasgow Scottish League Select against the League of Ireland in Dublin, then left Third Lanark and concluded his career with a season at Albion Rovers. He joined the RAF in 1944 as a Physical Training Instructor and returned to his native Lochgilphead after the War, where he donated the Neil Dewar Cup for clubs in Argyllshire. In his later years he worked as a hotel porter, died in 1982 and is buried in Achnabreac Cemetery.

Matt DICKIE (3/0, 1897-1900)
Matthew Dickie
Born 19 August 1873 James Street, Helensburgh, Dunbartonshire
Died 30 December 1959 Northern Hospital, Dunfermline, Fife
Scotland v Ireland 1897, 1899; Wales 1900.
Helensburgh Arthurlie; Helensburgh Victoria; Renton 1894-96; Rangers 1896-1904 (Scottish League 1899, 1900, 1901, 1902; Scottish Cup 1897, 1898, 1903); Clyde 1904-07 (Second Division 1905).

One of the finest goalkeepers of the late Victorian era, Dickie grew up in Helensburgh where he played for local sides and signed for Renton in 1894. He helped the village team to reach the Scottish Cup final of 1895, which they lost to St Bernard's, and the semi-final the following season. His move to the First Division with Rangers in 1896 opened the door to a wealth of honours, and he was in goal when they created the record of winning every league match in 1898/99, and repeated their title triumph for the next three seasons. He also won the Scottish Cup three times and five Glasgow Cups. There was scant international recognition, however, and he played just three times for Scotland, with one appearance for the Scottish League in 1898 when the Football League was defeated for the first time in England. He left Rangers in 1904 and joined Clyde where he won the Second Division title and then promotion, but gave up the game in 1907, although he nearly made a comeback in April 1909 when Clyde had a goalkeeping crisis. He was a well-known figure in Helensburgh, and with his sons he ran a tobacconist shop in Sinclair Street, with a snooker hall upstairs. He was involved in running Helensburgh football club, which played briefly in the Scottish League in the 1920s, and was four times champion of Helensburgh Bowling Club. He lived in the town for the rest of his life, but died in a Fife hospital.

Billy DICKSON (1/4, 1888)
William Alexander Dickson
Born 5 July 1866 Rattray, Perthshire
Died 1 June 1910 Liverpool Road, Stoke-on-Trent, Staffordshire
Scotland v Ireland 1888 (4).
Strathmore (Dundee) 1885-89 [trials for Sunderland Aug-Oct 1888]; Aston Villa 1889-1892; Stoke 1892-97.
Born as William McFarlane, his surname became Dickson when his mother married in 1871. He developed a talent for scoring goals with Strathmore and played several times for Forfarshire before he was called up in March 1888 for his international debut as a late replacement for Sandy Higgins. He had the distinction of being the first Dundee-based player to be capped for Scotland and certainly made an impression by scoring four goals against Ireland, but he was never selected again. In the autumn of 1888 he was offered a job as a boilermaker in the Sunderland shipyards

and played several times for the club before deciding to return home, and Strathmore were so pleased to welcome their captain back that they presented him with a purse of sovereigns when he got married later that year. However, in 1889 he did leave for good and turned professional with Aston Villa, scoring regularly in the league and playing in the FA Cup final in 1892. He moved on to Stoke that summer then started to put on weight and was even described as 'elephantine' in 1895, weighing in at nearly 14 stone. It is little surprise that speed was not his greatest asset but he could pass accurately, had a strong shot and was a good mentor for Stoke's younger players including fellow internationalist Willie Maxwell. After hanging up his boots in 1897 he remained in Stoke where he ran the Prince of Wales Inn on Liverpool Road, and became a director of the football club. His early death aged 43 left his widow Jessie with six children, and she and their eldest son continued to manage the pub until at least the 1940s.

John DIVERS (1/1, 1895)

John Divers
Born 19 January 1874 Calton Entry, Calton, Glasgow
Died 13 March 1942 Baltic Street, Dalmarnock, Glasgow
Scotland v Wales 1895 (1).
Vale of Clyde; Benburb; Celtic 1893-97 (Scottish League 1894, 1896); Everton 1897-98; Celtic Oct 1898-1901 (Scottish Cup 1899, 1900); Hibernian Sep 1901-04 (Scottish Cup 1902).

A centre forward or left winger, Divers won many honours in his career but could have achieved so much more. He represented the Glasgow Junior League in 1893 while at Benburb, signed for Celtic that summer and came into the team in November to played through the run-in of a title-winning campaign. Celtic discovered that he could be a great asset, his apparently fragile physique masking a terrific work rate and a ferocious shot. In 1895 he won his first Scotland cap, scoring in the 2-2 draw with Wales, and did well enough to be selected for the Scottish League the following month, but that was the end of his international career. Inconsistency was his downfall and at Celtic he was in and out of the side, never really establishing himself and played only five games in the 1895-96 championship season. Then in November 1896 he was one of the Celtic players who refused to play in protest against certain reporters being present, and was summarily dropped. He went to Everton for a season but was happy to be recalled a year later, joined the fledgling Scottish Players Union, and finally he got an extended run in the Celtic team. This culminated in a Scottish Cup victory of 1899 and he won the trophy again in 1900 with Celtic, scoring twice against Queen's Park, then lost the 1901 final to Hearts. His move to Hibs that year gave him the opportunity to put one over his old team with another Scottish Cup victory in 1902, his fourth consecutive final. He retired in 1904 and went to Dublin as trainer of Bohemians, where he was held in such high esteem that in 1906 the club presented him with a gold signet ring and other gifts.

Johnny DIVERS (1/0, 1938)

John Divers
Born 6 August 1911 Glasgow Road, Clydebank, Dunbartonshire
Died 8 June 1984 Western Infirmary, Glasgow
Scotland v Ireland 1938.
Rothesay Royal Victoria; Renfrew Juniors 1932-33; Celtic 1932-45 (Scottish League 1938) [guest for Morton 1942-43]; Morton Oct 1945-47; Oldham Athletic Aug-Oct 1947; Morton Oct 1947-50 player-coach; Portadown Sep-Nov 1950 player-coach.

Divers was capped by the Scottish Junior League while at Rothesay, and seemed destined for great things when he stepped up from Renfrew to Celtic. However, he took several years to find a regular place in the Celtic team, with manager Willie Maley concerned at his light-hearted approach to the game. Initially an inside left, he had a run in the team at the end of the 1933-34 season, but by the end of 1937 had barely featured and was on the point of being transferred. Then fate took a hand as Jimmy McGrory retired, Divers was given his chance and burst into action. He scored in ten of his first eleven starts, making such an impact that he was second top scorer as Celtic won the league title in 1938, not to mention the Empire Exhibition Trophy and the Glasgow Charity Cup. That autumn he earned a Scotland cap against Ireland, but had a disappointing match in Belfast, suffering the after-effects of sea sickness according to press reports. A year later, the nation went to war and he lost his best years during the conflict, as he worked in the shipyards and found little time for training. He went on loan to Morton for a season, where he showed that a lack in fitness was more than made up for in his reading of the game as he dropped to half-back, where he could control the game with his pinpoint passing. Back at Celtic, however, he struggled again to fit in and they gave him a free transfer in the autumn of 1945. He found a new lease of life at Morton, returning to full fitness and turning in a series of inspirational performances. He was also elected chairman of the Scottish Players Union. In the summer of 1947 he signed for Oldham Athletic, who made him captain, yet he only played one game as he could not find somewhere to live. Even aged 36 he had plenty of offers and chose a return to Morton, where he was desperately unlucky to miss their Scottish Cup final due to injury. In March 1949, just before the team was relegated, he was appointed player-coach and featured little as they bounced back with the Second Division championship, although he did play once in goal in a reserve match. Freed in 1950, he tried a move to Portadown as player-coach but after two months he decided to return home. He was a nephew of the great Patsy Gallagher, and his son John played for Celtic in the 1960s.

Joe DODDS (3/0, 1914)
Joseph Dodds
Born 14 July 1887 Kirk Road, Carluke, Lanarkshire
Died 14 October 1965 Govan Road, Govan, Glasgow
Scotland v Wales 1914; Ireland 1914; England 1914.
Carluke Milton Rovers; Celtic 1908-1920 (Scottish League 1909, 1910, 1914, 1915, 1916, 1917, 1919; Scottish Cup 1911, 1912, 1914); Cowdenbeath 1920-21; Celtic 1921-22 (Scottish League 1922); Queen of the South Oct 1922-26.
Brought up in Carluke where his father worked in the brickworks, Dodds was one of five brothers. A speedy left back, so fast that he once won a UK-wide footballers' race, he signed for Celtic in 1908 and soon had his opportunity when Willie Loney was injured, playing the second half of the 1908-09 season. He was an asset as Celtic lifted the title and the *Athletic News* assessed him that year that he 'carries 11½ stone of bone and muscle, lacks the finer points but a rare honest worker'. He might have done the double had it not been for the Hampden Park riot. Club honours continued to come thick and fast, and he made the first of eight appearances for the Scottish League. Then he made the full national team and played in all three of Scotland's games of 1914 but was denied any further caps due to the War. He worked in a munitions factory during WW1 until he lost his military exemption in 1917 and served in France with the Stirlingshire Territorials. After returning to Celtic at the end of 1918 he was selected for the Victory International against England, then had to call off due to injury. In the summer of 1919 he was arrested on a charge of desertion from the army but was able to prove his innocence. He fell out with Celtic in 1920 over his financial terms and refused to sign, preferring instead to have a year at Cowdenbeath in the Central League, before returning to the fold for a final championship-winning season in 1922. Later that year he made a surprise move to Queen of the South, then in the Western League, attracted by a higher wage and the opportunity to become host of the Victoria Bar in the town centre. He helped Queens to enter the Scottish League then to win promotion from the Third Division, although illness and injury restricted his appearances. He did not retire until the autumn of 1926 and a couple of years later he bought the King's Arms Hotel in Lochmaben, only to give it up to become a farmer. When that did not work out he returned to Glasgow in 1936 as Celtic's assistant trainer, a post he held until the club let him go on the outbreak of war in 1939. His son, also Joe, played junior football and was a wartime guest for Cardiff City.

Ned DOIG (5/0, 1887-1903)
John Edward Doig
Born 29 October 1866 The Square, Letham, Angus
Died 7 November 1919 Miriam Road, Anfield, Liverpool
Scotland v Ireland 1887, 1889; England 1896, 1899, 1903.
St Helena; Arbroath 1885-90 [trial for Blackburn Rovers Nov 1889]; Sunderland 1890-1904 (Football League 1892, 1893, 1895, 1902); Liverpool 1904-08 (Division 2 1905); St Helens Recreation 1908-10.
A legendary goalkeeper, Doig's five caps were spread out over a 16 year period and no other Scotland player had such a long international career until his record was broken by David Marshall and Craig Gordon in the 21st century. Famed for his ability to punch a ball, and easily recognised for his flat cap which covered his baldness, he started with seven years at Arbroath, where he won his first two Scotland caps as well as playing for the county select and lifting the Forfarshire Cup twice. Clearly destined for a bigger stage, Blackburn Rovers gave him a trial in 1889 but could not agree terms, and the following year he signed for Sunderland where he became the final line of defence in the 'team of all the talents' which won three league titles in four years. He spent 14 years at Roker Park, part of the defence of Doig, McCombie and Watson which also did duty for Scotland. He came back to the national team against England in 1896 and 1899, then played in the Ibrox Disaster match in 1902, although a sprained wrist kept him out of the rearranged fixture. Having secured another league title in 1902, he earned his final cap the following year with a victory over England at Sheffield. He was in his late thirties when he moved to Liverpool in 1904, but showed his worth by helping them to the Second Division title in his first season and he carried on playing well past his 40th birthday. After departing Anfield in 1908 he signed for St Helens in the Lancashire League, and was reportedly still keeping goal for a local team in 1914. He worked as an insurance agent for the Royal Liverpool Friendly Society until his early death aged 53 in the Spanish flu epidemic. Known as Ned or Teddie, he left a widow, five sons and three daughters.

Alex DONALDSON (6/1, 1914-22)
Alexander Pollock Donaldson
Born 4 December 1890 Trees Lodge, Barrhead, Renfrewshire
Died 1 January 1972 Hulton Hospital, Bolton, Lancashire
Scotland v Wales 1914; Ireland 1914, 1920, 1922; England 1914, 1920 (1).
Belgrave; Balmoral United; Ripley Town and Athletic [trial for Sheffield United Mar-May 1911]; Bolton Wanderers Dec 1911-22 [guest for Leicester Fosse 1915-19]; Sunderland Mar 1922-23; Manchester City 1923-25; Chorley Feb 1925-27.
Born in Barrhead, Donaldson's father died when he was seven and he moved with his mother to Leicester, where he grew up. He won a bravery award in 1907 for saving two little boys who had fallen into a canal and meanwhile he started out in football with local teams. He suffered a broken collar bone at Ripley Town early in 1911 but was soon attracting professional interest, and while a trial with Sheffield United came to nothing Bolton were sufficiently impressed to sign him. He was soon putting in an impressive shift for them on the right wing and did so well that he nearly played for England, who chose him for an international trial in January 1914 before it was pointed out that he was actually born in Scotland. This alerted the Scottish FA, who promptly sent a selector whose assessment was so enthusiastic that the player was awarded his first cap a month later, against Wales. Although he was something of an unknown quantity in Scotland he retained

his place for all three matches that year. During the War he returned home and played as a guest for Leicester Fosse for four seasons, and was selected for three of Scotland's 1919 Victory Internationals. Then, back at Bolton, he won two more full caps the following year, scoring against England. A broken knee cap in a match at Preston in 1921 put him out for several months, but he came back to make his final Scotland appearance in 1922. Shortly afterwards he was transferred to Sunderland, where he spent a year, then Manchester City, falling out with the club early on because he was still living in Sunderland and they insisted he move closer. He finished his career with a couple of years at Chorley in the Lancashire Combination and opened a sports shop in Manchester's Hyde Road, which was so prominent that the location became known as Donaldson's Corner. He sold the business when he retired about 1960 and latterly lived in Bolton.

Joe DONNACHIE (3/1, 1913-14)
Joseph Donaghy or Donnachie
Born 18 December 1882 Greenhead, Kilwinning, Ayrshire
Died 31 December 1966 Broadway East, Chester, Cheshire
Scotland v England 1913, 1914; Ireland 1914 (1).
Rutherglen Glencairn; Morton 1903-04; Albion Rovers 1904-05; Morton Apr-May 1905; Newcastle United 1905-06; Everton Feb 1906-08; Oldham 1908-19 [guest for Everton 1915-19; Liverpool Nov-Dec 1916]; Rangers Mar-May 1919; Everton 1919-20; Blackpool 1920-21; Chester 1921-24 player-manager.
Born in Kilwinning and brought up in Paisley with the surname Donaghy, he changed it to Donnachie when his playing career began. A clever player who could operate on either wing, he did well at Morton and had an opportunity to go to England in 1904 but turned down an offer from Middlesbrough and preferred to bide his time in Scotland. However, after another season with Albion Rovers and a brief return to Morton he joined Newcastle United, the league champions, in the summer of 1905. He went straight into the first team but it was a brief association, as was his subsequent spell at Everton. He finally settled at Oldham in 1908, doing so well that he made his Scotland debut at outside right in 1913, aged 30, and won two more caps against Ireland and England the following season at outside left before the War intervened. Throughout his time at Oldham he lived in Liverpool, and during the conflict he worked there in a munitions factory which led to him playing regularly as a guest for Everton and occasionally for Liverpool, as well as sometimes back at Oldham. When the War finished he moved to Scotland with Rangers for a reported fee of £800, then a few months later he was back at Goodison Park. There was a season at Blackpool before he was appointed player-manager of Chester, and he spent the rest of his life in the city, managing the Mariners' Arms pub for a decade from 1934. His son Joe, who played for Everton, Bolton and Chester in the 1930s, was killed in an RAF training flight crash in 1944.

Jimmy DOUGAL (1/1, 1939)
James Dougal
Born 3 October 1913 Stirling Avenue, Denny, Stirlingshire
Died 17 October 1999 Hurstfield Road, West Molesey, Surrey
Scotland v England 1939 (1).
Kilsyth Rangers; Falkirk 1932-34; Preston North End Jan 1934-46 [guest during WW2 for Blackburn Rovers 1942-44, Liverpool Apr 1944; Southport May 1944]; Carlisle United Nov 1946-48; Halifax Town Oct 1948-49.
Initially a right winger or even a right half, Dougal could play in any of the forward positions. From junior football, a year and a half with Falkirk was enough to confirm his potential and Preston took him south early in 1934. He slotted right into the team which won promotion to the First Division a few months later, and his close dribbling on the wing became a feature of Preston's play. He helped to take them to the 1937 FA Cup final, which was lost to Sunderland, and he really came into his own the following season when Frank O'Donnell was transferred to Blackpool. Dougal moved to the centre forward position and his goals took the club to third place in the league and another FA Cup final, but unfortunately he missed their victory due to a knee injury which required an operation. He was top scorer again in 1938-39 which led to his selection for Scotland against England and he rewarded that faith by scoring the opener, although ultimately Scotland went down to two second-half goals. It turned out to be his only full cap as war intervened, but he did score another against England a year later in a wartime international. What could have been his best years in football were lost while he worked in Civil Defence as an air raid warden. He continued to play for Preston while he could, and when they withdrew from league football he guested with Blackburn Rovers and played sporadically for a couple of other clubs, even winning a Lancashire Senior Cup medal with Southport in 1944. While he still had some legs left after the War he was happy to wind down his career at Carlisle and Halifax. In 1953 he took over the Moor Park Hotel in Preston from his wife's parents, and ran it for over ten years. He retired to Surrey, where he died in 1999. He came from a large football family, his brothers Peter and Willie played professionally and he was uncle of Neil Dougall, a post-war internationalist, who spelled the surname with a double L.

Angus DOUGLAS (1/0, 1911)
Angus Douglas
Born 1 January 1889 Railway Cottage, Lochmaben, Dumfriesshire
Died 14 December 1918 Station Road, Gosforth, Newcastle
Scotland v Ireland 1911.
Lochmaben Rangers; Dumfries 1905-08 [trial for Rangers May 1908]; Chelsea 1908-13; Newcastle United Oct 1913-15.
A talented all-round athlete, Douglas was sports champion of Lockerbie Academy and won numerous prizes at local athletics meetings. He focussed on football, joining Lochmaben Rangers as a schoolboy, then stepped up to Dumfries in the Scottish Combination, where he won the Southern Counties Cup and other local trophies. Outside of football, he worked as a sheriff's clerk in Dumfries and was initially reluctant to turn professional. However, he was much in demand and played a couple of trial matches for Rangers in the Glasgow Charity Cup in May 1908. That summer, Everton and Bolton Wanderers made him offers but he chose to sign for Chelsea, making his debut sooner than expected when William Brown scalded his foot with

boiling water from a kettle. Renowned for his speed in attack, he played at outside right where he won his one Scotland cap in 1911 against Ireland. If he had a weakness, it was a reluctance to shoot at goal. Newcastle paid £2,000 for him in 1913, and he played there until his playing career ended in 1915 when football was halted in the north-east due to the War. In wartime he worked as a machinist in the Armstrong Whitworth shell-making works in Newcastle, where he contracted blood poisoning which resulted in a finger being amputated in 1917. He recovered from that but died the following year of double pneumonia following an attack of flu, shortly before his 30th birthday. He is buried in Lochmaben Cemetery.

Jimmy DOUGLAS (1/0, 1880)
James Douglas
Born 3 September 1859 Meadowside Street, Renfrew, Renfrewshire
Died 13 September 1919 High Street, Renfrew, Renfrewshire
Scotland v Wales 1880.
Renfrew 1877-80; Barrow Rangers Sep-Nov 1880; Blackburn Rovers Nov 1880-92 (FA Cup 1884, 1885, 1886).

Douglas was clearly a forward of talent from an early age, and while at Renfrew he was selected for his first international trial early in 1879, then represented Renfrewshire and Scotch Counties before he won his Scotland cap against Wales in 1880, aged 20. He was also a reserve for the England game. That summer he went south to work in the shipyards of Barrow-in-Furness, where he was recruited by Barrow Rangers and played for them for a couple of months before he was invited by Hugh McIntyre to come to Blackburn Rovers. The club found him a job at Yates's Iron Foundry and gave him the opportunity to perform on a much greater stage, alongside McIntyre and the other 'Scotch professor', Fergie Suter. This trio were the backbone of Rovers' inexorable rise over the coming decade, as they progressed to top club in Lancashire then top club in England, winning the FA Cup three times in succession and becoming founder members of the Football League in 1888. Douglas, known as 'Black Jimmy', was key to all of this: small and brave, his dash and skill on the right wing added a vital dimension to the Blackburn attack, although later in his career he dropped to right half. He was a near constant presence in the first team until he was dropped in the autumn of 1889, and he only made a handful more appearances until his retirement in 1892. He ran a pub in the town for a while but after his playing days were over he went back to Renfrew and reverted to his old trade as a wood pattern maker in the shipyard. He died of heart disease shortly after his 60th birthday and is buried in Arkleston Cemetery.

Peter DOWDS (1/0, 1892)
Peter Douds
Born 24 August 1871 Grahame Street, Johnstone, Renfrewshire
Died 3 September 1895 Grahame Street, Johnstone, Renfrewshire
Scotland v Ireland 1892.
Broxburn Shamrock; Celtic Feb 1889-92 (Scottish Cup 1892); Aston Villa 1892-93; Stoke 1893-94; Celtic May-Dec 1894.

A left-sided player, Dowds was versatile enough to play wherever he was wanted and was synonymous with the earliest successes of Celtic. He made his debut in the spring of 1889, aged 17, and was an almost constant presence in the forward line over the next three years. He was the club's top scorer in the first season of the Scottish League, won the Glasgow Cup in 1891, and then in 1891/92 added another Glasgow Cup, the Charity Cup and the club's first Scottish Cup victory. When English money came calling he spent a season each at Aston Villa and Stoke then returned to Celtic Park in 1894 once professionalism had been legalised in Scotland. However, rather than it being a triumphant return, he managed just four matches before he became ill and was unable to play on. His health continued to decline and he died of tuberculosis in September 1895, having just turned 24. NB his name was spelled Doud at birth, and Douds on his marriage and death certificates, but generally the press referred to him as Dowds.

Bob DOWNIE (1/0, 1892)
Robert Downie
Born 9 September 1866 Lennoxtown, Stirlingshire
Died 27 July 1893 The Crescent, Dalmuir, Dunbartonshire
Scotland v Wales 1892.
Woodvale 1885-86; Thornliebank 1886-88; Third Lanark Feb 1888-93 (Scottish Cup 1889).

Downie was an accomplished goalkeeper whose play as the final line of defence was crucial in Third Lanark's Scottish Cup campaign of 1889, which required no less than 12 matches before ending in victory over Celtic. He had first come to notice with Thornliebank, and had already been selected for Renfrewshire when he moved to Third Lanark early in 1888. He slotted into the team immediately and was ever-present for Thirds in their Scottish Cup victory of 1889, and also in their first two Scottish League campaigns. He was selected once for Scotland, against Wales in 1892, and was being considered for further honours when he fell ill in the spring of 1893. He played his last match in March and died that summer, aged 26, after suffering several months of heart and kidney disease. Ironically the news of his demise reached Cathkin just as Third Lanark were playing their annual football tournament, casting a shadow over the day. The *Athletic News* paid a fine tribute: 'He was most popular with his club companions, a popularity which had its origins in genuine personal qualities as well as in his all-round excellence as a player.' Downie worked in Thornliebank as a calico printer and sketch maker but died at his brother's house in Dalmuir.

Dan DOYLE (8/0, 1892-98)
Daniel Doyle
Born 16 September 1864 Queen Street, Paisley, Renfrewshire
Died 8 April 1918 Royal Glasgow Cancer Hospital, Hill Street, Glasgow
Scotland v England 1892, 1894c, 1895, 1897, 1898; Wales 1893; Ireland 1895, 1898.
Rawyards Juniors; Slamannan Barnsmuir; Broxburn Shamrock 1886-87; Hibernian Feb 1887-88; East Stirlingshire 1887-88; Sunderland Albion Aug 1888; Grimsby Town 1888-89; Bolton Wanderers Apr-May 1889; Everton 1889-91 (Football League 1891); Celtic 1891-99 (Scottish Cup 1892; Scottish League 1893, 1894, 1896, 1898).

Doyle was one of the outstanding personalities of the late Victorian era and became Celtic legend, even though by the time he arrived at the club he had already packed in as much adventure as some players manage in a full career. Brought up in Rawyards, near Airdrie, where his family went when his father died, he worked as a coal miner from an early age which added toughness to his talent for football. He played where his work was, and while at Broxburn he was selected for Linlithgowshire (now West Lothian) in 1887. Shortly afterwards he joined Hibs, making his debut the week after the Edinburgh club won the Scottish Cup. He spent over a year with Hibs, also playing occasionally for East Stirlingshire, until he tried his luck in England as a professional. A short trial with Sunderland saw him described in the *Northern Echo* as 'a tremendous kicker with the hind-quarters of a dray horse' but he did not stay and was invited south by former Hibs colleague Jimmy Lundie, who offered him a job at Grimsby docks if he would play alongside him at full back. His time at Grimsby Town was marked by a tragedy in January 1889 when his heavy challenge on Staveley's William Cropper, a prominent Derbyshire cricketer, led to the death of his opponent. Although Doyle was cleared by a coroner's jury of blame, he moved on, playing briefly for Bolton Wanderers before landing at Everton. Here, he featured in almost every match as they finished second in the league, and then as they lifted the title in 1891. Despite being paid as a star professional with Everton, he was tempted back to Scotland in the summer of 1891 to sign for Celtic, notionally as an amateur, with the carrot being the tenancy of a pub in Bellshill, the Horse Shoe Bar. After all his wandering, this was where he played the rest of his career and he was a pivotal figure as Celtic won the Scottish Cup in his first season, and four league titles in the next few years. Meanwhile, he was selected for Scotland to face England in 1892, and was a regular in the national team for the rest of the decade, captaining the side once. His robust no-nonsense style brought regular brushes with authority but also made him the darling of the Celtic fans. He retired in 1899 to concentrate on his pub, using his spare time to play quoits with great skill and was an active member of Bellshill Bowling Club. However, his love of gambling was his downfall and he was forced to sell the pub in 1910. Within a few years he was dead. For a full account of his life read his biography, *Life and Death of a Wild Rover* by Marie Rowan.

Jock DRUMMOND (14/0, 1892-1902)
John Drummond
Born 13 April 1870 Stirling Street, Alva, Clackmannanshire
Died 23 January 1935 Royal Infirmary, Falkirk
Scotland v Ireland 1892, 1894, 1895c, 1896, 1897c, 1902, 1903c; England 1895, 1896c, 1898, 1900, 1901, 1902; Wales 1902.
Falkirk 1886-92; Rangers Apr 1892-1904 (Scottish League 1899, 1900, 1901, 1902; Scottish Cup 1894, 1897, 1898, 1903); Falkirk 1904-05.

An outstanding right back, Drummond was famed for wearing a peaked 'bunnet' throughout his career, and was apparently the last outfield player in Scotland to wear a cap in games. Born in Alva but brought up in Falkirk, he joined the town's football club in 1886 as soon as he left Liddle's School, and came to the fore while serving his apprenticeship in the local branch of the National Bank. His first representative match was in 1889 for Stirlingshire, and he went on to win his first Scotland cap as a Falkirk player in March 1892, as a late replacement after four Renton men refused to play. He turned down offers to turn professional with Everton and that summer he joined Rangers and spent over a decade at Ibrox where he was a model of consistency in defence alongside Nick Smith. As their partnership grew, so did the team and they won four league titles and as many Scottish Cups, although Drummond missed much of the 1898/99 season through injury, making only five appearances in the 'invincible' team that won every league match. He brought his Scotland caps total up to 14, as captain in four of them, and also made three appearances for the Scottish League, all against the Football League, in 1895, 1896 and 1901. He returned to Falkirk in 1904 and helped them to win promotion to the First Division before retiring, and immediately stepped up to become a club director. Outside football, he was an enthusiastic bowler with the Falkirk Adrian club and for 20 years he was a janitor at Falkirk Science and Art School. Tragically, he died in hospital after he was found with 'wounds in the throat' at his home in Albert Road, Falkirk; as there were no suspects it indicates suicide. By coincidence, he died a few hours before Jacky Robertson, with whom he played at Rangers and for Scotland.

Mick DUNBAR (1/1, 1886)
Michael Dunbar
Born 30 October 1863 Sheddens, Cathcart, Glasgow
Died 6 September 1921 Royal Infirmary, Glasgow
Scotland v Ireland 1886 (1).
Busby Linwood; Cartvale 1882-86; Cowlairs 1886-87; Hibernian Apr 1887-88; Celtic 1888-93.
Tall and thin, Dunbar was nevertheless strongly built and a hard worker, whose clever play at inside left created many opportunities for his fellow forwards. His only international cap was won early in his career in 1886 while still at Cartvale, and he scored one of the goals in a 7-2 victory against Ireland, but he was never consistent enough to warrant another call-up. He still managed to give good service to all his clubs and after four years at Cartvale he moved with his right wing partner Bobby Calderwood to Cowlairs where they had a season together. Dunbar joined Hibs shortly after their Scottish Cup win in 1887, and soon won a Rosebery Charity Cup medal with them, then a year later he was one of several players tempted to Glasgow by the newly-formed Celtic. He played in their inaugural game in May 1888 and was in the team which reached the Scottish Cup final in their first season, scoring a hat-trick against his former club Cowlairs along the way. He remained a regular in the Celtic team until he lost his place through injury in 1891, shortly after he won his last trophy, the Glasgow Cup. He took a season out to recuperate and only managed a couple of league games in 1892-93, both alongside his younger brother Tom, before retiring. He formed a lifelong attachment to Celtic and served on the committee then as a club director. He never married and ran a couple of successful pubs in Glasgow's East End until his death from Bright's Disease (kidney failure) in 1921. He is buried in St Peter's Cemetery, Dalbeth.

'Dally' DUNCAN (14/7, 1932-37)
Douglas Duncan
Born 14 October 1909 Linksfield Place, Aberdeen
Died 2 January 1990 Victoria Place, Brighton, Sussex
Scotland v Wales 1932 (1), 1933 (1), 1934 (1), 1935 (1), 1936, 1937; England 1933, 1935 (2), 1936, 1937; Austria 1933; Ireland 1935 (1), 1936; Germany 1936.
Aberdeen Richmond 1927-28; Hull City 1928-32; Derby County Mar 1932-46 (FA Cup 1946) [guest during WW2 for Notts County 1939-41; Reading Apr 1940; Nottingham Forest 1941-42]; Luton Town Oct 1946-48 (player-coach).
A Scotland schoolboy internationalist in 1924, Duncan was nicknamed Dally due to his calm and unhurried manner, although that belied a keen football brain. After a season in Aberdeen junior football he went south in 1928 and spent all his senior career in England. He was a regular with Hull City in his four years there, then joined Derby County in 1932, where he defined his career and made the club a force to be reckoned with. He was seen as a natural successor to Alan Morton on the wing for Scotland and featured regularly for the national team, gaining 14 caps and scoring seven goals over a five-year period. During the War he worked in Derby but when the club closed down for three seasons he guested for the two Nottingham clubs, also making a single appearance for Reading in April 1940. He returned to the Baseball Ground when his club resumed in 1942 and four years later he left the club on a high, having won the 1946 FA Cup, making the opening goal when his shot was deflected in off Charlton's Bert Turner. That autumn he was appointed Luton Town player-coach and gave up playing in 1948 after being appointed manager. He remained at the club for a decade, taking them to the First Division in 1955. His next job was with Blackburn Rovers but he left under a cloud in the summer of 1960, despite reaching the FA Cup final, as a disastrous run of league form had seen relegation narrowly avoided. He was asked to resign, refused, and was sacked. At that point he moved to Brighton, where he ran a boarding house and coached a schools team.

James DUNCAN (2/0, 1878-82)
James Sibbald Robertson Duncan
Born 4 February 1859 Greenvale Street, Bridgeton, Glasgow
Died 3 January 1936 Elsinore, Largs, Ayrshire
Scotland v Wales 1878, 1882.
Eastern; Alexandra Athletic 1878-82; Rangers 1882-85.
A full back, Duncan was reportedly taught how to tackle as a young man at Eastern by Alexander Kennedy. He developed a strange method of kicking the ball, swinging his leg full length like a sledge hammer, which gave him wonderful leverage and distance although not necessarily direction. He had his best days with Alexandra Athletic, where he played for four years and won two caps, the first coming in 1878 a month after his 19th birthday. Alexandra Athletic was a multi-sports club, reportedly the first to lay down a cycle track around the pitch, and the first to introduce cross-country running to keep its members fit. Duncan was the backbone of the club, so when he left in 1882 to join Rangers, along with James Gossland, it prompted an exodus that soon brought the demise of his old club. He only had two full seasons in the Rangers team and gave up playing in 1885, but remained to serve on the club committee. He worked in the Glasgow meat market and had a business partnership, Duncan & Taylor.

Johnny DUNCAN (1/1, 1925)
John Duncan
Born 15 February 1896 Auchterderran Road, Lochgelly, Fife
Died 14 March 1966 Royal Infirmary, Leicester
Scotland v Wales Oct 1925 (1).
Lochgelly Thistle; Denbeath Star 1914-15; Lochgelly United 1915-18; Raith Rovers Feb 1918-22; Leicester City 1922-30 (Division Two 1925).
Brought up in Lochgelly, where he was known as 'Tokey', as a young man Duncan carved out a reputation in whippet racing, training many dogs to victory in local races. Meanwhile, he did well in Fife football during the war

years with Denbeath Star and Lochgelly United. He joined Raith Rovers early in 1918 and spent four years with the Kirkcaldy side, much of it partnering his brother Tommy on the right wing, winning the Fife Cup in 1921. The brothers moved together to Leicester in July 1922 and although Tommy left after a season, Johnny would finish his career there. He immediately settled at inside right with 20 goals in his first season and by his third season the team won the Second Division title; along the way he set a record with six consecutive goals against Port Vale on Christmas Day 1924. The ball from that match is now on display at Leicester's King Power Stadium along with his international cap. He was selected against Wales in October 1925 and scored the opener of a 3-0 win in Cardiff, but it turned out to be his only cap. Leicester came close to winning the league title in 1929, missing out by a point, by which time Duncan had switched to right half. He retired in 1930 to take over the Turk's Head pub in Welford Road, which he ran for the rest of his life. However, he was tempted back to manage Leicester in the post-war years and took them to the FA Cup final in 1949, but they also narrowly avoided relegation to the Third Division and he was sacked during the following season.

'Daddy' DUNLOP (1/0, 1890)
James Dunlop
Born 17 May 1870 Railway Tavern, Quay Street, Gourock, Renfrewshire
Died 11 January 1892 Greenhill Road, Paisley, Renfrewshire
Scotland v Wales 1890.
Blackstoun Rangers; Sandyford; Underwood Strollers; Westmarch; St Mirren 1888-92.
Dunlop was a precocious talent who tragically never had the opportunity to realise his potential. He joined St Mirren from juvenile football and quickly came through the ranks with the third team (Underwood Strollers) and reserves (Westmarch), and did so well when he arrived in the first team that he was capped by Scotland aged 19 in a comfortable 5-0 win over Wales. An inside forward, he was a natural leader who earned the nickname Daddy for his ability to organise, and was appointed team captain in 1890. There were offers to move south, but he was fiercely loyal to his club and said he would 'Live and die a Saint', which turned out to be sadly prescient. He clearly had ability off the field, too, as he was working as a telephone company manager at the time of his early death aged just 21. He contracted tetanus after cutting his knee on a piece of broken glass in match at Abercorn on New Year's Day 1892 and died ten days later. There was a great outpouring of grief in Paisley at his loss, and local people subscribed for a monument over his grave at the town's Woodside Cemetery, which was erected later in the year. Fellow internationalist William Paul of Dykebar wrote an emotional poem in memory of his friend, which was published in the *Glasgow Evening Post*.

Billy DUNLOP (1/0, 1906)
William Peden Dunlop
Born 11 August 1874 Riccarton Road, Hurlford, Ayrshire
Died 28 November 1941 Horn Hall Hospital, Stanhope, Co Durham
Scotland v England 1906.
Hurlford 1890-93; Kilmarnock Jan-May 1893; Abercorn 1893-95; Liverpool Jan 1895-1911 (Second Division 1896, 1905; Football League 1901, 1906).
A strongly built, no-nonsense left back, Dunlop was approaching the veteran stage when he won his only Scotland cap, aged 31. It would have been hard for the selectors to ignore him, as Liverpool were on the cusp of winning the Football League title in 1906, having topped the Second Division the previous season. He had already been chosen five times for the Anglo-Scots trial match, and was even named in two Scotland teams in 1905 but his club denied him leave of absence. It was worth the wait, as he was praised in the *Scottish Referee* as a 'very solid and resolute back' in the 2-1 victory over England. The cap was the icing on the cake of a long career which started in his home town of Hurlford, where he joined the village club and played in the Ayrshire Cup final of 1891 as a 16-year-old. He had a few months at Kilmarnock, then experienced Scottish League football at Abercorn for a couple of years. He moved to Liverpool early in 1895 and spent the rest of his playing career with the club, a model of consistency, rarely missing a match. In 16 seasons at Anfield he won two league titles as he amassed over 320 league appearances. When he retired in 1911, having played most of the last couple of years in the reserves in the Lancashire Combination, he was appointed assistant trainer to Sunderland, a post he held until his death in 1941. There was tragedy in his life as his first wife died in 1903, a 26-year-old son died in 1922, and his second wife died in 1934; he married for a third time in 1938. He qualified as a masseur and worked in WW1 treating injured troops at Jeffrey Hospital and in WW2 with the ARP casualty services. He lived in Dene Lane, Fulwell, at the time of his death in hospital. NB he should not be confused with another William Dunlop, who went from Annbank to Sunderland in the 1890s.

Jimmy DUNN (6/2, 1925-28)
James Dunn
Born 25 November 1900 King Street, Trongate, Glasgow
Died 20 August 1963 Aintree Hospital, Liverpool
Scotland v Wales Feb 1925, 1928 (1); Ireland 1925 (1), 1927, 1928; England 1928.
St Anthony's; Hibernian 1920-28; Everton Apr 1928-35 (Second Division 1931, First Division 1932; FA Cup 1933); Exeter City 1935-36; Runcorn 1936-39 player-coach.

A Scotland junior internationalist at St Anthony's in 1920, Dunn was signed that summer by Hibs, at the time a mid-table side. He soon proved himself as a superb playmaker at inside right, passing with precision and making runs to create goals, which helped Hibs to make two outstanding cup runs and reach the Scottish Cup finals of 1923 and 1924. Although both finals were lost the prospects were bright for the Edinburgh side. Dunn scored

25 goals in 1924/25 and that was enough to win him his first Scotland cap against Wales, and later in the year he found the net against Ireland. It was the prelude to him achieving immortality in 1928 as a Wembley Wizard, and within weeks he was on his way to Everton, one of the richest clubs in England, together with clubmate Harry Ritchie. Despite the presence of Dixie Dean at centre forward, Everton struggled and were relegated in Dunn's second season at Goodison, but this proved to be a springboard to greater things. With Dean back to top form and Dunn in active support, the club won the Second and First Division titles in successive seasons, then the FA Cup in 1933. In the final, Dunn headed the third in a 3-0 victory over Manchester City, which was his first match at Wembley since the 1928 triumph. With age catching up, he slipped out of the side and moved to Exeter in 1935 but found life hard at the foot of the Third Division. A year later he was back on Merseyside as player-coach of Runcorn and guided them to three Cheshire League titles until he retired in 1939, and even in his final season he played in their memorable FA Cup third round tie against cup-holders Preston North End. He lived in Hawthorne Road, Bootle at time of death from cancer in Aintree Hospital. His sons played professionally and one of them, also Jimmy, won the FA Cup with Wolves in 1949.

Jimmy DYKES (2/0, 1938)

James Dykes
Born 12 October 1916 Kinloch Cottage, Law, Lanarkshire
Died 16 May 1974 Royal Hobart Hospital, Tasmania, Australia
Scotland v Netherlands 1938; Ireland 1938.
Heart of Midlothian 1934-47 [guest during WW2 for Third Lanark 1939-40; Ayr United May-Jun 1940, Charlton Athletic Mar 1942, Chelsea Apr-May 1942, Glentoran 1942-45; Dundalk Dec 1945-47]; Portadown 1947-50; Banbridge Town 1950-51; Ross County Jan-May 1951.
Brought up in the small Lanarkshire town of Law, Dykes learned his football at Wishaw High School and signed for Hearts straight from school. At six foot four and with a head of blond hair, he certainly stood out and was the ideal build for a centre half. He soon came to prominence and was selected for the Scottish League in October 1936, just after his 20th birthday. He subsequently won two Scotland caps in 1938 and went on the SFA tour of USA and Canada in 1939, but like so many others of his generation his career was disrupted by the Second World War. A plumber to trade, he continued to live in Lanarkshire and was rarely able to play for Hearts because of travel difficulties, and during the conflict he turned out for other clubs. Among his adventures he won a Scottish Second Eleven Cup winner's medal with Ayr United. He did manage a year with Hearts and was selected for wartime internationals against England but then he joined the RAF in 1942 and was posted to London where he played for Charlton and Chelsea. However, he was discharged a few months later, got married and went to Belfast on what was reported as 'essential work'. He appeared in two Irish Cup finals with Glentoran and played across the border with Dundalk, then after the War he decided to remain in Belfast and purchased a bookmaker's business in the city. He negotiated his formal release from Hearts in 1947 to sign for Portadown, who appointed him in 1948 as their manager on a temporary basis, and concluded his career with short spells at Banbridge Town and back in Scotland at Ross County. Then he decided to emigrate and he lived the rest of his life in Tasmania.

E

Jimmy EASSON (3/1, 1931-33)

James Ferrier Easson
Born 3 January 1906 City Road, Brechin, Angus
Died 20 May 1983 Ransom Road, Erdington, Birmingham
Scotland v Austria 1931; Switzerland 1931 (1); Wales 1933.
Carnoustie Panmure 1924-26; East Craigie 1926-28; Portsmouth 1928-39; Fulham Mar 1939-40 [loan to Dundee Oct 1939-40]; Carnoustie Panmure 1940-45 [trial for Dundee United Mar 1943].
A fine all-round sportsman, Easson could have made it as a cricketer or a golfer, but chose football and had the advantage of a family background in the game, as his father David had played for Brechin City, Forfar Athletic and Arbroath before the First World War. He went on to a fine career as a goal-scoring inside left although he turned professional relatively late at the age of 22, having waited until he completed an engineering apprenticeship. Meanwhile, he played for local junior sides before accepting a trial at Portsmouth in 1928, following which they offered him a contract. He went on to score more than a hundred league goals in just over 300 games, and the highlight of a decade with the Fratton Park side was perhaps the FA Cup final in 1934, which ended in a narrow defeat to Manchester City. Meanwhile he was selected for Scotland on the continental tour of 1931, as part of an entire forward line who made their debuts against Austria, only to be outclassed as the national team slumped to a 5-0 defeat. He was dropped for the match in Rome four days later, but returned at centre forward for the final match in Geneva where he achieved a measure of redemption by scoring the opening goal in a 3-2 win over the Swiss. It was not enough to secure a regular place in the Scotland team and just one more cap followed in 1933, against Wales. By the end of the decade he had faded out of the picture at Portsmouth and in March 1939 he moved on to Fulham but when the War intervened he came home to Carnoustie for 'vital war work'. He had a season on loan with Dundee before being freed by Fulham and he contented himself with junior football for Carnoustie Panmure, where he also started coaching. In 1945 he returned to Portsmouth as assistant trainer, and helped to coach the team which won the Football League twice in succession. In 1950 he joined Southampton, then went to Aston Villa as head coach in 1953, and back to Portsmouth in 1957, before retiring to live in Birmingham.

David ELLIS (1/1, 1892)

David Thomson Ellis
Born 10 April 1869 Front Street, Mossend, West Lothian

Died 29 January 1940 Sighthill View, Edinburgh
Scotland v Ireland 1892 (1).

Mossend Swifts 1886-92 [trials for Heart of Midlothian Jan & Mar 1892, St Bernard's Mar 1892]; Heart of Midlothian 1892-93; Mossend Swifts 1893-98.

Mossend Swifts, from a small mining community near West Calder, had a strong team for a while, including five brothers from the Ellis family. This has led to considerable confusion in record books which have credited David's brother James as the man who won the international cap in 1892; however, there is no doubt from local newspapers and obituaries that it was David who won the honour. Mossend Swifts rose and fell with equal rapidity, joining the East of Scotland FA in 1882 and the Scottish FA in 1886, the year David started out in the Swifts' reserves, known as the Lancers. By 1888 he had earned promotion to the first team, which had just won the East of Scotland Shield, beating Scottish Cup holders Hibs in the final. Along with two of his brothers, Alex and Jim, he represented the East of Scotland in 1891 and had trials for Hearts and St Bernard's but was not immediately tempted to leave his parent club. In 1892 he became the second Mossend player (after Bob Boyd) to be selected for Scotland, and he is credited with the winning goal in the 3-2 victory over Ireland, although it was highly controversial as reports claimed that his shot passed through the side netting. That summer a sudden economic downturn in West Lothian led to Mossend Swifts disbanding and their best players left, with Ellis joining Hearts. A season later, Mossend started up again and he returned to his home town team where he remained for the rest of his career, crowned by another East of Scotland Shield victory in 1896, in which he partnered his brother Jim on the right wing. He worked all his life in the shale oil industry, starting aged 13 as a pony driver with Young's Paraffin Light and Mineral Oil company, and worked his way up to mine manager. He was in charge of Newliston Mine in Broxburn, Roman Camp Mines and Duddingston Mines near Winchburgh until he retired in 1938. He died two years later in Edinburgh from a chill which he caught while attending a mine disaster inquiry.

Jock EWART (1/0, 1921)
John Ewart
Born 14 February 1891 Oakbank, Straiton, Midlothian
Died 22 June 1943 Motherwell Road, Bellshill, Lanarkshire
Scotland v England 1921.

Bellshill Rovers; Bellshill Athletic; Larkhall Thistle; Airdrieonians Mar 1909-1912; Bradford City 1912-23; Airdrieonians 1923-27 (Scottish Cup 1924); Bradford City 1927-28; Preston North End 1928-30.

Ewart was a fine goalkeeper who spent most of his career gravitating between two unfashionable clubs, Airdrieonians and Bradford City, which perhaps restricted his international honours to just one Scotland cap. At least he had the satisfaction of a clean sheet in the comprehensive 3-0 win over England in 1921. Born in a small mining community near Edinburgh, his family soon moved to Lanarkshire and he was brought up in Bellshill. Having started out in junior football, he signed for Airdrie aged 18 and over the next three years was almost ever-present and was selected twice by the Scottish League. In 1912 Bradford City, then in the First Division, paid £1,200, a record fee for a goalkeeper, to take him to Yorkshire, and despite an interruption for war service he made over 300 appearances for the club over the next decade. He served in WW1 with the Prince of Wales' Own (West Yorkshire) Regiment and later with the Training Reserve. After Bradford were relegated in 1922, he spent one more season before returning to Airdrie where he played a key role in Airdrie's greatest triumph, the Scottish Cup victory of 1924, keeping his goal intact in the final. Bradford took him back in 1927 but it turned out a disastrous season, which saw them relegated to Division 3 North. Ewart was released and wound up at Preston North End. Approaching the age of 40, his career came to an abrupt end in 1930 when he was given a surprise free transfer and subsequently an FA commission banned him for life from football after finding him guilty of trying to bribe opposition players. Ewart was unusually well-educated, apparently speaking French and German and a skilled musician. He also had a reputation for eccentricity on and off the field: once when he failed to stop a fierce shot he quipped 'Rather mourn a goal than a goalkeeper'; another time he was stopped at night by police in Bradford and gave the excuse that he was looking for ghosts. On leaving the game he returned to Lanarkshire where he worked as a hotel manager and newsagent, and for the Co-operative Society, whom he sued unsuccessfully for unpaid commission. He suffered poor health and in a gesture of compassion the FA lifted his ban, but he died of tuberculosis soon afterwards at his home in Bellshill, aged just 52.

F

Johnny FERGUSON (6/5, 1874-78)
John Ferguson
Born 22 June 1848 Alexandria, Dunbartonshire
Died 6 September 1929 Glebe Road, Kilmarnock, Ayrshire
Scotland v England 1874, 1876, 1877 (2); Wales 1876 (1), 1877, 1878 (2).

Vale of Leven 1872-80 (Scottish Cup 1877, 1878, 1879).

Ferguson was an established athlete by the time Vale of Leven formed a football club in 1872, having won prizes in local sports from 1868 onwards. He took to the new game so well that he became the goalscoring star of the team, but his athletic success proved something of a hindrance as the cash prizes he had won saw him branded a professional. The accusation forced Vale to withdraw from the first two Scottish Cups, as the competition had a rule that anyone who had ever won money in any sport could not take part. Vale stood by their man rather than accept the rule and in the middle of this dispute, somewhat hypocritically, the Scottish FA selected him to become the first provincial player to be capped in 1874. With the professionalism charge quietly dropped after Vale's AS McBride was elected SFA President, Ferguson went on to play an integral part in the club's rise to the top of Scottish football. That prowess was reflected in three consecutive Scottish Cup victories as Queen's Park were deposed from their pedestal as Scotland's champions. What is more, after the third of those victories, Vale were invited to London to meet their English counterparts, Wanderers, and Ferguson scored all three goals in a 3-1 win at Kennington Oval that crowned the Scots as champions of Britain. Meanwhile he won six Scotland caps, notably scoring twice against England in 1877. After he gave up playing in 1880 he maintained a lifelong association with his club, and met up with his fellow former players on their annual cruise on Loch Lomond. In latter days, he was the elder statesman of the gathering, and hosted the event until his death in 1929. He ran a wine and spirit business in Prestwick.

Bob FINDLAY (1/0, 1898)
Robert Findlay
Born 29 March 1877 Orchard Street, Galston, Ayrshire
Died 13 August 1926 Bayonne, New Jersey, USA
Scotland v Wales 1898.
Rugby XI; Kilmarnock 1897-1900 (Second Division 1898, 1899); Celtic 1900-01; Kilmarnock Nov 1901-04; Dundee Nov 1904-05; Motherwell 1905-07; Hamilton Academical 1907-08; Port Glasgow Athletic 1908-11.

An outside left, Findlay was playing in the Second Division when he was selected for Scotland against Wales in 1898, the last year the SFA chose 'second string' players for the lesser internationals. It was his first season as a professional and the excitement continued as a week later he was in the Kilmarnock side which contested the Scottish Cup final. They would soon clinch the Second Division title, although the team was denied promotion until they repeated the feat the following season. Sadly Findlay's potential was never realised as he suffered a knee injury in 1899 which troubled him for the rest of his career. Celtic took a gamble on him but released him after a season, and his knee continued to restrict his opportunities back at Kilmarnock. In despair, he gave up the game for six months before Dundee offered him a chance in the autumn of 1904 and the respite must have done him good as he went on to play for several more years at a variety of clubs, without ever reaching the same heights. When he retired in 1911 he was interviewed for the Motherwell manager's position but was beaten to it by Sailor Hunter. Instead, he emigrated with his family to USA in 1914 and, having been an iron turner in Scotland, he worked for Babcock & Wilcox in Bayonne where he managed the company soccer team, taking them to the American FA final in 1918. He died there in 1926, aged 49, after a short illness. His younger brother Tom played alongside him at Kilmarnock, Motherwell and Port Glasgow, while his son William played football for USA at the 1924 and 1928 Olympic Games.

Tom FITCHIE (4/1, 1905-07)
Thomas Tindal Fitchie
Born 11 December 1881 Orwell Terrace, Dalry, Edinburgh
Died 17 October 1947 Oakdale Road, Streatham, London
Scotland v Wales 1905, 1906, 1907; Ireland 1906 (1).
West Norwood 1897-1904 [guest for Woolwich Arsenal Feb 1902-03]; Tottenham Hotspur Jan-Aug 1904; Fulham Aug-Dec 1904; Woolwich Arsenal Dec 1904-06; Queen's Park 1906-08; Woolwich Arsenal 1908-09; Pilgrims 1909; Glossop 1909-12; Fulham Nov 1912-13; English Wanderers 1913; London Caledonians 1913-14.

The son of an accountant, Fitchie was born in Edinburgh but grew up in London where his precocious talent was clear to see: he once scored 20 goals in a game when South London Schools won 32-0 against Westminster Schools on 5 December 1896. He played primarily with West Norwood in his early years, and was selected for the London FA, where his amateur status allowed him considerable leeway to move between clubs and he would often find a guinea in his boots after the game if he scored. He made guest appearances for Arsenal from February 1902 onwards and then Spurs early in 1904, followed by Fulham that summer, and would often play midweek with the professionals and at weekends with the amateurs. By now he was a salesman with Jaques of London, a sports goods manufacturer, who actively encouraged his football career as it opened doors to clubs and players. They allowed him to travel the country, and for two years from 1906 he headed north each weekend to Glasgow to play for Queen's Park. A family anecdote relates how he was playing against Hearts at Tynecastle, facing the great Charlie Thomson who joked that Fitchie should not be playing inside left as he was not naturally left-footed, whereupon Fitchie proceed to nutmeg him twice in a row. Back in London, in 1909 his friend Vivian Woodward, an England internationalist, invited him to go on a lengthy tour to the USA with the Pilgrims select team. Some of the matches were tougher than expected and mid-tour Fitchie broke his ankle badly enough to threaten his playing career but he did recover and played three seasons for Glossop. He went on a European tour with English Wanderers in 1913 and concluded his football days with London Caledonians. In the First World War he served with the Argyll & Sutherland Highlanders, then in 1918 was transferred to the Royal Army Service Corps as a driver, initially in France and then with the army of occupation in Germany. When he was discharged in 1919 he was in poor shape, suffering from sciatica caused by the uncomfortable vehicles he drove, exacerbated by a painful knee from an old football injury. He lived in later years at Clapham Park and suffered from a lung disorder which eventually killed him in 1947. His grandson Andrew was a soccer blue at Cambridge in the 1970s.

Jimmy FLEMING (3/3, 1929-30)
James Nicholson Fleming
Born 29 May 1903 Kyle Street, Townhead, Glasgow
Died 13 May 1969 Hairmyres Hospital, East Kilbride, Lanarkshire
Scotland v Germany 1929; Netherlands 1929 (1); England 1930 (2).
Shettleston; St Johnstone Sep 1923-25 (Second Division 1924); Rangers Oct 1925-34 (Scottish League 1927, 1928, 1929, 1930, 1931, 1933, 1934; Scottish Cup 1928, 1930, 1932); Ayr United Nov 1934-36.

Fleming started out in Glasgow junior football with Shettleston and was already 20 when he turned senior with St Johnstone in 1923. He made an immediate impact with 16 goals in his first 14 matches and this helped Saints to win the Second Division championship, gaining promotion to the top league for the first time. He kept on scoring in the First Division and it was little surprise when Rangers bought him in the autumn of 1925, with three players going to Perth as part of the deal. It was a fine time to play for Rangers who had an almost unbroken record of success in Fleming's nine years there, winning seven league titles and three Scottish Cups. He notched up no less than 27 hat-tricks for Rangers, a club record, and among his scoring feats was nine in a 14-2 win over Blairgowrie in 1934, then five against Dundee the following week. However, at a time when Scotland had a wealth of attacking talent his national team opportunities were limited to just three caps. He was selected for Scotland's continental tour of 1929, playing twice against Germany and the Netherlands, and the following year he scored two second-half goals against England, which would normally have been acclaimed but the damage had already been done with Scotland losing 4-0 at half-time. He also played once for the Scottish League in 1934. His career ended with a couple of seasons at Ayr United and he retired when they were relegated in 1936. A trained accountant, he was an agent for a manufacturer.

Bob FLEMING (1/0, 1886)
Robert Fleming
Born 11 March 1860 Ingleston Road, Greenock, Renfrewshire
Died 9 January 1950 Hill Crest, Truro, Cornwall
Scotland v Ireland 1886.
Wellington Park 1878-79; Oakfield 1879-80; Morton 1880-90.
Fleming was Morton's first internationalist in 1886, and it would be another decade before Rab Macfarlane became the club's second. Brought up in Greenock, he played for local juvenile clubs before he joined Morton in 1880 and soon established himself as an excellent inside right. For much of his ten years with them he was captain and his determined expression stares out from the earliest known team photo, after Morton lifted their first trophy, the Greenock & District Charity Cup in 1885. He was then in his prime and that autumn he scored a hat-trick for Renfrewshire against Nottinghamshire, the first of several county honours, and later in the season the Scotland selectors rewarded him with his full cap against Ireland, a 7-2 victory. His younger brother Alex was a half-back for the club. After he retired from football in 1890 he played cricket for local clubs, including Morton. A foreman coppersmith, he retired to Cornwall and died in Truro but was buried back home in Greenock.

Johnny FORBES (5/0, 1884-87)
John Forbes
Born 13 January 1862 Bridge Street, Alexandria, Dunbartonshire
Died 31 January 1928 Wellington Street, Blackburn, Lancashire
Scotland v Ireland 1884; England 1884, 1887; Wales 1884, 1887.
Star of Leven; Vale of Leven 1881-88 [guest for Rangers Feb-Mar 1887]; Blackburn Rovers Nov 1888-93 (FA Cup 1890, 1891).

One of the top full backs of his era, Forbes was fast, agile and a fearless tackler. He started out in Alexandria with Star of Leven before the town's leading club saw his potential and he had seven outstanding years with Vale of Leven. After two fine matches for Scotch Counties he was selected to play against England in 1883 but was prevented by injury. A year later he made his Scotland debut in Ireland, partnering Walter Arnott in defence, and retained his place for that year's England and Wales games. He was selected again in 1885 and 1886 but turned down the honour, perceiving a snub against the Vale of Leven team as he was the only one chosen, and remained firm even after one newspaper challenged him 'to come out like a man and do battle for his country'. However in 1887, after he played for Rangers in the quarter-final and semi-final of their FA Cup run, he came back into the Scotland fold for the England and Wales games, making it five wins out of five in his internationals. He had less success with Vale of Leven, reaching three consecutive Scottish Cup finals but not winning any of them: those in 1883 and 1885 were lost in replays, while Vale refused to play the 1884 final, in part due to a Forbes family bereavement. As Vale declined, there was much speculation about a move to England and he turned professional with Blackburn Rovers in November 1888. At the peak of his powers, he was elected club captain the following summer and played a leading role as they won the FA Cup twice in succession. He retired from playing in 1893, apart from the occasional benefit match, and spent the rest of his life in Blackburn, having set up a gentleman's outfitters in Victoria Street, later in Lord Street. The business continued to sell sports gear and to advertise in Blackburn Rovers programmes long after his death in 1928.

Bobby FOYER (2/0, 1893-94)
Robert Foyer
Born 22 June 1868 Burnbank Road, Hamilton, Lanarkshire
Died 16 August 1942 Alexandra Parade, Dennistoun, Glasgow
Scotland v Wales 1893, 1894.
Burnbank Swifts; St Bernard's 1889-95 (Scottish Cup 1895) [guest for Heart of Midlothian Aug 1890]; Newcastle United 1895-97; St Bernard's Apr-May 1897; Clyde Aug-Oct 1897; Wishaw Aug-Nov 1899.
A junior internationalist and Junior Cup winner with Burnbank in 1889, Foyer started out as a winger but was later reckoned to be one of the lightest and smallest full backs ever to represent Scotland. He did not turn senior with St Bernard's until he was 21, and soon made up for lost time and was selected for the East of Scotland side just a couple of months later. His consistency brought him a Scotland call-up, although he had little to do at right back in his first cap, an 8-0 win in Wales in 1893, then he was

selected against the same opposition the following year, and was travelling reserve for the England match in 1895. That was also the year of St Bernard's Scottish Cup win, which no doubt prompted his transfer that summer to Newcastle. It didn't work out on Tyneside and when he was released by Newcastle in the spring of 1897 he was greeted like the prodigal son on his return to Saints, but surprised many by signing for Clyde in the summer. However, he soon dropped out of the picture at Clyde and disappeared from view before returning to action briefly at Wishaw in 1899. He lived throughout his football career in Bothwell, where he was a blacksmith and hammerman, and later in life he worked as an engineer with Plean Coal Company, living in Bannockburn, near Stirling. He died suddenly on a visit to his daughter in Glasgow. NB Foyer is the correct spelling of his surname although it was frequently recorded as Foyers.

'Sydney' FRASER (1/0, 1891)

James Fraser
Born 26 November 1868 Causeway Street, Moffat, Dumfriesshire
Died 25 March 1945 Gourlay Street, Springburn, Glasgow
Scotland v Ireland 1891.
Moffat 1888-91; Northern 1891-94; Leith Athletic 1894-95; Airdrieonians 1895-96.

Although christened James, Fraser was always known as 'Sydney' as he was born on the day that Sir Sydney Waterlow won the Dumfriesshire seat at the 1868 general election, and the boy's father was such a dedicated supporter of the philanthropist politician that he never called him anything else. Fraser was mentored by Moffat's greatest footballer, the internationalist James Niven, and his selection for Scotland to face Ireland in 1891 was perhaps fortunate as that year the SFA refused to pick players from league clubs who had declined to take part in the trial match. James Niven happened to be in Glasgow and told the selectors that Moffat was the best left forward in Scotland. They duly acted on his advice and selected Fraser on the left wing, although the *Scottish Referee* was not impressed: 'Fraser is a splendid man but somewhat selfish, and this will not do in an international.' Nevertheless, he passed to Jimmy Low for the winning goal as the weakened Scotland team scraped a narrow 2-1 win. At the time, Fraser was a porter at the Hydropathic Hotel in Moffat, but not long afterwards he married and moved to Glasgow, to work in the iron forge at North British Locomotive Works in Springburn, where he spent the rest of his life. He joined Northern and was clearly still a decent player as he featured in the Scottish Alliance select at the end of his first season, then when Northern got into the Scottish League he was twice chosen for Glasgow against Sheffield. In 1894 he joined Leith Athletic for a season in Division One, and finally spent a year at Airdrie.

Jack FRASER (1/0, 1907)

John Fraser
Born 10 November 1876 West Bridgend, Dumbarton
Died 30 September 1952 Northumberland House, Green Lanes, North London
Scotland v Ireland 1907.
Dumbarton 1896-97; Motherwell 1897-98; Notts County Feb 1898-99 [loan to Morton 1898-99]; Newcastle United 1899-1901; St Mirren 1901-02; Southampton 1902-05 (Southern League 1903, 1904); Dundee 1905-12 (Scottish Cup 1910).

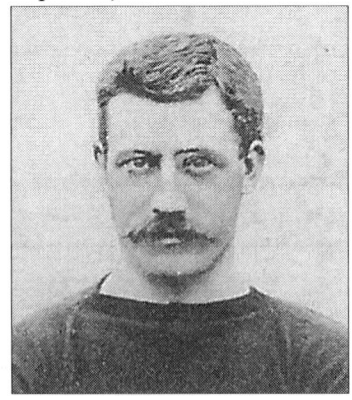

An outside left who was powerfully built and an excellent dribbler, Fraser had an eventful career on both sides of the border. He reached the Scottish Cup final in his first season as a professional with Dumbarton, although the club finished at the bottom of Division 2. He then had a few months at Motherwell, also at the foot of Division 2, before Notts County took him south, but he failed to settle and spent a season on loan at Morton before Newcastle signed him in 1899. He blossomed on Tyneside and was a regular in the team over two seasons, playing on the left alongside Sandy Macfarlane, then came back to Scotland with St Mirren for a year, where he was capped by the Scottish League. Next came a fruitful three year stay at Southampton, which included two Southern League titles, and finally he settled at Dundee where he resumed his left wing partnership with Macfarlane to outstanding effect. Already in the veteran category, he crowned his career by winning a Scotland cap in 1907, aged 30, and then the Scottish Cup in 1910. After hanging up his boots in 1912 he remained at Dens Park as team manager but during the War he combined his football with work as a shipwright, and was badly injured on Christmas Day 1915 at Camperdown docks when an anchor chain broke. After his recovery he moved to London to work as a masseur, and for many years he was chief scout for Chelsea, with his highest profile capture being Hughie Gallacher in 1930. He continued to live in Fulham until his death in a Finsbury Park nursing home in 1952, aged 75.

Eadie FRASER (5/3, 1880-83)
Malcolm John Eadie Fraser
Born 4 March 1860 Goderich, Ontario, Canada
Died 8 January 1886 Prince Alfred Hospital, Sydney, Australia
Scotland v Wales 1880, 1882 (2), 1883 (1); England 1882, 1883.
Kerland; Queen's Park 1879-84 (Scottish Cup 1881, 1882).

One of Scotland's most gifted footballers, the 'Graceful Eadie' was born in Canada and died in Australia, quite an unusual journey. The third and youngest son of Rev John Fraser and Sarah Ann Lawrie, his father was a native of Grantown-on-Spey but trained for the ministry in Canada. The boy was named after Dr John Eadie, professor of biblical literature, who was a leading Presbyterian. The family returned to Scotland in 1862 when his father was appointed as minister of the new Cumberland Street UP church in Glasgow's Gorbals, so Eadie grew up on the south side of Glasgow. He became a fine footballer with Kerland, a team in Crosshill, and was just the right kind of player for Queen's Park, the pre-eminent club in Scotland. Talented and gentlemanly, he made his international debut a year later, aged 20, and went on to win five caps for Scotland between 1880 and 1883, scoring three times against Wales in the process. At Queen's Park he enthralled spectators with his effortless dribbling, and according to the Queen's Park history: 'Scotland never had a better forward than Eadie Fraser, known to everybody as the Graceful Eadie. His movements were perfect. His popularity was extraordinary. On the field and off it he was a thorough gentleman, and never descended to those tricks which tend to bring the game into disrepute.' He won two Scottish Cups in 1881 and 1882 with Queen's Park and was club secretary for a year, then in 1884, at the peak of his powers and just before his 24th birthday, he left Scotland to take up a job in West Africa with Miller Brothers, Glasgow-based traders in palm oil. After a year he became ill with tuberculosis and returned to Scotland to convalesce in a nursing home, before being advised to try the dry climate of Australia to effect a cure. He departed in September 1885 as the sole paying passenger on the cargo ship *Ardmore*, and endured an utterly miserable three month journey. On arrival at Sydney he was taken straight to the Prince Alfred Hospital where, reviving briefly, he wrote what turned out to be his last letter home and died a few days later. He was buried in the city's vast Rookwood Cemetery and some Australian friends launched a memorial fund to erect a suitable headstone to this great footballer. Unfortunately, not enough money was raised and his grave remains unmarked.

William FULTON (1/0, 1884)
William Fulton
Born 1 April 1857 Garthland Lane, Paisley, Renfrewshire
Died 14 January 1941 Makerston Nursing Home, Paisley, Renfrewshire
Scotland v Ireland 1884.
Abercorn 1877-86.

A founding member of Abercorn in 1877, Fulton played for the club at half back for ten years in a fairly unremarkable career apart from his national team selection. He was chosen for Scotch Counties in 1883, then the following year was named in the Scotland team for the first ever international against Ireland, as was his club mate John Goudie. Having endured a stormy crossing to Belfast and a gale blowing throughout the match, the Scots carved out a 5-0 win. Fulton retired from the game around 1886 but remained involved with Abercorn after his playing days and occasionally acted as umpire. From a weaving family, he worked from a young age in the Paisley cotton mills, starting out as a bobbin polisher and rising to the more skilled role of cloth finisher. By the turn of the century he had put together enough money to open a tobacconist and newsagent shop in Causeyside Street, Paisley, which he ran for many years. He never married.

Bertie FYFE (1/0, 1895)
John Herbert Fyfe
Born 18 March 1873 Dounepark, Girvan, Ayrshire
Died 18 February 1950 County Hospital, Hertford, Hertfordshire
Scotland v Wales 1895.
South Western [trial for St Mirren Feb 1893]; St Mirren 1893-94; Third Lanark 1894-96; Rangers Apr 1896; Clyde 1896-97; Ayr Parkhouse 1897-98; Calcutta 1898-1906.
Fyfe was a Scotland junior internationalist with South Western, playing against Ireland in 1893, and after he scored twice for St Mirren in a trial he was asked to sign for the Paisley club. He had just a season at St Mirren and was good enough to play for Renfrewshire, then spent two years at Third Lanark where he won his full Scotland cap in 1895, at outside right against Wales. It appears his work started to take priority as he left Third Lanark the following spring, made a single guest appearance for Rangers in a friendly, had a season with Clyde, and ended his football

days with Ayr Parkhouse where he won the Ayr Charity Cup in 1897. Throughout his football career he worked as a commercial clerk and in the autumn of 1898 he went out to Calcutta for a new job. He continued to play football and in 1904 the *Scottish Referee* reported that Fyfe 'has for the past three years captained the leading Association team in India, and easily tops the list of goalscorers'. This was probably Calcutta FC, which won the Indian FA Shield several times in this era. In time he became a partner in the Gray Dawes shipping agency, then a director of Gray Mackenzie, and although he returned to the UK in 1914 for the duration of the War, he went back to Calcutta where he remained in business until the 1930s. He retired to Hertfordshire, first at Mangrove Hall, then the Old Vicarage in Ware. His son Kenneth was a Scotland rugby internationalist in the 1930s.

G

Hughie GALLACHER (20/24, 1924-35)
Hugh Kilpatrick Gallacher
Born 2 February 1903 Cleland House, Main Street, Bellshill, Lanarkshire
Died 11 June 1957 Low Fell, Gateshead, County Durham

Scotland v Ireland 1924, 1925 (1), 1926 (3), 1927, 1929 (5), 1930 (2); Wales Feb 1925 (2), Oct 1925, 1926 (1), 1927 (1), 1928 (3), 1929 (2); England 1925 (2), 1926, 1927, 1928, 1929, 1934, 1935; France 1930 (2).
Tannochside Athletic 1918-19; Hattonrigg Thistle 1919-20; Bellshill Athletic Feb 1920-21; Queen of the South Jan-May 1921; Airdrieonians 1921-25 (Scottish Cup 1924); Newcastle United Dec 1925-30 (Football League 1927); Chelsea 1930-34; Derby County Nov 1934-36; Notts County Sep 1936-38; Grimsby Town Jan-Jun 1938; Gateshead 1938-39.

One of the greatest Scottish goalscorers of all time, Gallacher had humble origins in Lanarkshire where he kicked the ball around in the streets of Bellshill as a boy with his chum Alex James. He started playing the game properly with local juvenile sides then Bellshill Athletic juniors and was only 17 when he was capped by the Glasgow Junior League. In January 1921 Queen of the South, newly formed and still only playing friendlies, signed the talented forward and he gave a taste of his prowess by scoring four on his debut. He went on to net 19 in nine games for the Dumfries side before being hospitalised with pneumonia. While recuperating he was signed by Airdrieonians without the knowledge of his own club, the start of an extraordinary professional career that saw Gallacher score with abandon. He netted no less than 24 times in 20 Scotland appearances, including a record five in one international against Ireland (some reports said four), although surprisingly he failed to find the net in the Wembley Wizards match of 1928. There is no doubt he could have achieved even more in the game and there is a telling gap of four years between his 18th and 19th caps, largely thanks to his erratic personal life which did not appeal to the selectors. He spent four years at Airdrie, at that time one of Scotland's top sides, crowned by their Scottish Cup success in 1924. English clubs were queuing up to sign him and Newcastle United dug deepest to take him south in December 1925 for a fee reported at around £7,000. He was idolised on Tyneside, piling on the goals with abandon as Newcastle won the league in 1927. However, his constant brushes with referees and officials caused a rift with the club directors and when Chelsea offered £10,000 in the summer of 1930 they accepted it without even consulting the player. He duly went to London and although the goals continued to flow in a side which flirted with relegation, his discipline was his downfall, compounded by a divorce and bankruptcy. Further arguments about money created a rift with Chelsea and he moved on again in 1934, this time to Derby County. Newly remarried, it was a chance for a fresh start and he nearly won honours as Derby finished second in the league in both years he was there. Now at the veteran stage he dropped to the Third Division with Notts County and early in 1938 was recruited to save Grimsby Town from relegation. He ended his career back in the north-east with Gateshead, where his return to Tyneside was greeted with huge enthusiasm. He felt at home there, and showed he still had the skills with 18 goals in one season, including five in one game, playing his last match as a professional on 2 September 1939. He drove an ambulance during the War and worked in local factories, but apart from a bit of coaching and sports writing was unable to get a job in football, although his eldest son Jackie played for Celtic in the 1940s. His final years were depressingly sad: after his second wife died he turned to alcohol, and in May 1957 he was charged with assaulting his youngest son. The day before he was due in court, he threw himself in front of the York to Edinburgh express train near his home at the ironically-named Dead Man's Crossing. See his biography, *The Hughie Gallacher Story* by Paul Joannou.

Patsy GALLACHER (1/1, 1934)
Patrick Gallacher
Born 21 August 1909 Kirkinner Place, Bridge of Weir, Renfrewshire
Died 4 January 1992 Orangefield Place, Greenock, Renfrewshire
Scotland v Ireland 1934 (1).
Linwood St Conval's; Bridge of Weir Thistle; Sunderland 1928-38 (Football League 1936; FA Cup 1937); Stoke City Nov 1938-46 [guest for Dundee United Nov-Dec 1941]; Coleraine Dec 1946; Cork United Jan-Mar 1947; Cheltenham Town 1948-49.

An inside forward who could play on the left or right, Gallacher was discovered by Sunderland playing juvenile football in his home town of Bridge of Weir and went south just after his 18th birthday in 1928. Taken under the wing of Tommy McInally, he took to English football well and made his first team debut a year later. His skills as a ball player made him a great favourite with the fans, helped by his knack of scoring goals, and he was called into the international team in October 1934, scoring Scotland's goal in a 2-1 defeat to Northern Ireland, but was not capped again as Sunderland consistently refused to release him. However, he could bask in the glory of their momentous league title win in 1936, in which he played in a superb forward line that included Raich Carter and fellow Scot Jimmy Connor. That was followed a year later by the FA Cup, with Gallacher scoring a precious winner in the semi-final to take them to Wembley, where they beat Preston North End 3-1 to lift the cup for the first time. One year on, his Roker love affair was over and halfway through his tenth season at Sunderland he moved to Stoke City, but due to injury he only managed four games for them before war broke out. He joined the RAF in 1940 and served as a PT instructor, playing little competitive football apart from guest appearances for Dundee United while stationed on Tayside. After being demobbed in 1946 he returned to Stoke but an Achilles tendon injury ended his time there. He had a month's trial at Coleraine and a brief spell as player coach at Cork United, then was out of the game for a while at home in Bridge of Weir before a swansong season at Cheltenham Town. He settled back in Scotland and spent his twilight years in Jericho House nursing home in Greenock, where he died in 1992.

Jamie GALT (2/1, 1908)
James Hill Galt
Born 11 August 1885 Vernon Street, Saltcoats, Ayrshire
Died 17 November 1935 Burnside Road, Whitecraigs, Glasgow
Scotland v Wales 1908; Ireland 1908 (1).
Stevenston; Ardrossan Winton Rovers; Ardeer Thistle; Rangers Jan 1906-14 (Scottish League 1911, 1912, 1913); Everton 1914-19 (Football League 1915) [guest for Fulham 1915-17; Partick Thistle Dec 1916]; Alloa Athletic Dec 1919.

A cultured half back who played on the left or in the centre, Galt was signed by Rangers in 1906 from Ardeer Thistle and within two years he was in the Scotland team, winning two caps in 1908 against Wales and Ireland, scoring in the latter. He also made two appearances for the Scottish League in 1912. Tall and bursting with enthusiasm, he was a mainstay of a fine Rangers team that won three consecutive league titles. However, he left Rangers under a cloud in 1914, telling the press he felt insulted that after captaining the team to the championship in 1912-13 he was dropped without any reasonable explanation. There was a further rift when the club charged him for three cups of tea while the team was on a training visit to Rothesay. Reluctantly he asked for a transfer and Everton were delighted to take him to Goodison Park. He captained the side to the English title in his first season but WW1 intervened and in 1915 he joined the Machine Gun Corps, playing for Fulham during his training. He later transferred to the Flying Corps and the Argyll & Sutherland Highlanders, rising to the rank of Lieutenant, until he was gassed and suffered from shell shock. After the War he serialised his story in the *People's Journal*. Released by Everton, he signed for Third Lanark, decided not to carry on playing, then changed his mind and tried to make a comeback with Alloa in December 1919 but was unable even to finish his first match. He became Third Lanark's honorary manager for a few years, although his main focus was a business partnership with Jimmy Gordon, which had started some years earlier in Glasgow, as sales agent for Alvis cars. He was a scratch golfer and took part in the Amateur Championship in 1913; not surprisingly, he won the annual Footballers' Golf Championship. He died aged just 50 in Glasgow and is buried in Eastwood Cemetery.

Dave GARDNER (1/0, 1897)
David Richmond Gardner
Born 31 March 1873 Caledonia Road, Gorbals, Glasgow
Died 5 November 1931 Longcliffe Golf Course, Loughborough, Leicestershire
Scotland v Wales 1897.
Cathcart; Third Lanark 1893-99; Newcastle United 1899-1902; Grimsby Town 1902-04; West Ham United 1904-07; Croydon Common Oct 1907-12.

A gifted defender, Gardner was appointed captain at all of his senior sides in recognition of his leadership qualities and thoughtful play. He had a speciality of back-heeling the ball, a rare trick in those days, which endeared him to the crowds. Brought up in the southside of Glasgow, he trained as a joiner while his football career slowly got under way. He was already 20 when he joined Third Lanark in 1893 and spent a couple of years in the reserves before breaking into the first team. Once established, he became an outstanding back and was rewarded with his one Scotland cap against Wales in 1897. However, although he played for Glasgow against Sheffield he was passed over for more representative honours. He left Third Lanark in the summer of 1899 when Newcastle United paid £200 for his signature, and captained his new side over three seasons on Tyneside. In 1902 he moved on to Grimsby, then a couple of years later to West Ham, at that time in the Southern League, where he played in their first match at Upton Park. His last club was Croydon Common, which had just turned professional and joined the Southern League, and he soon helped them to win promotion. He continued playing until around 1912, by which time he was team trainer, a role he continued until the club closed down in WW1. After the War, when Leicester City was reconstructed in 1919 from the ashes of Leicester Fosse, he was appointed trainer there and took the team into the First Division in 1924-25. He was still in post at Filbert Street when he died suddenly of a heart attack while playing golf with the team staff, aged 58.

Bob GARDNER (5/0, 1872-78)
Robert Gardner
Born 31 May 1847 Glasgow
Died 28 February 1887 High Street, South Queensferry, West Lothian
Scotland v England 1872c, 1873c, 1874, 1875, 1878.
Queen's Park 1867-74; Clydesdale 1874-80.

Scotland's first captain, Gardner was a redoubtable pioneer who had helped to establish Queen's Park in 1867, one of the few founders who had grown up in Glasgow. In that first international against England in 1872 he played the first half in goal, then swapped places with Robert Smith at half time to play up front, before reverting to goal later in the game. He was a fearsome opponent with his wild eyes and bushy beard, and he could be just as troublesome off the pitch, renowned for his short temper. Early in 1874 there was an almighty bust-up within the ranks of Queen's Park, after which several key players including Gardner and David Wotherspoon stormed out. They joined Clydesdale, and as fate would have it they soon faced their former colleagues in the first Scottish Cup final of 1874, when Queen's Park showed they could manage quite well without them and lifted the trophy. Gardner played with Clydesdale into his thirties, and continued to earn Scotland caps against England, the last being the extraordinary 7-2 victory in 1878. Uniquely, at the time he was also President of the Scottish FA, having spent several years as an enthusiastic administrator, and in that role he was referee of Scotland's match against Wales match the same year. Away from football his life was beset with difficulties. He worked as a grain salesman in Glasgow but lost his job, and as his wife was a cousin of the great industrial contractor William Arrol he appears to have used that family connection to find a position as a clerk on the Forth Bridge construction project. Sadly he fell ill with tuberculosis while working in South Queensferry and died there in 1887, before the bridge was completed.

William GIBB (1/1, 1873)
William Gibb
Born 8 January 1852 Glasgow
Died 26 May 1888 Watt Street, Glasgow
Scotland v England 1873 (1).
Queen's Park 1871-72; Clydesdale 1872-76.

Gibb's early sporting experiences were with Clydesdale as a cricketer, playing his first match for them in 1870. He was a decent batsman as well as a swift round-arm bowler, good enough to be selected for Gentlemen of Scotland in August 1873. He also developed into a fine footballer and joined Queen's Park, playing against Wanderers in the FA Cup semi-final of 1872. When Clydesdale adopted association football as a winter recreation for the cricketers, he was a founding member of the football section and soon established himself in their side. He was, however, still a member of Queen's Park, and on that basis was invited to make the journey to London to play against England in the 1873 international, in which he scored Scotland's second goal. He was not selected again despite playing in two trials in 1873-74, but did feature for Clydesdale in the first Scottish Cup final of 1874 and represented the club on the Scottish FA committee until work commitments effectively ended his football career in 1876. He was a legal clerk for shipping company Henderson Brothers and was posted abroad, probably to India as he was reported as having died there, but in fact he had returned to Glasgow where he died in 1888 of tuberculosis. He did not marry.

Jimmy GIBSON (8/1, 1926-30)
James Davidson Gibson
Born 5 June 1901 Raploch Street, Larkhall, Lanarkshire
Died 1 January 1978 Hesketh Crescent, Erdington, Birmingham
Scotland v England 1926, 1927, 1928; Wales 1926, 1927, 1929 (1); Ireland 1927, 1930.
Kirkintilloch Rob Roy; Ashfield; Partick Thistle 1921-27; Aston Villa 1927-36.

Son of Scotland legend Neil (see below), Gibson managed to eclipse his famous father as one of the Wembley Wizards who defeated England 5-1 in 1928. The youngest of three footballing sons, he grew up in Larkhall and had a solid grounding in junior football at Kirkintilloch Rob Roy and Ashfield, playing for the latter against the former in the 1921 Scottish Junior Cup final. His skills were enough to persuade Partick Thistle, one of his father's old clubs, to take him to Firhill and he starred for them over the next six years. Standing over six feet tall, he made an impact at right half or centre half, and as well as being a capable defender he knew the way forward, scoring over 40 goals for the club. International honours started to come his way in 1925 for the Scottish League, and the following spring he won his first Scotland cap, starring in a fine 1-0 win over England at Old Trafford. By 1927 he was such a prominent figure that he was chased by several English clubs, with the winners being Aston Villa, who set a transfer record by paying £7,500 for his signature. He took a while to settle into English football and had to sit on the sidelines after he broke a bone in his foot, but when he was fit again the Villa side made huge strides and were runners-up in the league in 1931 and 1933. Meanwhile, despite his Wembley Wizard status, he started to drift out of contention for the national team although he still managed a superb 25-yard goal against Wales in 1929 and his final appearance in dark blue was in 1930. When Jimmy McMullan was appointed manager at Villa Park in 1934, he judged Gibson to be past his best and the same could be said for the team which was relegated two years later. It was time for Gibson to retire from the game, although he remained in Birmingham with a job in industrial relations at ICI. NB his date of birth is widely recorded as 12 June, but his birth was registered on 5 June.

Neilly GIBSON (14/1, 1895-05)
Neil Gibson
Born 23 February 1873 Drygate Street, Larkhall, Lanarkshire
Died 30 January 1947 Muir Street, Larkhall, Lanarkshire
Scotland v Ireland 1895, 1896, 1897 (1), 1899, 1900, 1905c; England 1895, 1896, 1897, 1898, 1899, 1900; Wales 1899, 1901.
Larkhall Thistle; Royal Albert 1891-94 (Scottish Alliance 1894); Rangers Nov 1894-1904 (Scottish League 1899, 1900, 1901, 1902; Scottish Cup 1897, 1898); Partick Thistle 1904-09; Royal Albert 1909-13; Wishaw Thistle 1913-14 player-coach.

A wonderful talent, Gibson was described by Steve Bloomer as 'the greatest footballer I ever saw' and by Ivan Sharpe as 'the greatest half-back of Victorian times'. His early football successes were in his native Larkhall, where he worked as a coal miner, and at Royal Albert he won the Lanarkshire Cup and the Scottish Alliance championship in 1894. His outstanding ball control attracted a number of offers before he was persuaded by William Wilton to choose Ibrox, signing for Rangers aged 21 in November 1894. Within three months he had won the first of his 14 Scotland caps against Ireland, and did so well that a week later he was considered good enough to play against England. Although he scored an own goal in that match, he kept his place in the team for six years, culminating in the iconic 4-1 victory in 1900; he was also selected the following year but had to call off due to a family funeral. In addition, he played eleven times for the Scottish League. With Rangers, his first national trophy was the Scottish Cup in 1897, which they retained the following year, then he was an ever-present in the glorious season of 1898-99 when Rangers won every league match to take the first of four consecutive league titles. He missed a third Scottish Cup medal in 1903 as, having played in two draws against Hearts, he was injured for the second replay when Rangers lifted the trophy. He won the Glasgow Cup five times, the Charity Cup twice and the Glasgow Exhibition trophy in 1901. When he left Rangers for Partick Thistle in 1904 he captained them for several seasons, and was recalled to lead the Scotland team one last time in 1905, four years after his previous cap. In 1909 he returned to his roots in Larkhall, and despite his veteran status played for another five years in the Scottish Union, four of them with Royal Albert and then a final season at Wishaw Thistle aged 40, where he also coached. Meanwhile, he started a football dynasty as three sons were footballers: Willie, an FA Cup winner with Newcastle, Neil who played for Clyde and Wembley Wizard Jimmy (above). He spent all his life in Larkhall, mainly living in High Miller Street, and died there in 1947.

Jock GILCHRIST (1/0, 1922)
John Gilchrist
Born 15 April 1900 Avondale Place, Kirkintilloch, Dunbartonshire
Died 27 January 1950 Church Road, Birkenhead, Cheshire
Scotland v England 1922.
St Anthony's; Celtic 1919-23 (Scottish League 1922); Preston North End Jan 1923-24; Carlisle United Jan-Jul 1924; Third Lanark Aug-Sep 1924; Dunfermline Athletic Sep-Oct 1924; Brooklyn Wanderers 1925-26; Pawtucket Rangers 1926-27.

The story of Scottish football is littered with tales of wasted talent and falls from grace, yet few can match Gilchrist who, within a year of helping Scotland to a victory over England, found himself banished from Parkhead, and effectively out of the game before his 25th birthday. He came to Celtic in 1919 from St Anthony's, having been capped at junior level, and had the skill and physique to be a really impressive half-back. He went straight into the first team, won his Scotland cap at right half in a 1-0 win over England at Villa Park in 1922, and was an ever-present the following season until January. Then, after several warnings for failing to listen to those in authority, Celtic lost patience with his 'wilful inattention to training' and lost no time in selling him to Preston North End. It was the start of a very slippery slope. Despite a big transfer fee, reported as £4,500, he was a disaster at Preston and almost exactly a year later the club cut their losses and terminated his contract. His next stop was Carlisle United, then in the North-Eastern League, where he was player-coach till the end of the season. In the summer of 1924 he returned to Glasgow with Third Lanark, who soon regretted the move and sold him to Dunfermline after only three league games; this was initially seen as a good bit of business but he lasted less than a month in Fife. Salvation (of sorts) came from across the Atlantic in the summer of 1925, when he sailed to New York and joined Brooklyn Wanderers but made just six appearances, then played three games in a year at Pawtucket Rangers. That was that, as far as his football career was concerned, and he was divorced by his wife. He came home in 1931 after six years in America, remarried and lived on Merseyside, although he returned to Glasgow during WW2 to serve as a Royal Navy stoker. After the War he worked in construction in Birkenhead and died there early in 1950 of pancreatic cancer, aged 49.

Mick GILHOOLEY (1/0, 1922)
Michael Gilhooley
Born 26 November 1894 Pentland Rows, Lasswade, Midlothian
Died 17 May 1969 Ballochmyle Hospital, Troon, Ayrshire
Scotland v Wales 1922.
Glencraig Celtic; Celtic Nov 1913-18 [loan to Abercorn Dec 1913-14; Vale of Leven 1914-15; guest for St Bernard's Mar-May 1917; Raith Rovers Apr 1917]; Clydebank 1918-20; Hull City 1920-22; Sunderland Mar 1922-25; Bradford City 1925-27; Queen's Park Rangers 1927-28; Nithsdale Wanderers Oct 1928.

Born near Edinburgh to Irish parents who then moved to Fife to follow the shale mining industry, Gilhooley grew up in impoverished surroundings near Lochgelly. He started his football career with local junior club Glencraig Celtic and after showing signs of being a fine centre half, he was signed by Willie Maley for their Glasgow namesakes in November 1913 after impressing in a trial match. Too young and raw for the first team, he was farmed out to Abercorn and then Vale of Leven to gain experience. In WW1 he signed up with the 17th Highland Light Infantry for the duration and was on active service at the front line for much of the conflict, promoted to Corporal. He lost a couple of fingers and a thumb, but survived and kept fit by playing Army football and occasionally for clubs in Scotland. Released by Celtic when he was demobbed in 1918 he was signed by Alec Maley for Clydebank and soon earned a reputation as a resolute tackler and a good distributor of the ball. Hull City recognised his worth and paid nearly £2,000 to take him south in 1920, with his first season in the Second Division so impressive that he was made club captain. He was selected for the Anglo-Scots in the international trial in 1921, then won his Scotland cap in 1922 against Wales. Two weeks later, after months of transfer rumours, he was signed by Sunderland for around £5,000 but his time there was blighted by a serious knee injury and he played just 20 matches in three seasons. Moving on to Bradford City, he returned to regular action for a couple of years although he was unable to prevent them sinking to the Third Division in 1927. Next he joined Queen's Park Rangers, where his injury jinx returned as he broke three toes early in the season and he chose to retire at the end of the season. He did try a brief comeback with Nithsdale Wanderers the following year which came to nothing. He worked as an insurance inspector in the Glasgow area and died in 1969.

Geordie GILLESPIE (7/0, 1880-91)
George Gillespie
Born 1 April 1858 Carrick Street, Anderston, Glasgow
Died 3 February 1900 Radnor Street, Kelvinhaugh, Glasgow
Scotland v Wales 1880, 1881, 1886, 1890c; England 1881, 1882; Ireland 1891c.
Rangers 1876-84; Queen's Park Jan 1884-93 (Scottish Cup 1886, 1890) [guest for Corinthians Jan 1886; St Bernard's Dec 1887].

Brought up in Glasgow, the son of a steamship engineer, Gillespie started out in football as a full back with Rangers before finding his vocation as a goalkeeper. He enjoyed a particularly long career, spanning almost two decades, and it got off to an exciting start as his first season concluded with the 1877 Scottish Cup final, which Rangers lost to Vale of Leven in a second replay. By the time the teams met again in the 1879 final, Gillespie had dropped back to goalkeeper and was denied the chance of glory as Rangers refused to replay following a 1-1 draw. He did at least win a medal the following month with victory in the Glasgow Charity Cup. In the following years he played mainly in goal but still made occasional appearances in outfield. Halfway through the 1883-84 season he joined Queen's Park, in time to take part in their legendary FA Cup campaigns which concluded in two finals at Kennington Oval, which were both lost to Blackburn Rovers. However, he earned two Scottish Cup winners' medals in 1886 and 1890. On the Scotland front, he enjoyed victories in all seven of his internationals, some of them comprehensive, but only kept a clean sheet in one of them. He captained Scotland on his last two appearances. A wine and spirit merchant, he gave up the game in 1893 to focus on his business commitments although he continued to play recreationally for a couple of years. His early death aged 41 was caused by flu which developed into pneumonia, and he is buried in Glasgow's Western Necropolis.

Jimmy GILLESPIE (1/3, 1898)
James Gillespie
Born 22 March 1868 Hospital Street, Gorbals, Glasgow
Died 5 August 1932 Victoria Infirmary, Glasgow
Scotland v Wales 1898 (3).
Star; Clyde 1888-91; Sunderland Albion Mar 1891-92; Sunderland 1892-97 (Football League 1893, 1895); Third Lanark 1897-1902; Ayr 1902-03.

A speedy outside right with a powerful shot, Gillespie learned his football with a club called Star on Glasgow Green, with whom he played in the Glasgow Junior Cup final and was spotted by Clyde. Renowned for his muscular body, which he put down to regular exercise with dumb-bells, he spent three years at Shawfield until he accepted an offer in March 1891 from the short-lived Sunderland Albion club, who set him up with an attractive job as a cabinet maker and upholsterer. When they folded the following year he was taken on by their erstwhile rivals Sunderland, initially as a dependable reserve, but within a few months he had forced his way into the first eleven. He helped them to win the Football League in 1893 and again two years later. On deciding to return home to Glasgow in 1897, he had his pick of clubs and chose Third Lanark, where he spent the rest of his playing career. His first international honour came with a Scottish League appearance in January 1898 and he was then called into the full national team against Wales a few weeks later, scoring a hat-trick on his debut, three days short of his 30th birthday. It was to prove his only cap as age was not on his side and he hardly played after 1899 although he did not retire from the game until 1903. He returned to the upholstery trade and carried on a business at Hillfoot, Bearsden, until he died in 1932.

Jock GILLESPIE (1/0, 1896)
John Gillespie
Born 15 November 1870 Kerse Lane, Falkirk, Stirlingshire
Died 4 September 1933 Lynedoch Nursing Home, Drumsheugh Gardens, Edinburgh
Scotland v Wales 1896c.
Comely Park; Falkirk 1888-92; Queen's Park Feb 1892-1902 (Scottish Cup 1893) [guest for Camelon Apr 1894; Celtic Apr 1897; Rangers Sep 1897; Falkirk Amateurs 1898-99]; St Johnstone Feb 1902-03 [guest for Partick Thistle Mar 1902; Everton Apr 1902]; Partick Thistle 1903-04; Scottish Amateurs Jan 1904; Queen's Park Jan 1904.

An amateur throughout his playing career, Gillespie started with his local club Falkirk as a solid defender although he actually made his first team debut as an emergency goalkeeper. In his first season as a regular he won the Stirlingshire Cup and the Falkirk District Charity Cup in 1890 before his 20th birthday. He was invited to join Queen's Park early in 1892 and immediately fitted in, playing in the Scottish Cup final that year and then winning the trophy in 1893. He impressed the selectors with his performances and was made captain of Scotland against Wales in Dundee, leading the team to a convincing 4-0 win which turned out to be his only honour. Queen's Park were still holding back from Scottish League membership but were strong enough to win the Glasgow League in 1896/97 and the Glasgow Cup in 1898. Gillespie signed up to fight in the Boer War and went to South Africa early in 1900 as a Sergeant in the Imperial Yeomanry, having been presented with a purse of sovereigns by his team mates. He was ill with rheumatism when he came home, returned briefly to the QP team in October 1901 then his work with a brewery took him to Perth and he played for St Johnstone, winning Perthshire Cup medals in 1902 and 1903. He was also available as a guest for other sides, including an appearance for Everton on their Scottish tour in 1902. He gave up playing for refereeing for a few months, then returned to action, assisting Partick Thistle for a few matches and even made a surprise final reappearance for Queen's Park in a Scottish Cup tie against Dundee in January 1904. That was his last senior match although he continued his involvement in football by playing locally in Falkirk and was a committee member of Queen's Park. He came from a sporting family: his father John was a noted athlete and his brothers Alex, William and Robert were all footballers.

Bob GILLESPIE (4/0, 1926-33)
Robert Gillespie
Born 3 December 1900 Pollokshaws Road, Strathbungo, Glasgow
Died 11 August 1960 Courthill Avenue, Cathcart, Glasgow
Scotland v Wales 1926, 1930c; France 1932c; England 1933c.
Battlefield Juniors; Queen's Park 1919-33 (Second Division 1923).

A natural leader, Gillespie was the epitome of the amateur game in the inter-war years and played all his senior career with Queen's Park. Brought up in the southside of Glasgow, he started at Battlefield Juniors, where he was selected for the Scottish Junior League shortly before stepping up to Hampden in the summer of 1919. He made his debut as an 18-year-old and from 1920 was an almost constant presence in the side for over a decade, mostly at centre half although in the spring of 1925 he proved equally adept at centre forward. He not only won eleven amateur caps for Scotland, he made four appearances for the national team. His first full cap in 1926 was as a late replacement for the injured Willie Summers, but he proved his worth and was named as captain in his other three internationals. The most remarkable of these was the memorable 2-1 victory over England in April 1933, as he captained Scotland against England on two consecutive Saturdays, with the amateurs and then the full national team. He had actually retired from football the previous summer but was persuaded to return in November and he ended the season with a long run in the Queen's Park team. The international was his last major appearance before he hung up his boots and he remained committed to Queen's Park, serving as club secretary until 1940 and later as President. He was a partner in a Glasgow chartered accountancy firm, and a JP.

Torry GILLICK (5/3, 1937-38)
Torrance Gillick
Born 19 May 1916 Gartness, Airdrie, Lanarkshire
Died 15 December 1971 Royal Infirmary, Glasgow
Scotland v Austria 1937; Czechoslovakia May 1937 (1); Ireland 1938; Wales 1938 (1); Hungary 1938 (1).
Petershill 1931-33; Rangers 1933-35 (Scottish League 1935; Scottish Cup 1935); Everton Dec 1935-45 (Football League 1939) [guest during WW2 for Airdrieonians 1939-40; Rangers 1940-45]; Rangers Nov 1945-51 (Scottish League 1947; Scottish Cup 1948; Scottish League Cup 1947, 1949); Partick Thistle 1951-52.

A product of Airdrie Academy, Gillick joined Rangers in 1933 from Petershill aged 17 and saw limited action in his first season at Ibrox with just two league appearances, although he did win a Glasgow Cup medal. He was given an extended run the following year and played his part in a league and cup double in 1935, ending as second highest scorer behind Billy McPhail. Towards the end of the year, still only 19, he was transferred to Everton who paid £8,000 for the skilful left winger, who told them he wanted to play on the right instead. He settled immediately into English football and was almost ever-present over for Everton the next four seasons, winning five Scotland caps and helping his side to lift the league title in 1939. However, he was upset at being dropped for the Scotland team to face England that year and told the press that he never wanted to play international football again. Then, of course, the Second World War intervened and he returned home and spent a season at Airdrie before reaching an agreement with Everton to play for Rangers while he worked in the Clydeside shipyards. He settled in well at Ibrox and was a constant presence through the war years as Rangers he won six consecutive Southern League titles, the Southern League Cup three times and the Summer Cup in 1942. He also made three wartime appearances for Scotland. After football returned to normal, rather than go back to Everton he signed for Rangers on a formal basis just in time to play in the famous match against Moscow Dynamo in November 1945. Further successes included a league title in 1947, the Scottish Cup the following season, and two League Cup victories. He had a final season with Partick Thistle, making only a few appearances before retiring in 1952. He ran a scrap metal business in Airdrie and died in 1971, the day after Alan Morton, another Rangers great from the town.

Jock GILMOUR (1/0, 1930)
John Rooney Gilmour
Born 19 June 1900 Old Orbiston Rows, Bellshill, Lanarkshire
Died 26 February 1963 Maryfield Hospital, Dundee
Scotland v Wales 1930.
Orbiston Celtic; Bathgate 1921-23; Dundee 1923-36; Ross County Nov 1936; Montrose Jan-May 1937; Brechin City Sep-Nov 1937; Dundee United Feb-Apr 1938; Yeovil & Petters United Sep 1938.
Left back and occasional left winger who spent most of his career with Dundee, Gilmour used football to escape a tough life as a miner in Bellshill. He was born as John Rooney to an unmarried mother and although his parents did not marry he later adopted his father's surname of Gilmour. Brought up in Orbiston, the same mining community as Matt Busby, he progressed from local juvenile football to Bathgate, then in the Second Division, and two years later joined Dundee in 1923. It was the start of a lifelong association with the city, and he was a model of consistency in defence, a clean and decisive tackler, with the ability to play in midfield or even in attack. In fact, he played on the left wing in the Scottish Cup final of 1925, hitting the bar with a shot which led to Dundee taking a half-time lead, which they eventually lost to Celtic. That was the nearest he came to club honours, but he was touted for international recognition long before he was finally capped aged 30 by Scotland against Wales in October 1930. That came three weeks after he represented the Scottish League, a game in which he scored a rare goal by accident, his long ball from midfield being completely misjudged by the Irish League goalkeeper. His first class career was effectively ended by a serious knee injury at Dundee in his mid-thirties, but he fought back to fitness and persevered for a couple of years in the lower leagues before retiring in 1938. An excellent golfer, he won the Caird Park GC championship in 1930. After football he worked for Dundee Corporation Transport as a bus conductor and driver, and died in a city hospital aged 62.

Bob GLEN (3/0, 1895-1900)
Robert Glen
Born 16 January 1875 Waterside, Renton, Dunbartonshire
Died 16 July 1953 Langley Avenue, Toronto, Ontario, Canada
Scotland v Wales 1895, 1896; Ireland 1900.
Renton 1891-93; Sheffield Wednesday 1893-94; Renton Feb 1894-97; Rangers Jan 1897-98; Hibernian 1898-1907 (Scottish Cup 1902); Renton Oct 1908.
Glen joined Renton as a young man and made his Scottish League debut aged 16. He was soon recognised as a talented left back and after being named as a reserve for the Scottish League eleven, Sheffield Wednesday took him south in 1893 but he made just one appearance for their first team and returned after a few months. In his second spell for Renton, now in the Second Division, he won his first Scotland cap against Wales, and shortly afterwards played in the 1895 Scottish Cup final which Renton lost to St Bernard's. He signed for Everton that summer but changed his mind and came home, which effectively removed any further temptation to play in England. A year later he was playing in a Renton defence with former internationalist John Lindsay in goal, and future cap Donald Colman at full back. With a second cap under his belt, he was signed by Rangers early in 1897 as a reserve to full backs Nicol Smith and Jock Drummond, whose prowess meant he made only a handful of first team appearances. Next stop was Hibs where his experience was valued and he spent nearly a decade at Easter Road at left back, winning a third cap while contributing to their great successes that included the Scottish Cup in 1902 and the Scottish League the following year, although he missed out on a league medal through injury which restricted him to just three appearances that season. He left Hibs in 1907 and made a brief return to Renton, by this time in the Scottish Union. With limited work prospects locally, he emigrated to Canada in 1909, followed a year later by his wife and children, and worked as a bricklayer in Toronto, where he spent the rest of his life.

Jimmy GORDON (10/0, 1912-20)
James Eadie Gordon
Born 23 July 1888 Chapelwell Street, Saltcoats, Ayrshire
Died 22 November 1954 Royal Beatson Memorial Hospital, Glasgow
Scotland v Ireland 1912, 1913, 1914, 1920; England 1912, 1913, 1914c, 1920; Wales 1913, 1920.
Thornwood Athletic; Renfrew Victoria 1904-07; Rangers Apr 1907-20 (Scottish League 1911, 1912, 1913, 1918, 1920) [guest during WW1 for Fulham 1916-17; Hearts Apr 1917]; Dunfermline Athletic 1920-23.
Gordon was a precocious talent in the Renfrew Victoria team which reached the Scottish Junior Cup final of 1905, and was still only 18 when he captained Scotland at junior level in 1907. Immediately afterwards he joined Rangers which marked the start of a long and prosperous relationship, usually at right half although Sir George Graham, secretary of the SFA, recalled 'He was an

outstanding football player, not least because he was so versatile. He played for Scotland as a forward, half-back and back, and on one occasion I remember when the goalie was injured he went into goal'. Gordon's first season at Ibrox was spent largely in the reserves, but he did end it with the first of several Glasgow Charity Cup medals. In the next 13 years he made over 300 league appearances for Rangers, winning the league title five times but to his regret he never won the Scottish Cup, although he was in the side which reached the Scottish Cup final in 1909, which was abandoned after a riot. He made his Scotland debut against Ireland in 1912 and went on to be capped ten times on both sides of the War; in fact his honours are much greater than at first glance as he played in all four Victory internationals in 1919 and made 14 appearances for the Scottish League. During WW1 he joined up in 1916 and served with the Highland Light Infantry, reaching the rank of Sergeant. He ended his playing career with three seasons at Dunfermline Athletic, and went on the 1921 tour of North America with the Scottish select team masquerading under the Third Lanark banner. Meanwhile he went into business in Glasgow with Jamie Galt, in a variety of enterprises including the motor trade, cinemas and entertainment, which were not all successful as his Union Billiard Hall in Govan Road went bust in 1930. He lived in Milngavie until he retired to Largs, and died in hospital after a lengthy illness in 1954.

Jimmy GOSSLAND (1/2, 1884)
James Gossland
Born 1 July 1859 Comely Park Street, Dennistoun, Glasgow
Died 8 September 1944 Standerton, Mpumalanga, South Africa
Scotland v Ireland 1884 (2).
Dennistoun; Alexandra Athletic 1878-82; Rangers 1882-87.
Gossland first came to notice with Alexandra Athletic, based in Dennistoun, and in his first season was selected for a Glasgow trial match, aged 18, although he did not represent the city until 1882. That was shortly before Athletic suffered a sudden decline, which prompted him to throw in his lot with Rangers that summer. It was a good decision as he was their top scorer in his first season, playing on the left side of the forward line, and in 1884 he was called up for the Scotland team. He scored twice against Ireland on his debut which turned out to be his only international appearance. He lost his regular place in the Rangers side towards the end of 1885 and gave up top level football in 1887, but remained involved with Rangers as match secretary and club secretary until 1895. Then he emigrated with his wife to the Transvaal, where he was manager of the New Scotland Land Company in Ermelo district. This was on the front line of the Boer War and he was called up to fight in 1899, survived unscathed and remained on his farm in East Transvaal for the rest of his long life. His younger brothers Alex and Archie were also with Rangers, then Alex played for Northern and Leith Athletic, Archie for Northern and Clyde.

John GOUDIE (1/1, 1884)
John Wilson Goudie
Born 5 July 1857 Wardrop Street, Paisley, Renfrewshire
Died 23 April 1921 Gauze Street, Paisley, Renfrewshire
Scotland v Ireland 1884 (1).
Abercorn 1877-87; Everton Sep-Nov 1887.
A founding member of Abercorn in 1877, Goudie played for the team for ten years and also took an active role as club trainer in the 1880s. A speedy right-sided forward, he captained Renfrewshire in 1881 and played regularly for the county in succeeding years, then his international chance came when he was selected for the first Scotland side to face Ireland, in 1884. He scored the third goal of a 5-0 win in atrocious conditions in Belfast. In 1887 he was tempted to move south to Everton, probably because, as a plumber, he hoped to follow his trade on Merseyside while earning money as a footballer. However, after a few months he (and others) fell foul of the English laws on professionalism and when Everton were disqualified from the FA Cup he returned home. He opened a plumbing and electrical business in Paisley's Causeyside, and continued his involvement with Abercorn as a committee member and for a while was club President. In 1909 he performed the ceremonial kick-off when Abercorn opened a new ground. He was keen on other sports, notably bowls and golf. He met a sudden end in 1921 when he collapsed and died in a Paisley tramcar as it trundled along Gauze Street, on his way home from playing a round of golf. His son James was awarded the Military Medal in WW1.

James GOURLAY (1/1, 1886)
James Gourlay
Born 30 October 1862 Kirkhill, Cambuslang, Lanarkshire
Died 8 June 1926 Main Street, Cambuslang, Lanarkshire
Scotland v Ireland 1886 (1).
Cambuslang 1884-92.
An inside left or left winger, Gourlay appears to have spent all his playing career with Cambuslang at a time when they were one of the leading teams in Scotland. In his first season at the club they won the Lanarkshire Cup in 1885, and reached the Scottish Cup semi-final. He was soon in line for representative honours and after being selected by Scotch Counties he was capped for Scotland against Ireland in Belfast in March 1886, scoring once in an 8-2 victory that turned out to be his only international cap. Shortly afterwards his namesake joined the club, and because there were two players of the same name this has led to confusion in some records which have conflated the Gourlays, who were not related. To distinguish them, the press referred to him as Gourlay (1). Cambuslang's successes continued and in 1888 they had a surprise victory over Rangers in the Glasgow Cup final and reached the finals of the Scottish Cup and Glasgow Charity Cup but went down heavily to Renton in both of them. Gourlay was in the Cambuslang team on the opening day of the Scottish League in August 1890, and carried on playing until he retired in 1892. He spent his whole life in Cambuslang, where he worked in the steel industry, and sadly was killed by a bus in 1926 while crossing the main road in the town.

James 'White' GOURLAY (1/0, 1888)
James McCrorie Gourlay
Born 1 November 1860 Thornton Rows, Annbank, Ayrshire
Died 10 March 1939 Weston Avenue, Annbank, Ayrshire

Scotland v Wales 1888.
Annbank 1877-86; Cambuslang 1886-89 [guest for Ayr May 1888, Sunderland Sep 1888]; Annbank 1889-97 (Scottish Qualifying Cup 1895).

A robust centre half, although he sometimes played in the forward line, Gourlay had a terrific career with two clubs which were dominant in their local spheres in the 1880s. He started as a young man with Annbank and took part in their Ayrshire Cup victory of 1881, also playing for Ayrshire several times. In 1886 he moved to Cambuslang to work in the Lanarkshire coal mines, and joined the town's team, where they already had a player with the same name so he was known as Gourlay (2). His three years with Cambuslang coincided with the club's peak, and in 1888 they beat Rangers in the Glasgow Cup final, but lost heavily to Renton in the finals of the Scottish Cup and Glasgow Charity Cup. Gourlay was selected at half back for Scotland against Wales in 1888 and played twice for Glasgow against Edinburgh. There were offers from other clubs, and he played a trial for Sunderland in September 1888 against the touring Canadian side, but he chose to remain in Scotland. On returning to Annbank in 1889 he won the Ayrshire Cup two more times, had success in the Kilmarnock and Ayr Charity Cups, and most memorably he led Annbank to victory in the Scottish Qualifying Cup in 1895 at the age of 35. He tried to retire in 1896 and there was a fulsome tribute in the *Scottish Referee*, saying 'Had he been a Glasgow player, nothing short of his cap against England would have been his portion, but located in the province he was overlooked'. The club held a benefit match for him then he was persuaded to play one more season. He came from a large sporting family with many football connections, the most famous being his son James (1888-1970) who scored the goal that won the Scottish Cup for Morton in 1922, having previously played for Port Glasgow Athletic and Everton.

Donald GOW (1/0, 1888)
Donald Robertson Gow
Born 8 February 1868 Bridge of Tilt, Perthshire
Died 11 October 1945 St Luke's Hospital, Middlesbrough, Yorkshire
Scotland v England 1888c.
Cessnock Bank; Rangers Apr 1886-91 (Scottish League 1891); Sunderland 1891-92 (Football League 1892); Rangers 1892-93; Sunderland 1893-97; New Brighton Tower 1897-98; Millwall Athletic 1898-99; Girvan 1899-1901.

Born on a farm near Bridge of Atholl, where Gow's father was a tenant of the Duke of Atholl, the family moved to Glasgow after their father died and he grew up in the Ibrox area. Here he was introduced to football, showed his worth with a juvenile side in Cessnock then worked his way up the ranks at Rangers, where he joined his younger brother John (below) in April 1886. Donald was a good sprinter although not quite at the same standard as his brother, and focussed on his football, developing into a superb left back, occasionally playing at centre forward. He was good enough to be made captain of Scotland on his debut, aged only 20, but it was a disastrous 0-5 defeat to England. The honour probably came too soon for him, and he was never selected again for Scotland although he had a long and successful club career. He became the first man to win a league title on both sides of the border, starting with his success with Rangers in 1891 (albeit shared with Dumbarton), and the following season he was in the Sunderland team which won the English title. He was also good enough to be selected to play for the Football League in 1892. He came back to Ibrox that summer for another season before deciding to devote himself to English football, and had four more years with Sunderland, leaving them in 1897 when they reneged on a promise to give him a benefit match. He joined the newly-formed New Brighton Tower for a season and then had a year at Millwall where he coached the team. His final senior appearances were for Girvan in Ayrshire football. In later life he worked as a general labourer in Middlesbrough and died in hospital there after suffering from cancer.

John GOW (1/0, 1885)
John James Gow
Born 4 October 1859 Houston Street, Kinning Park, Glasgow
Died 25 April 1932 Norham Street, Crossmyloof, Glasgow
Scotland v England 1885.
Maxwell; Parkgrove 1878-80; Pilgrims Apr-Jun 1880; Queen's Park 1880-87 (Scottish Cup 1884, 1886); Battlefield 1887-88; Cathcart 1889-90.

Gow started out on Glasgow Green with Maxwell then moved in 1878 to Parkgrove, where he partnered Andrew Watson in defence and sat on the club committee. Then when Parkgrove foundered in 1880 after Watson's departure, Gow and the remaining players initially formed a club called Pilgrims, also based in Govan, then a few months later he was persuaded to follow Watson to Queen's Park. He flitted in and out of the team at left half for a couple of years, winning the Glasgow Charity Cup in his first season but missing the Scottish Cup victories of 1881 and 1882. Then he formed a fearsome midfield partnership with Charlie Campbell and although they lost the 1883 Scottish Cup final they won the trophy in 1884 and 1886. Gow was selected alongside Campbell to face England in 1885 at the Oval, a ground he knew well, having played there for Queen's Park in February 1881 in a meeting of the Scottish and English cup holders, as well as in the 1884 FA Cup final. The 1-1 draw turned out to be his only international although he was selected for Glasgow against Sheffield and London. He was forced to give up top level football in 1887 due to illness, but after recovering he played with Battlefield and then helped to establish a new club at Cathcart in 1889, earning a selection for

Renfrewshire before retiring. A wine and spirits traveller in Glasgow, he was a member of Merrylea Golf Club, where he donated a medal in 1897 just before the club changed its name to Cathcart Castle.

John GOW (1/0, 1888)
John Robertson Gow
Born 17 April 1869 Bridge of Tilt, Perthshire
Died 12 November 1931 Shanghai, China
Scotland v Ireland 1888.
Glasgow Fairfield; Rangers 1885-91.
Gow had a brief but eventful football career which was effectively over before his 20th birthday. Born in Perthshire, his family moved to Glasgow after their father died and he grew up in the Ibrox area. He joined Rangers as a 16-year-old athletics member in 1885, and soon showed he could also play football, making his debut for the team in November that year on the left wing. A few months later his elder brother Donald (above) joined the club. In 1888, a week after Donald captained Scotland, Gow was capped against Ireland aged just 18 but was the only forward to fail to score in Scotland's 10-2 win. He made his last competitive appearance for the Rangers first team in October 1888, when he was injured, but he remained a club member to concentrate on his athletics, becoming Scottish hurdles champion over 120 yards in 1893. Meanwhile he turned out regularly for the Rangers reserves, the Swifts, and made one more first team appearance in a friendly in April 1891. He was of much greater value to the club as honorary secretary and was elected President of Rangers from 1896-98. For many years he was the Glasgow branch manager of an insurance company, the Ocean Accident and Guarantee Corporation. He lived in Cardross and latterly Millport, but died in Shanghai on a business trip to China. He is commemorated on the family grave in Pitlochry.

Alex GRAHAM (1/0, 1921)
Alexander Graham
Born 11 July 1889 Knowehead Rows, Galston, Ayrshire
Died 9 August 1972 Whittington Hospital, Islington, London
Scotland v Ireland 1921.
Larkhall United; Arsenal Jan 1912-24 [guest during WW1 for Royal Albert 1915-16; Vale of Leven Aug-Dec 1916; Hamilton Academical Jan 1917-18, Third Lanark 1918-19]; Brentford Dec 1924-26; Folkestone 1927-28 player-manager.

Brought up in Ayrshire, Graham moved to Larkhall as a young man where he followed his father into the coal mines. He played in Lanarkshire junior football with Larkhall United until he was snapped up by Arsenal after impressing in a trial, aged 22. He arrived in London early in 1912 and went on to spend over a decade with the club at right half, sometimes centre half, and if required as a centre forward. It was a momentous time as he played in Arsenal's last match at Woolwich before the club went to Highbury in 1913. When football was suspended in England for the War he returned to Larkhall to work down the pit, playing as a guest for several Scottish sides including Hamilton and Third Lanark. When he came back to Arsenal in March 1919, he showed he had lost none of his power as in his first match, against Fulham in the London Victory Cup, he broke the net with a fierce penalty. In fact, he had an excellent record with penalties and hardly ever missed. Under Michael Knighton the Arsenal team was not a great success but Graham stood out, 'tall, powerfully-built and a man of deliberate calculation'. His form was noticed by the Scotland selectors and he made his international debut in 1921 against Ireland, when the *Dundee Courier* described him as 'a young player who has come greatly to the front this season', seemingly unaware he was 31. He performed well in the 2-0 victory but was not given another chance although named as a reserve the following year. He was appointed Arsenal captain for a while and scored key goals in 1921/22 as the team just escaped relegation by winning four of their last five matches, then was dropped from the first team in 1924. He walked out on the club briefly and was placed on the transfer list, so he was glad to move on to Brentford, where the following year he also became assistant manager. He developed appendicitis in the summer of 1926 which required hospital treatment and effectively ended his top-level career, then after recuperating he had a season with Folkestone as player-manager, and coached Botwell Mission in the Great Western Suburban League. He spent the rest of his life in London, ran a confectionary shop on Brentford High Street and later worked as a security guard.

Johnny GRAHAM (1/0, 1884)
John Graham
Born 23 February 1857 Craighall, Coylton, Ayrshire
Died 24 February 1927 Main Street, Ochiltree, Ayrshire
Scotland v Ireland 1884.
Lanemark 1875-82; Kilmarnock Portland 1882-83; Annbank 1883-84; Preston North End 1884-90 (Football League 1889, 1890; FA Cup 1889); Annbank 1892-93.
Graham was one of the great early exports from Ayrshire and became one of the 'Invincibles' of Preston North End. His first experience of football came as a founder member of Lanemark in his home village of New Cumnock in 1875 and he developed into a fine half back, first selected for Ayrshire in 1882. When Lanemark started to decline he moved to Kilmarnock Portland for a season and then in 1883 to Annbank, which was one of the strongest teams in the county. Physically robust thanks to his work in a quarry and mine, he played for Scotch Counties which was a stepping stone to national recognition and a Scotland cap against Ireland in 1884. That was enough to persuade Preston to sign him that summer, albeit professionalism was not yet legal, and he helped the team develop into the strongest in England. He was known as the 'safety valve' of the team for his coolness under pressure, and was famed for his long throw-ins. His first FA Cup final experience in 1888 ended in defeat but the following season Preston not only lifted the FA Cup without losing a goal, they won the inaugural Football League title with an unbeaten record to earn that 'Invincible' tag. They retained their league title in

1890 but a broken collar bone forced Graham's retirement and he returned to Scotland. However, two years later he was persuaded to resume playing with Annbank and to his delight he finally won an Ayrshire Cup winner's medal with them in 1893, at the age of 36, alongside another former international, 'White' Gourlay. Graham kept in close touch with his former colleagues in the 'Invincibles', attending a celebration dinner in Preston in 1922. He lived in Cumnock and worked in the mines until shortly before his death, the day after his 70th birthday. His younger brother Willie played alongside him at Preston and later went to Newcastle United.

Archie GRAY (1/0, 1903)
Archibald Gray
Born 18 April 1877 Mossvale, Cadder, Lanarkshire
Died 29 July 1943 Glasgow Road, Paisley, Renfrewshire
Scotland v Ireland 1903.
Columba; Ashfield; Hibernian 1899-1904 (Scottish Cup 1902; Scottish League 1903); Woolwich Arsenal 1904-12; Fulham Apr 1912-15.

Gray moved around a lot as a child because of his father's industrial work until the family settled in Govan where he played juvenile football for Columba, then for Ashfield as a junior. The talented defender became a professional with Hibs in the summer of 1899 and played a major role in the club's successes, winning the Scottish Cup in 1902 and the Scottish League title the following year. He could be summed up as 'hard but fair', described in the *Athletic News* as 'a firm believer in the doctrines of the sturdy shoulder charge, he has an utter abhorrence of dirty play', an attitude he claimed to have learned from his full back partner Bobby Glen at Hibs. His ability was recognised with a Scotland cap in 1903 against Ireland, but the match was lost 2-0 and he was not selected again. When Hibs manager Phil Kelso went to Arsenal in 1904 he paid £425 for Gray to follow him, the highest fee ever received by the Edinburgh club. He made his debut in Arsenal's first game in the First Division and went on to make over 200 appearances at right back in eight years, with Arsenal giving him a benefit match in 1909 against Everton. He was allowed to leave in 1912 and joined Fulham, where his old boss Phil Kelso was now the manager, and continued to feature until the outbreak of WW1, albeit mainly in the reserves. He left in 1915 to come back to Scotland and used his savings to set up a dairy business in Govan, although he was also an assistant trainer with Third Lanark in the 1920s. In later years he was working as a chauffeur when his car crashed into a tramway stop sign in 1943, killing himself and injuring four others. His elder brother John played briefly for Celtic in 1900.

Dougie GRAY (10/0, 1928-32)
Douglas Herbert Gray
Born 4 January 1905 Bydand, Alford, Aberdeenshire
Died 19 May 1972 Southern General Hospital, Glasgow
Scotland v Wales 1928, 1929, 1930, 1932; Ireland 1929, 1930, 1932; Germany 1929; Netherlands 1929; England 1930.
Mugiemoss; Rangers 1925-47 (Scottish League 1927, 1928, 1929, 1930, 1931, 1933, 1934, 1935, 1937, 1939; Scottish Cup 1928, 1930, 1932, 1934, 1935, 1936).

Gray was born in Alford where his father William was a Colour Sergeant with the Gordon Highlanders, and his family moved to Aberdeen two years later, where he was brought up. A highly promising right back with Mugiemoss, where he earned two Scotland junior caps against Wales and England in 1925, he was signed by Rangers that summer and travelled to Glasgow to embark on his senior career. He made his first team debut after just a couple of months in the reserves, and by the turn of the year had made the right back position his own. Hardly missing a match for 20 years, he had an outstanding record of success at Ibrox, winning ten league championships and six Scottish Cups, followed by numerous honours in wartime football. He was utterly reliable rather than spectacular, with an uncanny ability to anticipate danger, intercept, and use the ball intelligently to start an attack. His Scotland caps were limited to ten because of the strong competition from Jimmy Crapnell and Andy Anderson, but he also made six appearances for the Scottish League and went on the SFA tour of America in 1939. By the time of his last competitive appearance in December 1945 he had nearly 1,000 senior games under his belt including wartime competitions, although he did not officially retire until 1947. He later ran the Pavilion pub and lived in Cardonald until his death in 1972 after a long illness.

Woody GRAY (1/0, 1886)
Woodville Gray
Born 10 June 1866 Firbank, Pollokshields, Glasgow
Died 28 February 1938 General Hospital, Birkenhead, Cheshire
Scotland v England 1886.
Pollokshields Athletic 1882-88 [guest for Queen's Park May 1883, Apr & Oct 1885]; Battlefield Nov 1888-90.

A precocious talent on the left wing, Gray has the unique claim of being selected to play for Glasgow while a schoolboy. He had an unusual back story as the son of William Gray, the proprietor of Gray Dunn & Co, a well-known Glasgow biscuit maker with a factory in Kinning Park. The family were Quakers, and the boy was sent to board for three years at the Bootham School in York, a Quaker establishment, where he learned to play association football. In 1882, he returned home for the final year of his education at Glasgow Academy, but as it was a rugby-playing school he joined Pollokshields Athletic to continue playing soccer. He was clearly a great talent and was still at school when he represented Glasgow against Edinburgh in April 1883, aged 16. After he left the Academy that summer the recognition continued and he scored twice for Glasgow against London at the Oval in December, then was named in the Scotland team to face Ireland in Belfast on 26 January 1884. He would have been 17 years and 230 days but was 'compelled to decline the honour' according to the *Scottish Athletic Journal*. He was named as a reserve for two more internationals before finally winning his solitary Scotland cap against England in 1886, three months before his 20th birthday. Meanwhile, although he remained loyal to Pollokshields Athletic he played as a guest for Queen's Park from time to time, winning the Glasgow Charity Cup in 1883 as a 16-year-old. Queen's also took him to London to face Blackburn Rovers in the FA Cup final of 1885 as a replacement for the injured William Harrower, a perfectly acceptable ploy under the rules of the time. When Pollokshields Athletic foundered in 1888, he played rugby briefly for Glasgow Academicals in October, then returned to the round ball the following month when his old side amalgamated with Battlefield. He married in 1891 and moved to the Wirral where he worked as a printer. He lived at Ravenswood Avenue in Rock Ferry until his death in 1938.

Willie GROVES (3/4, 1888-90)
Patrick William Groves
Born 20 August 1868 Hallside Street, Gorbals, Glasgow
Died 13 February 1908 Longmore Hospital, Edinburgh
Scotland v Wales 1888 (1); Ireland 1889 (3); England 1890.
Leith Harp; Thistle; Hibernian 1885-88 (Scottish Cup 1887); Celtic 1888-90 [guest for St Bernard's Apr 1890]; West Bromwich Albion Oct 1890-93 (FA Cup 1892); Aston Villa 1893-95 (Football League 1894); Hibernian 1895-96; Celtic Nov-Dec 1896; Rushden Town Dec 1897-99.

Groves was rated one of finest players ever to come out of Leith, but poor health brought a sorry end to his career after successes on both sides of the border. Born in Glasgow, his family moved to Leith when he was a baby, and he grew up in the port. After making his mark with local juvenile and junior sides his talent made him a target for Hibs, where he made his first team debut in February 1886. He was only 18 when he scored the winner as Hibs lifted the Scottish Cup in 1887, and scored again when he was first capped for Scotland against Wales a year later. His mazy runs, his dribbling, his speed and his shooting ability made him the darling of the Easter Road crowds, and in fact his nickname was 'Darling'. Tempted west to join newly-founded Celtic in 1888, he was in the team which reached the Scottish Cup final in their first season and returned to the Scotland team, scoring a hat-trick in a 7-0 win over Ireland in 1889. After his third international, against England the following year, he joined West Bromwich Albion, helping them to win the FA Cup in 1892, and was selected for the Football League. He moved in 1893 to near rivals Aston Villa in the first £100 transfer, and had further success as they took the Football League title, then the first signs of ill health materialised. He was diagnosed with tuberculosis and returned to Edinburgh, reportedly 'to die at home', but after a year of convalescence he was well enough to open a small tobacconist's shop in Forrest Road. He even fought back to a semblance of fitness and made a handful of appearances for Hibs including their Scottish Cup final defeat of 1896, but there were only flashes of his old brilliance. Celtic also offered him an opportunity which stretched to just two matches. After a year out of the game he had a bizarre swansong in England with Rushden Town, in the Midland League, which ended in the spring of 1899 with him lying in a Northampton hospital which confirmed his playing days were over. Back home in Edinburgh, he was forced to give up his shop and worked as a casual labourer. Although Hibs tried to look after him financially, his health continued to decline and he died before his 40th birthday. NB at birth and baptism he was registered as Patrick William Groves.

Willie GULLILAND (4/0, 1891-95)
William Gulliland
Born 3 January 1871 Hospital Street, Gorbals, Glasgow
Died 13 March 1928 Princes Square, Glasgow
Scotland v Wales 1891; Ireland 1892; England 1894, 1895.
Myrtle; Victoria; Rawcliffe; Queen's Park 1889-95 (Scottish Cup 1890, 1893) [guest for St Bernard's May 1893, Bridge of Allan May 1895]; Scottish Amateurs 1897-98.

An outside right with great mastery of the ball, Gulliland was a deadly finisher with a terrific shot, but was sometimes criticised for not working hard enough. He grew up in the shadow of Hampden and was educated at Glasgow High School, along with Tom Waddell and Willie Lambie, who played with him in juvenile football at Victoria. They were considered such a good team that the entire Victoria eleven joined Queen's Park, although Gulliland found time to play for Rawcliffe where he was selected for a South Glasgow junior select. When he arrived at Queen's Park in 1889 he went straight into the team, winning the Glasgow Cup and the Scottish Cup in his first season, aged 19, and had further successes in the Glasgow Charity Cup in 1891 and another Scottish Cup in 1893. He also played as a guest for St Bernard's in a Rosebery Charity Cup final. For Scotland, he was capped for the first time in 1891 against Wales, and against Ireland the following year, then was twice chosen to face England, in 1894 partnering Jimmy Blessington on the wing in a 2-2 draw, then the following year rather less successfully with his old friend Tom Waddell. To his chagrin, in the summer of 1895 he was voted off the Queen's Park committee and at the age of 24 he gave up from football for a while and played tennis. However, he returned to action briefly in 1897 with the Scottish Amateurs touring team. He was an auctioneer with McTear's in Glasgow, following in the footsteps of his father who was a partner in the business.

H

Davie HADDOW (1/0, 1894)
David Haddow
Born 11 October 1867 Whifflet, Lanarkshire
Died 17 March 1949 Crown Street, Newcastle-upon-Tyne
Scotland v England 1894.
Caldervale; Albion Rovers 1886-90; Derby County 1890-91; Royal Albert May-Jun 1891; Rangers 1891-95 (Scottish Cup 1894); Motherwell Aug-Nov 1895; Burnley Dec 1895-98 (Second Division 1898); New Brighton Tower 1898-99; Tottenham Hotspur 1899-1901 (Southern League 1900); Albion Rovers 1901-02.

A goalkeeper with an eventful career on both sides of the border, Haddow had a tough start in life as he was only two when his father died. He grew up near Coatbridge and took up football with such a passion that he was fined in 1886 for arguing vociferously in the street about a game he had just played. Having embarked on an engineering apprenticeship, he signed for Albion Rovers that summer and made a strong impact in four years with the club, playing twice for Lanarkshire. He turned professional with Derby County in 1890 and featured in most of their league matches that season, but let in goals at an alarming rate and decided to return home. After winning the Airdrie Charity Cup with Royal Albert that summer, he was given a fresh opportunity at Rangers, and did so well that he was ever-present in his first two seasons, winning his first national medal in the Scottish Cup final of 1894 when he kept Celtic at bay until his forwards got the goals in the second half. He was capped against England a month later but had to accept criticism for letting Goodall score after knocking the ball out of his hands: 'I suppose the first goal I lost looked a soft thing for me, but the ball was in my hands before I knew of it, my view being obscured, and I had no time to do anything ere Goodall was on me.' He was the last Rangers goalkeeper to play against England until 1932, although he did face the Football League two weeks later, and won the Glasgow Cup twice before leaving in 1895 to join Motherwell. It was a brief association as in the autumn he was sent by his employer to work on an engineering contract and signed for Burnley, where he experienced relegation and then promotion in 1898. He spent a year at New Brighton, then had an outstanding season at Tottenham Hotspur where his 16 clean sheets in 20 appearances went a long way to them winning the Southern League title in 1900. However, in his second season at Spurs he was largely confined to the reserves and he missed their FA Cup triumph. He came home to Coatbridge in 1901 and gave up the game after a brief swansong with Albion Rovers to focus on his engineering career. He joined the Salvation Army and told *War Cry* newspaper that he had once been a 'professional drunkard', perhaps alluding to a couple of prosecutions as a young man. His work as a metal fabricator took him back to England and he settled before WW1 in the Newcastle area, remaining there for the rest of his life.

Alick HAMILTON (4/0, 1885-88)
Alexander Hamilton
Born 17 December 1864 Naburn Street, Gorbals, Glasgow
Died 11 June 1946 Stobhill Hospital, Glasgow
Scotland v England 1885, 1886, 1888; Wales 1885.
Carradale Overnewton; Rangers 1881-84; Queen's Park 1884-89 (Scottish Cup 1886).

The eldest of three brothers capped for Scotland, in fact the eldest of no fewer than nine brothers in total, Hamilton was born and brought up in Glasgow where his father ran a business as a builder. The family home was in Kelvinhaugh, and the young Alick progressed from his local juvenile team to Rangers, where he played for the Swifts before being promoted to the first team in the autumn of 1882. Over the next two seasons he proved himself on the right wing, being selected for Glasgow against Sheffield in 1884, the first of five games for the city. That summer he joined Queen's Park where he partnered Willie Anderson on the wing, and in his first season the team reached the FA Cup final while he made his Scotland debut alongside Anderson, a 1-1 draw with England at the Oval, then played two days later against Wales. A year later he won his first major trophy as Queen's Park defeated Renton in the 1886 Scottish Cup final, and was again in the team to face England. His fourth and final cap, however, was a disaster as the game as England dished out a crushing 5-0 defeat in 1888. That autumn, the month after he played for the Scotland eleven against Canada in September and at the peak of his powers, he twisted his ankle in a cup tie against Third Lanark so badly that he was forced to retire from the game aged 24. Rather than give up football entirely, he moved into legislative work and was elected President of Queen's Park 1893-94. He was also invited to become a member of the Corinthians. Having originally trained as a bricklayer with his father's company, he became an inspector of sanitary works for the local council in Hamilton. He did not marry and lived in Knightswood at the time of his death in 1946.

'Gladys' HAMILTON (1/0, 1906)
Gladstone Hamilton
Born 23 July 1879 Dumbarton Road, Glasgow
Died 12 December 1961 Millport Hospital, Isle of Cumbrae
Scotland v Ireland 1906.
Queen's Park 1895-1901 [guest for Partick Thistle Apr 1900]; Ayr Mar 1901-02; Port Glasgow Athletic 1902-06; St Mirren 1906-07; Port Glasgow Athletic 1907-08; Brentford 1908-09; Port Glasgow Athletic 1909-10 [guest for Morton Feb 1910].

The youngest of three Hamilton brothers capped by Scotland (in three different decades), he followed in Alick and Jamie's footsteps at Queen's Park, playing for several years at outside right in the Strollers reserve eleven. He barely troubled the first team so he decided to move in 1901 to Ayr, where he started to find his feet. A year later he joined Port Glasgow Athletic, at the time in the First Division albeit in the lower reaches, and did well enough at centre forward to be selected on the right wing of the Scotland team to face Ireland in 1906. However, despite a competent performance there were comments in the press which alluded to his selection being for sentimental reasons due to his brothers' reputations. The tag of internationalist earned him a season at St Mirren, and later a surprise transfer to Brentford in the Southern League, but each time he failed to impress and returned to Port Glasgow where he worked in the shipyards as a steel plater. He retired from the game in 1910. A younger brother, David, played briefly for Port Glasgow while he was there.

Jamie HAMILTON (3/3, 1892-93)
James Hamilton
Born 7 June 1869 Naburn Street, Gorbals, Glasgow
Died 20 December 1951 Govandale, Kilchattan Bay, Isle of Bute
Scotland v Wales 1892 (2); Ireland 1893 (1); England 1893.
Queen's Park 1885-1894 (Scottish Cup 1890, 1893) [guest for Cowlairs Sep 1888, Rangers Aug 1889]; Rangers 1894-95.

The second of the three Hamilton internationalists, Jamie started out at Queen's Park alongside his elder brother Alick. A centre forward with a reputation for putting himself about physically, at the age of 18 he won two prestigious honours, the first as a guest for Cowlairs when they won the Glasgow Exhibition Cup, and later in the year he scored as Queen's Park won the Glasgow Cup. The next season, 1889-90, he scored one of the goals that retained the Glasgow Cup, then headed an equaliser in the Scottish Cup final replay that set up Queen's Park for victory over Vale of Leven. As the goals continued to flow, international recognition followed. He scored a hat-trick for the Scotland eleven against the touring Canadians in October 1891, and another two on his full Scotland debut against Wales in 1892. However, it was not all rosy as Queen's Park lost the Scottish Cup final of 1892 to Celtic and at the end of the season he was sent off in a Charity Cup tie with Rangers. This did not go down well with the Hampden hierarchy and he was admonished, but he buckled down and his form the next season was so good that Queen's Park won the Scottish Cup again in 1893. He also took his caps total to three, playing against Ireland and England. To general surprise he left Queen's Park in 1894 and played briefly for Rangers, making a couple of league appearances, but then stepped back from top class football while keeping fit enough to make occasional appearances in scratch teams. He worked as a shipyard manager for William Beardmore & Co in Dalmuir.

Jimmy HAMILTON (1/0, 1924)
James Hamilton
Born 16 June 1901 Drumpark, Coatbridge, Lanarkshire
Died 21 September 1972 Belvidere Hospital, Glasgow
Scotland v Ireland 1924.
Vale of Clyde; St Mirren Apr 1922-25; Rangers Sep 1925-28; Blackpool Sep 1928-29; Barrow Nov 1929-30; Armadale Dec 1930-Jan 1931.

Hamilton was a Scotland junior internationalist with Vale of Clyde, playing against Ireland and Wales in the spring of 1922, and no fewer than eight clubs were reported to have made him an offer before he chose St Mirren. Going straight into the first team, he soon developed a reputation as a talented and dependable left back, and was in such outstanding form that he was capped for Scotland against Ireland in March 1924. He also played for the Scottish League two weeks later but there were no further international honours and his career never reached such heights again due to injury. When Rangers needed to bolster their defence after a shaky start to the 1925/26 season, Bill Struth paid a substantial fee to take Hamilton to Ibrox, where he made a good initial impression and replaced Billy McCandless in the side. However, he injured his knee towards the end of the season and had to undergo a cartilage operation, after which he barely played in the first team. Rangers allowed to him to leave in 1928 to join Blackpool, where at least he featured regularly but was clearly past his best. A year later he moved on to Barrow, who finished last in the Third Division North, then when he was released in November 1930 he returned to Scotland where Armadale signed him on a one-month contract as they had been drawn to face Rangers in the Scottish Cup. They lost 7-1 and his football career was over.

Bob HAMILTON (11/15, 1899-1911)
Robert Cumming Hamilton
Born 13 May 1877 Auchry House, High Street, Elgin, Moray
Died 2 May 1948 North Street, Elgin, Moray
Scotland v Wales 1899, 1900c (1), 1902, 1911 (2); Ireland 1899 (2), 1901c (4), 1902 (3), 1904 (1); England 1899 (1), 1901 (1), 1903.
Elgin City 1893-96; Queen's Park 1896-97; Rangers 1897-1906 (Scottish League 1899, 1900, 1901, 1902; Scottish Cup 1898, 1903); Fulham 1906-07 (Southern League); Rangers 1907-1908; Heart of Midlothian Feb-Aug 1908; Morton 1908-10; Dundee 1910-13; Elgin City 1913-14 [guest for Buckie Thistle Feb 1914].

Hamilton's exceptional scoring talent was recognised early by Elgin City, who he joined aged 16, and by the time he won a scholarship to train as a teacher at Glasgow University in 1896 he had represented Morayshire and the North of Scotland. On arrival to study in Glasgow he was recruited by Queen's Park, and when he scored all four goals in a 4-0 defeat of Celtic in a Glasgow League match, he was signed as a professional with Rangers, still a student. At Ibrox he had a remarkable record as top scorer for Rangers in nine consecutive seasons, averaging over a goal a game most years. He also created many opportunities for his team mates, as the side won four league titles and two Scottish Cups, scoring in both finals in 1898 and 1903. When he was still only 20 the *Press and Journal* wrote: 'His play is characterised by both dash and judgement. Possessed of speed and good dribbling and shooting powers, he has proved himself a very dangerous centre forward.' He came into the Scotland team in 1899, featuring in all three internationals that year, and scored fifteen times for his country, albeit ten of them came in four matches against Ireland. He would have played against England in 1900 but ruled himself out as he had an important graduation exam, and that summer he qualified as a school teacher, continuing to teach throughout his playing career. He also played seven times for the Scottish League, netting nine times, the highlight being a hat-trick in a crushing 6-2 win over the Football League in 1901. Rangers allowed him to leave in 1906 for a season at Fulham, where he won the Southern League title. He returned to Ibrox for one more year, and then moved around Scotland with a variety of clubs, notably at Dundee where he was again top scorer and earned a recall to the Scotland team in 1911, seven years after his previous cap. He responded with two goals, including a last-minute equaliser, against Wales. In 1913 he went home to Elgin in 1913 where he took over the family fishing net manufacturing business while enjoying a final season with his home town club, although right at the end of his career he guested for Buckie Thistle in the 1914 Aberdeenshire Cup final, which was lost to Aberdeen. In April 1915 he was commissioned in the Cameron Highlanders with the rank of Lieutenant, and saw considerable active service in France until he was gassed in the summer of 1918. Happily, he recovered and went on to be a prominent figure in Elgin, sitting on the town council for over two decades, as Lord Provost for 1931-37, and was captain of Elgin Cricket Club.

Thomas 'Kiltie' HAMILTON (1/0, 1891)

Thomas Hamilton
Born 22 March 1872 Ash Street, Lochee Road, Dundee
Died 17 October 1942 Kilmarnock Infirmary, Ayrshire
Scotland v Ireland 1891.
Hurlford 1889-91; Nottingham Forest 1891-93; Hurlford 1893-95; Clyde Dec 1894-Nov 1895; Hurlford 1896-1901.

Born in Dundee, Hamilton moved to Kilmarnock at an early age and the story goes that he was spotted playing in a local park and was offered a game with Hurlford, where he developed into a forceful right half. Small but powerfully built, he stood out for his white hair as well as his fine positional sense and staying power. At Hurlford he represented Ayrshire and was then capped by Scotland against Ireland in 1891, the week after his 19th birthday, coming into the side as a late replacement for Tom MacMillan. That summer he went to England to turn professional with Nottingham Forest, who offered him £2 15s a week, and he soon reported home how he was getting on: 'Wish I had gone sooner: fed on the best, drink of the best, smoke of the choicest – quite lionised. Never was so happy. Glad to stay.' However, he never really hit it off in Nottingham and made just seven league appearances in two years before coming back to Hurlford in 1893. He picked up where he left off, selected again for Ayrshire and also being touted for further international honours by the *Scottish Referee*, which praised him as the best half-back in the county. He joined Clyde but a serious leg injury in 1895 put him out of football for several months and it was thought he might not play again. He reverted to amateur status and rejoined Hurlford, where he continued to play for another five years until 1901. He was fondly remembered after he retired and the club held a benefit match for him in 1907 when he was unable to work. A plasterer to trade, he emigrated to America then returned after the War, and spent the rest of his life in Kilmarnock, where he died in 1942 aged 70.

Tom HAMILTON (1/0, 1932)

Thomas Hamilton
Born 1 January 1902 Ward, Strathaven, Lanarkshire
Died 1 July 1964 Sharphill Road, Saltcoats, Ayrshire
Scotland v England 1932.
Kirkintilloch Rob Roy; Rangers 1924-34 (Scottish League 1927, 1928, 1929, 1930, 1931, 1933; Scottish Cup 1928, 1930, 1932, 1934); Falkirk 1934-35.

Rangers signed Hamilton from Kirkintilloch Rob Roy in 1924 as goalkeeping understudy to Willie Robb, and he had to wait until May 1925 to make his debut in the Glasgow Charity Cup final, which earned him his first medal. He came into the league side halfway through the following season, and by the time Rangers embarked on their run of five consecutive titles from 1927-31 he was first choice in goal. Despite his consistent form, there were limited representative opportunities but he did go on the Scottish FA tour of North America in 1927, playing in all 20 matches as he was the only goalkeeper, and was selected twice for Glasgow against Sheffield. He finally won a Scotland cap in 1932, aged 30, a forgettable 3-0 defeat to England. He lost his place in the Rangers team after the arrival of Jerry Dawson in 1931, although he did make enough appearances in 1932-33 to win a sixth league medal. Essentially a reserve after that, he secured a fourth Scottish Cup medal in 1934 when Dawson, who had played in every previous round of the competition, was injured for the final. Hamilton moved on that summer to Falkirk but was unable to prevent them being relegated and retired in 1935. He went into business as a caravan site owner in Ayrshire, where he died of a heart attack in 1964.

Andy HANNAH (1/0, 1888)

Andrew Hannah
Born 17 September 1864 Main Street, Cardross, Dunbartonshire
Died 29 May 1940 Western Infirmary, Glasgow
Scotland v Wales 1888.
Renton 1882-89 (Scottish Cup 1885, 1888) [guest for West Bromwich Albion Sep 1888]; Everton 1889-91 (Football League 1891); Renton 1891-92; Liverpool 1892-95 (Second Division 1894); Callander Rob Roy 1895-96; Clyde Oct 1896-97.

A great full back, a superb tackler with good speed, Hannah came to the fore when he won the Scottish Cup with Renton in 1885. Having been brought up locally, he was immensely proud to captain the side in their greatest year in 1888, when Renton won the Scottish Cup for a second time, lifted the Glasgow Charity Cup for the third year in a row, and most famously were declared the unofficial Champions of the World by defeating the FA Cup holders, West Bromwich Albion. On top of that, Hannah made his international debut for Scotland, against Wales. West Brom were so impressed that they invited him to play for them, but he agreed only one match and immediately returned home for another season at Renton. By 1889 the inducements were too great to resist and he moved to Everton where he had two successful years, with the club finishing second in the Football League before he captained them to the title in his second season. Again he came home to Renton, who had just joined the Scottish League and reached the Scottish Cup semi-final; for good measure he was selected for the Scottish League team in their first meeting with the Football League. Then it was back to Merseyside as newly-formed Liverpool persuaded him to return to the city and he not only played in their first-ever competitive match, he captained the side for three years as they entered the Football League and won the Second Division title in 1894. It was a short-lived promotion as they finished bottom in 1895 and he retired from top level football. He planned to go into the hotel business and initially considered Callander, where he played for the local Rob Roy, but instead he took over the Albion Hotel in Lanark early in 1896. He made a surprise return to league action with Clyde before finally hanging up his boots. In 1898 he took over the Black Bull Inn at Kirkintilloch, and three years later another pub in Forfar, before finally settling back at Dumbarton with his second wife Mary. He was living in Clydebank where he was a shipyard detective when he died aged 75. Hannah was an athlete as well as a footballer with a talent for jumping which earned him many prizes throughout his playing career: in 1886 he made 48 feet in the hop, step and leap, and his best long jump at the Renton Games was 20 feet 10 inches. His 'party piece' was to kick the cross bar of the goal while wearing his football kit. Perhaps his greatest exploit was winning a gold medal for entering a lion's den and the *Blackburn Standard* told the story on 25 November 1893: 'On Friday evening Andrew Hannah, captain of the Liverpool Football Club, entered the den of forest bred lions and lionesses in Wombwell's Royal Menagerie. The daring act was to decide a wager and Messrs Wombwell, upon Hannah completing his daring enterprise, handed to him the wager deposited with them, and also presented him with a gold medal, value £5.' Other footballers later did the same, but he was the first. NB a middle name Boyd, often quoted, was his mother's maiden name but did not appear on his official certificates.

Jimmy HANNAH (1/0, 1889)
James Hannah
Born 17 March 1869 Gilmour Street, Gorbals, Glasgow
Died 1 December 1917 Cromwell Street, Millfield, Sunderland
Scotland v Wales 1889.
Elmwood; Third Lanark 1887-89 (Scottish Cup 1889) [guest for St Bernard's Apr 1889]; Sunderland Albion 1889-91; Sunderland 1891-97 (Football League 1892, 1893, 1895); Third Lanark 1897-99; Queen's Park Rangers 1899-1900; Sunderland Royal Rovers Jan-May 1901.

A left-sided forward who was two-footed, 'Blood' Hannah started as a full back with Glasgow juvenile side Elmwood and was recruited by Third Lanark in 1887. They moved him upfield to the left wing and scored at least half a dozen goals in their Scottish Cup campaign which ended in victory over Celtic in the 1889 final, followed shortly afterwards by his international debut against Wales, which turned out to be his only Scotland cap. He was hot property and that summer the two rival clubs in Sunderland vied for his signature, with Albion bidding the most, and he joined two other Third Lanark cup-winning heroes, John Oswald and John Rae. The club also set him up as landlord of a pub, which he relinquished after a couple of years (in favour of Rae) when he moved on to local rivals Sunderland, who had a coveted place in the Football League. Unusually he announced his intention several months in advance, and before he left Albion he played for the Football Alliance against the Football League in April 1891. He recovered from a bout of typhoid to make his Sunderland debut in September, and became a part of the 'team of all the talents' that won the league in his first two seasons at Roker Park, with a third title in 1895. Meanwhile, he managed another pub in Sunderland, the Free Gardener's Arms. After the team slumped badly, having to win a test match in 1897 to retain their place in the First Division, Hannah returned to Third Lanark for another couple of seasons. Then at the age of 30 he was tempted south once again for a final payday at QPR, who had just turned professional and were determined to make a splash in the Southern League. He retired in 1900 and returned to Sunderland to run the Smyrna Hotel and kept involved in football by coaching local side Sunderland Royal Rovers in the Wearside League. He later worked behind the bar at the Mountain Daisy Hotel, and his life was cut short after a lengthy illness which led to his death in 1917 from cirrhosis of the liver, just days after his former club and international teammate John Rae.

Jack HARKNESS (12/0, 1927-33)
John Diamond Harkness MBE
Born 27 September 1907 Preston Street, Govanhill, Glasgow
Died 6 October 1985 Briar Road, Newlands, Glasgow
Scotland v Ireland 1927, 1929, 1933; England 1927, 1928, 1929, 1930; Wales 1928, 1929, 1931, 1933; France 1932.
Queen's Park 1925-28; Heart of Midlothian 1928-37.

An outstanding goalkeeper for club and country, Harkness will forever be remembered as a Wembley Wizard. Growing up in the shadow of Hampden Park, his first international experience came in 1922, keeping a clean sheet for Scotland schoolboys against England and Wales while at Mount Florida School. He progressed to Queen's Park School, winning the Scottish Intermediate Shield, and was then invited to join the Hampden club. He quickly worked his way up through the elevens and after he made his first team debut in December 1925 he never looked back, not missing a single game for over two years and helping the club to reach the Scottish Cup semi-final for the first time in a generation. He won his first two Scotland caps in 1927 as a teenage amateur and went on to become first choice goalkeeper for the national team for many years. His third cap was at Wembley in 1928 and he had two unique souvenirs from the 5-1 victory: as the only amateur in the team he received a gold medal, while he also had the presence of mind to hold on to the match ball, which is now in the Scottish Football Museum. Four weeks later he had another victory over England, this time in an amateur international. Queen's Park had persuaded him to stay with them longer than he intended so it was little surprise that he then decided to turn professional. As an amateur there was no transfer fee so he could negotiate his own terms and opted for Hearts who were reported to have paid him £3,000 for his signature, on top of a weekly wage and a job on the side. In nine seasons at Tynecastle he played over 300 games and the team consistently finished near the top of the league but did not win any national trophies. He continued to play for Scotland until 1933 although curiously he never played for the Scottish League, selected just once when he had to withdraw through injury. He retired in 1937 at the relatively young age of 29 due to persistent knee injuries, and started writing reports and an entertaining column for the *Sunday Post*. During the War he served with the Royal Army Service Corps then when the conflict was over he became a full-time journalist, becoming the doyen of Scottish football writers. He was made an MBE for services to football in the New Year honours list of 1971, but sadly any celebrations were forgotten in the aftermath of the Ibrox Disaster.

Bill HARPER (11/0, 1923-26)
William Harper
Born 19 January 1897 Tarbrax, Carnwath, Lanarkshire
Died 25 April 1989 Rochester Road, Plymouth, Devon
Scotland v Ireland 1923, 1924, 1925, 1926; Wales 1923, 1924, Feb 1925; England 1923, 1924, 1925, 1926.
Winchburgh Thistle; Edinburgh Emmet; Hibernian 1920-25; Arsenal Nov 1925-27; Fall River Marksmen 1927-29; Boston Soccer Club 1929; Boston Bears 1929; New Bedford Whalers 1929-30; Arsenal 1930-31 (Football League 1931); Plymouth Argyle Dec 1931-40.

Harper was a late starter in professional football due to war service with the Scots Guards. A blacksmith to trade, his muscular build helped him to become regimental heavyweight boxing champion and he was also in his brigade's rugby team, but football was his first love and he kept goal for his battalion team. After being demobbed he played for Winchburgh Thistle, which had been his team before the War, and briefly for Edinburgh Emmet until he was signed by Hibs as a safe pair of hands in 1920. He was already 23 when he started his professional career and soon made up for lost time, being selected for the Scottish League in 1922. The following year he won the first of eleven Scotland caps, keeping a clean sheet in seven of them. There were to be no major honours with Hibs, who lost the Scottish Cup finals of 1923 and 1924 and he found a greater stage with his transfer to Arsenal in November 1925 which cost them £4,000, a record for a goalkeeper. However, after he was left out of their FA Cup final team in 1927, he decided to cross the Atlantic and spent three years with a variety of east coast clubs. When he returned to Highbury he was initially consigned to the reserves but became first choice midway through the season and played his part in their league title win of 1931. Later that year he joined Plymouth Argyle, and settled in the town for the rest of his life. After he retired from regular action in 1934 he stayed with the club as a coach, and was appointed trainer three years later. He kept in trim and, amazingly, in April 1939 he was recalled to the team for his first game in three years, a 1-1 draw with Sheffield Wednesday. He made two further appearances as an emergency early in 1940. During WW2 he came back to Scotland to work at Rosyth Dockyard, then returned to Plymouth in 1946 to resume his duties as trainer. After he collapsed in 1949 he spent a year out of action and took over the less onerous role of club groundsman. He was such a legendary figure at Plymouth that in 1972 they held a testimonial in his honour, against Arsenal, and the club's training ground, Harper's Park, is named after him.

Joe HARRIS (2/0, 1921)
Joseph Harris
Born 19 March 1893 Mordaunt Street, Dalmarnock, Glasgow
Died 29 October 1933 Royal Infirmary, Glasgow
Scotland v Wales 1921; Ireland 1921.
Strathclyde; Partick Thistle 1913-23 (Scottish Cup 1921); Middlesbrough Mar 1923-25; Newcastle United Sep 1925-31; York City 1931-33.

A strong and uncompromising half back who could play on the left or right, Harris had a raft of senior clubs chasing his signature in 1913 but Partick Thistle beat them to it. His cousin Neil (below) also signed for the club that summer. He spent ten years at Firhill, making well over 240 appearances despite the disruption of the war years when he featured sporadically through the conflict. Returning to regular action, he was in top form as he played in every match of Thistle's Scottish Cup triumph of 1921, not to mention winning two Scotland caps that year against Wales and Ireland. In the spring of 1923, Middlesbrough were enamoured enough to pay £4,200 for the 30-year-old veteran's services in their successful bid to avoid the drop, and he continued to play for almost a decade south of the border. His first full season with Boro ended in relegation and after a year in the Second Division he moved on to nearby Newcastle United where he had a brief reunion with his cousin. He was largely a reserve in Newcastle's league winning season of 1926/27 but proved himself an effective replacement during the title run-in and thereafter played regularly in the side. Aged 38 he joined York City in the Third Division North, and although he left the club in the summer of 1933 to return to Glasgow, he was still their registered player when he died a few months later, aged 40, from an acute intestinal obstruction. Outside football, he had a trade as a French polisher.

Neilly HARRIS (1/0, 1924)
Neil Harris
Born 30 October 1894 Dunlop Street, Tollcross, Glasgow
Died 3 December 1941 Swindon Hospital, Wiltshire
Scotland v England 1924.

Wellshot Albion; Vale of Clyde 1912-13; Partick Thistle 1913-20 [guest during WW1 for Kilmarnock Apr 1917, Rangers Apr 1917, St Mirren Oct 1917, Distillery 1918-19, Fulham Jan-Apr 1919]; Newcastle United 1920-25 (FA Cup 1924); Notts County Nov 1925-27; Oldham Athletic 1927-29; Third Lanark Mar-May 1929; Burton Town 1929-32 player-manager; Distillery 1932-34 player-manager; Swindon Town Jan 1940.

A prolific centre forward with an eye for a chance and a ferocious shot, Harris joined Partick Thistle in 1913 after an impressive season with Vale of Clyde who won the Glasgow Junior League. His cousin Joe (above) also signed for Thistle that summer. He went straight into the first team at Firhill in 1913 and scored goals throughout the war years when his work as a shipyard hammerman allowed, making occasional guest appearances elsewhere. For much of the 1918/19 season he was away, playing for Distillery and then Fulham, sometimes under the assumed name of G Hudson, then returned to Glasgow with a vengeance. He notched over 30 goals for Thistle in the first post-war season, which was sufficient for Newcastle United to snap him up for a substantial fee, reported to be over £3,000. Although it took him a while to adjust to English football he went on to score over 100 times in five seasons, the highlight being the breakthrough goal with seven minutes left in Newcastle's 1924 FA Cup victory over Aston Villa. It was a good month for him as two weeks earlier he had been Scotland's centre forward against England, his only international cap. Later in his career he had a couple of years each at Notts County and Oldham Athletic, then played briefly for Third Lanark before going into management with Burton Town, who he guided to the third round of the FA Cup in 1932. Next stop was Distillery in Belfast, playing a few games before concentrating on management, and he took them to the Irish Cup final in 1933 then won the City Cup in his second year. He managed Swansea Town from 1934-39, keeping them in the Second Division, and was appointed at Swindon Town in the summer of 1939, even playing once for them in an emergency in January 1940, aged 45. Swindon closed for the War that summer and he was still in post when he died in hospital in December 1941, aged 47, a fortnight after undergoing an operation. As well as his internationalist cousin Joe, he had a notable football family, with his elder brother Joshua at Bristol City and Leeds United, while his son John was a Chelsea legend and was capped in a Scotland wartime match.

William HARROWER (3/4, 1882-86)
William Harrower
Born 9 October 1861 Castle Street, Townhead, Glasgow
Died 27 October 1910 King Street, Paisley, Renfrewshire
Scotland v England 1882 (1); Ireland 1884 (2); Wales 1886 (1).
Crosshill; Queen's Park 1881-88 (Scottish Cup 1882, 1884, 1886).

Harrower followed in the great Queen's Park tradition of centre forwards and scored in all three of his internationals. The son of a foreman engine fitter, he was bright enough to go to Glasgow University but does not appear to have graduated. He started out in football with Crosshill, which played on the Queen's Park Recreation Ground near his home in Cathcart, and modelled himself on the determined dribbling style of JB Weir. Described as 'plucky, untiring, resourceful and gritty', his first season at Queen's Park was a huge success as he not only won a Scotland cap, scoring in the 5-1 win over England, he scored twice in the 1882 Scottish Cup final and got another in the replay. In 1884 he was capped for a second time, getting two goals against Ireland, and was awarded another Scottish Cup medal when Vale of Leven failed to turn up. He also played in the FA Cup final which QP lost to Blackburn Rovers. Two years on, he scored another important goal in the 1886 Scottish Cup final to help secure his third winner's medal, and against Wales on his third and final cap. His top-level involvement was ended brutally in October 1886 in an FA Cup defeat to Preston North End when he was repeatedly fouled by Jimmy Ross and had to be carried to the pavilion, suffering from a severe neck and shoulder injury. He didn't touch a ball for a year and a half, and then only for the Strollers, but did play one more first team match in the autumn of 1888. He remained involved with QP and took charge of the reserves for a while. For a while he ran a pub in Beith, Ayrshire, but his wife died in 1902 and he himself succumbed to asthma in 1910, aged 49, leaving a son and daughter. He was working at the time as a commercial clerk.

Alex HASTINGS (2/0, 1935-37)
Alexander Cockburn Hastings BEM
Born 17 March 1912 Gairdoch Terrace, Falkirk
Died 26 December 1988 Adelaide Hospital, South Australia
Scotland v Ireland 1935, 1937.
Carron Welfare; Rosewell Rosedale; Dunblane Rovers; Stenhousemuir 1929-30; Sunderland 1930-45 (Football League 1936) [guest for Hartlepools United 1939-40].

A left half with superb ball control, adept at creating goalscoring opportunities, Hastings was an inspirational captain for Sunderland in the 1930s. Born into a football family (his father James was a goalkeeper and trainer with East Stirlingshire for many years), Hastings had a short spell in juvenile football and even more briefly with Dunblane Rovers in the juniors, then joined Stenhousemuir as a 17-year-old. He did so well that in 1930 he was snapped up by Sunderland, whose manager John Cochrane came to the Stenhousemuir pre-season trial game to open negotiations. Hastings, who had already gone home, was recalled by taxi to sign on the spot. He spent the rest of his career at Roker Park, much of it as club captain, and led the side to the league title in 1935-36, making his Scotland debut during the campaign. However, his appearances were curtailed the following season through injury, and he missed Sunderland's FA Cup victory in 1937 with Sandy McNab taking his place. Back in the side, he made one more Scotland appearance in November 1937 against Ireland. On the outbreak of war, Sunderland took an enforced break from football for two years and Hastings played briefly for Hartlepools but did not return to regular action until 1941. Meanwhile he had gone into business, running Seaburn Post Office, and served as a commissioned officer in the Home Guard Ack Ack division. He then played until the end of the conflict before retiring from the game. After the War he expanded his business at Seaburn and even tried to build an ice-skating rink but when that came to nothing he was appointed manager of Kilmarnock in March 1948. He remained for two years with moderate success then resigned in April 1950 to focus on running the Park Hotel in Prestwick. Next, he came home to Falkirk in 1953 to run the R B Buffet, a café and cocktail lounge, and scouted for Stoke City. He emigrated to Australia in 1965 where he went into football administration, was elected President of the South Australia Soccer Federation in 1971, and was awarded the British Empire Medal in 1981 for services to association football. He died in an Adelaide hospital and is buried in Centennial Park cemetery.

Jimmy 'Dun' HAY (11/0, 1905-14)
James Hay
Born 9 February 1881 Woodside, by Annbank, Ayrshire
Died 4 April 1940 Marchfield Road, Ayr
Scotland v Ireland 1905, 1909, 1910c, 1911, 1914; Wales 1910c, 1912; England 1910, 1911c, 1912, 1914.
Woodside; Annbank 1899-1902; Ayr Jan 1902-03; Celtic Mar 1903-11 (Scottish Cup 1904, 1907, 1908, 1911; Scottish League 1905, 1906, 1907, 1908, 1909, 1910); Newcastle United 1911-15; Ayr United 1915-20 [guest for Heart of Midlothian Apr-May 1918; Clydebank Jan 1919].
Born in the tiny mining village of Woodside, now disappeared, Hay would have been destined for a life down the pit, like his father, until football came along. From the local juvenile team he progressed to nearby Annbank where he did well at half back. He was provisionally signed by Glossop North End before deciding to stay at home, then Ayr came calling early in 1902 to ask him to fill a gap in their team, although the discovery that he had once signed a form for Glossop cost them a £5 transfer fee. They got their money back a year later in the spring of 1903 when Celtic saw his worth and invested £100 in his signature, which marked the start of a wonderful top-level career. He won the first of four Scottish Cups in his first season at Parkhead, and went on to captain of one of the great Celtic sides, winning the Scottish League championship in six consecutive seasons. By 1907, after leading the team to a league and cup double, the *Scottish Referee* hailed him as one of the great team captains, praising him for 'ability, tact and geniality'. He played regularly for Scotland over a decade, having made his debut in 1905, and had the honour of captaining the side three times. In 1911, after Celtic gave him a benefit, he moved to Newcastle United and continued to perform at the highest level until war intervened. On the suspension of football in England in 1915 he went back to Ayrshire and worked in a coal mine while playing for Ayr United, but was called up in the last year of the conflict and served as a Gunner in France with the Royal Field Artillery. When he was demobbed he worked for a while as a sports journalist and appears to have kept playing in a small way. He took over the management of Clydebank in 1922, where he had a young Jimmy McGrory in his side, and after two years there he was appointed manager of Ayr United in 1924. His first season ended in relegation on goal difference, and a match in the closing stages of the campaign prompted Hay to accuse one of his own club directors of attempting to bribe the referee. When the story came out a year later, instead of his allegation being taken seriously he was sacked by the club and then suspended by the Scottish FA for refusing to apologise. The ban was later lifted, and he was Newcastle United's Scottish scout while he worked as an insurance agent. He died in Ayr aged 59 after a long illness. See his biography *James 'Dun' Hay, the Story of a Footballer* by his grandson, Roy Hay.

Charlie HEGGIE (1/4, 1886)
Charles Winton Heggie
Born 26 September 1862 Kinning Street, Kingston, Glasgow
Died 15 July 1925 Perth Hospital, Western Australia
Scotland v Ireland 1886 (4).
Ailsa; South Western 1879-82; Rangers 1882-87 [guest for St Bernard's Apr 1886]; St Bernard's Jan 1887-88.
Initially a half-back, Heggie grew up in the Govan area and started out at South Western where his talent was recognised and he made the first of his two appearances for Glasgow in 1881, aged 18. He moved down the road to Rangers the following summer, and after switching to the forward line late in 1883 he became an accomplished centre forward or inside right. Twice he finished top scorer and notably in 1885-86 he scored 29 goals for the club. This brought him into the international reckoning and although he was initially chosen as a reserve for the Ireland game in 1886, he came in for the injured Harrower. He grabbed the

opportunity and scored four times in Scotland's 7-2 victory but it proved to be his only cap (a similar fate befell William Dickson two years later, when he also scored four against the Irish). At the end of that year he left Rangers, just after scoring the winner in an FA Cup tie against Everton, and spent a season and a half in Edinburgh with St Bernard's before retiring as a player. An ironmonger to trade, he married in 1886 but the marriage did not last and his wife emigrated to Detroit in 1892, taking their son with her. He went in the opposite direction to Western Australia and ran a bar in his new home of Perth, where he remarried and brought up a second family.

George HENDERSON (1/0, 1904)
George Turnbull Henderson
Born 8 June 1879 McKinlay Street, Gorbals, Glasgow
Died 23 January 1930 Albert Road, Stechford, Birmingham
Scotland v Ireland 1904.
Queen's Park 1900-02; Dundee Jan-Nov 1902; Rangers Nov 1902-1905 (Scottish Cup 1903); Middlesbrough 1905-06; Chelsea Apr 1906-09; Glossop 1909-10.

Henderson was brought up in Cathcart and joined Queen's Park in 1900, but barely featured for the side in two years. However, he was a talented right half and when he was given a trial at Dundee early in 1902, they were only too keen to sign him and he made his debut against none other than his old team Queen's Park. He was ever-present through the rest of his brief stay in Dundee and by the end of the year several clubs were after him. He chose to go back to Glasgow with Rangers and had played just a couple of league matches when he was drafted into the side for the second replay of the Scottish Cup final in 1903, in place of the injured Neil Gibson, and came away with a winner's medal. This turned out to be his only major club honour as Rangers lost the finals of 1904 and 1905. In the meantime he won his single Scotland cap against Ireland in 1904. He went to Middlesbrough in the summer of 1905 but his debut was delayed for several months due to an attack of pneumonia, and towards the end of the season he moved on again, to Chelsea. Although signed as a reserve, when George Key was injured he was given a chance in the first team and did so well that he retained his place for over a year. In all he played 60 league matches over three years for the Stamford Bridge side. Having reverted to the reserves, he left to spend a final season at Glossop before retiring from football in 1910. He settled in the Stechford area of Birmingham, and died there aged 50.

Jock HEPBURN (1/0, 1891)
James Hepburn
Born 18 January 1865 Kelty, Parish of Cleish, Kinross-shire
Died 2 August 1925 Gaberston Park, Alloa, Clackmannanshire
Scotland v Wales 1891.
Alloa Athletic 1879-1892.

Hepburn has a unique place in the history of Alloa Athletic, not just as the club's only internationalist, but for his lifetime devotion as a founding member, player and administrator. He was only 14 when the club was established in 1879 and he played regularly through the next decade at full back or half back as the team grew in stature. He was so dedicated that in 1884, at the age of 19, he gave a talk to Alloa Literary Society about the football club, and was appointed as the club's secretary and treasurer that summer. When Alloa won their first honour, the Fife Cup in 1885/86, he scored one of the goals in a 4-0 victory over Cowdenbeath, and followed that with victories in the first three editions of the Clackmannanshire Charity Cup. His skill was recognised with a regular place in the Fife FA team, then the East of Scotland, and he was finally given the ultimate honour of a full Scotland cap against Wales in 1891. He gave up playing in 1892 after his marriage, but continued to be involved on Alloa's selection committee. In summer, he was a playing member of Clackmannan County Cricket Club and served as its secretary from 1892 to 1920, while in his professional life he worked for George Younger's brewery in Alloa for 45 years, rising to chief accountant and then company secretary. He also sat on Alloa Town Council from 1910 until his death and was a Dean of Guild. He died at his home in Gaberston Park, which had been Alloa's ground in the 1880s and which he bought in 1918. His grave is in Sunnyside Cemetery in Alloa.

Bob HEPBURN (1/0, 1931)
Robert White Hepburn
Born 17 December 1901 Eddlewood Rows, Hamilton, Lanarkshire
Died 27 November 1976 Edgware General Hospital, Hendon, Middlesex
Scotland v Ireland Sep 1931.
Quarter 1921-24; Third Lanark 1924-25; Dykehead 1925-26; Ayr United Feb 1926-36 (Second Division 1928).

Born in Eddlewood mining village in Lanarkshire, Hepburn followed his father and brother into the Neilsland pit, which meant he had few opportunities to develop his skill as a goalkeeper until the First World War was over. He had three years with Quarter Juniors then signed for Third Lanark in May 1924, but only played once for the first team in a Charity Cup tie, letting in six. On his release he joined Dykehead in the Scottish Third Division, then halfway through the season he had the unique experience of signing for Ayr United down the pit, balancing the contract on a slab of coal. He really found his feet at Ayr where he spent ten years, winning the Second Division title in 1928 and then enjoying First Division football for the rest of his career. His skills and consistency were recognised with a Scotland cap against Ireland in September 1931, although the circumstances were not what he would have wished, standing in for the recently killed John Thomson. He scored one goal in his career, in a Scottish Cup tie against Clackmannan in 1931, when he used his captain's privilege to take a penalty in an 11-2 rout. In 1934 Ayr gave him a benefit match against Manchester City, in which Frank Swift and Matt Busby played for the visitors. His final season with Ayr ended in relegation in 1936 and he gave up playing at this point. All this time he lived in Eddlewood, where he was known as

'Hep' and was very active in community affairs. However in WW2 he joined the RAF and worked as an aircraft metal polisher, a role which included landing in France shortly after D-Day. After the conflict he settled in north London with his second wife Elizabeth, and continued in the aircraft industry with De Havilland. He died in London but his ashes are buried in Ayrshire at Prestwick Cemetery.

Andy HERD (1/0, 1934)
Andrew Clark Herd
Born 4 October 1903 Jamphlars, Auchterderran, Fife
Died 1 December 1984 Preston, Victoria, Australia
Scotland v Ireland 1934.
Bowhill Star; Dundee Feb 1923-24; Dunfermline Athletic 1924-27 (Second Division 1926); Heart of Midlothian 1927-37; East Fife 1937-39 (Scottish Cup 1938).

As a promising left half in Fife junior football, Herd joined Dundee in the spring of 1923 but was largely confined to the reserves and only made one first team appearance before being released the next year. He found his feet at Dunfermline, who won the Second Division title in 1926 and then retained their place in the top league (only just, escaping on goal average after winning their last three matches). He deserved a bigger stage and joined Hearts in 1927, spending the next decade there as part of a fine team which almost always finished in the top six but did not win any major trophies. His consistency was finally recognised at the age of 31 with a Scotland cap in October 1934 against Ireland, and he was also honoured by the Scottish League against the English ten days later. When he was released by Hearts in 1937 his experience was valued by East Fife to steady their defence, and he captained the Second Division side to a sensational Scottish Cup success. He scored four key goals on the way, including a last-minute penalty winner against Raith Rovers in the quarter final, and although he was injured in the final and had to miss the replay, he was given a medal nonetheless. He gave up playing on the outbreak of the Second World War and remained in Methil but his two sons were evacuated to Australia and in 1946 he followed them by emigrating to Melbourne with the rest of the family. He found work there as a panel beater, and remained in football as a coach, being in charge of the Victoria state team for a while. His brother Alec (1911-82) was a Scotland wartime cap, and Alec's son David was capped five times by Scotland.

Sandy HIGGINS (1/4, 1885)
Alexander Higgins
Born 7 November 1863 Braehead, Kilmarnock, Ayrshire
Died 17 April 1920 Richardland Road, Kilmarnock, Ayrshire
Scotland v Ireland 1885 (4).
Kilmarnock 1880-88 [guest for Hibernian Apr 1887; Preston North End Jun 1888]; Derby County 1888-90; Nottingham Forest 1890-94 (Football Alliance 1892); Kilmarnock 1894-95.

A prolific centre forward from an early age, Higgins led the line at Kilmarnock and his potential was soon recognised as he was selected numerous times for Ayrshire and his club won the Ayrshire Cup three years in a row, 1884-86. He was made club captain and was presented with a gold chain in appreciation of his service in 1884, the year before he became Kilmarnock's first internationalist. He more than proved his worth on his Scotland debut by scoring four goals against Ireland but was not selected again. Higgins worked as a coal miner while playing as an amateur, and while he played trials and had numerous offers to turn professional he held out until joining Derby County in 1888. He played up front for them in the opening two seasons of the Football League, and two years later he moved a few miles down the road to Nottingham Forest where he galvanised the team's attack as they reached the FA Cup semi-final in 1892 and won the Football Alliance. This was enough to secure their election to the First Division where he continued to star, although he dislocated his shoulder in the spring of 1893 which put him out for a while. He came back to Kilmarnock in 1894 as a professional and played out a final season, mainly in the reserves. He took over as licensee of the Star Inn and returned to the coal mines, being seriously injured in an accident in 1911. He died in 1920 on the day Kilmarnock won the Scottish Cup. His son Sandy (see below) was an internationalist while a younger son, Nicholas, joined Newcastle United but did not make the first team.

Sandy HIGGINS junior (4/1, 1910-11)
Alexander Higgins MM
Born 4 November 1885 Robertson Place, Kilmarnock, Ayrshire
Died 15 March 1939 The Fossway, Newcastle-upon-Tyne
Scotland v Ireland 1910, 1911; England 1910, 1911 (1).
Belle Vue; Kilmarnock 1904-05; Newcastle United 1905-19 (Football League 1909; FA Cup 1910) [guest for Clydebank 1918-19]; Kilmarnock 1919-20; Nottingham Forest 1920-21; Jarrow Sep-Nov 1921 player-coach; Norwich City Nov 1921-22; Wallsend Dec 1922; Preston Colliery Nov 1926.

Higgins followed in the footsteps of his illustrious father and spent much of his childhood in Derby and Nottingham until the family returned to Kilmarnock in 1894. He developed into a skilful inside forward, playing on left or right, with a silky left foot and the ability to glide past defenders with ease. He was a provider rather than a goal taker and could pass with accuracy, although sometimes he wasted the opportunity by waiting too long. From local junior football he had a season with the Kilmarnock reserve team before being signed in 1905 by Newcastle, who gave him an early opportunity by taking him on tour to Europe that summer but he rarely featured in the first team in his first three years there. His career finally took off in 1908-09 which ended in Newcastle winning the league, and the following year he played in every cup-tie as United won the FA Cup after several failed finals. Meanwhile he won four Scotland caps in a two-year spell and scored a late equaliser against England in 1911, which turned out to be his last international. He fell out of favour at Newcastle in 1913 and hardly played for them again until the club closed down for the War in 1915. During the conflict he saw active service with the Yorkshire Regiment and Durham Light Infantry and was awarded the Military Medal. When he came home he was not wanted by Newcastle so he guested for Clydebank and then joined Kilmarnock for the 1919-20 season but was injured in February and missed their 1920 Scottish Cup victory; by a terrible coincidence his father died the same day as the final. Back in England he had a full season at Nottingham Forest then made a gradual move from playing to coaching, initially at lower league sides. He was Kilmarnock's trainer for a year and then went to coach FC Bern in Switzerland in 1925. He settled back on Tyneside where he ran a grocery shop in Byker and a pub in the city, making a surprise final appearance for North Shields side Preston Colliery in 1926.

Tom HIGHET (4/1, 1875-78)
Thomas Cochrane Highet
Born 16 August 1853 Cathcart Street, Ayr
Died 26 January 1907 Victoria Infirmary, Glasgow
Scotland v England 1875, 1876 (1), 1878; Wales 1876.
Queen's Park 1873-80 (Scottish Cup 1875, 1876, 1880).
One of seven brothers who gained a fine grounding in football at Ayr Academy, Highet moved to Glasgow when he left school to train as an ironmonger. He joined Queen's Park and soon showed his abilities as a versatile forward, winning numerous honours. The fact that three of his four caps were against England showed how highly he was thought of, although he scored just once, in the 3-0 win of 1876 when Scotland raced into a three goal lead within the first twenty minutes. He also played for Glasgow against Sheffield in 1877. He will probably best be remembered for his excellent record of Scottish Cup final goals, getting one in Queen's Park's 3-0 defeat of Renton in 1875, and the following year he scored both as Third Lanark were defeated 2-0 in a replay. In his third final in 1880 he scored another double to see off Thornliebank. That was his last serious football action as, having finished his apprenticeship, he went into business as an ironmonger. He lived in the southside of Glasgow and died relatively young in 1907 aged 53.

Davie HILL (3/1, 1881-82)
David Hill
Born 12 July 1858 Mill Street, Perth
Died 3 February 1920 Ann Street, Hillhead, Glasgow
Scotland v England 1881 (1); Wales 1881, 1882.
Rangers 1875-84.
One of the earliest Rangers stars, Hill was born in Perth but his family moved to Glasgow when he was a baby. He first appeared in the Rangers team at the end of 1875, initially at full back, then switched to the forward line where he was versatile enough to play on the left or right. He was still only 18 when he took part in the momentous Scottish Cup final of 1877 which was lost to Vale of Leven in a second replay. Two years later, another shot at glory came to nothing in 1879 when Rangers refused to participate in a replay. However, Hill did win a medal that season as Rangers won their first-ever trophy, the Glasgow Charity Cup. He had grown in stature sufficiently to be selected against England in 1881, and scored Scotland's second goal in the astonishing 6-1 victory at the Oval. He also played in Wales two days later, and the following year against Wales as well as for Glasgow against Sheffield. From then on his appearances in the Rangers team were sporadic and he played his last match in April 1884. He worked as a clerk in a cotton warehouse, and later moved to East Kilbride where he married and worked as a yarn salesman. He is buried in East Kilbride cemetery.

David HILL (1/0, 1906)
David Alexander Hill
Born 16 December 1881 Hawkhill, Ayr
Died 30 April 1928 Shaughnessy Military Hospital, Vancouver, Canada
Scotland v Ireland 1906.
Ayr Parkhouse 1900-05; Third Lanark 1905-09; Vancouver Celtics.
Hill was a dashing left back who trained as an architect, a career which enabled him to remain amateur throughout his football career. Educated at Ayr Academy, he played in local junior football before signing in 1900 for Ayr Parkhouse, whose Beresford Park was just around the corner from his family home. He played with them for three seasons in the Ayrshire League, and was selected for Ayrshire, before Parkhouse joined the Scottish League in 1903. They had an inauspicious start, finishing bottom on their first season, and dropped back to the Scottish Combination. Hill, who played alongside his brother Willie in the Parkhouse side, was clearly deserving of a higher stage as he was selected for a Scotland international trial in 1905. Shortly afterwards he joined Third Lanark, whom he had already guested for in a couple of league games, and his first season with them saw a number of career highlights. In the spring of 1906 he was capped for Scotland against Ireland, and the following month he played for Glasgow against Sheffield then for Third Lanark in the Scottish Cup final which was lost to Hearts. He was a regular in the Thirds team until 1909 when he decided to emigrate to Canada, where he continued to play in local football with Vancouver Celtics. On the outbreak of WW1 he signed up for the Canadian Expeditionary Force and served at the front as a Sapper attached to the Royal Scots Fusiliers, rising to the rank of Sergeant. However, he suffered from the effects of gas and shock, which contributed to his early death from pneumonia, aged 46.

Frank HILL (3/0, 1930-31)
Frank Robert Hill
Born 21 May 1906 North Street, Forfar, Angus
Died 26 August 1993 Lafayette, California, USA
Scotland v France 1930; Wales 1930; Ireland Feb 1931.
Forfar West End; Forfar Athletic 1924-28; Aberdeen 1928-32; Arsenal 1932-36 (Football League 1933, 1934, 1935); Blackpool 1936-37; Southampton 1937-38; Preston North

End 1938-44 player-coach [guest for Wrexham 1942-44]; Crewe Alexandra 1944-48 player-manager.

Hill was an uncompromising half-back, nicknamed 'Tiger' for his dogged persistence. He started his career with a lengthy apprenticeship at Forfar Athletic, spending four seasons in the lower reaches of Scottish football until a move to Aberdeen in 1928 gave him the opportunity to shine. He formed part of an excellent midfield at Pittodrie and won three Scotland caps, also playing once for the Scottish League. However, in 1931 he was one of five players implicated in a betting scandal and he never played for the club again. Aberdeen were happy to sell him to Arsenal for £3,000 in 1932 and at Highbury he was part of the magnificent team which won three consecutive league titles, as a regular in his first two seasons although he drifted out of the picture after that. He was sold to Blackpool in 1936 and captained their promotion-winning side, but rather than return to the First Division he transferred to Southampton. A qualified masseur, in 1938 he accepted a coaching post with Preston and wanted to continue playing, but Southampton churlishly refused to release his registration. His career was in any case interrupted by WW2, and he joined the RAF as a physical training instructor, serving in India as a Flight Lieutenant and playing some guest matches for Wrexham. Appointed player-manager of Crewe in 1944, he was unable to take up the job until he was demobbed in November 1945 and continued to play well beyond his 40th birthday. He had to work with small budgets at Crewe, operating the transfer system, then resigned from the job when the directors refused to give him a pay rise. He returned to the First Division as manager of Burnley and spent six years there before going back to Preston North End in 1954. When he was sacked in 1956, he accepted a coaching job in Iraq and spent 18 months in charge of the Army team, leaving the country after the 1958 revolution to manage Notts County 1958-61 and Charlton Athletic 1961-65. He scouted for Manchester City for a year before emigrating to California, where he ran a fish and chip shop in Lafayette with his family.

Johnny HILL (2/0, 1891-92)
John Jack Hill
Born 3 July 1862 Plains, Airdrie, Lanarkshire
Died 29 December 1930 Wilson's Place, Glengowan, Lanarkshire
Scotland v England 1891; Wales 1892c.
Plains Bluebell 1882-84; Glengowan 1884-85; Airdrieonians 1885-87; Queen's Park 1887-88; Heart of Midlothian Apr 1888-93 (Scottish Cup 1891) [guest for St Bernard's Dec 1888]; Airdrieonians 1893-94.

A left half with the power to really influence a game, Hill was capable of shoring up the defence or adding to the attack, and was fast enough to win sprint prizes. He always carried a handkerchief in his pocket, and was known to celebrate a goal by giving it a little twirl. His first major honours came with Airdrieonians in 1886 and 1887 when they won the Lanarkshire Cup twice, and his team also recorded a remarkable 10-2 victory over Rangers at Kinning Park in a friendly. He had a year at Queen's Park before moving to Edinburgh to join a Hearts side which was rapidly growing in stature. He must have been impressed when he married in 1889 that Hearts presented him with a gold watch, and a gold bracelet for his new wife. Playing with Hearts as they entered the newly-founded Scottish League, he won the Scottish Cup in 1891 as part of a famous half-back trio alongside Isaac Begbie and John McPherson, and all three were selected together a few weeks later to face England. The following year he was made captain of Scotland for a victory over Wales. He was regularly capped throughout his career by regional teams, including Lanarkshire with both Glengowan and Airdrieonians, by Glasgow while at Queen's Park, and by East of Scotland at Hearts. A papermill worker in his younger days, he became a publican in Edinburgh with a hotel at Juniper Green, and was elected President of Hearts in 1899. However, after experiencing business problems he returned to Plains and his old trade in the textile industry, working for J Glen and Son. He was also a prominent member of Glengowan Bowling Club.

Geordie HOGG (2/0, 1896)
George Hogg
Born 2 December 1869 East Street, Mossend, West Lothian
Died 22 May 1939 Gwanda Hospital, Rhodesia
Scotland v Ireland 1896; England 1896.
West Calder; Mossend Swifts 1889-92; Heart of Midlothian 1892-1904 (Scottish League 1895, 1897; Scottish Cup 1896, 1901); Bathgate Jan-May 1905.

A left half who grew up in West Calder, Hogg worked there as a shale miner before football gave him the means to set up in business as a fishmonger. He first came to attention with Mossend Swifts, and was selected to play for the Edinburgh select, but when the club got into difficulties in 1892 he moved to Hearts and spent the rest of a very successful career at Tynecastle. With Hogg partnering Isaac Begbie and either Johnny Russell or Harry Marshall in the half-back line, Hearts were a dominant side in the 1890s, winning league titles in 1895 and 1897. However, his most memorable month came in 1896 when Hogg captained the Hearts team which beat city rivals Hibs in the Scottish Cup final of 1896, then played for Scotland on each of the following two Saturdays, against Ireland and England, and a week after that for the Scottish League against the Football League. He later won another Scottish Cup medal in the 1901 defeat of Celtic but by the time Hearts gave him a benefit match in 1903 he was starting to drift out of the team. He had a brief swansong with Bathgate in 1905 before retiring. He emigrated to Rhodesia (now Zimbabwe), and although he returned briefly with his son George in 1913, he settled permanently to assist his brother who owned the Jessie Gold Mining Company in Matabeleland.

Jimmy HOGG (1/0, 1922)
James Hogg
Born 16 June 1896 Springs, Coylton, Ayrshire
Died 11 February 1974 Lansdowne Road, Ayr
Scotland v Ireland 1922.
Shettleston 1915-17; Vale of Clyde 1917-18; Ayr United 1918-25; Clydebank 1925-27.
A model of consistency at right half, Hogg had a longer than usual period in the juniors due to WW1. He had a reserved occupation as a coal miner while he played for Shettleston, representing the Glasgow Junior FA, then Vale of Clyde for a season, before he joined Ayr United in 1918 aged 22. Ayr may not have been the most fashionable club but in the early 1920s they had a fearsome defence and Hogg played in front of the formidable partnership of Jock Smith and Phil McCloy, who were capped together against England. Hogg got there first, however, and was selected for Scotland against Ireland in 1922. It was to prove the only major honour of his career, and when Ayr were relegated on goal difference in 1925 he moved on to Clydebank, who had just gone up to the First Division. He ended up suffering relegation for the second season in a row, and after persevering for a year in the lower league he decided to retire in 1927. He returned to the Ayrshire coal mines, and was latterly a mine training officer.

Bobby HOGG (1/0, 1937)
Robert Brown Hogg
Born 10 May 1914 Elmbank, Burnhead, Lanarkshire
Died 14 April 1975 Maxwellton Road, Paisley, Renfrewshire
Scotland v Czechoslovakia May 1937.
Royal Albert; Celtic 1931-48 (Scottish League 1936, 1938; Scottish Cup 1933, 1937); Alloa Athletic Dec 1948-49.
Hogg had won three junior caps with Royal Albert by the time he turned 17, which Celtic recognised as a clear indication of his outstanding potential. He signed at Celtic Park in the summer of 1931 and spent almost all his career with the club, winning many honours in a career that was heavily interrupted by the Second World War. After making his entry to the Celtic team late in 1932 at right back in place of Willie Cook, he was virtually ever-present for the next six years until the outbreak of war. Even through the war years he remained first choice until 1947 by which time he had played well over 500 games for Celtic, although he never scored a goal. Quick, perceptive and a great tackler, his first major trophy was the Scottish Cup of 1933, then he went on to lift the league title twice and another Scottish Cup in 1937, not to mention the prestigious Glasgow Exhibition Trophy in 1938. He was regularly named as a travelling reserve for the national team but surprisingly he only played once for Scotland, an end-of-season friendly in Prague in 1937. However, he did represent the Scottish League six times and made one wartime appearance for Scotland against England in 1941. When age started to catch up with him he was not only given a free transfer from Celtic, the club paid him £500 as a parting gift, and he played for Alloa for a few months before retiring from football in 1949. He married a sister of fellow internationalist George Walker, and worked as a welder in Paisley until his death from lung cancer in 1975.

Andrew HOLM (3/0, 1882-83)
Andrew Hair Holm
Born 4 November 1859 Kelvingrove Street, Glasgow
Died 8 January 1934 Kilmarnock Road, Giffnock, Renfrewshire
Scotland v Wales 1882, 1883; England 1883c.
Shaftesbury; Ayr Thistle; Queen's Park 1879-84 (Scottish Cup 1881, 1882, 1884).
Holm joined Queen's Park from Ayr Thistle in 1879 and soon made his presence felt as a solid and dependable left back. He partnered Andrew Watson in defence for Queen's Park's Scottish Cup victories in 1881 and 1882, then when Watson went south his next partner was Walter Arnott, so he was in excellent company. Highly respected, he made his Scotland debut in 1882 and was made captain of the side to face England in 1883, which was applauded by the *Athletic News*: 'The honour will sit gracefully on the shoulders of such a gentleman'. He led Scotland to a glorious 3-2 victory in Sheffield, and carried on for another solid victory in Wales two days later. He also played three times for Glasgow. He was awarded a third Scottish Cup medal in 1884 after Vale of Leven refused to appear, then was left out of Queen's Park's FA Cup final team against Blackburn Rovers despite playing in most of the earlier ties. He never appeared for the first team again but there does not appear to have been a fall-out as Queen's Park presented him with a gold watch when he married three years later and he continued to socialise with his former colleagues. It seems likely that his business as a whisky distiller became too pressing as he was a director of Mackie & Co, whose best-known brand was White Horse. He had a villa in Cathcart and a second home on the Ayrshire coast where he was a member of Troon Golf Club. When he died in 1934, he left over £200,000 in his will. His brothers John and William also played for Queen's Park.

Willie HOWDEN (1/0, 1905)
William Howden
Born 11 November 1879 Dovecothill, Barrhead, Renfrewshire
Died 27 January 1937 Oshawa General Hospital, Ontario, Canada
Scotland v Ireland 1905.

Benburb [trial for Celtic Apr 1898]; Rutherglen Glencairn 1898-99; Rangers 1899-01; Partick Thistle Oct 1901-08 [guest for Rangers Jan 1903]; Abercorn 1908-09; Partick Thistle 1909-11; Abercorn 1911-13; Arthurlie 1915-17.

A dependable goalkeeper, Howden started in junior football with Benburb and had a trial with Celtic in a friendly in April 1898, but a year later he signed as a professional for Rangers. As reserve to Matt Dickie he made just one competitive appearance in two years at Ibrox and asked to be reinstated as an amateur in December 1900. He was released at the end of the season to join Partick Thistle and went on to spend the bulk of his career with them, playing over 250 games, apart from one friendly for Rangers as a guest in January 1903. His consistency was rewarded in 1905 with a single Scotland cap, keeping a clean sheet against Ireland, when *Scottish Referee* described him as 'a daring, clever resourceful keeper'. He played for Glasgow v Sheffield in 1906 but suffered a fractured collar bone early in 1907 which forced him to miss the rest of the season. When he returned to action he found it difficult to secure his place in the team, and although Thistle granted him a benefit match against Celtic, he moved on to Abercorn in 1908. A season later Thistle asked him to return and he remained first choice until October 1910. Then, rather than sit on the sidelines, he wound down his career with a couple more seasons at Abercorn and after a break from football he played for Arthurlie during the War. A joiner in his native Barrhead, he emigrated with his wife and daughter to Canada in 1924 and worked for General Motors in Oshawa until his death from cancer in 1937.

Bobby HOWE (2/0, 1929)
Robert Howe
Born 6 August 1903 Levenhaugh Street, Dumbarton
Died 20 June 1979 Castlemilk Road, Glasgow
Scotland v Norway 1929; Netherlands 1929.
Shotts United; Petershill; Hamilton Academical 1927-32; Heart of Midlothian 1932-34; Third Lanark Feb 1934-36 (Second Division 1935); Queen of the South Dec 1936-37; St Johnstone 1937-38; Dundee United 1938-39.

Howe was a late developer who was already 24 when he turned senior with Hamilton in the summer of 1927, after a lengthy football apprenticeship in the juniors at Shotts and Petershill. He showed some sparkling form and in his second season, despite being a winger, was Hamilton's top scorer. He was an obvious choice for Scotland's continental tour in 1929, and played in the matches against Norway and Netherlands. Back home, he retained his position as top scorer for Hamilton for another season, but after that his career seemed to drift along and he was ousted from the first team by Jimmy King. He joined Hearts in 1932 and was mainly a reserve, then went to Glasgow early in 1934 as Third Lanark made a desperate bid to avoid relegation. The attempt failed but he helped them to win the Second Division the following season and they reached the Scottish Cup final in 1936 only to lose narrowly to Rangers. Dropped from the first team at Cathkin, he had short spells at Queen of the South, St Johnstone and Dundee United before retiring in 1939. He acted as match secretary of Petershill during the war years, then applied for management jobs in football without success and reverted to his profession as an engineer turner.

Jimmy HOWIE (3/2, 1905-08)
James Howie
Born 19 March 1880 Old Manse Close, Galston, Ayrshire
Died 13 December 1962 Central Middlesex Hospital, London
Scotland v England 1905, 1906 (2), 1908.
Galston Athletic; Kilmarnock 1898-1902 (Second Division 1899); Bristol Rovers 1902-03; Newcastle United 1903-10 (Football League 1905, 1907, 1909; FA Cup 1910); Huddersfield Town Dec 1910-13.

Known as 'Gentleman Jim', Howie was an effective inside right who not only created goals, he also knew how to score them and perhaps his greatest career achievement was scoring both Scotland goals in the 2-1 victory over England in 1906. With an unconventional running style, which made him appear slower than he really was, he grew up in Galston where he started out with local side which reached the Ayrshire Junior Cup final. Moving on to Kilmarnock aged 18, he won the Scottish Second Division title and enjoyed three seasons in the First Division, playing once for the Scottish League against the Irish in 1901. A year later he was transferred to Bristol Rovers, in the Southern League, where his potential and style was recognised by Newcastle United who signed him at the end of the season. He spent seven excellent years on Tyneside and played his part in three league championships, establishing an effective partnership with Jock Rutherford which concluded in their elusive FA Cup victory in 1910 after losing finals in 1905 and 1906. He left Newcastle later that year and spent three seasons at Huddersfield, in Division Two, before retiring in 1913. Going straight into management at Queen's Park Rangers, he took the Southern League side to the FA Cup quarter final in his first season, and remained with them until 1920. He then moved north to Middlesbrough for three seasons with a mid-table finish in the First Division each time; a year after he left they were relegated. He returned to London where he ran a tobacconist's shop in Aldersgate Street and lived in Holland Road. His brother David played for Kilmarnock, then Brentford.

Jimmy HOWIESON (1/0, 1927)
James Howieson
Born 7 June 1900 Victoria Street, Rutherglen, Lanarkshire
Died 28 May 1971 Victoria Infirmary, Glasgow
Scotland v Ireland 1927.
Port Glasgow; Rutherglen Glencairn; Airdrieonians Oct 1921-24; St Johnstone 1924-25 [loan to St Mirren 1924-25]; Dundee United May-Oct 1925; St Mirren Oct 1925-27 (Scottish Cup 1926); Hull City Mar 1927-28; New Bedford Whalers 1928-29 [loan to New York Giants 1929]; Hull City 1929-30; Shelbourne 1930-32 (Free State League 1931); Clyde 1932-34; Alloa Athletic Sep 1934; Glenavon Oct-Dec 1934; Belfast Celtic Feb 1935.

An inside forward, Howieson played for over a dozen teams in several countries over the course of an eventful career. Yet he was a late starter to football, and worked as a marine engineer on leaving school until an accident that crushed his fingers led him to join the Royal Navy in 1918. He had never played organised football before then, but with the ship's team it was soon clear that he had talent, and in 1921, on shore leave at home, he played a few games for Port Glasgow juniors. Realising he had a possible career in the game, he purchased his release from the Navy for £48 and joined Rutherglen Glencairn, before being snapped up by Airdrieonians. He scored regularly for Airdrie over three seasons until his poor disciplinary record led to him falling out of favour just before the side lifted the Scottish Cup. He moved to St Johnstone in the summer of 1924 and in a strange season he played for the Perth side in league games but was loaned to St Mirren for cup ties. After a short spell at Dundee United he joined St Mirren on a formal basis and by the end of the season was a hero. In the Scottish Cup final of 1926 he was a decisive figure, as his corner kick was headed home early on to give St Mirren the lead against Celtic, and he finished off a passing move himself after half an hour's play to clinch a 2-0 victory for the Paisley side. He was selected for Scotland against Ireland in February 1927 and a month later Hull City paid over £3,000 to take him to England but he found it hard to settle and crossed the Atlantic for a year until Hull persuaded him to return. He managed another season then from the summer of 1930 he resumed his wandering. He won an Irish league title with Shelbourne, and had a couple of years with Clyde, the team he had supported as a boy. By 1934 his options were limited, he played a trial with Alloa and ended his career with a couple of short contracts in Northern Ireland before hanging up his boots. After retiring, he followed in his father's footsteps as a publican and ran the Railway Tavern in Glasgow's Rutherglen Road with his brother. He served as a merchant seaman in WW2, and afterwards coached Strathclyde Juniors.

Jack HUNTER (4/0, 1874-77)
John Hunter
Born late 1854 Hole Farm, Coylton, Ayrshire
Died 2 November 1881 Barns Street, Ayr, Ayrshire
Scotland v England 1874, 1875, 1876; Wales 1877.
Third Lanark 1873-75; Eastern Mar 1875; Third Lanark 1875-78.

Born into a fairly well-off family, Hunter's father managed a 100 acre farm in Coylton, but after his father died in 1866 the family moved to Ayr where his widowed mother ran a small pub. Hunter studied as an engineer and went to Glasgow where he took up football, and first came to notice as a full back with Third Lanark. He was so impressive that in 1874 he won his first Scotland cap against England, aged just 19. He appears to have briefly joined Eastern in the spring of 1875 before returning to his parent club and he captained Third Lanark in the 1876 Scottish Cup final, which was lost to Queen's Park in a replay. Two years later he scored the winner in the 1878 Scottish Cup final, but it was not a cause for celebration as he deflected a shot past his own goalkeeper. Meanwhile, his international record was exemplary as he played in 1875 and 1876 against England at a time when it was the most important match on the calendar, and he was selected against Wales in 1877. He appears to have given up the game in 1878, and was working as engine fitter when he caught a cold which spread to his lungs. After a year's struggle he succumbed to pneumonia in his mother's house in Ayr, aged just 27. His fame in the game was somewhat overshadowed by his footballing brothers Andy and Archie, who played with distinction for Aston Villa and who both also died young.

'Sailor' HUNTER (1/0, 1909)
John Hunter
Born 6 April 1878 High Street, Johnstone, Renfrewshire
Died 12 January 1966 Cleland Hospital, Lanarkshire
Scotland v Wales 1909.
Westmarch XI; Abercorn Jan 1898-99; Liverpool 1899-1902; Heart of Midlothian 1902-04; Woolwich Arsenal 1904-05; Portsmouth 1905-07; Dundee 1907-10 (Scottish Cup 1910); Clyde Oct 1910-11; Motherwell Apr 1911-12 player-manager.

Known as Sailor from an early age, Hunter started at Westmarch XI, a Paisley junior nursery with strong links to St Mirren, yet he chose to join their local rivals Abercorn at the start of 1898 after a couple of successful trials. He had developed a fine reputation at inside right by the time he joined Liverpool in 1899, but although they tried him on both wings and at centre forward he never really established himself in the team and was released after three seasons. He chose to return to Scotland with Hearts where the highlight was a Scottish Cup final in 1903, lost after two replays. Twelve months later, Phil Kelso persuaded him to join Arsenal, then after an erratic year he was on the move again to Portsmouth, in the Southern League. Approaching the veteran stage with plenty of experience but little to show for it, he was recruited by Dundee in 1907 and here he finally found success, leading the forward line for three seasons. His sparkling performances and goals took Dundee to within a point of the league title in 1909, then culminated in a Scottish Cup victory the following year. The final went to two replays and he emerged triumphant, with the additional kudos of scoring Dundee's winning goal in the third match against Clyde. He was also capped by Scotland in 1909, having travelled to Wales as a reserve, and was called into the side at the last moment due to Jimmy Quinn's ankle giving way; however, the match was a forgettable 3-2 defeat. As his powers started to wane he joined Clyde, which was closer to his home in Hamilton where he worked as an iron turner. In April 1911 he applied for the vacant post of manager at Motherwell and was selected from 70 applicants, an inspired appointment that would see him go on to serve the club for almost five decades. He continued to play occasionally for one last season before focussing on management duties and while his early years at Fir Park gave little indication of the triumphs to come, the club kept faith in him. Under his guidance, Motherwell became one of Scotland's outstanding teams, winning the League Championship in 1931-32. When Hunter stepped down as manager in 1946 he continued as club secretary until his retirement in 1959, aged 80. Married three times, he died in 1966. NB many modern sources mistakenly give him a middle name of Bryson, but he was plain John Hunter.

Dick HUNTER (1/0, 1890)
Richard Dunn Hunter
Born 16 March 1865 Ardnacaple Toll, Rhu, Dunbartonshire
Died 10 September 1910 Northern Hospital, Liverpool, Lancashire
Scotland v Ireland 1890.
Yoker 1881-87 [trial with Burnley Dec 1884]; St Mirren 1887-1892 [guest for Dumbarton May 1892].

A full back, Hunter had several years with Yoker, where he was club secretary as a 16-year-old in 1881. In 1884, just after Yoker were put out of the Scottish Cup by eventual finalists Vale of Leven, he was given a trial by Burnley. This was still in the era when professionalism was illegal and he returned after one match. Capped by Renfrewshire while at Yoker, he signed for St Mirren in 1887, and at Saints he captained his county and eventually won his international cap against Ireland in 1890, a 4-1 win in Belfast. He was selected again for Scotland the following year but had to drop out at the last minute. Shortly before he retired from the game in 1892 he was a guest for Dumbarton in a Glasgow Charity Cup tie. During his playing career he ran the Ferry Inn at Erskine, taking over from his father, then when his lease was terminated early in the new century he moved to Birkenhead on Merseyside and was working as a billiard hall proprietor in Rock Ferry at the time of his death in 1910. He was aged 45, leaving a widow and five children.

Jamie HUTTON (1/0, 1887)
James Lockerby Hutton
Born 12 January 1865 Rankeillor Street, Edinburgh
Died 8 February 1947 Marton Road, Middlesbrough, Yorkshire
Scotland v Ireland 1887.
Northern; St Bernard's 1884-91; Stockton 1891-93.

Hutton started with a juvenile club called Northern in the Stockbridge area of Edinburgh, which was the heartland of St Bernard's territory, and it was no surprise that he stepped up to the senior club in 1884. A small but forceful half-back, he quickly established himself in the Saints team at a time when they were one of the leading city clubs. In 1887 he became the first St Bernard's player to win international honours, alongside his clubmate James Lowe, when he was selected for Scotland at left half in a 4-1 victory over Ireland at Hampden Park. His worth to Saints was recognised when he was presented with a gold watch and chain to mark five years with the club in 1889. However, in the summer of 1891 he moved south as a professional with Stockton, and played for the club for a couple of years while he established himself in the brewing industry there. He spent the rest of his life in the north-east and became a brewery manager, and when he died he left £20,000 in his will. He was also an accomplished piano player.

Jock HUTTON (10/1, 1923-28)
John Hutton
Born 29 October 1898 Calder Street, Motherwell, Lanarkshire
Died 2 January 1970 Sandringham Street, Belfast, Northern Ireland
Scotland v Ireland 1923, 1924c, 1926, 1927, 1928; Wales 1923, Oct 1925, 1927 (1); England 1923, 1926.
Motherwell Hearts; Larkhall Thistle; Hall Russell; Bellshill Athletic; Aberdeen Apr 1919-26; Blackburn Rovers Oct 1926-33 (FA Cup 1928).

Hutton was one of the finest right backs of his generation, although he was originally signed by Aberdeen as a centre forward. His arrival in the north-east of Scotland was almost an accident, as in 1918 he joined the Gordon Highlanders who were recruiting in his home town of Motherwell. He was stationed in Aberdeen, where he played for the depot team, then he was released to work in one of the local shipyards and turned out for the Hall Russell works team until he was demobbed early in 1919. Returning to Motherwell, he played a couple of games for Bellshill Athletic but Aberdeen remembered him and was invited him back for a trial in a friendly against Partick Thistle. They liked what they saw and a few days later he signed for them as a professional. In his first full season he played in the forward line and at centre half, then he was tried at full back and that is where he remained. Not particularly tall, he was heavily built and that made him a fearsome opponent, added to which he had a cannonball shot. He won his first Scotland cap in 1923 when it was unusual for an Aberdeen player to be honoured (the previous one was Donald Colman in 1913) and he did so well that he retained his place for all three home internationals, concluding with the England match. His stature was such that Liverpool provided the opposition for his benefit match in April 1924, and he was named Scotland captain against Ireland; he would have played against England too but had to withdraw through injury. Not surprisingly, a number of clubs were after him, and likewise he wanted to move, with Blackburn Rovers winning the race by paying around £4,000 for him in the autumn of 1926. He had six years as a regular for them in the First Division, the highlight being their FA Cup victory in 1928, the year he also made his final Scotland appearance. He played his last first team game in 1932 and retired in March 1933. He returned to Aberdeen where he drove a fish lorry (not particularly well, he crashed twice!), and in 1939 he joined the Admiralty as a fitter and worked for them until 1948 in many countries. He travelled to Spain for coaching assignments and was appointed Linfield manager in March 1948 but resigned that summer and went back to Spain for another couple of years. Next, he was a fitter for Daimler in Coventry, where he coached the works football team, and finally he lived in Belfast until his death.

'Tom HYSLOP' (2/1, 1896-97)
Bryce Scouller
Born 20 August 1871 Main Street, Auchinleck, Ayrshire
Died 21 April 1936 Royal Alexandra Infirmary, Paisley, Renfrewshire
Scotland v England 1896, 1897 (1).
Elderslie; 2nd Scots Guards 1890-94 [Millwall Athletic trial Apr 1893]; Sunderland Jan 1894-95 (Football League 1895); Stoke Feb-May 1896; Rangers 1896-98 (Scottish Cup 1897, 1898); Stoke 1898-99; Rangers 1899-00; Partick Thistle 1900-01; Dundee Wanderers Sep-Nov 1902; Johnstone Nov 1902-04; Abercorn 1904-05; Philadelphia Thistle 1907-09; Tacony 1909-12 (American Cup 1910).

An unusual character, Hyslop played his entire career under an assumed name. With a powerful stature, standing 6ft 3in, he had a shot to match, and once broke two ribs of the great Jimmy Trainer, Preston's goalkeeper. Born in Ayrshire and brought up in Renfrewshire, he joined the Argyll and Sutherland Highlanders in 1888 under his real name, Bryce Scouller, but disappeared from the records after a year. Then in 1890, presumably to cover his tracks, he used the name Thomas Hyslop to join the Scots Guards. Based at the Victoria Barracks, near Windsor Castle, he was centre forward in the 2nd Scots Guards football team which won the Army Cup twice, the Middlesex County Cup twice, and took part in the FA Cup. He represented the Army against the famous Corinthians, also scoring seven goals for Middlesex in a victory over Sussex. Not surprisingly, he was sought by professional clubs, and equally the Army wanted to keep him. In April 1893 he was granted home leave but instead played a trial for Millwall, and at the end of the game was arrested by the military authorities and taken to Wellington Barracks where he was charged with disobeying orders. Despite being given a lenient punishment, he was obliged to remain in the Army for a further two years. This seems to have been a ploy to keep him in uniform, so when Sunderland expressed an interest in signing him it took several months of protracted negotiations before they finally bought out his contract in January 1894 for the princely sum of £18. He then embarked on his professional football career, although he found it hard to establish himself in the Sunderland side. They let him move to Stoke early in 1895 and he made a solid impact, scoring 24 goals in a season and a half, the highlight being a hat-trick from three cannonball shots against West Brom. This brought him into the sights of the international selectors, which used English-based players for the first time in 1896 and Hyslop was one of five Anglos to face England. Despite some press criticism for his awkward style, he was signed by Rangers that summer and played a key role in the team which won the Scottish, Glasgow and Charity Cups in 1896/97. It was enough to ensure he retained his Scotland place against England, and while Scotland were given little chance at Crystal Palace, Hyslop headed an equaliser before Scotland's late winner from Jimmy Miller, who knocked himself out in the process. England defender Howard Spencer later recalled: 'Tom Hyslop was a thorn in our side, not because he was a particularly skilful forward, but because he was so deadly in his shooting.' The same month he sprinted to victory in the 220 yards race for professional footballers at the Rangers Sports, and went on to another successful season at Ibrox, winning the Scottish Cup again in 1898. Thereafter his career slid downhill. He returned to Stoke where he had a disastrous run of form, failing to score even once in a full season, and then came back to Rangers in 1899 but was soon out of the team, playing only a small part in the league title win. Moving to Partick Thistle, he scored in his first five matches but none of them was won, and although he was top scorer the club was relegated. In any case, he left before the end of the season as he was called up to fight in South Africa. On his return in 1902 he played a few games for Dundee Wanderers, then returned home to Renfrewshire and joined Johnstone, moving to full back, and finally Abercorn. By the end of 1905 he was reported to be appearing in a music hall in London, then he emigrated to USA in March 1906 and worked as a carpet weaver in Philadelphia. He took up football again and played for Philadelphia Thistle, then remarkably won the American Cup with Tacony in 1910 and appears to have continued playing past his 40th birthday. During the last year of WW1 he served in Europe with the Canadian Expeditionary Force, then went back to Philadelphia where he applied for US citizenship. For unknown reasons, he returned to Scotland in 1922 and worked as a carpet weaver in Elderslie until his death from a perforated ulcer in 1936, when obituaries revealed his true identity.

I

Bill IMRIE (2/1, 1929)
William Noble Imrie
Born 4 March 1908 Crossroads, Methil, Fife
Died 26 December 1944 Windygates Hospital, Fife
Scotland v Norway 1929; Germany 1929 (1).
East Fife Juniors; Dunnikier; St Johnstone 1927-29; Blackburn Rovers Sep 1929-34; Newcastle United Mar 1934-38; Swansea Town 1938-39; Swindon Town Aug-Sep 1939; East Fife Nov 1939-40.
Imrie grew up in Methil where his performances in local junior football attracted St Johnstone in 1927 and he quickly settled into the team at half-back. As well as his commanding displays which made him a natural captain, he developed a talent for penalties (reportedly missing just one during his career) and long throw-ins. He was playing so well that he was called into the Scotland travelling party for the continental tour of 1929 and won two caps, scoring a rare goal from open play to rescue a draw in his second match against Germany. That was the last of his international honours, but he clearly deserved for a bigger stage and early in the new season Blackburn Rovers paid a substantial fee to take him to Ewood Park. Five years later, although he was club captain, Rovers sold him to Newcastle for £6,000 as the north-east side made an unsuccessful attempt to avoid relegation. He spent the next four seasons in the Second Division, narrowly avoiding a drop into the Third in 1938. He moved on to Swansea that summer and Swindon a year later but on the outbreak of war he returned home to Methil where he was fixed up by East Fife. He joined the RAF and had reached the rank of Corporal when he was struck down by stomach cancer and died aged just 36. He was a steel moulder to trade.

Jock INGLIS (2/0, 1883)
John Inglis
Born 17 June 1859 Loch, Kilwinning, Ayrshire
Died 16 August 1920 Cheviot Street, Preston, Lancashire
Scotland v England 1883; Wales 1883.

Partick 1879-80; Rangers Oct 1880-84; Blackburn Rovers Feb-May 1884 (FA Cup 1884); Great Lever Nov 1884-87 [guest for Blackburn Olympic Feb 1885, Preston Swifts Nov-Dec 1885]; Preston North End 1888-90.

Brought up in Kilwinning, Inglis came to Partick to work as a carpenter and started playing for the local football side, with whom he made his first trips to Lancashire. However he really came to prominence as an inside forward at Rangers and won two Scotland caps in 1883, against England and Wales. He was at the centre of a storm early the next year when he was induced to play for Blackburn Rovers in the FA Cup quarter final, as Rangers had been knocked out of the Scottish Cup. The circumstances upset some people as he was working as a mechanic in Glasgow at the time, so there was deep suspicion as to how and why he made what was perceived as a mercenary move, although he was far from being the first Scot to join Blackburn, with Fergie Suter, Hugh McIntyre and Jimmy Douglas well established there. Not only did Rangers cancel his club membership, a protest by Notts County after the semi-final prompted an FA investigation into possible professionalism at Blackburn. No evidence was found, however, and he was in place to help Rovers win the FA Cup for the first time, defeating his fellow Scots Queen's Park in the 1884 final. With the job done, he returned to work in Glasgow for the summer, only to be lured back to Lancashire to play for Great Lever, who set him up with a job in Bolton. When Great Lever faded, he found work in Preston and in 1888 was appointed to coach their reserves, although he did make a handful of appearances for the first team. After his football days were over he remained in Preston, working as a foreman at Margerison's soap works. Later in life he was dogged by ill health for many years and died of dropsy aged 61.

John INGLIS (1/0, 1884)

John Inglis
Born 16 September 1857 Dykehead Colliery, Riccarton, Ayrshire
Died 30 October 1942 Howard Park Drive, Kilmarnock, Ayrshire
Scotland v Ireland 1884.
Kilmarnock Athletic 1878-84.

A goalkeeper with Kilmarnock Athletic, Inglis had his first success in 1879 when Athletic won the Ayrshire Cup, and he was still in the team when they won the trophy a second time in 1883. Representative honours followed and he played for Ayrshire against Edinburgh in 1883 before winning his sole international cap the following year, keeping a clean sheet in Scotland's first meeting with Ireland, a straightforward 5-0 win in Belfast. That was effectively his last major match as he appears to have given up the game in 1884. He worked as a stone mason and builder in Kilmarnock, and survived a serious accident at Ballochmyle Quarry in 1887 when a chain snapped and hit him on the arm, breaking it badly. He recovered to live a long life in the town and died in 1942 aged 85.

James IRONS (1/0, 1900)

James Hay Irons
Born 30 October 1874 Bayview Terrace, Leven, Fife
Died 22 October 1957 Mansewood Road, Glasgow
Scotland v Wales 1900.
Queen's Park 1894-1901.

Born in Fife, Irons grew up in Cathcart on the southside of Glasgow after his accountant father moved there to work. A solid half back, he was recruited by Queen's Park and came up through the ranks before making his first team debut in 1896, which was too just late for the Hampden club's glory days but he did win one club honour, the Glasgow Cup of 1899. He was consistent enough to be selected for Glasgow against Sheffield in the autumn of 1899 and was brought into the Scotland team to face Wales later that season when a Scottish Cup replay forced Barney Breslin to withdraw. It proved to be his only cap. He was on the losing side in the Scottish Cup final of 1900 and although Queen's Park then entered the Scottish League he found that work commitments made it difficult to commit his time and he gave up playing football in 1901. He was a talented golfer, winning the Pollok GC championship five times, and was a member of the Pollok pair which won the Evening Times trophy in 1907, as well as winning the Glasgow city championship in 1912. In his professional life he was an electrical engineer in Glasgow.

J

Alex JACKSON (17/8, 1925-30)

Alexander Skinner Jackson
Born 12 May 1905 Hall Street, Renton, Dunbartonshire
Died 15 November 1946 19th General Hospital, Cairo, Egypt
Scotland v Wales Feb 1925, Oct 1925, 1926 (2), 1927, 1928, 1929; Ireland 1925, 1926, 1927, 1929 (2), 1930; England 1925, 1926 (1), 1928 (3), 1929, 1930; France 1930.
Renton Victoria; Dumbarton 1922-23; Bethlehem Star 1923-24; Aberdeen 1924-25; Huddersfield Town 1925-30 (Football League 1926); Chelsea Sep 1930-32; Ashton National 1932-33; Margate Feb-Apr 1933.

Hat-trick hero of the Wembley Wizards, Jackson packed a great deal into his fascinating career. Born in the football town of Renton, the youngest son of a tinsmith, he showed early promise in local juvenile football and signed his first professional contract with Dumbarton aged 17. A year later, he and his elder brother Walter decided to try their luck in America, and spent a season with New York side Bethlehem Star. This alerted an old Aberdeen player to their potential and when he recommended the brothers to his former club, they were both invited back to Scotland and the Jacksons made their

Aberdeen debuts in August 1924. They exceeded all expectations, and while Walter banged in the goals and was top scorer, Alex was such a revelation on the right wing that by the end of a brilliant first season he had been capped three times for Scotland, all before his 20th birthday. He was so highly regarded as a young talent that Huddersfield Town, the champions of England, splashed out £5,000 for his signature in the summer of 1925, and he soon proved his worth. In his first season his new team retained the Football League title and he went on to be a regular fixture not just with Huddersfield, reaching two FA Cup finals, but also in the Scotland team. The highlight was clearly the 5-1 win over England at Wembley in 1928, when he produced an extraordinary performance with three goals from the wing. However, after he played against France in 1930, in what turned out to be his last game for Scotland, it all started to unravel. He signed for Chelsea for a reported £8,500 in September 1930 and scored 30 times in two seasons, then in 1932 he had a major dispute with the club over the maximum wage, which stood at £8 per week. Rather than cave in, at the age of 27 and at the peak of his powers, he simply walked out and dropped into non-league football with Ashton National in the Cheshire League, then briefly for Margate in the Kent League before a knee injury ended his season. In 1933 he was courted by several clubs, including Roubaix and Nice in France and Streatham Town at home, but could not agree terms with any of them. As Chelsea continued to demand a transfer fee there was no prospect of him returning to the English game and his football career was over, essentially on a point of principle. He went into the hotel business and became a partner in the Queen's Hotel in London's Leicester Square. In the Second World War he served in the Middle East as a Second Lieutenant in the Pioneer Corps, and did make something of a football comeback as a regular participant in services matches. He survived the conflict and was promoted to Major, but never returned home as in 1946 the three-ton lorry he was driving near Cairo skidded and overturned. He was fatally injured and died in hospital shortly afterwards.

Andrew JACKSON (2/0, 1886-88)

Andrew Jackson
Born 26 April 1856 High Street, Airdrie, Lanarkshire
Died 3 December 1930 Gordon Street, Paisley, Renfrewshire
Scotland v Wales 1886; Ireland 1888.
Excelsior; Cambuslang 1876-91 [guest for St Bernard's Apr 1886].
Acknowledged as the father of football in Cambuslang, Jackson joined the fledgling club in 1876 and rose to prominence through his hard work and physical presence. Born in Airdrie, he moved to Cambuslang as a boy and followed his father's trade as an engine driver throughout his playing career. Initially a full back, he switched to half back in the early 1880s when William Semple arrived at the club, and in that position he led the team through its most successful period. Cambuslang won the Lanarkshire Cup in 1884 and 1885, while Jackson was made captain of the Lanarkshire team, and was then selected for his Scotland debut in 1886 against Wales. He led Cambuslang as they won the first Glasgow Cup in 1888, beating Rangers 3-1 in the final, but a week later came the humiliation of a 6-1 defeat to Renton in the Scottish Cup final. Later that spring, Jackson won his second cap, a 10-2 drubbing of Ireland which remains Scotland's record away win. He carried on playing for Cambuslang until 1891, when he was presented with a purse of sovereigns and given a benefit match between Cambuslang and a Scottish League Select. He departed for Australia, where much of his family had already gone, but returned home after a year. He served on the Cambuslang committee, and later moved to Paisley where he managed a brickworks. His family had a number of sporting connections: his son Andrew captained Middlesbrough before being killed in action during WW1 while his younger brother James (1874-1966) played for Arsenal and Newcastle. Among his nephews were several professional footballers and the famous cricketer Archie Jackson of Australia.

Johnny JACKSON (8/0, 1931-35)

John Jackson
Born 29 November 1905 Springbank Street, Maryhill, Glasgow
Died 10 June 1965 Victoria General Hospital, Halifax, Nova Scotia, Canada
Scotland v Austria 1931; Italy 1931; Switzerland 1931; England 1933, 1934, 1935; Wales 1935; Ireland 1935.
Kirkintilloch Rob Roy; Partick Thistle 1926-33; Chelsea 1933-45 [guest during WW2 for Portsmouth Dec 1939; Brentford Mar 1940-43 and 1944-45]; Guildford City Sep 1945.

A fine goalkeeper, Jackson started out with Kirkintilloch Rob Roy and played for the Glasgow Junior League against the Irish in 1926, moving to Partick Thistle that summer. He was a model of consistency with the Firhill club, and from the day he made his debut in August 1926 to his departure for England in 1933 he did not miss a single first team match. He went on the Scotland tour of Europe in 1931, playing in all three matches, and was selected twice for the Scottish League, really coming to the fore in 1933 with his first appearance against England. He moved to Chelsea that summer in a big money transfer but in just his fourth match he was hospitalised with a kick to the head, and by the time he was ready to play again he had lost his place to Vic Woodley. However, he did retain his place in the Scotland goal and despite being in the middle of a spell with Chelsea reserves he was selected against England in April 1935, keeping a clean sheet in a 2-0 win. He won his last two caps that autumn, against Wales and Ireland. For all his efforts to regain the Chelsea jersey, he never got his permanent place back in the team and although he had a good run in 1934/35 he played only rarely for the first team after that. During the war years, while serving as a Special Constable, he was first choice at Stamford Bridge until 1942 and was regularly loaned to Brentford, winning the London War Cup with them in June 1942. After he completed the 1943-44 season with Chelsea, he reverted to his loan to Brentford, and retired in 1945 following a few matches with Guildford City. Meanwhile, in 1941 he had been appointed golf professional at the Wyke Green Club at Osterley, near his London home. He was ambitious enough to enter several times for the Open Championship but each time failed to qualify. In 1951 he emigrated to Canada where he was the professional at White Point Golf and Country Club in Nova Scotia until he died in hospital after a heart operation, aged 59.

Tom JACKSON (6/0, 1904-07)
Thomas Alexander Jackson
Born 12 November 1876 The Baths, Thornliebank, Renfrewshire
Died 9 October 1916 killed in action on the Somme, France
Scotland v Wales 1904, 1905c, 1907; Ireland 1904, 1907; England 1904.
Summerlee Juveniles; Thornliebank 1896-98; St Mirren 1898-1908; Clyde Aug-Nov 1908; Bathgate Nov 1908-10; St Johnstone 1910-12.

A right back, Jackson's first honour came at Thornliebank when he represented Renfrewshire, and in 1898 he signed for St Mirren, going on to become one of their finest ever defenders. He spent a decade with the Paisley side and in 1904, at the peak of his powers, he was capped in all three Scotland matches, two Scottish League internationals and the Anglo-Scots match, a rare feat for which he was given a special medal by the SFA. In two of those games he was partnered by his teammate Jack Cameron. The following year he captained Scotland against Wales, and he won two more caps in 1907. He was linked with a transfer to several English clubs, and West Ham tried to sign him that summer, but he told them he had decided to remain in Paisley and headed off to the USA on holiday. He looked set to spend the rest of his career with St Mirren until he injured his knee in a Scottish Cup tie which kept him out for several weeks, and as soon as he returned he suffered an accident to his eye. In the summer of 1908 he parted from Saints, but his options were limited as they demanded a heavy transfer fee, which left him little option but to leave league football. He played a few times for Clyde in the Qualifying Cup, then joined Bathgate in the Scottish Union. In September 1910 he moved to St Johnstone, at that time in the Central League, and was made captain as they won the Perthshire Cup, Dewar Shield and Scottish Consolation Cup, the prelude to their election to the Scottish League. He retired from the game in 1912 having won another Dewar Shield and focused on his job as a commercial clerk in Thornliebank. Unmarried, he was called up to fight after the outbreak of war and served as a Private with the Argyll and Sutherland Highlanders. He had only just returned to the front after suffering wounds when he was killed in action in the final weeks of the Battle of the Somme and is buried in northern France at Adanac Military Cemetery, Miraumont. There is also a memorial in Eastwood Cemetery.

Alex JAMES (8/3, 1925-32)
Alexander Wilson James
Born 14 September 1901 Caledonian Row, Mossend, Lanarkshire
Died 1 June 1953 Royal Northern Hospital, Holloway Road, London
Scotland v Wales Oct 1925, 1929 (1), 1932; England 1928 (2), 1929, 1930; Ireland 1929, 1930.
Orbiston Celtic; Bellshill Athletic; Ashfield 1921-22; Raith Rovers 1922-25; Preston North End Sep 1925-29; Arsenal 1929-37 (Football League 1931, 1933, 1934, 1935; FA Cup 1930, 1936).

Described by George Allison as 'the greatest exponent of all the arts and crafts known to association football', James was a legendary figure for his trademark long baggy shorts, an almost comic look which belied the extraordinary skill that made him a Wembley Wizard. Born into a coal-mining community, he went to Bellshill Academy, the same school as Hughie Gallacher who was two years younger. He worked in a munitions factory during WW1, where he picked up a facial scar and was moved to an office job, and played juvenile and junior football locally before being signed by Glasgow junior side Ashfield in 1921. His ball skills were soon noticed and he had trials for Motherwell and Hearts, but his lack of height was against him until Raith Rovers took a chance and his professional career started in 1922. While his ability was not in doubt, they put him on a special diet to bulk him up. Raith was one of the top Scottish sides at the time, and fielded an inspirational forward line with James the star of the team thanks to his sharp-shooting, elaborate dribbling and ball control. In September 1925 he was bought for around £3,000 by Preston North End, which was not the most glamorous of destinations as his four years at the club were all spent in the Second Division. However, it was a springboard to international recognition and within a month of going south he won his first Scotland cap against Wales. He had to wait almost three years for his second cap, when he wrote himself into legend by scoring twice as England were humbled 5-1 at Wembley. A full set of home internationals followed in 1929 and it was only a matter of time before a bigger club came calling. That club was Arsenal, on the verge of an extraordinary decade thanks to the management of Herbert Chapman, and James played a major part in that success. To secure his services, they not only paid him the maximum wage as a player, but gave him the freedom to undertake a number of well-paid jobs outside football, as a newspaper columnist and a 'demonstrator' for Selfridge's department store. On the field, at Chapman's behest he changed from goal scorer to goal provider, and although it took time to adapt he became the mastermind of Arsenal's dominance. Four league titles in five years, as well as two FA Cups, were testament to that. Eventually age caught up with him, not to mention the early death of Chapman, his mentor, and he retired in 1937. He remained in London, where he had a number of business interests on top of his journalism, and served with the Maritime Royal Artillery Regiment during WW2. He coached Arsenal's third team then sadly he fell victim to cancer and died in 1953, aged just 52. See his biography *Alex James, Life of a Football Legend* by John Harding.

Tom JENKINSON (1/1, 1887)
Thomas James Jenkinson
Born 21 April 1865 Buccleuch Street, Edinburgh
Died 2 May 1952 Homebush, Sydney, Australia
Scotland v Ireland 1887 (1).
Mayfield; Avondale; Heart of Midlothian Nov 1884-91 [guest for Clyde Nov 1886; Hibernian Aug 1887]; Thistle (Sydney) 1893; Granville 1894; Pyrmont Rangers 1894-96.
A zippy outside right who provided a potent goalscoring threat, Jenkinson joined Hearts from local juvenile side Avondale in the autumn of 1884, and soon settled into the team. He was a consistent and loyal performer for seven years, resisting any attempts to persuade him to move to England, his only 'departures' being one appearance for Clyde when they were a man short at Easter Road, and once for Hibs in a charity cup-tie. He was the first Hearts player to be capped although he only made the Scotland team once, scoring and hitting the post in a 4-1 win over Ireland in 1887. He was not selected again but did play several times for Edinburgh, captaining the side against Glasgow in 1888. Fast and clever, he also won prizes at athletic meetings. He had been dropped from the Hearts team by 1891, when they won the Scottish Cup, and decided to emigrate to Australia, where he continued his football career in New South Wales. Initially he captained Thistle, a newly-formed team in Sydney, then played briefly for Granville and had three seasons for the city's top team Pyrmont Rangers, where he won the Gardiner Cup and the local league championship. With his international pedigree he stood out and was selected to represent 'Scotland' in May 1894 in a match against 'England', also playing for the Sydney city team. Later in the decade he returned to Edinburgh for a few years to follow his old trade as a tinsmith before taking his family with him to Australia on a permanent basis. He settled in the Homebush area of Sydney where he worked as a gas engineer. He died there in 1952, aged 87.

Jimmy JOHNSTON (1/0, 1888)
James Johnston
Born 16 September 1866 High Street, Johnstone, Renfrewshire
Died 10 February 1952 Pawtucket, Rhode Island, USA
Scotland v Wales 1888.
Johnstone; Abercorn 1886-91; Pawtucket Free Wanderers 1892-93.
Johnston only had a brief career in Scottish football as he emigrated when he was just 26. Described by John McCartney in his *Story of the Scottish Football League* as 'a really classic and stylish half-back', he first played for Renfrewshire in 1885 while with Johnstone, and continued to represent the county after moving to nearby rivals Abercorn the following summer. His good form at right half resulted in a Scotland cap in 1888, when he was one of ten debutants who had little problem in carving out a 5-1 win against Wales in Edinburgh. He left Scotland for good in 1891 to go to the USA and played for the local football team in the Rhode Island community of Pawtucket, where he worked as a machine tool maker. He married in 1904 and had two children, spent the rest of his life in Pawtucket and died there in 1952. He is buried in Swan Point Cemetery, Providence.

Johnny JOHNSTON (3/0, 1929-32)
John Ainslie Johnston MA
Born 17 November 1902 Thistle Cottage, Stevenston, Ayrshire
Died 12 October 1987 Ayrshire Central Hospital, Kilwinning, Ayrshire
Scotland v Wales 1929, 1932c; Ireland 1932.
Ardeer Thistle; Heart of Midlothian Nov 1921-35 [loans to Stevenston United Feb-May 1922; Cowdenbeath Jan-May 1926]; Arbroath 1935-36.
A commanding centre half, six feet tall, Johnston joined Hearts aged 19 and was almost immediately sent back to Ayrshire junior football to gain experience, then spent most of the next three years at Hearts in the reserves. He may have thought his time at the club was over when he was loaned to Cowdenbeath for the second half of the season in 1926, but after he returned to Tynecastle that summer he hardly looked back. He was a fixture in the Hearts side for the next eight seasons, and although it was not a time for club honours they generally finished in the top half of the league. He made the first of three appearances for the Scottish League against the Irish in 1928, and the following year won his first full cap against Wales, with another League appearance a week later. Three years later he was recalled to the Scotland team for two autumn internationals, enjoying a win over Ireland but then he captained Scotland for the disastrous 5-2 home defeat to Wales in October 1932, at his home ground of Tynecastle to boot. His reputation was not too badly damaged as he was in the Scottish League eleven the following month, when some pride was restored with a 3-0 win over their English counterparts, but there were no more honours. After leaving Hearts in 1935 he had a season with Arbroath before retiring. During his playing career he studied for a university degree and qualified as a school teacher, the profession he followed for the rest of his life. He taught PE and Maths at Stevenston Higher Grade school, where he himself had been educated as a boy. An excellent golfer, he reached the fourth round of the Scottish Amateur Championship in 1925.

Bert JOHNSTON (1/0, 1937)
Robert Johnston
Born 2 June 1909 Mungall Mill Cottage, Falkirk, Stirlingshire
Died 27 September 1968 Hywell Avenue, Sunderland, County Durham
Scotland v Czechoslovakia Dec 1937.
Strathallan Hawthorn; Bothkennar United; Alva Albion Rangers; Sunderland 1929-1946 (Football League 1936, FA Cup 1937) [guest during WW2 for Hartlepools United 1939-40; Lincoln City 1940-45].
Johnston went almost directly from Stirlingshire juvenile football to Sunderland, as he only played a few games with Alva and never signed a contract. It was two years before he made his first team debut at centre half, and he had stiff competition for the position with Jack McDougall before he could become a regular in a fine Sunderland side. Then he was largely understudy to Jimmy Clark in the team that won the league title in 1936, making only nine appearances that season, but there was no doubting his contribution to their FA Cup success the following year. In the final

against Preston, Sunderland were one down to a Frank O'Donnell free kick when O'Donnell raced through again. Johnston brought him down just outside the box, knowing that a second goal would prove too much, and as the resulting free kick came to nothing it gave his team hope at half-time. Sunderland regrouped after the break and eventually ran out 3-1 winners to lift the cup. His one international was a late call-up to face Czechoslovakia in December 1937 after the first two choices for centre half, Jimmy Simpson and Jimmy Dykes, both pulled out. Johnston himself was not fully fit, having just missed three matches due to a thigh strain, but was determined to win his cap. During the war years he was unable to play for Sunderland after 1940, serving with the Sunderland Constabulary Emergency Reserve, and then with the RAF. Instead, he played as a guest for Lincoln City until 1945, and by the time he returned to Roker Park he was too old to make an impact beyond a couple of matches before retiring. He went straight into coaching at Sunderland, being promoted to senior trainer in 1951, and spent his summers in charge of the Norwegian national team from 1947-49. He also coached the England B team for a couple of matches against Scotland in the 1950s. After he was sacked by Sunderland in 1957 he was appointed manager of Horden Colliery Welfare, leaving after 18 months for a full-time post at Consett in the Midland League. Two unusual incidents of note: on Sunderland's tour of Spain in 1935 he suffered an attack of malaria, while in July 1938 he made the news for spending a night in a Dartmoor bog after losing his way in the dark.

Billy JOHNSTON (3/1, 1887-90)
William Johnston
Born 29 April 1865 Dalrymple Street, Girvan, Ayrshire
Died 21 December 1950 Argyle Street, Finnieston, Glasgow
Scotland v Ireland 1887 (1); Wales 1889; England 1890.
Govanhill; Third Lanark 1884-1895 (Scottish Cup 1889) [guest for St Bernard's Apr 1889]; Bute Casuals 1896-97; Partick Thistle Jan 1898.

Johnston was a sparkling forward, mainly at inside left or on the left wing, who spent almost all his career with Third Lanark despite many tempting offers from English clubs. In 1889 he went as far as signing a form for Sunderland Albion, then changed his mind which brought a suspension from the English FA, and in 1890 he turned down a bid from Notts County which was described as 'the biggest ever offered to a Scotch player'. Known as 'William the Silent' because of his quiet off-field demeanour, he was born in Girvan and brought up in Glasgow, playing for Govanhill before joining Third Lanark in 1884. Praised in the *Scottish Referee* for 'great judgement and is equally good at dribbling, shooting and charging', he was selected several times for Glasgow and won his first Scotland cap in 1887, scoring on his debut against Ireland. Then in 1889 he helped Third Lanark win the Scottish Cup at the second attempt after the original final with Celtic was declared void because of snow, and played his second international against Wales. His third cap in 1890 completed the home nations set, at centre forward in a 1-1 draw with England, and Johnston is credited in some reports with Scotland's equalising goal. The season ended with Third Lanark's first Glasgow Charity Cup victory. When he stopped playing in 1895 the club made him a life member and gave him a benefit match although it did not take place until September 1896, against Hibernian. By then he had moved to Rothesay where he played for local side Bute Casuals, and made a brief return to top league action with Partick Thistle, scoring in his one appearance against Rangers in January 1898. In Rothesay he worked as a slater, surviving a fall from a roof in 1903 which left him with a badly broken arm, and in 1909 was reported as training Bute Athletic. He returned to Glasgow soon afterwards and spent the rest of his life in the city.

Jocky JOHNSTONE (1/0, 1894)
John Johnstone
Born 11 April 1868 Robertson Place, Kilmarnock, Ayrshire
Died 6 February 1953 Grange Street, Kilmarnock, Ayrshire
Scotland v Wales 1894.
Riccarton Victoria; Kilmarnock 1889-1901 (Scottish Qualifying Cup 1896; Second Division 1898, 1899) [guest for Rangers Feb 1894].

Despite a lack of inches at 5 feet 5, Johnstone gave great service over a decade at Kilmarnock and was made an honorary life member of the club when he retired in 1901. At left half, he played a key role in the club's rise to national importance, as they entered the Scottish League in 1895, won the Scottish Qualifying Cup in 1896 reached their first Scottish Cup final in 1898, and won two consecutive Second Division titles which earned promotion in 1899. He played once for Rangers in 1894, a league game against Celtic. He was touted for international honours long before his sole cap in 1894, which happened to be played on his home ground, Rugby Park. Despite contributing to a 5-2 win over Wales, he did not play particularly well and was not selected again. He worked for many years as a brass finisher for the engineering company Glenfield and Kennedy, and lived in Kilmarnock until his death aged 84.

K

Johnny KAY (6/5, 1880-84)
John Leck Kay
Born 6 September 1857 Port Dundas Road, Cowcaddens, Glasgow
Died 1 March 1933 Western Infirmary, Glasgow
Scotland v England 1880 (1), 1882 (1), 1883; Wales 1882 (1), 1883, 1884 (2).
Wellpark; Third Lanark 1876-79; Queen's Park 1879-84 (Scottish Cup 1880, 1881, 1882); Third Lanark Apr-May 1884; Pollokshields Athletic 1884-85.

Born in north Glasgow, Kay's family moved to Crossmyloof in the south of the city when he was a small boy. Inspired by the first Scotland match in 1872, he was in the ideal environment to take up football and started out with junior side Wellpark, where his team included another future internationalist, John Marshall. He joined Third Lanark in 1876, when the club was so closely allied to the Volunteer regiment that rifle drill at Cathkin Park was as much part of their activities as football. Tall and slimly built, he soon progressed to the first team where his height and ball control made him a great asset. Along with other Thirds players, notably David Davidson, he was persuaded to join Queen's Park in 1879 and within a season he had won his first cap for Scotland, scoring against England. He ended up playing six times for the national team, all of them ending in victory for Scotland and he scored five goals along the way. With Queen's Park, he partnered James Richmond on the left wing and was an integral player in a fine team that won three consecutive Scottish Cups. After leaving the club in the spring of 1884 he made a few appearances for Third Lanark, including the Charity Cup final, then played a season with Pollokshields Athletic. He gave up the game at this point but kept fit and appeared occasionally for veteran teams until at least 1888. He went into the drapery business in Glasgow as a manufacturer of buttons and garments, while he played bowls as a member of Shawlands club, and was a devoted fan of Robert Burns and loved to sing. He died in hospital in 1933 after an operation.

Sandy KEILLER (6/2, 1891-97)

Alexander Keiller
Born 15 November 1867 Murray Street, Montrose, Angus
Died 16 June 1960 Montrose Royal Infirmary, Angus
Scotland v Wales 1891, 1895, 1896 (1), 1897; Ireland 1892 (1), 1894.
Crown; Montrose 1884-93; Dundee 1893-1902; Montrose 1902-06 (Northern League 1904).

From local junior side Crown, Keiller joined Montrose in 1884 at a time when they still played on open ground. He grew along with the club over the next decade as they progressed to winning the Forfarshire Cup for the first time in 1892, by which time he had been capped twice on the left wing by Scotland against Wales and Ireland, not to mention numerous county caps. It was little surprise that he turned professional in 1893 when he moved to the newly-formed Dundee team. After a couple of seasons at outside left, he dropped to midfield and helped to form the powerful half-back line of Dundas, Longair and Keiller. Although there were offers to go south, he had a steady job and preferred to remain at home, which meant he continued to be selected by Scotland, taking his caps total to six. He also played once for the Scottish League in 1897, a 3-0 victory over the English that ended with him being carried shoulder-high from the pitch. After nine years with Dundee, in 1902 he returned to Montrose and despite being in his mid-thirties he had several years of football left in him, with the club winning the Northern League flag in 1904. His other sport was golf, and as a member of Mercantile GC in Montrose he won the links championship six times. A master slater, he inherited his father's business in Montrose, and lived in the town all his life until he died there, aged 92. NB note the correct spelling of his surname, Keiller not Keillor.

Leitch KEIR (4/1, 1886-88)

Leitch Keir
Born 22 June 1861 Lower Coalgate, Alloa, Clackmannanshire
Died 29 June 1922 Meadowbank Street, Dumbarton
Scotland v Ireland 1886; England 1887 (1), 1888; Wales 1887.
Dumbarton 1881-97 (Scottish Cup 1883; Scottish League 1891, 1892).

A left half who was fierce and fearless in the tackle, with a prodigious throw-in, the only club Keir ever played for was Dumbarton, where he partnered Peter Miller in the side which won the Scottish Cup in 1883. Keir is credited in most books as making his international debut against Wales in 1885, but newspaper reports show that he called off late and his place in the Scotland team was taken by Hugh Wilson, also of Dumbarton. He did play for Scotland the following year against Ireland, and was then selected to face England in 1887, part of the first team to feature three half-backs, and may have scored in the 3-2 victory at Blackburn, with reports crediting a 'scrimmage' after he took a free kick. However, he had the embarrassment of a 5-0 home defeat to England the following year and was not capped again. He played in Dumbarton's Scottish Cup final defeats of 1887 and 1891, and enjoyed further highlights with two Scottish League titles in 1891 (shared with Rangers) and 1892. Although he gave up playing on a regular basis in 1893 he remained on Dumbarton's roster and as late as 1897 was asked to play in an emergency against Leith Athletic in a Scottish Cup tie. Born in Alloa, he had moved to Glasgow as an infant and then on to Dumbarton where he worked as a fitter and plater in the shipyards. He spent all his adult life in the town until he died of stomach cancer in 1922. Tragically his eldest son Henry died just two weeks later, killed in an accident at Leven shipyard in Dumbarton.

James KELLY (9/2, 1886-96)

James Kelly
Born 25 January 1865 Burns Street, Renton, Dunbartonshire
Died 20 February 1932 Thornhill, Blantyre, Lanarkshire
Scotland v Ireland 1886 (1), 1893c (1), 1896c; England 1888, 1889, 1890, 1892, 1893c; Wales 1894c.
Renton 1883-88 (Scottish Cup 1885, 1888) [guest for Hibernian Oct 1886]; Celtic 1888-97 (Scottish League 1893, 1894, 1896; Scottish Cup 1892).

An immensely important figure for Scottish football in the late Victorian era, Kelly was a leading light at Renton then a founding father of Celtic, where he laid down the foundations of a club dynasty. He joined Renton as a young man and won the Scottish Cup twice with them, the first as a forward in 1885 against fierce local rivals Vale of Leven, then at centre half in the crushing 6-1 defeat of Cambuslang in 1888. He made a scoring debut for Scotland against Ireland in 1886 as a late replacement for Johnny Lambie, and was recalled in 1888 to face England. A few weeks later he played his last game for Renton in their victory over West Bromwich Albion which saw the village side declared 'world champions'. That summer he was a star signing for newly-formed Celtic, where he was appointed captain and played in their first ever match, the start of a lifelong association on and off the field. He dominated Celtic's first decade, leading them to their earliest successes in the Scottish Cup and Scottish League. Meanwhile, he went on to take his Scotland caps total to nine, four of them as captain, and played seven times for the Scottish League. When he gave up playing in 1897 it was to become a club director, secure in the knowledge that he had helped to establish Celtic as a major force. He remained a director for the rest of his life, and was chairman from 1909-14. The Kelly family continued to run Celtic for generations, notably his son Sir Robert Kelly, although another son Francis was a casualty in WW1, killed in a train collision in 1919 while serving in France.

Bob KELSO (7/0, 1885-98)
Robert Robison Kelso
Born 2 October 1865 Thimble Street, Renton, Dunbartonshire
Died 19 November 1950 Lomond Drive, Dumbarton
Scotland v Ireland 1885, 1898c; Wales 1885, 1886, 1887; England 1887, 1888.
Renton 1883-88 (Scottish Cup 1885, 1888); Newcastle West End 1888-89; Preston North End 1889-91 (Football League 1890); Everton 1891-96; Dundee 1896-98; Bedminster 1898-99.

Kelso was a star right back for Renton in the 1880s at their peak, including the Championship of the World. He was in the Renton side which won the Scottish Cup in 1885, reached the final in 1886 and won it again in 1888, and this was closely followed by the victory over West Bromwich Albion which saw them proclaimed 'world champions'. By then, Kelso had won six Scotland caps, the first two in 1885 while he was just 19, and as an established international he was a target for ambitious English clubs. Like many Renton players, he was tempted to turn professional, initially joining Newcastle West End where he switched to half back. Then he moved to the all-conquering Preston team for two years, winning the Football League in 1890. His next stop was Everton where he reverted to full back and he spent five years on Merseyside, reaching the FA Cup final in 1893. He was a seasoned veteran by the time he came back to Scotland in 1896, signing for Dundee who made him club captain, and clearly had retained all his powers as he was selected to lead Scotland one last time in 1898, fully ten years after his sixth cap. He wound up his playing career with a brief spell at Bedminster, then came home to Dumbarton where he worked as a ship plater. His brother James played for Renton and briefly for Liverpool, while his nephew Tom (see below) was capped in 1914.

Tom KELSO (1/0, 1914)
Thomas Kelso
Born 5 June 1882 Catherine Place, Renton, Dunbartonshire
Died 29 January 1974 Vale of Leven Hospital, Alexandria, Dunbartonshire
Scotland v Wales 1914.
Dumbarton Union; Clydebank Juniors; Dumbarton Corinthians 1903-04 [trial for Rangers Jan 1904]; Third Lanark Jan 1904-1906; Manchester City 1906-13 (Second Division 1910); Dundee Feb 1913-14; Rangers 1914-15; Dumbarton Oct 1915-18; Abercorn Sep 1919-20; Aberdare Athletic 1920-21 player-coach.

A solid and reliable full back, Kelso had football in the blood, growing up in the heartland of Renton where his uncle Bob (see above) was a famous player. He started out as a junior with Clydebank and Dumbarton Corinthians while he finished his apprenticeship as an engine fitter, a trade he followed throughout his playing career. He had a trial at Rangers shortly before signing for Third Lanark early in 1904 but could not break into the first team and missed out on the club's successes in league and cup. Frustrated at the lack of opportunity, in the summer of 1906 he was allowed to leave and joined Manchester City where he slotted in immediately, proving himself fearless and dashing, with a powerful kick that meant he took the side's penalties. He was also a prominent member of the Players' Union. City were relegated in 1909 but bounced back to win the Second Division a year later, then he fell out of favour and was in the reserves until he moved on to Dundee in February 1913. He scored what was described as one of the greatest goals ever scored at Ibrox (albeit against Rangers), a ferociously powerful free kick from well outside the box which flew through the goalkeeper's hands. He finally achieved international recognition aged 31, after seeming destined to be forever a reserve, and his one Scotland cap was a 0-0 draw against Wales in 1914. That summer he joined Rangers although the War restricted his appearances as he was working in a Clydeside shipyard as an engine fitter. He signed for Dumbarton but had to give up competitive football for a long time and only returned to action in December 1918 when Dumbarton had an emergency. In 1919 he joined Abercorn and wound up his career with a season as player-coach of Aberdare Athletic, guiding his team to second place in the Welsh section of the Southern League. In 1921 he settled back in his home town of Cardross where he opened a fish and chip restaurant in partnership with his brother-in-law Johnnie Miller, a former goalkeeper with Bo'ness and Dumbarton. He remained a keen supporter of Dumbarton until his death, age 91.

Joe KENNAWAY (1/0, 1933)
James Kennaway
Born 21 January 1907 Pointe St Charles, Montreal, Canada
Died 7 March 1969 Johnston, Rhode Island, USA
Scotland v Austria 1933.
Montreal Star; Gurney; Canadian Pacific Railway; Providence Clamdiggers/ Providence Gold Bugs 1927-30; Montreal May-Aug 1930; Fall River 1930-31; Canadian Nationals Jun 1931; New Bedford Whalers Sep 1931; Celtic Oct 1931-39 (Scottish League 1936, 1938; Scottish Cup 1933, 1937); SA Healey 1940; Montreal Wings 1941-42; Montreal Vickers 1943-44; Fall River 1946.

Born in Montreal to Scottish parents who had emigrated there from Dundee, Kennaway was a rare double international for Canada and Scotland. Slightly built, weighing just ten and a half stone, he had considerable strength and agility which made him an outstanding goalkeeper. His football career was impressive from the start, and he was only 19 when he was capped by Canada against USA in November 1926, a 6-2 defeat in Brooklyn. He moved around several clubs in the US professional league and had just signed for New Bedford when fate took a hand in October 1931. Celtic needed an emergency replacement when John Thomson was tragically killed, and the club signed him having admired his performance when playing a friendly against them for Fall River that summer. He spent eight successful years with Celtic, winning two league titles, two Scottish Cups and the Empire Exhibition trophy in 1938. A week after lifting the Scottish Cup for the second time, he was goalkeeper in Celtic's extraordinary 8-0 defeat to Motherwell in April 1937, when a shoulder injury forced him to leave the field in the first half, with his side already four down. He was called up to the Scotland team once, to face Austria in 1933, but there was controversy over his selection, to the extent that the Celtic handbook called him 'the despised and rejected of the Scottish international selectors'. He also played for the Scottish League. He left Scotland when war broke out, and continued to play until at least 1946 while he worked as a carpenter and lived in Rhode Island, USA. He later coached the Brown University football team for 13 years before retiring in 1960. He was inducted into Canada's Soccer Hall of Fame in 2012.

Sandy KENNEDY (6/0, 1875-84)
Alexander Kennedy
Born 13 March 1853 Alexandria, Dunbartonshire
Died 26 December 1944 City Hospital, Belfast, Northern Ireland
Scotland v England 1875, 1876, 1878; Wales 1876, 1882, 1884.
Eastern 1873-76; Third Lanark 1876-85.
Kennedy presented a formidable defensive barrier to his opponents, with the *Glasgow Evening Post* describing him as 'a man with a strong grip of mother earth, and a deep affection for a forward's shins'. A half back, weighing 13 stone with tree-trunk thighs, he was not a speedy mover but made up for it by reading the game well and passing the ball accurately once he had won it. Brought up in the Vale of Leven, he came to Glasgow as a young man and took up football on Glasgow Green where he was asked to make up the numbers with Eastern. They soon recognised his talent, invited him to join the club and he became one of the country's leading players. In 1875 he played for Glasgow against Sheffield and won his first cap for Scotland in the 2-2 draw with England in London. He was capped twice more the following year, against England and Wales, then joined Third Lanark where he spent the rest of his playing career, sometimes alongside his younger brother James. He was in the Third Lanark team which lost the 1878 Scottish Cup final to Vale of Leven, and won three more Scotland caps as well as making another four appearances for Glasgow. He gave up playing in 1884, the year of his final Scotland cap, but was brought out of retirement a year later for a Scottish Cup tie, and remained active in Scotland as a referee for several years. A skilled calico engraver, he moved to Belfast in 1892 and spent the rest of his life there with his wife Isabella and their nine children. He is buried in the City Cemetery, Belfast.

Jack KENNEDY (1/0, 1897)
John Kennedy
Born 18 June 1870 Vennel, Greenock, Renfrewshire
Died 24 September 1940 Main Street, Shotts, Lanarkshire
Scotland v Wales 1897.
Bathgate Rovers 1889-92; Broxburn Shamrock Nov 1892-93; Hibernian Mar 1893-98 (Second Division 1894, 1895); Stoke Mar 1898-1900; Glossop 1900-02; Bathgate Sep 1902; Dykehead 1904-06.
Born in Greenock, Kennedy grew up in Dykehead where he worked down the pit but played his early football in West Lothian after he moved there to work in the mines. He was capped by the county and won the Linlithgowshire Cup with Bathgate Rovers, and had recently joined Broxburn Shamrock when the newly reformed Hibernian came calling in 1893. He proved an excellent signing at inside right for the Edinburgh side, as they won two consecutive Second Division titles to earn promotion, reached the Scottish Cup final of 1896, and consistently finished in the top three in the higher league. Kennedy was good enough to be selected for Scotland and won his single cap against Wales in 1897. The following March he went to Stoke along with Alec Raisbeck to help their fight against relegation, and while Raisbeck left after the test matches were successfully negotiated, Kennedy remained in the Potteries and had a couple of years in the English First

Division. His next stop was with Glossop, who had just been relegated to the Second Division, then in 1902 he returned to Scotland and was reported to have signed for Bathgate and later for Dykehead. He resumed his trade as a miner and settled in Shotts, where he spent the rest of his life. However, he kept in touch with his former Edinburgh colleagues and made a brief return to action in 1912 for the Auld Hibs. His younger brother James signed for Hibs in 1897 but did not make the first team.

Sam KENNEDY (1/0, 1905)
Samuel Watson Kennedy
Born 8 April 1881 Nelson Street, Girvan, Ayrshire
Died 31 August 1955 Marine Gardens, Stranraer, Wigtownshire
Scotland v Wales 1905.
Ayr 1899-1902; Partick Thistle 1902-10; Girvan 1910-14.

Brought up in Girvan, where his parents worked in a cotton mill, Kennedy served an apprenticeship as a plumber. Meanwhile, he embarked on his football career as a centre forward with Ayr in lower reaches of the Second Division. Fast and dashing with a nose for a goalscoring opportunity, he stepped up to newly-promoted Partick Thistle in 1902 and led their attack for seven good seasons, as their top scorer in the first four years. He made his sole Scotland appearance in Wales in 1905 as a late replacement for Jimmy Quinn, but failed to impress in a disappointing 3-1 defeat. As he slowed down, Thistle did likewise and finished bottom of the First Division in 1909. He drifted out of the team, made only two more appearances, and returned to his native Girvan in 1910, continuing to play for them until the First World War. He worked as a plumber throughout his life and retired to Stranraer, where he died in 1955 aged 74.

Geordie KER (5/10, 1880-82)
George Ker
Born 26 February 1860 Hillhead Place, Partick, Lanarkshire
Died 26 February 1922 Moxee, Washington, USA
Scotland v England 1880 (3), 1881 (2), 1882 (2); Wales 1881 (2), 1882 (1).
Kerland; Alexandra Athletic 1876-77; Queen's Park 1877-82 (Scottish Cup 1880, 1881, 1882).

Ker was an outstanding goalscorer in his brief but stellar football career. The younger brother of William (below), he rose quickly through the ranks of minor sides in Glasgow, joined Queen's Park aged 17 and went on to make a huge impact in his five years at the club. One reporter commented after an outstanding performance against Blackburn Rovers: 'The wonderful way in which Geordie slipped the ball round and through his opponents was worth going a long way to see, whilst his fearfully strong shooting at goal was a treat to all.' His first trophy came when he scored the only goal of the game as Queen's Park won the Glasgow Charity Cup in 1878, and he went on to win three consecutive Scottish Cups. More impressively, he scored a hat-trick against England on his Scotland debut in 1880, and went on to record ten in just five internationals. The accuracy and power of his shooting, allied to tactical awareness and combination play, made him one of the greatest of his generation. Then tragically he was forced to give up the game aged just 22 due to injury. He did play one more game in April 1884, for Glasgow against Edinburgh, then that summer he emigrated to America. He learned cattle herding skills at a ranch in Texas before travelling to join his brother in the Yakima Valley in Washington state. He assisted in the management of the Moxee Company before buying his own farm nearby, growing hops, and remained in Yakima for the rest of his life. He married just a few weeks before his death in 1922.

William KER (2/0, 1872-73)
William Ker
Born 21 March 1852 Edinburgh
Died 3 December 1925 Q Street, Washington DC, USA
Scotland v England 1872, 1873.
Granville; Queen's Park 1870-73.

The second son of Scottish physicist John Kerr, William and his brothers changed their surnames to Ker on the insistence of their mother, who asserted it was the correct traditional spelling. Born in Edinburgh but brought up in Mount Florida, he was in the right place at the right time to become involved in the early development of football. He captained Granville (based at Myrtle Park) as well as joining Queen's Park (based at the Recreation Ground) and at the time of the first international in 1872 he was listed as a member of both clubs. He had already travelled to London with Queen's Park for the semi-final of the first FA Cup competition against Wanderers. A natural leader, he worked hard to promote the game and football historian DD Bone wrote: 'William Ker did much by his tact and ability to bring on our senior club to seek new conquests in England. He was a most gentlemanly young fellow and made himself respected by companions and opponents alike'. He was selected to face England again in the return match in 1873, and was elected honorary treasurer of the newly-founded Scottish Football Association a couple of weeks later, but emigrated towards the end of the year. First, he worked in Ontario, where he married a cousin of Alexander Graham Bell, the inventor of the telephone. This led to him returning to Britain to help launch the new technology, and for over a year he lived in Leeds, where he managed the opening of the first telephone exchanges in Yorkshire. In 1881 he crossed the Atlantic again to become the general manager of Pennsylvania Telephone Company, then five years later headed over to Washington state on the west coast, where he established a 7,000 acre farm in the Yakima Valley. He later handed over the management of the farm to his younger brother George (above) so that he could move back east to become a real estate broker in Washington DC. He died there in 1925 and is buried in the city's Rock Creek cemetery.

Peter KERR (1/0, 1924)
Peter Simpson Dennitts Kerr
Born 20 June 1891 Wallyford, Inveresk, East Lothian
Died 24 April 1969 Amisfield Mains Cottage, Haddington, East Lothian
Scotland v Ireland 1924.
Prestonpans; Wallyford Bluebell; Wemyss Athletic Aug-Dec 1910; Hibernian Dec 1910-26; Heart of Midlothian 1926-31; Leith Athletic Dec 1931-32.
After a grounding in local juvenile football, Kerr spent just six months in the juniors with Wemyss Athletic before signing for Hibs and made his debut in a league match at Hampden Park, aged 19. Few would have thought he would still be playing at the top level two decades later. A solid right half, although he played once in goal for Hibs and kept a clean sheet, he remained with Hibs for over 15 years, playing in three Scottish Cup finals in 1914, 1923 and 1924 (the latter two as captain) without winning any of them. There was a brief interruption to his career in WW1 when he signed up for the Royal Field Artillery in 1918, but he was soon back in action. He seems to have improved with age as his one Scotland cap came late in life, aged 32 against Ireland in 1924, and he was also capped twice by the Scottish League in his thirties, against the Irish in 1923 and 1926. The latter came after he was given a free transfer by Hibs and made a surprise move across the city to join Hearts. He played regularly for Hearts for three seasons, and he was 40 when he joined Leith Athletic midway through the 1931/32 season. They were relegated a few months later and he gave up playing at that point but remained to manage Leith Athletic until the Second World War. His son Jimmy played for Leith Athletic and Raith Rovers. NB he was born as Peter Simpson Dennitts, then his mother married Thomas Kerr five months later and he adopted his surname

George KEY (1/0, 1902)
George Key MM
Born 7 February 1878 Slatefield Street, Dennistoun, Glasgow
Died 17 November 1958 Royal Alexandra Infirmary, Paisley, Renfrewshire
Scotland v Ireland 1902.
Parkhead; Heart of Midlothian 1899-1905 (Scottish Cup 1901); Chelsea 1905-09.
Reputed to be the smallest-ever Scotland internationalist at just 5ft 3in, which led to his nickname of 'Chicken', Key was renowned for his energy and tackling, although his distribution of the ball was not always the best. Elder brother of Willie (below), he proved his worth with Parkhead, winning the Scottish Junior Cup in 1898 and then for Scotland juniors against England in 1899. He joined Hearts shortly afterwards although their first impressions were that he was too small and light to be a half-back, and he was initially consigned to the reserves. However in 1901 he was given his chance in the latter stages of the season which culminated in a Scottish Cup victory, and his performance in the final against Celtic sealed his elevation to the first team. A year later he had his cap, playing in Scotland's 5-1 defeat of Ireland in Belfast. He came desperately close to another Scottish Cup victory in 1903 against Rangers when Key's shot appeared to cross the line in the replayed final with the score at 0-0 in the closing stages, but the referee refused to award a goal. Hearts lost the second replay a week later. He was signed by Jacky Robertson for Chelsea when the club was formed in 1905, and adapted well to English football. An excellent performer from the outset, he played in Chelsea's first league match and remained with the club until he retired from the game in 1909. He returned to Barrhead where he worked as a labourer in a gasworks, while in the First World War he served with the 2nd Highland Light Infantry, being awarded the Military Medal in 1918 for his bravery in extinguishing a fire in a bomb store which was being shelled. His youngest brother Walter had been killed in action a few months earlier. He never married and spent the rest of his life in Barrhead. NB he was wrongly identified in Doug Lamming's book as George Brown Key born 1882.

Willie KEY (1/0, 1907)
William Key
Born 18 August 1881 Cathkin Place, Shettleston, Glasgow
Died 5 June 1951 Western Infirmary, Glasgow
Scotland v Ireland 1907.
Parkhead; Vale of Clyde 1900-06; Queen's Park 1906-07; St Mirren 1907-10; Beith Nov 1910-11; Royal Albert 1911-12.
Younger brother of George (above), Key was a fine right half who spent much longer than usual in the juniors, and did not step up to play senior until he was 25. In six years with Vale of Clyde he reaped a number of honours and won the Scottish Junior Cup in 1904, played several times for the Glasgow Junior League and was capped for Scotland at junior level in 1906. He joined Queen's Park that summer and showed such good form that he was selected for Scotland against Ireland in a 3-0 win at Celtic Park, just a year after his junior honour. Shortly afterwards he turned professional with St Mirren and in his first season he played in the 1908 Scottish Cup final, although it ended in a heavy defeat to Celtic. He was released by St Mirren in 1910 after three seasons, and as they demanded a fee for his Scottish League registration he had little option but to play for Beith and then Royal Albert in the Scottish Union before retiring in 1912. A foreman in a bakery, he lived in Paisley until his death in a Glasgow hospital in 1951.

Alex KING (6/1, 1896-99)
Alexander King
Born 18 June 1871 Dykehead, Shotts, Lanarkshire
Died 11 December 1957 Hunter Street, Shotts, Lanarkshire
Scotland v Wales 1896, 1899; England 1896; Ireland 1897 (1), 1898, 1899.
Burnbank Juveniles [trials for Airdrieonians Mar 1893; Albion Rovers Apr 1893]; Wishaw Thistle 1893-94; Darwen 1894-95; Dykehead Apr 1895; Rangers May 1895; Heart of Midlothian 1895-96 (Scottish Cup 1896); Celtic 1896-1900 (Scottish League 1898, Scottish Cup 1899); Dykehead Sep 1900; St Bernard's Oct 1900-01; Dykehead 1901-03; Airdrieonians 1903-04; Dykehead 1904-05.
Man of many clubs, King was an attacking left half or inside left, noted for hard work and an ability to read the game, which made up for his lack of speed. A coal miner, his performances for Wishaw Thistle earned him a cap for

Lanarkshire in 1893, and then he was offered a professional contract by Darwen, newly relegated to the Second Division. He played in most of their matches in 1894/95 and scored ten goals, but returned home at the end of the season and spent the rest of his career with Scottish clubs. He had trials with Dykehead and Rangers, for whom he played in a Glasgow Charity Cup final, then joined Hearts which gave him a chance to show his worth. He really blossomed at Hearts, scoring in their Scottish Cup final victory against city rivals Hibs, closely followed by two Scotland caps against Wales and England, not to mention an appearance for the Scottish League. He was clearly hot property and Celtic snapped him up in the summer of 1896. He had four years with Celtic, the longest he spent with any club, winning further honours for club and country, including the Scottish League title in 1898, the Scottish Cup in 1899, four more Scotland caps and three more appearances for the Scottish League. However, he then appeared to lose confidence and Celtic allowed him to leave in 1900. He returned home to Shotts and played almost by default for local side Dykehead, but also took the opportunity to turn out for St Bernard's and Airdrie before retiring in 1905. Throughout his playing career he worked in the coal mines, and spent the rest of his long life in the Shotts area.

Jimmy KING (2/1, 1932-33)
James King
Born 8 August 1906 Overjohnstone Place, Craigneuk, Lanarkshire
Died 18 July 1985 Law Hospital, Carluke, Lanarkshire
Scotland v Ireland 1932 (1), 1933.
Carfin Emmet; Carluke Rovers 1927-29; Hamilton Academical 1929-39; Alloa Athletic 1939-40.
King started his career in the juveniles near his home in Craigneuk, then had two seasons in junior football with Carluke Rovers where he played for Lanarkshire and was a reserve for the Scotland team. His last games for Carluke in the summer of 1929 brought him a flurry of cup medals with victories in the Lanarkshire League Cup, the Lanarkshire Central Cup and the Glasgow Junior Cup. He immediately signed for Hamilton, although he did not become a first team regular until late in 1931 when he replaced Bobby Howe at outside left. An astute tactical thinker, he soon became known as 'King James' in acknowledgement of his cool and calculating play. In 1932 he was called up to the national team against Ireland and scored after three minutes of his debut in Belfast, setting Scotland on the road to a 4-0 victory, but his second cap a year later was a huge let-down as the Irish won at Celtic Park. He also played once for the Scottish League against the Irish in 1932. He was two-footed which enabled him to switch to the right wing in 1934, and it worked a treat as Hamilton went on to finish fourth in the league and reached the 1935 Scottish Cup final, which they narrowly lost to Rangers. When he was released in 1939 he was signed by former team-mate Jimmy McStay for Alloa but the outbreak of war a few weeks later effectively ended his playing days. He continued to live in Wishaw and worked for many years in Motherwell as senior foreman in the repair department of a mining equipment manufacturer, retiring in 1972. His son Johnny played for Hamilton in the 1960s and two other sons, Jimmy and Eddie, both featured for local junior teams.

Willie KING (1/0, 1928)
William Walter Stewart King
Born 1 February 1898 Craig Park Street, Dennistoun, Glasgow
Died 10 March 1962 Victoria Infirmary, Glasgow
Scotland v Wales 1928.
Queen's Park 1920-32.
King was a one club man for Queen's Park, a half back who could play left right or centre. Educated at Whitehill Secondary School in Dennistoun, his early football experiences are unclear but he was with Queen's Park by 1920, playing for the Strollers, the club's reserve side. He made two first team appearances in October that year then promptly went back to the Strollers for the next couple of years, reappeared in the first team in January 1923 and did not become a regular until 1926. He therefore definitely falls into the 'late starter' category but made up for lost time with a number of representative honours. He was 30 when he won his Scotland cap against Wales in the autumn of 1928, called into the side as a late replacement for the injured David Meiklejohn, and although this was his only full international he went on to win five Scotland amateur caps, once as captain, and played twice for Glasgow against Sheffield. When he gave up playing in 1932 he remained on the club committee and was elected President of Queen's Park in 1939 for two years. In his professional life he was a distillery manager and was later a director of White Horse Distillers. He died of cirrhosis of the liver in 1962, just three weeks before he was due to retire.

Jimmy KINLOCH (1/0, 1922)
James Kinloch
Born 14 April 1898 Houston Street, Govan, Glasgow
Died 21 October 1962 Canniesburn Hospital, Bearsden, Glasgow
Scotland v Ireland 1922.
Anderston Thornbank; Parkhead 1917-18; Queen's Park 1918-20; Partick Thistle 1920-28 (Scottish Cup 1921).
Kinloch represented Glasgow Juveniles with Anderston, then had a season in junior football with Parkhead where he was sufficiently well regarded to be made an offer to turn professional. Instead, he chose to remain amateur with Queen's Park and picked up valuable experience with them over two seasons while he finished his studies. Partick Thistle therefore signed a mature inside right in 1920, and he proved his worth in a marathon eleven-match Scottish Cup campaign in his first season at Firhill, culminating in an unexpected victory over Rangers in the final. His fine attacking partnership with Johnny Blair earned him praise as 'the man with the twinkling feet' and he remained a key part of the Thistle team for several years. International recognition came in 1922 for Scotland against Ireland and he played five times for Glasgow against Sheffield, scoring in three of them. He was probably running out of steam by the time he missed Thistle's only other cup success of the decade, the Glasgow Charity Cup in 1927, and he played his last game for the club in September that year. On retiring from playing in 1928 he went straight onto the Partick Thistle board of directors, serving for a while from

1936 as chairman. He also sat on the Scottish League management committee and was a selector for the League eleven. He lived in Girvan and was a director of Archibald Bryce & Co, wholesale electrical suppliers, until his death.

Arthur KINNAIRD (1/0, 1873)

Hon. Arthur Fitzgerald Kinnaird, later Lord Kinnaird KT
Born 16 February 1847 Hyde Park Gardens, Kensington, London
Died 30 January 1923 St James's Square, London
Scotland v England 1873.
Old Etonians 1865-87 (FA Cup 1879, 1882); Wanderers 1866-78 (FA Cup 1873, 1877, 1878); Cambridge University 1865-68; Gitanos 1868-76; West Kent 1869-71; Hanover United 1885-86.

Kinnaird was a giant of football as a player and administrator. He not only played in nine FA Cup finals, a record to this day, he was capped by Scotland and served the Football Association for 55 years, most of it as President. Educated at Eton College, where he won the House Football Cup, he was adept at the school's Field Game and was introduced to association football after leaving school. As a member of several clubs, he soon became a prominent player and was selected for London against Sheffield in the first representative match in 1866. Off the field, he was brought onto the FA committee in 1868 and helped to instigate the series of unofficial international matches between England and Scotland which started in 1870, playing in three of them. When international matches started in earnest, he represented the full Scotland team against England in 1873, his only cap. However, he is remembered mainly for his prowess in the FA Cup, winning the trophy five times with Wanderers and Old Etonians. In his first final in 1873 he captained Wanderers, and in the decade that followed he switched between them and Old Etonians, playing for the latter in their cup finals of 1875 and 1876 then winning the cup with Wanderers in 1877 and 1878. The newly-reconstituted Old Etonians took almost all his attention thereafter and he won the FA Cup with them in 1878 and 1882, as well as playing in losing finals in 1881 and 1883. By then he was 36 and withdrew from top level football at that point but continued to play regularly for many years, and his last recorded match was in 1898, when he was 51 years old. He was much in demand at many different clubs through his lengthy career, either as a member or a guest. Outside football, Kinnaird was a talented sportsman in many fields: he was a Cambridge University tennis blue, a prize-winning athlete, swimmer and canoeist, and he played competitive cricket in his fifties. He became Lord Kinnaird in 1887 on the death of his father, and was elected President of the Football Association three years later, a position he held for 33 years until his death. In recognition of his unrivalled stature in the game, he was presented with the original FA Cup in 1911 when the design was retired. For his full life story see *Arthur Kinnaird, First Lord of Football* by Andy Mitchell.

Davie KINNEAR (1/1, 1937)

David Kinnear
Born 22 February 1917 Sinclairstown, Dysart, Fife
Died 3 February 2008 Mearnskirk House, Newton Mearns, Renfrewshire
Scotland v Czechoslovakia Dec 1937 (1).
Burntisland United; Raith Rovers Oct 1933-34; Rangers 1934-46 (Scottish League 1937, 1939) [guest during WW2 for Queen of the South Apr 1940, Hamilton Academical Jun 1941, Dunfermline Athletic 1941-42, Northampton Town 1943-44]; Third Lanark Aug-Oct 1946; Dunfermline Athletic Oct 1946-49; Stirling Albion Oct-Nov 1949.

Brought up in Kirkcaldy where he played for Scotland Schools, Kinnear progressed from local amateur football to Raith Rovers in the autumn of 1933 as a 16-year-old. He not only scored on his league debut, he found the net regularly from the left wing through the season and ended it as Raith's top scorer. Rangers recognised his potential and although it took a couple of years to break into the first team, he spent his best years at Ibrox in the fine side of the late 1930s. Fast and direct, he played in two title-winning sides but only won one Scotland cap, scoring the final goal in the 5-0 defeat of Czechoslovakia in December 1937. He was also honoured twice by the Scottish League against the Football League, in 1936 and 1938, and played once for Glasgow against Sheffield. His career was interrupted by the Second World War, and as a Physical Training Instructor with the Army he played as a guest for clubs around the country as well as various Services selects, but only a handful of times for Rangers. After the War he had a brief spell at Third Lanark then three good seasons with Dunfermline until he was freed in 1949. His final senior appearance was at Ibrox for Stirling Albion shortly before a knee injury forced him to retire, although he later played for Cowdenbeath's reserve side which he was coaching. He used his professional skills as a remedial physiotherapist at Bridge of Earn Hospital before being invited back to Ibrox in the mid-1950s as trainer (and briefly as acting manager), and stayed until 1970. Offered the chance to coach Galatasaray, he preferred to remain in Scotland and was an occupational therapist at Leverndale Hospital in Glasgow until he retired. He was 90 when he died in 2008, Scotland's last surviving pre-WW2 internationalist.

L

Johnny LAMBIE (2/0, 1887-88)
John Alexander Lambie
Born 18 December 1868 Cavendish Street, Gorbals, Glasgow
Died 25 December 1923 Tufnell Park Road, London
Scotland v Ireland 1887c; England 1888.
Victoria; Queen's Park 1884-88 (Scottish Cup 1886); London Caledonians 1888-95 [guest for Queen's Park Apr 1892, Corinthian 1890-94]; Queen's Park Jan-May 1894.
Lambie was a precocious talent who holds the records of being Scotland's youngest internationalist and youngest captain. He achieved this aged just 18 when he faced Ireland in 1887, yet he was also selected the previous year as a 17-year-old but withdrew from the side at the last minute. Despite his youth, he was already an experienced player having made his Queen's Park debut in an FA Cup tie in January 1885, just after his sixteenth birthday. A year later scored the opening goal of their Scottish Cup final victory over Renton. He owed his prowess to his powerful athletic build, which enabled him to simply plough his way through the opposition. Shortly after winning his second cap, against England in 1888, he left Scottish football to move to London on business. Still a teenager, he joined London Caledonians and within a few months was selected to represent London against Sheffield, and featured regularly in the city team. As a top-class amateur, he was invited to join the Corinthians and enjoyed several New Year tours with them in the early 1890s. In 1892 he made a single appearance for Queen's Park in the Scottish Cup final, which was lost to Celtic, then when he came back to Glasgow on business for a few months in 1894 he turned out regularly for the Hampden side. He gave up football after a serious injury, but remained heavily involved as a committee member of London Caledonians and sometimes turned out as a recreational player, his last match coming in December 1898 when he featured alongside 51-year-old Lord Kinnaird in a team of Old Internationals. A manufacturer's agent and later a journalist, he lived in Islington and died suddenly at home on Christmas Day 1923, age 55. He was the elder brother of Willie (below).

Willie LAMBIE (9/5, 1892-97)
William Allan Lambie
Born 10 January 1873 Langside Road, Crosshill, Glasgow
Died 16 June 1936 Nithsdale Road, Pollokshields, Glasgow
Scotland v Ireland 1892 (1), 1895 (1), 1896, 1897; Wales 1893 (1); England 1894 (1), 1895, 1896 (1), 1897c.
Queen's Park 1889-1900 (Scottish Cup 1893) [guest for Corinthian Jan 1893].
Lambie was a free-scoring centre forward, rated more highly than his elder brother Johnny (above) and this was reflected in the number of caps he accumulated. He was brought up in Cathcart and went to Glasgow High School along with Willie Gulliland and Tom Waddell. Having joined Queen's Park aged 16 he made his first team debut in May 1890, just after the club had won the Scottish Cup. Because of his youth he had to wait a year for another appearance, but it brought him a medal and considerable kudos as he scored four goals in the Glasgow Charity Cup final of 1891, when Northern were defeated 9-1. Not surprisingly he was an ever-present for Queen's Park the following season and made a scoring debut for Scotland against Ireland when David Baird called off. Then in 1893, shortly after a guest appearance alongside his brother for the Corinthians, he won the Scottish Cup in the 2-1 defeat of Celtic, recovering just in time from an injury in the semi-final. Described in the press as 'a left wing of the highest class, quick on the ball and a deadly shot at goal', he went on to win nine caps, scoring in five of them including his first four. After professionalism was legalised in Scotland he was often the only amateur in the national team and showed his worth by captaining the side to victory over England in his final international in 1897. His only other winner's medal for Queen's Park was another Charity Cup in 1898, and he gave up playing for the first team the following season. He ran a business as a muslin manufacturer in Glasgow.

William LAMONT (1/0, 1885)
William Lamont
Born 28 August 1862 Eglinton Street, Gorbals, Glasgow
Died 22 March 1938 Bridge Hotel, Irvine, Ayrshire
Scotland v Ireland 1885.
Pollok 1882-83; Queen's Park 1883-84; Pilgrims 1884-86.
Son of a warehouse goods agent, Lamont was brought up in the southside of Glasgow and played for local football teams but his career is difficult to follow as he was never a high profile player. He was initially with Pollok, then had a year at Queen's Park without appearing for the first team, and two seasons with Pilgrims, a short-lived club which played at Copeland Park in Govan (the former home of Parkgrove). Playing on the left side of the forwards, in 1885 he was the only Pilgrims player to win international recognition in Scotland's 8-2 victory against Ireland, and some reports credit him with the opening goal. He

disappears from football records after 1886 although his obituaries claim he also played for Renton and Third Lanark. He was a book-keeper for Archibald Arrol's brewery for many years, and latterly he ran the Bridge Hotel in Irvine, which was owned by the brewery. He died in tragic circumstances, stumbling into his fireplace and being fatally burned; sadly, his wife had died just a few weeks before. His son Alfred, who had played for Alloa, Clackmannan and Third Lanark, took over the running of their hotel.

Archie LANG (1/0, 1880)
Archibald Lang
Born 13 December 1859 High Street, Dumbarton
Died 23 January 1925 Gasworks House, Alexandria, Dunbartonshire
Scotland v Wales 1880.
Dumbarton 1877-81 & Dec 1886; Shanghai Marine Engineers' Institute.

A fine full back who showed great early promise, Lang was selected for the Scotland trial matches in 1878 aged just 18, and his reputation was enhanced the following year when Dumbarton put the cup-holders, Vale of Leven, out of the Scottish Cup. He was capped for Scotland against Wales in 1880, when along with Joe Lindsay he became the club's first internationalist, but just as Dumbarton were emerging as a major force he left the country. Early in 1881 he sailed for China, shortly after helping his team to reach their first Scottish Cup final, in which his place was taken by Michael Paton, another future cap. Lang followed his father's profession as a marine engineer, and worked for many years in Shanghai where he played for and captained the Marine Engineering team founded by fellow Scots and which was, bizarrely, a member of the Scottish FA. He did play once more for the Dumbarton team in 1886 while home on leave.

Jamie LANG (2/2, 1876-78)
James Joseph Lang
Born 20 March 1851 Main Street, Lennoxtown, Stirlingshire
Died 14 July 1929 Stobhill Hospital, Balornock Road, Glasgow
Scotland v Wales 1876 (1), 1878 (1).
Eastern; Jamestown 1873; Clydesdale 1873-76; Sheffield Wednesday 1876-78; Spital Dec 1876; Third Lanark 1877-79; Sheffield Wednesday 1879-82; Third Lanark 1882-83; Farnworth Feb-Sep 1883; Great Lever Oct 1883, Jan 1884; Preston North End Nov 1883, Jan 1884; Sheffield Wednesday Jan 1884; Northwich Victoria Nov 1883, Feb 1884; Airdrieonians 1884-85; Mellor's Limited (Nottingham) Nov 1885.

Lang claimed to be the first professional footballer in 1876, and said 'I crossed to England to play football and for no other purpose. I was the first to do that.' Although the supporting evidence is inconclusive, what is certain is that he made many appearances for Sheffield Wednesday with no obvious link to the city, and was able to travel to Sheffield without any financial concerns. What makes his story even more incredible is that he lost an eye aged 18 in an accident at work in John Brown's shipyard on the Clyde. Even though he was officially classified as disabled, he kept the impairment a closely-guarded secret throughout his football career. He witnessed the first international in 1872 and recalled playing for Eastern and Jamestown, but the first club he was closely involved with was Clydesdale, for whom he played in the Scottish Cup final in 1874, which was lost to Queen's Park. He was growing in reputation when his life changed in 1876, with two visits to Sheffield in quick succession, the first for the Glasgow select in February, then again in April for Clydesdale against Wednesday, a week after scoring a goal against Wales on his Scotland debut. Later that year he turned up in Sheffield, the cover story being that he had found a job in a knife factory run by Walter Fearnehough, who happened to be a Wednesday committee member. Over the next six years Lang gravitated between Glasgow and Sheffield, popping up in both cities on a regular basis. He played in the 1878 Scottish Cup final for Third Lanark which they lost to Vale of Leven, and won his second Scotland cap the same year, scoring another against Wales. He left Sheffield in 1882, apparently for good, but was tempted back south in 1883 to train the football and cricket teams at Farnworth, and the following season he played for a bewildering number of English clubs on a match-by-match basis (even the above list may not be complete). He eventually returned to Glasgow in 1886 where he was appointed as trainer to Third Lanark, and worked as a boiler maker until his death in 1929. He was interviewed several times in old age about his pioneering football career.

Alec LATTA (2/2, 1888-89)
Alexander Latta
Born 7 September 1867 Church Street, Dumbarton
Died 25 August 1928 Cavendish Drive, Rock Ferry, Cheshire
Scotland v Wales 1888 (2); England 1889.
Dumbarton Athletic 1883-89 [guest for Leith Athletic Apr 1889]; Everton 1889-96 (Football League 1891); Liverpool Oct 1896-97.

Brought up in Dumbarton, Latta served an apprenticeship as a carpenter before following his father into the boat-building trade, a career he followed all his life. Showing talent as a footballer, he joined Dumbarton Athletic as a young man, did well in the club's second eleven, and unusually he resisted the temptation to join the senior club in the town. Promoted to Athletic's first team in 1885, he made the first of several appearances for Dunbartonshire, and as he rose to prominence it was inevitable that he would win international honours. An excellent outside right, powerfully built and a hard worker, his long stride allowed him to race down the wing and place an accurate ball into the centre. He made his Scotland debut against Wales in 1888, scoring twice in a 5-1 win, then the following year was impressive in the side which beat England 3-2 at the Oval. That summer Dumbarton Athletic merged with Dumbarton but by then Latta had gone south to join Everton as a professional. He formed a right-wing partnership with his great friend Joe Brady, backed up by Dan Kirkwood at right half, and their combination and understanding played a major part in Everton winning the Football League title in 1891. Sadly, that turned out to be their only major honour as they lost the 1893 FA Cup final. Latta was given a lucrative benefit match against Celtic at the end of that season, and in total he made 148 appearances for Everton, scoring 70 goals including six hat-tricks. He retired in the summer of 1896 to focus on his business as a yacht builder in Hoylake, although he made a surprise return to action with near rivals Liverpool later that year, playing several times for their reserves. He spent the rest of his life on Merseyside where he married and raised a family of seven children.

Geordie LAW (3/0, 1910)
George Law
Born 13 December 1885 Kinnaird Street, Arbroath, Angus
Died 9 September 1969 Western Infirmary, Glasgow
Scotland v Wales 1910; Ireland 1910; England 1910.
Lochside; Dauntless; Arbroath 1905-07; Rangers Feb 1907-1912 (Scottish League 1911, 1912); Leeds City 1912-16; Rangers 1916-19 [loan to Partick Thistle Mar-Apr 1917]; Arbroath 1919-22.

A determined defender with a fine turn of speed, Law was an outstanding right back. Having started out in local junior football, he had a couple of seasons at Arbroath before being transferred to Rangers early in 1907 for a fee reported at £55. As it took a year to settle into the first team at Ibrox, he was allowed to return to Arbroath a couple of months later for the Forfarshire Cup final, and came away with a winner's medal. By the end of the decade he was rated one of the best backs in the country, and it was little surprise when he made the Scotland team in 1910 and did well enough against Wales to be retained for the Ireland and England games. He won the league title with Rangers in 1911 and again the following season, although by then his appearances were constrained by a leg injury and competition for the full back role. A move to Leeds City in 1912 saw him shift to right half, but when football in England was suspended due to the War, he returned to Glasgow and worked in the Clyde shipyards. He rejoined Rangers, making only limited first team appearances, then went home to Arbroath in 1919 where he and his brother took over their father's garage business. He still had three years of football left in him with his old club Arbroath, returning to Ibrox in a Scottish Cup tie but suffering a 5-0 defeat. However, he did pick up another Forfarshire Cup medal, captaining the side to victory in 1921. After retiring from the game in 1922, he remained in Arbroath where he ran the family motor business for the rest of his working life.

Tommy LAW (2/0, 1928-30)
Thomas Law
Born 1 April 1908 Lancefield Street, Finnieston, Glasgow
Died 17 February 1976 Acfold Road, Wandsworth, London
Scotland v England 1928, 1930.
Claremont Union; Bridgeton Waverley; Chelsea 1925-39.
Law grew up in Finnieston where he started work in the shipyards, and only took to football seriously after leaving school, playing at juvenile and junior level. After just five games for Bridgeton Waverley, Chelsea took him south in the spring of 1925 and he spent the rest of his career in England. A fierce tackler who was renowned for sliding in to win the ball, and an accurate passer, he made his first team debut at left back in September 1926 and kept his place in the team for the rest of the season. As Chelsea were then in the Second Division he was still virtually unknown when selected for Scotland in 1928, an inspired choice as he achieved legendary status as a Wembley Wizard, the day before his 20th birthday. He was resolute in defence in the 5-1 win but recalled that the Scottish FA was in no mood to reward the players: 'I asked for £1 expenses to cover taxi fares and lunch; all I got was 8d to cover two bus fares – to my London home and back!' Chelsea won promotion in 1930, as runners-up, which heralded his second and final appearance for Scotland although the 5-2 defeat to England was far from a memorable return to Wembley. Chelsea spent big in the 1930s to consolidate their return to the First Division, but the one constant in their team was Tommy Law although an FA Cup semi-final in 1932 was the nearest he came to a major honour. He missed all of the 1934-35 season due to a serious injury, after which he spent most of his remaining years in the reserves before Chelsea gave him a free transfer in 1939. He retired at that point and remained in London, coaching various non-league sides after the War, including Tooting and Mitcham, Carshalton and Ware Town, and continued to support Chelsea whenever he could.

Jimmy LAWRENCE (1/0, 1911)
James Lawrence
Born 16 February 1879 Stewartville Street, Partick, Lanarkshire
Died 21 November 1934 Victoria Infirmary, Glasgow
Scotland v England 1911.
Partick Athletic 1900-02; Glasgow Perthshire 1902-04 [guest for Rangers Apr-May 1903; Hibernian Mar-Apr 1904]; Newcastle United 1904-22 (Football League 1905, 1907, 1909; FA Cup 1910) [guest for South Shields 1915-16; Sunderland Rovers Feb-May 1917; Glentoran Dec 1918].

Lawrence holds Newcastle United's appearance record, with 496 first team games, but throughout his career he kept his age a secret. In all documentation including registration forms and travel documents he gave his birthdate as 16 February 1885 but he was actually born six years earlier, arriving forty-five minutes after his twin sister Margaret. The origin of the deception probably lies in his late arrival in football, as when he joined Newcastle from Glasgow Perthshire in 1904, newspaper reports mentioned that he had only taken up the game four years earlier with Partick Athletic, which would have led many observers to think that he was around 19. In fact he was 25 and had, by then, represented Scotland at junior level and made guest appearances for Rangers and Hibernian. He spent his entire senior playing career on Tyneside and was one of the country's top goalkeepers, winning numerous honours including three Football League titles and the FA Cup in 1910 but just a single Scotland cap in 1911 against England, aged 32. When Newcastle United shut down for WW1 he remained in the town and worked at the Armstrong Whitworth munitions factory, playing for local sides in the Tyneside League. He picked up again with his club in 1919 and by the time of his last appearance in April 1922 he was 43, which makes him Newcastle's oldest-ever first team player. Yet that summer, when he made his annual visit to see his mother in Canada, he claimed to be only 37 on his immigration papers. A tinsmith before he became a full-time professional, Lawrence was a passionate trade unionist and was a leading light in the Players' Union, eventually becoming chairman in 1921. He contributed a column to the *Yorkshire Weekly Record* which helped to put his views across. Having hung up his boots he was appointed manager of South Shields (from 60 applicants) but the job only lasted six months. He then had a couple of years coaching Preston North End, and in 1925 began a successful six-year spell in Germany with Karlsruhe, winning several regional championships. When ill health forced his return to the UK in 1931 he settled in Stranraer and was chairman of the football club there until angina and heart disease led to his premature death.

Denis LAWSON (1/0, 1923)
Denis Lawson
Born 11 December 1897 Main Street, Lennoxtown, Stirlingshire
Died 23 May 1968 Shamrock Street, Cowcaddens, Glasgow
Scotland v England 1923.
Kirkintilloch Hearts; Kirkintilloch Rob Roy 1915-16; Kilsyth Emmet Mar-Nov 1919 [trial for Celtic Aug 1919]; St Mirren Nov 1919-23; Cardiff City Nov 1923-26; Springfield Babes Sep-Oct 1926; Providence Clamdiggers Nov 1926-27; Wigan Borough Oct 1927-28; Clyde Dec 1928- Jan 1929; Brechin City 1930-31.
Lawson had to wait for WW1 to finish before he could embark on his football career. A nippy outside right, he was playing well for Kirkintilloch Rob Roy when he enlisted in 1916 and saw active service with the 14th Highland Light Infantry until he was captured in November 1917 at the Battle of Cambrai. He spent the last year of the conflict as a Prisoner of War and after being released towards the end of 1918 he joined Kilsyth Emmet where his good form soon attracted senior clubs. Celtic gave him a trial, then in November he was given a game by St Mirren, scored on his debut and was signed on the spot. St Mirren finished last in 1921 but escaped relegation due to league reconstruction, and Lawson's displays on the wing were so impressive that he was selected for Scotland against England in 1923. Later that year Cardiff City splashed out a hefty fee to take him south but he struggled to make an impact, and when he decided Cardiff's terms were not good enough, he embarked in September 1926 for the USA. It was not a success and he came home after playing for less than a year with Springfield Babes and Providence Clamdiggers. He found it difficult to land another club and joined Wigan Borough in the Third Division North, then came back to Scotland for a brief spell with Clyde. A year later he made a surprise return at Brechin City, his final club before he retired in 1931. He worked as an engineer's checker and spent the rest of his life in Glasgow.

Robert LECKIE (1/0, 1872)
Robert Leckie
Born 19 October 1846 Spittal Farm, Killearn, Stirlingshire
Died 25 November 1886 Olifants Bosch, Mankazana, South Africa
Scotland v England 1872.
Queen's Park 1867-75 (Scottish Cup 1874).
Leckie played an important role in the early years of Queen's Park, as a club founder in 1867 and as the scorer of the clinching goal in the first Scottish Cup final of 1874. He played in Scotland's first international match in 1872, but was unable to get to London for the return. Small and powerful, he had a distinctive running style that made him difficult to tackle, as described by DD Bone: 'While dribbling past an opponent with the ball at his toe, his peculiarity asserted itself in such a way that, once seen, could never be forgotten. When he obtained possession of ball, he guarded his body with extended arms drooping from his side, with the back of his hands in front of the thighs, and thus formed a barrier to an opponent who attempted to tackle or take the ball from him.' He played in the Scottish Cup semi-final in 1875 then gave up the game to emigrate to Port Elizabeth in South Africa. It was a major trading port and he appears to have done well in business until he contracted tuberculosis. He went inland to seek a cure in the dry Mankazana Valley but it was to no avail and he died in the small Scottish community at Olifants Bosch, leaving a wooden chest containing his clothing, a few books and a gold watch and chain.

Willie LENNIE (2/1, 1908)
William Lennie
Born 26 January 1882 New City Road, Cowcaddens, Glasgow
Died 24 August 1954 Balgownie Eventide Home, Bridge of Don, Aberdeenshire
Scotland v Wales 1908 (1); Ireland 1908.
Maryhill; Queen's Park 1901-02; Rangers 1902-03; Dundee 1903-04; Fulham 1904-05; Aberdeen 1905-13; Falkirk 1913-14; St Johnstone 1914-15.

Aberdeen's first internationalist, Lennie had already had an interesting career before he won his Scotland caps. An outside right with Maryhill, where he played alongside Donald Colman, he represented Scotland at junior level before turning senior with Queen's Park in 1901. The following summer he became a professional with Rangers but despite scoring twice on his debut he failed to displace Alec Smith in the team and played just five league games. Next stop was Dundee where he started to show his true form and held down a regular place, then moved to Fulham in the Southern League in 1904. Again he only lasted a year, before he finally settled at Aberdeen in 1905. He established a great partnership on the left with Charlie O'Hagan and played over 250 matches in his eight years at Pittodrie, and despite being a winger was twice top scorer for the club. He was selected for Scotland in 1908, scoring a late winner against Wales and then playing his part in a 5-0 win over Ireland a week later, when Jimmy Quinn scored four. He was also capped twice by the Scottish League. He joined to Falkirk in 1913 and had a final season with St Johnstone before he gave up professional football in 1915, although he played during the War for his munitions works team in Aberdeen. He remained in the city for the rest of his life and ran a newsagent shop at Hilton Road. He died in 1954, aged 72.

Dan LIDDLE (3/0, 1931)
Daniel Snedden Hamilton Liddle
Born 17 February 1912 Richmond Terrace, Bo'ness, West Lothian
Died 9 June 1982 Holmdene Avenue, Wigston, Leicestershire
Scotland v Austria 1931; Italy 1931; Switzerland 1931.
Castlepark Thistle; Wallyford Bluebell; East Fife 1929-32; Leicester City 1932-46 (Second Division 1937) [guest during WW2 for Northampton Town 1939-40, Notts County 1942-43 and Mansfield Town 1944-45]; Mansfield Town 1946-47; Hinckley United 1947-48.
Brought up in Bo'ness, where his father Jock and brother John had both played for the local senior team, Liddle's potential was recognised early on, winning a Scotland junior cap in 1929 when he was just 17 and playing for Wallyford. He had several offers to turn senior and surprised many by choosing East Fife, but it proved an inspired decision as the Methil club won promotion in his first season, narrowly missing the Second Division title on goal average. Sadly they were relegated in 1931 but Liddle was their outstanding performer at outside left and he was selected for Scotland's end of season tour to Europe. Aged just 19, he was East Fife's first internationalist and played in all three games, although he was injured against Austria and could not complete the match. Even though several clubs were on his tail, to enable him to complete his apprenticeship as a carpenter he signed on for another season, and did not leave East Fife until the summer of 1932. He chose to go to Leicester City and spent almost all the rest of his career at Filbert Street. Moving to inside left, a personal highlight was scoring four in a First Division match against Sheffield United in 1933 and he was the club's top scorer for two seasons but it was not enough to save them from relegation in 1935. However, they won the Second Division in 1937 and at the end of their first season back he scored the goal against Charlton which secured Leicester's place in the top division, while the club gave him a benefit match against Manchester City. It proved a false dawn and they finished at the bottom of the league in 1939, the last pre-war season. In wartime he remained in the area and played over a hundred games for Leicester, also guesting for other Midland sides. By the time the conflict was over he was in his mid-30s and he wound down his career at Mansfield Town and Hinckley United. He lived in the area for the rest of his life and died in 1982.

David LINDSAY (1/0, 1903)
David Lindsay
Born 27 December 1877 Old Linn, Dalry, Ayrshire
Died 31 October 1950 West Bowling Green Street, Leith, Edinburgh
Scotland v Ireland 1903.
Rutherglen Glencairn; St Mirren Dec 1899-1905; Heart of Midlothian 1905-06; West Ham United 1906-08; Leith Athletic 1908-11 (Scottish Qualifying Cup 1909, Second Division 1910).
An outside right, quick off the mark and with excellent ball control and a fierce shot, Lindsay played for Scotland as a junior in March 1899 while at Rutherglen Glencairn, and signed for St Mirren towards the end of the year. Turning professional meant escaping life as a shale miner and he enjoyed five good years in Paisley. He was capped for Scotland against Ireland in 1903 and entered the record books in 1904 as the first player ever to score a hat-trick of penalties, with Rangers the opposition. However, he fell out with the club manager John McCartney over his poor timekeeping and was sold to Hearts in 1905 for £100. His season at Hearts was not a great success despite being paired on the wing with Bobby Walker, as both players were too individualistic to combine well. By the time Hearts won the Scottish Cup in 1906 he was out of the team and he moved that summer to West Ham, in the Southern League. He was first choice for two seasons in London before coming back to Edinburgh to join Leith Athletic who were enjoying a successful but ultimately frustrating time, being in the shadow of the big Edinburgh teams. In 1909-10 they won the Scottish Qualifying Cup and shared the Second Division title with Raith Rovers, but while the Fife team was elected to promotion, Leith stayed where they were. Lindsay gave up playing in 1911 when he was appointed trainer of Leith Athletic and remained in the post until WW1. He continued to live in the port until his death, latterly working as a labourer. His son John was also with Leith Athletic, winning the Qualifying Cup in 1925, and another son, Hugh, won three Scotland junior caps.

John LINDSAY (3/0, 1888-93)
John Lindsay
Born 16 January 1862 Burns Street, Renton, Dunbartonshire
Died 16 October 1932 Glasgow Road, Dumbarton
Scotland v England 1888, 1893; Ireland 1893.
Renton 1883-89 (Scottish Cup 1885, 1888); Accrington 1889-90; Renton 1891-93; St Bernard's 1893-94; Renton 1896-97.
An outstanding goalkeeper in Renton's halcyon days, Lindsay won the Scottish Cup in 1885 and 1888 and was in the team declared 'Champions of the World' after the latter success. It was not all glory that year as he had a disastrous first cap for Scotland, losing 5-0 to England, but he was actually praised for keeping the score down. In 1889 he turned professional with Accrington and played a full season with them in the Football League before returning home, only to find himself banned by the Scottish FA for professionalism. He was forced to take a year out until given an amnesty in 1891, when he took up again with Renton, and was clearly still in top form as he came back into the reckoning for Scotland. Although selected against

Ireland in 1892, he refused to play along with the other Renton players, but was forgiven and called up for two more internationals, against England and Ireland, the following year. His final season should have been with St Bernard's in the Scottish League before retiring in 1894. However, after a couple of years refereeing he made a surprise return to action in 1896 with Renton in several league matches alongside a youthful Donald Colman. Relatively short for a goalkeeper at 5 feet 6, he made up for it with his powerful build, weighing 12 stone. He was a lifelong abstainer and spent all his working life in Dumbarton where he was a locomotive driver.

Joe LINDSAY (8/6, 1880-86)
Joseph Lindsay
Born 13 November 1858 Levenshaugh Street, Dennystown, Dunbartonshire
Died 12 October 1933 Lennox Street, Renton, Dunbartonshire
Scotland v Wales 1880 (1), 1881, 1884 (1), 1885 (3); England 1881, 1884, 1885 (1), 1886.
Dumbarton 1877-86 (Scottish Cup 1883); Rangers Dec 1886-87; Dumbarton Athletic 1887-89; Dumbarton 1889-91; Renton 1891-93.

Lindsay was an outstanding forward at a time when Scottish football was dominant,, playing at centre or inside right and was a real asset to his home town of Dumbarton. With a great turn of speed, he scored on his international debut in 1880 and went on to win eight caps, notably as one of the attacking spearhead which faced England at the Oval in 1881, when Scotland won 6-1. He did not score in that game but in 1885 he got a precious goal against England and then a hat-trick against Wales two days later. His final cap in 1886 was also against England although he should not have played as he had been injured the previous week and was a virtual passenger throughout the match. For Dumbarton, he played in the Scottish Cup finals of 1881 and 1882 before finally lifting the trophy in 1883. He was asked to assist Rangers late in 1886 and took part in their memorable run to the FA Cup semi-final, then found he had lost his place in the Dumbarton side. Instead, he signed up for their local rivals Dumbarton Athletic, then when the two clubs merged in 1889 he was again frustrated at the lack of opportunities and left in March 1891 for a job as a painter on board the SS Tanui which was heading for New Zealand. When he came home six months later he resumed his football with Renton and showed he was still capable by playing for them in the Scottish League for two more years. Although he retired in 1893 he kept fit and as late as 1916 he played in a veterans match for an 'Old Dumbarton' side. When he died in 1933 a minute's silence was held at Dumbarton's next home match.

Geordie LIVINGSTON (2/0, 1906-07)
George Turner Livingston
Born 5 May 1876 Ballingall's Land, Risk Street, Dumbarton
Died 15 January 1950 Bellevue, Helensburgh, Dunbartonshire
Scotland v England 1906; Wales 1907.
Sinclair Swifts; Artizan Thistle; Parkhead; Heart of Midlothian 1896-1900; Sunderland 1900-01; Celtic 1901-02; Liverpool 1902-03; Manchester City 1903-06 (FA Cup 1904); Rangers Nov 1906-09; Manchester United Jan 1909-14 (Football League 1910-11).

An inside left with a great physical presence, Livingston had a remarkable career at top clubs in Scotland and England, and almost uniquely he played for both sides of the divide in Glasgow and Manchester. His earliest success was winning the Dunbartonshire Juvenile Cup with Artizan Thistle, and he had a brief trial with Parkhead juniors before crossing the country to join Hearts in 1896. In four seasons in Edinburgh he established himself as a significant talent, and he embarked on his travels with Sunderland in 1900, the first of four clubs in four years. While at Celtic he was capped against England in 1902 in the Ibrox Disaster match, which was declared void and he was injured when the countries met a few weeks later in Birmingham. He had to wait a further four years before his international chance came again, by which time he was at Manchester City. He left Celtic shortly after the 1902 Scottish Cup final, in which he hit the post with a shot that could have saved defeat from Hibs. Next stop was Liverpool, and then he finally won a major medal as Billy Meredith's wing partner in Manchester City's FA Cup triumph of 1904. He left City in 1906 when he was caught up in a bribery scandal and suspended for six months, forcing him to return to Scotland where he joined Rangers. He returned to the national team against Wales, and was selected once by the Scottish League in 1907. His final club was Manchester United, and although he was already at the veteran stage when he went to Old Trafford early in 1909 he played his part in the title-winning season of 1910-11 with ten appearances. After that he focussed on training the reserves but made at least one first team appearance each season until he retired in 1914. He served during WW1 with the RAMC in Palestine and Egypt then when he was demobbed he resumed coaching, taking charge of Dumbarton for a season before he was appointed in 1920 as trainer to Rangers under Bill Struth. He left them in 1927 for health reasons, and worked in a similar capacity for Bradford City from 1928-35, after which he gave up football entirely and ran a plumbing business in Dumbarton.

Alex LOCHHEAD (1/0, 1889)
Alexander Lochhead
Born 27 June 1863 Stewart's Land, Neilston, Renfrewshire
Died 9 January 1939 Craw Road Institution, Paisley, Renfrewshire
Scotland v Wales 1889.
Neilston Victoria; Abercorn 1881-84; Arthurlie 1885-86; Morton 1886-87; Notts Castle Feb 1887; Arthurlie 1887-88; Third Lanark 1888-91 (Scottish Cup 1889); Everton Feb-Nov 1891; Third Lanark 1892-93; Neilston 1896-97; Cartvale 1897-98; Barrhead Amateurs 1898-99.

A half back, Lochhead had represented Renfrewshire while with Morton and Arthurlie, before trying his luck as a professional in a brief trial in 1887 with the short-lived Notts Castle club. He came back to Arthurlie but it was really at Third Lanark that he made his name, notably for being one of the few footballers to be prosecuted for his actions on the field. He was convicted of assault in Govan Police Court in December 1888 for fighting with Robert Buchanan of Abercorn. That was all forgotten when Thirds won the Scottish Cup in 1889 in the so-called 'snow final', and a couple of months later Lochhead was capped against Wales, playing alongside no fewer than five other Third Lanark men. With Scottish football still nominally amateur, he took another chance on English football and joined Everton in February 1891 with an £80 signing fee in his pocket and a £3 weekly wage on top. He left after a year but had to wait for an amnesty the following summer before he could resume playing with Thirds. Scottish football was still a tough prospect, as he found out in an early match when he was knocked out by a Rangers player, and he had a further injury later in the season. He appears to have stopped playing in the summer of 1893, then picked up again three years later and turned out for a variety of local sides in Renfrewshire. He was much admired in football circles and when he was in poor health in 1910 a benefit match was played for him at Barrhead. He spent the rest of his life in Barrhead with a home in Main Street until his death in hospital in 1939.

Jimmy LOGAN (1/1, 1891)
James Logan
Born 24 June 1870 Portland Street, Troon, Ayrshire
Died 25 May 1896 Leopold Street, Loughborough, Leicestershire
Scotland v Wales 1891 (1).
Ayr 1889-91; Sunderland 1891-92; Ayr Aug-Oct 1892; Aston Villa Oct 1892-93; Notts County Oct 1893-95 (FA Cup 1894); Dundee Mar-May 1895 [guest for Ayr Apr 1895]; Newcastle United 1895-96; Loughborough Athletic Jan-Apr 1896.
Brought up in Troon, Logan was a talented but erratic centre forward. He was capped early in his career while with Ayr, scoring Scotland's opening goal on his debut against Wales in 1891, which would prove to be his only international honour. He moved to Sunderland that summer although he was largely a reserve and only played a couple of times as they won the league. He returned to Ayr to weigh up his options and tried again at Aston Villa, where opportunities were limited and he left them just after the start of a league-winning season. He finally found his niche at Notts County, at that time in the Second Division, scored freely and played a key role in their FA Cup run in 1893-94, the undoubted highlight being his hat-trick against Bolton Wanderers in the final, a feat which was described as 'one of the most wonderful exhibitions ever given by an individual in a big game.' Sadly his form did not last, and he played briefly back in Scotland with Dundee and Ayr before Newcastle took a chance on him, then six months later he was passed on to Loughborough Athletic. They were in the lower reaches of the Second Division and he played well enough but soon died in tragic circumstances. On Easter Saturday, 4 April 1896, he played for Loughborough at Newton Heath in torrential rain, wearing his own clothes as the team kit had failed to arrive. With nothing to change into for the journey home, he contracted a chill which developed into pneumonia and a few weeks later he was dead, aged just 25.

Tom LOGAN (1/0, 1913)
Thomas Logan
Born 17 August 1888 Grahamston, Barrhead, Renfrewshire
Died 21 June 1962 Altgolach, Pirnmill, Isle of Arran
Scotland v Ireland 1913.
Barrhead Fereneze; Arthurlie 1908-10; Falkirk 1910-13 (Scottish Cup 1913); Chelsea 1913-21 [loan to Dunfermline Athletic Apr 1916, Falkirk 1917-18]; Arthurlie 1922-23.
Logan won the Scottish Consolation Cup in 1910 with his local team Arthurlie, then joined Falkirk that summer. He played at inside right alongside his brother Alec, who was centre forward and despite finishing as top scorer in his first season, he dropped back to centre half and steadily improved to international class. He won his Scotland cap in March 1913 as a late replacement for Charlie Thomson, who had to drop out because of a cup replay, and the following month he had further cause for celebration as Falkirk won the Scottish Cup, with Logan scoring the second and clinching goal that saw off Raith Rovers. That summer he moved to Chelsea for a fee of over £2,000 and had two seasons in London, reaching the FA Cup final in 1915 which was lost to Sheffield United, before war intervened. He got married a few days after the final and returned to Scotland where his club gave him permission to join Partick Thistle but he did not play any matches, having joined the Argyll & Sutherland Highlanders. In 1916 he was injured on active service in France, and later returned to the UK to train for a commission, which gave him the opportunity to play for Falkirk again. In 1919 he was posted to India for several months, and after he was demobilised in October he returned to Chelsea where, despite standing six feet tall, he found himself the smallest of their half-back line alongside Nils Middelboe and Harry Wilding. He last played for Chelsea in the autumn of 1920 and spent over a year on the transfer list before ending his career where it began, at Arthurlie. A scratch golfer, he took part in the 1922 Amateur Championship. He worked for many years as a commercial traveller in Barrhead until he retired to a farm in Arran, where he died. He had two well-known footballing brothers, James of Aston Villa and Rangers, and Alec of many clubs including Hibs, Aston Villa and Falkirk.

Willie LONEY (2/0, 1910)
William Loney
Born 31 May 1879 Stirling Street, Denny, Stirlingshire
Died 6 March 1956 Halgreen Avenue, Drumchapel, Glasgow
Scotland v Wales 1910; Ireland 1910.

Denny Athletic; Celtic 1900-13 (Scottish League 1905, 1906, 1907, 1908, 1909, 1910; Scottish Cup 1904, 1908, 1912); Motherwell Oct 1913-14; Partick Thistle 1914-15 [guest for Clydebank 1915-16].

A versatile player who joined Celtic as a centre half, Loney was tough enough to be known as 'the obliterator' in the famous six-in-a-row team. He had the dribbling skills to feature on the right wing and was later quoted as saying 'I was practically a sixth forward and it was a poor season when I did not score a number of goals.' He won six league titles and two Scottish Cups with Celtic but injury and illness caused him to miss much of the 1906-07 season, while he was ruled out of Celtic's cup victories of 1907 and 1912. Although he had represented Glasgow against Sheffield in 1902, his first international experience did not come until 1909 when he was selected for the Scottish League, then the following year he was finally capped twice by Scotland at the age of 30, against Wales and Ireland. He played twice more for the League that year. When he left Celtic in 1913 he still had a couple of years left in him and played for Motherwell, Partick Thistle and Clydebank before retiring; his last match was the Dunbartonshire Charity Cup final of 1916 which Clydebank lost to Renton. A saddler by trade, he was brought up in Denny, where his uncle was Provost, and later lived in Glasgow. His brother James played for Clyde and Dundee United.

'Plum' LONGAIR (1/0, 1894)
William Longair
Born 19 July 1870 Laing Street, Hilltown, Dundee
Died 28 November 1926 Royal Infirmary, Dundee
Scotland v Ireland 1894.
Rockfield; Dundee East End 1888-93; Dundee 1893-96 [guest for Newton Heath Apr 1895]; Sunderland Aug-Dec 1896; Burnley Dec 1896-97; Dundee 1897-98; Brighton United 1898-99; Dundee 1899-1902.

A no-nonsense half back who was described in the *Scottish Referee* as 'burly, brusque and fearless', Longair was one of the early success stories of football in the city of Dundee. He had five years as captain of East End, where he earned several selections for Forfarshire, before his club merged with Our Boys to form Dundee in 1893. A year later he was one of three Dundee players to be capped in the win over Ireland in Belfast, but that turned out to be his only selection although he later played in several international trials. His career was punctuated with several short spells in England, including single appearances for Newton Heath and Sunderland and a few months at Burnley, but each time he came home to Dundee. Towards the end of the decade he also had a season in the Southern League with Brighton United, who bought no less than six Dundee players for their first season, then had to release them after a year for financial reasons. He developed a lifelong devotion to his club and after he retired in 1902 he was appointed Dundee trainer, a role he held until 1922, and then remained on the staff as groundsman until his death from cancer aged 56. He had an interesting family background, as his uncle was Lord Provost of Dundee while his son Alexander was a nuclear scientist in WW2 and worked on the first atom bombs.

Andy LOVE (3/1, 1931)
Andrew Robb Love
Born 26 March 1905 Hairst Street, Renfrew, Renfrewshire
Died 3 November 1962 Tor-na-Dee, Hilltimber, Aberdeen
Scotland v Austria 1931; Italy 1931; Switzerland 1931 (1).
Kirkintilloch Rob Roy 1923-25 [trials for Rangers & Dundee]; Aberdeen Mar 1925-35; Aldershot 1935-36; Montrose Dec 1936-Jan 1937.

An attacking winger, Love was well regarded as a junior in Kirkintilloch and played trials for Rangers and Dundee before Aberdeen signed him in the spring of 1925. Although it took a couple of years for him to become established in the first team, he went on to spend ten years at Pittodrie, usually on the left and sometimes on the right. He scored many goals, generally reaching double figures each season, although his primary role was to provide crosses for the prolific Benny Yorston in the centre forward position. He made one appearance for the Scottish League against the Irish in 1929, and was then selected for Scotland's tour of Europe in May 1931, playing in all three matches, with the satisfaction of scoring a last-minute winner against Switzerland, but that was to prove his final cap. He barely featured in the Aberdeen side after 1933 and was given a free transfer in 1935, which gave him the opportunity to go south for a season at Aldershot in the Third Division South. A brief connection with Montrose on his return came to nothing and he retired from the game in 1937. He remained in the north-east and was a caretaker at King's College in Aberdeen when he died of a brain tumour aged 57.

Alex LOW (1/0, 1933)
Alexander Innes Low
Born 12 December 1908 Greenhill, Bonnybridge, Stirlingshire
Died 22 February 1994 Falkirk Royal Infirmary, Stirlingshire
Scotland v Ireland 1933.
Bonnybridge Caledonia; Bankfoot; Falkirk Nov 1929-35; Workington 1935-38; Raith Rovers 1938-46 [guest for Dundee United May 1942].

Low came from junior football to Falkirk in late 1929 and went straight into the team where he developed a reputation as a thoroughly reliable, if unspectacular, centre half. He was rated highly enough to be capped against Ireland in the autumn of 1933 but it was not a match to remember as Scotland slumped to a home defeat and he was heavily criticised for his performance. It was to prove the highpoint of his career as he left Falkirk in the summer of 1935 when the club was relegated, following a disagreement about a benefit match. He spent the next three years at Workington in the obscurity of the North-Eastern League until Sandy Archibald brought him back to Scotland with Raith Rovers in 1938. He played for the Fife club throughout the Second World War while working in the shipyards, playing his last match in December 1945. He lived in his native Bonnybridge until his death in 1994.

Jimmy LOW (1/1, 1891)
James Low
Born 1 June 1863 Silvergrove Street, Bridgeton, Glasgow
Died 29 January 1939 Main Street, Cambuslang, Lanarkshire
Scotland v Ireland 1891 (1).
Cambuslang 1883-96.

A centre forward or inside right, Low scored for Scotland after just six minutes of his only international, against Ireland in 1891. By then he had ample experience of representative football, having played regularly for Lanarkshire since 1884. His only senior club was Cambuslang, then a force in the game and a founding member of the Scottish League, although he missed their Scottish Cup final defeat of 1888. After a long playing career with the club he retired in 1896 and served on the committee. He spent all his life in the town and was still employed as a greenkeeper at Kirkhill Golf Course when he died of a heart attack at home aged 72. The elder brother of Tommy (below), his 19-year-old son Thomas Pollock Low was killed in action on 16 June 1917.

Tommy LOW (1/0, 1897)
Thomas Pollock Low
Born 3 October 1874 Rosebank Buildings, Cambuslang, Lanarkshire
Died 11 December 1938 La Jolla, San Diego, California, USA
Scotland v Ireland 1897.
Cambuslang Rangers; Cambuslang Hibs; Parkhead [trial for Blackburn Rovers Sep 1896]; Rangers 1896-99 (Scottish Cup 1897); Dundee 1899-1900; Woolwich Arsenal 1900-01; Falkirk 1901-02; Abercorn Feb-Mar 1905; Rangers Mar-Nov 1905; Dunfermline Athletic Nov 1905-06; Morton 1906-07.

The younger brother of Jimmy (above), Low was a lively outside right who had a lengthy apprenticeship in the junior game and did not turn senior until he was 22. While at Parkhead he won a Scotland junior cap in 1896 against England, partnering Bobby Walker on the right wing. That autumn he played a trial at outside right for Blackburn Rovers at Ibrox and so impressed the home side that he signed for Rangers right after the game. He made his debut in October, with half the league season already played, and quickly formed a terrific wing partnership with John McPherson which was so effective that in his first season with Rangers he won three winners' medals in the Scottish Cup, Glasgow Cup and Charity Cup. He was also good enough to be selected for Scotland against Ireland and for the Scottish League against the English, scoring the opening goal in a 3-0 win. It was an impressive start to his career but unfortunately he could not maintain his form and made only sporadic appearances for Rangers in 1897-98, winning another Glasgow Cup but missing the Scottish Cup final. He went almost completely off the radar at Ibrox after that and took the opportunity to move on, first to Dundee in 1899 and then to Arsenal for a year before arriving at Falkirk in 1901. They played in the Scottish Combination, and when they released him at the end of the season he was left in limbo as Arsenal still held his registration and he could not sign for anyone else without their permission. He wasted almost three years out of the game until Abercorn negotiated his release in February 1905. A few weeks later he found himself back at Rangers, who signed him in an emergency to pitch him into the Scottish Cup final replay against Third Lanark, but he was out of condition and the game was lost. He only played three league matches for Rangers before they released him that autumn, and he wound up his career at Dunfermline and Morton. He emigrated in 1910 and found work in Los Angeles as a shipping clerk for AG Spalding, the sports manufacturer, then became a golf pro at La Jolla Country Club near San Diego. He became a US citizen and remained in California until his death in 1938.

Wilfy LOW (5/0, 1911-20)
Wilfrid Lawson Low
Born 8 December 1885 Stafford Street, Aberdeen
Died 30 April 1933 Royal Victoria Infirmary, Newcastle-upon-Tyne
Scotland v Wales 1911; England 1911, 1920; Ireland 1912, 1920.
Abergeldie [trial for Montrose May 1904]; Aberdeen 1904-09 (Scottish Qualifying Cup 1904); Newcastle United 1909-24 (FA Cup 1910) [guest during WW1 for Hartlepools United 1915-16, Huddersfield Town Sep-Nov 1916, Rotherham County Nov 1916, Fulham Dec 1916-19].

An apprentice stonecutter, Low was described as 'best Aberdeen granite' when joined Aberdeen from Abergeldie juniors in the summer of 1904. A muscular centre half who was not afraid to use his strength against opposition forwards, he had five years at Pittodrie. After spending most of his first season in the reserves, he had an early success in the Scottish Qualifying Cup in November 1904 and was soon impressing in Division One with his hard work and strong performances. He was sold to Newcastle in the summer of 1909, and at the end of his first season he had an FA Cup winner's medal, while he also played in the 1911 final. He came into the national team, winning his first Scotland caps against Wales and England in 1911 while the following year against Ireland he gave away a penalty, although it mattered little in Scotland's 4-1 win. When Newcastle United shut down in 1915 he played as a guest for various teams while serving with the Anti-Aircraft Corps and Royal Engineers. Then, when he was posted south, he played for Fulham until he was demobbed in 1919. When he returned to action for Newcastle he had clearly lost none of his power and was recalled to the Scotland team for two internationals in 1920, eight years after his previous cap. He retired in 1924 and remained at St James' Park as assistant trainer and then groundsman until 1933 when he was knocked down by a car in St Thomas Street, near his home in Leazes Terrace. He was admitted to hospital in a critical condition, suffering from a fractured skull, but could not be saved and died 24 hours later. Newcastle staged a benefit match in aid of his family that autumn. His brother Harry played for Sunderland, also at centre half.

Jimmy LOWE (1/1, 1887)
James Lowe
Born 26 November 1863 South Richmond Street, Southside, Edinburgh
Died 17 July 1922 Mertoun Place, Merchiston, Edinburgh
Scotland v Ireland 1887 (1).
Brunswick 1881-82; St Bernard's Nov 1882-92.
An excellent left-sided forward, Lowe represented Edinburgh no less than 19 times, the first three appearances coming in 1882 while he was still at Brunswick. Later that year he joined St Bernard's, who were so keen to recruit him that they abandoned their own rule that players must live in Stockbridge, and he spent a fine decade with Saints. Although he did not win any trophies with the club, his talent was recognised in 1887 when he was selected for Scotland, and he scored the final goal in the 4-1 win over Ireland at Hampden Park. He played well and was named as a reserve for the other internationals that season, but was not chosen again. The year after winning his cap he was appointed captain of St Bernard's, and he carried on playing until 1892. He followed an unusual trade, being a bell hanger in the city. He died in 1922 and was buried in North Merchiston Cemetery.

Jimmy LUNDIE (1/0, 1886)
James Lynden or Lundie
Born 3 September 1861 The Green, Kilwinning, Ayrshire
Died 16 August 1942 Cleethorpes Road, Grimsby, Lincolnshire
Scotland v Wales 1886.
Lugar Boswell 1880-83; Hibernian 1883-87 (Scottish Cup 1887) [guest for St Bernard's Apr 1885]; Grimsby Town 1887-96.
Lundie was one of several Lugar Boswell players who moved to Edinburgh in 1883 to transform the fortunes of Hibernian. He already had an excellent reputation, having won the Ayrshire Cup in 1881 and was seen as a powerful right back. In 1886, he and Jimmy McGhee became the first Hibs players to be capped by Scotland and he strolled through a 4-1 win over Wales at Hampden Park, but unfortunately headed an own goal towards the end. According to the *Edinburgh Evening News* he otherwise played a capital game but it was his only international honour. The following season he won the Scottish Cup as Hibs beat Dumbarton 2-1 in the final, the first time the cup came east, and he used that as a springboard to turn professional with Grimsby Town. It was not quite the football backwater that it sounds, as the club was investing heavily in new players and they reached the last 16 of the FA Cup in 1889, then were founder members of the Football League Second Division in 1892. Lundie became an integral part of the team and an early history of Grimsby Town paid him fulsome praise: 'It is exceedingly doubtful when he was at his best whether there was another back in the country to equal him. Cool, gentlemanly on the field to a degree, he scored to take advantage of a foe, and never during his career with the Fisheries was he known to give a foul.' He settled permanently in the town, working as a labourer for a fish merchant in the docks until his death in 1942. He is buried in Scartho Road Cemetery with his wife Catherine, whom he married in 1902. His younger brother John also played for Hibs in 1886. NB he is recorded at birth and in census returns as James Lynden, but changed his surname to Lundie about 1880.

Jack LYALL (1/0, 1905)
John Lyall
Born 16 April 1881 Alexander Street, Hilltown, Dundee
Died 12 February 1944 Washtenaw Street, Detroit, Michigan, USA
Scotland v England 1905.
Jarrow 1899-1901; Sheffield Wednesday Feb 1901-09 (Football League 1903, 1904; FA Cup 1907); Manchester City 1909-11 (Second Division 1910); Dundee Apr 1911-14; Ayr United Jan 1914-15; Jarrow 1915-16; Sheffield Wednesday 1916-17; Palmers Mar 1920.

Born in Dundee, Lyall moved to Jarrow as a young boy when his father found work there, and grew up in the north-east of England. He worked as a plasterer while playing football for Jarrow, who won the Durham Cup in 1900, and signed full-time for Sheffield Wednesday early the following year. Standing at 6 feet 2 inches, he had the ideal build for a goalkeeper and in eight years with Wednesday he won two league titles and the FA Cup. He was selected just once for Scotland, 1905, and was partly blamed for the defeat to England after conceding a late goal. Curiously it was said in his obituaries that he had previously been picked for England before it was discovered he was born north of the border, but this appears to be apocryphal. After falling out with Wednesday over the terms of a benefit, he moved on to Manchester City in 1909, helping them to promotion and the Second Division title in his first season, then lost his place the following year and joined Dundee in April 1911. Early in 1914 he joined Ayr United, then returned to Jarrow in 1915. He played for them when he could in the North Eastern League during WW1 while he served with the Royal Engineers although at one point, finding himself based in Yorkshire, he spent the best part of a season with Sheffield Wednesday. He served abroad from early 1917, in South Africa and then India, once travelling 2,000 miles to play in an Army cup-tie. When he came home to Jarrow in 1919 he played briefly with the Palmers company team, and went into business with his brothers as Lyall Brothers, plasterers. With his health failing, in 1925 he emigrated with his family to Michigan, where he continued to work as a plasterer and later as a janitor. Interviewed by a local paper he was asked what it was like to be a star footballer and responded: 'It was grand to be in it, and I guess I was pretty good. I must have been pretty good, but I never knew it. I was too busy playing soccer.' He died in Detroit in 1944.

M

James McADAM (1/1, 1880)
James McAdam
Born 30 March 1860 Thornliebank, Renfrewshire
Died 16 October 1911 Manhattan State Hospital, New York, USA
Scotland v Wales 1880 (1).
Kerland; Third Lanark 1878-81; Cumbrae 1881-84.
McAdam joined Third Lanark as an 18-year-old student teacher in 1878 and played as a forward for the club for three years. He won a single Scotland cap against Wales in 1880, three days before his 20th birthday, scoring one of the goals in a 5-1 victory. Then, having qualified as a teacher, he left Glasgow in September 1881 to take up an appointment as assistant master at Cumbrae Public School in Millport. He continued to play football and organised a team on the island, leading Cumbrae to victory in the Rothesay Challenge Cup in 1882, as well as returning occasionally to turn out for Third Lanark. In 1884 he was described as 'the presiding genius of football in Millport' but in October that year something went seriously wrong at work. The school board took a unanimous decision to suspend him, for reasons not stated in their minutes, and he immediately resigned. That appears to have prompted him to leave Scotland to emigrate to the USA, and although his movements are hard to track he worked as a bookkeeper clerk in Philadelphia. However, his health went downhill and he died aged 51 after a lengthy spell in a New York hospital that specialised in mental illness. He never married.

Dan McARTHUR (3/0, 1895-99)
Daniel McArthur
Born 9 August 1867 Bargeddie, Lanarkshire
Died 11 November 1943 Crail Street, Parkhead, Glasgow
Scotland v Ireland 1895; England 1895; Wales 1899.
Parkhead; Celtic 1892-1902 (Scottish League 1896, 1898; Scottish Cup 1899, 1900); Clyde 1903-04.

McArthur did not join a senior club until he was 25, having spent several years as a goalkeeper in the junior ranks with Parkhead. He had other things to worry about as his wife Mary died aged 24, leaving him with two young daughters. What is more, even after he arrived at Celtic in 1892 he was a reserve to Joe Cullen and did not establish himself as first choice for a couple of years. Making up for lost time, he was soon among the honours, and in his first full season made his international debut against Ireland in 1895. A week later, he found himself facing England at Goodison Park and was on the end of a 3-0 defeat; it was another four years before the selectors chose him for the third and last time. However, he had plenty of success with Celtic, winning two league titles and two Scottish Cups, not to mention several Glasgow Cup medals. He also made four appearances for the Scottish League but was heavily criticised for letting in four to the English in 1899. Although on the small side, reported as 5 feet 6 inches, he was brave with a reputation for throwing himself about in an era when goalkeepers had no protection apart from their own toughness. He was given a benefit match against Rangers in 1901 which raised about £150 for him, and retired due to his cumulative injuries in 1902. He was coaxed back a year later by Clyde then broke a rib in only his third match and that was that. A steel dresser, he worked on the Celtic ground staff for a while then emigrated to Canada in 1922. He returned to Scotland in 1935 and in his later years was given a weekly pension by the club in recognition of his fearless contributions. He died in 1943 and was buried in the Eastern Necropolis, in the shadow of Celtic Park.

Andy McATEE (1/0, 1913)
Andrew McAtee
Born 2 July 1888 Smithston Row, Smithston, Dunbartonshire
Died 14 July 1956 Dalshannon View, Condorrat, East Dunbartonshire
Scotland v Wales 1913.
Smithston Hibs; Smithston Albion; Kilsyth Harp; Kilsyth Emmet; Mossend Hibernian; Celtic 1910-24 (Scottish League 1914, 1915, 1916, 1917, 1919, 1922; Scottish Cup 1911, 1912, 1914, 1923); New Bedford Whalers 1925-26; Newark Skeeters 1926.
A coal miner, McAtee followed in the footsteps of Jimmy Quinn, who also came from the mining village of Smithston, which was demolished in the 1930s. He had a lengthy apprenticeship in the juvenile and junior ranks, where he scored many goals, and was already 22 when he was given a trial with Celtic in September 1910. His speed and strength were so impressive that he was immediately signed by the Parkhead club and spent the rest of his professional career there, starring on the right wing as the team won six league championships and four Scottish Cups. His one Scotland cap in 1913 was scant reward for his talent, although he did play seven times for the Scottish League. In January 1914 McAtee was on his way with the Celtic team to play in Dundee when he heard his father had been killed by a train, and returned home. As a miner he was initially exempted from military service in WW1 due to being engaged on work of national importance, but he finally signed up with the Royal Field Artillery in February 1918 and saw action in France in the last year of the War.

He was back at Parkhead early in 1919 and slotted straight into a league-winning side, remaining a first team regular until he was released by Celtic in 1924. Although several clubs wanted to sign him, he was out of football for a year before being persuaded to try his luck in America and he spent 18 months there with appearances for New Bedford Whalers and Newark Skeeters. He returned to Scotland in December 1926 and went back to the coal mines. His nephew, Anthony McAtee, signed for Celtic in 1942 but only made four appearances.

Jimmy McAULAY (9/1, 1882-87)
James McAulay
Born 28 August 1860 Balagan, Bonhill, Dunbartonshire
Died 13 January 1943 Bellsdyke Hospital, Larbert, Stirlingshire
Scotland v Wales 1882 (1), 1883, 1885, 1887c; England 1883, 1884, 1885, 1886, 1887c.
Albion; Dumbarton 1878-87 (Scottish Cup 1883).

McAulay started out as a centre forward and played up front in the Scottish Cup finals of 1881 and 1882, as well as his first international in 1882, when he scored for Scotland against Wales. However, that summer he made an inspired move into goal and remained there, performing so well that he earned the title Prince of Goalkeepers. In his first season in goal, he was capped against Wales and England, as well as winning his only major domestic honour, the Scottish Cup, when Dumbarton defeated Vale of Leven in the replayed final of 1883. He retained his place in the Scotland team facing England for five consecutive years and one of his opponents, Charles Wreford-Brown, recalled one outstanding save in 1884 and wrote of his talents in glowing terms: 'He was a wonderful keeper, with the eye of a hawk, the agility of a cat and the power of using his feet as readily as his hands. Some of his performances partook of the nature of conjuring, so marvellous did they appear to be.' A marine engineer, McAulay's football career came to an abrupt end in April 1887, just a month after captaining Scotland to two fine victories over England and Wales, when he went to Burma to work for the Irrawaddy Flotilla Company, which operated steamers on the Irrawaddy River. He later returned to live in Dumbarton and was appointed an Honorary Sheriff Substitute. In 1930 he was invited to the England v Scotland match at Wembley, which was reported to be the first international he had seen since 1887. He died in hospital in 1943 after several years' illness.

John MACAULAY (1/0, 1884)
John Macaulay
Born 3 October 1860 Main Street, Barrhead, Renfrewshire
Died 4 December 1942 Lower Black Moss Farm, Barley, Lancashire
Scotland v Ireland 1884.
Barrhead Rangers 1879-81; Arthurlie 1881-84; Padiham 1884; Union Star 1884-87; Brierfield 1887-89; Union Star 1889-91.

Macaulay was established as a talented right winger with Arthurlie and had already represented Scotch Counties when he won his Scotland cap against Ireland in 1884, a late selection after Woody Gray pulled out. That summer, in the face of industrial unrest locally in Barrhead, he was attracted south by the prospect of a secure job in a cotton mill in Lancashire, and unusually he did not go to one of the bigger teams and settled down to spend the rest of his life in Burnley. In 1937 the *Burnley Express* reported on his golden wedding celebration, and revealed that he was still working as a beamer in Emmott's Stanley Mill at the age of 76. The article gave a fascinating account of his move south: 'He was a brass moulder by trade, but as a dispute arose at the Scottish works at which he was employed he obtained a travelling card from his union and came to England in search of work in 1884. After visiting several towns he called upon an old chum at Padiham, none other than Billy McFetridge, who was then playing for the Padiham team. McFetridge and Jim McConnell, the Padiham goalkeeper, prevailed upon Mr Macaulay to play for Padiham, and he agreed to do so on condition that they found him work. This was found for him and he played for Padiham for about three months, teams he played against including Blackburn Rovers and Bolton Wanderers. The following season he joined up with Burnley Union Star and he obtained employment at Grey's mill, where he was taught to beam.'

Bob MacAULAY (2/0, 1931)
Robert MacAulay
Born 28 August 1904 Bell's Row, Wishaw, Lanarkshire
Died 25 January 1994 Royal Edinburgh Hospital, Edinburgh
Scotland v Ireland Sep 1931; Wales 1931.
Wishaw YMCA; Lachine; Grenadier Guards; Montreal Carsteel 1925-27; Providence Clamdiggers 1927-28; Fall River Marksmen 1928-30 (US Challenge Cup 1930); Rangers 1930-32 (Scottish Cup 1932); Chelsea 1932-36; Cardiff City Dec 1936-37; Sligo Rovers 1937-38 player-manager; Workington 1938-39; Raith Rovers 1939-40.

MacAulay grew up in Wishaw and emigrated to Montreal in 1922 when he was 17, after a few appearances on the wing for Wishaw YMCA. He worked as a machinist in Montreal while he played in Canadian soccer until he was 26, at first with local side Lachine, then he joined Grenadier Guards (which had no military connection) where he developed into a fine left back and was coached by England internationalist Steven Bloomer. Although he sometimes appeared ponderous he could put on a great burst of speed when required. He was offered an expenses-paid trial in England with Everton in 1925, but decided to remain in Canada and turned professional with Montreal Carsteel. Meanwhile he had married but when his wife died tragically young in the summer of 1927, soon after he played for Montreal All Stars against the touring Scottish FA side, he moved to the USA. He had a season with Providence Clamdiggers, then joined Fall River, winning the US National Challenge Cup in 1930; they won the Eastern Cup to qualify for a play-off with Western winners Bruell Insurance, and took the title on a 9-3 aggregate. That summer, Rangers played against him on their transatlantic tour and were impressed enough to invite him to Ibrox, and he accepted their offer. It took some time to adjust to Scottish football and he spent most of his first year in the reserves before coming into the side late in the season as part of the Charity Cup-winning eleven in May. He secured a regular first team place at the start of the following season but it was a major surprise that he was considered for honours so quickly, winning his first Scotland cap in September. In fact all his international appearances came in a six-week spell in the autumn of 1931, for Scotland against Ireland and Wales, either side of a game for the Scottish League. A notable campaign ended with a Scottish Cup victory over Kilmarnock then Chelsea paid a substantial fee to take him south in 1932. He had four years at Stamford Bridge before winding up with a series of short contracts in Wales, Ireland, England and Scotland. He returned to live in Edinburgh, where he worked as a warehouse foreman, coached Dalkeith Thistle for a while, and was chief scout for Rangers until 1979. NB his name is widely spelled McAuley but all his certificates say MacAulay.

Eddie McBAIN (1/0, 1894)
Edward Cunningham McBain
Born 30 April 1869 Old Smithhills, Paisley, Renfrewshire
Died 13 April 1911 Cotton Street, Paisley, Renfrewshire
Scotland v Wales 1894.
St Mirren 1887-98.

A right half-back, McBain followed his elder brother William into the St Mirren ranks (which also had an Alex McBain, no relation) and soon rose from the third team to the first. He found almost immediate success by winning the Renfrewshire Cup in 1888, just before his 19th birthday, and became a mainstay of the team over the following decade. A newspaper praised him as an 'out-and-out Saint', describing him as 'like a running stream, his play always pleases the eye and keeps his opponents on the move'. It was an exciting era for St Mirren which included taking part in the inaugural season of the Scottish Football League in 1890, and they held their own in the division throughout the decade. McBain captained Renfrewshire on numerous occasions, and made a single Scotland appearance in 1894 against Wales; he was later capped twice by the Scottish League. In his final year as a player he won the Renfrewshire Cup for the fifth time, shortly before retiring in the summer of 1898. A riveter in a shipyard, he was just 41 when he died after a long illness.

Neil McBAIN (3/0, 1922-24)
Neil McBain
Born 15 November 1895 Kinloch Road, Campbeltown, Argyllshire
Died 13 May 1974 Ailsa Hospital, Ayr
Scotland v England 1922; Ireland 1923; Wales 1924.
Kintyre; Campbeltown Academicals Mar 1913-14; Ayr United 1914-21 [guest during WW1 for Portsmouth 1916-17]; Manchester United Nov 1921-23; Everton Jan 1923-26; St Johnstone 1926-28; Liverpool Mar-Nov 1928; Watford Nov 1928-31; New Brighton Mar 1947 [emergency].

Neil McBain's great claim to fame is that he is the oldest player ever to appear in a Football League match. On 15 March 1947, aged 51 years and 120 days, he kept goal for New Brighton against Hartlepools United after two players failed to turn up. What is more, it was almost exactly 32 years after he made his professional debut for Ayr United, another record. Initially an inside left until he found his natural position at centre half, McBain learned his football in the Kintyre peninsula and joined an ambitious Campbeltown Academicals side, playing alongside Peter Pursell, another future internationalist. In June 1914, just after playing in the Renfrewshire Junior Cup final, he signed for Ayr United but as a member of the Territorial Force since 1912, when war broke out he was immediately called up for service with the Argyll and Sutherland Highlanders. This delayed his first senior match until March 1915, when – somewhat surprisingly – he was discharged from the Army for flat feet. He was later recalled, this time to the Royal Navy, which took him to the south coast, where he played for Portsmouth. He resumed at Ayr after being demobbed, still part-time while he worked as a joiner, until his mature performances persuaded Manchester United to pay £4,600 for him in 1921, and towards the end of the season he made his Scotland debut against England. Everton forked out another large fee in 1922, and his talent was rewarded with two more international caps in successive years. In 1926 he came back to Scotland with St Johnstone but there was a surprise move to Liverpool in March 1928, when they were desperately fighting relegation and needed his experience. Mission accomplished, he only stayed for a few months and his last club was Watford, initially as player-manager until he hung up his boots in 1931. This marked the start of a lengthy managerial career and he remained at Vicarage Road until 1937, then Ayr United for a season and Luton Town for 1938-39. After the War he managed New Brighton 1946-48, Leyton Orient 1948-49, coached in Argentina with Estudiantes 1950-52, Ayr United again 1955-56, Watford 1956-59 and finally Ayr United once more in 1962-63. Between posts he scouted for a variety of clubs.

Peter McBRIDE (6/0, 1904-09)
Peter Fisher McBride
Born 16 November 1874 Main Street, Newton-on-Ayr, Ayrshire
Died 3 January 1951 Sharoe Green Hospital, Preston, Lancashire
Scotland v England 1904, 1906, 1907, 1908; Wales 1907, 1909.
Westerlea; Fairfield; Westerlea; Ayr 1892-96; Preston North End Dec 1896-1913 (Division 2 1904); Fulwood Garrison Dec 1913.

Nearly six feet tall and weighing over 14 stone, McBride had the ideal build for a goalkeeper, although he was quoted as saying 'the eye has mair to dae wi' goalkeeping than inches'. He started out in junior football with Westerlea, and briefly with Fairfield, before joining Ayr in the summer of 1892. His first season was a strange introduction to senior football as Ayr played only cup-ties and friendlies, then when they entered the Ayrshire Combination he moved to centre forward with reasonable success. He reverted to goal in 1894 and despite Ayr's lowly status, he did well enough to play an international trial in 1895 and clearly he deserved a bigger stage. Late in 1896 he was transferred to Preston, where he spent the rest of his career. He was signed as a replacement for the great James Trainer and the terms of his transfer were reported as McBride earning £3 a week while Ayr were paid £55 for his release. Preston were fading from their glory days and were relegated in 1901, but McBride missed the last few games of the season after being injured in a Scotland trial, and his deputy conceded 15 goals. He remained loyal to the club in the Second Division, and helped them win the championship in 1904, the year he made his first Scotland debut. He went on to secure six caps, four of them against England. With Preston, his goalkeeping helped them to finish second in the First Division in 1906, with the best defensive record in the league, and he was first choice for 13 years, barring occasional accidents and internationals, and he still holds the club appearance record with 442 league matches. He made a brief comeback for Fulwood Garrison in December 1913. A slater to trade, he worked for the local council and lived in Ribbleton, on the outskirts of Preston.

'Baldie' McCALL (1/0, 1888)
Archibald McCall
Born 21 July 1861 Main Street, Renton, Dunbartonshire
Died 17 April 1936 Dumbarton Hospital, Dunbartonshire
Scotland v Ireland 1888.
Renton 1883-95 (Scottish Cup 1885, 1888) [guest for Celtic Apr 1892].

McCall played at right back through Renton's halcyon years, when the 'chicken bree' team won the Scottish Cup twice and were proclaimed as Champions of the World in 1888. He was capped by Scotland against Ireland that year, and later made two appearances for the Scottish League. His last big match before retiring was the Scottish Cup final of 1895 which Renton lost to St Bernard's. Later in life, while working as a bricklayer in Renton, he had the strange experience in 1928 of helping to build over the club's old ground at Tontine Park, which was being covered in houses. However, he refused to be sentimental and said: 'We must move with the times. Today there is no necessity for the old football ground in Renton as a football enclosure; and there is a crying need for new houses. There is none prouder than me of what the old club did. The Renton champions were certainly the superiors of many Glasgow senior clubs in their heyday. But money, or the lack of it, made it impossible for us to compete with the town clubs once they made the game a business.' He was elder half-brother of Jimmy McCall (below), and they both guested in a friendly for Celtic against Nottingham Forest in April 1892, having already played in a league match for Renton against Clyde the same day.

Jimmy McCALL (5/1, 1886-90)
James McCall
Born 2 March 1865 Main Street, Renton, Dunbartonshire
Died 16 February 1925 Leven Street, Renton, Dunbartonshire
Scotland v Wales 1886, 1887; England 1887 (1), 1888, 1890.
Renton 1883-99 (Scottish Cup 1885, 1888) [guest for Celtic Apr 1892].

A fine dribbler, McCall played at inside left for the great Renton side of the 1880s and was a mainstay of the team for almost two decades. The younger half-brother of Archie (above) by his father's second wife, his first triumph came in the Scottish Cup of 1885 when he scored the opening goal of the replayed final, setting Renton on the way to victory over local rivals Vale of Leven. A year later he made his Scotland debut against Wales, and went on to win five caps by the end of the decade, three of them against England. Meanwhile he scored another goal in the final as Renton won the Scottish Cup for a second time in 1888, and again found the net as West Bromwich Albion were defeated 4-1 to secure the title of World Champions for the village club. He remained resolutely amateur despite the best efforts of English clubs to tempt him south, and in 1890 Preston North End reportedly offered him £250 just to play two matches. He refused, and Renton rewarded his loyalty by staging a benefit match against Celtic that summer which earned him over £100 and a gold watch. This generosity backfired as McCall was suspended by the SFA for professionalism. Nevertheless, he returned to the team as it entered the Scottish League, and made two appearances for League eleven in 1893 and 1894. He was also a champion of Renton Bowling Club. A builder to trade, he never married.

Neilly McCALLUM (1/1, 1888)
Neil (or Cornelius) McCallum
Born 3 July 1868 Braehead, Bonhill, Dunbartonshire
Died 5 November 1920 Barnhill Poorhouse, Edgefauld Road, Glasgow
Scotland v Ireland 1888 (1).
Renton 1885-88 (Scottish Cup 1888) [guest for Rangers Feb 1888; guest for Bohemians Jun 1888]; Celtic 1888-90; Blackburn Rovers Feb-Jul 1890; Nottingham Forest 1890-91; Celtic 1891-92 (Scottish Cup 1892); Nottingham Forest 1892-94; Newark 1894-95; Notts County 1895-96; Heanor Town 1896-97; Middleton 1897-98; Folkestone 1898-1902.
An obituary described McCallum as 'one of the cleverest, trickiest and brainiest outside rights that the Vale of Leven ever produced'. A precocious talent, before he was 20 he scored twice in Renton's Scottish Cup final victory of 1888 and once for Scotland as they beat Ireland 10-2. That summer, shortly after Renton won the 'World Championship' by beating West Bromwich Albion, he joined the newly-formed Celtic and scored the club's first ever goal, against Rangers Swifts. He was struck down by blood poisoning in January 1889 and reported to be dangerously ill, but a month later he was playing in the Scottish Cup 'snow final', which Celtic lost to Third Lanark. He was tempted south to Blackburn Rovers early in 1890, had a season with Nottingham Forest, then came back to Scotland in 1891 and played on the right wing in Celtic's first Scottish Cup victory the following spring. Although he was often mentioned as worthy of international honours his only further selection was for the Scottish League against the English in April 1892. That summer he went south for a second time and spent the rest of his playing career in England, moving around clubs in Nottinghamshire, at Forest for two years and a season each at Newark, Notts County and Heanor Town. After a short spell at Middleton, in Lancashire, he headed to Kent, where he captained Folkestone in the Kent League. He remained there for four years while he worked as a general labourer, but after a conviction for being drunk and disorderly in 1902 he returned to Glasgow. He worked as a motor machineman and did some odd jobs for Celtic as his life went downhill and he died in a Glasgow poorhouse in 1920. His family ensured he was given a decent burial and he lies in Vale of Leven Cemetery. NB at birth and death he was recorded as Neil but he sometimes used the forename Cornelius, such as when he married a Nottingham girl in September 1893; the marriage appears not have lasted as his death certificate said he was unmarried.

Billy McCARTNEY (1/0, 1902)
William McCartney
Born 30 April 1879 St Phillans, Largs, Ayrshire
Died 14 November 1945 Dunard Road, Rutherglen, Lanarkshire
Scotland v Ireland 1902.
Rutherglen Glencairn; Hibernian 1899-1903 (Scottish League 1903); Manchester United 1903-04; West Ham United 1904-05; Lochgelly United Oct 1905-07; Clyde 1906-08; Broxburn Sep-Nov 1908; Clyde Nov 1908-12.
Born at a country house near Largs, where his father was a coachman, McCartney moved to Rutherglen as a boy where he trained as a mechanical engineer. He was spotted playing junior football by Phil Kelso, who snapped him up for Hibs in September 1899 and he went straight into the first team at inside left. Hibs were on the cusp of success and McCartney played a major role in that, but a serious injury curtailed his chances of glory: in March 1902, just after his Scotland debut against Ireland and a Scottish League cap, he suffered a broken leg from a collision with Nicol Smith in the cup semi-final against Rangers. This caused him to miss not only a second Scotland cap as he had already been selected to face England, but also the famous Hibs victory in the Scottish Cup. However, a year later (having made a second appearance for the Scottish League) he was an integral part of the Hibs team which won the Scottish League. That side promptly broke up as the top talent were tempted south of the border, with McCartney joining Manchester United, but the move was not a great success and they let him go after one season. He went on to West Ham in the Southern League for a year, and returned to Scotland in the autumn of 1905 with Lochgelly United in the backwater of the Northern League, as Manchester United still held his league registration. It was not until the following year that Clyde formally negotiated his transfer from Old Trafford, although somewhat bizarrely in 1906 he reached an agreement which allowed him to play for Clyde in league matches, and for Lochgelly in cup ties. That arrangement only lasted one season, after which he focused on Clyde apart from a brief spell at Broxburn. He reached a second Scottish Cup final in 1910 but his chances of finally gaining a winner's medal were dashed when Clyde threw away a two goal lead in the last five minutes of the final, and eventually lost to Dundee in a second replay. A serious knee injury in late 1911 required an operation which meant the end of his playing career and Clyde held a benefit for him in July 1912. He was a storeman with a tube manufacturer in Rutherglen until he died suddenly in 1945 of a heart attack while on his way to work. His son Charlie played for Morton and Cowdenbeath in the 1930s.

Allan McCLORY (3/0, 1926-34)
Allan McClory
Born 11 November 1899 Bathville Row, Armadale, West Lothian
Died 10 July 1983 Fairmile Nursing Home, Edinburgh
Scotland v Wales 1926, 1934; Ireland 1928.
Bathville United; Harthill Athletic 1921-22; Bathville United 1922-23; Shotts United 1923-24; Motherwell 1924-37 (Scottish League 1932); Brideville player-manager 1937-38; Albion Rovers Nov 1938-40; Motherwell 1940-46; Montrose Sep-Dec 1946.

McClory was goalkeeper in the great Motherwell side which broke the Glasgow monopoly on the league title in 1932, the only time the championship left the city between the wars. He was brought up in a West Lothian mining community where his father was killed in an underground accident in 1916, and he also worked in the mines in his early years. His football career was almost over before it began as he had to take a year out through injury, and he was already 24 when he turned senior with Motherwell, having just won the Lanarkshire League with Shotts United. He spent the best years of his career at Fir Park yet despite his consistency he was only capped three times by Scotland, making his debut in 1926 against Wales, then a second cap in 1928 resulted in a home defeat to Ireland and he had to wait six years for his third. He also played twice for the Scottish League. In 1937 he thought about retiring but was hired by Brideville in Dublin as player-manager, then signed for Albion Rovers on his return. Remarkably he came back to Fir Park in 1940, although he was rarely in action at Motherwell during the war years. Finally in 1946 he made a surprising move to play for Montrose, then in Division C, but decided after three months that the travel was too much for him. He had just passed his 47th birthday when he played his final league game. Latterly he worked as a night watchman in a papermill.

Phil McCLOY (2/0, 1924-25)
Philip McCloy
Born 18 April 1896 Clova Terrace, Uddingston, Lanarkshire
Died 26 November 1971 St Bride's Way, Bothwell, Lanarkshire
Scotland v England 1924, 1925.
Uddingston St Johns; Mossend Hibs 1915-16; Kilsyth Emmet 1916-17; Parkhead 1917-18; Ayr United Sep 1918-25 [loan to Clyde Jan 1919]; Manchester City 1925-30 (Second Division 1928); Chester 1930-31; Cork Nov 1931-32; Stade Rennais Aug-Sep 1933; Workington Mar 1934; Kidderminster Harriers Jan-Feb 1935.

McCloy grew up in Uddingston and worked in the Lanarkshire coal mines during the First World War, having to wait until the conflict was over before his senior football career got underway. After a variety of junior clubs he signed in 1918 for Ayr United, where he formed a successful partnership at full back with Jock Smith, both of them winning their first caps together for Scotland against England in 1924. A year later in 1925 McCloy was initially named as a reserve but the late withdrawal of Jock Hutton earned him a second cap. Ayr were relegated that summer and he was transferred to Manchester City where he had an eventful five years, reaching the FA Cup final in his first season and suffering his second successive relegation. Subsequently City missed out on promotion on goal average but returned to the top flight as champions in 1928. He was 34 when he moved to Chester for a season in the Cheshire County League alongside Dave Morris, who had also been in the Scotland team against England in 1925. Subsequently, he struggled to find a club and over the next few years he had trials in the League of Ireland with Cork, in France with Rennes and briefly for Workington and Kidderminster. A joiner to trade, he returned to Lanarkshire when his playing days were over.

Bob McCOLL (13/13, 1896-1908)
Robert Smyth McColl
Born 13 April 1876 Holmhead Street, Townhead, Glasgow
Died 25 November 1958 Ayr Road, Newton Mearns, Renfrewshire
Scotland v Wales 1896, 1899 (3), 1900, 1901; Ireland 1896 (2), 1897 (1), 1898 (1), 1899 (3), 1908; England 1899, 1900 (3), 1901, 1902.
Benmore; Queen's Park Jan 1894-1901; Newcastle United Nov 1901-04 [guest for St Bernard's Dec 1901]; Rangers 1904-07; Queen's Park 1907-10.

A prince among centre forwards, McColl remains one of the most famous Scottish footballers thanks to his chain of newsagents. He was not powerfully built but had a lightning turn of speed with reflexes to match, and developed his talents with Queen's Park. He made his first team debut in the Glasgow Charity Cup as an 18-year-old and was consistently the club's top scorer for the rest of the decade. He could shoot powerfully with either foot, and won his first caps in 1896 while still a teenager. Although best remembered for his treble against England in 1900, in the famous 4-1 victory known as the 'Rosebery International', uniquely he scored a hat-trick against all three of the home nations, performing the feat against Wales and Ireland in 1899. At Queen's Park he was resolutely amateur, and it came as something of a surprise when he went to Newcastle United as a professional in the autumn of 1901. His Scotland career seemed to be over in 1902, but remarkably he was recalled in 1908 after a gap of six years. He also played once for the Scottish League. He returned to Scotland with Rangers in 1904, then rejoined Queen's Park in 1907 where he was considered such a special talent that the club made an exception to their rules and allowed him to revert to amateur status. He retired in 1910, although he could probably have carried on as he was Queen's Park's top scorer that season and notched a goal in each of his last three games. By then his business was taking up more of his time: together with his brother Tom, he had set up a chain of newsagents and confectioners and used his fame to publicise their growing portfolio by calling the shops RS McColl, earning him the nickname 'Toffee Bob'. They sold to Cadbury in 1933, and it has since changed ownership again, but the McColl name survives into the modern era. Another brother, Willie, was a Scottish boxing champion in the 1920s.

Will McCOLL (1/0, 1895)
William McColl
Born 19 February 1865 Drymen, Stirlingshire
Died 20 August 1903 District Asylum, Larbert, Stirlingshire
Scotland v Wales 1895.
Jamestown 1884-85; Vale of Leven 1885-87; Morton 1887-89; Burnley Dec 1889-90; Ardwick 1890-91; Jamestown 1891-93; Vale of Leven Oct 1893-94; Renton Oct 1894-95.
Born in Drymen with his mother's surname McMillan, he adopted McColl after his parents married in 1867. They moved to Jamestown in Dunbartonshire in the mid-1870s, where he lived for the rest of his short life and worked as a ham curer. He first made his mark at Vale of Leven at inside forward, where he was selected for the Dunbartonshire county team, then had a couple of years at Morton. Tall and strongly built, he turned professional with Burnley in December 1889 but only made five appearances and was mainly a reserve, so he signed for Ardwick the following summer and won a Manchester and District Cup medal in April 1891, defeating Newton Heath in the final (Manchester City v Manchester United in modern parlance). He returned to Scotland, was reinstated as an amateur, and rejoined Jamestown but appears to have played little football for the next couple of years. He had dropped back to centre half by the time he signed for Vale of Leven in the autumn of 1893. A year later he moved to neighbours Renton who, although in the Second Division, had some talent and reached the Scottish Cup final of 1895, losing to St Bernard's. That achievement was recognised when McColl was one of three Renton men to be capped against Wales, a few weeks past his 30th birthday, as a late replacement when Barbour dropped out. Not long afterwards, his career was ended abruptly by a badly broken leg in a match at Greenock in November 1895 which forced him to spend over a month in hospital. This may have contributed to his early death in 1903 aged just 38 of 'general paralysis of the insane', a medical term which refers to acute mental illness, although it is thought his death was hastened by a spinal injury incurred while playing. Through his son William (born 1897), he was grandfather of Ian McColl, Scotland internationalist in the 1950s and later national team manager.

Andy McCOMBIE (4/0, 1903-05)
Andrew McCombie
Born 30 January 1877 Leopold Place, Dingwall, Ross-shire
Died 28 March 1952 Lovaine Avenue, North Shields, Northumberland
Scotland v Wales 1903, 1905; England 1903, 1905.
Inverness Thistle 1893-99 (Highland League 1894); Sunderland Feb 1899-1904 (Football League 1902); Newcastle United Feb 1904-10 (Football League 1905, 1907).
As a young defender, McCombie won his first title in 1894 when Inverness Thistle topped the Highland League but it would take a few more years before his talent at right back was spotted by a bigger club. Sunderland signed him early in 1899 and he soon became an automatic choice, making over 160 appearances in five years, which include the league title in 1902. However, amid a wrangle with the club over money, he was transferred in 1904 to near rivals Newcastle United for what was then a record fee of £700. There, he had a key role in winning two Football League championships, played in the FA Cup finals of 1905 and 1906 which were both lost, and was still on the fringes of the team when they won the title again in 1909. On retiring from playing in 1910 he was appointed Newcastle's assistant trainer and he spent the rest of his life with the club, becoming head trainer in 1928. He stepped down from the role after a couple of years and ran an off licence in North Shields, but stayed on the club's staff until his death in 1952 – in fact he had been at St James' Park earlier on the day he suffered a fatal heart attack.

John McCORKINDALE (1/0, 1891)
John McCorkindale
Born 30 August 1867 Dalmuir, Dunbartonshire
Died 24 May 1953 Andrew Drive, Clydebank, Dunbartonshire
Scotland v Wales 1891.
Dalmuir Thistle; Partick Thistle Feb 1888-91 [guest for Rangers Feb 1890]; Clyde Jan 1892-94.
A well-respected goalkeeper, McCorkindale played over 130 matches in four years for Partick Thistle, and helped them reach the Glasgow Cup final in his first season although it was not a day to remember as he conceded eight goals. He also played once as a guest for Rangers in a friendly at Everton in February 1890 but again suffered the humiliation of letting in eight. Nevertheless, he won his Scotland cap against Wales the following year. After Thistle entered the Scottish Alliance in 1891, he left midway through the season to join Clyde, making his debut on New Year's Day 1892 in a friendly at Newcastle West End. After retiring from playing in 1894, he became a referee in the Scottish League but gave it up shortly after he was attacked by a mob following a Morton v Rangers match in December 1905; the ground was closed for a month as punishment. He lived in Clydebank, where he followed his trade as a joiner in a shipyard.

Robert McCORMICK (1/1, 1886)
Robert McCormick
Born 26 November 1864 Newton Street, Paisley, Renfrewshire
Died 28 July 1928 Halfway Street, West Kilbride, Ayrshire
Scotland v Wales 1886 (1).
Abercorn 1884-89; Stoke 1889-90; Abercorn Oct 1892.

A speedy right-sided forward with Paisley side Abercorn, McCormick represented Renfrewshire before going on to be selected for Scotland in April 1886, scoring the opening goal in a 4-1 win over Wales. He also made a name for himself by winning numerous local athletic competitions as a middle-distance runner. In the summer of 1889 he turned professional with Stoke but in December of his first season, playing against Burnley on a heavy pitch, he suffered such a serious leg break that his football career was effectively ended at the age of 25. He returned to Paisley and although he attempted a comeback with Abercorn in 1892 it came to nothing. He worked as a ceramic potter in the sanitaryware industry.

Davie McCRAE (2/0, 1929)
David McCrae
Born 24 February 1901 Gateside Cottage, Bridge of Weir, Renfrewshire
Died 24 October 1976 Royal Alexandra Hospital, Paisley, Renfrewshire
Scotland v Norway 1929; Germany 1929.
Kilmacolm; Bury Jan-May 1922; Denaby United 1922-23; Beith 1923-24; St Mirren Jan 1924-34 (Scottish Cup 1926); New Brighton Aug-Nov 1934; Queen of the South Nov 1934-35; Stranraer Jan 1935; Darlington Feb 1935; Beith Sep 1935; Glentoran Oct 1935-36.

A bustling centre forward, McCrae holds the record as St Mirren's all-time top scorer, netting 222 league goals over ten years, yet his career took some time to get under way. He started out with Kilmacolm Amateurs, and early in 1922 signed for Bury, where his brother was half-back. However, he never got further than the reserves, moved over to Denaby United for a season then returned to Scotland at Beith, who had just entered the Scottish Third Division. His big break came when he scored for Beith against St Mirren in a Scottish Cup tie early in 1924, and the Paisley club was so impressed by his performance that they wasted no time in securing his signature. As soon as he made his debut, it was clear he was the 'real deal' and he became a fixture in the side for a decade. The summit was reached in 1926 when St Mirren won the Scottish Cup for the first time, with McCrae heading the opener in their 2-0 win over Celtic. By 1929, he had reportedly scored an average of 38 goals a season in all matches over a five year period, an astonishing record which finally won him a call-up to the national team's summer tour of the continent. He duly scored twice in an unofficial game with a Norwegian select, then failed to find the net in two full internationals against Norway and Germany. Despite continuing his scoring form at home, he was not selected again, but there were many tempting offers to go south which his club resisted. He did eventually leave Paisley, having fallen out with the club hierarchy over money, a dispute that saw him suspended for two months, and he was dropped for the disastrous 1934 Scottish Cup final which was lost 5-0 to Rangers. He signed for New Brighton but could not settle, and over the next two years he played for a dizzying array of clubs, all on short contracts or on trial. Finally at Glentoran he concluded his playing career in some style by scoring sixteen goals in eight games, including five against Ards and two hat-tricks. After hanging up his boots in 1936 he joined the coaching staff at St Mirren, initially as assistant trainer then as trainer from 1939 to 1941. After that he had no direct involvement in the game but remained interested in football and was a regular spectator. He continued to live in Paisley where he was a fitter for Wimpey, and later a lathe operator in a steel factory. His elder brother James also had a long football career, playing for Clyde, West Ham and Bury among others, and coaching Egypt at the 1934 World Cup.

Andy McCREADIE (2/0, 1893-94)
Andrew McCreadie
Born 19 November 1870 Arch, Girvan, Ayrshire
Died 4 April 1916 Bain Street, Calton, Glasgow
Scotland v Wales 1893; England 1894.
Maybole; Cowlairs 1889-90; Rangers Mar 1890-94 (Scottish League 1891; Scottish Cup 1894); Sunderland 1894-96 (Football League 1895); Rangers Mar 1896-98 (Scottish Cup 1897); Bristol St George 1898-99.

Born and brought up in Girvan, McCreadie first played at Maybole where he represented Ayrshire before coming to Glasgow in the autumn of 1889. He was briefly with Cowlairs, where he was selected for the Glasgow North-Eastern Association team, then followed his elder brother Hugh (1867-1931) to Rangers in March 1890. The brothers played together at Ibrox for four seasons, with Andy at centre half and Hugh in the forward line, and they both won the shared league title of 1891 and the Scottish Cup in 1894. However, while Hugh was capped for the Scottish League, Andy went one better and was twice picked for the national team; he also played against Canada in 1891. Fast and direct, after his second cap in 1894 he moved to Sunderland where he won another league title. He came back to Rangers in the spring of 1896 and another Scottish Cup success followed in 1897, but then he fell out of contention and played his last match in September that year. He went south for a second time in 1898 when Bristol St George spent heavily on an ill-fated experiment of recruiting a team of professionals to play in the Western League. At the end of the season he retired, still only 28, and returned to Glasgow where he worked as a pattern weaver until he died in 1916 of a cerebral haemorrhage at his sister's house.

Dave McCULLOCH (7/3, 1934-38)
David McCulloch
Born 5 October 1912 Brown Street, Hamilton, Lanarkshire

Died 21 June 1979 Murdoch Road, East Kilbride, Lanarkshire
Scotland v Wales 1934, 1936, 1938; England 1936; Ireland 1936 (1); Czechoslovakia Dec 1937 (2); Hungary 1938.
Hamilton Amateurs; Shotts United; Third Lanark 1932-34; Heart of Midlothian 1934-35; Brentford Nov 1935-38; Derby County Oct 1938-46 [guest for Hamilton Academical 39-40; Motherwell 39-41; Falkirk 39-40; Brentford 39-43; Aldershot 40-44; Chelsea 41-42; Bournemouth 41-42; Swansea Town 43-44; Bath City 43-44]; Leicester City Jul-Dec 1946; Bath City Dec 1946-49; Waterford 1949-51 player-coach; Alloa Athletic 1951-52 player-manager.

McCulloch was a tall and direct centre forward who joined Third Lanark in 1932 from Shotts United, but when they were relegated two years later they sold him to Hearts, where he became an outstanding success. He was selected for the Scottish League in October 1934, scoring against the English, and the following month won his first Scotland cap against Wales. His scoring average in his first season was over a goal a game, and he was on course to repeat the performance when Brentford paid over £5,000 for him in November 1935. They deemed it money well spent as he made a huge impact in England, and was acclaimed as the best header of the ball in the country, scoring 78 goals in his first hundred games. Unfortunately, he could not reach such heights in his international appearances, managing just three in seven caps. Brentford rated him so highly that in 1937 they turned down a bid of £15,000 from Blackpool, which would have been a British record. A year later, with the side struggling at the foot of the First Division and in financial difficulties, they sold him to Derby County for just under £10,000. Unfortunately the goals dried up in his new environment, and in the summer of 1938 Derby offered him just £6 a week to re-sign. When war broke out Derby ceased operations and he returned home to Hamilton, where Accies were delighted to use his services as a guest in Scottish wartime competitions, and he won the Lanarkshire Cup into the bargain. By the end of the 1939-40 season he had played as a guest for Brentford, Motherwell and Falkirk, and for Scotland against England. He continued at home for a further season at Motherwell, but after that his role in the Army as a Sergeant PT Instructor took precedence, and he played for a number of clubs wherever his postings took him, with Aldershot getting the most use out of him. There were also sporadic appearances for Derby County after they restarted in 1942. In autumn 1944 he went over to France on active service and missed most of the domestic football season, and by the time he returned to Derby in 1945-46 he was largely out of the picture and did not feature in their FA Cup victory. He toured Czechoslovakia with Derby County in the summer of 1946, and shortly afterwards was transferred to Leicester City. Six months later he moved on to Bath City, one of his wartime clubs, and in 1949 he embarked on a coaching career with Waterford and then Alloa. He was not a success as a coach and he returned to Lanarkshire, where he worked as a material controller in an engineering company.

John MACDONALD (1/0, 1886)
Dr John Macdonald
Born 24 December 1861 Bridge Street, Inverness
Died 29 August 1938 Marchhall Nursing Home, Edinburgh
Scotland v England 1886.
Edinburgh University 1879-86; Queen's Park Mar 1884-85; Northern Counties (rugby) 1886-89.

Originally a rugby player at Inverness Royal Academy, Macdonald took up association football on going to Edinburgh University in 1879 and soon became an accomplished full back. However, his first national honour was in cricket, playing for Scotland against the Australians in 1880, and he went on to captain the University cricket team. Meanwhile, the University football eleven was one of the strongest in Edinburgh at that time and he won the East of Scotland Shield with them in 1883. In his final two years as a student he also played for Queen's Park, having initially been invited to bolster the team for the FA Cup semi-final and final in March 1884. The following season he played in another FA Cup final for Queen's Park, which again ended in defeat to Blackburn Rovers, and his last competitive appearance for the club was in August 1885. After he graduated in medicine from Edinburgh in 1886 he was appointed resident surgeon at Inverness Royal Infirmary and resumed his football but reverted to the oval ball, playing rugby for Northern Counties. In 1889 he took up a post in West Calder for 18 months, then spent the rest of his working life in Inverness, rising to become Chief Medical Officer of Health. For a while he continued to be involved in football as a referee, and gave further evidence of his sporting ability by winning the Inverness Tennis Club championship in 1892. His home in Inverness was at Old Edinburgh Road, although he died in an Edinburgh nursing home.

Jimmy McDOUGALL (2/0, 1931)
James McDougall
Born 23 January 1904 Ivy Bank, Port Glasgow, Renfrewshire
Died 3 July 1984 Allerton, Liverpool
Scotland v Austria 1931; Italy 1931c.
Port Glasgow Athletic; Partick Thistle Jan 1925-28; Liverpool 1928-38; South Liverpool 1938-39 player-coach.
McDougall started out in junior football with Port Glasgow, as did his elder brother Jack (below), and was a slow starter as he did not sign for Partick Thistle until he was 21, and had to wait until the following season for his debut. He appeared only 11 times for Thistle in 1925/26, and only for half of the succeeding season, but finally blossomed superbly in 1927/28 when he was second top scorer. He was transferred to Liverpool in the summer of 1928, and although he had played mainly at inside left for Partick Thistle he dropped to half-back soon after going south. He remained for a decade, making over 350 appearances and later said: 'Coming to Anfield was the best move I ever made. I thoroughly enjoyed all the years I had with the

club.' His two internationals came on Scotland's 1931 tour of Europe, and could hardly have been more chastening experiences. His debut was a 5-0 defeat to Austria, and he was appointed captain for the second match, against Italy, which ended in another heavy loss, this time 3-0. In 1938 he was appointed coach of South Liverpool in the Lancashire Combination, retiring when war broke out, and he remained in the city for the rest of his life, running a chandlery business.

Jack McDOUGALL (1/0, 1926)
John McDougall
Born 21 September 1901 Ivy Bank, Port Glasgow, Renfrewshire
Died 26 September 1973 Harelaw Reservoir, Port Glasgow, Renfrewshire
Scotland v Ireland 1926.
Port Glasgow Athletic; Airdrieonians 1921-29 (Scottish Cup 1924); Sunderland 1929-34; Leeds United Nov 1934-37.

A quiet giant, once described as 'six feet of silence', McDougall earned immense respect by his performances at centre half. Elder brother of Jimmy (above), he joined Airdrie in 1921 from his home town junior side and played his part as the team became a real power in the 1920s, finishing second in the league for four seasons in a row, with their greatest triumph the Scottish Cup victory in 1924. An excellent header of the ball, he could be a real attacking danger at corner kicks, and Airdrie resisted numerous offers for his transfer before they finally allowed him to go to Sunderland in 1929. He was only capped once for Scotland, against Ireland in 1926, although he was later a reserve and turned down the opportunity to tour Europe with the Scotland team in 1931 (while his brother Jimmy did go). He also played twice for the Scottish League. He spent five years at Sunderland then moved to Leeds United in the autumn of 1934 where he was immediately appointed captain. He had coached in Norway in the summer of 1927 but did not go into coaching after his retirement from playing in 1937 and returned to Port Glasgow. He was found drowned in 1973 in Harelaw Reservoir, near his home, on the day Scotland qualified for the World Cup finals by beating Czechoslovakia at Hampden.

John McDOUGALL (5/4, 1877-79)
John Smith McDougall
Born 9 April 1854 Bonhill, Dunbartonshire
Died 16 May 1925 Alexander Street, Renton, Dunbartonshire
Scotland v England 1877, 1878 (3), 1879 (1); Wales 1877, 1879c.
Vale of Leven 1874-79 (Scottish Cup 1877, 1878, 1879).

A versatile forward with Vale of Leven in the club's prime, a brilliant dribbler, McDougall won the Scottish Cup in three consecutive years, although he nearly spoiled the first triumph in 1877 by heading an own goal which earned Rangers a replay. He scored for his own side in the second match, also drawn, before the trophy was lifted at the third attempt. In the 1878 and 1879 finals he captained the side, such was his stature at the club. His five caps came in the same years, and in 1878 (according to some reports) he became the first man to score a hat-trick against England, in a crushing 7-2 victory. In 1879 he was forced to give up the game in his prime, aged 25, due to a knee injury. He was in business in Renton as a wine and spirit merchant until his death in 1925, and is buried in Vale of Leven Cemetery.

Willie MACFADYEN (2/2, 1933)
William Macfadyen
Born 23 June 1904 Bentfoot, Overtown, Lanarkshire
Died 31 October 1972 Dudley Road Hospital, Winson Green, Birmingham
Scotland v Wales 1933 (1), Austria 1933 (1).
Colville's Welfare; Wishaw YMCA; Motherwell 1921-36 (Scottish League 1932) [loans to Bo'ness Jun-Dec 1922; Dykehead Jan-May 1923; Clyde Oct 1924-25]; Huddersfield Town Dec 1936-39; Clapton Orient 1939-42 [guest during WW2 for Wishaw Juniors 1940-41; Blackpool Apr 1941; Nottingham Forest Nov 1941; Huddersfield Town 1941; Rochdale Jan-Feb 1942; Halifax Town 1941-2; Raith Rovers Sep 1942].

Macfadyen's family moved from Overtown to Wishaw when he was a boy, and his first job at Dalzell Steel Works offered him an opportunity to play football at Welfare level. At Wishaw YMCA he reached the Lanarkshire Cup final in 1921 and he signed for Motherwell that summer, notionally as understudy to Hugh Ferguson, but he was sent on loan to Bo'ness and Dykehead to gain experience and did not break into the first team until 1923. He was then sent on loan again to Clyde, and only really became a regular in 1925 after Motherwell bounced back from a year in the Second Division. From then on, he became an integral part of the club's most successful era that saw them finish in the top three for eight consecutive seasons. In 1928 he impressed many in the club's tour of Argentina and on another summer tour to South Africa in 1931 which must have done wonders for team spirit. When Motherwell won the Scottish League title in 1931-32, Macfadyen scored 52 goals in 34 league matches, a record that included one five, four 4s and three hat-tricks. The only major disappointments were the Scottish Cup finals of 1931 and 1933, both lost to Celtic. Despite his scoring prowess, he won just two Scotland caps in 1933, scoring in both, and represented the Scottish League once, scoring twice against the Irish. In December 1936, aged 32, he moved to Huddersfield Town in a swap deal for Duncan Ogilvie and played in their FA Cup final of 1938 but his career was starting to wind down. He had just signed for Clapton Orient the following summer when war broke out and he returned to Scotland, stationed at Arbroath, where he was a PT instructor in the RAF with the rank of Corporal. He continued playing until 1942 and made guest appearances for several English clubs while stationed down south, while he also coached Arbroath and was appointed manager of Dundee United in 1945, remaining in the role for nine years. After that he worked as a physiotherapist and finally as an accounts clerk in Birmingham. His family was steeped in football: in 1929 he married Jean Crystal, daughter of a Motherwell director, while his brother Ian played alongside him at Fir Park and his son, also Ian, played for the club in the 1950s.

Sandy MACFARLANE (5/1, 1904-11)
Alexander Macfarlane
Born 6 August 1878 Elderslie Street, Anderston, Glasgow
Died 22 December 1945 Market Street, Preston, Lancashire
Scotland v Wales 1904, 1906, 1908, 1911; Ireland 1909 (1).
Baillieston; Airdrieonians 1895-96; Woolwich Arsenal Nov 1896-97; Airdrieonians 1897-98; Newcastle United Oct 1898-1901; Dundee Nov 1901-13 (Scottish Cup 1910); Chelsea 1913-15.

As a promising centre forward or inside left at Airdrie in the Second Division, Macfarlane's first venture south of the border aged 18 ended in disappointment when Arsenal let him go after a season. Undaunted, he returned to Airdrie for another year and scored 17 league goals, which was enough for Newcastle to offer him another opportunity in 1898. In three years on Tyneside he proved himself as an effective forward in every position, notably alongside Jack Fraser on the left, but was allowed to go in 1901 when new recruits pushed him to the margins. Newcastle's loss was Dundee's gain, as he had a marvellous decade at Dens Park, later resuming his wing partnership with Fraser, and became a legend for his part in their famous Scottish Cup victory of 1910. He came into the international reckoning and won his first cap against Wales in 1904, going on to take his total to five, but could never replicate his club form in a Scotland jersey. He also played twice for the Scottish League against the English, in 1904 and 1911. His career ended at Chelsea, who appointed him coach of the reserve side in 1913 although he was available for the first team and made a handful of competitive appearances. His contract was ended by the outbreak of war. In 1919 he was appointed manager of Dundee, holding the position for five years, and again for six months in 1928. He managed Charlton Athletic twice, winning the Third Division South title in 1929, and Blackpool from 1933-35 before he left the game to take over a hotel next to White Hart Lane in London. He managed two pubs in London which were destroyed in the blitz, then ran the Market Inn in Preston from 1940 until his death.

Rab MACFARLANE (1/0, 1896)
Robert Macfarlane
Born 6 January 1874 Roxburgh Street, Greenock, Renfrewshire
Died 27 July 1943 Newton Street, Greenock, Renfrewshire
Scotland v Wales 1896.
Greenock Rosebery; Greenock Volunteers; Morton Oct 1894-96; Third Lanark 1896-97; Everton 1897-98; Bristol St George 1898-99; East Stirlingshire 1899-1900; New Brompton Aug-Dec 1900; Grimsby Town Dec 1900-01 (Second Division 1901); Celtic 1901-02; Middlesbrough 1902-04; Aberdeen 1904-08 (Scottish Qualifying Cup 1905); Motherwell Feb-Mar 1909.

Macfarlane was an effective journeyman goalkeeper who played for ten clubs in ten years, moving regularly across the border. He won international honours early in his career, playing for Scotland against Wales in 1896 while with Morton, and for the Scottish League against the English a year later while at Third Lanark, keeping a clean sheet in both games. After establishing a solid reputation he made his first foray to England in 1897 with Everton, then left after a season and had a year in Bristol. A season at East Stirlingshire led in 1900 to him signing for New Brompton but he never played for them due to a cycling accident that summer, and in December he moved on again to Grimsby Town, who had to pay Everton £20 as a transfer fee for his Football League registration. An eventful few months concluded with him winning a Second Division championship medal. Back in Scotland, he came close to further honours in a season at Celtic as the club finished a close second to Rangers in the Scottish League and lost the Scottish Cup final to Hibs. He could not be persuaded to stay and went to Middlesbrough for two seasons, then spent four years at Aberdeen, helping them to win their first national trophy, the Scottish Qualifying Cup. He tried to retire in 1908 but Motherwell coaxed him back to action in February 1909. Unfortunately a month later his career ended definitively when he broke a finger in two places trying to save a shot. He was subsequently reported to have emigrated to Australia, but he soon returned to Scotland. An apprentice ship plater in his younger days, he later opened a newsagent in Greenock.

Alexander McGEOCH (4/0, 1876-77)
Alexander McGeoch OBE
Born 23 September 1854 Hamilton Crescent, Partick, Lanarkshire
Died 24 January 1922 Sherbourne Road, Acocks Green, Birmingham
Scotland v England 1876, 1877; Wales 1876, 1877.
Glasgow Wanderers 1873; Dumbreck 1875-78 and 1880.
McGeoch started out in 1870 as a rugby player with West of Scotland, whose ground in Partick was overlooked by his family home, and he represented Glasgow against Edinburgh at rugby in December 1875. At the same time he played the occasional game as goalkeeper for Glasgow Wanderers and then Dumbreck, and was selected for Glasgow against Sheffield at the association game in February 1876, just two months after his rugby honour for the city. He was good enough to win four Scotland caps in 1876 and 1877, conceding just one goal in his four appearances, then gave up football in 1878 but it proved to

be temporary as he returned in 1880 to represent the Scotch Canadian team in three of their matches in England. He was also a useful cricket player for West of Scotland. McGeoch had a successful career in the family firm of William McGeoch & Co of Glasgow, a brass foundry which specialised in shipping hardware, and which had works at Small Heath in Birmingham, where he moved around 1882. He became a company director and during the First World War he was responsible for important contracts carried out by his firm for the Admiralty, for which he was made an OBE in March 1920.

Jimmy McGHEE (1/0, 1886)
James McGhee
Born 2 April 1862 Lugar, Ayrshire
Died 30 July 1941 Fourth Street, Philadelphia, Pennsylvania, USA
Scotland v Wales 1886.
Cronberry; Lugar Boswell 1880-83; Hibernian 1883-1890 (Scottish Cup 1887) [guest for St Bernard's Mar-May 1889; Corinthian Apr 1889; Celtic Aug 1889]; Celtic Dec 1890-91; Abercorn Nov 1891-92.
Brought up in the mining rows of Ayrshire, McGhee followed his father into the ironstone mines until he was one of several players from Lugar Boswell who were recruited by Hibs in 1883. In Edinburgh he became an outstanding right-half (and occasional inside right) and was one of the first players from the club to win international honours, the other being Jimmy Lundie, in the Scotland team against Wales in 1886. A year later, he captained Hibs to their Scottish Cup triumph in 1887, with victory in the final over Dumbarton to take the trophy east for the first time. While several of his colleagues soon departed for the newly-formed Celtic, he remained loyal to Hibs until the club had virtually expired at the end of 1890. He went to Celtic but had only a few months in the first team, his last match coming in August 1891. He then joined Abercorn, and although unable to play league games because Celtic still held his registration, he was excellent in local cup-ties and was selected as captain of Renfrewshire. He retired from the game in 1892 and settled in Edinburgh where for several years he ran a pub, the Athletic Arms in the Pleasance. He made a surprise return to football as secretary of Hearts in 1908 then resigned in December 1909 after a player dispute and decided to emigrate to the USA, settling in Philadelphia where he worked as a plasterer, and in his later years as a barman. His son Bart played for USA in the 1930 World Cup finals. NB his death certificate contained the middle name Joseph, but this does not appear on any other documentation.

Peter McGONAGLE (6/0, 1933-34)
Peter William McGonagle
Born 30 April 1905 Glasgow
Died 19 December 1956 Royal Crescent, Cheltenham, Gloucestershire
Scotland v England 1933, 1934; Ireland 1933c, 1934; Austria 1933; Wales 1934.
Duntocher Hibs; Celtic 1926-36 (Scottish Cup 1931, 1933); Dunfermline Athletic Mar-July 1936; Hamilton Academical 1936-37; Cheltenham Town 1937-39.
McGonagle's original identity may never be known was adopted by his parents in 1905 a few months after they lost an infant son called William. Born in Glasgow, he was christened Peter after his adoptive father, and took William as a middle name. Brought up in the Lanarkshire mining community of Eddlewood, he was discovered in junior football by Willie Maley who signed him for Celtic in 1926 but he was far from the finished article and the *Evening Times* described him as 'plucked off the trees at Duntocher'. However, he made up for his rawness with enthusiasm and determination, exemplified by one early match at Motherwell where he suffered a head wound and had six stitches inserted, but was soon back on the field, wearing a rugby scrum cap. With his rugged features, tall and strongly built, he was beloved of cartoonists. He developed into a fine full back and helped Celtic to Scottish Cup victories in 1931 and 1933 against Motherwell. He played six times for Scotland, once as team captain against Northern Ireland in 1933 (although he missed a penalty in the match), as well as winning five caps for the Scottish League. After he left Celtic in 1936 he had brief spells at Dunfermline and Hamilton before heading south to Cheltenham where his playing days were ended in 1939 by a kick on the knee that almost resulted in his leg being amputated. He remained in Cheltenham for the rest of his life, working as a fitter in the engineering department of the National Coal Board research establishment until his death aged 51. His son Peter played water polo for Scotland and captained the Great Britain team.

John McGREGOR (4/1, 1877-80)
John Cunningham McGregor
Born 20 February 1851 Bridge Street, Alexandria, Dunbartonshire
Died 3 January 1930 Bridge Street, Alexandria, Dunbartonshire
Scotland v England 1877, 1878 (1), 1880; Wales 1877.
Vale of Leven 1872-81 (Scottish Cup 1877, 1878, 1879).
One of the founders of football in Vale of Leven in 1872, McGregor was devoted not only to his club but to his town of Alexandria, where he was born and died in the same street. Despite playing for a provincial club he was quickly recognised as one of the most talented forwards in the country, and was invited to play in the match which launched association football in Edinburgh in December 1873. A right-sided attacker, he went on to play his part in Vale's three successive Scottish Cup victories in 1877 to 1879, although he did not score in any of the finals. He also took part in their memorable wins in London against FA Cup-holders Wanderers and Old Etonians. For the national team he scored just once in four appearances, in Scotland's famous 7-2 victory over England in 1878. When he gave up playing in 1881 he remained involved in the football club as a referee, and was an enthusiastic participant in the annual reunions of the old Vale team right into the 1920s. A printfield foreman in the local turkey dye works, he was a member of Vale of Leven's cricket club and golf club.

His daughter Jessie has a place in art history as she was painted by her sweetheart, the artist John Munnoch, who was killed in WW1; her portrait known as 'The Chinese Coat' now hangs in Stirling Smith Art Gallery.

Jimmy McGRORY (7/6, 1928-33)
James Edward McGrory
Born 26 April 1904 Millburn Street, Garngad, Glasgow
Died 20 October 1982 Southern General Hospital, Glasgow
Scotland v Ireland 1928, Sep 1931 (1), 1932 (1), 1933; England 1931 (1), 1933 (2); Wales 1931 (1).
St Roch's; Celtic 1922-37 (Scottish Cup 1925, 1931, 1933, 1937; Scottish League 1926, 1936) [loan to Clydebank 1923-24].

McGrory was a scorer without peer, recording 550 goals in first class matches, including 410 in 408 league games at an extraordinary average of over a goal a game. He excelled with his head, able to direct the ball so powerfully and accurately that he earned the nickname 'the Golden Crust'. Even so, it took a little while for Celtic to appreciate his full potential and after he signed from junior side St Roch's in 1922 he was farmed out to Clydebank for a season. Then in 1924 he burst onto the scene and spent the next decade breaking scoring records, such as eight in one game against Dunfermline and a three minute hat-trick against Motherwell. It is astonishing, with hindsight, that a man who had so many goals in him notched up only seven caps, even in the era of Hughie Gallacher. He could at least be content with four Scottish Cups and two league titles for Celtic. Throughout his career he resisted overtures from English clubs, and when he finally left Parkhead it was to be manager of struggling Kilmarnock from December 1937. His first game ended in an embarrassing 8-0 defeat to his old club but he turned things around, and they not only escaped relegation but had an amazing run to the Scottish Cup final which included defeats of both Celtic and Rangers. When war broke out Kilmarnock closed and he spent the next few years working for ICI as a head storeman. Then in 1945 he was invited to return to Celtic as manager and he was in charge for two decades. Although there were few highlights he did guide them to a league and cup double in 1954. He remained in post until 1965 but even when he was replaced by Jock Stein his devotion to the club was such that he continued to be involved with a PR role. His biography was titled, appropriately enough, *A Lifetime in Paradise*. He died in Glasgow in 1982 and is buried in St Peter's Cemetery, Dalbeth.

William McGUIRE (2/0, 1881)
William McGuire
Born 24 March 1860 Head Street, Beith, Ayrshire
Died 14 March 1925 Kingcarse Cottage, High Road, Prestwick, Ayrshire
Scotland v England 1881; Wales 1881.
Beith Thistle; Beith 1878-82; Darwen Jan 1882-83.

McGuire was the scoring power which made Beith one of the top sides in Ayrshire. He helped them to win the Ayrshire Cup in 1880, and was selected several times for Ayrshire and Scotch Counties, then stepped up to the full national team for both matches in 1881. Although he did not score, he was one of four centre forwards as Scotland blew England away by a record 6-1 score, then Wales 5-1 two days later. He had already played in Lancashire for Ayrshire, and when he performed well for Beith in a friendly against Blackburn Rovers, Darwen offered him a job in the town if he would also play for them. He accepted in early 1882 and was the only Scot in the side, which was now playing second fiddle to local rivals Blackburn Rovers. However, he was bedevilled by injuries: he broke a leg in October 1882 playing against Bolton, and the clubs staged a benefit match for him the following month. He was not fit to play until March, when he scored in the Lancashire Cup final, which his team lost to Blackburn Rovers. Unfortunately he was badly hurt again in November 1883, and that appears to have ended his football career prematurely aged just 23. He returned to Beith where he worked as a wood carver, and was an elder in the local church. His football injuries may have developed into something more serious as his death certificate stated he had suffered from paraplegia for over 20 years.

Frank McGURK (1/0, 1933)
Francis Reynolds McGurk
Born 15 January 1909 Eddlewood Rows, Hamilton, Lanarkshire
Died 2 March 1978 General Hospital, Birmingham
Scotland v Wales 1933.
Blantyre Celtic; Clyde 1931-33; Birmingham City 1933-35; Bristol City 1935-36; Whittaker Ellis 1936-39.

McGurk had a fleeting career at the top of football, which was enough to win him a Scotland cap but little else. Brought up in Eddlewood, the same small Lanarkshire mining community as Peter McGonagle, he was already 22 when he joined Clyde from junior side Blantyre Celtic and was soon recognised as a great find. After a good second season in which he scored 24 goals for Clyde at outside right, Birmingham signed him in 1933 and he had a whirlwind start that earned him a cap against Wales in October that year. However, he soon fell out of favour with his club and by the end of his first season he was put on the transfer list, then given a free transfer a year later. In all, he only played 19 games for Birmingham, and made just three more appearances for Bristol City before he quit senior football in 1936 at the age of 27, barely three years since he was deemed international quality. He continued to play football in the Birmingham Works League and spent the rest of his life in the city, where he worked as a compressor driver.

Hugh McHARDY (1/0, 1885)
Hugh McHardy
Born 22 November 1860 Catherine Street, Anderston, Glasgow
Died 30 May 1912 Broomlands, Paisley, Renfrewshire
Scotland v Ireland 1885.
Rangers 1880-86; Partick Thistle May 1886; St Mirren 1886-90.

McHardy started out as a forward, making his Rangers debut in 1880 but only established himself as a first team regular early in 1883. The following year he dropped to full-back and quickly made his mark as a defender, gaining his first representative honours that season. He played for Glasgow against London and Birmingham, and did well enough to come into the full international team against Ireland in 1885. However, the following year his time at Rangers came to an end after he was criticised for 'rash kicking'. He played a trial for Partick Thistle in May 1886 but that summer decided to join St Mirren, where he was appointed club captain. He was effective, too, leading the team to victory in the Paisley Charity Cup in his first season, followed by the Renfrewshire Cup in 1888. He retired from the game around 1890 and remained in Paisley where he worked as a joiner. He died there aged just 51.

Tommy McINALLY (2/0, 1926)
Bernard McInally
Born 18 December 1899 Main Street, Barrhead, Renfrewshire
Died 29 December 1955 Paisley Road, Barrhead, Renfrewshire
Scotland v Ireland 1926; Wales 1926.
Croy Celtic; St Anthony's 1917-19; Celtic 1919-22 (Scottish League 1922); Third Lanark 1922-25; Celtic 1925-28 (Scottish League 1926; Scottish Cup 1927); Sunderland 1928-29; Bournemouth Nov 1929-30; Morton Nov-Dec 1930; Derry City Jan-Feb 1931; Coleraine Mar 1931; Armadale Jan 1933.

Known to everyone as Tommy although his real name was Bernard, McInally's first experience of junior football came in 1917 when his local side Croy Celtic were a man short and he was roped into to play in a Dunbartonshire Cup tie. He was clearly a talented forward and had a couple of years at St Anthony's, where he became a junior internationalist before signing for Celtic in June 1919, in the same week as John Gilchrist. He was an immediate sensation, with a hat-trick in his first senior match and scored 15 goals as Celtic won their opening nine games of the season. An expert at corner kicks, with excellent ball control and the vision to place a telling pass, he was the club's top scorer in his first two seasons, but by the third his temperament came into play. He was a hugely frustrating player to manage, being brilliant one week and invisible the next, compounded by a short fuse, all of which combined to persuade Celtic to drop him for the last two months of a championship-winning season. They decided he could leave in 1922 and he moved across the city to Third Lanark where he had three years, during which time he fell out with the club directors and was suspended for a month by the SFA. Celtic hankered after his goals and took another chance on him in 1925, even appointing him captain, and for a while it looked like he had matured as he had his best season and Celtic won the league flag in 1926. On top of that, the Scotland selectors rewarded him with two international caps against Ireland and Wales. Celtic followed up with a Scottish Cup victory in 1927, but he was becoming a liability. That autumn he was sent off against Rangers for speaking back to the referee, which brought a two-week SFA ban, then he was suspended by Celtic in November for 'a breach of training rules' and again in March 1928. Things also went wrong off the field as he bought a car and a few months later was fined for drink driving. Following the disastrous Scottish Cup final defeat to Rangers in 1928, the club had had enough and was happy to transfer him to Sunderland, who paid almost £3,000. It was a poor investment for the Wearside club, who gave him a free transfer in November 1929, after which he took on a series of short-term contracts at the tail end of his career. He made a surprise reappearance for Armadale in a Scottish Cup tie in 1933, when he was clearly overweight, and as late as 1946 he played in a charity match at Govan. He ran a betting shop in Paisley for a while, worked as a travelling salesman, and did some scouting for Celtic. He never married and died in 1955, aged just 56.

Tommy McINNES (1/1, 1889)
Thomas McInnes
Born 22 March 1869 Possil Road, Maryhill, Glasgow
Died 17 January 1939 Hart Lane, Luton, Bedfordshire
Scotland v Ireland 1889 (1).
Ashfield; Cowlairs 1887-89; Notts County Dec 1889-92; Rangers May-Sep 1892; Notts County Sep 1892-93; Third Lanark 1893-94; Everton 1894-97; Luton Town 1897-1900; Bedford Queen's Engineers 1900-01.

McInnes made his name at Cowlairs as a talented young inside forward, winning the Glasgow Exhibition Cup in 1888 and he was still only 19 when he was selected for a Scotland cap against Ireland in March 1889, scoring in the final minutes of a 7-0 win. He also represented Glasgow later the same month. He turned professional with Notts County in December that year and continued his good form, playing in the 1891 FA Cup final which they lost to Blackburn Rovers, and was selected for the Football League in their first match against the Scottish League on 11 April 1892. The following month he returned to Scotland and signed for Rangers, playing in their end-of-season Charity Cup ties and the opening four league matches of the new season but in September he was welcomed back at Notts County. First, however, he had to serve a month's FA suspension for having played in Scotland (those were the rules at the time!). In summer 1893 he went north for a season with Third Lanark, and was again selected for an international trial but did not make the Scotland team. He then joined Everton where he spent three seasons, was at Luton Town for another three years and wound up his career at Bedford Queen's Engineers before retiring in 1901. Although he went home to Scotland, following the death of his wife he returned to Luton in the late 1920s and worked in an iron foundry in the town until his death from a stroke, aged 69. NB he is sometimes confused with another Tommy McInnes (1873-1937) who won the FA Cup with Nottingham Forest in 1898.

Willie McINTOSH (1/0, 1905)
William Forbes McIntosh
Born 2 January 1879 Cowane Street, Stirling
Died 15 January 1973 52nd Street, Edmonton, Alberta, Canada
Scotland v Ireland 1905.
King's Park 1898-1901; Third Lanark Nov 1901-10 (Scottish League 1904; Scottish Cup 1905); Vale of Leven 1910-11; Edmonton Caledonians 1912-14.
McIntosh was an unsung hero in the great Third Lanark team of the 1900s, at left back and then left half, gaining scant international recognition with just one Scotland cap. Brought up in Stirling, where he worked as a joiner and carpenter, he played as an amateur with King's Park in the Scottish Combination, winning the Stirlingshire Cup and Dewar Shield in 1899. He moved to Third Lanark in November 1901 and from then until the end of the decade he missed few games, as the Scottish League title was secured in 1904, followed by the Scottish Cup in 1905. He missed the following year's final, which was lost to Hearts, but won the Glasgow Cup three times, even scoring a rare goal in the 1902 defeat of Celtic and going on to win further medals in 1903 and 1908, the last after Third Lanark needed no less than nine matches to win three ties. Thirds gave him a benefit match against Celtic in January 1910, before allowing him to leave. He had a season at Vale of Leven, who were struggling at the foot of Division Two, despite having to recover from an accidental collision in a match at Dumbarton which resulted in a broken shoulder blade and put him out for two months. After retiring in 1911 he emigrated with his family, initially to New Jersey before heading to Canada and he spent the rest of his life in Edmonton where he played for the Callies football team and worked as a carpenter for the local government for many years. In 1966, when he was 87, he made a return trip to Scotland and was a guest of Third Lanark at a match in their final season.

Andy McINTYRE (2/0, 1878-82)
Andrew McIntyre
Born 9 August 1855 Main Street, Alexandria, Dunbartonshire
Died 30 March 1941 Middleton Street, Alexandria, Dunbartonshire
Scotland v England 1878, 1882.
Vale of Leven 1874-85 (Scottish Cup 1877, 1878, 1879)
McIntyre was full back in the successful Vale of Leven side that won the Scottish Cup for three years in succession, He was powerfully built, a particular asset in those muscular days, and worked well in partnership with Sandy McLintock in defence while his younger brother James was a half-back in their third Scottish Cup success, which saw the cup awarded by default when Rangers refused to replay. At a time when Vale usurped Queen's Park as the dominant side, McIntyre won only two Scotland caps four years apart, but both saw extraordinary results: his first international in 1878 saw England beaten 7-2, and when he was selected again, this time England lost 5-1. The four year gap can be explained by a dip in his form but reports in 1881-82 indicated he was back at the top of his game, and he partnered Andy Watson at full back. Along the way, he had other honours, being selected several times for Dunbartonshire from 1876 onwards, and for Scotch Counties in 1883. An engineer, he spent his whole life in Alexandria and kept in close touch with football, enjoying the annual reunions of the Vale of Leven team on Loch Lomond in the 1920s; indeed, he was the last survivor when he died in 1941.

Hugh McINTYRE (1/0, 1880)
Hugh McIntyre
Born 16 January 1857 Dumbarton Road, Milton, Glasgow
Died 25 June 1905 King's College Hospital, London
Scotland v Wales 1880.
Lancelot; Northern 1876-77; Rangers 1877-80 [guest for Partick Jan 1879; Blackburn Rovers Mar-Apr 1879]; Blackburn Rovers Jan 1880-86 (FA Cup 1884, 1885, 1886); Darwen 1886-87; London Caledonians 1887-89 [guest for Grimsby Town Dec 1887]; Warwick County Sep 1889.
A vigorous full-back, the elder brother of Tuck (below), McIntyre was a pioneering professional footballer as one of the first to seize the opportunity to make a living from the game in England. He probably became aware of the potential in his early years with Rangers when he made regular trips to England to play friendlies, and played as a guest for Partick at Darwen, where he would have encountered Fergie Suter and Jimmy Love. Meanwhile he enhanced his reputation in the Rangers side which reached the Scottish Cup final of 1879 and won the Glasgow Charity Cup. He was invited to play a couple of games for Blackburn Rovers, who decided to take the plunge and emulate their near rivals Darwen by signing Scottish 'professors' after McIntyre played an outstanding game for the Scotch-Canadian eleven which came to Blackburn in

January 1880. He was persuaded to stay on in Lancashire, albeit he did not make the move permanent until he had won his Scottish cap against Wales that spring, and spent six hugely successful years with Rovers, which rose to become the dominant team in England and won the FA Cup three times in a row. He settled well into the city's sporting life and developed into a fine cricketer, making one first class appearance for Lancashire in 1884 as wicket keeper. Two weeks later, in a club game, a ball struck him in the face and broke his nose so severely that his life was reported to be in danger; however, he recovered and was playing football again within a couple of months. He also enjoyed amateur dramatics, and even appeared on stage with his wife at Blackburn's Theatre Royal. After his third FA Cup win in 1886 he joined Darwen for a season, playing in goal. He moved to London in 1887 where he played for London Caledonians and became a committee member, while he also turned out for Grimsby Town when visiting a friend in the town, and played once for a team in Warwick after he took over the George Inn at Wolverhampton. Then his life unravelled in 1893 with a messy divorce case, in which his wife Marie claimed he was 'given to drink and ill-treated her', and his evidence in court about his financial circumstances gave a fascinating insight to his life as a professional footballer. After the divorce he went back to London to work as an upholsterer and died there in hospital, aged 48.

'Tuck' McINTYRE (1/0, 1884)
James McIntyre
Born 11 August 1858 Dumbarton Road, Milton, Glasgow
Died 17 March 1943 Paisley Road West, Glasgow
Scotland v Wales 1884.
St Andrew's; Alexandra Athletic 1877-80; Rangers 1880-92 (Scottish League 1891).

McIntyre started with Dennistoun side Alexandra Athletic, where he was a good enough half back to play in an international trial in 1880. Known as Tuck because of his generous build, he followed his elder brother Hugh (above) to Rangers but they only played a handful of games together before Hugh departed for Blackburn. Tuck remained in Glasgow and established himself in the Rangers team, spending 12 years with the club where he formed an excellent half back partnership with James Cameron, was appointed club captain, served as ground convenor and sat on the club selection committees. He was selected for Scotland just once, against Wales in 1884, and represented Glasgow on several occasions. By the time the Scottish League was founded in 1890 he was a veteran and only played in half of the matches as Rangers shared the league title with Dumbarton. He retired the following season, but remained dedicated to Rangers and was awarded life membership. He took over the running of the Angel Bar at Paisley Road Toll, although it later got into financial difficulties and in his twilight years he was described as a cargo checker.

Johnny McKAY (1/0, 1924)
John Reid McKay
Born 1 November 1899 Carbeth Street, Possilpark, Glasgow
Died 6 February 1970 Carbeth Street, Possilpark, Glasgow
Scotland v Wales 1924.
St Anthony's; Celtic 1919-21; Blackburn Rovers Nov 1921-27; Middlesbrough Mar 1927-36 (Second Division 1927, 1929); Hibernian 1936-37.

McKay saw war service with the Royal Scots Fusiliers and played for St Anthony's in the Junior Cup final before signing for Celtic in 1919. An inside right, much was promised but two years at Parkhead saw only sporadic first team appearances and his only medal was a Glasgow Charity Cup success. He was allowed to leave in the autumn of 1921 for Blackburn Rovers where he blossomed and was highly rated for his clever play. This resulted in international recognition in 1924, but Scotland went down to a disappointing defeat to Wales and he was not called upon by the selectors again. He moved to Middlesbrough in 1927 and had nine good years at Ayresome Park, helping his new side to win the Second Division title shortly after his arrival, and again two years later. When he dropped out of the picture he came back to Scotland for a season with Hibs before deciding to retire in 1937. A storeman with the Admiralty, he was born and died in the same Glasgow street (although not the same house). His younger brother Tom played for Queen of the South.

Bobby McKAY (1/0, 1927)
Robert McInnes McKay
Born 2 September 1900 Salamanca Street, Parkhead, Glasgow
Died 10 June 1977 Royal Infirmary, Glasgow
Scotland v Wales 1927.
Parkhead White Rose; Vale of Clyde; Parkhead; Neilston Victoria; Morton 1921-25 (Scottish Cup 1922); Rangers 1925-26; Newcastle United Nov 1926-28 (Football League 1927); Sunderland Oct 1928-30; Charlton Athletic Dec 1930-32; Bristol Rovers Nov 1932-35; Newport County 1935-36.

McKay did the rounds of several junior sides before Morton took him on in 1921, and he had little cause to regret it with their unexpected Scottish Cup win in his first season. He proved himself to be a marvellous inside right and in 1925 Rangers paid a fee of just under £2,000 to take him to Ibrox. He scored in his first couple of matches but the goals soon dried up and he found himself in the reserves, so there was relief all round in November 1926 when Newcastle United paid an even higher fee to sign him. Suddenly, everything clicked and he had a whale of a time on Tyneside, scoring in the first minute of his debut against West Brom and finishing the game with a hat-trick, while he scored another treble in just five minutes against Derby County. His speed and goals not only helped United to the league title in 1927, they earned him a Scotland cap against Wales that year. It was too good to last and when his form dipped the following year he was exchanged for Bob Thomson, a fellow Scotland internationalist at Sunderland. The pattern of early promise and loss of form continued and he bounced around at Charlton, Bristol Rovers and Newport County before retiring in 1936. He was appointed manager of Dundee United in July 1939 but his contract was terminated after just six weeks because of the outbreak of war, although in that time he did sign future United manager Jerry Kerr. After the War he coached Ballymena United 1947-49 then left football and worked in Glasgow in the steel-making industry, which had been his original trade before going full-time in football.

'Doctor' McKEE (1/2, 1898)
James McKee
Born 18 March 1871 Tullyard, Moira, County Down, Ireland
Died 12 May 1949 Old Eastfield, Harthill, Lanarkshire
Scotland v Wales 1898 (2).
West Benhar Violet; Dykehead 1894-95; Heart of Midlothian 1895-96; Darwen 1896-97; East Stirlingshire 1897-1900 (Scottish Qualifying Cup 1898); Bolton Wanderers 1900-03; Luton Town 1903-04; New Brompton 1904-06; East Stirlingshire 1906-07.

Born in Ireland, McKee's family moved to Shotts when he was a child and he grew up in the Lanarkshire mining town where he learned his football with local junior side West Benhar Violet. Known as 'Doctor', he carved out a career as a goal-scoring journeyman centre forward. From Dykehead he joined Hearts in 1895 but played just a couple of first team games, scoring in both, signed for Darwen in the English Second Division a year later, and came back to Scotland with East Stirlingshire in 1897. Here, he benefited from the Scottish FA's policy at the time of putting out three distinct elevens for the home internationals, with the players chosen to face Ireland and Wales regarded as 'second strings', deserving of recognition but not really good enough to face England. McKee, who had won county caps for Stirlingshire, came into the reckoning as the SFA appeared unaware of his birthplace in Ireland, and even though he had to withdraw from an international trial through injury, he was included in the Scotland team to face Wales in 1898. He scored twice in a relatively straightforward 5-2 victory, and like almost all of the team was never selected again. Meanwhile, he won the Scottish Qualifying Cup with East Stirlingshire and signed for Bolton Wanderers in 1900 where he was first choice centre forward for three years. He played 81 First Division matches, scoring 19 goals, then went to Luton Town in the Southern League for a year, and had two seasons at New Brompton (Gillingham). He returned to Scotland and a brief reunion with East Stirlingshire while he resumed work as a miner in Harthill, where he spent the rest of his life. He never married and was a keen supporter of the local junior team, Polkemmet.

Duncan MacKENZIE (1/0, 1937)
Duncan MacKenzie
Born 10 August 1912 Couper Street, Townhead, Glasgow
Died 15 May 1987 El Cajon, San Diego, California, USA
Scotland v Ireland 1937.
Milton Parish Church; Albion Rovers Apr 1930-32; Brentford 1932-38 (Third Division South 1933, Second Division 1935); Middlesbrough 1938-45 [guest during WW2 for Brentford 1939-45; Worcester City May 1940; Brighton & Hove Albion 43-45].

MacKenzie jumped from the Glasgow Churches League straight into the Albion Rovers team in the spring of 1930, aged 17, and developed into such a talented right half over the next two years that he was sold for a 'substantial' fee to Brentford just before his 20th birthday. He had six successful years in London, helping Brentford to two promotions as they stormed from the Third Division South to become the top team in London, finishing fifth in the First Division in 1936. He won just one international cap, Scotland's 1-1 draw with Ireland in November 1937, and the following summer was given a surprise transfer to Middlesbrough. His first season at Ayresome Park was disrupted by flu and a broken bone in his foot, then war broke out and he returned to his home in Osterley, near London, for war work as a mechanic. However, Middlesbrough retained his registration, so he needed their permission to play for Brentford, which was not always forthcoming. Nevertheless, he devoted himself to the Griffin Park club as a guest throughout the war years, winning the London War Cup in 1942, and also made a few guest appearances for Brighton. He steadfastly refused to return north and was finally released by Middlesbrough in December 1945, six years after his last match for them, as his career was over and he wanted to be free to live in London. He later emigrated to California and died there in 1987.

Mick McKEOWN (2/0, 1889-90)
Michael McKeown
Born 24 January 1869 Craigmark, Dalmellington, Ayrshire
Died 25 October 1903 Broad Street, Camlachie, Glasgow
Scotland v Ireland 1889; England 1890.
Lugar Boswell; Hibernian 1887-88; Celtic 1888-91; Blackburn Rovers 1891-92; Cowlairs Aug-Sep 1892; Fair City Athletic Sep-Nov 1892; Motherwell Nov 1892-Jan 1893; Fair City Athletic Feb-Mar 1893; Victoria United Mar 1893; Morton Sep 1893; Hamilton Harp Feb 1896; Lugar Boswell Sep 1896-97; Hibernian May 1897; Carfin Shamrock Oct 1897; Camelon Mar 1898; Lugar Boswell Oct 1899.

Turbulent is perhaps the best word to describe McKeown's life, with his football talent negated by a self-destructive streak, compounded by alcohol, that effectively ended his top-level career in his early twenties. He grew up in Lugar Boswell which was, at the time, a hotbed of football talent having already produced a number of future internationals (such as McGhee, McLaren and Lundie) and he followed in their footsteps to Hibs as an 18-year-old. A year later he was recruited by the newly-formed Celtic, and did so well in his first season that he was selected for Scotland against Ireland in March 1889. He won a second cap against England the following year, as a late substitute for Bob Smellie who was ill. He was in the Celtic team that won the Glasgow Cup in 1891 and soon after departed for Blackburn Rovers, who needed a replacement for Tom Brandon. He did reasonably well on the pitch but his off-field behaviour proved too much and Rovers released him after a season. From that point his career rapidly went downhill and he featured for a bewildering succession of clubs, playing for anyone who would pay him. On his return to Scotland he signed for Cowlairs, then found a job in Perth with Campbell's Dye Works and joined local team Fair City Athletic. He was selected for the Perthshire county team yet within six weeks he had gone to Motherwell, and when they dismissed him he returned to Perth and won another county cap. His career is difficult to follow after this but he played briefly for Morton before enlisting in the Royal Scots Fusiliers in April 1894. In less than a year he was kicked out of the Army, who deemed him 'incorrigible and worthless'. His past reputation still induced a few clubs to take a chance on him, although none of them managed to shake him out of his wayward ways. In

April 1898 he was suspended by the SFA for signing forms for two clubs, and by the time Lugar Boswell applied 18 months later to have the suspension lifted, his career was over. Meanwhile, his life was spiralling out of control, with several convictions for drunkenness, and he lived on charity and temporary jobs until his death aged just 34. By then he was no longer capable of working and was allowed to sleep rough at a bottling works in Camlachie, where his body was found in an empty lime kiln after he fell in and suffocated. In memory of his fleeting greatness, Celtic quickly stepped in to pay for his funeral.

Tom McKILLOP (1/0, 1938)
Thomas Boyd McKillop
Born 27 October 1917 Drybridge, Dundonald, Ayrshire
Died 14 February 1984 Masons Hill, Bromley, Kent
Scotland v Netherlands 1938.
Dreghorn; Rangers Feb 1935-46 (Scottish League 1937, 1939) [guest during WW2 for Arsenal Sep 1942, Portsmouth Jan 1943, Birmingham City Feb 1944]; Asturias 1946-47; Rhyl 1947-53.

McKillop was educated at Irvine Academy, where he shared the school sports championship with his friend David Wallace and both of them stepped up from Dreghorn Juniors to Rangers in 1935. While Wallace made just one league appearance, McKillop spent a decade at Ibrox and made his first team debut shortly before his 18th birthday. He was given an extended run in the team at right half the following season which ended in the league championship. His continued good form resulted in a Scotland call-up and he won a cap in Amsterdam in May 1938 but had a poor match and there were no more opportunities. After a second league title in 1939 he wanted to leave Rangers but was refused a free transfer and an appeal to the League Management Committee was turned down. Then the War intervened and he joined the Royal Navy in 1940, which meant that service commitments restricted his football. He played only rarely for Rangers after that, appearing mainly for services teams and occasionally on loan to other clubs with one game each for Arsenal, Portsmouth and Birmingham City. He was demobbed in November 1945 and returned to Ibrox for the last time but only played two more first team matches. In 1946 he went to Mexico to join Asturias, who were managed by a Scot, William Raeside, for an adventurous season with Jackie Milne and Jimmy Hickie until the trio were abandoned the following summer and returned to the UK. With several teams to pick from, he made the surprising choice of Rhyl in North Wales where he captained and then managed the team in the Cheshire League, enjoying the company of a large Scottish contingent. He was still with the club in the 1960s, and later retired to Bromley in Kent.

Donald McKINLAY (2/0, 1922)
Donald McKinlay
Born 25 July 1891 Boghall, Broomhouse, Lanarkshire
Died 16 September 1959 Broadgreen Hospital, Liverpool
Scotland v Wales 1922; Ireland 1922.
Newton Swifts; Newton Villa; Liverpool Jan 1910-29 (Football League 1922, 1923); Prescot Cables 1929-30.

Born near Baillieston, McKinlay was brought up in Newton, a suburb of Cambuslang, and played his early football there. He was performing well as a left back with Newton Villa in the Lanarkshire Junior League when Liverpool signed him in January 1910, aged 18, and within three months he made his first team debut. He spent the rest of his senior career with the Merseyside club and recorded almost 400 league appearances, mainly at left half. Renowned for his powerful kick, he was often entrusted with free kicks and that brought him a number of spectacular goals, but surprisingly he only occasionally took penalties. He was one of seven Scots in Liverpool's FA Cup final team of 1914 which was lost to Burnley, and plenty of success came in the following decade. He remained in the city during WW1, despite limited competitive football, and was appointed club captain in 1922, leading the team to two successive league titles. This brought him into the international fold and in 1922 he made two appearances for Scotland aged 30, against Wales and Ireland. When he finally left Anfield in 1929 he had a season with Prescot Cables in the Lancashire Combination before retiring. He went into the hotel business and ran several pubs, including one in East Prescot Road.

Angus McKINNON (1/1, 1874)
Angus McKinnon
Born April-July 1851 Cowcaddens, Glasgow
Died 24 July 1880 Kingston, Ontario, Canada
Scotland v England 1874 (1).
Queen's Park 1870-78 (Scottish Cup 1874, 1875).

In March 1874, McKinnon became the first man to score the winner in a Scotland match, with a shot which slipped through the hands of England goalkeeper Welch to secure a 2-1 victory. Sadly, his scoring ability did not earn him any more caps and this was his only appearance for the national team. However, it was just the start of a remarkable month for McKinnon, as the following Saturday he travelled south with the Glasgow select team to face Sheffield, and the week after that he took part in the inaugural Scottish Cup final, which Queen's Park won by defeating Clydesdale. And just to complete a season of firsts, a few months earlier he had scored the first goal in the exhibition match which introduced association football to Edinburgh. He won a second Scottish Cup winner's medal for Queen's Park the following season then suffered a serious illness which kept him out for the 1875/76 season. He worked for Glasgow merchants West Watson & Son and returned to action for Queen's Park (sometimes using the pseudonym AL Senior), also serving as club secretary for a few months. Then in 1878 he decided to emigrate to Canada which proved an ill-fated decision as he was working as a labourer in Kingston, Ontario when he died aged just 29. McKinnon's father had died when he was an infant, and after his mother remarried he sometimes used his stepfather's surname of Taylor.

Billy MACKINNON (9/5, 1872-79)
William Muir Mackinnon
Born 18 January 1852 Eglinton Street, Gorbals, Glasgow
Died 24 May 1942 Hamilton Road, Mount Vernon, Glasgow
Scotland v England 1872, 1873, 1874, 1875, 1876 (1), 1877, 1878 (1), 1879 (2); Wales 1876 (1).
Queen's Park 1870-80 (Scottish Cup 1874, 1875, 1876) [guest for Rangers May 1872].

Mackinnon was perhaps the most respected centre forward of the 1870s, as he led Scotland's attack in the first eight matches against England, as well as once against Wales in 1876. He is one of the few people who can be identified from the drawings of the 1872 international, pictured in mid-air for his overhead kick, an athletic clearance which took the English by surprise and was the talk of the match: 'Mackinnon, who is not tall, here made a very clever kick. The ball was on the bound higher than his head, when he leaped up and to the surprise of his opponent, who was waiting till the ball came over Mackinnon, kicked it well up the hill. The kick was much admired, and lustily applauded.' Growing up in the southside of Glasgow, he had joined Queen's Park in 1870 and played a part in their early successes, including the first three Scottish Cup victories from 1874-76. In fact he scored the opening goal of both the 1874 and 1875 finals. Although this was his only club, he has another claim to fame as he played as a guest for Rangers in their very first match in May 1872, on Glasgow Green against Callander. Away from football he was an engineer for P&W MacLellan, a major concern which owned the Clutha Iron Works in Glasgow. His passion was music and as a young man he was an outstanding tenor, so much so that he auditioned for La Scala Opera in Milan and was invited to join them. However, rather than leave his family he decided to stay at home and devoted himself to the Glasgow Choral Union, becoming a tenor soloist in 1882. In the course of my research I met his nephew Walter, who recalled meeting his famous uncle and offered an anecdote about the pioneering days: 'After the match on Saturday, the Queen's Park players would head to the nearest pub for their dinner and came out well stewed. Willie would stagger home to Cambuslang, but had to be in a fit state to walk all the way back to Glasgow Cathedral to sing in the choir on the Sunday morning.' When he died in 1942, aged 90, he was by far the longest-lived of the original Scotland football internationalists but his obituary in the *Glasgow Herald* was headed 'Veteran Glasgow Musician'.

Willie McKINNON (4/0, 1883-84)
William Neilson McKinnon
Born 6 June 1859 Main Street, Bonhill, Dunbartonshire
Died 14 October 1899 Little's Hospital, Dumbarton
Scotland v England 1883, 1884; Wales 1883, 1884.
Alclutha; Dumbarton 1880-86 [guest for St Bernard's Apr 1886]; Hawick Rugby Club 1884-86.

A versatile left winger, good at dribbling and with a keen eye for goal, McKinnon was well known for his boundless enthusiasm and energy. Spending most of his career with Dumbarton, he had little to show for it in terms of medals, as he played in the Scottish Cup finals of 1881 and 1882, both of which were lost in replays, and missed the club's triumph in 1883. His stature was recognised with four Scotland caps, playing against England and Wales in 1883 and again in 1884, without scoring. He studied at the Free Church Training College in Glasgow to become a school teacher, like his teammate Michael Paton, and left Dumbarton in 1884 to take up a post at the Buccleuch School in Hawick. Although he set up a football team he also took up rugby and was good enough to play for Hawick at half back, and was in their team which won the Hawick Sevens tournament in 1886. He was so well respected that when returned to Dumbarton to teach at Knoxland School in November 1886 the rugby club members presented him with a gold scarf pin as a farewell gift. His new teaching post prompted his retiral from playing, but he remained involved in football for many years as a Dumbarton official and occasional referee, ultimately becoming chairman. However, he died at 40 from liver disease, which was reportedly exacerbated by an injury he had sustained while playing rugby. His fellow teachers and pupils paid for a memorial at his grave in Dumbarton Cemetery.

Sandy McLAREN (5/0, 1929-32)
Alexander McLaren
Born 25 December 1910 Tulloch Terrace, Tibbermore, Perthshire
Died 5 February 1960 Dunkeld Road, Perth
Scotland v Norway 1929; Germany 1929; Netherlands 1929; Ireland 1932; Wales 1932.
Tulloch; St Johnstone 1927-33; Leicester City Feb 1933-45 (Second Division 1937) [guest for Morton 1940-41, Airdrieonians Mar 1941]; St Johnstone Oct 1945-46.

McLaren was the first St Johnstone player to be capped by Scotland when he was an 18-year-old goalkeeper, and went on to a long career on both sides of the border. Six feet tall, he had been spotted in Perth juvenile football and made his first team debut in April 1927 aged just 16, becoming regular halfway through the next season. By the time the SFA selected an experimental squad for its first ever continental tour in 1929, he had come into contention after an excellent season which included one spell of seven shut-outs in eight games. The youngest member of the group which headed for Norway, Germany and the Netherlands, he held down his place for all four games including the first against a regional select in Bergen. Back home, Saints were relegated in 1930, taking two years to come back up, but his performances were good enough to win two more caps in 1932. Unfortunately, his international career was ended by a horrendous 5-2 home defeat to Wales. Nonetheless, early in 1933 a bid of £2,500 came in from Leicester City who were in a desperate fight to avoid relegation, and although he made a shaky start, conceding six on his debut, he soon settled in. His side won their last three league matches to avoid the drop by two points and he was virtually ever-present at Filbert Street for the rest of the decade, as the side bounced between divisions. In 1935 they went down and the Foxes spent a couple of years in Division Two until they won the title in 1937 with the reward of a tour to Eastern Europe. Another relegation followed in 1939 but war broke out and he played his last match for Leicester in 1940. Although he remained their player throughout the war years, he came back to Perth and joined the Royal Navy, serving as a gunner in a variety of theatres including the Russian convoys and the Middle East. After being demobbed he returned briefly to St Johnstone, and worked with the Ministry of Defence as a policeman at the Naval Stores Depot in Almondbank until his early death from bronchial pneumonia, aged 49. His eldest son Sandy was also a goalkeeper and played for Dundee United in the 1950s. Another son, Garrow, wrote his biography, *Of Saints and Foxes*.

Jimmy McLAREN (3/1, 1888-90)
James McLaren
Born 27 April 1861 Durhamtown, Bathgate, West Lothian
Died 3 January 1927 Royal Inland Hospital, Kamloops, British Columbia, Canada
Scotland v Wales 1888; England 1889 (1), 1890c.
Cronberry Eglinton; Lugar Boswell; Hibernian 1883-88 (Scottish Cup 1887) [guest for St Bernard's Apr 1885]; Celtic 1888-91; Clyde 1891-92.
Known as the 'Grand Auld Gineral', McLaren was a natural leader and a hugely popular figure in Scottish football. He started life in straitened circumstances as the illegitimate son of Mary Gallacher, a coal pit labourer in Bathgate, and only acquired his surname after she married James McLaren two years later. He grew up in the Ayrshire coalfields and started playing football aged about 15 when he helped to found the Cronberry club on the Eglinton Estates. Three years later he joined Lugar Boswell which was an outstanding nursery of talent and won the Ayrshire Cup in 1881. A raid on the team by Hibs in 1883 opened the door to a wonderful football career, as McLaren was one of five Lugar players who moved to Edinburgh. Heavily built and cumbersome, he hardly looked like a top-level footballer but he had a fine football brain and tactical awareness. Featuring on the left side of midfield, he played a key role as Hibs won the Scottish Cup in 1887, and had won his first Scotland cap against Wales, when he was one of several players poached by Celtic in 1888. The following year, he scored a rare goal in glorious circumstances, netting a late winner after Scotland were losing 2-0 to England at half-time. Asked to speak at the celebratory dinner afterwards, he was terrified at the prospect and instead he convulsed the room by simply planting his large left foot on the table and saying 'There's the fut that bate England!'. He was appointed captain of Scotland against England the following year for his third and final cap. His time at Celtic was turbulent but he was popular with the fans. He was in the side which reached the Scottish Cup final in 1889 and he played in Celtic's first Scottish League match in August 1890, then by January he was dropped from the team. Although he was selected to captain Scotland against Ireland in March, he had to withdraw. In the summer he joined Clyde, who had just been admitted to the League, but his powers were diminishing and he retired from playing in 1892. He remained involved in the game as an occasional referee, also going on tour in the summer of 1893 with Ginnett's Circus which had a football show. He worked for several years for Glasgow Corporation then emigrated to British Columbia in 1912 where he established a ranch farm at Lac du Bois, near Kamloops. Like many other exiles he signed up with the Canadian Forces in WW1 and served in France, and even attended a match at Celtic Park in 1918 dressed in Canadian Foresters uniform. After the conflict was over he returned to his ranch, and died in hospital in 1927 from injuries received in a fall at his daughter's house during a Christmas visit.

Adam McLEAN (4/1, 1925-27)
Adam McLean
Born 27 April 1898 Mackenzie Street, Greenock, Renfrewshire
Died 29 June 1973 Western Infirmary, Glasgow
Scotland v Wales Oct 1925 (1), 1926; Ireland 1926; England 1927.
Broomhill YMCA; Anderston Thornbank; Celtic Jan 1917-28 (Scottish League 1919, 1922, 1926; Scottish Cup 1923, 1925, 1927); Sunderland 1928-30; Aberdeen Oct 1930-33; Partick Thistle 1933-34.
Born in Greenock, McLean spent part of his childhood in Belfast where his father worked in the shipyards. When he returned to Glasgow, he showed early promise as an outside left and joined Celtic in 1917 directly from a juvenile side. Pitched into the first team aged 18, he held his place at outside left for the next decade, notably in a wing partnership with Tommy McInally, making over 400 appearances as he featured in Celtic's championship-winning sides of 1919, 1922 and 1926 (he only made six appearances in 1917, not enough for a medal). He also won the Scottish Cup three times, not to mention numerous successes in the Glasgow Cup and Charity Cup. International recognition followed and he made the first of three appearances for the Scottish League in 1923, before finally breaking into the Scotland team in the autumn of 1925, scoring against Wales. It was the first of four caps over the next two seasons while he was at his peak. He might have stayed at Celtic Park for the rest of his career but a dispute about terms prompted his reluctant departure in 1928 to Sunderland. His two seasons in England were fruitful, keeping the side in the top half of the first division, and he came back to Scotland to conclude his career with three years at Aberdeen and a final season with Partick Thistle. On retiring he took up coaching and was appointed trainer of Brann Bergen in the summer of 1936 on the recommendation of Donald Colman. Back home, he scouted for Huddersfield then from 1938 was assistant trainer at Partick Thistle, a role he held until the 1950s.

Davie McLEAN (1/0, 1912)
David Prophet McLean
Born 13 December 1890 John Street, Forfar, Angus
Died 21 December 1967 Craig o' Loch Road, Forfar, Angus
Scotland v England 1912.

Forfar Celtic; Forfar Athletic Mar-May 1907; Celtic 1907-09; Preston North End Nov 1909-11; Sheffield Wednesday Feb 1911-13; Forfar Athletic May-Dec 1913; Sheffield Wednesday Dec 1913-19 [guest in WW1 for Dykehead Sep-Dec 1915; Third Lanark Dec 1915-18 and Rangers 1918-19]; Bradford Oct 1919-22; Dundee 1922-26; Forfar Athletic 1926-31.

McLean was one of the most prolific scorers Scotland has ever seen, with over 500 senior goals. He could shoot with accuracy and power from any distance and any angle, prompting Alan Morton to say 'For kicking a dead ball with power, I never saw the equal of Davie McLean. He had as strong a shot for goal as any man I knew'. Yet he won just one cap in the course of an exceptionally long career, which saw him play into his forties. From a family of footballers, with six brothers who played the game, McLean's peripatetic career started in Forfar where his fine form quickly attracted several clubs. In 1907 he was taken to Parkhead where he scored the winner on his Celtic debut against Rangers to win the Glasgow Cup, then hit a hat-trick the following week against Port Glasgow Athletic on his first league start. However, he was never given an extended run in the team, being an understudy to Jimmy Quinn, and reportedly he fell out with Willie Maley. In 1909, the club was all too happy to sell him to Preston, and two years later they transferred him to Sheffield Wednesday. In each of his two seasons there he was top scorer in the Football League, the latter with 30 goals, yet incredibly in the summer of 1913 he refused terms with Wednesday, and when Forfar Athletic (in the Central League, no less) made him an offer he took the opportunity. It was a sensational ploy but he stuck to his guns and eventually won his point in December when Wednesday, by now battling against relegation, persuaded him to return; they also had to pay a hefty fee to Forfar. When competitive football in England was suspended due to the War, he returned to Glasgow to work in a munitions factory, and played briefly for Dykehead before joining Third Lanark for three seasons. In 1918 he moved to Rangers for a season in which he averaged over a goal a game and won a second Glasgow Cup medal. He went back to Wednesday in 1919 but they soon sold him to Bradford, and when that club suffered a double relegation he decided to return to Scotland with Dundee, and the nearest he came to national silverware was their Scottish Cup final defeat in 1925, despite his goal against Celtic. He left them the following summer and wound down his playing days with five more years at his beloved Forfar Athletic, crowning his career in his final season by captaining the side to a rare victory in the Forfarshire Cup. Even after retiring he kept fit and played in charity matches as late as 1945. He was an important figure in the town and was elected a town councillor in 1938, while he ran the Strathmore Bar in the High Street, donated a charity cup for local sides and indulged his passion for cricket by playing many years for Strathmore. McLean has legendary status in Forfar but is, unjustly, rarely mentioned among the game's greats.

Duncan McLEAN (2/0, 1896-97)

Duncan McLean
Born 20 January 1868 Back Street, Renton, Dunbartonshire
Died 17 November 1941 Lennox Street, Renton, Dunbartonshire
Scotland v Wales 1896; Ireland 1897.
Renton Union; Renton 1888-90; Everton 1890-92 (Football League 1891); Liverpool 1892-95 (Second Division 1894); St Bernard's Oct 1895-98.

McLean is thought to be the first footballer ever featured on a cigarette card, the 'Field Favorites' card which was issued about 1895. He grew up in the football hotbed of Renton, and played two seasons at right back with his local team which had recently been crowned 'World Champions'. Although their glory days were largely behind them, Renton became founders of the Scottish League in 1890 then were expelled after five games for professionalism. Left without a club, McLean was offered a contract at Everton where he was initially the understudy to Andrew Hannah, then played a significant part as his new club won the Football League title. He was first choice for his second season but after club turmoil in 1892 he joined the newly-founded Liverpool where, in partnership with Hannah who had returned from Renton, he travelled on the new club's journey from Lancashire League to Second Division title and into the First Division. Following their relegation in 1895 he returned to Scotland to play for St Bernard's and was recognised with two international caps, against Wales in 1896 and Ireland in 1897. He retired from the game in 1898 and went back to Renton where he worked in a cotton dye factory.

Donnie McLEOD (4/0, 1905-06)

Donald McLeod
Born 28 May 1882 St Mary's Square, Laurieston, Stirlingshire
Died 6 October 1917 Poperinge, Flanders, Belgium
Scotland v Ireland 1905, 1906; Wales 1906; England 1906.
Stenhouse Thistle; Stenhousemuir 1901-02; Celtic 1902-08 (Scottish Cup 1904, 1907; Scottish League 1905, 1906, 1907, 1908); Middlesbrough Oct 1908-13.

A full back who was fast and two-footed, McLeod was brought up in Larbert where he played for a local juvenile team and had a superb season at Stenhousemuir, who won the Central Combination as well as the Scottish Qualifying Cup and the Stirlingshire Cup, although he did not play in either final. He joined Celtic in 1902 and played in all but two of their league matches in his first season there, then his first triumph came in the Scottish Cup final of 1904, alongside Willie Orr in defence, as Rangers were beaten 3-2. The following year he won his first Scotland cap against Ireland, a week after playing for the Scottish League, and then featured in all three internationals of 1906, plus another appearance for the Scottish League. Those years encompassed the start of Celtic's six consecutive league titles, and McLeod combined the championship of 1907 with another Scottish Cup win. However, it was not all rosy as he had a tendency to put on weight and when he was left out of Celtic's cup final team in 1908 it was perhaps an early sign of the fall-out that led to his transfer to Middlesbrough that autumn. At Ayresome Park he was later reunited with his former Celtic partner Jimmy Weir, who had been alongside him for his final year in Glasgow, and they picked up where they left off to make a fearsome defensive combination. He won no further honours but McLeod helped to keep Middlesbrough in the First Division until he retired in 1913, and he stayed in the town where he ran the Lord Byron Hotel. He enlisted early in 1916 as a gunner in the Royal Field Artillery and saw active service on the front line until sadly he died of wounds received at the Battle of Passchendaele. He is buried in Dozinghem Military Cemetery by Poperinge, Belgium.

John McLEOD (5/0, 1888-93)
John McLeod
Born 12 March 1866 High Street, Dumbarton
Died 4 February 1953 Cottage Hospital, Dumbarton
Scotland v Ireland 1888, 1890c; Wales 1889, 1893; England 1892.
Dumbarton Athletic 1885-89; Dumbarton 1889-95 (Scottish League 1891, 1892); Rangers 1895-96.

A reliable goalkeeper, McLeod started with Dumbarton Athletic and was picked to represent Dunbartonshire in 1886, then won his first two Scotland caps in 1888 and 1889. He was clearly destined for better things and in summer 1889 he joined the town's leading club, Dumbarton and played nearly every match as the club won the inaugural two Scottish League titles (albeit the first was shared with Rangers) and reached the 1891 Scottish Cup final. For his third Scotland match he was appointed captain, an unusual honour for a goalkeeper in those days, and he eventually took his caps total to five. He also played twice for the Scottish League and against the Canadian touring team in 1891. A move to Everton in 1892 fell through at the last minute and he remained first choice at Boghead until 1895 when he went to Rangers, but he only played a handful of games at Ibrox before retiring. A naval architect, he worked in the Dumbarton shipyards throughout his long life.

'Wiggy' McLEOD (1/0, 1886)
William McLeod
Born 24 December 1860 Springvale, Springburn, Glasgow
Died 8 November 1943 Royal Infirmary, Glasgow
Scotland v Ireland 1886.
Cowlairs 1881-86 [guest for Queen's Park Feb-Apr 1885]; Aston Villa Aug-Oct 1886; Cowlairs Oct 1886; Blackburn Olympic Oct-Nov 1886; Jardine's XI Nottingham Nov 1886-87; Nottingham Forest Jan 1887; Cowlairs 1887-92 [guest for St Bernard's Apr 1890].

McLeod was a classy full back known as 'Wiggy' because of the wig he wore to hide his baldness, which playful opponents would try to knock off. He devoted most of his football career to Cowlairs, and found time for some great adventures along the way. He played several times for Glasgow from 1884 onwards, and his reputation was such that he was roped in for Queen's Park's FA Cup campaign in 1885, partnering Wattie Arnott at full back in the latter stages of the competition which ended in defeat to Blackburn Rovers at the Oval. It was no surprise that he won a Scotland cap in the 1886 victory over Ireland and that summer, along with Tom Robertson, he went south to Aston Villa whose club President, George Kynoch MP, found them work at his ammunition factory. They did not remain long in Birmingham and McLeod played for Cowlairs when they came south for an FA Cup tie at Darwen in October, then stayed locally to feature briefly for Blackburn Olympic. In November he moved to Nottingham where Jardine's machine factory had a team and he also made an appearance for Nottingham Forest. After an adventurous year he came home to Scotland in the summer of 1887 and devoted the rest of his football days to Cowlairs, right up to the opening year of the Scottish League. After finishing playing in 1892 he remained active in the game for many years as a referee and club official. He narrowly escaped death in a tragedy on Loch Lomond in February 1895, when he and others went skating and fell through the ice, but while McLeod was rescued by rope, another man was not so fortunate and drowned. By career, he worked as a brass finisher and spent the rest of his life in Glasgow where he married late, in 1903, but still found time to have six children.

Sandy McLINTOCK (3/0, 1875-80)
Alexander McLintock
Born 1853 Paisley, Renfrewshire
Died 17 May 1931 Wilson Street, Dumbarton
Scotland v England 1875, 1876, 1880.
Vale of Leven 1875-84 (Scottish Cup 1877, 1878, 1879); Burnley 1884-86.

Although born in Paisley, McLintock was brought up in Bonhill and spent almost all his life in the area. A brilliant half back, he was 'hard as nails, dour as a bulldog' according to the *Scottish Referee*. His method of charging could put an opponent into the air, a skill which once nearly caused a riot at Hampden as he flung his great rival Jamie Weir over his back into a pool of water. He formed a formidable defensive partnership with Andy McIntyre in the triumphant Vale of Leven side which became the first Scottish team to defeat Queen's Park on 30 December 1876 and went on to win the Scottish Cup three times in a row. The third cup final victory in 1879 was somewhat hollow, however, as Vale refused to allow Rangers additional time for their players to recover from injury, and the Glasgow side refused to play. Around 1882 he dropped back to goalkeeper, and in that position he won the Glasgow Charity Cup and played in the 1883 Scottish Cup final defeat. He would have played in the 1884 final but was unwell, one of the factors which caused Vale to refuse to play. That summer he went to Burnley as a professional and during his two years there he was set up with a pub, The Marlborough. After he retired he took up refereeing and early in 1887 his pub was threatened with a boycott by supporters who were furious about a decision he gave to allow a goal for Accrington. He came back to Scotland in the summer of 1888 as trainer to Rangers and returned to his old trade as a tinsmith and gasfitter in Dumbarton. He took part in the Vale of Leven reunions on

Loch Lomond through the 1920s and died in 1931. His son James was also a player with Vale of Leven.

Jimmy McLUCKIE (1/0, 1933)
James Sime McLuckie
Born 2 April 1908 Miller Street, Stonehouse, Lanarkshire
Died 6 November 1986 Royal Infirmary, Edinburgh
Scotland v Wales 1933.
Tranent Juniors; Hamilton Academical Sep 1928-33; Manchester City Feb 1933-34; Aston Villa Dec 1934-36; Ipswich Town 1936-46 (Southern League 1937) [guest for Chelmsford City 1940-44, Clapton Orient Mar-Sep 1943].
Born in Lanarkshire and brought up in Edinburgh, McLuckie showed early promise at inside right with Craiglockhart School and was a Scotland schoolboy international in 1922 in the same team as Jack Harkness. He graduated via Tranent Juniors to Hamilton Accies in September 1928, and went straight into their league team. A versatile forward, he could play in the inside positions or on the right wing and was regarded highly enough for Manchester City to pay around £4,500 for the double transfer of himself and Alex Herd in February 1933. However, while Herd went into the City team, McLuckie was an understudy to Jimmy McMullan and did not play a first team match until the following season when McMullan moved on. Once given the opportunity he had such a great start that he was called up for a Scotland cap against Wales in October 1933. He played most of City's league matches but his form drifted and he was not only left out of their FA Cup winning team in 1934, he had to settle for being largely a reserve again in the following campaign. In search of regular football, he went to Aston Villa in December 1934 but after just one match they were so aggrieved at his apparent lack of fitness that they asked the Football League Management Committee to investigate his transfer. Although the probe found nothing wrong, he played less than half the games as Villa were relegated in 1936. Keen to move on, he was recruited by Ipswich Town, then in the Southern League and newly turned professional, able to pay the maximum wage of £8 a week. He dropped to the halfback line, was made club captain, and helped them achieve election to the Football League two years later, playing in every match of their first league season. Unfortunately, war intervened and as Ipswich closed down for the duration he played as a guest for Chelmsford City, and a few times for Orient while in London as a member of the Home Guard. He was appointed coach at Ipswich when they restarted and played a few times as an emergency before retiring in 1946. For a couple of years he managed Clacton Town in the Eastern Counties League, then resigned in 1949 and returned to Edinburgh.

Sandy 'Duke' McMAHON (6/4, 1892-1902)
Alexander McMahon
Born 16 October 1870 Whithillbrae, Kirkhope, Selkirkshire
Died 25 January 1916 Royal Infirmary, Glasgow
Scotland v England 1892, 1893, 1894; Ireland 1893 (1), 1901 (3); Wales 1902.
Leith Harp 1886-89; Hibernian Jan 1889-90 [guest for St Bernard's Apr-May 1890]; Celtic Dec 1890-1903 (Scottish League 1893, 1894, 1896, 1898; Scottish Cup 1892, 1899, 1900); Partick Thistle 1903-04.

McMahon was born in the Borders at a farm near Selkirk, the son of Irish immigrant labour, and the family moved to Edinburgh when he was a boy. He played for juvenile sides Woodburn and Leith Harp, a nursery side for Hibs who called him up early in 1889. He did well in their forward line but the club was in crisis, struggling to survive after an exodus of players to newly-formed Celtic, and about to collapse entirely. McMahon left the sinking ship and reportedly played for Darlington St Augustine's in November 1890 under an assumed name before choosing to follow his former colleagues to Celtic, where he made his debut on New Year's Day 1891. He went on to spend more than a decade with Celtic, a glorious period in which he won numerous honours for club and country. In his first full season he was Celtic's top scorer as they won the Scottish Cup, Glasgow Cup and Charity Cup. Nottingham Forest tried to lure him south in the summer of 1892 but such was his worth that Celtic sent a deputation to find him and persuaded him to return without playing a match. He struck up a devastating attack partnership with Johnny Campbell, scoring the goals that secured the club's first Scottish League title in 1893, and McMahon went on to win a further three titles while also lifting the Scottish Cup twice more, scoring in all his finals. However, there were long periods when he was out of the side due to injury, notably in November 1896 when he had to sit out the rest of the season after undergoing treatment at Matlock House in Manchester, an early football treatment centre. Meanwhile he won his first Scotland cap in 1892 against England, having already faced the Canadian touring team in 1891. He went on to win six caps, although he had to wait seven years after his fourth, then made up for lost time by scoring three (according to most reports, some say four) against a hapless Ireland side in 1901. He also made eight appearances for the Scottish League. With age catching up, Celtic allowed him to leave in 1903 and he had a brief swansong at Partick Thistle, but his knees were giving way and he only played four times for them before he was forced to retire. He invested his money from a benefit match into the Duke Bar in Gallowgate, but sadly he died aged 45 of kidney disease. Known for his intellectual abilities as he could recite Burns and Shakespeare, he was nicknamed 'the Duke', probably after the French President, Duc de Mac Mahon, or perhaps from a supposed resemblance to the Duke of Wellington. NB there is some confusion over his early career as Leith Harp had another McMahon, whose first name was Ross, a defender who had a season at Burnley.

'Napoleon' McMENEMY (12/5, 1905-20)
James McMenamin
Born 11 October 1880 King Street, Rutherglen, Lanarkshire
Died 23 June 1965 Robroyston Hospital, Glasgow
Scotland v Ireland 1905, 1909 (2), 1911 (1), 1914, 1920; Wales 1910, 1911, 1912, 1914; England 1910 (1), 1911, 1914 (1).
Cambuslang Hibernian 1900-01 [trial for Celtic Aug 1900]; Rutherglen Glencairn 1901-02 [trials for Everton Apr 1902, St Mirren Apr 1902]; Celtic 1902-20 (Scottish League 1905, 1906, 1907, 1908, 1909, 1910, 1914, 1915, 1916, 1917, 1919; Scottish Cup 1904, 1907, 1908, 1911, 1912, 1914); Partick Thistle 1920-23 (Scottish Cup 1921).

Jimmy McMenemy's real surname was McMenamin, as recorded on his birth, marriage and death certificates, but he was universally known as 'Napoleon' (or Nap for short) in tribute to his leadership qualities and battling style. He had a strong grounding in junior football and although he was given a trial by Celtic in an August 1900 friendly, they decided to wait. However, after he won the Scottish Junior Cup with Rutherglen Glencairn in 1902, playing alongside Alex Bennett and scoring the only goal of the final, Celtic made sure he signed for them that summer. It marked the start of nearly two decades with the club, a fruitful career which saw him playing well into his forties. He won an extraordinary number of trophies in over 500 appearances for Celtic, mainly at inside right where his speed, ball control, powerful shot and heading ability made him the perfect leader of an attacking side. He ended with no fewer than eleven league titles to his name, including six in a row in 1905-10, another four from 1914-17 and a final championship in 1919. There were also six Scottish Cups with Celtic, alongside numerous Glasgow trophies. On the Scotland front, he won 12 caps over a fifteen-year period, played 14 times for the Scottish League and in two Victory internationals in 1919. A paragon of fitness, he was selected against Ireland in March 1920 for his final cap and played just one more game for Celtic before he was released to Partick Thistle. It may have seemed like his career was virtually over but at the age of 40 in 1921 he won a seventh Scottish Cup as Thistle secured a 1-0 win over Rangers. He was still not done and carried on for another couple of seasons, with his final year largely spent coaching the reserves. He took over the Duke Bar from Sandy McMahon and remained active in football, coaching Partick Thistle and then Celtic in the 1930s. He was the father of John (below) and Harry of Newcastle United, as well as two junior internationalists, James and Frank.

John McMENEMY (1/0, 1933)
John McMenemy or McMenamin
Born 25 April 1906 Greenhill Road, Rutherglen, Lanarkshire
Died 5 February 1983 Royal Infirmary, Glasgow
Scotland v Wales 1933.
St Anthony's; St Roch's; Celtic 1926-28 (Scottish Cup 1927); Motherwell Oct 1928-36 (Scottish League 1932); Partick Thistle 1936-37; St Mirren 1937-39.

Son of Jimmy (above), McMenemy joined Celtic just six years after his father left Parkhead and perhaps his father's shadow was still too strong as he did not really fit in. He barely played in his three years at the club, although he did come away with a medal when an injury to Jimmy McGrory gave him a place in the Scottish Cup final team in 1927. He moved on to Motherwell in 1928 where he found his true form, providing the ammunition for Willie Macfadyen and scoring quite a few himself, notably with his performances at inside right in the side which won the Scottish League in 1932, the only time in a generation that the title left Glasgow. Motherwell were models of consistency and did not finish outside the top three positions in his first six seasons and there were two Scottish Cup finals, in 1931 and 1933, both of which were lost to Celtic. His only full international cap in 1933 was a real family affair as his brother Harry was originally selected to face Wales, but when he called off through injury his place went to John and poor Harry never got the call again. McMenemy also played three times for the Scottish League. He wound down his career at Partick Thistle and St Mirren, and retired on the outbreak of WW2. He worked during the War in an aircraft production factory and in his father's pub, and was later a clerk, spending all his life in Glasgow. He was born as a McMenamin, but by the time of his marriage he had adapted it to McMenemy.

James McMILLAN (1/0, 1897)
James Andrew McMillan
Born 11 April 1869 Campbell Street, Bonhill, Dunbartonshire
Died 20 February 1937 Bedford Road, Bootle, Lancashire
Scotland v Wales 1897.
Vale of Leven 1888-90; Everton Oct 1890-96; St Bernard's 1896-98.

An inside left or left winger, McMillan started at Vale of Leven and played in their Scottish Cup final of 1890, which was lost to Queen's Park after a replay. He played in the opening league matches of the following season for Vale then was signed by Everton, but made little impact there and only played seven league games in six years, spending most of his time with the reserves in their Combination team. He came back to Scotland with St Bernard's in 1896 and was playing well enough to be called up for the international against Wales in 1897 as a late replacement for Alex King. Meanwhile, he opened a cycle shop in Edinburgh but when he gave up the game in 1898 he returned to Liverpool where he married and found a job in Liverpool Docks as a porter. He lived in Bootle for the rest of his life and is buried in Anfield Cemetery. His eldest son George was killed in France in 1918 with the RAF.

Tom MacMILLAN (1/0, 1887)
Thomas MacMillan
Born 27 April 1864 Mauchline, Ayrshire
Died 2 January 1928 Glasgow Road, Dumbarton
Scotland v Ireland 1887.
Mauchline; Dumbarton Athletic 1884-85; Dumbarton 1885-95 (Scottish League 1891, 1892).

After playing originally for his home town team of Mauchline, MacMillan went to Dumbarton in 1884 to find work with his brother John, and both of them joined Dumbarton Athletic which was founded that year. A season later, Tom moved to Dumbarton where he was a mainstay of the team for ten glorious years, captaining them to two Scottish League titles (one shared), and he also played in the Scottish Cup finals of 1887 and 1891. Their half-back line of MacMillan, Dewar and Keir was legendary. Renowned for his all-round abilities including tackling, heading, accurate passing and sheer hard work, he won just one Scotland cap, against Ireland in 1887, although he was selected again in 1891 but had to decline. He played once for the Scottish League in 1894. He remained in Dumbarton as a joiner and cabinetmaker in the shipyards.

Jimmy McMULLAN (16/0, 1920-29)
James McMullan
Born 7 February 1894 Stirling Row, Denny, Stirlingshire
Died 27 November 1964 Carrville Drive, Sheffield, Yorkshire
Scotland v Wales 1920, 1921, Oct 1925, 1926, 1927c, 1928c; Ireland 1921, 1924, 1929c; England 1921, 1924c, 1925, 1926, 1927, 1928c, 1929c.
Denny Hibernian 1911-13; Partick Thistle Oct 1913-21; Maidstone United 1921-23 player-manager; Partick Thistle 1923-26; Manchester City Feb 1926-33 (Second Division 1928); Oldham Athletic 1933-34 player-manager.

Captain of the Wembley Wizards, McMullan was a massive figure for club and country in the inter-war years. He started at Denny Hibs, which already had a centre-half called James McMullan, and played alongside his namesake in the 1912 Junior cup final, which was lost 5-0 to Petershill. He was signed by Partick Thistle in October 1913 after a couple of trials with the reserves, went straight into the first team, and was not called up for wartime service as he was a miner, which enabled him to play throughout the First World War. This led inadvertently to him making his international debut in June 1918, not in the blue of Scotland but as a late substitute for England in a charity match at Celtic Park. The following year he appeared for Scotland in all four Victory Internationals, and finally won his first full cap in 1920 in Wales. He missed Partick Thistle's Scottish Cup victory of 1921 as he had been injured playing for Scotland against England the previous week, but was presented with a medal nonetheless for his contributions in the previous rounds. That summer he made a surprise move to Maidstone, in the Kent League, who recruited him as captain and team manager. They won every local competition going for a couple of years, then in 1923 Maidstone's benefactor, Herbert Sharp, withdrew his funding and McMullan returned home to Denny to consider offers. With some reluctance, he rejoined Partick Thistle and spent another three seasons at Firhill, showing such fine form that he captained Scotland against England in 1924 and played in six consecutive matches against the English, the most famous being the 5-1 victory of 1928. He also played four times for the Scottish League. He won a total of 16 Scotland caps, six as captain, although it could have been more as he withdrew from the team to face Ireland in February 1926 to devote his time to his new club, Manchester City, who were fighting to stay in the top division. He had some success as City reached the FA Cup final, but more importantly they were relegated. He remained with City for seven years, leading them back to the top division in 1928, where they stayed. In the autumn of 1931 he missed three months of the season when he was seriously ill with pneumonia. He reached a second FA Cup final in 1933 which again ended in defeat, and a week later he played his last match for the club before he was appointed player-manager of Oldham Athletic. A year later he took the reins at Aston Villa but resigned in October 1935 to go into business, only to be tempted back into management with Notts County, then at Sheffield Wednesday until 1942. He settled in Sheffield and strangely he died there in 1964 on the same day as another former Sheffield Wednesday manager, Billy Walker.

Alec McNAB (2/0, 1921)
Alexander McNab
Born 27 December 1894 Ann Place, Kempock Street, Gourock, Renfrewshire
Died 3 April 1960 Creve Coeur Country Club, St Louis, Missouri, USA
Scotland v Ireland 1921; England 1921.
Gourock Woodvale; Morton 1914-24 (Scottish Cup 1922); Boston 1924-28 (American Soccer League 1928); Fall River Marksmen 1928-31 (American Soccer League 1929, 1930; US National Challenge Cup 1930); New York Yankees 1932; New Bedford Whalers 1932-33; Stix Baer & Fuller 1933-34; St Louis Central Breweries 1935; St Louis Shamrocks 1936-37; South Side Radio 1937; St Matthew's 1937-38; Burke's Undertakers 1938-39.

McNab spent nearly a decade with Morton, a talented winger who playing consistently through the First World War and was capped twice for Scotland in 1921 before being a part of the team which famously won the Scottish Cup in 1922. Understandably he was keen to capitalise on his talents but Morton refused to raise his wages or countenance his departure so in 1924, in protest at the prohibitively high transfer fee on his head, he simply walked out and crossed the Atlantic to treble his wages in Boston while Morton, who retained his registration, got nothing. He found a new lease of life in the USA and never came home. At Boston he played alongside Barney Battles junior, a future Scotland cap, and won the League Cup twice then the League title in 1928. With Fall River Marksmen he won the league twice more and won the US title in a play-off against Cleveland; he was in line for a repeat the following year but broke his arm the day before the final. Fall River merged to become the New York Yankees then the New Bedford Whalers in a time of great upheaval in US soccer. In 1933 McNab moved to St Louis where he was offered a job with Stix, Baer and Fuller at their sporting goods store, while he also played for the company team in the western championship; it was renamed twice in succeeding seasons before disbanding. He took up coaching, and concluded his career with South Side Radio, St Matthew's and finally the wonderfully named Burke's Undertakers. He remained in St Louis until his sudden death from a heart attack while playing golf in 1960. His contribution to the growth of the game in America was recognised by his induction in the US Soccer Hall of Fame in 2005.

Sandy McNAB (2/0, 1937-39)
Alexander McNab
Born 27 December 1911 Rutherglen Road, Glasgow
Died 12 September 1962 Cloverhill View, East Kilbride, Lanarkshire
Scotland v Austria 1937; England 1939.
Pollok; Sunderland 1932-38 (Football League 1936; FA Cup 1937); West Bromwich Albion Mar 1938-46 [guest for Nottingham Forest 40-41 (one app), Walsall Sep 1945, Northampton Town Oct 1945, Newport County 45-46]; Newport County Apr-Dec 1946; Dudley Town Dec 1946-47; Northwich Victoria 1947-49.

A red-headed dynamo with Pollok juniors, who found him playing in the shopkeepers' midweek league, McNab attracted the attention of Sunderland and moved south in 1932. He developed into a constructive left half on Wearside but was slow to reach his potential and by 1935 he was flitting in and out of the reserves. He played just 13 times in their league winning season, and the following year he won an FA Cup medal only after he was brought into Sunderland's cup final team in place of injured captain Alex Hastings. However, he did enough for the Scotland selectors to pick him for the end-of-season visit to Austria in 1937. In March 1938 he reluctantly accepted a transfer to West Brom, who were fighting a desperate (and unsuccessful) battle against relegation, and was the first Scot to sign for the club in over 30 years. Despite playing in the Second Division the following season he was capped against England at Hampden in 1939 and went on the Scottish FA tour of North America that summer. A few months later, war broke out and he started working nearby at the Accles and Pollock aircraft construction factory, which enabled him to continue playing for West Brom. After falling out of the first team picture in 1945 he guested for several sides and signed for one of them, Newport County, before finding the travel from his home too much. He came back to the West Midlands with Dudley Town then joined Northwich Victoria in the Cheshire League, spending his second season as player-manager before retiring in 1949.

Colin MacNAB (6/0, 1930-32)
Colin Duncan MacNab
Born 6 April 1902 East Main Street, Darvel, Ayrshire
Died 25 November 1970 Royal Infirmary, Dundee
Scotland v Wales 1930; England 1931, 1932; Austria 1931; Italy 1931; Switzerland 1931.
Musselburgh Bruntonians 1920-24; Dundee 1924-34; Arbroath Sep 1934-36; Forres Mechanics Oct 1937.

Born in Ayrshire, MacNab's family came to Portobello, near Edinburgh, when he was a baby and he was brought up there. His football career started with four years in the juniors, and he won the Scottish Junior Cup in 1923 with Musselburgh Bruntonians. He was 22 when he signed for Dundee in 1924, and spent ten years at Dens Park where he became such a dependable and creative right half that he not only won six Scotland caps he also made five appearances for the Scottish League. There was frequent transfer speculation at the peak of his career but he never left Tayside. He failed to agree terms with Dundee in 1932 and although that was resolved he fell out with the club again in 1934, which opened the door for him to move up the road to Arbroath, where he opened a tobacconist shop. He played for Arbroath for two years, and his final match before he retired from football earned him a medal as they won the Forfarshire Cup in 1936. While he remained on Arbroath's management committee for many years, he made a cameo appearance for Forres Mechanics in October 1937 while on holiday in the area, and played for his local Civil Defence team during the Second World War. Latterly he ran a licensed grocery store in Arbroath.

Jock McNAB (1/0, 1923)
John McNab
Born 17 April 1894 Cleland, Lanarkshire
Died 2 January 1949 Litherland Road, Bootle, Lancashire
Scotland v Wales 1923.
Bellshill Athletic; Liverpool Oct 1919-28 (Football League 1922, 1923); Queen's Park Rangers 1928-30; Higson's Athletic 1930-31.

A right half or centre half, McNab was six feet tall with a strapping physique to match. His professional career was delayed until he was 25 due to service in WW1, although according to one account he 'learned his football in the army'. His performances for Bellshill after he was demobbed soon made him a target and Liverpool took him south in October 1919, just after he was sent off in his final match in the Glasgow Junior League. He made his Anfield debut on New Year's Day 1920 but did not feature regularly in the first team until the 1921-22 season, when he provided a rock-solid presence in two consecutive championship winning sides. He was further rewarded with his first and only Scotland cap, a 2-0 victory over Wales in 1923. He spent most of the decade with Liverpool, although there was an enforced break in November 1923 when his car crashed and he was thrown through the windscreen, requiring 16 stitches on his face. He moved to QPR in 1928, who immediately appointed him club captain, and he spent a couple of years in London before returning to live in Liverpool for good, making a brief swansong with Higson's Athletic in the Liverpool Midweek League. He was a keen bowler at Derby Park BC and captained a 'Scotland' side in local fundraising matches. He ran the Jawbone Hotel in Bootle (named after a whalebone archway created from Liverpool's whaling factories), where he died aged 53. His younger brother David played for Fulham.

Alec McNAIR (15/0, 1906-20)
Alexander McNair
Born 24 December 1882 Church Street, Stenhousemuir, Stirlingshire
Died 18 November 1951 Rae Street, Stenhousemuir, Stirlingshire
Scotland v Wales 1906, 1908, 1910, 1912, 1920; Ireland 1907, 1912c, 1914c, 1920c; England 1908, 1909, 1912c, 1913, 1914, 1920c.
Stenhousemuir Hearts [trial for Celtic May 1903]; Stenhousemuir 1903-04; Celtic 1904-25 (Scottish League 1906, 1907, 1908, 1909, 1910, 1914, 1915, 1916, 1917, 1919, 1922; Scottish Cup 1907, 1908, 1911, 1912, 1914, 1923).

As the winner of eleven league titles and six Scottish Cups with Celtic, it is little wonder that McNair was regarded as one of the finest players of his generation. Known as 'the icicle' for his cool temperament, he was described by Hughie Gallacher as 'the greatest back I ever played against'. From his early performances with local sides in Stenhousemuir it was clear he had talent, and when he moved to Celtic in 1904 it marked the start of a twenty-year association with the Parkhead club. He made over 600 competitive appearances for Celtic and although notionally a right back, he could play anywhere and was a talented enough dribbler and passer to fill in occasionally on the wing. For Scotland, he made his debut in 1906 and went on to win 15 caps, and even after his career was interrupted by the First World War, he featured in three Victory Internationals, then captained his country in the 1920 British Championship. He also played 15 times for the Scottish League. He was 42 when he played his last game for Celtic in 1925, then was appointed secretary/manager of Dundee for a couple of years until he left the game in 1927 to set up as a stockbroker in Falkirk, turning down the opportunity to coach in Egypt. He became secretary of Falkirk Tryst Golf Club and lived all his life in Larbert, close to the Stenhousemuir ground, spending his last months in a nursing home in Glasgow although he returned home a few days before his death, aged 68.

Harry McNEIL (10/6, 1874-81)
Henry McNeil
Born about May 1850 Belmore, Garelochside, Dunbartonshire
Died 2 June 1924 Buchanan Drive, Rutherglen, Lanarkshire
Scotland v England 1874, 1875 (1), 1876 (1), 1878 (2), 1879, 1881; Wales 1876 (1), 1877, 1879, 1881 (1).
Third Lanark 1872-73; Queen's Park 1873-84 (Scottish Cup 1874, 1875, 1876, 1880) [guest for Rangers Apr 1882].

McNeil spent his early years at Belmore House, on the east side of Gare Loch, where his father was the estate gardener (and originally spelled the surname McNiel). Like his brothers, Harry was active in local sports as a youth, playing shinty and taking part in athletics, before heading to Glasgow in the 1860s to work as a commercial clerk. He first started playing football on Glasgow Green but not in a serious way until he joined the Volunteers and turned out for the new Third Lanark club. Preferring to concentrate on football rather than soldiering, he soon threw in his lot with Queen's Park where he became an immense figure for over a decade. Added to his talents as a goal-scorer, he was an astute passer of the ball with a reputation for selflessness and a cheerful nature which made him very popular. He won four Scottish Cups with Queen's Park, including the first three in a row, and would have won a fifth in 1881 but missed the replay through injury after captaining the side in the draw against Dumbarton. Meanwhile he was a proficient scorer for Scotland at a time when the national team was able to defeat England 7-2 and 6-1, with six goals in ten appearances, including the game against Wales in 1876 when he partnered his brother Moses (below) in attack. He also captained Glasgow against Sheffield. In the 1870s Harry and his brother Peter opened a successful sports shop in the city centre but when the venture started to fail his career took a new direction. He moved to Ireland and ran the Royal Hotel in the seaside resort of Bangor with his second wife then following her tragic death in 1895 he returned to Scotland, and later he worked as a travelling salesman and a florist.

Moses McNEIL (2/0, 1876-80)
Moses McLay McNeil
Born 29 October 1855 Belmore, Garelochside, Dunbartonshire
Died 9 April 1938 Central Hospital, Dumbarton
Scotland v Wales 1876; England 1880.
Rangers 1872-82 [guest for Queen's Park 1875-76].
The younger brother of Harry (above), Moses came to Glasgow around 1871 and a year later he and his brothers Peter and Willie formed a football club on Glasgow Green, which they called Rangers. In due course they played in the new club's first match, and Moses would remain with the club for ten years. In that time, he had the distinction of scoring the Rangers' first ever competitive goal, in a Scottish Cup tie against Oxford in October 1874. He took part in their first final, the 1877 Scottish Cup which went to two replays before being lost to Vale of Leven, and he was in the side which won the club's first trophy, the Glasgow Charity Cup in 1879. He could have been tempted away in 1875 as he played alongside brother Harry in Queen's Park's famous 5-0 victory over Wanderers and the return game in London a few months later, but although he remained a member of QP, he devoted himself to Rangers for the rest of his playing career. A wing forward, in 1876

he was selected for Glasgow against Sheffield, then alongside his brother for Scotland against Wales, his first cap. It would be four years before his second, and last, international honour against England in 1880. He worked for most of his life as a travelling salesman, apart from a couple of years in Ireland at the end of the century running a hotel in Bangor with his brother Harry. In his later years he lived quietly in retirement at Craig Cottage in Clynder until his death in 1938. Three years earlier, he was interviewed about the origins of Rangers for a fascinating article in the *Daily Record*, as the last survivor of the original 'gallant pioneers'.

Bob McPHAIL (17/7, 1927-37)
Robert Lowe McPhail
Born 25 October 1905 Paisley Road, Barrhead, Renfrewshire
Died 24 August 2000 Hillside Nursing Home, Paisley, Renfrewshire
Scotland v England 1927, 1931, 1933, 1935, 1937 (2); Wales 1928, 1931, 1937; Ireland Feb 1931, Sep 1931 (1), 1932 (2), 1933 (1), 1937; France 1932; Austria 1933; Germany 1936; Czechoslovakia May 1937 (1).
Pollok [trial for Arthurlie Nov 1923]; Airdrieonians Jan 1924-27 (Scottish Cup 1924); Rangers Apr 1927-40 (Scottish League 1928, 1929, 1930, 1931, 1933, 1934, 1935, 1937, 1939; Scottish Cup 1928, 1930, 1932, 1934, 1935, 1936); Queen of the South Jan 1941; St Mirren Jan-May 1941 [guest for Falkirk May 1941].

A legendary figure for Rangers, McPhail came to Ibrox in 1927 with a terrific reputation. He was a Scottish Schools internationalist in 1919 while at Barrhead and had only a brief spell in junior football before joining Airdrie early in 1924. His first season concluded with their victory in the Scottish Cup when he was just 18 and over the next three years his goals tally rose significantly each season until he scored 34 in 31 games in 1926/27, the season he made his Scotland debut against England, two weeks after scoring on his first Scottish League appearance. Airdrie could not afford to keep him and he was transferred to Rangers in April 1927, playing for them in the Glasgow Charity Cup. His first full season at Ibrox ended with a glorious success as he not only won the first of nine league championships, he scored in the Scottish Cup final as Rangers defeated Celtic 4-0 to end their cup hoodoo. He went on to win another five Scottish Cups with Rangers, taking his overall tally to seven. On the international front he played regularly for a decade without ever really being first choice for Scotland. It seemed he could only score against Ireland but he finally hit the spot with a late double against England in 1937 to secure a 3-1 victory, and scored once more the following month in Prague. To his regret he never played at Wembley as all five of his caps against England were at Hampden. He also made six appearances for the Scottish League. When war was declared in 1939 he had reached the veteran stage and he left Rangers early in 1941, spending his last few months as a player with St Mirren. Curiously however, he played his final senior game at Ibrox in a Second XI Cup tie with Falkirk Reserves on a temporary transfer. After the War he went into business and ran an electrical equipment supply company, keeping involved with Rangers as trainer of the reserves for many years. In 1988 he wrote an autobiography, *Legend, Sixty Years at Ibrox*. His brother Malcolm won the Scottish Cup with Kilmarnock in 1920.

Davie McPHERSON (1/0, 1892)
David Murray McPherson
Born 22 August 1872 Grange Street, Kilmarnock, Ayrshire
Died 24 July 1942 Craighall Road, Kilmarnock, Ayrshire
Scotland v Ireland 1892.
Kilmarnock 1891-92 [trial for Rangers Apr 1891]; Rangers May 1892-93; Kilmarnock 1893-1904 (Scottish Qualifying Cup 1896; Second Division 1897, 1898); Beith 1904-06.
When McPherson signed for Kilmarnock in 1891, he must have felt at home as his father John was club trainer. A powerful and skilful inside right, he soon attracted attention and like his elder brother 'Kitey' (below), he was only 19 when capped for Scotland in 1892, but despite a fine career was never selected again. He had impressed Rangers while playing against them in a Scottish Cup tie and two replays, and joined his brother at the Ibrox club in May 1892, but only spent one season there before returning to his home town. He played in Kilmarnock's first League match in 1895 and they went from strength to strength, winning the Scottish Qualifying Cup in 1896, and then the Second Division title two years running. At a time when promotion was not automatic, by 1898 their claim was irresistible after the second title, not to mention reaching the Scottish Cup final, and the club was elected into the top league. He played on for several years then left after Kilmarnock finished bottom of the First Division in 1904 (but escaped relegation). He was given a benefit match against Ayr, and spent his last couple of years playing for Beith.

John MACPHERSON (1/0, 1875)
John Douglas Macpherson
Born 15 September 1853 Dingwall, Ross-shire
Date of death unknown
Scotland v England 1875.
Clydesdale 1873-76.
As with many Clydesdale players, Macpherson was adept at both cricket and football. He had an unusual background, born in Dingwall he went as an infant to Inveraray where his father had just taken over the Argyll Arms Hotel. DD Bone, writing of Macpherson in 1890, said he 'did much for football and cricket at Inveraray', and that he had acted as outrider to Her Majesty in the Highlands. This was presumably a reference to Queen Victoria's visits to the Duke and Duchess of Argyll at Inveraray Castle in 1871 and 1875, when his father's hotel provided a team of horses to convey the Queen's carriage. It is not clear why he was living in Glasgow in the early 1870s, but while there he played for Clydesdale and featured in the 1874 Scottish Cup final (lost to Queen's Park) as part of a strong forward line that included fellow internationalists Fred Anderson,

William Gibb, James Lang and David Wotherspoon. He was praised for his speed and dribbling, and although his passing sometimes fell short he did well enough to be selected for Glasgow to face Sheffield in February 1875 and then for Scotland against England the following month. He appears to have left Glasgow soon afterwards to return to Inveraray. He later moved with his father to the Queen's Hotel in Rothesay in 1882 but there was a scandal that year when he was named in a paternity suit back in Inveraray, and was successfully sued for child maintenance. There is no further trace of him which indicates he may have left the country, and currently his fate is unknown.

John McPHERSON (1/0, 1891)
John McPherson
Born 1 March 1863 Jerviston Square, Motherwell, Lanarkshire
Died 2 April 1957 Royal Jubilee Hospital, Victoria, British Columbia, Canada
Scotland v England 1891.
Alpha 1880-85; Cambuslang Dec 1885-86; Motherwell 1886-88; Heart of Midlothian 1888-91 (Scottish Cup 1891); Nottingham Forest 1891-92; Heart of Midlothian May-Sep 1892; Nottingham Forest 1892-1901 (FA Cup 1898); Motherwell 1901-02.
McPherson started out as a centre forward but found his vocation when he dropped back to centre half. A coal miner, he began with Alpha, the side which later merged with Glencairn in 1886 to form Motherwell FC. Having gone to play for Cambuslang for a few months, he returned in time for the new club's first match and stuck with them for a couple of years, during which he was picked several times for Lanarkshire. His career really took off when he signed for Hearts in 1888, playing at the heart of their defence as they entered the Scottish League in 1890 and won the Scottish Cup the following year. His success led to a move south that summer when he was recruited by Nottingham Forest as successor to David Russell, and he was joined there by Hearts team-mate Willie Mason, who had scored the cup-winning goal. Although he returned to Edinburgh after a season it was a brief reunion and by September he was back in Nottingham where he spent a fine decade at Forest, and will chiefly be remembered for captaining them to victory in the FA Cup final of 1898, when they beat Derby County 3-1; he even scored the final goal. He was a veteran of 35 by then, but still had a few years of football left in him. In 1900 he was involved in a bribery case after reporting a Burnley player to the FA for offering £5 to lose a match. He returned to Motherwell in 1901, making a handful of appearances before he retired a year later. He remained in the town, where he was a prize-winning enthusiast for homing pigeons, then emigrated to Canada in 1910, settling in Regina, Saskatchewan, where he worked as an engineer for the city. In 1938 he was robbed at gunpoint in his home by three youths who stole his FA Cup medal and had thrown it away by the time they were caught. However, he kept the ball with which Forest had won the cup and was very proud of it. He moved to Victoria on the west coast in 1951 to escape the harsh winter climate, and died there aged 94. NB his birth name was registered as Peter but was later changed to John.

John 'Kitey' McPHERSON (9/6, 1888-97)
John McPherson
Born 19 June 1868 Grange Street, Kilmarnock, Ayrshire
Died 31 July 1926 Shawfield Stadium, Rutherglen, Lanarkshire
Scotland v Wales 1888, 1892 (2); England 1889, 1890 (1), 1894 (1), 1895; Ireland 1890, 1895, 1897 (2).
Britannia; Kilmarnock 1886-88; Cowlairs 1888-90; Rangers 1890-1902 (Scottish League 1891, 1899, 1900, 1901; Scottish Cup 1894, 1897, 1898).

McPherson played with local junior side Britannia before joining Kilmarnock in 1886, and was such a success that he won his first Scotland cap in 1888 against Wales, aged 19. A versatile forward who usually played inside left, he went on to win further international honours after moving to Glasgow, playing twice against England while at Cowlairs, and continued to be capped at Rangers after he went to Ibrox in 1890. His nine Scotland caps were spread over a ten-year period, and he also made five appearances for the Scottish League. He played in every match as Rangers shared the first Scottish League title with Dumbarton, scoring five in one match against St Mirren and four against Cambuslang, and captained Rangers to their first Scottish Cup success in 1894. That was followed by further cup victories in 1897 and 1898, then the league championship three times in a row starting with the unbeaten season of 1898-99. After the turn of the century he played only a handful of matches and strangely his last appearance for Rangers before retiring in 1902 was in goal when Matt Dickie was injured. He came from a great football family and at Cowlairs he played alongside his brother Jimmy, while his younger brother Davie (above) was also an internationalist. He worked as an engine fitter but was also a Rangers director from 1907 until his death in 1926, when he collapsed while watching the Clyde sports at Shawfield Stadium.

Jack McPHERSON (8/1, 1879-85)
John Campbell McLeod McPherson
Born summer 1854 Balloch Park, Dunbartonshire
Died 14 March 1934 Keir Terrace, Dumbarton

Scotland v England 1879, 1880, 1883, 1884; Wales 1879, 1881, 1883; Ireland 1885c (1).
Vale of Leven 1876-85 (Scottish Cup 1878, 1879).

A robust half back, described in *Athletic News* as 'cautious, good and at times brilliant', McPherson was born on the Balloch estate where his father was a gardener. He spent all his playing career with Vale of Leven and had a great start in his first full season as he won the Scottish Cup in 1878, when Third Lanark were defeated, and then travelled to London to face the FA Cup winners Wanderers at the Oval. He played magnificently in defence, although injured, as Vale beat the English champions 3-1. A year later, he won another Scottish Cup medal when Rangers refused to replay the final. The same year he earned his first national team selection, and played alongside Charles Campbell at the Oval in a 5-4 defeat. However, that was to prove his only international reverse as Scotland won all his other seven matches. Vale continued to be a force in Scotland football and reached the Scottish Cup finals of 1883, lost to Dumbarton, and 1884, when they refused to play against Queen's Park because of illness and injuries. He was appointed club captain for his last season as a player, helping to bring through young talent, and reached the Scottish Cup final yet again in 1885, only to lose to Renton in a replay. He was a successful businessman in the Dunbartonshire shipyards and spent most of his working life as manager of Dennystown Brass Works, which closed shortly after his death in 1934. He was a good tennis player, winning the Vale of Leven championship, and a president of Dumbarton Bowling Club.

Robert McPHERSON (1/1, 1882)
Robert McPherson
Born 15 June 1858 Barrhead, Renfrewshire
Died 15 September 1921 Saltcoats, Ayrshire
Scotland v England 1882 (1).
Arthurlie 1879-87 [guest for Third Lanark May 1884].

A leading figure at Arthurlie, his only senior club, McPherson helped them to win the Renfrewshire Cup in 1881 and 1882. Known as 'the baker', his first representative selection came in 1879 for Renfrewshire and in 1882 he became his club's first internationalist, shortly after playing for Scotch Counties. Partnering Johnny Kay on the left wing, he was the only non-Queen's Park player in the Scotland forward line that faced England, and rewarded that faith by scoring one of the goals in a 5-1 victory. Despite that impressive result there were no more honours, although he was named as a reserve in 1884, the year he made a guest appearance for Third Lanark in the Glasgow Charity Cup final. He retired from playing in 1887. He worked as a power loom weaver and calico machine printer in Barrhead but there was tragedy lurking. His marriage broke up acrimoniously in 1903, to the extent it was covered in the press, and ultimately he took his own life in 1921, when he hired a rowing boat at Saltcoats and threw himself into the sea; he was later found drowned on the foreshore. NB his parents were not married and he was registered in his mother's name, Esdon, but subsequently took his father's surname.

Matt McQUEEN (2/0, 1890-91)
Matthew McQueen
Born 8 May 1863 Harthill, Lanarkshire
Died 29 September 1944 Kemlyn Road, Anfield, Liverpool
Scotland v Wales 1890, 1891.
West Benhar 1882-85; Bo'ness 1885-86; Champfleurie 1886-87; Heart of Midlothian 1887-88; Champfleurie 1888-89; Leith Athletic 1889-92 [guest for St Bernard's Apr-May 1890]; Liverpool Oct 1892-99 (Second Division 1894, 1896).

Born in Harthill to a pit worker, McQueen went down the coal mines and grasped the opportunity which football provided to better himself. He first played for West Benhar, a mining team, and then moved to Bo'ness where he worked in an oil factory. After a season with the local club he joined Champfleurie, a Linlithgow side; he was also selected for West Lothian with both clubs. He had a season with Hearts without really making an impression, but after another spell at Champfleurie he was recruited by Leith Athletic in 1889, with the incentive of a job in a warehouse. He really made his name with the port club, playing three times for Edinburgh in his first season, and was capped in Scotland's 5-0 win over Wales in 1890. A year later he faced the Welsh again, and played against the touring Canadians in October 1891. He played at half back in his internationals, but was versatile enough for any other position and with a wealth of experience he was recruited by Liverpool, along with younger brother Hugh, shortly after the club was formed in 1892. Matt was paid £100 and Hugh got £70, according to reports. After a season in the Lancashire League, they both played in the club's first ever Football League match the following year, and Matt developed a lifelong attachment to the Anfield side. He went on to win two Second Division titles, and played not just in all the outfield positions but regularly as goalkeeper. After he retired from the game in 1899 he became a referee and was on the Football League list from 1904-08. He remained in Liverpool, with a home right outside Anfield, and worked as an insurance agent. He was appointed a Liverpool director in 1918 and became the club's manager in 1923, overseeing the final stages of a league title win. However, in December 1923 he was knocked down by a taxi while on a scouting excursion to Sheffield, and had to have his leg amputated, with two months in hospital. His disability ultimately prompted his retiral four years later and he continued to live in the shadow of Anfield until his death in 1944, age 81.

Dan McRORIE (1/0, 1930)
Daniel McRorie
Born 25 June 1906 Jamieson Street, Govanhill, Glasgow
Died 26 July 1963 Mearnskirk Hospital, Newton Mearns, Renfrewshire

Scotland v Wales 1930.
Queen's Park; Airdrieonians 1925-27; Stenhousemuir 1927-28; Morton 1928-30; Liverpool Nov 1930-33; Millwall Sep 1933; Rochdale Oct-Dec 1933; Morton Dec 1933-34; Runcorn Aug-Nov 1934; Morton Feb 1938.

McRorie went to Queen's Park School and naturally joined his nearest club but left before making a first team appearance. He turned professional with Airdrieonians in 1925 and was mainly a reserve as he developed a knack of scoring goals from the right wing, netting seven in one game. He dropped a division to Stenhousemuir to get first team football, and then blossomed at Morton. In the autumn of 1930 he was top of the scoring charts in Scotland, which won him an appearance for the Scottish League and then two weeks later a Scotland cap against Wales. Liverpool were persuaded to pay a fee of £1,200 for his services but although he made an early impact at Anfield he never really settled and after drifting out of the picture was released in 1933. He played for a series of clubs on short trials without establishing himself and his last attempt was back on Merseyside with Runcorn, before he retired from the game. He returned to Scotland and went into the insurance business but kept fit and, when Morton were short of players for a Second Eleven cup tie in 1938, he was persuaded to turn out for them one more time. He lived in the southside of Glasgow in Kingswood Drive until his early death at the age of 57.

Alex McSPADYEN (2/0, 1938-39)
Alexander McLuckie McSpadyen
Born 19 December 1914 Main Street, Holytown, Lanarkshire
Died 31 October 1978 Sunnyside Crescent, Holytown, Lanarkshire
Scotland v Hungary 1938; England 1939.
Holytown United; Partick Thistle Mar 1935-48 [guest for Aberdeen Sep 1943]; Portadown 1948-49.

In many ways, McSpadyen's life was shaped by the two world wars: when he was born his father was away serving with the Scottish Rifles in WW1, while his playing career was interrupted by the outbreak of WW2. Having represented Scotland as a juvenile with Holytown, his village side, the flying winger was signed by Partick Thistle in March 1935 and went straight into the first team, spending almost all of his playing career with them. He came into contention for a Scotland call-up after an appearance for the Scottish League, but even so he was capped almost by accident against Hungary in December 1938: Jimmy Delaney called off late and reserve Alec Munro was too far away in Blackpool, so McSpadyen got a last-minute call to play. He did well and featured against England in the spring, as well as playing again for the Scottish League. He would no doubt have added to his caps tally had the War not broken out. He remained in Scotland for the opening years of the conflict but in 1943 was fined for failing to attend his essential war work and soon afterwards he joined the Army. By the time he was demobbed in 1946 he had fallen out of the reckoning at Firhill and only played a handful more games, then in 1948 he signed up at Portadown for a final year. He returned to his home town and in 1953 was appointed trainer of Holytown United until the club folded a year later.

Willie McSTAY (13/0, 1921-28)
William McStay
Born 21 June 1892 Netherburn, Dalserf, Lanarkshire
Died 3 September 1960 Shettleston Road, Glasgow
Scotland v Wales 1921, Feb 1925, Oct 1925, 1926c, 1927; Ireland 1921, 1925, 1926c, 1927c, 1928; England 1925, 1926c, 1927c.
Netherburn Juniors; Larkhall Thistle; Celtic 1912-29 (Scottish League 1917, 1919, 1922, 1926; Scottish Cup 1923, 1925, 1927) [loan to Vale of Leven Jan-Apr 1912, Ayr United 1912-16; Belfast Celtic 1917-18 (Irish Cup 1918); trial for New York City May 1923]; Heart of Midlothian 1929-30; Kirkmuirhill Juniors 1931-32.

An outstanding left back who was a major force with Celtic in the 1920s, McStay signed from Larkhall Thistle in 1912 but had few opportunities to play for the team until the end of the decade. He was almost immediately sent on loan to Vale of Leven, then later to Ayr United to gain experience and he remained there until 1916 when he was recalled to Celtic Park. He won a league title in his first season but then his career was interrupted by war service as a Trooper with the North Irish Horse. Based in Northern Ireland at Antrim camp, he played as a guest for Belfast Celtic and even won the Irish Cup with them. On being demobbed he returned to action with Celtic in December 1918, featured in every match till the end of the season for another title win, and his career really took off. His first international honours came in 1921, selected against Wales and Ireland, and he went on to play 13 times for Scotland, five as captain. He also made ten appearances for the Scottish League. Celtic won the league again in 1922 and the Scottish Cup in 1923 but when the club reduced player wages he walked out and decided to try his luck in American soccer. After two games with New York City he was persuaded to come home, having made his point. He went on to win the Scottish Cup twice more and the league in 1926, and by the time he was released in 1929 he had played well over 400 matches for the club. He was succeeded as Celtic captain by his younger brother Jimmy. He had a season with Hearts before retiring, and took over a pub in the Lanarkshire village of Kirkmuirhill, where he made a brief reappearance on the field the following year. After the pub went bust he managed Glentoran and Coleraine during the 1930s, then returned to Glasgow where he worked as a factory security officer. In 1960, suffering from chronic bronchitis, he collapsed in Shettleston Road and was taken to Glasgow Royal Infirmary where he was found to be already dead. NB McStay's birth name was registered as Hugh, and remarkably it was only formally corrected by him in 1957, although he spent his life known as Willie.

Jock McTAVISH (1/0, 1910)
John Kay McTavish
Born 7 June 1885 McLean Street, Govan, Glasgow
Died 4 April 1944 Grahams Road, Falkirk
Scotland v Ireland 1910.
Ibrox Roselea; Petershill 1904-05; Falkirk 1905-10; Oldham Athletic Jun-Dec 1910; Tottenham Hotspur Dec 1910-1912; Newcastle United Apr 1912-13; Partick Thistle 1913-19 [guest during WW1 for Heart of Midlothian Aug-Nov 1917, Falkirk Nov 1917-18); Bo'ness 1919-20 (Central League); East Fife Aug-Oct 1920; Dumbarton Oct 1920-21; East Stirlingshire 1921-22; Arbroath Athletic 1922-23 player coach.

A fleet-footed inside forward, McTavish joined newly-promoted Falkirk in 1905 from Petershill and formed a highly effective right wing partnership with Jock Simpson. In their five years at Brockville their attacking play took Falkirk to unprecedented heights and twice they were runners-up in the league, missing out on the title in 1910 by just two points. By then McTavish had played twice for the Scottish League against the Football League in 1907 and 1908, then won his only Scotland cap in 1910 against Ireland, as a replacement for the injured Jimmy McMenemy. Although that game ended in a disappointing 1-0 defeat, his reputation earned him a transfer to England that summer, initially with First Division side Oldham Athletic who splashed out to sign him, then after a few months he moved on to Spurs, following his younger brother Robert. He played regularly without making a major impression and was transferred in the spring of 1912 to Newcastle where he did well enough to be selected for the Anglo-Scots in the international trial. However, his three years in England could not be judged a great success and he returned to Scotland in 1913 with Partick Thistle, in an exchange deal. He remained with Thistle throughout the war years, playing once for Glasgow against Sheffield in 1914, and at times he went out on loan. Then after the conflict he signed for Bo'ness, who won the Central League in his season there, had short spells at East Fife and Dumbarton, and in 1921 was signed by East Stirlingshire who made an ambitious move to get Jock Simpson at the same time, but Blackburn Rovers refused to let him go. His final club was Arbroath Athletic, a short-lived rival to the senior Arbroath side, who played in the Eastern League. He returned to Falkirk where he played in occasional veterans matches and worked as a repairman in the Corporation Gas Department. He died in 1944 after he collapsed on a bus in Grahams Road, Falkirk, near his home in Brown Street.

'Joe' McWATTIE (2/0, 1901)
George Chappell McWattie
Born 22 April 1875 Commerce Street, Arbroath, Angus
Died 3 July 1952 Princes Street Station, Edinburgh
Scotland v Ireland 1901; Wales 1901.
Ardenlea; Alpine; Arbroath 1894-98; Hibernian Mar 1898-1900; Queen's Park 1900-01; Heart of Midlothian 1901-04.

McWattie, known as 'Joe' or 'Geo', was a fine goalkeeper who remained amateur throughout his career. One of four brothers who played for Arbroath, his father James was a well-known local tobacco manufacturer and a town Bailie. He was educated at the prestigious Harris Academy in Dundee, where he played as a forward for the school team, then took up goalkeeping with Arbroath junior side Ardenlea and was such a success that they won their league. He caught the eye of his town's senior club and joined them in 1894, taking part in their memorable Forfarshire Cup win of 1896 with another future internationalist, Albert Buick, in the team. When his work as an assurance agent took him to Edinburgh early in 1898 he signed for Hibs, and in 1900 was recruited by Queen's Park for their first season as a league team. He was only there for a year, but was good enough in this time to win two Scotland caps against Ireland and Wales. He also made appearances for the Scottish League against the Irish and the Football League, although the latter ended in a 6-3 defeat. Finding the travel between Edinburgh and Glasgow was too much, he left Queen's Park and joined Hearts. He played in the 1903 Scottish Cup final, which was lost in a second replay to Rangers, and gave up the game the following season. He took up cricket with Edinburgh side Clarendon, a sport he had played in Arbroath as a young man, and spent the rest of his life in the city, with a home in Mayfield Road, until he died suddenly of a heart attack in Princes Street Station in 1952.

Peter McWILLIAM (8/0, 1905-11)
Peter McWilliam
Born 21 September 1879 Argyle Street, Inverness
Died 1 October 1951 Corporation Road, Redcar, Yorkshire
Scotland v England 1905, 1906, 1907, 1909, 1910; Wales 1907, 1909, 1911c.
Heatherly; Inverness Thistle 1899-1902; Newcastle United 1902-11 (Football League 1905, 1907, 1909; FA Cup 1910).

From humble origins in the Highland League, 'Peter the Great' was nearly 23 when he was recruited by Newcastle United from Inverness Thistle, the same club which had produced Andy McCombie. The story goes that McWilliam was on his way to a trial with Sunderland (who had tried to sign him in 1899) when he was effectively hijacked by United officials at Newcastle Central Station, and they persuaded him to sign at St James' Park instead. It took him a couple of years to establish himself in the first team, but he went on to be a hugely effective half back who could read and dictate the play. His style of passing and careful possession was the key to Newcastle's success in the Edwardian era, and he enjoyed three league titles and a much-vaunted FA Cup triumph in 1910 (after three final defeats). He was a mainstay of the Scotland team for the second half of the decade, making five appearances against England and three against Wales. However, he sustained a nasty knee injury in the last of these, while captaining Scotland, and was forced to give up playing in 1911. He then embarked on a lengthy managerial career and in 1913 secured his first management post with Tottenham Hotspur, where he suffered relegation in his second season. He worked in a Woolwich munitions factory during WW1 then came back to the club and won the FA Cup in 1921, becoming one of the few men to win the trophy as player and manager. Remembering his roots, he took Spurs on a short tour to Inverness that autumn. When Middlesbrough offered him a higher salary he joined them in 1927, remaining for seven years and winning two Second Division championships. He was sacked in 1934, and after a spell scouting for Arsenal he was appointed manager again at Spurs from 1938-42. He then retired to his wife's home town, Redcar, where he died in 1951.

Johnny MADDEN (2/5, 1893-95)
John Madden
Born 11 June 1865 High Street, Dumbarton
Died 17 April 1948 Dobrovského, Prague, Czechoslovakia
Scotland v Wales 1893 (4), 1895 (1).
Dumbarton Albion; Dumbarton Hibs 1885-86; Dumbarton 1886-87; Gainsborough Trinity 1887-88; Celtic May 1888; Dumbarton 1888-89; Celtic 1889-97 (Scottish League 1893, 1894, 1896; Scottish Cup 1892); Dundee Aug-Dec 1897; Tottenham Hotspur Jan-Apr 1898.
Madden had a fine playing career in Scotland, but is nothing short of a legend in the Czech Republic where he is known as the father of Czech football. Brought up in Dumbarton, he soon developed a reputation as a goal-scoring centre forward and was nicknamed was 'the Rooter', apparently for his ability to backheel a ball. He had a box of tricks in his repertoire which endeared him to fans at all his clubs, although in his first season at Dumbarton his form deserted him at the worst possible time when he missed a host of chances in the 1887 Scottish Cup final. He tried his luck down south with Gainsborough Trinity, playing alongside future England star Fred Spiksley, then decided to return home after a year and was recruited to play in Celtic's first-ever match in 1888. However, he spent another season at Dumbarton before throwing in his lot with the Glasgow side and had eight successful years at Celtic which brought three league titles. He won the Glasgow Cup four times, but had misfortune in the Scottish Cup, missing Celtic's replay victory of 1892 after featuring in the first match, and then experiencing defeat in 1893 and 1894. He played for Scotland just twice, despite scoring four against Wales on his debut in 1893, and another goal two years later on his final cap. He also made four appearances for the Scottish League and had a lucrative side-line winning five-a-side tournaments which brought many prizes including gold watches. When he left Celtic in 1897 he went to Dundee for a few months, then to Spurs until the end of the season before retiring. He worked as a riveter in the Clydeside shipyards until his life was transformed in 1905 when he was invited to Prague, at that time in Bohemia, to coach Slavia, shortly before his 40th birthday. He stayed the rest of his life and was in charge of Slavia until 1930, revered not just as a trainer but for his healing powers, treating injuries with skill and care. He coached the Bohemia national team which faced England in 1908 and was with the Czech team at the 1919 Inter-Allied Games and the 1924 Olympics. Known as 'Dedek', the 'old man', his death in 1948 was widely mourned and his grave in Prague remains a place of pilgrimage. NB he is widely credited with a middle name William but I have found no documentary evidence of this.

Jimmy MAIN (1/0, 1909)
James Main
Born 27 May 1886 Stewart Street, West Calder, Midlothian
Died 29 December 1909 Royal Infirmary, Edinburgh
Scotland v Ireland 1909.
West Calder Swifts 1903-04; Hibernian Sep 1904-09.

Main grew up in the village of Mossend, where he was a shale miner, and followed in the sporting footsteps of two elder brothers Willie and Alex who had already made a name for themselves as athletes, the latter as a footballer for Arsenal. Hibs coach Dan McMichael spotted his ability and snapped him up from West Calder Swifts to play for the Edinburgh side in 1904 and he made his league debut the following week, aged 18. Despite his youth he was a regular in the Hibs team for over five years. With a powerful physique and excellent temperament, he developed into an international full-back, made one appearance for the Scottish League in 1908 against the Football League, then played in Scotland's 5-0 win over Ireland in March 1909. He was rumoured to be signing for an English club that summer but chose to stay at Hibs, with fatal consequences. On Christmas Day he was knocked in the stomach while playing against Partick Thistle in Glasgow, and although he had to go off, initially it seemed not to be serious. He was able to return home to Mossend, but the pain became so severe that a doctor was called and on Sunday he was taken to hospital where he was diagnosed with a ruptured bowel. He died three days later, aged just 23, and huge crowds followed his funeral procession to West Calder Cemetery. A granite memorial was erected in his honour a year later, paid for by Hibs supporters.

Bobby MAIN (1/0, 1937)
Robert Frame Main
Born 10 February 1909 Hallcraig Street, Airdrie, Lanarkshire
Died 30 March 1985 Monklands General Hospital, Airdrie, Lanarkshire
Scotland v Wales 1937.

Lochburn; Baillieston Juniors 1926-29; Rangers 1929-39 (Scottish League 1934, 1935, 1937; Scottish Cup 1934, 1935); New Brighton 1939-41 [guest for Airdrieonians Dec 1939]; Dunfermline Athletic 1941-42.

An unsung hero of the Rangers team of the 1930s, Main was a talented right winger who only won one Scotland cap but came away with several club honours. The son of a former Albion Rovers player, he was educated at Airdrie Academy and played for three seasons with Baillieston, winning the Scottish Intermediate League in 1929. He signed for Rangers that summer but had to be patient and spent most of his first four years in the reserves as understudy to Sandy Archibald. He was finally given an extended run in 1933-34 and proved his worth in a season that ended in a league and cup double, and he chipped in with one of the goals in the 5-0 Scottish Cup final win over St Mirren. He played in another double-winning side the following season, and in most of the matches as another league title was secured in 1937. Having made three appearances for the Scottish League, all against the English, and being invited on the SFA tour of North America in 1935, he was finally capped for Scotland in October 1937, a disappointing defeat to Wales. From the autumn of 1938 he faded out of the picture at Ibrox and at the end of the season was given a free transfer. He went to New Brighton and had played just one competitive game before war broke out in September and he returned to Scotland. He managed to play in occasional matches for the Lancashire club and made a guest appearance for Airdrie but that was essentially all until he signed for Dunfermline in 1941 for a final season before retiring.

Willie MALEY (2/0, 1893)
William Patrick Maley
Born 25 April 1868 Newry Barracks, County Down, Ireland
Died 2 April 1958 Bon Secours Hospital, Mansionhouse Road, Glasgow
Scotland v Ireland 1893; England 1893.
Hazelbank Juniors; Third Lanark 1887-88; Celtic 1888-97 (Scottish Cup 1892; Scottish League 1893, 1894, 1896) [guest for Manchester City 1896].

If there is one man who embodied Celtic in the club's early years, it was Willie Maley.

Born in Ireland, where his father was a physical training instructor with the Army, he moved to Scotland as a one-year-old and was brought up in Cathcart, on the south side of Glasgow. A champion athlete with Clydesdale Harriers, winning the Scottish Amateur Athletic Union 100 yards title in 1896, he really made his mark in football and played briefly for Third Lanark before helping to found Celtic. He had just turned 20 when he played in their very first match in May 1888, together with his brother Tom, and would spend the rest of his life with the club. He was no mean player at half back, and was appointed club secretary, the start of over 50 years as an administrator with Celtic. On the field, he took part in their earliest adventures and successes, including the Scottish Cup final of 1889 and the first victory of 1892, and had a significant role in their league-winning teams of 1893 and 1894, with a lesser part in 1896. His Irish birth should have ruled him out of contention for Scotland, under the rules of the time, but he was called up in 1893 for two matches with differing fortunes, a thumping defeat of Ireland followed a week later by a heavy loss to England. When he retired from playing in 1897 he was appointed secretary-manager of Celtic, a post he held until 1940, and shortly before he retired he wrote the club history, *The Story of the Celtic*. He presented trophies for junior and schools football, and the Willie Maley Trophy is still contested by Fife schools. Outside football he was a company director in a drapery business until his death, a few weeks before his 90th birthday. See his biography *Willie Maley, the man who made Celtic* by David Potter.

Harry 'Beef' MARSHALL (2/1, 1899-1900)
Henry James Hall Marshall
Born 24 November 1873 Bridge Street, Portobello, Midlothian
Died 16 September 1936 Eastern General Hospital, Leith, Edinburgh
Scotland v Wales 1899 (1); Ireland 1900c.
Portobello Thistle; St Bernard's Apr-May 1892; Heart of Midlothian Aug-Oct 1892; Blackburn Rovers Oct 1892-94; temporary retirement; Heart of Midlothian 1896-99 (Scottish League 1897) [loan to Blackburn Rovers Apr 1898]; Celtic Feb 1899-1903 (Scottish Cup 1899, 1900) [loan to Alloa Athletic Sep-Oct 1900, Raith Rovers Oct 1900-01]; Clyde 1903-04.

Marshall was not the quickest of half backs but made up for that with his powerful build that he used to subdue tricky opponents and was sufficient to earn the nickname 'Beef'. Also known as the Portobello Boatman, he followed his father into the boat hiring business at the seaside resort near Edinburgh where he grew up. As an 18-year-old he had brief spells with St Bernard's and Hearts before joining Blackburn Rovers in the autumn of 1892. The team had had a woeful start to their season and he not only helped to haul them to safety, they reached the FA Cup semi-final in both years he was there. For two years he gave up football to focus on his boat hire business in Portobello, then returned to action with Hearts in 1896 and won the league in his first full season at Tynecastle. He spent another two years there, interrupted by a month in Blackburn in April 1898 when they were in trouble again and threatened by relegation. They lost three out of four test matches but were ultimately saved from the drop by league expansion. He had an unusual season in 1898-99, playing the full league campaign for Hearts then transferring to Celtic in February for their successful attempt on the Scottish Cup. Meanwhile he scored on his Scotland debut against Wales in 1899, and captained the side in a 3-0 win over Ireland the following year. He also won four caps for the Scottish League, three of them against the English in consecutive years from 1898. Unable to agree terms with Celtic in 1900, he was sent out on loan for a full season at Alloa and Raith Rovers, then they called him back for another couple of years, before he ended his career at Clyde. He went back to Edinburgh, and later in life he ran the Spylaw Tea Room in Colinton with his third wife, until he died of lung cancer in 1936.

Jimmy 'Doc' MARSHALL (3/0, 1932-34)
Dr James Marshall MB, ChB, DPh
Born 3 January 1908 Avonbridge, Stirlingshire
Died 27 December 1977 Hothfield Hospital, Ashford, Kent
Scotland v England 1932, 1933, 1934.

Shettleston; Rangers 1925-34 (Scottish League 1927, 1929, 1930, 1931, 1933, 1934; Scottish Cup 1930, 1932, 1934); Arsenal 1934-35; West Ham United 1935-37.

Marshall was a rare example of a player who combined top level football with a demanding professional career, qualifying as a doctor while a committed member of the Rangers team. Educated at Airdrie Academy, as were his Rangers team mates Jimmy Smith, Torry Gillick and Bobby Main, he came to Ibrox as a 17-year-old from Shettleston Juniors, and made a scoring debut at centre forward in April 1926. He showed such exceptional talent that he remained in the side and in his first full season he finished top scorer as Rangers won the league. The following couple of years he barely played as his medical studies at Glasgow University took priority, but he fought his way back into the team in early 1929. Having moved to inside right he remained a fairly constant presence for the next five years, with occasional absences for exams. After he qualified as a doctor in October 1933, his time with Rangers concluded marvellously in 1934 with a league and cup double, with the Glasgow Cup and Charity Cup thrown in. Meanwhile he played three times for Scotland between 1932 and 1934, all of them against England, and made one appearance for the Scottish League. His medical career then took him to London and he signed for Arsenal but found it hard to break in to a brilliant team and only played four times in their title-winning season. He was more at home with West Ham where he made over fifty appearances in Division Two before retiring from the game in 1937. He remained in the south of England and rose to the top of his profession as Principal Medical Officer of Health for Kent County Council.

Johnny MARSHALL (4/0, 1885-87)
John Marshall
Born 28 April 1859 Crossmyloof, Cathcart, Glasgow
Died 23 May 1938 Rutherglen Road, Glasgow
Scotland v Ireland 1885; Wales 1886, 1887; England 1887.
Wellpark; Cowlairs; Harmonic; Third Lanark 1883-90 (Scottish Cup 1889) [guest for St Bernard's Apr 1889].

Marshall played full back at Wellpark, a Glasgow Green junior side who had another future internationalist, Johnny Kay, in the team, then at Cowlairs and Harmonic (of Dennistoun), so he was already well experienced by the time he joined Third Lanark in 1883. There, he blossomed into a top class forward with pace and shooting power which made him a national team contender. The Scottish Football Annual of 1884 described him as 'a brilliant right-wing forward; dribbles and dodges well, with good speed; splendid shot at goal'. He enjoyed an excellent wing partnership over several years with Billy Thomson but only Marshall played for the national team. He made his Scotland debut against Ireland in 1885, and all four of his internationals were victories although he was unable to find the net (some reports say he scored against Ireland and England). He also played nine times for Glasgow. His career highlight was Third Lanark's marathon Scottish Cup win in 1889, in which he played in all 12 matches up to their final victory over Celtic, which itself had to be replayed because of a snowstorm on the original date. He retired a year later and Third Lanark staged a benefit match for him against Rangers in March 1891. He kept closely involved in the game as a referee until 1905, taking charge of significant matches including Scottish League v Football League in 1893, the Scottish Cup final of 1894 and Ireland v England in 1900. He lived in Glasgow where he worked as a spirit salesman.

Jack MARSHALL (7/0, 1921-24)
John Marshall
Born 24 April 1892 Braehead, Baillieston, Lanarkshire
Died 7 October 1964 South Amboy Memorial Hospital, New Jersey, USA
Scotland v Wales 1921, 1922c, 1924; Ireland 1921, 1922; England 1921c, 1922.
Saltcoats Victoria 1911-14; Shettleston Aug 1914; St Mirren 1914-19 (Victory Cup 1919); Middlesbrough Nov 1919-23; Llanelly 1923-24; Brooklyn Wanderers 1924-25; Newark Skeeters 1925-27; Brooklyn Wanderers 1927-28; Bethlehem Steel 1928-29 [loan to Philadelphia Centennials Nov 1928].

Marshall was an uncompromising defender whose varied career included a Scotland cap while with a Welsh non-league side and another cap for the USA. Born near Baillieston, where his miner father worked at the Braehead pit, the family soon moved to the Ayrshire coalfields at Saltcoats. Jack followed his father underground while starting to make a name for himself with Saltcoats Victoria, where he did well enough to play trials for the Scotland junior team and for Rangers Reserves. Then, in August 1914, after only three games for Shettleston, St Mirren signed him and although the War had just broken out, Marshall was exempt from military service as a miner and he established himself as one of the country's top right backs through the war years. He won a Victory Cup medal in 1919 and, a few weeks later, played for Scotland in a Victory International against Ireland. Saints gave him a benefit match as a reward but he wanted a greater stage and fell out with the management when Middlesbrough wanted to sign him. Marshall insisted on a share of the fee, refusing to play for Saints until he got his way. He duly went to Teesside, where he was soon dubbed the 'ferro-concrete full-back' by the press, and made over 100 league appearances for Middlesbrough in four seasons.

He was called into the Scotland team for six consecutive matches, making his full debut in 1921 aged 28. After captaining the nation to an impressive 3-0 win over England at Hampden which clinched the British Championship, a new comic called *The Dandy* gave away a colour card with his picture. His temperament made him a difficult employee, however and in 1921, the FA banned him for four weeks for playing football in Scotland during the close season, while early in 1923 Middlesbrough suspended him for going home without permission. Despite an apology from the player, they placed him on the transfer list at a substantial fee. With no takers, to avoid the transfer fee he took the radical step of signing for Llanelly in the Southern League. The little Welsh club had ambitions to reach the Football League and Marshall was their star signing, leading them to FA Cup triumphs over two Third Division teams before they lost to Fulham. To general surprise, the Scotland selectors picked him to face Wales at Cardiff in 1924, partnered at full-back by Jimmy Blair of Cardiff City. The gamble failed as Marshall was clearly off the pace and Scotland lost 2-0, but he remains the only Scotland cap of the modern era from a club outside the senior leagues. Now aged 32, his international career was over, or so it seemed. That summer he was one of many British players lured across the Atlantic by the prospect of steady work and paid part-time football. He found the slower pace suited him just fine, and he was considered one of the outstanding players in the American Soccer League. The highlight was a call-up to play for USA in 1926 against Canada and he even scored a rare goal in a 6-2 victory. In a strange quirk, the Canadian goalkeeper was Joe Kennaway, who later played for Scotland. After a season in Brooklyn, Marshall had two years at Newark, whose owner Tom Adams remarked: 'That fellow is worth his weight in gold to any team if he did nothing more than free kicking.' Then it was back to Brooklyn and finally to Bethlehem Steel, where, even in the twilight of his career, the local paper enthused: 'The players are rejoicing over the success in the satisfactory negotiations which will bring Jock Marshall, without a doubt the greatest right back in the country, to the Bethlehem team.' Marshall was 37 when he retired from football in 1929 but, unlike many British players, did not return home with his wife and six children. He worked in construction in New Jersey and lived in Kearny then Morgan until his death in 1964.

Bob MARSHALL (2/0, 1892-94)
Robert William Marshall
Born 30 October 1864 North Woodside Road, Kelvinbridge, Glasgow
Died 5 January 1924 Bank Street, Hillhead, Glasgow
Scotland v Ireland 1892, 1894c.
St Andrew's; Partick 1883-85; Partick Thistle 1885-89; Rangers 1889-96 (Scottish League 1891; Scottish Cup 1894); Abercorn 1896-97.
A right wing forward who later dropped to half back, Marshall first won representative honours for Glasgow while with Partick, and when that club folded in 1885 he jumped to near neighbours Partick Thistle where he spent four years. His career took off in 1889 when he joined Rangers, where he was a key part of the team over the next seven years. Playing mainly at right half, they won the first league championship (shared with Dumbarton) and challenged regularly for honours. He was called into the Scotland team against Ireland in 1892 and although he had to wait two years for a second cap it contributed to a momentous year. In 1894 he won the Scottish Cup in February as Rangers defeated Celtic 3-1 in the final, then in March he captained a winning Scotland team in Belfast while on his honeymoon, having got married the day before. He also made one appearance for the Scottish League against the English in 1895. When he left Rangers in 1896 he had a season with Abercorn before giving up playing. In his working life he was a plumber.

Alex MASSIE (18/1, 1931-37)
Alexander Massie
Born 13 March 1906 Morrin Street, Springburn, Glasgow
Died 20 September 1977 Rolls Wood, Welwyn Garden City, Hertfordshire
Scotland v Ireland Sep 1931, 1932, 1933, 1934c, 1935, 1936; Wales 1931, 1934, 1935, 1936, 1937 (1); France 1932; England 1934c, 1935, 1936, 1937; Germany 1936; Austria 1937.
Petershill 1923-24; Benburb 1924-25; Ashfield Aug-Dec 1925; Ayr United Dec 1925-27; Bury Jan 1927-28; Bethlehem Steel Aug 1928-30; Dolphin Aug-Oct 1930; Heart of Midlothian Oct 1930-35; Aston Villa Dec 1935-45 (Second Division 1938) [guest for Birmingham City Sep-Nov 1939, Nottingham Forest Nov-Dec 1939; Solihull Town Jan-Apr 1940; Notts County Apr 1940-41, Heart of Midlothian Jan-May 1941].

Brought up in north Glasgow, Massie had a solid football background as his father Willie played for Partick Thistle. A stylish right half despite starting out as an inside left, he was 24 before his professional career really got underway, by which time he had played for clubs in four countries. He gained experience at three Glasgow junior teams then bounced around at Ayr United, Bury, Bethlehem Steel and Dolphin until Hearts brought him back from Ireland in the autumn of 1930. This finally provided him with the stage he needed and within a year he had won his first Scotland cap, going on to become a regular international over the next six years. He also made six appearances for the Scottish League while at Hearts, where he was regarded as 'the complete footballer'. He left in December 1935 when Aston Villa were in a dogfight to avoid relegation and paid £6,000 to take him south. Curiously, the day he left Hearts he was in court, accused of throwing mud at a spectator after a match against Kilmarnock in which he had been barracked; he was found not guilty. Villa failed to avoid the drop but he retained his place in the Scotland team until 1937, and in his final appearance he scored the only goal of his international career, against Wales. In 1938, Villa swept to the Second

Division title and returned to the top flight but after the club decided to close down on the outbreak of war, he played as a guest for a variety of clubs while he worked for ICI and opened a newsagent shop in Sheldon. Villa started up again in 1942-43 and he was immediately appointed club captain, returning to top form. Although very much at the veteran stage, he captained a Scotland eleven against the RAF in 1943, and at the age of 38 he won his final trophy, the Football League North Cup of 1944. After retiring from the game the following year he was appointed manager of Aston Villa, holding the post until the summer of 1949 when he resigned, apparently because the board would not give him control over team selection. He had short spells as manager of Torquay United 1950-51 and Hereford United 1951-52, where he ran a pub, before moving to Hertfordshire for an engineering job. There, he remained involved in football as coach of Hertford Town and Welwyn Garden City, taking the latter to the South Midlands League title in 1973. He serialised his life story in the Birmingham *Sports Argus* in 1962.

Willie MAXWELL (1/0, 1898)
William Sturrock Maxwell
Born 21 September 1875 Victoria Street, Arbroath, Angus
Died 14 July 1940 Leighton Road, Southville, Bristol, Gloucestershire
Scotland v England 1898.
Ardenlea 1890-93; Arbroath 1893-94; Heart of Midlothian Aug-Oct 1894; Dundee Nov 1894-95; Stoke 1895-1901; Third Lanark 1901-02; Sunderland 1902-03; Millwall 1903-05; Bristol City 1905-09 (Second Division 1906).

Maxwell had a long and eventful career which culminated in an Olympic gold medal as coach of the Belgian national team. An inside right, his first senior club was Arbroath, where he was selected for Forfarshire aged 18, and he had short spells with Hearts then Dundee, playing in their run to the Scottish Cup semi-final in 1895. He was a part-time footballer while working as a solicitor's clerk until he joined Stoke in 1895, where he went on to be the club's top scorer in five out of his six seasons there. Rated one of the best forwards in the country, Stoke turned down serious money to hold on to him. However, when he won his Scotland cap against England in 1898 he failed to live up to his reputation. He was selected for a second cap versus Ireland in 1900 but was forced to withdraw because of a knee injury, and the following summer he came back to Scotland for a season at Third Lanark. He spent the rest of his playing career in England, and although a year at Sunderland was not a great success, at Millwall in the Southern League and then at Bristol City in Division Two he maintained an excellent goalscoring average of one every two matches. He helped City to win promotion in 1906 and they even came close to the league title the following season. On retiring in 1909 he went to Brussels as a coach, taking charge of Leopold and then Daring, leading the latter to the Belgian championship in 1914. He started coaching the national team in the summer of 1911, came home during the War and returned to Belgium after the conflict. He retained the national team position until 1928, with his team winning the 1920 Olympic gold medal and taking part in the 1924 and 1928 Olympic Games. Reverting to club football, he coached Mechelen (Malines) from 1925 for a decade, and finally Cercle Bruges, who he led to the Belgian Second Division title in 1937-38. He eventually returned to his wife's home town of Stone, Staffordshire, where he is buried although he died in Bristol. He was also an excellent batsman and played cricket for Arbroath, Staffordshire and Bedminster while in June 1913, uniquely for a Scottish footballer, he represented Belgium at cricket against Holland.

Johnny MAY (5/0, 1906-09)
John May
Born 15 April 1878 Dykehead, Shotts, Lanarkshire
Died 24 July 1933 Western Infirmary, Glasgow
Scotland v Wales 1906, 1909; Ireland 1906c, 1908; England 1908.
Rising Blues; Bo'ness 1895-96; Wishaw Thistle 1896-97; Abercorn 1897-98; Derby County 1898-1904; Rangers 1904-10; Morton 1910-15.

Born in Dykehead, May spent some of his youth in the Linlithgow area, which explains his first senior club being Bo'ness, which he joined from a local juvenile team. A left half, always in the thick of the action, he had a season at Wishaw Thistle and another as captain of Abercorn in Division Two, when the *Scottish Referee* first suggested he might be worthy of a Scotland trial. He had just turned 20 when he moved to Derby in the summer of 1898 and his team reached the FA Cup final of 1899, but their hopes of lifting the trophy were dashed when May was injured with his side winning 1-0 against Sheffield United, and in his absence Derby conceded four goals. Despite having the likes of Archie Goodall and Steve Bloomer in the team, their next cup final was even worse, losing 6-0 to Bury in 1903. There were no further chances of a medal, as Derby were a mid-table side throughout his six years there, and after a fine performance in an international trial in Glasgow he came back to Scotland with Rangers in 1904. In his first season he was unlucky enough to miss out on honours as Rangers lost a league play-off to Celtic and he missed that year's cup final through injury. He played in the 1909 final when the cup was withheld due to a riot, and his only medals with Rangers were in the Glasgow Charity Cup, which he won three times. Although he was bald, which made him look older than he was, his maturity paid dividends while he was at Rangers as he was selected five times for Scotland, once as captain, and also made three appearances for the Scottish League, captaining the side which met the Football League in 1907. He moved to Morton in 1910 and spent his twilight years with the Greenock club before retiring in 1915. A scratch golfer, he worked as a mechanical engineer and ran a billiard saloon near his home in Maryhill. Sadly, he took his own life by cutting his throat, aged 55. His brother Hugh (1882-1944) also played for Derby and Rangers.

Peter MEEHAN (1/0, 1896)
Peter Meehan
Born 28 February 1872 Holygate, Broxburn, West Lothian
Died 26 June 1915 Port Morien, Nova Scotia, Canada
Scotland v Ireland 1896.
Broxburn Shamrock 1890-93; Hibernian Feb-May 1893; Sunderland 1893-95 (Football League 1895); Celtic 1895-96 (Scottish League 1896); Everton Jan 1897-98; Southampton 1898-00 (Southern League 1899); Manchester City 1900-01; Barrow 1901-02; Broxburn 1902-03; Clyde Aug-Oct 1903; Broxburn Oct 1903-04; Broxburn Shamrock 1904.

Meehan was an excellent right back who could appear just a bit too relaxed, which was a reflection of his confidence but sometimes came across as indifference. He grew up in Broxburn where he worked in the shale mines, like his father, and played for Broxburn Shamrock. He had already represented Linlithgowshire when he was recruited by the newly reformed Hibernian in February 1893, but did not stay for long. That summer he accepted a good financial package to join Sunderland and he slotted straight into the team, revelling in the higher standard. His side were league runners-up in his first season then won the title the following year in 1895. He was persuaded to come back to Scotland with Celtic, where he partnered fellow Broxburn product Dan Doyle in defence, and they had a great season as Celtic won the league title as well as the Glasgow Cup and Charity Cup. While this was going on Meehan made an appearance for the Scottish League then earned his one Scotland cap against Ireland in March 1896. Unfortunately the game, played in a snowstorm, was a personal disaster as he not only played poorly but was injured in a heavy tackle and had to sit out most of the second half. Things really went wrong for him at the end of the year when Meehan was one of three Celtic players (the others were Barney Battles and John Divers) who refused to play in a league game against Hibs unless two critical journalists were removed from the press box. The club refused to accede to their demands and he was offloaded to Everton the following month, in return for a substantial fee of £450 (of which £250 went to Celtic and £200 to Sunderland, who still held his Football League registration). He had an early shot at glory, playing in the FA Cup final of 1897 which Everton lost narrowly to Aston Villa, and won no medals in his time at Goodison Park. He moved in 1898 to Southampton, where he won the Southern League title in his first season and reached another FA Cup final in his second. Next stop in 1900 was Manchester City, were he only played half a dozen games as the competition for places was fierce, and then he wound down his career at Barrow before coming home in Scotland. With Broxburn in 1903 he captained the team to the Linlithgowshire Cup, he had a few games for Clyde and played his last games with the two Broxburn senior sides. In 1906 he emigrated to Canada and settled in Nova Scotia where he worked as a miner, and died there in 1915 of pleurisy and pneumonia. NB his name was widely reported in the press as Meechan but the correct spelling was Meehan.

Davie MEIKLEJOHN (15/3, 1922-33)
David Ditchburn Meiklejohn
Born 12 December 1900 Sharp Street, Govan, Glasgow
Died 22 August 1959 Broomfield Park, Airdrie, Lanarkshire
Scotland v Wales 1922, 1924, Feb 1925 (1), 1927, 1931c; Ireland 1925 (1), 1928, 1929, 1930c, Sep 1931c; England 1925, 1929, 1930c, 1931c; Austria 1933c (1).
Greenfield United; Maryhill 1918-19; Rangers Oct 1919-36 (Scottish League 1921, 1923, 1924, 1925, 1927, 1928, 1929, 1930, 1931, 1933, 1934, 1935; Scottish Cup 1928, 1930, 1932, 1934, 1936).

One of Rangers' greatest ever players, 'Meek' created an extraordinary record by winning 12 league titles, and for good measure played more than a bit part in a thirteenth. He played over 500 games at centre half or right half during a period of almost uninterrupted success for the Ibrox club, which he joined from Maryhill Juniors in 1919. There were only three years during his career that Rangers did not win the league, and he also won five Scottish Cups, the most important being that of 1928 which banished the club hoodoo which had run for 25 years; he was only too conscious of the record having played in the losing finals of 1921 and 1922. With the score 0-0 in the 1928 final, when Rangers got a penalty against Celtic, team captain Meiklejohn was brave enough to step up, despite not being a regular taker of spot kicks. He knew the significance and admitted afterwards: 'If I scored we would win, if I failed we could be beaten. It was a moment of agony.' The sense of relief when he found the net was palpable and set Rangers on course for a 4-0 win. Strangely the following year's final was lost to Kilmarnock, but Rangers then won the cup regularly in the 1930s. On the international front, he won 15 caps for Scotland over a decade, and unusually for a half back he scored in three of them, twice in 1925 and the other in his last match against Austria in 1933; however, he missed a penalty against Northern Ireland in 1931. He made six appearances for the Scottish League, five of them against the English, and went on tour with the Scottish FA to North America in 1935. He retired in 1936 shortly after winning the Scottish Cup and became a sports writer with the *Daily Record*. After the War he was appointed Partick Thistle manager in 1947 and remained in post until his sudden death in 1959 when he collapsed while watching a match in the director's box at Broomfield Park in Airdrie. He was pronounced dead on arrival at Glasgow Royal Infirmary.

Alex MENZIES (1/0, 1906)
Alexander William Menzies
Born 25 November 1882 Allison Place, Blantyre, Lanarkshire
Died 24 November 1964 Orchard Drive, Blantyre, Lanarkshire
Scotland v England 1906.
Blantyre Victoria; Heart of Midlothian Dec 1902-06 (Scottish Cup 1906) [loans to Motherwell 1903-04, Arthurlie 1904-05]; Manchester United Nov 1906-08; Luton Town 1908-09; Dundee 1909-10; Hamilton Academical Mar-May 1910; Port Glasgow Athletic Aug-Dec 1910; Dumbarton Dec 1910-12.

A centre forward who never really hit the heights, Menzies really only had one great season in his career. Son of a Blantyre blacksmith, he did well enough with the local junior team to represent Lanarkshire, and was signed by Hearts in December 1902. Much of his four years at Hearts were spent on loan to other clubs, but in 1905-06 he scored 18 goals as Hearts came second in the league and won the Scottish Cup, although he missed much of the final due to a second half injury. Earlier that month, to general surprise, he had made his Scotland debut against England, and did well in a 2-1 win. Manchester United took him south later in the year, paying around £500 to Hearts, but although he was a regular at Old Trafford in his first season, he failed to live up to his reputation and in 1907-08, when United won the Football League, he played just six times without scoring. He was allowed to leave for Luton Town of the Southern League that summer, and spent the rest of his career drifting around a variety of clubs, never staying for long and usually in the reserves. He retired in 1912 and reverted to his old job as a coal miner in Blantyre.

Bob MERCER (2/0, 1912-13)
Robert Mercer
Born 21 September 1889 Avonbridge, Stirlingshire
Died 23 April 1926 Ettrick Park, Selkirk, Selkirkshire
Scotland v Wales 1912; Ireland 1913.
Gala Hailes Villa; Selkirk 1907-08; Leith Athletic 1908-09; Heart of Midlothian 1909-21 [guest for Luton Town Aug-Oct 1917]; Dunfermline Athletic 1921-24.

Born in Stirlingshire, Mercer came to Edinburgh as a boy and his talent as a footballer was recognised early, while playing for his school in Leith Walk. He represented Edinburgh Schoolboys against London in 1902, then when he went to Galashiels to work in a textile mill he did well enough at Gala Hailes Villa to be selected twice for a Borders select. He continued to progress, with a season each at Selkirk and Leith Athletic before joining Hearts in 1909, just before his 20th birthday. A strapping centre half, six feet tall, his influence helped Hearts to develop into a team that challenged for honours and he was recognised first by the Scottish League against the Football League in February 1912 then two weeks later he made his Scotland debut in a 1-0 win over Wales. He played the following year versus Ireland, and made a further four appearances for the Scottish League. However, just as the promising Hearts eleven looked like winning the league, the team was broken up by the War. Mercer was initially excused from military service up because of a knee injury and continued to play regularly, but he was called up in 1917 to the Royal Garrison Artillery as a Bombardier. During his training he played a few matches for Luton Town and for the British Army against the Belgian Army, then went to the front. He was gassed in France and although he resumed football at Hearts and was given a benefit match, he never fully recovered, falling victim to recurring attacks including one in November 1919 that caused pneumonia. With his health compromised he still felt capable of playing for Dunfermline in Division Two until he retired in 1924. Working as a clerk in the tramways office in Edinburgh, in 1926 he was asked to play for Hearts in a friendly at Selkirk, where his career began. Tragically, he collapsed after only a few minutes and died on the spot. The match was abandoned. He was not forgotten in Selkirk and a stand was named in his honour in 2013, although when the club folded it was sold to Gala Fairydean Rovers.

Bob MIDDLETON (1/0, 1930)
Robert Connon Middleton
Born 24 January 1904 Crocketts Buildings, Montrose Street, Brechin, Angus
Died 19 May 1984 Brechin Infirmary, Angus
Scotland v Ireland 1930.
Brechin Comrades; Edzell; Brechin City; Brechin Victoria 1924-28; Brechin City Aug-Dec 1928; Cowdenbeath Dec 1928-30; Sunderland Nov 1930-33; Burton Town 1933-34; Chester Mar 1934-38.

Middleton originally played at right back for local sides around his native Brechin before going between the posts in a junior match when another player was injured. Already in his early twenties, he found his true vocation as a goalkeeper and made such an impression when he rejoined Brechin City in 1928 that he was soon on the road to a full-time career. A few months later he was signed by Cowdenbeath, who needed a replacement goalkeeper in a hurry for the injured John Falconer, and they could hardly have suspected that his replacement would be adept enough to win a Scotland cap. Yet in February 1930 Middleton was the first Cowden player to represent his country, holding the line in a 3-1 victory over Ireland. As the scouts took an interest there were several bids from England and he was transferred to Sunderland, with Cowdenbeath pocketing £2,000. At Roker Park he had a good start then faded and was playing largely in the reserves by 1932. He wanted away but with a heavy transfer fee on his head, he moved into non-league football with Burton Town in the Birmingham and District League. By the end of the season he was signed by Chester in the Third Division North, and was an excellent stopper for them until he retired in 1938. He took over the Olde Custom House Inn in Chester for a while but gave it up during the War, in which he served in France, and returned to Brechin for the rest of his life. He was on the committee at Brechin City, and worked locally as janitor of Damacre School. His Scotland cap and jersey are on display in the boardroom at Glebe Park.

Archie MILLER (1/0, 1938)
Archibald Miller
Born 5 September 1913 Academy Street, Larkhall, Lanarkshire
Died 14 July 2006 Orbiston Nursing Home, Motherwell, Lanarkshire
Scotland v Wales 1938.
Royal Albert; Heart of Midlothian Oct 1932-47 [guest for Falkirk Jan-May 1940]; Blackburn Rovers Nov 1947-48; Kilmarnock 1948-49; Workington 1949-50 player-coach; Carlisle United 1950-51; Heart of Midlothian 1951-52; Workington Feb-May 1952 player-manager.

A hard-tackling left half or left back, Miller joined Hearts from a Larkhall junior team in the autumn of 1932 and made a scoring debut in December but was rarely first choice during his early years at the club. It was not until 1937 that he became established, and then his performances as Hearts finished runners-up in the league brought him to the attention of the selectors. He was called up for the Scottish League in September 1938, then to the full national team two months later to face Wales, although somewhat bizarrely he won his Scotland cap while he was dropped from the Hearts team. Later, he played in one wartime international in 1943 but unfortunately it was the 8-0 defeat to England in Manchester when he was up against Stanley Matthews. He continued to play for Hearts through the War years, apart from a spell on loan at Falkirk where he lived, although by the time the conflict was over his best years were behind him. After 15 years with Hearts, he was allowed a free transfer and moved around in the veteran stage, with spells at Blackburn Rovers and Kilmarnock before a coaching post came up at Workington in 1949. He made a single appearance for Carlisle United and had a few months back at Hearts coaching the reserves before winding up his career at Workington. He was 92 when he died in 2006.

Jimmy MILLER (3/2, 1897-98)
James Miller
Born 10 February 1871 Annbank, Ayrshire
Died 5 February 1907 Chiddingstone Street, Fulham, London
Scotland v England 1897 (1), 1898 (1); Wales 1898.
Primrose; Annbank; Sunderland 1890-96 (Football League 1892, 1893, 1895); Rangers 1896-1900 (Scottish League 1899, 1900; Scottish Cup 1897, 1898); Sunderland 1900-04 (Football League 1902); West Bromwich Albion 1904-05.
An dashing inside forward, Miller was an integral part of Sunderland's 'team of all the talents' which won three Football League titles in the 1890s, then he went on win to a similar wealth of honours with Rangers. He was recruited by Sunderland manager Tom Watson in 1890 having just won the Ayrshire Cup with Annbank and went straight into an all-Scottish attack which developed into a superb combination and won the league in 1892, 1893 and 1895. After six years on Wearside he returned to Scotland to join Rangers and was again in an outstanding team, winning the Scottish Cup in his first two seasons, and the Scottish title in the next two years including the famous unbeaten season of 1898-99. His long overdue international debut came in 1897 when he scored a late winner for Scotland against England at Crystal Palace, and although he scored against Wales the following year he drew a blank in his third and final appearance against England. He was also selected three times for the Scottish League. His standing in the game was such that in 1898 he was founding secretary of the Scottish section of the Football Players' Union, but he stepped down in December 1899 at a time when he was thinking of giving up the game entirely, having had a debilitating attack of pleurisy. However, he recovered well and returned to action with a vengeance in the summer of 1900, scoring for Rangers as they beat Celtic in the Glasgow Charity Cup final then moving back to Sunderland for four more years. He won another league title in 1902, and as age started to catch up with him he concluded his playing career at West Bromwich Albion, where he focused on training duties and only played one first team match. The newly-formed Chelsea appointed him trainer in 1905, and he was still in post when tragedy struck and he died of tuberculosis early in 1907. Chelsea played a benefit match to raise funds for his widow Marion (sister of his former team-mate Will Gibson) and their children. He had another family connection at Sunderland, his uncle Billy Dunlop (not the internationalist) who was also from Annbank.

Johnny MILLER (5/0, 1931-34)
John Miller
Born 8 November 1903 Denmark Street, Maryhill, Glasgow
Died 11 December 1981 Stobhill Hospital, Glasgow
Scotland v England 1931, 1934; Italy 1931; Switzerland 1931; France 1932.
Renfrew; Yoker Athletic; St Mirren Feb 1925-39.
Miller joined St Mirren in 1925 after gaining experience in junior football at Renfrew and Yoker, but had to wait patiently for a chance in the first team. He was not in the team for their 1926 Scottish Cup final victory and did not

establish himself as first choice left half until 1929. However, he then became a fixture in the side for the next decade, a model of consistency as he played over 350 league matches. He made his Scotland debut in a 2-0 win against England in 1931, and went on the continental tour that summer, also travelling to France the following year. In 1934 he made a return to the national side which lost 3-0 to England, and a week later he was unlucky enough to play in St Mirren's 5-0 defeat to Rangers in the Scottish Cup final. He might have been consoled by a benefit match against Kilmarnock in the autumn, but it was poorly attended. When he retired in 1939 after 14 years as a Saints player he was offered the post of assistant trainer to Dave McCrae, which he accepted, while keeping up his day job in a bakery.

Peter MILLER (3/0, 1882-83)
Peter Miller
Born 2 February 1858 Glenkin, Kilmun, Argyllshire
Died 11 October 1914 Western Infirmary, Glasgow
Scotland v England 1882, 1883; Wales 1883.
Dumbarton 1877-84 (Scottish Cup 1883); Partick Thistle Mar-May 1885; Dumbarton 1885-89; West Hartlepool NER 1889-91.

Born on the shores of Loch Long, where his father was a ploughman, Miller's family moved to Dumbarton when he was a child to find work in the shipyards. A hard-working and effective half back, he first came into the Dumbarton side in 1877 and was good enough to be selected for an international trial the following spring. Although that did not lead to a Scotland cap, he made several appearances for Dunbartonshire and Scotch Counties before earning his deserved Scotland debut in the 5-1 win of 1882 against England. He won two more caps the following year in England and Wales, both of which were won. At club level he was an integral part of the great Dumbarton side of the 1880s, and played in the Scottish Cup finals of 1881 and 1882, both lost to Queen's Park, before captaining his side to victory over Vale of Leven in 1883. In 1885 he had a brief spell with Partick Thistle while he worked in the Govan shipyards but a few months later was persuaded to return to play for Dumbarton and he had another four years at the club, reaching one more cup final in 1887, lost to Hibs. In 1889, when he was 31, he went to England with the offer of work as a skilled ship plater, plus the added financial incentive of playing for West Hartlepool NER. He captained the side for two years until his retirement and liked the town so much that he settled in West Hartlepool for the rest of his life. However, he died back in Glasgow where he was being treated in hospital for a gastric obstruction and is buried in Dumbarton. The *Scottish Referee* remembered him as 'a perfect specimen of the footballer of his times, who never used physical strength against an opponent to gain an advantage.'

Tom MILLER (3/2, 1920-21)
Thomas Miller
Born 30 June 1890 Windmillhill Street, Motherwell, Lanarkshire
Died 3 September 1958 Montgomery Street, Girvan, Ayrshire
Scotland v England 1920 (2), 1921; Ireland 1921.
Larkhall Hearts; Larkhall United 1909-11; Hamilton Academical Mar 1911-12; Liverpool Feb 1912-20 [guest for Royal Albert Aug-Nov 1915]; Manchester United 1920-21; Heart of Midlothian 1921-22; Torquay United Aug-Dec 1922; Hamilton Academical 1923-26 [guest for Royal Albert Apr 1924]; Raith Rovers Dec 1926-27.

Miller's long and wandering career was curtailed by the First World War but he proved himself an adept scorer at many clubs. From his earliest days in the juveniles with Larkhall Hearts and then junior side Larkhall United, he scored with regularity, winning the Lanarkshire Junior Cup and Lanarkshire League. In 1911 he joined Hamilton as a 20-year-old and after less than a year of impressive performances at inside left Liverpool came calling early in 1912. He was in the side which reached the FA Cup final in 1914 and the following year was involved in what became known as the 'scandal match', a rigged league game between Liverpool and Manchester United. By the time news came through in December that he had been banned for life from the FA, he had returned to Scotland and was playing for Royal Albert of Larkhall in the Western League. He then signed up to fight with the Glasgow Highlanders and had no more senior football until the War was over but was allowed to return to Merseyside in August 1919 when the FA lifted the suspension in recognition of his service to his country. Fully rehabilitated, he did well enough for Liverpool to earn a call-up to the national side, making an impressive Scotland debut in 1920 with two goals against England. He then moved to Manchester United for a season and won two more caps in 1921. Back at Hearts, he fell out with the club in 1922 and signed for Torquay United, newly admitted to the Southern League, but returned after six months. Hearts were in no mood to make up, and as they had retained his registration they froze him out of football until September 1923 when they agreed to release him. He went back to Hamilton Accies and had three seasons at Douglas Park, then signed for Raith Rovers late in 1926 where he continued to score goals for a few months before hanging up his boots in 1927. That summer he was selected from over 200 applicants as manager of Dunfermline, and coached the side until the end of 1929. He went to Barrow as trainer before being promoted to team manager in 1930 then left after a few months and that appears to be the end of his football career. He had strong family connections in the game, as uncle of internationalist Jock Govan, while his brothers Adam played for Hamilton and John for Aberdeen and Partick Thistle, among others.

William MILLER (1/0, 1876)
William Miller
Born 19 May 1854 Govan, Glasgow
Died 1 May 1894 Doune Quadrant, Kelvinside, Glasgow
Scotland v England 1876.
Third Lanark 1872-79.

A founding member of Third Lanark in 1872, Miller was a forward whose peak came in March 1876. He started the month earning his sole international cap in a winning Scotland team which beat England 3-0, then he returned to the Hamilton Crescent ground on each of the following two Saturdays to represent Third Lanark in the Scottish Cup final and replay, which was ultimately lost to Queen's Park. He was also in the Thirds team which lost the 1878 final to Vale of Leven, and gave up the game the following year. He worked as a buyer in the flannel department of Stewart & Macdonald, a major clothing wholesaler in Glasgow, and died after a long illness just before his fortieth birthday.

Willie MILLS (3/0, 1935-36)
William Mills
Born 28 January 1915 Dillichip Terrace, Bonhill, Dunbartonshire
Died 26 May 1990 Woodend Hospital, Aberdeen
Scotland v Wales 1935, 1936; Ireland 1935.
Bridgeton Waverley; Aberdeen 1932-38; Huddersfield Town Mar 1938-47 [guest for Dumbarton Nov 1939-Jan 1940; Aberdeen Jan-Apr 1940; Clyde 1940-44; East Fife 1944-45; Dundee May 1945]; Queen of the South Sep 1947; Aberdeen Oct 1947; Lossiemouth player-manager Nov 1947-49; Huntly player-manager Jan 1949-50; Hamrun Spartans player-manager 1950-51; Keith player-manager 1951-52; Huntly player-manager 1952-53.

Mills was discovered with Bridgeton Waverley by Pat Travers, who took him to Aberdeen in the summer of 1932, and after only one game in the reserves he made his first team debut aged 17. He became a fixture in the Aberdeen team for the next six years at inside left, thanks to his creative play and ability to seek out the long pass, not to mention an eye for goal that saw him reach double figures each season. He toured the USA with Scotland in the summer of 1935 and was soon in the reckoning for further honours, playing in the Jubilee international against England then winning three full caps. The nearest he came to a major medal with Aberdeen was the Scottish Cup final of 1937, which was lost to Celtic and he moved to Huddersfield in March 1938 for a substantial fee of around £6,500 but only played one match that season and was not in their team for the FA Cup final. A year later, when war was declared he returned to Scotland and joined the Infantry Training Centre in Perth, later serving with the BAOR in Germany, making guest appearances for a number of clubs around the country when available. At one of his stops, he won the Forfarshire Cup with Dundee in May 1945. Released by Huddersfield in 1947, he played a trial with Queen of the South and a few reserve matches with Aberdeen before being appointed player-manager of Highland League sides Lossiemouth and Huntly. In 1950 he went to Malta to coach Hamrun Spartans, then returned to the north-east with Keith and Huntly again. After hanging up his boots he continued to coach, and was fit enough to appear in charity matches into the 1970s. He worked as a machine operator in Aberdeen.

Jackie MILNE (2/0, 1938-39)
John Vance Milne
Born 25 March 1911 Upper Castle Hill, Stirling
Died 29 August 1959 Ballochmyle Hospital, Mauchline, Ayrshire
Scotland v England 1938, 1939.
Ashfield; Blackburn Rovers Feb 1932-35; Arsenal 1935-37 (Football League 1938); Middlesbrough Dec 1937-45 [guest for St Mirren Oct 1939; Dumbarton Nov 1939-45]; Dumbarton player-manager 1945-46.

Born in Stirling and brought up in Cathcart on the south side of Glasgow, Milne came through at Ashfield where his performances on the wing put him in contention for a junior cap until Blackburn Rovers signed him in the spring of 1932. He launched a solid career in England although initially he had a frustrating couple of years as understudy to Jack Bruton before getting his chance at outside left early in 1934, and did so well that he kept his place in the side. Arsenal paid £5,000 to take him to Highbury in the summer of 1935, but again he was mainly a fringe player so he moved to Middlesbrough in December 1937; however, Arsenal did win the league after he left, and he had already made 16 league appearances, enough to earn a championship medal. At Middlesbrough he was in fine form and was called up to make his Scotland debut against England at Wembley at outside right. He did well enough to be retained for the same fixture in 1939, this time at outside left, much to the chagrin of Torry Gillick who had played in every other international that season. When war broke out, he returned to Scotland and was loaned to Dumbarton for pretty much the full duration. He won one wartime cap for Scotland against England in February 1941, a rare victory at Newcastle, while technically he remained a Boro player. When Dumbarton decided to make the transfer permanent in 1945 and appoint him as player-manager, they were obliged to pay a transfer fee to Middlesbrough. It did not last long as in June 1946 he signed a lucrative contract to coach Asturias in Mexico, going over with fellow internationalist Tom McKillop and Jimmy Hickie of Clyde. After one season the club hit financial problems and all three had to return home. He gave up football and ran the Wee Thackit Inn at Carluke, and was proprietor of the Fullarton Hotel in Irvine at the time of his death aged just 48 from kidney failure.

Davie MITCHELL (5/0, 1890-94)
David Mitchell
Born 29 April 1866 Titchfield Street, Kilmarnock, Ayrshire
Died 6 December 1948 Cunninghame Hospital, Irvine, Ayrshire
Scotland v Ireland 1890, 1893; England 1892, 1893, 1894.
Britannia 1885-86; Kilmarnock 1886-89; Rangers 1889-1900 (Scottish League 1891, 1899; Scottish Cup 1894, 1897, 1898).

Mitchell had a solid grounding in the game in his native Kilmarnock and had played for Ayrshire before signing for Rangers in 1889. Over the following decade he held down the left half position at Ibrox and helped to establish Rangers as one of the top teams in Scotland, winning two league titles (the first of them shared with Dumbarton) and captaining them to three Scottish Cups. He made his international debut in a 4-1 win over Ireland in 1890 and was later selected to face England three years in a row, added to another cap against Ireland and two appearances for the Scottish League against the English. A year after his second league title he retired in 1900 and went back to work in Kilmarnock as an engineering draughtsman. However, he also had an interesting appointment to coach with the Danish FA, who invited him over in 1903 for several months to ensure their players would be prepared for a visit from Queen's Park, making him one of the earliest British coaches to pass on his skills abroad. He spent all his life in Kilmarnock until his death in an Irvine hospital in 1948.

Jamie MITCHELL (3/0, 1908-10)
James Mitchell
Born 21 January 1880 Gatehead, by Kilmarnock, Ayrshire
Died 1 April 1958 Merrick Road, Kilmarnock, Ayrshire
Scotland v Ireland 1908, 1910; Wales 1910.
Crosshouse; Kilmarnock Nov 1900-20 [loan to Hurlford 1904-06].

Brought up in Crosshouse, Mitchell was originally a left half with his local Ayrshire junior team and joined Kilmarnock in 1900, while still working as a coal miner. He suffered a serious injury in the 1903/04 season which threatened to end his career and played a couple of seasons at Hurlford before he was ready to return to Rugby Park in 1906. At that point he moved to left back where he excelled, and won deserved recognition on the international front. He won his first Scotland cap in 1908 when Alec McNair withdrew, playing alongside club partner Bill Agnew in a 5-0 win over Ireland, and that was followed by two more caps against Ireland and Wales in 1910, as well as a Scottish League honour against the Irish. By then he was the oldest and longest-serving player on Kilmarnock's books, yet he completed another decade at the club. He only played rarely after 1918 but he soldiered on and by the time he made the last of over 400 first team appearances in September 1919 he was nearly 40. Even then, he continued to play in the reserve team which won the Scottish Alliance title in 1920, and was given a second benefit match. After his football career was over, he worked as a railway wagon painter.

Hughie MORGAN (2/0, 1898-99)
Hugh Morgan
Born 7 August 1874 Shettleston, Glasgow
Died 30 June 1938 Stobhill Hospital, Glasgow
Scotland v Wales 1898; England 1899.
Longriggend Wanderers [trials for Airdrieonians 1894-95; Motherwell 1895-96]; St Mirren 1896-98; Liverpool 1898-1900; Blackburn Rovers 1900-03; Dundee Sep 1903-04; St Mirren 1904-06; King's Park 1906-7.

Capped for Scotland at junior level with Longriggend, the mining village near Airdrie where he was brought up, Morgan had trials at Airdrie and Motherwell before signing up at St Mirren. He had an impressive couple of seasons at inside left and in 1898 won his first cap for Scotland, a victory over Wales. This came shortly after he played for the Scottish League against the Irish League, a match in which he caught the eye of Liverpool's Tom Watson, who took him south that summer. He partnered Tom Robertson on the left wing at Anfield, successfully enough to earn a second Scotland cap in 1899, this time against England. Moving on to Blackburn, he formed an inside forward partnership with Peter Somers and thanks to their creative passing the team came close to winning the league title, eventually finishing fourth in 1902. After Somers left, the team struggled and Morgan decided to come back to Scotland, joining Dundee for a season before heading to St Mirren, completing a full circle in his playing career. However, his powers were declining and after a short spell with King's Park in the Scottish Union he retired in 1907.

Davie MORRIS (6/1, 1923-25)
David Main Liston Morris
Born 21 August 1897 Ann Street, Newhaven, Edinburgh
Died 27 November 1971 Hamilton Crescent, Leith, Edinburgh
Scotland v Ireland 1923, 1924 (1), 1925c; England 1924, 1925c; Wales Feb 1925c.
Leith Hawthorn; Newtongrange Star; Raith Rovers Dec 1920-25; Preston North End Dec 1925-30; Chester 1930-31; Dundee United Dec 1931-32; Berwick Rangers Mar 1934.

The son of a merchant seaman, Morris worked as a shipwright in Leith Docks until he became a full-time footballer. He was already 23 when he joined Raith from Newtongrange Star in December 1920 as a replacement centre half for Willie Porter and went straight into the team, playing over 260 games for the Kirkcaldy side, mostly as captain. He won his first international cap in 1923 against Ireland, then five more caps over the next two years and in doing so, he became the first and only Raith Rovers player to captain Scotland. What is more, he did so in all three matches in Scotland's unbeaten British Championship campaign in 1925. He also played once for the Scottish League. There were foreign adventures with Raith along the way, including a tour of Denmark and a famous trip to the Canary Islands when the team's ship ran aground. He was sold for £4,200 to Preston North End three days before Christmas 1925, and duly captained the Deepdale side as well, but while he was selected for the Anglo-Scots the nearest he came to further honours was as a reserve. By 1930 he had dropped out of the team and was placed on the transfer list, with Preston placing a prohibitive fee on his head which gave him little choice but to play in non-league football with Chester until he was released in December 1931. He had six months at Dundee United before retiring, although he did make a surprise appearance for Berwick Rangers in 1934, having come home to his native Leith.

Tom MORRISON (1/0, 1927)
Thomas Kelly Morrison
Born 21 July 1904 Crookedholm, Kilmarnock, Ayrshire
Died 17 March 1980 Bedford General Hospital, Bedfordshire
Scotland v England 1927.
Troon Athletic; St Mirren 1924-28 (Scottish Cup 1926); Liverpool Feb 1928-35; Sunderland Nov 1935-36 (Football League 1936); Gamlingay Aug-Dec 1936; Ayr United Mar-Aug 1937; Drumcondra 1938-39.

Signed in 1924 from Troon Athletic juniors, Morrison went straight into the St Mirren first team, and was immense at right half in the side which lifted the Scottish Cup in 1926, beating Celtic 2-0 in the final, with the first goal resulting from his corner kick. He made an appearance for the Scottish League, and was then capped for the national team against England in 1927. That summer he went with the Scottish FA team on its tour of USA and Canada and with continued good form, and with St Mirren in debt, he was sold to Liverpool in February 1928 for £4,100, their record signing. Morrison himself was given £400. He played over 250 games for the Reds who were a mid-table First Division side at the time but after a few years of dependable defending there were signs of the trouble to come. He was dropped from the team, failed to report for a reserve game, went missing, and was twice suspended by the club. With their patience exhausted, a year after his last appearance Liverpool sold him to Sunderland in November 1935 and the new surroundings gave him a new lease of life for a while. He played 23 times as Sunderland romped to the league title with an eight point margin. Then something extraordinary happened: he attended a celebration dinner and simply disappeared without waiting for his championship medal or bonus money. Nobody, least of all his wife, knew where he was. However, a week or two later a man was found sleeping rough in the Cambridgeshire village of Gamlingay. Calling himself Jock Anderson, he took on seasonal work such as picking peas and apples for local growers. He was given a trial for the Gamlingay football team who immediately recognised his ability and with 'Anderson' playing superbly, they went on a winning streak in the Cambridgeshire League and topped the league with a played nine, won nine record. The fame of their mystery centre forward spread, attracting scouts, but then 'Anderson' disappeared. The reason was that Tom Morrison, under his real name, was appearing in court in Sunderland, accused of deserting his wife and child. His absence was sorely felt by Gamlingay who went on a run of five defeats, eventually finishing third. Sunderland, having found their man, gave him a free transfer. He returned to Ayrshire and was given training facilities by Ayr United, playing in a few reserve games. They signed him in the summer of 1937 but he went off the rails again, failed to turn up for pre-season training, and was convicted of housebreaking. His contract was quickly cancelled although it was not quite the end of his playing career as he turned up in Dublin at Drumcondra and played for several months until he suffered a compound fracture of his leg in February 1939. That summer he was appointed team coach and worked as groundsman before being dismissed in 1942. He later returned to Gamlingay and coached the village juniors, worked at the Greene King Brewery in Biggleswade, and remained in the area for the rest of his life.

Alan MORTON (31/5, 1920-32)
Allan Lauder Morton
Born 24 April 1893 Skaterigg Farm, Jordanhill, Glasgow
Died 14 December 1971 Victoria Place, Airdrie, Lanarkshire
Scotland v Wales 1920, 1922, 1923, 1924, Feb 1925, 1927, 1928, 1929, 1930, 1931; Ireland 1920 (1), 1923, 1924, 1925, 1927 (2), 1928, 1929, 1930, Feb 1931c; England 1921 (1), 1922, 1923, 1924, 1925, 1927 (1), 1928, 1929, 1930, 1931, 1932; France 1932.
Queen's Park 1913-20; Rangers 1920-33 (Scottish League 1921, 1923, 1924, 1925, 1927, 1928, 1929, 1930, 1931; Scottish Cup 1928, 1930).

One of the finest wingers ever produced by Scottish football, Morton was known as the 'Wee Blue Devil', a title conferred on him by the English football writer Ivan Sharpe. Born in a cottage at Skaterigg Farm, roughly where Glasgow High School now stands, his name was originally registered as John Archibald Morton but changed two months later to Allan Lauder Morton (note the spelling of Allan). He moved to Airdrie as a boy when his father, a colliery manager, took over a coal mine there, and lived all his life in the town. He won his earliest honours in the game at Airdrie Academy and when he left school he studied to become a mining surveyor, a profession he followed with United Collieries Ltd during his football career. Thanks to his studies he was already 20 when he made his debut for Queen's Park in November 1913, in the same team as his younger brother Robert. He kept his place for the rest of the season, indeed he was virtually ever-present for seven seasons through the war years, until he was persuaded to turn professional with Rangers in the summer of 1920. By then he was 27 and had played in three Victory internationals and won his first Scotland cap while still an amateur. He also made the first of 15 appearances for the Scottish League. However, that was just the start and he won a wealth of honours with Rangers, including nine league titles and two Scottish Cups. Perhaps his greatest year was 1928, when Rangers won the League and Cup double, and he became one of the Wembley Wizards, the oldest man in the team that beat England 5-1. A year after his last of 31 appearances for Scotland in 1932, and with almost 500 first team matches for Rangers, he retired on his 40th birthday. He was immediately taken onto the Rangers board and remained a director until 1971, when he resigned after several years of ill health which saw him confined to a wheelchair. He died a few months later. His extraordinary contribution to the club is recognised by having his portrait at the top of the marble staircase at Ibrox. See his biography, *Blue Devil with a Briefcase*, by Brian Morton.

Hugh MORTON (2/0, 1929)
Hugh Auld Morton
Born 25 November 1902 Jeffrey Place, Newmilns, Ayrshire
Died 23 April 1980 Ranoldcoup Road, Darvel, Ayrshire
Scotland v Germany 1929; Netherlands 1929.
Darvel Juniors; Kilmarnock 1922-32 (Scottish Cup 1929); Galston Aug-Dec 1932; Morton Dec 1932-33; Kilmarnock 1933-37.
A right half who spent almost his entire senior career with Kilmarnock, Morton made his debut in 1922 and played steadily throughout the decade until he reached his peak. He had already represented the Scottish League against the English when he took part in Kilmarnock's Scottish Cup final victory over Rangers in 1929, which was followed by his selection for Scotland's summer tour to the continent. He played in the internationals against Germany and the Netherlands as well as the match with a Norwegian select. After appearing in the 1932 Scottish Cup final defeat he could not agree terms with Kilmarnock and sought pastures new, but as they placed a hefty transfer fee on his head he simply signed for Galston in the Scottish Alliance and threatened to give up football altogether. Eventually Kilmarnock relented and transferred him to Morton, where he returned to excellent form until he suffered a knee injury in April 1933 which put him out until the end of the season. To general surprise, he was accepted back in the Rugby Park fold that summer and, dropping to full back, remained there until he retired in 1937. He coached the younger players during this spell and returned to take charge of Kilmarnock's reserves in the late 1940s. He later served as a club director from 1951 until he was voted off the board in 1958. He was a partner in a lace manufacturing business in Darvel.

Willie MUIR (1/0, 1907)
William Muir
Born 17 January 1876 Coalburn, Lesmahagow, Lanarkshire
Died 18 October 1941 Sandbank, Dunoon, Argyllshire
Scotland v Ireland 1907.
Glenbuck Athletic [trials for Third Lanark Feb-Apr 1896]; Kilmarnock Jan-Apr 1897; Everton Apr 1897-1902; Dundee 1902-1907; Bradford City 1907-08 (Second Division 1908); Heart of Midlothian 1908-10; retired; Dumbarton Nov 1911-12.
An excellent goalkeeper, Muir was born into a mining family which moved to Glenbuck when he was a boy and he was soon immersed in the village's extraordinary football culture. In time he became one of five players from Glenbuck to be capped by Scotland but that was far in the future when he first came to notice as a junior internationalist in 1896 against England. By then he had started to make steps in the professional game, with three trial appearances for Third Lanark, although he didn't formally make the step up until he signed for Kilmarnock early in 1897. A few months later he went south to Everton for a £45 fee and had four successful seasons with the First Division club. His fifth season, however, saw him largely in the reserves and he returned to Scotland with Dundee where he had his best period and gained two Scottish League caps in 1903 and 1907, both against England, before finally making his full Scotland debut in March 1907 against Ireland, aged 31. Despite keeping a clean sheet, it was his only cap. That summer he went south for a fine season at Bradford City, helping them to win the Second Division title, and in 1908 joined Hearts. At the same time he opened the Grey Horse Inn in Musselburgh, which prompted him to retire in 1910 while he was still a first team player. Hearts retained his registration, which meant that offers from Dundee Hibs and Leith Athletic fell through as they were put off by the transfer fee. However, in November 1911 he was tempted out of retirement by Dumbarton, who duly paid a fee to Hearts, and Muir returned to action before hanging up his boots definitively two months later. He ran his pub in Musselburgh High Street until 1930, when he took over the Ardnadam Hotel near Dunoon but gave it up in 1935 after it suffered extensive damage in a fire, when he rescued several trapped guests by helping them to escape from the first floor. He remained in the area and died there in 1941.

Tommy MUIRHEAD (8/0, 1922-29)
Thomas Allan Muirhead
Born 24 January 1897 Park Street, Cowdenbeath, Fife
Died 27 May 1979 Victoria Infirmary, Helensburgh, Dunbartonshire
Scotland v Ireland 1922, 1927, 1928c, 1929; England 1923; Wales 1924, 1928, 1929c.
Hearts of Beath 1913-16; Hibernian Apr 1916-17; Rangers 1917-24 (Scottish League 1920, 1921, 1923, 1924); Boston Wonder Workers May-Dec 1924 (player-manager); Rangers Dec 1924-30 (Scottish League 1927, 1928, 1929, 1930).
An inside right or right half, Muirhead could (and did) play anywhere in the forward line or half-back line. He started in Fife junior football but his early career was interrupted by the War and his work for the Army Pay Corps. While still serving he joined Hibs in April 1916 and then moved on to Rangers in the summer of 1917, the club where he would spend almost all his career. There were few opportunities to appear for them in his first two years as he took up an Army commission but after he was demobbed in 1919, still only 22, he played a key role as Rangers dominated the decade in Scottish football. In his time there he won eight

league medals, interrupted by an American interlude in 1924 when he spent six months as player-manager of the cash-rich Boston club. Apart from that, despite regular offers from big English clubs, he remained loyal to Rangers. His only regret was never lifting the Scottish Cup as he missed the victories of 1928 (through injury) and 1930, and lost the finals of 1922 and 1929. On the international front he amassed eight Scotland caps, twice as captain, without ever establishing himself as a regular, and he also represented the Scottish League six times. Immediately after retiring in 1930 he wrote for the *Evening Citizen* as a journalist but gave management a try at St Johnstone from 1931-36 then Preston North End in 1936-37. At that point, to widespread surprise, he decided to return to journalism with the *Scottish Daily Express*, where he was later sports editor.

Alec MUNRO (3/1, 1936-38)
Alexander Dewar Munro
Born 6 April 1912 Fordale Terrace, Carriden, West Lothian
Died 27 August 1986 Thirsk Grove, Blackpool, Lancashire
Scotland v Ireland 1936 (1); Wales 1936; Netherlands 1938.
Bo'ness United; Champfleurie; Newtongrange Star; Heart of Midlothian 1932-37; Blackpool Mar 1937-50 [guest for Middlesbrough Aug-Sep 1940, Brighton 1945-46].

Munro signed for Hearts as an outside left in 1932 but they converted him into a right winger so effectively that he was called into the Scotland team in the autumn of 1936. His first international against Ireland ended in a fine 3-1 victory, with the bonus of a goal, but his second against Wales a few weeks later was a disappointing home defeat. A subsequent loss of form saw him dropped to the reserves, which led to a transfer request and a move to Blackpool in March 1937 for their final push to win promotion to the First Division. A year later he was back in the Scotland team for a third and final cap against Netherlands. He joined the Royal Tank Regiment shortly after the outbreak of war and saw active service in Palestine then North Africa, where he was captured in 1942. He spent three difficult years in German prisoner of war camps, and when he returned to Blackpool he was so weak that many thought his playing days were over. However, he fought back to fitness so successfully that he made it back into the side and played for a couple more seasons. At the age of 36 he achieved a long-held ambition to play at Wembley when he was a surprise pick for the 1948 FA Cup final, which Blackpool lost to Manchester United, and that was virtually the end of his involvement in the first team. Thereafter he coached their third eleven until his retirement from playing in 1950. He ran a hotel in Blackpool and applied to manage clubs including Scunthorpe, Halifax Town and Carlisle United, without success.

Neil MUNRO (2/2, 1888-89)
Neil Munro
Born 27 September 1868 Newhouses, Dalry, Ayrshire
Died 4 September 1948 Abbot Street, Paisley, Renfrewshire
Scotland v Wales 1888 (1); England 1889 (1).
Abercorn 1887-90; Pawtucket Free Wanderers 1890-91; Abercorn 1891-94.

Born in Ayrshire, Munro moved to Paisley as a child, and started his football career with Abercorn where he played initially in the third eleven, soon working his way up to the top team where he excelled on the wing. He won his first Scotland cap in 1888 aged 19, scoring against Wales, while a year later in England he played a superb game on the left with John McPherson of Cowlairs, and scored the goal which started a memorable comeback that converted a two-goal deficit into a 3-2 win. Despite being at the top of the game, he decided to emigrate to the USA with his wife in 1890 and was presented with a purse of sovereigns as a farewell gift from his Abercorn colleagues. Having joined the Pawtucket club in New England, a year later he returned to the UK as part of the 1891 Canadian touring party (which was in fact half Canadian and half American) and played *against* Scotland at Ibrox, as well as against Ireland and Wales. The tour lasted from August to January, but Munro only took part in matches up to November as Abercorn persuaded him to desert the tourists and return to Paisley. Whether he repaid the sovereigns is not recorded, but he played in Abercorn's Scottish League campaigns until 1894. He spent the rest of his life in Paisley, where he worked as a general labourer for a starch manufacturing company and then for the local council.

Johnny MURDOCH (1/0, 1931)
John Livingstone Murdoch
Born 6 February 1901 Clydesdale Buildings, Holytown, Lanarkshire
Died 7 September 1964 Grange Road, Stanion, Northamptonshire
Scotland v Ireland Feb 1931.
Clydesdale Wanderers; Kirkintilloch Rob Roy 1920-21; Airdrieonians 1921-28; Motherwell Oct 1928-33 (Scottish League 1932); Dundee 1933-34; Dunfermline Athletic 1934-35; Stewarts & Lloyds 1935-36.

An outside right with an eye for goal, Murdoch had a reputation for popping up in unexpected places, either to nick a goal or to surprise an opposing full-back. Brought up in New Stevenston, he appeared in the Scottish Juvenile Cup final with his home town team Clydesdale before an eventful season for Kirkintilloch Rob Roy where he won the Scottish Junior Cup in 1921, was selected for the Glasgow Junior League and Dunbartonshire, and was a reserve for the Scotland team. He signed that summer by Airdrieonians, although it took him several years to fully establish himself in a top-class side, which had stars such as Hughie Gallacher and Bob McPhail. Airdrie finished second in the league for four consecutive seasons and won the Scottish Cup in 1924 but unfortunately for Murdoch, he was a reserve on that occasion, with his place in the team going to Jimmy Reid. Airdrie gave him a benefit match in 1927, with Rangers providing the opposition, but deplorable weather kept the crowd down to just 200 and the game was abandoned in the second half. The following autumn he moved to Motherwell, who were on the cusp of glory and he played a significant role in their league-winning season with ten goals in 26 appearances. By then he had won a Scotland cap, a disappointing scoreless draw against Ireland. He played in two Scottish Cup finals, in 1931 and 1933, both lost to Celtic and was then given a free transfer by Motherwell as a thank-you for his service. Next, he spent a season each with Dundee and Dunfermline, then went south to go into business as a stationer and newsagent in Corby where he played for Stewarts & Lloyds in the United Counties League and continued to enjoy works football into his forties. He remained in the town until his death.

Frank MURPHY (1/1, 1938)
Francis Murphy
Born 6 December 1913 Brickwork Rows, Gartcosh, Lanarkshire
Died 12 February 1984 Sinclair Place, Airdrie, Lanarkshire
Scotland v Netherlands 1938 (1).
St Patrick's Boys Guild; Croy Celtic 1931-32; Maryhill Hibernian 1932-33; St Roch's 1933-34; Celtic 1934-46 (Scottish League 1936, 1938; Scottish Cup 1937) [guest during WW2 for Albion Rovers 1942-43; Tranmere Rovers Nov 1943; Aldershot 1943-44]; Limerick 1946-47.

An outside left with the capacity to deliver pinpoint crosses, Murphy played a major role in Celtic's successes of the late 1930s, winning two league titles and the Scottish Cup, not to mention the Empire Exhibition trophy of 1938 and three Glasgow Charity Cups. He first signed a provisional form for Celtic in 1931 but was allowed to develop in junior football at Croy Celtic and Maryhill Hibs (winning a Scottish junior cap) then at St Roch's before he was called back to Parkhead in April 1934. He was soon hailed as the solution to a long-standing problem for Celtic in finding a good left winger. As well as creating goals, he scored a fair number, his powerful shot making him adept at penalties and free kicks. He netted a wonderful strike for Scotland against Netherlands in May 1938 in what proved to be his only cap, as WW2 intervened just as he was coming into his finest form. He joined the Royal Navy early in 1943 and that effectively ended his connection with Celtic although he played regularly as a guest for Albion Rovers and later at Aldershot. After the War he had a season in Ireland with Limerick, showing he had not lost his touch by scoring four goals in one league game against Drumcondra. Back in Scotland after retiring from the game, he ran a pub in Airdrie.

Johnny MURRAY (1/0, 1895)
John Murray
Born 29 March 1874 Back Street, Renton, Dunbartonshire
Died 17 October 1933 Western Infirmary, Glasgow
Scotland v Wales 1895.
Renton 1891-97; Dundee 1897 (did not play).
Murray joined Renton as a young man and played inside right for the team in the 1895 Scottish Cup final, which was lost to St Bernard's. He had proved his worth over several seasons and the previous month won his only Scotland cap in a 2-2 draw with Wales in Wrexham. Some reports credit him with the first goal, although it is usually allocated to Johnny Madden. He appeared to have a fine career ahead when he signed for Dundee in May 1897, and a local paper referred to him in glowing terms: 'He holds a first class football certificate, is a hail fellow, well met, a capital after-dinner speaker'. He was also reportedly a strict teetotaller. However, he was laid low by a serious bout of influenza that summer, which prevented him from ever playing for his new team and his football career was over at the age of 23. An engineer and iron turner, he spent the rest of his life in Renton, but died in a Glasgow hospital.

John MURRAY (1/0, 1890)
John Winning Murray
Born 24 April 1865 Union Place, Lennoxtown, Stirlingshire
Died 16 September 1922 Victoria Hospital, Accrington, Lancashire
Scotland v Wales 1890.
Vale of Leven Wanderers; Vale of Leven 1885-90; Sunderland Sep 1890-92 (Football League 1892); Blackburn Rovers 1892-96.
Born in Lennoxtown, Murray moved to Bonhill as a baby when his father started work at one of the local calico mills, and grew up in one of Scotland's most fervent football villages. In time he joined Vale of Leven Wanderers and stepped up to Vale of Leven in 1885. Six feet tall and with a muscular physique, he was soon playing for the Dunbartonshire county team, although some considered him to be too gentlemanly and even 'too fair in tackling an opponent'. He played initially as left half then found his best position when Johnny Forbes went south in 1888 and he switched to left back in partnership with Andy Whitelaw, a combination which helped Vale to reach the Scottish Cup final in 1890. The same year he was a late selection for his only international, partnering Whitelaw at full back for Scotland against Wales after Mick McKeown pulled out due to a bereavement. At the peak of his powers, but with a secure job in the print works and newly married, it took a leap of faith to turn professional that autumn, when Sunderland tempted him with a good wage and a daytime job. He had two excellent years in the north-east which concluded with the Football League title in 1892, but he did not settle locally. That summer Blackburn Rovers found him a skilled job as a pattern maker and engraver in a Brinscall cloth factory which was enough to persuade him to move to Lancashire. Even better, he was reunited in a full back partnership with his old team-mate Johnny Forbes, and later with Tom Brandon, playing almost every match for Rovers over a four year period before work commitments prompted him to conclude his football career in 1896. Teetotal and an amateur sprinter of note, he remained in Lancashire and was manager of the engraving department at Broad Oak Printworks in Accrington, living at Hollins Hill Cottage. He died in hospital aged 57 after an operation for appendicitis.

Paddy MURRAY (2/0, 1896-97)
Patrick Murray
Born 6 May 1874 Lennoxtown, Stirlingshire
Died 25 December 1925 Albion Road, Edinburgh
Scotland v Ireland 1896; Wales 1897.
Campsie Black Watch; Campsie 1891-93; Hibernian Feb 1893-1901 (Second Division 1894, 1895).

In his first season as a senior player, Murray won the Stirlingshire Cup with Campsie in 1892, when they defeated Falkirk in the final. He was recruited by the newly resurrected Hibs in February 1893 and played in their very first match as well as in their first game after entering Scottish League that summer. It proved to be a successful campaign with the title won, although there was no automatic promotion and the club was forced to play another season in the Second Division, which they promptly won again. This time they were elected to the top league, finishing third at the first attempt and reaching the 1896 Scottish Cup final, which was lost to city rivals Hearts. Two weeks later, Murray made his international debut against Ireland, and the following year he picked up his second cap versus Wales, which ended in another draw. He was also selected for the Scottish League. Playing on the right side of the forward line, Murray was a consistent scorer throughout the decade, and despite offers to move to other clubs he remained loyal to Hibs. However, he fought a losing battle against putting on weight and was only 27 when he decided to hang up his boots in 1901. As a thank-you farewell Hibs gave him a benefit match against Celtic and he was presented by his fellow players with a gold albert watch. He continued his devotion to the club as a director and was still in that role when he collapsed and died of a heart attack one Christmas morning while at work at Redpath Brown's steel works in Albion Road, just round the corner from the Hibs ground. His son John played for Falkirk in the 1920s. NB confusingly, Hibs had another Patrick Murray in the mid-1890s, who went on to play for several clubs including Darwen, Preston, Nottingham Forest, Celtic, Portsmouth and East Stirlingshire.

George MUTCH (1/0, 1938)
George Mutch BEM
Born 21 September 1912 Walker Road, Torry, Aberdeen
Died 1 April 2001 Royal Infirmary, Aberdeen
Scotland v England 1938.
Avondale; Banks o' Dee; Arbroath 1933-34; Manchester United 1934-37 (Second Division 1936); Preston North End 1937-46 (FA Cup 1938) [guest during WW1 for Manchester City 40-41; Liverpool 41-42; Aberdeen 41-42; Everton 41-44; Southport 43-45; Blackburn Rovers 44-45]; Bury 1946-47; Southport 1947-48 player-manager.

As a junior with Banks o' Dee, Mutch scored two goals in a trial for Aberdeen reserves but was not signed, and joined Arbroath instead as a part-timer, which allowed him to complete his apprenticeship as a printer. Several clubs were after his signature by the following summer and the race was won by Manchester United, whose manager Scott Duncan got him to sign a contract just an hour before the representatives of Hearts and Chelsea arrived at his front door. He fitted straight into the team at Old Trafford and helped United to win the Second Division title in his second season. When they were immediately relegated, however, he was transferred to Preston North End which allowed him to remain in Division One. He had a momentous month in April 1938 when he not only played in a winning Scotland side at Wembley, his only full cap, he returned to the stadium three weeks later and scored the only goal of the FA Cup final with a penalty in the last minute of extra time. He later recalled that he did not want to take the kick as he was hurt in the tackle that brought the award, but nobody else wanted the responsibility: 'I was very undecided. I made up my mind to kick the ball as hard as I could, keep my head down and hope for the best. I was afraid to look up after I kicked the ball and the next thing I saw was it hitting the underside of the crossbar. I wasn't sure if it was going into the net or back into play, but the ball went into the back of the net.' A year later, war broke out and he went to work in a Preston aircraft factory, taking the opportunity to play for a range of other teams as a guest, including a few games back home in Aberdeen, and he won the Football League War Cup with Preston in 1941. By the time the War ended his best playing years were over and he wound down his career at Bury and then Southport, where he was also manager. In 1950 he came back to Aberdeen where he opened a grocer's shop and coached Banks o' Dee, leading them to the Scottish Junior Cup in 1957. He had a long-term interest in teaching handicapped children to swim, and eventually worked full time at special schools in Peterhead and Inverurie, for which he was awarded the British Empire Medal in 1978.

N

Charlie NAPIER (5/3, 1932-37)
Charles Edward Napier
Born 8 October 1910 Gowan Avenue, Falkirk
Died 5 September 1973 School Road, Laurieston, Stirlingshire
Scotland v England 1932, 1935; Wales 1934 (2); Ireland 1936 (1); Austria 1937.
Bonnybridge; Maryhill Hibernian; Celtic 1929-35 (Scottish Cup 1931, 1933); Derby County 1935-38; Sheffield Wednesday 1938-45 [guest for Falkirk 1939-41, 1943, 1945]; Falkirk 1945-46; Stenhousemuir 1946-48.

Napier was born into football as his father was a former referee and, for a while, secretary of Falkirk. Known as 'Happy Feet' at Celtic, he joined the club from Maryhill Hibs in 1929 and his first medal came in the Scottish Cup final of 1931 when two late goals earned a replay, and ultimately victory, against Motherwell. In 1932 he made his Scotland debut in a defeat to England at Wembley, and that summer toured Canada and America with Celtic. In Montreal the players visited the Kit Kat Club where there was a dance competition which Charlie and his partner won. The same tour also nearly brought disaster at a swimming pool in New York when his team mates pushed Charlie, a non-swimmer, into the water. He had to be rescued and said afterwards 'I shall never forget the terrifying experience of choking. It reduced me to panic. [Peter] McGonagle came to the rescue but I was in such a desperate state that he had all his work cut out to save me.' After winning his second Scottish Cup in 1933 he had two cartilages removed and feared his top level career might be over, but he made a fine recovery and was overjoyed to win his second Scotland cap in the autumn of 1934 against Wales, more so as he scored twice. He went on to win five international caps in all, and made two appearances for the Scottish League. In his latter days at Celtic he suffered a series of injuries, then moved to Derby County in 1935 where he was again bedevilled by time on the treatment table. However, he had a steady run after his transfer to Sheffield Wednesday in 1938 and it was only the outbreak of war that ended his time there. He returned immediately to Falkirk and played for the club as a guest through the war years. Bizarrely, because he was still registered in England, his poor disciplinary record while playing for Falkirk led to a sanction from the FA in London, who in February 1941 announced he was suspended *sine die,* for a sending-off and two cautions in Scottish football. This put him out of the professional game for over two years until he was reinstated in July 1943, and he resumed playing with Falkirk. Then he was called back to his parent club for the Wednesday v Grimsby match on 23 October 1943 and as a result of an incident in that game he was suspended again from January 1944 until August 1945. It was rough justice on the player. After finally returning to the Falkirk side as a guest in early season games of 1945, he was signed formally in September but his lack of pace limited his appearances and he was allowed to move on to Stenhousemuir the following summer. He retired in 1948 and coached his local side Bonnybridge Juniors. A qualified electrician, latterly he worked as a hospital storekeeper.

Bobby NEILL (2/2, 1896-1900)
Robert Scott Gibson Neill
Born 24 September 1875 James Street, Greenhead, Glasgow
Died 2 March 1913 Holmfauldhead Drive, Govan, Glasgow
Scotland v Wales 1896 (2), 1900.
Gartmore; Ashfield; Hibernian 1894-96 (Second Division 1895); Liverpool 1896-97; Rangers 1897-1904 (Scottish League 1899, 1900, 1901, 1902; Scottish Cup 1898).

Lightly built and small for a centre half, Neill was still 19 when he was described as a 'little wonder' by the *Scottish Referee*, which admired his cleverness and deceptive power. He had been signed by Hibs from Glasgow junior side Ashfield in 1894, and soon had a brush with controversy in December when he played in a Hibs victory over Celtic in the Scottish Cup, after which the losers put in a successful protest that he was ineligible; Hibs lost the replay without him. There was the consolation of the Second Division title that season, and Hibs proved a major force in the First Division, finishing third and reaching the Scottish Cup final. Neill was considered good enough for the national team, and scored twice on his Scotland debut in a 4-0 win over Wales in 1896. He was hot property, and was tempted south for a season with Liverpool before coming back to Scotland with Rangers in May 1897, just in time to win the Glasgow Charity Cup. He went on to have the best years of his career at Ibrox, securing the Scottish Cup in his first season, then four consecutive league titles and of those, the best was in 1898-99 when Rangers won every league match with a midfield backbone of Gibson, Neill and Robertson. For a half back he scored more goals than might be expected, as he took penalties and was not afraid to shoot from distance. International recognition was barely forthcoming, however, and he won only one more cap in 1900, four years after his first, also against Wales, although he did make a memorable appearance for the Scottish League, a record 6-2 victory against the English in 1901. He retired in 1904 and became a restauranteur in Glasgow, but died of chronic alcoholism aged 37.

Robert NEILL (5/0, 1876-80)
Robert Walker Neill
Born 4 August 1853 Clelland Street, Gorbals, Glasgow
Died 19 August 1928 Treasury Buildings, Perth, Australia
Scotland v Wales 1876, 1877, 1878c; England 1877, 1880c.
Queen's Park 1872-80 (Scottish Cup 1874, 1875, 1876, 1880).

Neill was a fairly typical Queen's Park player of the pioneer days: the son of a head teacher in the southside of Glasgow, he pursued a professional career as a commercial agent for an engineering company. His football was exemplary and he was described in the Scottish Football Annual as 'one of the finest backs Scotland ever produced'. That was in 1880, the year in which a knee injury in the Glasgow Charity Cup final, when he captained QP to victory over Rangers, ended his playing days prematurely. He played for Scotland five times, all on the winning side, making his debut against Wales in 1876 and going on to captain the side twice. He was also in four Queen's Park Scottish Cup winning sides of 1874, 1875 (as goalkeeper!), 1876 and 1880. After giving up football, in the 1880s he spent a couple of years working in South America and married Janet Johnston on his return. He and his wife had four children, although only two survived to adulthood, and in the 1911 census the family are at 106 Kilmarnock Road in Shawlands, where he is recorded as a 58-year-old machine maker and employer. Then something strange happened: there is nothing in the press about it, but the indications are that he simply walked out one day and never returned. A year later, he arrived on the SS Monaro in Fremantle, Western Australia, where he found work as a station hand, in other words a general labourer. He had no financial resources and lived in the Salvation Army 'Palace'. When war broke out, Neill was in his sixties, far too old for the Anzac forces, which had an upper age limit of 45, although for those with mining and engineering experience an exception was made up to 50. However, on 17 May 1917 he walked into the recruiting office at Blackboy Hill camp, near Perth, declared himself to be 48 years old with no next of kin, and signed on the dotted line. Private Neill passed the physical examination and was taken into the Mining Corps. He underwent his initial training and was appointed as a Sapper on 31 July, then a week later the ruse was discovered and he was summarily discharged for being over age. It was a brave attempt, and in fact other Australians in their 60s managed to keep up the deception and saw active service in Europe, but for him the War was over. He went back to the Salvation Army hostel, and worked as its caretaker until his death in 1928. His funeral at Karrakatta Cemetery drew a good crowd and the *Daily News* reported: 'The respect and esteem in which the deceased was held was demonstrated by the number of friends who attended at the graveside and the beautiful wreaths and floral tributes received.' His younger brothers were footballers, George with Airdrieonians, Quintin with Queen's Park and Lincoln City.

Peter NELLIES (2/0, 1913-14)
Peter Nellies
Born 4 September 1885 Kingseat, Fife
Died 15 July 1930 Royal Infirmary, Glasgow
Scotland v Ireland 1913; Wales 1914c.
Douglas Water Thistle; Heart of Midlothian 1908-21; King's Park 1921-22; Berwick Rangers 1922-23 player-manager.

Born near Dunfermline, Nellies moved to Lanarkshire when his father found work in the coal mining community of Ponfeigh, close to Douglas Water. He remained in the area all his life, and started his football career with a lengthy apprenticeship with Douglas Water Thistle, where he was captain not only of his club but also the Lanarkshire League and the Scotland junior team against England in the last of his three caps, in 1908. With a good turn of speed and an astute tackler that made him a fine all-round footballer, his talents as a half back were recognised by Hearts in 1908 and they took him to Tynecastle. It was the start of a lengthy association which saw him captain the side through a momentous era. He made eight appearances for the Scottish League, the first in 1911, and it was only a matter of time before he was selected for Scotland, making his debut against Ireland in 1913 and a year later he was made captain of the side that faced Wales. At that point the War intervened, and although he tried to enlist he was needed during the conflict in the coal mines. He also drove a taxicab in Edinburgh and played for Hearts when he could, remaining at the club until he was released in 1921. He still had some football in him, spent a year with King's Park, and was then appointed player-manager of Berwick Rangers, but towards the end of his first season he was sacked for failing to turn up at a match. He continued to live in Douglas Water, where he worked in a coal mine as a brusher, until his life ended tragically aged 44 when he fractured his skull after being thrown from a motorbike near his home and he died two days later in hospital.

Jimmy NELSON (4/0, 1925-30)
James Nelson
Born 7 January 1901 Wellington Street, Greenock, Renfrewshire
Died 8 October 1965 Sully Hospital, Barry, Wales
Scotland v Wales Feb 1925; Ireland 1925; England 1928; France 1930.
St Paul's; Glenarm; Crusaders 1919-21; Cardiff City 1921-30 (FA Cup 1927; Welsh Cup 1923, 1927, 1928, 1930); Newcastle United 1930-35 (FA Cup 1932); Southend United 1935-39; Ekco Sports 1939-45.

A Wembley Wizard of legend, Nelson had little connection to Scotland other than his birth and never played for a Scottish club. Born in Greenock, his family moved to Belfast when he was a boy and he was brought up in Ireland where he worked as an apprentice boilermaker while playing for local junior clubs. He joined Crusaders just after the War ended, captained an Irish Alliance XI and was being considered for an Ireland cap when the selectors were told of his birthplace. In 1921 he was recruited by Cardiff City, newly promoted to the First Division, and soon formed a defensive partnership with Scottish veteran Jimmy Blair. Cardiff was one of the top teams of the 1920s, packed with internationalists, and came desperately close to winning the league in 1924, lost the FA Cup final the following season, and finally won the trophy in 1927 with a famous 1-0 victory over Arsenal at Wembley. When Nelson made his Scotland debut in 1925 against Wales at Tynecastle it was the first time he had ever played football in the land of his birth. He did well enough to be retained for the subsequent match against Ireland in his 'home' town of Belfast but the best was yet to come, on a wet day in March 1928 at Wembley, with that astonishing 5-1 victory over England. Surprisingly he won only one more cap, an end of season friendly in France in 1930, although he did have the satisfaction of wins in all four matches. Meanwhile, Cardiff had been relegated in 1929 and Nelson secured his return to the top division a year later by signing for Newcastle for a substantial fee of around £7,000. He was badly injured in his very first match but returned to action in style, and in 1932 he captained the side to his second FA Cup success. When Newcastle were relegated in 1935 he went to Southend United for four years, and although he retired from senior football in 1939 he continued to live locally and played for and coached works side Ekco Sports through the war years, while working as a special constable. He went into the licensed trade, running the Spread Eagle in Southend then went back to Wales, where he was proprietor of the Plymouth Hotel in Penarth when he died. His son Tony played for Newport County and Bournemouth, and won Wales amateur international honours.

Tom NIBLO (1/0, 1904)
Thomas Bruce Niblo
Born 24 September 1878 Netherton, Dunfermline, Fife
Died 30 June 1933 City Hospital, Newcastle-upon-Tyne, Northumberland
Scotland v England 1904.
Cadzow Oak; Hamilton Academical Dec 1895-96; Linthouse 1896-98; Newcastle United Apr 1898-1902 [loan to Middlesbrough Apr 1900]; Aston Villa Jan 1902-04; Nottingham Forest Apr 1904-06; Watford 1906-07; Newcastle United 1907-08; Hebburn Argyle Aug-Dec 1908 (player-manager); Aberdeen Dec 1908-09; Raith Rovers 1909-10; Cardiff City Nov 1910-Feb 1911; Blyth Spartans Feb-May 1911; Newcastle City 1911-12; Fulham Nov 1915; Crystal Palace Dec 1916.
Brought up in various central Scotland towns wherever his father, a steel riveter, found work, Niblo continued to travel in his football career and was a man of many clubs on both sides of the border. He was briefly with Hamilton Accies before gaining a solid grounding at Linthouse, then in the Scottish Second Division, and was good enough to be recruited by Newcastle United in 1898 just as they were being promoted to the First Division. The move earned Linthouse a fee of £90 while the player was promised £2 10s a week and a job as a boilermaker so he could finish his apprenticeship. He found it hard to break into the Newcastle team and his time was spent mainly in the reserves, with a brief spell on loan to Middlesbrough, so it was with relief that he was transferred to Aston Villa early in 1902. There, he had his best years, showing that he could dribble through the tightest defence with his 'dandy left foot' although he had a tendency to try and beat one man too many. He was adept on either wing or in the middle, and could shoot and pass delightfully, sufficient for him to be considered for a Scotland cap, and there was little debate in 1904 when he was selected against England. However, he was fielded at outside right rather than his preference for the left, and he acknowledged that he did not perform to the best of his ability in Scotland's 1-0 win, and was not chosen again. Despite this honour he was out of favour at Villa and the following month they sold him to Nottingham Forest for £400. From that time on he never really settled with any club, and moved around the country with increasing rapidity until his apparent retirement in 1912. He signed up for active service in 1915 with the Royal Field Artillery and while training in London he made a couple of surprise appearances for Fulham in 1915 (scoring against Arsenal) and Crystal Palace the following year. He was wounded in France in June 1916, coming to Birmingham for treatment, then returned to the front and was not demobbed until the end of 1919. He settled in Newcastle in his trade as a boilermaker, and was a skilled golfer. He died aged 55 in hospital, where he had been receiving treatment for six months, apparently for the long-term effects of his war service.

Joe NIBLOE (11/0, 1929-32)
Joseph Nibloe
Born 23 November 1903 Pollok Buildings, Corkerhill, Renfrewshire
Died 25 October 1976 Stockarth Lane, Oughtibridge, Yorkshire
Scotland v England 1929, 1931, 1932; Norway 1929; Netherlands 1929; Wales 1929; Ireland Feb 1931; Austria 1931; Italy 1931; Switzerland 1931; France 1932.
Shawfield Juniors; Rutherglen Glencairn; Kilmarnock 1924-32 (Scottish Cup 1929); Aston Villa Sep 1932-34; Sheffield Wednesday 1934-39 (FA Cup 1935).
A powerfully built full back, nicknamed 'Stonewall', Nibloe was a Kilmarnock legend, a model of consistency who played 279 competitive matches for the club in eight seasons. The highlight was their Scottish Cup win of 1929, when Rangers were defeated 2-0, but the team could not repeat the success three years later against the same opponents. While at Kilmarnock he won eleven caps for Scotland, three of them against England while in the others he faced eight different countries. He also played twice for the Scottish League. Everything changed in the aftermath of the 1932 cup final, when Nibloe had a disagreement with Kilmarnock over a benefit match and was transferred to Aston Villa in September. He developed an outstanding partnership with Danny Blair in defence, but it was not to last as after a couple of years Villa sold him to Sheffield Wednesday. Here, in his first season he became one of the select few to add an FA Cup medal to his Scottish honour when Wednesday beat West Brom at Wembley in the 1935 final. He was even respected enough to play for Sheffield in their annual match against Glasgow. When he retired from playing in 1939 he remained with Wednesday as a reserve team coach and was still working part-time for the club into the 1950s. He lived in Wortley, just north of Sheffield, and worked in a Stocksbridge munitions factory during the

War, then as an electrician in the Samuel Fox steelworks, having trained as a brass moulder in a Govan shipyard while a younger man. His son John, who played for Stockport County and other clubs, was killed aged 22 in a car crash in 1964.

Jimmy NISBET (3/2, 1929)
James Nisbet
Born 27 August 1904 Grasshill Row, Glenbuck, Ayrshire
Died 18 November 1964 West Main Street, Broxburn, West Lothian
Scotland v Norway 1929 (2); Germany 1929; Netherlands 1929.
Glenbuck Cherrypickers; Cumnock; Ayr United Oct 1926-31 (Second Division 1928); Dalbeattie Star 1931-34.
One of many fine footballers to emerge from Glenbuck, Nisbet's father was killed in a mining accident before he was born. He had a remarkably short senior career, and only a couple of years after winning his Scotland caps he was playing in the South of Scotland League. He started in football with the legendary Glenbuck Cherrypickers before moving on to Cumnock and then Ayr United in the autumn of 1926 where he established himself on the left wing. The following season, centre forward Jimmy Smith stole the show with a record 66 goals as Ayr romped to the Second Division title, but all the team played their part and were rewarded with a summer tour to Norway. A year later, Nisbet was back in the same country as his fine form in Ayr's return to the First Division earned him a call-up for Scotland's first European tour. He scored a double in the opening match, a 7-3 victory in Bergen, and another in the defeat of a Norwegian select, but failed to find the net in the other two games. After that, his career went downhill and Ayr gave him a free transfer in 1931. He moved on to Dalbeattie Star, not entirely without success as the club reached the Qualifying Cup final, and he had a further brush with fame when his side hosted Celtic in the Scottish Cup in January 1934, shortly before he hung up his boots.

Jimmy NIVEN (1/0, 1885)
James Bryden Niven
Born 10 February 1861 Longbedholm Farm, near Moffat, Dumfriesshire
Died 28 July 1933 Mill Road Infirmary, Liverpool
Scotland v Ireland 1885.
Moffat 1880-85; Rangers 1885-86; Moffat 1886-92.
Niven was a founding member of Moffat when the club was formed in 1880, and became its most famous exponent. Elected captain early on, he was the first Southern Counties player to play for Scotland, winning his cap in the 8-2 victory over Ireland in 1885. He played a few matches for Rangers in 1885-86 while working in Glasgow, then returned to his home town for the rest of his playing career. He was Moffat's match secretary and a mentor to James Fraser, the club's only other international. Remarkably, he was one of the first players to write a book about his experiences, publishing *A Scottish Football Story* in 1906, which doubled as a detailed history of football in Moffat. He ran a grocer's shop in Moffat and was also an insurance agent, then moved to Liverpool where he again worked as a grocer. His son of the same name played for New Brighton and Tranmere Rovers in the 1920s.

O

Frank O'DONNELL (6/2, 1937-38)
Francis O'Donnell
Born 30 August 1911 Denbeath, Wemyss, Fife
Died 4 September 1952 Macclesfield Hospital, Cheshire
Scotland v England 1937 (1), 1938; Austria 1937 (1); Czechoslovakia May 1937; Wales 1937; Netherlands 1938.
Wellesley Juniors; Celtic 1931-35; Preston North End 1935-37; Blackpool Nov 1937-38; Aston Villa Nov 1938-46 [guest for Preston NE 1939-40, Blackpool Mar 1940 & 1943-46, Heart of Midlothian Apr 1940, Notts County Apr 1940, Liverpool Aug-Sep 1940, Wolverhampton Wanderers Dec 1941-Jan 1942, York City 1942-43, Fulham Jan 1943, Brentford Mar 1943, Tottenham Hotspur Dec 1943-Aug 1944, Brighton 1944-45]; Nottingham Forest Jan 1946-47; Raith Rovers Apr 1947; Buxton Dec 1948-51 player-manager.

O'Donnell had a great footballing brain, with an eye for a chance allied to accurate shooting. Standing over six feet tall, he sounds like the ideal forward, yet although he scored 58 goals in 83 competitive matches for Celtic, he was never really accepted by the fans, who considered him too slow and lacking incisiveness. For much of the time he had to play second fiddle to Jimmy McGrory and by 1935 there was little for it but to move on. He was transferred to Preston North End, where he was given the opportunity and encouragement to make the most of his gifts. He scored in every round of their FA Cup run in 1937, and in the final he netted with a free kick to give Preston the lead which they eventually lost to Sunderland. The same year he made his Scotland debut, scoring against England to set up a 3-1 victory, and found the net again on his second appearance, against Austria, but there were no more goals in his other four caps. Meanwhile, he had been transferred to Blackpool, and a year later went to Aston Villa. When war broke out he signed up for the RAF, and played regularly for services selects as well as making guest appearances for many clubs, according to where he was stationed. The only time he managed to play regularly for Villa was in 1943-44. Shortly after he was demobbed, in January 1946 Nottingham Forest bought him from Villa, despite him being a veteran of 34. They released him the following year and he came home to Fife, where Raith Rovers gave him a trial that came to nothing, then he seems to have been out of football for a year until Buxton appointed him player-manager towards the end of 1948. He played with Buxton until 1951, and the following season as manager took them to the third round of the FA Cup. However, that summer he fell ill and two months later he died, aged just 41. His career was sometimes mirrored by his brother Hugh who played alongside him at Celtic and Preston, while another brother, Dennis, was killed in WW2.

Duncan OGILVIE (1/0, 1933)
Duncan Henderson Ogilvie
Born 8 October 1912 Main Street, Shettleston, Glasgow
Died 6 May 1967 Victoria Hospital, Blackpool, Lancashire
Scotland v Austria 1933.
Alva Albion Rangers; Motherwell 1932-36; Huddersfield Town Mar-Dec 1936; Motherwell Dec 1936-42; Falkirk 1942-46; Hamilton Academical Dec 1946-48; Dundee United 1948-50.

Born in Glasgow and brought up in Alva, Ogilvie played for the local junior side before turning professional with Motherwell in the summer of 1932. He had such a good first season that he was capped against Austria on the right wing, and nearly scored with a header that hit the bar. That turned out to be his only international despite the press regularly suggesting he deserved further Scotland honours for the rest of the decade. His continued good form generated frequent transfer rumours and after four seasons with Motherwell in which he scored regularly he was sold to Huddersfield for a hefty fee of about £2,900 in the spring of 1936. However, although he did well in England and played regularly, after nine months he returned to Fir Park in exchange for veteran centre forward Willie Macfadyen. The highlight of his second spell at Motherwell should have been the 1939 Scottish Cup final, but his side lost heavily to Clyde. Meanwhile, in the summer months he used his speed to win many sprinting prizes at athletics meetings, running under the names of D Henderson or J Shepherd. During the War, to be closer to home and his protected job in engineering, he transferred to Falkirk in the summer of 1942, in exchange for Sammy Ross. Having been an outside right for much of his career, with a steady supply of goals at all his clubs, he dropped to the half-back line. After the conflict he had a year and a half at Hamilton, then a swansong with Dundee United which included a memorable Scottish Cup defeat of Celtic in 1949. When he retired he coached Falkirk's reserve team and served as a club director, while making a successful career in the building trade and the firm he established in Stirling with his father and brother, D&J Ogilvie, is still a major concern. He was chairman of the company when he suffered a fatal heart attack aged 54 on a holiday trip to Blackpool, and this provoked a double tragedy as his younger brother Jack fell ill on hearing the news and died five days later.

Frank O'ROURKE (1/1, 1907)
Francis O'Rourke
Born 5 December 1876 Omoa Square, Cleland, Lanarkshire
Died 24 December 1954 Monkland View Crescent, Bargeddie, Lanarkshire
Scotland v Ireland 1907 (1).
Kirkwood Thistle; Airdrieonians Jan-May 1899; Albion Rovers 1899-1900; Airdrieonians 1900-07 (Second Division 1903); Bradford City Apr 1907-14 (Second Division 1908; FA Cup 1911).

O'Rourke had a bleak start to life in a small coal-mining community, and when he was five his father died of exposure while intoxicated. He became a miner and it was only through his football talents that he managed to escape a tough life down the pit. Playing at centre forward, heavily built with a good turn of speed, he started out in junior football and was 22 when he made his senior debut at Airdrieonians in January 1899. That summer he moved to nearby rivals Albion Rovers, where he won the Lanarkshire Cup in 1900 and was then persuaded to return to Broomfield. One of the club directors later recalled that O'Rourke was reluctant to sign but agreed to do so if the club bought his mates a round of beer. It was a few shillings well spent, as Airdrie went on to win the Second Division title in 1903 as well as the Lanarkshire Cup, and then established themselves in the First Division, finishing in the top four for three consecutive seasons. Shortly after winning his Scotland cap at the age of 30, a scoring performance against Ireland in March 1907, he was sold to Bradford City, whose manager Peter O'Rourke (no relation) signed him in the middle of the night at a Leeds hotel where the Airdrie team were staying after a friendly at Valley Parade. He made an immediate impact and was top scorer as City won promotion to the First Division, then consolidated their place before going on to their greatest triumph in 1911, defeating Newcastle in an FA Cup final replay, with the only goal coming from fellow Scot Jimmy Speirs. O'Rourke played his final game in 1914 but remained at Bradford as reserve team coach, and was appointed first team trainer in 1922. He resigned in 1926 and returned to Lanarkshire where he spent the rest of his life. His younger brother Henry (Harry) played alongside him at Airdrie and had a season at Bradford's other club, Park Avenue.

Jimmy ORR (1/0, 1892)
James Orr
Born 11 December 1871 Mathieson Street, Gorbals, Glasgow
Died 2 October 1942 Eastpark Buildings, Knockentiber, Ayrshire
Scotland v Wales 1892.
Shawbank; Kilmarnock Athletic 1889-90; Kilmarnock 1890-92; Darwen 1892-95; Celtic 1895-98; Kilmarnock Athletic 1898-99; Galston May 1899-1900.

Known as 'Duster', Orr was born in Glasgow but moved to Kilmarnock as a boy when his father found work there. A solid and dependable full back, he played for Ayrshire in 1891 and won the Ayrshire Cup with Kilmarnock. However, he really came to notice for his performances in a twice-replayed Scottish Cup tie against Rangers in 1891-92. He was duly selected for Scotland and partnered Jimmy Adams of Hearts at full back in his one international against Wales. Having won his cap he turned professional with Darwen, who also raided Kilmarnock for two other players. After a slow start, Orr had three good seasons at the Lancashire club, at that time in the Football League, experiencing promotion and relegation. He came back to Scotland in 1895 but his three years at Celtic were spent mainly in the reserves and he only played seven league matches. He ended his career with a season each at Kilmarnock Athletic and Galston, reverting to his old trade as an iron turner in Knockentiber for the rest of his life.

Ronnie ORR (2/1, 1902-04)
Ronald Orr Gunion
Born 6 August 1876 Bartonholm Colliery, Ayrshire
Died 21 March 1924 Bartonholm, Ayrshire
Scotland v England 1902 (1), 1904.
Monkcastle 1894-96; Glossop North End 1896-97; Kilwinning Eglinton 1897-98; St Mirren 1898-1901; Newcastle United 1901-08 (Football League 1905, 1907); Liverpool 1908-12; Raith Rovers Jan-May 1912; South Shields Mar 1913-14.
Orr was part of an outstanding Newcastle forward line in the Edwardian era and made a lengthy career out his ability to score goals. Brought up in Bartonholm, an Ayrshire mining community, he was originally a winger with Monkcastle, a junior side in Kilwinning, then had a year in England with Glossop North End which did not work out. He came back to Kilwinning before signing for St Mirren in 1898, where his performances as top scorer prompted Newcastle to sign him in 1901, along with Bob Bennie. Small but powerfully built, he made a serious impact in his first season with several memorable goals: for Newcastle he scored four against Notts County and grabbed the winner in an FA Cup tie defeat of Sunderland, while he ended the season by finding the net on his international debut for Scotland against England in May 1902. He was selected as a replacement for George Livingston, who had played in the Ibrox Disaster match, and went on to win one more cap two years later, also against England. Featuring at inside right or left, he was a significant player in two league title wins for Newcastle but somehow never managed to become popular with the fans, and barracking from the terraces prompted him in 1908 to move to Liverpool. He used his experience to excellent effect at Anfield and in 1910 he was the club's top scorer, described as their 'navigating lieutenant'. Aged 35, he signed for Raith Rovers in January 1912 but made little impact and was dropped after a few games. He left the club and returned to Tyneside the following spring, spending a final season with South Shields in the North Eastern League. In the summer of 1914 he was a guest on Third Lanark's tour to Portugal and Spain, following which he retired from the game and went back to work in the mines in his home village in Ayrshire. He died there in 1924, aged 47. NB although he played under the surname Orr, he was born as Ronald Guinness Gunion, which he later changed to Ronald Orr Gunion.

Willie ORR (3/0, 1900-04)
William Orr
Born 17 December 1872 Crewe Cottages, Cramond, Edinburgh
Died 26 February 1946 George Street, Airdrie, Lanarkshire
Scotland v Ireland 1900, 1903; Wales 1904.
Airdrie Fruitfield 1890-93; Airdrieonians 1893-94; Preston North End Mar 1894-97; Celtic 1897-1908 (Scottish League 1898, 1905, 1906, 1907; Scottish Cup 1900, 1904, 1907).

Born in Edinburgh where his father was employed on the railways, Orr moved to Airdrie as a young man, working as a house painter before his football career took over. From junior side Fruitfield he did well in his first season with Airdrieonians and, together with team-mate Adam Henderson, earned a transfer to England with Preston North End in 1894. However, it was not until he joined Celtic in 1897 that he really achieved his potential at left half. He spent ten years with the Parkhead side, winning four league titles and three Scottish Cups, and was captain of the side for several of those triumphs including the first two of their six successive championships. He was an adept penalty taker, including the first ever awarded in a Scottish Cup final, in 1907. He was selected for Scotland three times, making his debut against Ireland in 1900. After he retired in 1908 he was appointed a director of Airdrieonians, stepping up in 1921 to be manager during the club's greatest era, encompassing their Scottish Cup win of 1924 and successive second place finishes in the League. He left in 1926 when he was appointed as Leicester City manager and stayed until he resigned early in 1932. He returned to Scotland to manage Falkirk, a position that came to a sudden end in 1935 when the SFA banned him from football following an allegation of bribery. Subsequently he worked as a bus depot manager in Crieff with Alexander's Buses and retired to Airdrie shortly before his death.

Bobby ORROCK (1/0, 1913)
Robert Abbie Orrock
Born 25 May 1885 South Overgate, Kinghorn, Fife
Died 6 July 1969 Coathill Hospital, Coatbridge, Lanarkshire
Scotland v Wales 1913.
Kinghorn Thistle; Forth Rangers; East Stirlingshire 1906-08; Falkirk 1908-17 (Scottish Cup 1913) [guest for East Stirlingshire Sep 1916]; St Mirren 1917-19 [guest for Third Lanark May 1918]; Alloa Athletic 1919-23 (Second Division 1922); East Stirlingshire 1923-25; Nairn County 1925-26 player-coach.
Small in stature for a centre half at 5 feet 6 inches, Orrock was described as 'the midget centre' but had a fine career, spent entirely in Scotland. He grew up in the Fife coastal town of Kinghorn, where he not only developed his football skills, he became a scratch golfer. From junior football with Forth Rangers, where he twice represented Stirlingshire, he joined East Stirlingshire in 1906 as a forward and soon found he was better suited as a half-back. Two years later he crossed the town to Falkirk, where he had the best years of his career and the undoubted highlight was captaining the side to their first Scottish Cup success in 1913. The story goes that he was handed a lucky horseshoe by a stranger who wished him luck at Grahamston Station as they set off for the final, and amazingly he brought it to

Hampden in 1957, presented it to team captain John Prentice and Falkirk again lifted the trophy. He was also capped for Scotland against Wales in 1913, at right back, and may well have won more honours if the War had not intervened. In 1917, after a lengthy illness, he managed to sign for both Clydebank and St Mirren, and it took an SFA enquiry before the decision went the Paisley club's way. A couple of years later he signed for Alloa, and aged 37 he led them to the Second Division title, before going on the 1923 tour of South America organised by Third Lanark. His career turned full circle as he made a successful return to East Stirlingshire, his first senior club, winning the 1924 Stirlingshire Cup as well as promotion from the Third Division. The following year he went north to Nairn County as a player coach but was badly injured after five games and that concluded his playing career at the age of 40. He returned to live in Coatbridge where he worked as a riveter.

Jimmy 'Tinny' OSWALD (3/1, 1889-97)
James Oswald
Born 3 January 1868 Wellington Street, Greenock, Renfrewshire
Died 26 February 1948 Aikenhead Road, Glasgow
Scotland v England 1889 (1), 1895c; Wales 1897.
Govanhill; Kelburne; Third Lanark 1888-89 (Scottish Cup 1889); Notts County 1889-93; St Bernard's 1893-95 (Scottish Cup 1895); Rangers 1895-97; Morton 1897-1902.

Renowned as a prolific centre forward, Oswald started out as a back before Third Lanark discovered he could be much more effective up front. Born in Greenock, he moved to the Gorbals in Glasgow as a small boy where he was known as Tinny, probably because his father was a tinsmith although he himself was a boilermaker. Unusually, he won three Scotland caps with three different clubs, scoring on his debut in the 3-2 victory over England at the Oval in 1889, and then had to wait six years before he captained an 'all tartan' side against England in 1895 as a St Bernard's player. He had moved to Rangers by the time he was selected to face Wales in 1896 then had to pull out, but won his final cap against them the following year. He also made three Scottish League appearances. He was no stranger to cup finals, and his first success was the 'snow final' of 1889 when Third Lanark beat the newly-founded Celtic. Moving to Notts County that summer, he captained them in the 1891 FA Cup final, which they lost heavily to Blackburn Rovers, and was reportedly such a bag of nerves before the match that his hands were trembling and he had to get someone to tie his shoelaces. He came back to Scotland in 1893 with St Bernard's and although he was seriously ill for several weeks in his first season, he recovered to be instrumental in their Scottish Cup victory in 1895. He moved to Rangers that summer and they won the Scottish Cup in 1897 but he missed the final as he had been dropped following an injury at work. Active in the Players Union, he concluded with five years at Morton and was still highly thought of, enough to be selected for the Home Scots in an international trial in 1901. After he retired from football in 1902, he continued to live on the southside of Glasgow, where he was a loyal supporter of Third Lanark. His younger brother John was also with Third Lanark, scoring the winner in the 1889 cup final, and followed him to Notts County.

P

Bob PARLANE (3/0, 1878-79)
Robert Parlane
Born 5 January 1847 Polmont, Stirlingshire
Died 13 January 1918 Springfield Road, Belfast, Ireland
Scotland v Wales 1878, 1879; England 1879.
Vale of Leven 1872-81 (Scottish Cup 1878, 1879); Cliftonville 1881-82.

Parlane literally stood head and shoulders above his contemporaries, a giant at six feet three at a time when the average male height was around five feet five, and his height was emphasised by a luxuriant beard. Born in Polmont while his father was working there, he was brought up in Bonhill and trained as an engineer. He went to work in New York aged 20 and married there, but when his wife died a couple of years later he returned to Scotland and became one of the founders of Vale of Leven football club in 1872. Serving on the committee, he played in their first match and soon developed into a fine goalkeeper, not afraid to venture upfield. He was thirty when he made his international debut against Wales in 1878, the year he first won the Scottish Cup with Vale of Leven, not to mention defeating English champions Wanderers in a 'championship of Britain' clash. Circumstances were somewhat different the following year in the eventful month of April 1879, as he let in five against England and was credited in some reports with an own goal as Scotland contrived to lose after holding a 4-1 advantage at half-time. Two days later he earned his third cap against Wales and then won his second Scottish Cup medal, but only after Vale were awarded the trophy by default when Rangers refused to replay; it was Parlane's mistake which had let in Struthers to score a disallowed goal in the first match, the source of the dispute. In 1881 he moved to Belfast to take up an engineering job and joined Cliftonville, keeping goal for them in the Irish Cup final of 1882, which his team lost 1-0 to Queen's Island. Although he then gave up playing football, he maintained a close interest in the game and in 1885, when he had a contract at the Alpha Engineering Works in Motherwell, he coached the players of Alpha, who merged the following year to form Motherwell FC. He also took up refereeing and was in charge of the Ireland v Scotland international in 1888, as well as that year's Irish Cup final. He lived in Belfast for the rest of his life and made a point of returning for Vale of Leven's annual reunions. He married three times, his first two wives dying young.

George PATERSON (2/0, 1938-46)
George Paterson
Born 26 September 1914 Stoneywood, Denny, Stirlingshire
Died 24 January 1986 Queen Street West, Hastings, New Zealand
Scotland v Ireland 1938; Belgium 1946.
Dunipace; Celtic 1932-46 (Scottish League 1936, 1938; Scottish Cup 1937) [guest during WW2 for Leicester City Apr & Sep 1941, Tranmere Rovers 1943-44, Blackpool 1944-45, Arsenal Jan 1946]; Brentford Oct 1946-49; Yeovil Town Oct 1949-51 player-manager.

Paterson scored for Celtic on his debut in April 1933, a year after he joined from Dunipace juniors, and established himself at left half in a fine side which won two league titles and the Scottish Cup. He was called into the Scotland team in 1938 against Northern Ireland and also made three appearances for the Scottish League before the War. He continued to play regularly for Celtic until he joined the RAF in November 1940, and during WW2 his duties as a Sergeant at RAF Cleveleys, near Blackpool, kept him away from Glasgow apart from occasional visits. Instead, he played for RAF sides and appeared as a guest for several English teams but was clearly still a significant talent as he was recalled to the Scotland team in January 1946 against Belgium, and for the Victory Internationals against Wales and Northern Ireland; he was also selected to face England but had to withdraw through injury. However, that summer he was harshly suspended by the SFA for three months after being sent off for dissent against Rangers in a Victory Cup semi-final. He decided there was no future for him in Scottish football and was all set to sign for Arsenal until Brentford put in a late offer to exchange Jerry McAloon for him, so he wound up at Griffin Park. Although he had to wait several weeks until his suspension expired, he settled well and spent three years in London, then had a swansong at Yeovil where he was player-manager. He was appointed Stirling Albion manager in November 1951 but resigned at the end of a disastrous season and was taken onto the Celtic coaching staff, during which time he won the Scottish Footballers' Golf Championship in 1954. When he parted company with Celtic in 1955, he left football altogether to take up a teaching post in Renfrewshire. A committed Christian, he lectured frequently at YMCA clubs around Scotland, sometimes using football as his theme, condemning the football pools for eliminating sporting feeling. He had an interesting side-line in film direction, and had at one point considered giving up football to enter the movie business. Late in life he emigrated to New Zealand and died there in 1986.

Jimmy PATERSON (3/0, 1931)
James Paterson
Born 15 June 1905 Foulford Road, Cowdenbeath, Fife
Died 30 December 1978 Fountain Road, Bridge of Allan, Stirlingshire
Scotland v Austria 1931; Italy 1931; Switzerland 1931.
Causewayhead; Camelon 1926-27; Everton Feb-May 1927; St Johnstone 1927-30; Cowdenbeath 1930-32; Leicester City 1932-35; Reading 1935-38; Clapton Orient 1938-39.

Born in Cowdenbeath, Paterson was brought up near Stirling and started to make a name for himself with prodigious scoring feats for Camelon Juniors. Everton took a chance on him early in 1927 but he never got past their Central League side and was released that summer. He was snapped up by St Johnstone and although it took him a while to break into the first team, he certainly made an impact when he got his chance, scoring four against Kilmarnock on his debut. Despite that, he never really established himself in the side and when Saints were relegated in 1930 he was released. He signed for Cowdenbeath, his birth town, and blossomed to the extent that everyone wondered how St Johnstone had let him go. After he scored 53 league goals in two seasons, he was rewarded with a call-up to the Scotland side in 1931 for three continental friendlies, albeit a squad without players from the top clubs. The tour was not a success and that was the end of his international honours. His scoring feats won him a transfer to Leicester City in the summer of 1932, but life near the bottom of the First Division was a struggle and his scoring ratio dropped, so when Leicester were relegated in 1935 he moved on to Reading in Division Three South, and ended up with a year at Clapton Orient. He was released in 1939 and was reportedly about to sign for Shelbourne when war broke out so he came back to Scotland and spent the rest of his life in Bridge of Allan.

Jock PATERSON (1/0, 1920)
John Paterson
Born 14 December 1897 William Street, Forebank, Dundee
Died 11 January 1973 King's Cross Hospital, Dundee
Scotland v England 1920.
Dundee Osborne; East Craigie; Dundee Violet; Dundee Mar-Dec 1919; Leicester City Dec 1919-22; Sunderland Mar 1922-24; Preston North End Oct 1924-25; Mid Rhondda Sep 1925-26; Queen's Park Rangers Jan 1926-28; Mansfield Town Jul-Oct 1928; Montrose Oct 1928-29.

The First World War not only delayed Paterson's introduction to senior football, he was wounded serving with the Black Watch 51st Division. Yet after he returned home from the War his first year in senior football was extraordinary: he signed for Dundee in March 1919 as the team started to rebuild after its wartime closure, but was not considered good enough for the first team and made just a single appearance. He was allowed to leave in December for Leicester City, a mid-table Second Division side and in the remaining four months of the season he scored 20 goals, making such an impact at centre forward that he was chosen to face England in April. It turned out to be the highlight of his career, his only Scotland selection, and he spent the rest of the 1920s as a journeyman footballer. He tried his luck at a variety of clubs, perhaps the most successful being Sunderland where he averaged a goal every second match, but never seemed to settle. A year at Preston was followed by a few months with Mid Rhondda in the Welsh League, then he moved to QPR and Mansfield Town, and ended his career back on Tayside with Montrose, at that time in the Scottish Alliance. After giving up the game he worked as a labourer in the Dundee Works Department.

Dan PATON (1/1, 1896)
Daniel John Ferguson Paton
Born 3 December 1871 Blairvault Cottage, Bonhill, Dunbartonshire
Died 9 August 1957 Wylie Avenue, Alexandria, Dunbartonshire
Scotland v Wales 1896 (1).
Vale of Leven Wanderers; Vale of Leven 1891-92; Aston Villa Jun-Dec 1892; Vale of Leven Jan 1893-94; St Bernard's 1894-98 (Scottish Cup 1895); Clyde 1898-00; Vale of Leven 1900-02 [loan to Dumbarton Oct 1900].
Having started at the lesser of the Alexandria teams, Paton stepped up to Vale of Leven in 1891 and after a season in which they finished rock bottom of the Scottish League, he turned professional with Aston Villa. However, his time in England was not a success and having failed to break into the first team he returned to Vale after just six months. His next move did the trick, and he proved his worth as an inside forward at St Bernard's, where he was in the team which lifted the Scottish Cup in 1895, defeating Renton in the final. He was called up for his only Scotland cap the following year and scored against Wales. In 1898 he left Edinburgh for Clyde, which turned out to be his final spell in the top flight, and saw out his playing days back at Vale of Leven, who were now a shadow of their former selves. He worked as a press printer in Alexandria, where he turned his hand to bowls with considerable success, winning the Scottish Bowling Association fours championship in 1910 and 1936 with Vale of Leven BC. Although too old to be called up in WW1, he had been in the Dunbartonshire Volunteer Rifles for many years and joined the Royal Defence Corps (the Home Guard of the day); he was even taken into the regular Army in the final year of the War, without seeing active service. His elder brothers James and Alex were both professionals in England with Bolton Wanderers, the former also playing for Aston Villa and Arsenal.

Michael PATON (5/0, 1883-86)
Michael Paton
Born 7 November 1859 Meadowside Street, Partick, Lanarkshire
Died 30 January 1948 Dinart Street, Riddrie, Glasgow
Scotland v England 1883, 1885c, 1886; Wales 1884c, 1885c.
Dumbarton 1880-86 (Scottish Cup 1883).

A solid left back, Paton packed a lot into a fairly short football career, all of it with Dumbarton where he replaced Archie Lang in the team. Easily distinguished because of his luxuriant beard, at his peak he was thoroughly dependable in defence, an astute tackler who knew how to distribute the ball intelligently once he had won it. In 1883 he won the Scottish Cup at the third attempt after two losing finals, and the same year he made his Scotland debut in challenging circumstances, as a late replacement for Johnny Forbes in the away game to England. He came up smiling after a 3-2 win in Sheffield and, having made a good impression, was selected four more times for his country. However, by the time he won his final cap in 1886, also against England, it was based on reputation rather than current form as he had hardly played all season, and his selection raised some eyebrows in the press. He gave up football in 1886 to focus on his career as a school teacher, as did his teammate Billy McKinnon. Following his teaching career he retired to the southside of Glasgow, where he was a member of Whitecraigs Golf Club into old age and a keen chess player.

Bobby PATON (2/0, 1879)
Robert Paton
Born early 1854 Bonhill, Dunbartonshire
Died 17 February 1905 Burnside Crescent, Jamestown, Dunbartonshire
Scotland v England 1879; Wales 1879.
Vale of Leven 1874-1881 (Scottish Cup 1877).

Paton is credited as the first man ever to score a goal against Queen's Park, heading in just before half-time in a friendly in January 1875. It was a clear sign that Vale of Leven were on the ascendant, and Paton played a vital role part in their halcyon period with numerous goals. His most notable success was their first Scottish Cup victory of 1877 when he scored in the final, which was drawn, and also fired the winner in the second replay against Rangers. That turned out to be his only medal as he missed the club's victories of the following two years. However, he was honoured with two Scotland caps in 1879 against England and Wales. Away from football, he spent all his working life in a drapery warehouse in Jamestown, rising from a humble dyer to a quality checker. He was a well-known figure in the local community as a parish councillor, President of the Jamestown Liberal Association, and a noted temperance speaker.

John PATRICK (2/0, 1897)
John Patrick
Born 10 January 1870 Kingston, Kilsyth, Stirlingshire
Died 30 November 1945 East Burnside Street, Kilsyth, Stirlingshire
Scotland v Wales 1897; England 1897.
Kilsyth Wanderers 1888-90; Grangemouth 1890-91; Falkirk 1891-92; St Mirren 1892-1901 [guest for Everton Nov 1896].

After starting out in junior football with his local team in Kilsyth, Patrick did well in goal for Grangemouth, where he represented Stirlingshire, and then had a season with Falkirk. Nearly six feet tall and weighing 14 stone, he had the ideal build for a goalkeeper at a time when they had little protection, and spent nine years as first choice for St Mirren, who he joined in 1892. He also had a single league match in England, as a guest for Everton when he kept a clean sheet against Burnley in November 1896. At the end of that season he was selected for Scotland versus Wales and then two weeks later was a late replacement for Ned Doig against England, performing superbly in a 2-1 win at Crystal Palace. Although those were his only full caps he played twice for the Scottish League, both against the Irish League in 1895 and 1898, and appeared in an international trial as late as March 1901, shortly before retiring from the game. He lived most of his life in Kilsyth, where he was a coal miner, but in his time with St Mirren he rented the club house at St Mirren Park.

Harry PAUL (3/2, 1909)
Harold McDonald Paul MRCVS
Born 31 August 1886 Sauchiehall Street, Glasgow
Died 19 April 1948 North Cliffs, near Camborne, Cornwall
Scotland v Wales 1909 (1); Ireland 1909 (1); England 1909.
Crieff Morrisonians 1904-05; Queen's Park May 1905-14.
Paul was brought up in Gourock and Glasgow, the son of a solicitor, and after his father's death he was sent as a boarder to Morrison's Academy in Crieff. An all-round sportsman, he represented the school at rugby, cricket and athletics, but in football he made his name by scoring six goals for local team Morrisonians against St Johnstone in the Perthshire Second XI Cup final of April 1905. He promptly joined Queen's Park while still a schoolboy, then later that summer he went to Glasgow as a student. Taken under the wing of RS McColl, he developed from a left-sided midfielder into a talented winger, operating to great effect for Queen's Park over the next decade, although as an amateur he occasionally returned to play for Morrisonians in local cup-ties. He was at the top of his form in 1909, winning five international honours within a six week period, starting with two selections for the Scottish League in February and then capped in all three Scotland internationals, scoring in two of them. His playing career was frequently interrupted by his studies to become a vet, and he finally qualified in 1913 at Glasgow Veterinary College. On the outbreak of WW1 he signed up immediately to the Scottish Horse and later served as a Captain in the Army Veterinary Corps, attached to the Royal Field Artillery. After the conflict he went into veterinary practice in Northumberland, based in Alnwick. In 1943 he retired to Redruth in Cornwall, where he ended his own life five years later on the cliffs of the appropriately named Deadman's Cove.

Willie PAUL (3/5, 1888-90)
William Paul
Born 7 February 1866 Merkland Street, Partick, Lanarkshire
Died 23 October 1911 Carmichael Street, Govan, Glasgow
Scotland v Wales 1888 (1), 1889, 1890 (4).
Partick Thistle 1885-90; Queen's Park 1890-91; Partick Thistle 1891-1899 (Second Division 1897); Hamilton Academical 1899-1900.
A stylish dribbler who led the forward line with enthusiasm and skill, Paul was one of Partick Thistle's early stars. In 1888 he became their first internationalist, and while with the side he won three Scotland caps, all against Wales, and achieved the rare feat of scoring four in his final international in 1890. That summer he was invited to join Queen's Park, but a season later he returned to his old club who had just entered the Scottish Alliance, and stayed with them as they entered the Scottish League in 1893, winning promotion four years later. He played eight times for Glasgow, the last in 1898, which indicates he remained at a high standard long after his international career was over. In the twilight of his career he signed for Hamilton Academical but did not make any first team appearances there. A foreman joiner, he moved around the country on contracts and was reported to be working in Grangemouth in July 1889 when he played for a Queen's Park four-a-side team. He died aged just 45 after a short illness.

Willie PAUL (1/0, 1891)
William Paul
Born 25 May 1867 Wester Crossflat, Paisley, Renfrewshire
Died 3 August 1932 Royal Alexandra Infirmary, Paisley, Renfrewshire
Scotland v Ireland 1891.
Dykebar 1885-94 [loan to Port Glasgow Athletic Jan 1892]; Paisley Academicals 1895-99.
Paul played at right back for nearly a decade at Dykebar, one of Paisley's lesser sides, with his brother Harry in midfield. They both represented Renfrewshire but Willie went one further and was the only Dykebar player ever to gain a Scotland cap, as one of ten debutants against Ireland in 1891. After Dykebar went defunct in 1894, he played in goal for Paisley Academicals and became a referee. He also sat on the SFA committee as secretary of the Renfrewshire FA. Away from football, he was devoted to bowling, winning the Paisley championship in 1895 and going on to serve as secretary of the Renfrewshire Bowling Association for over 30 years, then in the 1920s was elected President of the Scottish Bowling Association and a member of the International Bowling Board. He was also an authority on the care of bowling greens, published a guide to the treatment of turf and invented a specialist fork for ground maintenance. In his working life he managed the Larbert Laundry and was Chairman of the Scottish section of the National Federation of Launderers.

James PHILLIPS (3/0, 1877-78)
James Phillips
Born 1853 Bath Street, Gourock, Renfrewshire
Died 18 August 1932 West Side, Clapham Common, London
Scotland v England 1877; Wales 1877, 1878.
Blythswood; Queen's Park 1874-78 (Scottish Cup 1875, 1876).
Born in Gourock, Phillips was brought up in Glasgow where his father ran a building business, and trained as a joiner and carpenter. A robust half-back, and occasionally full back, he started out with Blythswood but was invited to

play for Queen's Park, where he was in the side which won the Scottish Cup in 1875 and 1876, as well as the Merchants' Charity Cup in the following two seasons. He represented Glasgow three times and then won three caps for Scotland in 1877 and 1878. His football career appears to have ended when he left Glasgow in October 1878, and his fellow players at Queen's Park recognised his contribution by presenting him with a gold watch, while he was elected a life member of the club. He spent the rest of his life in south London where he worked as a builders' manager and had a house overlooking Clapham Common.

Willie PORTEOUS (1/0, 1903)
William Porteous
Born 13 November 1878 Gatehead, Wamphray, Dumfriesshire
Died 9 April 1962 Bangour General Hospital, Broxburn, West Lothian
Scotland v Ireland 1903.
Vale of Grange; Bo'ness Sep-Nov 1899; Heart of Midlothian Nov 1899-1904 (Scottish Cup 1901); Portsmouth 1904-05; Falkirk 1905-07.

Born in rural Dumfriesshire, where his father was a blacksmith and postmaster, Porteous moved to Lochwinnoch and later settled in Linlithgow. A right winger or inside right, he made the step up from junior side Vale of Grange to Hearts in 1899 via a short spell with Bo'ness, and although he didn't establish himself in the Hearts side until the following year he soon developed a fruitful partnership with Bobby Walker. Together, they helped Hearts to win the Scottish Cup in 1901, with Porteous scoring the opening goal from 30 yards in the 4-3 defeat of Celtic. However, his shooting boots deserted him at other key moments, notably in 1903 when he failed to score on his only Scotland appearance, a disappointing defeat to Ireland. A month later, he missed a great chance for a second Scottish Cup winner's medal by blazing over with the goal at his mercy, and Hearts went on to lose to Rangers in a second replay. In 1904 he had a disagreement with Hearts and was persuaded to head south to Portsmouth by former teammate Albert Buick, who had joined the Southern League side a year earlier. Porteous returned after one season as he wanted to set up in business and opened a cycle shop in Bathgate, while he wound up his football career with Falkirk. He later expanded the cycling business into Edinburgh, although he continued to live in Linlithgow where he was a local bowling champion.

Charlie PRINGLE (1/0, 1921)
Charles Ross Pringle
Born 18 October 1894 Victoria Row, Nitshill, Renfrewshire
Died 12 December 1966 Fulwood Avenue, Linwood, Renfrewshire
Scotland v Wales 1921.
Inkerman Rangers; Maryhill; St Mirren 1916-22; Manchester City 1922-28 (Second Division 1928); Manchester Central 1928-29; Bradford Park Avenue 1929-31; Lincoln City 1931-33 (Third Division North 1932); Stockport County Feb-May 1933; Zurich Aug-Oct 1933 player-coach; Hurst Oct 1933-34; Waterford Aug-Dec 1934 player-coach.

Pringle signed for St Mirren in 1916 as an inside right from Maryhill juniors, but his career was soon interrupted by war service in France and he was not demobbed until 1919, which meant he missed their Victory Cup success. Flexible enough to play up front or in the half back line, he played once for Scotland at centre half in 1921, as a late replacement for Willie Cringan against Wales, but had a fairly anonymous game. He had played once for the Scottish League the previous month. A year after winning his cap, he refused terms with Saints and several English clubs bid for his signature, Manchester City winning the race with a fee of £1,410, of which the player got £300. He settled immediately into life at Maine Road at wing half or centre half and went on to captain City, then was relieved of the position late in 1924 after an unseemly argument with his clubmate Horace Barnes. His six years with City saw relegation and an FA Cup final in 1926, promotion denied by goal average in 1927 and the Second Division title in 1928. He made another close connection with the club by marrying Billy Meredith's daughter Lilian, but then, with a return to the top league in prospect, City decided they could do without Pringle and placed a high transfer value on him. In response, he took the novel step of helping to set up a new club, Manchester Central, for whom he played in the Lancashire Combination for a season. He had a couple of years as captain of Bradford City and then led Lincoln City to the Third Division North title. He left the club 'by mutual consent' the following February and wound up his career with a variety of clubs where he combined playing with coaching. He was 40 by the time he hung up his boots on his appointment as coach of St Mirren in December 1934. He also coached Arthurlie before he returned to Manchester in 1938 to take over his father-in-law's business, then after the War he came back to Renfrewshire where he worked in the boiler room of a local factory.

Peter PURSELL (1/0, 1914)
Peter Pursell
Born 1 July 1894 Burnside Street, Campbeltown, Argyllshire
Died 14 August 1968 Drymen Road, Bearsden, Dunbartonshire
Scotland v Wales 1914.
Campbeltown Academicals; Queen's Park 1913-14; Rangers 1914-19 (Scottish League 1918); Port Vale 1919-24; Wigan Borough 1924-26 player-coach; Congleton Town 1926 player-manager.

Following in the footsteps of his elder brother Bob, who went from Queen's Park to Liverpool, Pursell's defensive performances with Campbeltown Academicals brought him to wider attention. When he joined Queen's Park in 1913 they moved him to centre half, and he did so well that he was selected for Scotland to face Wales aged just 19. It was an extraordinary accolade for a young man in his first season in senior football and it was little surprise that a bigger club came calling. Rangers signed him that summer and he spent five years at Ibrox, winning the league title in 1918 as well as two Glasgow Cups. In 1919 he was transferred to Port Vale, where he formed a full-back partnership with his brother Bob, with Peter being appointed club captain. After five years in the Potteries, he had a couple of seasons playing and coaching with Wigan Borough in Division 3 North, did the same job at Congleton Town and then spent five years coaching Dordrecht in the Netherlands. From about 1932 he settled back in Hanley where, together with his brother, he ran a tobacconist shop in Tontine Street. He lived in the area for the rest of his life although he died on a return visit to Scotland. His son Bob was also a full back at Port Vale.

Q

league titles and five Glasgow Cup medals, most of them coming after he made the crucial switch from wing to centre forward in 1904 when Alec Bennett was injured. After scoring a hat-trick against Rangers in the Scottish Cup final that year, he never looked back. He was selected eight times (with as many goals) for the Scottish League and in 1905 he made his debut for Scotland, finding the net against Ireland. He became a Scotland regular over the next seven years, going out with a bang as he scored the winner against Wales just three minutes from the end of his final international in 1912. Powerfully built, he was said to go 'where angels fear to tread' and was such a popular figure that he was commemorated on a china plate. He resisted attempts by English clubs to sign him, and preferred to live all his days in Croy. A knee injury restricted his appearances after 1913 and he retired two years later, returning to life as a coal miner. He was much mourned when he died in 1945 and a galaxy of football personalities attended his funeral at Kilsyth Cemetery. His grandson, also James, played for Celtic in the 1960s.

R

John RAE (2/0, 1889-90)
John Rae
Born 27 December 1862 Burnbank, Rutherglen Road, Rutherglen, Lanarkshire
Died 20 November 1917 Hartwood Asylum, Shotts, Lanarkshire
Scotland v Wales 1889; Ireland 1890.
Burnbank; Rutherglen; Third Lanark 1887-90 (Scottish Cup 1889) [guest for St Bernard's Apr 1889]; Sunderland Albion 1890-92; Glasgow Thistle Dec 1892; Third Lanark Jan 1893-94.

Jimmy QUINN (11/7, 1905-12)
James Quinn
Born 8 July 1878 Smithston Row, Smithston, Dunbartonshire
Died 21 November 1945 Cuilmuir Terrace, Croy, East Dunbartonshire
Scotland v Ireland 1905 (1), 1906, 1908 (4), 1910; Wales 1906, 1910, 1912 (1); England 1908, 1909, 1910 (1), 1912.
Smithston Albion; Celtic Jan 1901-15 (Scottish League 1905, 1906, 1907, 1908, 1909, 1910; Scottish Cup 1904, 1907, 1908, 1911, 1912).

Born and brought up in the small coal-mining community of Smithston, near Croy, Quinn used football to escape from a life in the pits and developed into one of the finest scorers of the Edwardian era. He started as an outside left with local junior side Smithston Albion, alongside his brothers Peter and Philip, and represented Dunbartonshire. With several clubs after his signature he opted for Celtic and made a scoring debut for his new side in January 1901. At the end of the season he tasted the first of many Scottish Cup finals, but although he scored the match ended in a 4-3 defeat to Hearts. Nevertheless, he went on to lift the trophy five times with Celtic, and won numerous other honours including six

Rae was a robust full back who spent several seasons with his local senior club Rutherglen, where was captain and well respected. Known as 'Spriggy', his playing career really started to go places after he was selected for Lanarkshire in 1887, and that summer he joined Third Lanark where he continued to improve. In 1889 he started the year by playing for Glasgow against Sheffield, then captained his club to victory in the Scottish Cup in February and was capped for Scotland against Wales in April, alongside his club partner Andy Thomson. A year later he made his second Scotland appearance, against Ireland, and his international pedigree no doubt helped him to earn a bit of cash by signing for Sunderland Albion in the summer of 1890. They also set him up as manager of the Burton House Inn, taking over from Jimmy Hannah. Unfortunately Albion was a short-lived rival to Sunderland AFC and when the latter won the Football League title in 1892, Albion was wound up and Rae was left without a club. After regaining his fitness with Glasgow Thistle, Third Lanark took him back but his playing career was already drawing to a close and he retired in 1894 at the age of 31. He reverted to his old job as a colliery engine keeper, living in Rutherglen at Shawfield Bank House, opposite what is now Shawfield Stadium. He died in 1917 at Hartwood Asylum in Shotts of 'general paralysis of the insane', probably denoting the final stage of syphilis, which in the days before antibiotics was a killer disease with no effective treatment. Coincidentally, his death came just days before Jimmy Hannah.

James RAESIDE (1/0, 1906)
James Smith Raeside
Born 6 July 1879 East Wellington Street, Parkhead, Glasgow
Died 17 January 1946 Eastern District Hospital, Duke Street, Glasgow
Scotland v Wales 1906.
Parkhead [trial for Partick Thistle Apr 1899]; Third Lanark 1899-1906 (Scottish League 1904; Scottish Cup 1905); Bury 1906-13.

A safe if unspectacular goalkeeper, Raeside won a Scotland junior cap with Parkhead in March 1899 and had a trial with Partick Thistle, then ended up signing for Third Lanark that summer. Over the early years of the new century he played a significant role in the club's most successful era, which included a league title in 1904 followed by a Scottish Cup victory the next season. However, when international recognition came he was blamed for the 2-0 defeat to Wales in 1906, and according to one harsh judgement 'he has not the necessary nerve for international matches'. For a man who had done so well with Third Lanark this was hard to take, and that summer he moved to Bury, who were delighted with him. Unusually for a goalkeeper, he took penalties and in 1910 even scored twice against Sheffield United, the only goals of the game. He carried on playing well into his thirties but was let down financially by Bury when they offered him a reserve game as a benefit match. He also had to cope with personal tragedy when his wife and mother both died in 1908, although he remarried two years later. When he left Bury in 1913 he came back to Glasgow where he worked as a spirit salesman but by the time of his death he was living in the Great Eastern Hotel, a hostel for homeless working men in the east end.

Alec RAISBECK (8/0, 1900-07)
Alexander Galloway Raisbeck
Born 26 December 1878 Wallacestone, Polmont, Stirlingshire
Died 12 March 1949 Walton Hospital, Liverpool
Scotland v England 1900, 1901, 1902, 1903c, 1904, 1906c, 1907; Wales 1903c.
Larkhall Thistle; Royal Albert; Hibernian 1896-98; Stoke Mar-May 1898; Liverpool 1898-1909 (Football League 1901, 1906; Second Division 1905); Partick Thistle 1909-14 player-manager.

Born near Falkirk into a coal-mining family, Raisbeck moved to Cambuslang as a boy and then to Larkhall where he went down the pit himself from the age of 12. Like many others, he found an escape through football and enjoyed a lifetime in the game. He signed his first professional contract with Hibs in 1896 and after a couple of seasons he and his colleague Jack Kennedy left to join Stoke on a temporary transfer to assist them to retain their First Division status, a mission which was duly accomplished by finishing top of the play-offs. He came back to Edinburgh only for Hibs to immediately re-transfer him to Liverpool, this time on a permanent basis. His fair hair dominated the Anfield club for over a decade, playing at half back and captaining them to their first league title in 1901. Although they were relegated three years later, he led them to an instant return and then another championship in 1906. He had speed, a strong tackle and enormous enthusiasm, all of which contrived to make him a hero to the Liverpool fans, but he had something extra, as the *Liverpool Echo* recalled: 'He helped to create the soul, that inward sacred fire of zeal without which no club can thrive.' On the international front, he made his debut in the 4-1 defeat of England in 1900, and in fact all but one of his caps were against England, which says something of his stature in the game. He also played three times for the Scottish League, the first with Hibs in 1897, the other two with Partick Thistle in 1911 and 1912. Liverpool gave him a benefit match in 1904, and Partick Thistle did likewise after five seasons there as player-manager. When he finally hung up his boots in 1914 he was appointed manager of Hamilton Academical, then moved on to Bristol City in 1921, resigning in 1929. A year later he took the reins at

Halifax Town, managed Chester for two years, then Bath City until the outbreak of war. He retired to his home in Bingley Road, a five minute walk from Anfield, and lived there until his death in 1949.

Gil RANKIN (2/3, 1890-91)
Gilbert Rankin
Born 20 March 1870 Main Street, Alexandria, Dunbartonshire
Died 28 November 1927 Hornsey Central Hospital, London
Scotland v Ireland 1890 (3); England 1891.
Vale of Leven 1887-1892; Renton 1892-93; Vale of Leven 1893-95.

A baker, following in the footsteps of his father and grandfather whose hot pies were legendary, Rankin grew up in the football fervour of the Vale of Leven and developed into an excellent inside right. He played for Vale in Scottish Cup final of 1890, which was lost to Queen's Park after a replay, and the following month was selected for the national team, scoring a fine hat-trick in Scotland's convincing 4-1 victory over Ireland, just a few days after his 20th birthday. A year later, he won his second cap against England in curious circumstances, as it brought a suspension from the Scottish League which suspended Rankin and six other players for choosing to take part in an international trial rather than appear for their clubs in a league match. He was soon forgiven for doing his patriotic duty and when he left Vale in 1892 to join Renton he was selected as a reserve for a league international. He went back to Vale for a couple more years but the club was fading rapidly, which may have influenced his decision to give up the game entirely in 1895. He was still only 25, and appears to have focussed instead on playing bowls for Alexandria. He later moved to England and married in London in 1913, living in Rathcoole Gardens, Hornsey, until his death.

Bobby RANKIN (3/2, 1929)
Robert Rankin
Born 7 April 1905 Albert Street, Paisley, Renfrewshire
Died 25 August 1954 Paisley Royal Infirmary, Renfrewshire
Scotland v Norway 1929 (1); Germany 1929; Netherlands 1929 (1).
Kilwinning Rangers; Strathclyde; St Mirren Oct 1926-33; Beith Dec 1933; Dundee Jan 1934-35; Clyde 1935-37; St Mirren 1937-39.

Despite his international status, Rankin remained a part-timer throughout his football career, working as a clerk at Paisley Canal Street station. A clever inside forward, he was a reserve for the Scotland junior team while at Kilwinning, then had a few months at Strathclyde before turning senior in the autumn of 1926. Several clubs were after his signature but he chose St Mirren because he lived and worked locally. After an excellent season which saw him score 19 league goals and reach the Scottish Cup semi-final, he was called up for Scotland's 1929 tour of the continent, along with his strike partner Davie McCrae. Rankin scored within five minutes of his Scotland debut against Norway and played in all four matches of the tour, although only three of them are counted as full internationals by the SFA. However, all was not well at his club and in 1931 he refused to accept the terms being offered and nearly went to Spurs before an agreement was reached. He fell out again with St Mirren in the summer of 1933 and rejected a new contract, eventually moving on to Dundee after several months of inactivity, apart from a brief trial at Beith. After a year and a half of travelling to Dundee for matches only, because of his day job, he was glad to sign for Clyde in 1935, and finally made up with St Mirren in 1937 for the last two years of his career. He was brought onto the board of directors at Love Street in 1941 and was then appointed as St Mirren manager in 1945, remaining in post until his death from cancer, aged just 49.

Jimmy REID (3/0, 1914-24)
James Greig Reid
Born 1 May 1890 School Brae, Peebles, Peeblesshire
Died 21 April 1938 Wester Moffat Hospital, Airdrie, Lanarkshire
Scotland v Wales 1914, 1920; Ireland 1924.
Peebles Rovers 1906-10 [trial for Partick Thistle Jan 1910]; Lincoln City Apr 1910-12; Airdrieonians 1912-27 (Scottish Cup 1924); Clydebank 1927-28.

Reid was an outstanding centre forward in the fine Airdrie team of the 1920s which won the Scottish Cup and finished second in the league four times in a row. He started in football with Peebles Rovers in East of Scotland football, and by 1909 his scoring abilities were attracting bigger clubs. Celtic gave him a trial and then Partick Thistle tested him in three First Division matches, but he eventually signed for Lincoln City in April 1910. It was a tough introduction to English football as Lincoln finished bottom of the Second Division in his first season, then spent a year in the Midland League. He returned to Scotland in 1912 with Airdrie, and made such an impact that in November he made the first of three appearances for the Scottish League, scoring twice against the Irish. He ended the season with 30 league goals and the *Scottish Referee* rated him in the same class as Willie Reid of Rangers and Jimmy Quinn of Celtic, saying 'he has rare speed, a capital command of the ball, and at taking a chance he is second to none'. Early in 1914 he won his first Scotland cap, against Wales but failed to find the net in a disappointing 0-0 draw. His appearances in wartime were limited by his service with the Royal Engineers, in which he was a Sergeant, then after demob in 1919 he played for Scotland in a Victory International against England, and was back in the full national team to face Wales the following year. The next few years were an adventure at club level, as Airdrieonians developed into a superb team, while Reid was shifted to the right wing which drastically reduced his goalscoring contributions. However, his fine form did bring him one more Scotland cap in 1924 against Ireland. He eventually left Broomfield Park in 1926 after fifteen years and spent a season with Clydebank before retiring. Throughout his time in Airdrie he ran a tobacconist shop, and still had it when he died suddenly of pneumonia aged 47. Many former teammates attended his funeral at New Monkland Cemetery.

Bobby REID (2/0, 1937-38)
Robert Reid
Born 19 February 1911 Wylie Street, Hamilton, Lanarkshire
Died 16 November 1987 Hairmyres Hospital, East Kilbride, Lanarkshire
Scotland v Ireland 1937; England 1938.
Ferniegair Violet; Hamilton Academical 1931-36 [loan to Stranraer Jan 1933]; Brentford Jan 1936-39; Sheffield United Feb 1939-46 [guest for Hamilton Academical 1939-42, Airdrieonians May 1943]; Bury Nov 1946-47.

Reid came directly from juvenile football to Hamilton Accies in 1931 and developed mainly in the reserves for his first three seasons, which included a loan to Stranraer for a Scottish Cup tie. He finally got his chance on the left wing in 1934 when Jimmy King switched to the right and was such a success that within months he was honoured by the Scottish League against the Irish and the Football League. A lightning-fast winger with a powerful left foot shot, known as the 'flying Scotsman' he played in the 1935 Scottish Cup final which Hamilton narrowly lost to Rangers, then they sold him for £4,000 early in 1936 to Brentford, who were a top six side in the First Division. Although he had to take time out for appendicitis he adapted well to the faster pace and his continued good form earned two Scotland caps against Ireland and England. He joined Sheffield United in 1939 but played for Hamilton during the war years until 1943, when his wartime service kept him out of football for a couple of years. He was only able to play again from September 1945, and a year later he was transferred to Bury, where he played alongside George Mutch. He retired in 1947, qualified as a physiotherapist and set up a practice back in Hamilton. He also coached at Third Lanark and later helped other clubs including Ayr United, Airdrieonians and finally Hamilton Accies where he was assistant trainer at the time of his death.

Willie REID (9/4, 1911-14)
William Reid
Born 3 May 1884 Main Street, Baillieston, Lanarkshire
Died 13 May 1964 Calderbank Cottage, Baillieston, Lanarkshire
Scotland v Wales 1911, 1913; Ireland 1911 (1), 1912 (1), 1913 (1), 1914; England 1911, 1913, 1914 (1).
Baillieston Thistle; Morton Feb 1904-06 [loan to Third Lanark Apr 1906]; Motherwell 1906-08; Portsmouth 1908-09; Rangers Apr 1909-20 (Scottish League 1911, 1912, 1913, 1920); Albion Rovers player-manager 1920-22.

A prolific centre forward, Reid gained experience on both sides of the border before ending up at Rangers, where he spent the bulk of his career and won all his honours. He started at Morton and had a decent couple of seasons before leaving in a hurry in 1906 to help Third Lanark, who had a crisis at centre forward for their Scottish Cup final against Hearts. He was not able to provide the winning spark and the match proved to be his only appearance for the club. That summer he moved on to Motherwell, then had a season at Portsmouth in the Southern League before he was recruited by Rangers in April 1909. He made his debut in the Scottish Cup final replay which ended in a riot, so again he was denied a winner's medal. However, after that disappointment there were glory years ahead and he was top scorer for Rangers in six consecutive seasons, winning the league title three times before the War. He also established himself in the Scotland team and won nine caps in three years, scoring in four of them, as well as making ten appearances for the Scottish League. Then his career, like so many, was interrupted and in 1916 he joined the Royal Field Artillery as a Gunner. Apart from rare matches on leave he did not return to action until 1919, when he played his part in another league title for Rangers, appearing in nine matches. Now at the veteran stage he joined Albion Rovers in 1920 as player-manager and scored 36 league goals in two seasons. When he hung up his boots in 1922 he continued as manager, and despite relegation in his first season he remained in Coatbridge until 1931. He then spent three years as Dundee United manager but the team sank like a stone under his guidance and he was sacked in 1934. The son of a grocer, he returned to Baillieston where he ran a market garden.

Harry RENNIE (13/0, 1900-08)
Henry George Rennie
Born 1 June 1873 Barnhill Street, Greenock, Renfrewshire
Died 17 March 1954 Wellington Street, Greenock, Renfrewshire
Scotland v Ireland 1900, 1902, 1903, 1904, 1906, 1908; England 1900, 1901, 1902; Wales 1902, 1903, 1905, 1908.
Greenock Volunteers; Morton 1895-98; Heart of Midlothian 1898-1900; Hibernian 1900-08 (Scottish Cup 1902, Scottish League 1903); Rangers 1908-10 [guest for Inverness Thistle Apr 1910, Morton Apr 1910]; Kilmarnock 1910-11; Morton Sep 1911.
Scotland's outstanding goalkeeper of the Edwardian era, Rennie actually began as a half-back and was capped there at junior level in 1895 with Greenock Volunteers, where he won the Renfrewshire Junior Cup. It was not until 1897, two years into his senior career at Morton, that he switched position to goal when another player joined the Army. His

outfield experience influenced his playing style, as he was known for his tendency to wander up to the halfway line when his team was attacking, and he was one of the first to develop theories and strategies, which he published in *The Art of Good Goalkeeping* in 1904. Just one season of excellent performances persuaded Hearts to pay £50 for him in 1898, and within two years he made his debut for Scotland against Ireland. That summer he moved to city rivals Hibs and he had his best years at Easter Road, winning the Scottish Cup in 1902 and then the league title a year later. Instantly recognisable due to an abscess which distorted his face, he established himself in the national team, winning thirteen caps and in 1901 he was the first Scotland goalkeeper to save a penalty by blocking Ernest Needham's attempt for England. The following year he faced England again after missing the Ibrox Disaster match. He also represented the Scottish League seven times. In his mid-thirties he moved back to the west and had a season with Rangers which concluded with the abandoned Scottish Cup final of 1909, and a year later joined Kilmarnock where he effectively ended his playing career. However, after he settled back in his home town he did make a final appearance for Morton in an emergency, and turned out for their reserves as late as 1913. He also played cricket for Greenock and golf for Gourock. An engineer to trade, he was reported once to have created ornamental ironwork for a memorial bench in Greenock's George Square.

Henry RENNY-TAILYOUR (1/1, 1873)

Colonel Henry Waugh Renny-Tailyour
Born 9 October 1849 Neemuch, Madhya Pradesh, India
Died 15 June 1920 Newmanswalls, Montrose, Angus
Scotland v England 1873 (1).
Royal Engineers 1870-76 (FA Cup 1875).
A great sporting all-rounder, Renny-Tailyour played for Scotland at both rugby and association football and was a first class cricketer. Born in India, where his father was a surveyor with the East India Company, he spent much of his childhood in Scotland and was educated at Cheltenham College from the age of 10. When he left, he took up a commission in the Royal Engineers and during his training at the Royal Military Academy in Woolwich he played for their rugby team in the late 1860s, then switched to association football when his military career got under way. He was part of the outstanding Royal Engineers team that played in three FA Cup finals, losing in 1872 and 1874 before winning at the third attempt in 1875 thanks to his goals in the replay which saw off the Old Etonians 2-0. Meanwhile, uniquely he was selected for Scotland against England at rugby in 1872 and repeated the feat in the association game in March 1873, when he was the scorer of Scotland's first international goal. An outstanding cricketer, he played 28 first class matches over a decade, including three times for the Gentlemen against the Players at Lords, and turned out regularly for Kent. His military service took him to Ireland, Gibraltar and Australia, where he helped to map areas of New South Wales, and he rose to the rank of Colonel. After leaving the Army in 1899 he joined Guinness and Co in Dublin, becoming managing director, and retired to the family estate at Newmanswalls, near Montrose, shortly before his death in 1920. NB his birthplace in India is often quoted as Mussoorie but in fact it was further south, in Neemuch; when he was born his surname was Renny, but shortly afterwards it was altered to Renny-Tailyour in accordance with his late grandfather's wishes.

Alex RHIND (1/0, 1872)

Alexander Rhind
Born 20 September 1849 Thistle Street, Aberdeen
Died 13 December 1923 Lochalsh Road, Inverness
Scotland v England 1872.
Queen's Park 1870-73.
Perhaps the lowest profile of the original Scotland players in the first international against England in 1872, Rhind was in the right place at the right time, as until that summer he had played for the Queen's Park second eleven. Brought up in the north-east of Scotland, he had come to Glasgow as a young man to work in the drapery business, and soon joined the football club for recreation. He developed into a talented forward who was an excellent dribbler but his playing career was brief, and after his international debut he faded rapidly from the picture. He was reported as being too ill to travel to London for the return match against England in March 1873 and left Glasgow in November that year. He worked in Aberdeen until about 1892 as a commercial traveller in the drapery business, and thereafter opened a shop in Inverness, where he spent the rest of his life. He died there in 1923 and is buried in Tomnahurich Cemetery. His son Robert played for Caledonian and signed for Queen's Park in 1913.

Andy RICHMOND (1/0, 1906)

Andrew Richmond
Born 20 January 1882 Roseland, Erskine, Renfrewshire
Died 30 January 1967 Shieldhall Hospital, Glasgow
Scotland v Wales 1906.
Queen's Park; Parkhead; Queen's Park 1903-10 [guest for Celtic Dec 1907]; Rangers 1910-12 (Scottish League 1911, 1912).
Richmond's early football experiences were with Queen's Park but he was frustrated at being stuck in the third team, known as the Hampden eleven, so he decided to try his luck in junior football. He certainly proved his point as he won numerous honours with Parkhead, including the Scottish Junior Cup in 1903, and was selected twice for Scotland juniors. Despite inducements to turn professional, he chose to return to his old club and went straight into the first team at left back. A strong tackler who could pass the ball accurately and with intelligence, he held his own in the team for the rest of the decade, although strangely for a while in 1905 he reportedly played tennis with Bellahouston in preference to football. He was capped once by Scotland in 1906 in a disappointing defeat to Wales, and made two appearances for the Scottish League in 1909. He also played once as a guest for Celtic in a friendly v

Blackburn Rovers on Christmas Day 1907, then in 1910 turned professional when he joined Rangers. While he enjoyed a successful time at Ibrox and contributed to two league championship wins, he never really established himself in the side. He left in 1912 and only played recreationally after that. He served in World War One as a Bombardier in the Royal Field Artillery, rising to Corporal, then resumed his career as a travelling salesman in the paint industry. He spent the rest of his life in Glasgow and died there in 1967, aged 85.

James RICHMOND (3/1, 1877-82)
James Tassie Richmond
Born 22 March 1858 Sauchiehall Street, Glasgow
Died 13 January 1898 West Regent Street, Glasgow
Scotland v England 1877 (1), 1878; Wales 1882.
Towerhill; Northern; Clydesdale; Queen's Park 1877-82 (Scottish Cup 1880, 1882).
Richmond was an energetic and powerfully-built forward who found early acclaim as a Clydesdale player, making his debut for Scotland a few weeks before his 19th birthday, scoring the second goal in the 3-1 victory over England at the Oval in 1877. He was selected again the following year, by which time he had joined Queen's Park. He was with the club for five years, winning the Scottish Cup twice, in 1880 and 1882, scoring the opening goal in the first minute of the latter success against Dumbarton. A week earlier, he had won his third and final Scotland cap, against Wales. Despite being at the top of the game and only 24 years old, he then gave up football that summer to focus on his career as an accountant in Glasgow. He never married and died aged 39 of meningitis. He is buried at Glasgow Necropolis.

Archie RITCHIE (1/0, 1891)
Archibald Ritchie
Born 12 April 1872 Rose Street, Kirkcaldy, Fife
Died 18 January 1932 Greyfriar Gate, Nottingham
Scotland v Wales 1891.
East Stirlingshire 1889-91; Nottingham Forest 1891-99 (FA Cup 1898); Bristol Rovers 1899-1900; Swindon Town 1900-01.
Ritchie was a precocious talent at right back with East Stirlingshire, capped by his county in his first season at the age of 17. Only five feet six inches, he made up for his lack of height with determination and tackling ability. He was still only 18 when he made his Scotland debut in a 4-3 win against Wales in 1891, and concluded the season with wins for his club in the Stirlingshire Cup and the Falkirk Infirmary Shield. Not surprisingly a number of clubs were interested in his services and he joined Nottingham Forest as a professional that summer. He played over 200 matches in his eight years at Forest, mostly alongside Adam Scott who was even smaller, the highlight being their FA Cup victory of 1898, when near rivals Derby County were beaten 3-1 at Crystal Palace. The following summer he moved on to Bristol Rovers in the Southern League, and then had a year at Swindon Town before retiring in 1901. He returned to Nottingham where he was a pub landlord for many years, and became a top bowler, winning the Nottinghamshire championship among other prizes. He was still running the Sawyers Arms at the time of his death in 1932.

Harry RITCHIE (2/0, 1923-28)
Henry Ritchie
Born 18 February 1900 Laurieston Hall, Balmaghie, Kirkcudbrightshire
Died 3 July 1941 Nottingham General Hospital, Nottingham
Scotland v Wales 1923; Ireland 1928.
Perth Roselea; Hibernian Apr 1919-28; Everton 1928-30; Dundee Feb 1930-31; St Johnstone Oct 1931-34; Brechin City 1934-35; Arbroath Jan-Feb 1935.

Born in Kirkcudbright but brought up in Perth where he went to Caledonian Road School, Ritchie signed up for the Royal Navy during the First World War where he played his first serious football. After demob, he had only a brief period in junior football before he was signed by Hibs in the spring of 1919. Originally an outside left, he switched to the right wing and never looked back, becoming part of a legendary partnership with Jimmy Dunn as Hibs reached the Scottish Cup final in 1923 and 1924, only to lose them both. Ritchie was capped twice by Scotland, five years apart, against Wales in 1923 and Ireland in 1928, and also made five appearances for the Scottish League, including against the Football League in 1923 and 1927. In the summer of 1928 he resumed his partnership with Dunn, who had signed for Everton the previous year, and spent two seasons at Goodison Park. He then had a few months at Dundee without much success, but when he joined St Johnstone in his home town in October 1931 he found a new lease of life and his accurate crosses helped them to win promotion, missing out on the Second Division title on goal average, then finish in fifth place in the top league. Thereafter he only played occasionally, and had a final season at Brechin and briefly Arbroath before retiring in 1935. After giving up football he moved to Nottingham where he worked for as a cooper for Shipstone's brewery and died in hospital in 1941 following an operation.

John RITCHIE (1/1, 1897)
John Lindsay Ritchie
Born 25 November 1875 Main Street, Renton, Dunbartonshire
Died 30 April 1943 Findlay's Shipyard, Old Kilpatrick, Dunbartonshire
Scotland v Wales 1897c (1).
Tontine Juveniles; Renton 1894-96; Queen's Park 1896-98; Hibernian Oct-Nov 1898; St Mirren Aug 1899; Renton 1900-07.
Ritchie was born a twin but his brother, born half an hour later, did not survive. He grew up in the football heartland of Renton and progressed to the town's club, playing for them at full back in the Scottish Cup final of 1895, which was lost to St Bernard's. The following year he joined Queen's Park and in his first season the team won the Glasgow League, he represented Glasgow against Sheffield, and more importantly he was selected for Scotland. He was made captain on his debut against Wales,

a 2-2 draw, and had the honour of converting Scotland's first-ever penalty kick, but was never selected again. In the summer of 1898 he went on tour to Denmark with Queen's Park, the first foreign tour by a Scottish club, then moved on. He was briefly at Hibs alongside former Renton full back Bobby Glen, and appeared once for St Mirren, but seems to have played little serious football for a couple of years. Then in 1900 he returned to Renton, where he helped to run the club as vice-president. He retired from the game in 1906 then was pressed back into service in 1907, playing his part in a Scottish Cup victory over Dundee and remaining until the end of the season. He never married and lived all his life in Renton where he worked as a clerk for the British Linen Bank. In the Second World War he was a detective in Findlay's Shipyard in Old Kilpatrick, where he died suddenly of a heart attack in 1943. His younger brothers Sandy and George also played for Renton.

Willie ROBB (2/0, 1925-27)
William Robb
Born 20 March 1895 Mitchell Street, Rutherglen, Lanarkshire
Died 18 February 1976 Friend Avenue, Aldershot, Hampshire
Scotland v Wales Oct 1925, 1927.
Kirkintilloch Rob Roy; Birmingham Jan 1914-20 [guest for Vale of Leven Oct 1915; Royal Albert Dec 1915; Vale of Leven 1916-17; Third Lanark 1917-19; Armadale 1919-20]; Rangers 1920-26 (Scottish League 1921, 1923, 1924, 1925); Hibernian 1926-30; Aldershot 1930-37; Guildford City 1937-38.

Robb had a lengthy goalkeeping career which started in junior football with Kirkintilloch Rob Roy, where he represented the Glasgow Junior League. He moved to Birmingham early in 1914 and remained on the club's books until 1920, although in 1915 he returned to Scotland for military duties and he made just one more appearance for Birmingham in November 1918. Meanwhile he appeared for a variety of Scottish clubs, notably a couple of seasons with Third Lanark. He finally made a permanent transfer in 1920 to Rangers and remarkably did not miss a single league match in his first five years at the club. He was outstanding as they won the league in his first season at Ibrox and he went on to win three more titles, while he also appeared in the Scottish Cup finals of 1921 and 1922 but lost them both. On the international front he was selected twice for the Scottish League, both against the Irish League, then finally won his first Scotland cap aged 30 in his final season at Ibrox. Curiously that coincided with him losing his place in the Rangers team and the following summer he failed to agree terms with the club, who had Tom Hamilton as a ready replacement in goal. He chose to joined Hibs, where he won his second Scotland cap in 1927. When he was dropped early in 1930 after an injury, Hibs put a hefty transfer fee on his head, and to avoid that he made a surprise move into non-league football with Aldershot. He continued playing for them after they entered the Football League in 1932, until well into his forties, and his last matches were for Guildford City while working as a steward at their Supporters Club. He remained in the area for the rest of his life.

George ROBERTSON (1/0, 1937)
George Robertson
Born 7 September 1915 Bonnyton Square, Kilmarnock, Ayrshire
Died 24 January 2006 Crosshouse Hospital, Kilmarnock, Ayrshire
Scotland v Czechoslovakia Dec 1937.
Bartonholm Juveniles; Dalry Thistle; Irvine Meadow 1935-36; Kilmarnock 1936-39.

Robertson had a remarkably brief football career, with all the highlights coming in less than three years as a professional. A hard-working right half, he joined Kilmarnock from Irvine Meadow in 1936 and soon made his debut, retaining his place in the side until the end of the season. The 1937-38 season saw him selected for the Scottish League against the English in September, then called up to the full national team in December to face Czechoslovakia. He made a return to Hampden at the end of the season as Kilmarnock reached the Scottish Cup final, only to lose to East Fife in a replay. However, his football career then ended suddenly and prematurely. He had just finished his apprenticeship as a painter and early in the new season he asked the club to cancel his registration as he was planning to emigrate to Bulawayo, where he was setting up in business with his brother. It took a bit longer than planned, and he saw out the season in Kilmarnock's reserves with just four more first team games. Then in the summer of 1939 he left Scotland, although he continued to play in Rhodesia (now Zimbabwe) as an amateur. He later returned to Kilmarnock where he worked as a general manager for a dry-cleaning company and lived to the age of 90.

Geordie ROBERTSON (4/0, 1910-13)
George Clarke Robertson
Born 7 March 1885 Menstrie, Clackmannanshire
Died 10 May 1937 Osborn Street, Providence, Rhode Island, USA
Scotland v Wales 1910, 1912; Ireland 1913; England 1913.
Yoker Athletic; Motherwell 1906-10; Sheffield Wednesday Mar 1910-20; East Fife Oct 1920-22.
Robertson was brought up in the town of Menstrie where his father ran a joinery business but went to the west of Scotland to pursue his trade as a baker. He was a good enough right winger with Yoker to be given a junior international trial and signed for Motherwell in the summer of 1906. He played in almost every match for four years,

and as his reputation continued to grow in 1910 he was the first Motherwell player to be capped, playing for Scotland in a late 1-0 win against Wales. Within a few weeks he had been signed by Sheffield Wednesday and he was a prominent figure in their pre-war seasons. He went on to play three more times for Scotland, another dramatic last-gasp 1-0 win over Wales in 1912, then a victory in Dublin over Ireland in 1913 which saw him pursued by a mob who thought he had struck a spectator. In his last game against England the following month he played alongside his club strike partner Andy Wilson. He worked in a Sheffield munitions factory during WW1 and because of a knee injury was thought to have effectively retired from football in 1915, bar a few wartime appearances. However, after an operation in summer 1919 to remove his cartilages, he managed a final year with Wednesday in the first post-war season, although his movement was restricted. With the team being relegated, it was little surprise that he left Sheffield in 1920 and he came home to Scotland, helping East Fife to gain Scottish League status in 1921. He retired in 1922 and emigrated to USA, working as a house painter in Providence, Rhode Island, where he died of broncho-pneumonia in 1937, aged 52. See his biography *Wings of Steel* by Iain Paterson.

Jimmy ROBERTSON (2/0, 1931)
James Robertson
Born 19 June 1906 Coupar Street, Lochee, Dundee
Died 26 August 1982 Royal Lancaster Infirmary, Lancashire
Scotland v Austria 1931; Italy 1931.
Lochee United; Logie; Dundee 1928-33; Birmingham Dec 1933-34; Kilmarnock 1934-38; Elgin City Jul-Sep 1939 player-coach.
Inside left or centre forward, Robertson was one of the top players in the Dundee Junior League and played several times for the county select. He was already 22 when he joined Dundee in 1928 and went on to be an effective inside left for them over five years. In 1931, after a season in which he was their joint top scorer, he was called up for Scotland's continental tour, although his two caps both ended in heavy defeats, 5-0 to Austria and 3-0 to Italy. In 1932 he switched to centre forward and boosted his scoring rate, so much so that Birmingham bought him in December 1933. However, he failed to settle and moved on to Kilmarnock the following summer. He was top scorer in his first season at Rugby Park but then his strike rate declined dramatically and he made his last appearance in late 1937. He was not happy at being dropped and matters came to a head in a bizarre case in the spring of 1938 when he was suspended by Kilmarnock for refusing to act as linesman in a reserve match. Although he won an appeal to the SFA against the punishment, not surprisingly he was given a free transfer that summer and found himself out of the game. He kept fit and a year later was appointed player-coach of Elgin City but had only played a few games when war broke out and he gave up football, serving with the Army as a PT instructor during WW2. He was living in Kilmarnock and working as a jewellery salesman when his life took a dramatic turn in April 1947. He was found in a Glasgow city centre street, shot in the chest and bleeding heavily. His assailant Daniel Cronin was charged with attempted murder, yet the jury found the case not proven, as Cronin claimed that both men were very drunk and the gun went off accidentally during a struggle. Robertson subsequently abandoned his wife and children (he was described in the divorce papers as 'address unknown') and ended up in Lancashire, spending his final years living in a hotel in Morecambe.

Jacky ROBERTSON (16/2, 1898-1905)
John Tait Robertson
Born 25 February 1877 High Street, Dumbarton
Died 24 January 1935 Royal Cancer Hospital, Glasgow
Scotland v England 1898, 1899, 1900c, 1901c, 1902, 1903, 1904c; Wales 1900, 1901c, 1902 (1), 1903, 1904, 1905 (1); Ireland 1901, 1902, 1904c.
Pointfield; Sinclair Swifts; Morton 1894-96; Everton 1896-98; Southampton 1898-99 (Southern League 1899); Rangers 1899-1905 (Scottish League 1900, 1901, 1902; Scottish Cup 1903); Chelsea player-manager 1905-06; Glossop player-manager Dec 1906-09.
An outstanding left half, Robertson was a true athlete, full of running, who loved to drive forward with the ball at his feet and could finish off a move with a powerful shot, so much so that he sometimes played in the forward line. His senior career started at Morton as a 17-year-old, where two seasons in the lower reaches of the Second Division gave him a good grounding in the game until Everton saw his potential and signed him in 1896. In two years at Goodison continued to progress and won the first of 16 caps for Scotland, against England in 1898. That summer Southampton induced him to join them and he won the Southern League title in his one season there. By the time he came to Rangers in 1899 he was at the top of his game, and helped the team to three straight league titles and the Scottish Cup of 1903. Perhaps the greatest testimony to his ability was seven consecutive selections against England, and in 1900 he was made captain for the first time, an inspired decision as it was the memorable 'Rosebery International' when Scotland beat England 4-1. The following year he was the first Scotland player ever to miss a penalty, shooting wide in the 11-0 win over Ireland, but he did score against Wales in 1902, and again in the closing minutes of his sixteenth and final cap in 1905. He also made six appearances for the Scottish League. By then he was looking to extend his career with a coaching position, and there were rumours about him going to Prague, but he really landed on his feet as the first player to sign for the newly created Chelsea, who also appointed him as coach. He even scored the London side's first-ever goal, away to Blackpool in September 1905, and led them to

third place in their inaugural year in the Second Division. However, he decided to leave midway through the next season for the somewhat less glamorous surroundings of Glossop, where he had two and a half years as player-manager, before leaving in 1909 to coach Manchester United's reserves. He then coached MTK Budapest for a couple of years and came home to Glasgow in 1913. He worked as a sports writer, living in Greenhead Street, overlooking Glasgow Green, until his death from cancer in 1935, the day after his former Rangers and Scotland team mate Jock Drummond.

Peter ROBERTSON (1/0, 1903)

Peter Neilson Robertson
Born 24 September 1875 Rosewell, Midlothian
Died 4 February 1929 St Francis Hospital, Litchfield, Illinois, USA
Scotland v Ireland 1903.
Polton Vale; Burnley Aug-Nov 1895; Polton Vale Nov 1895-96; St Bernard's Mar-Apr 1896; Polton Vale 1896-98; Cowdenbeath 1898-99; Raith Rovers 1899-1901; Dundee 1901-04; Nottingham Forest 1904-05.

Born into a mining family, Robertson found a partial escape through football although his career was slow to take off. He played for his local side in Loanhead and in 1895 was one of three Polton Vale players signed by Burnley but he only made a single first team appearance before returning home. Apart from a brief spell at St Bernard's he was at Polton Vale until 1898 when he moved to Cowdenbeath, where he won four local trophies in a season there. Next, he joined local rivals Raith Rovers in the East of Scotland League and by the time he signed for Dundee in 1901 he had developed into an excellent half back. He was good enough to keep internationalist Sandy Keiller out of the team, and in his second season was appointed club captain. He also earned international recognition, selected for the Scottish League in 1902 and then for Scotland against Ireland a year later, but it was not a day to remember as the visitors won 2-0 at Celtic Park. Otherwise it was a good season, with Dundee coming second in the league and reaching the Scottish Cup semi-final. However, a serious knee injury in the summer of 1903 virtually ended his career, forcing him to undergo surgery and specialist treatment. He tried to make a comeback at Nottingham Forest the following season, but only managed a handful of games before giving up. With his football days over, he emigrated to the USA in 1905 to find work as a miner and settled in Illinois where he lived in the curiously named town of Benld (derived from its founder Ben L Dorsey), and worked for the Superior Coal Company of Sawyerville until his death aged 53.

Tom ROBERTSON (4/0, 1889-92)

Thomas Robertson
Born 9 December 1863 West Bogside, Baldernock, Stirlingshire
Died 25 January 1924 Kirkintilloch Road, Bishopbriggs, Dunbartonshire
Scotland v Ireland 1889c, 1892c; England 1890; Wales 1891c.
Possil Bluebell; Northern 1881-82; Cowlairs 1882-86; Aston Villa Aug-Dec 1886; Jardine's XI Dec 1886-Feb 1887; Notts Castle Feb-Mar 1887; Cowlairs 1887-88; Queen's Park 1888-94 (Scottish Cup 1890) [guest for Corinthian Jan 1889, Jan 1890; Nottingham Forest Apr 1891, Nov 1892]; St Bernard's Jan-Nov 1895 (Scottish Cup 1895).

Son of a Stirlingshire farmer, Robertson came to Glasgow to work as an engineer and developed into an outstanding half-back for Cowlairs. In 1885 he made the first of ten appearances for Glasgow, but the following year he decided to pursue his career in England, having been offered a job along with Cowlairs team mate 'Wiggy' McLeod. Unusually he remained an amateur in Birmingham where he turned out for Aston Villa, and then Nottingham where he played for Sir Ernest Jardine's works team as well as the short-lived Notts Castle club. He returned to Cowlairs after a year and won the Glasgow Exhibition Cup in 1888, then embarked on the next stage of his football adventure at Queen's Park. He had a distinguished few years with the Hampden club, where he won the Scottish Cup in 1890 and captained Scotland in three of his four internationals, including his debut against Ireland in 1889. As an amateur he could move freely, and returned on occasion to Nottingham, even playing a league match for Nottingham Forest in November 1892. Early in 1895 he was asked to help out St Bernard's following the tragic death of their left back William Cowan. Robertson assumed the centre half position, with fellow internationalists William Baird moving to left back and Bobby Foyer to right back to accommodate him. Out of adversity came a remarkable triumph, as two months later, St Bernard's won the Scottish Cup and Robertson added a second winner's medal to his collection. His last match for St Bernard's was in November 1895 and he immediately took up refereeing, reaching the top level with his assertive control, although it was said that he was quick to penalise acts that he himself had been prone to commit when playing! He took charge of numerous international matches, as well as the Scottish Cup finals of 1899, 1903, 1904, 1905 and 1913, and continued to referee until 1919 when he was 55. Meanwhile he was a committee member of Queen's Park, and was elected President of the Scottish Football League 1919-21. He worked as an iron turner and died suddenly of heart failure in 1924.

Tommy ROBERTSON (1/1, 1898)

Thomas Robertson
Born 17 October 1876 East Benhar, West Lothian
Died 13 August 1941 Stanley Road, Harthill, Lanarkshire
Scotland v Ireland 1898 (1).
East Benhar Heatherbell [trial for Motherwell Apr 1896]; Heart of Midlothian 1896-98 (Scottish League 1897); Liverpool Apr 1898-1902 (Football League 1901); Heart of Midlothian May-Oct 1902; Dundee Oct 1902-3; Manchester United 1903-04; Bathgate Aug 1905.

Born into a coal mining family in the now-disappeared community of East Benhar, near Fauldhouse, Robertson followed his father down the pits before embarking on a highly successful football career, winning league titles north and south of the border. An outside left, fast and direct, he was noticed by Hearts in 1896 when they played a reserve match in Fauldhouse and as they were a man short he was asked to make up the numbers. He did so well that they brought him to Tynecastle and although he only played eight games in his first season he helped the club to win the league title, notably scoring four against Clyde in one match. He was almost ever-present the following year and his form was good enough to earn a Scotland cap, which he marked with a goal against Ireland in March 1898. A few days later, Tom Watson paid £350 to take him to Liverpool in time for the last three games of the season, and he scored on his debut. He spent four years at Anfield, becoming a key part of the team which won the Football League title in 1901. He returned to Hearts in May 1902 as the season was winding up, and took part in the first three league games of the next before moving to Dundee, but again it was a brief association of less than a year, although his last matches included winners' medals in the Forfarshire Cup and Dewar Shield. He made another foray into England in 1903 with Manchester United but only appeared in three league matches and returned home to end his career with a brief spell at Bathgate. He resumed his work in the coal mines and never married.

William ROBERTSON (2/1, 1887)
William Robertson
Born 24 March 1866 High Street, Dumbarton
Died 9 December 1926 Machrins, Kirktonhill, Dumbarton
Scotland v England 1887; Wales 1887 (1).
Dumbarton 1886-93; Roamers 1893-94.
Educated at Blair Lodge, a rugby-playing boarding school in Polmont, Robertson was a sporting all-rounder who played rugby at Glasgow University and was selected for Glasgow at the oval ball; he was also a university sprint champion. He was a late conversion to association football, only taking up the game in 1886 in his final year as a student, after Dumbarton offered him the captaincy if he would join them. Initially he declined but changed his mind when he was selected for Dunbartonshire in October 1886, and adapted so well to the association game that his speed on the right wing brought him into the international reckoning. Shortly after playing in Dumbarton's Scottish Cup final defeat to Hibs in 1887, he won two Scotland caps in the space of three days at Blackburn and Wrexham. Both games were won and he scored the opening goal against the Welsh, but he was not selected again. After graduating from university, his legal career took off and he drifted out of the Dumbarton first team, playing no part in their league title successes, and in 1893 he became a founder of a short-lived recreational amateur club called Roamers, intended to be on the lines of the Corinthians. He played no more football but was a leading light in Dumbarton tennis, reaching the West of Scotland championship semi-final, and was secretary and treasurer of Dumbarton Golf Club. Having qualified as a lawyer, he was made a partner in the firm of McArthur, Brown and Robertson. He was an agent for the Unionist party, agent for the Bank of Scotland, and secretary of several bodies including the Dunbartonshire Red Cross, and Dunbartonshire NSPCC. During the War he served with the Dunbartonshire Territorials, with the rank of Captain. He died suddenly at home in 1926, aged 60, having been at work the previous day.

Archie ROWAN (2/0, 1880-82)
Archibald Rowan
Born 4 October 1855 Westmuir, Parkhead, Glasgow
Died 14 November 1923 Delaware, Mansewood, Glasgow
Scotland v England 1880; Wales 1882c.
Caledonian 1875-80; Queen's Park 1880-88 (Scottish Cup 1881, 1882).
Rowan was one of the most active sportsmen of his generation, excelling at cricket, football and golf. He first came to notice as a batsman with Caledonian Cricket Club, then took up the winter game when they founded a football section in the early 1870s. He played initially as a back before moving into goal, where he developed a special talent for the role, and although he became a member of Queen's Park in 1877, apart from the occasional friendly he continued to play for Caledonian until 1880, and his first cap that year against England was earned as a Caledonian player. The club then folded, and in any case his reputation was now sufficient for him to become first choice at Queen's Park where he won two Scottish Cups in 1881 and 1882. He took part in their FA Cup campaigns before he was deposed as goalkeeper by George Gillespie, although he continued to play for several years after that. Often he used the pseudonym of McCallum, and confusingly Queen's Park had another goalkeeper later in the decade whose real name was Peter McCallum. Rowan served as President of Queen's Park twice, from 1883-85 while still a player and again in 1890-91. In cricket, after Caledonian CC collapsed in the late 1870s he played for Drumpellier and West of Scotland, and represented Glasgow against the Australian touring side in 1880. In golf he was a regular on the Troon course and a founding member of Stoke Poges Golf Club when it was established by his good friend Pa Jackson, of Corinthians fame. A marine insurance underwriter, he never married.

Davie RUSSELL (6/1, 1895-1901)
David Russell
Born 9 January 1871 Shotts Iron Works, Lanarkshire
Died 8 November 1952 Croftfoot Drive, Fauldhouse, West Lothian
Scotland v Ireland 1895, 1898, 1901 (1); England 1895; Wales 1897, 1901.
East Benhar Heatherbell; Broxburn; Heart of Midlothian 1890-92 (Scottish Cup 1891) [guest for St Bernard's Aug 1892]; Preston North End Sep 1892-93; Heart of Midlothian Apr 1893-96 (Scottish League 1895, Scottish Cup 1896); Celtic 1896-98 (Scottish League 1898); Preston North End 1898-99; Celtic 1899-1903 (Scottish Cup 1900); Broxburn 1903-04.

Originally from Shotts, Russell grew up in nearby Fauldhouse where he worked as a coal miner (like his father) and started out in junior football with East Benhar Heatherbell. He then stepped up to Broxburn, where he represented East of Scotland at centre half, and joined Hearts in the autumn of 1890. He was clearly in demand as he signed a form for Burnley in November 1890 but never played for the club. Hearts turned the 'fair haired laddie' into a centre forward and he had an immediate impact as they won the Scottish Cup in his first season but his early form soon deserted him, and an injury late in 1891 was followed by a transfer to Preston the following autumn. After a season in England he returned to Edinburgh and reverted to his original position at centre half, where he excelled at a time when Hearts were the top team in Scotland. In 1895 he won the league with them and was selected for his first two international caps against Ireland and England, despite suffering from sciatica. Another Scottish Cup success followed in 1896, after which he was tempted over to Glasgow to play for Celtic. He continued to add to his Scotland caps, represented the Scottish League against the English in 1897, and played a major role as Celtic won the league in 1898. Preston, who still held his Football League registration, came calling again and he spent another season in England, before settling back at Celtic Park where he won his final major honour, the Scottish Cup in 1900. There was still time for two more caps, in one of which he scored his only international goal in an 11-0 win over Ireland. Celtic gave him a benefit match in August 1902 and the following summer his career turned full circle as he returned to his first senior club, Broxburn, for a brief swansong. Returning to life in the coal mines, he survived serious injury in October 1906 when he was badly crushed in a roof fall at Greenriggs Colliery, and he spent the rest of his life in Fauldhouse. NB He is often confused in the record books with another Scot called David Russell, from Stewarton, who also played for Preston.

Johnny RUSSELL (1/0, 1890)
John Russell
Born 19 July 1868 Bell's Rows, Wishaw, Lanarkshire
Died 5 March 1945 Belhaven Terrace, Rutherglen, Lanarkshire
Scotland v Ireland 1890.
Cambuslang 1887-1891.
Born in a mining community in Wishaw, Russell moved to Cambuslang as a boy when his father started working in the coal mines there. He first came into the Cambuslang team in the spring of 1887, and in January 1888 he was their full back for a magnificent tour of north-east England when Cambuslang crushed Newcastle West End 4-0, Sunderland 11-0 and Middlesbrough 8-1 on consecutive days. However, after that he was out of the team for several weeks and missed their Glasgow Cup success over Rangers as well as the Scottish Cup final defeat to Renton in February, although he returned to the side for the Glasgow Charity Cup final in May, which was also lost to Renton. The following season he established himself in a fine Cambuslang half-back line, alongside internationalists Andrew Jackson and John Buchanan, and was selected for Glasgow against Edinburgh in February 1890. The following month he was initially named as a reserve for the Scotland team to face Ireland in Belfast, and was capped when Third Lanark's Bob McFarlane had to pull out. He played in most of Cambuslang's matches in 1890/91, the inaugural season of the Scottish League, scoring once against Hearts, and appeared for Glasgow against Sheffield early in 1891, but after the end of that season he appears to have given up football. He lived in Flemington, an industrial suburb of Cambuslang, and was a fitter in the steel industry, probably for the Lanarkshire Steel Company which had its works there, then after his marriage in 1900 he lived in Rutherglen where he had a business as an ironmonger, while his wife Jeanie ran a dairy next door. His younger brother James (1874-1929) also played for Cambuslang and went on to Grimsby Town, St Bernard's and Motherwell, successfully suing the latter for unpaid wages in 1900.

Willie RUSSELL (2/0, 1924-25)
William Fraser Russell
Born 15 December 1897 Risk Street, Calton, Glasgow
Died 30 November 1944 Springbank Terrace, Aberdeen
Scotland v Wales 1924; England 1925.
Benburb; Airdrieonians Dec 1920-25 (Scottish Cup 1924); Preston North End 1925-31; Shelbourne 1931-32.
A sparky inside right and occasional right half, Russell spent several years in junior football and was already 22 when he joined Airdrie from Benburb. He went on to play his part in the marvellous Broomfield side of the early 1920s and notably entered into legend in the Scottish Cup-winning team of 1924, when his two first-half headers proved enough to defeat Hibs. Playing alongside Hughie Gallacher, this was just reward for Airdrie, who consistently finished in second place in the league until the side was broken up as the stars were transferred. Russell won two Scotland caps, the first against Wales in 1924, the second alongside Gallacher in a 2-0 win over England, and was also selected twice for the Scottish League. He moved on to Preston shortly after the start of the 1925/26 season for a 'substantial fee' and was a first team regular for most of his six years at Deepdale, all of them in the Second Division, but there were regular reports that he was not happy there. By 1931 he was on the fringes of the team and wanted to leave, but as he was not granted a free transfer he went over to Ireland where Shelbourne could avoid paying a fee. However, he had to return home in February of his first season for a stomach operation, and although he recovered it was the end of his football career. He became an inspector with Liverpool Victoria Insurance, based in Glasgow, but died of a heart attack three weeks after being transferred to Aberdeen in 1944. He was just 46.

S

Billy SAWERS (1/0, 1895)
William Sawers
Born 4 January 1868 St Marnoch Street, Kilmarnock, Ayrshire
Died 24 October 1927 Western Infirmary, Glasgow
Scotland v Wales 1895.
Kilmarnock South-Western; Clyde 1888-90; Sunderland Albion Jan 1890; Clyde 1890-92; Blackburn Rovers Sep

1892-93; Stoke 1893-94; Dundee 1894-95; Stoke Sep 1895; Dundee Sep 1895-96; Kilmarnock Feb-Apr 1896; Clyde 1896-97.

Sawers moved from Ayrshire junior football in 1888 to Clyde, where his elder brother Alex was already playing in defence, and soon established himself as a lively inside left or centre forward. Praised as a clever dribbler, he was criticised for hanging onto the ball too long but was certainly in demand and played for a bewildering variety of clubs on both sides of the border, rarely staying more than a season. He left Clyde for Sunderland Albion early in 1890 and played against Bootle in the FA Cup, but immediately fell foul of professionalism rules and his side were thrown out of the cup, while he himself was suspended for months. After biding his time back at Clyde, his next attempt in England in 1892 was more successful, scoring 11 goals in a season with Blackburn Rovers. He then had a year at Stoke, also in the First Division before returning to Scotland and was capped against Wales in the middle of a purple patch with Dundee, which included a memorable cup-tie winning goal against Celtic. However, he blotted his record by missing a penalty against Renton that would have seen his club into the Scottish Cup final. He went back briefly to Stoke before changing his mind after just one match, then lost his form at Dundee and fell out with the management who were exasperated by his attitude. They let him go to Kilmarnock in the spring and he ended his playing days back at Clyde in 1897. He decided to focus on running his sports shop in Glasgow's Eglinton Street, then when the business failed he returned to his old trade as a cabinet maker, the same as his father. He died of cancer in Glasgow shortly before his 60th birthday.

Peter SCARFF (1/0, 1931)
Peter Scarff
Born 29 March 1909 Napier Street, Linwood, Renfrewshire
Died 9 December 1933 Bridge of Weir Road, Linwood, Renfrewshire
Scotland v Ireland Feb 1931.
Linwood St Conval's; Celtic 1928-32 (Scottish Cup 1931) [loan to Maryhill Hibernian 1928-29].

A prolific goalscorer at inside left or centre forward, Scarff's life was tragically cut short and his senior career lasted just three years. He joined Celtic from a Linwood juvenile team in 1928 and was farmed out to Maryhill Hibs for a few months to gain experience. When he was recalled to Parkhead in January 1929 for a Scottish Cup tie he did so well that he retained his place for the remainder of the season. His form dipped in his second season but he was scoring regularly again in 1930-31 and won his international cap against Ireland in February 1931. A couple of months later he helped Celtic to their Scottish Cup victory over Motherwell, and that summer he went to America with Celtic, a tour that saw him score five goals in one game, and ordered off in another for a shoulder charge that would have been perfectly acceptable in Scotland. His health started to give concern in the autumn and he played his last game in December, when his career came to an abrupt halt after he coughed up blood and was diagnosed with pulmonary tuberculosis. He went into a sanatorium in Bridge of Weir and spent time on the Ayrshire coast, and although his illness appeared for a time to be in remission, his condition then went downhill. Two years after his last match he succumbed in his native Linwood, aged just 24. The full Celtic team and thousands of fans attended his burial at Kilbarchan Cemetery.

Matt SCOTT (1/0, 1898)
Matthew McLintock Scott
Born 11 July 1872 Aitchison Street, Airdrie, Lanarkshire
Died 14 August 1941 Royal Cancer Hospital, Glasgow
Scotland v Wales 1898c.
Airdrieonians 1889-1900; Newcastle United Oct 1900-01; Albion Rovers Oct 1901-03; Airdrieonians 1904-06.

Scott had early success when he won the first Airdrie Schools Cup in 1886 with Victoria School, and developed into a powerful full back and dependable leader during a decade at Airdrieonians. Playing alongside his brother Bob (below) his side won the Lanarkshire Cup four times in the 1890s and won a place in the Second Division in 1894. He had several international trials but was selected just once for Scotland in 1898, when he was captain of the team which beat Wales 5-2 and was praised by the *Scottish Referee* for 'a clean, cool style and a tower of strength'. In October 1900 he made a surprise move to Newcastle United, who needed an experienced man as defensive cover for Dave Gardner, and he made just five appearances in his one season in English football. He returned home to Airdrie and signed for local rivals Albion Rovers, who were in the Scottish Combination at the time. He considered retiring after a serious leg break playing for Rovers against Renton in February 1903, but fought his way back to fitness and joined Airdrieonians again in the summer of 1904, proving himself a useful asset in their First Division campaigns until he retired in 1906. He spent the rest of his life in Airdrie, where he worked as a dispatch clerk in a tubeworks. He died of cancer in 1941 and his grave is in New Monkland Cemetery.

Bob SCOTT (1/0, 1894)
Robert Scott
Born 2 October 1870 Aitchison Street, Airdrie, Lanarkshire
Died 25 August 1952 Torrisdale Street, Coatbridge, Lanarkshire
Scotland v Ireland 1894.
Airdrieonians 1888-1900 [guest for Third Lanark Oct 1889; Celtic Apr 1893].

Scott had a powerful shot and was an early specialist at taking penalty kicks. An inside left, he played throughout the 1890s alongside his younger brother Matt (above) at a time when Airdrieonians were in the Second Division, but good enough to win the Lanarkshire Cup several times. He devoted his entire career to the club apart from a guest appearance for Third Lanark and another for Celtic in April 1893, when he acquitted himself well in a 3-0 win over Rangers. A year later he won his sole international honour in Scotland's narrow 2-1 win over Ireland, when the *Scottish Referee* said he was in such good form that he deserved to play against England. However, there were no more caps and his career was essentially ended by a broken ankle in a league match against Motherwell in December 1898, although he managed to return to fitness and was able to play just one more league game exactly two years later, against Hamilton. He lived all his life in the Airdrie area, where he worked as a foreman engine fitter.

Bill SELLAR (9/3, 1885-93)
William Sellar
Born 21 October 1864 Gallowhill, Kirkintilloch, Dunbartonshire
Died 10 June 1914 Ashgrove, Millport, Isle of Cumbrae
Scotland v England 1885, 1886, 1887, 1888, 1891, 1892c, 1893 (1); Wales 1887; Ireland 1892 (2).
Battlefield 1882-88 [guest for Queen's Park 1884-85; Rangers Sep 1887]; Queen's Park 1888-94 (Scottish Cup 1890, 1893).

Sellar emerged with Battlefield, at the time one of the city's most prominent sides, although he was also a member of Queen's Park from 1882 which gave him the opportunity to make occasional guest appearances, including their Glasgow Charity Cup final victory of 1884, when he scored four against Third Lanark. The following season he took part in their FA Cup campaign, including the final which was lost to Blackburn Rovers. He later played one match as a guest for Rangers in September 1887, against Queen's Park. Best known as a forward, he was versatile enough to fill almost any position and was selected regularly for the Glasgow team and then for Scotland, facing England for the first time in 1885. However, he was largely ineffective as a centre forward for the national team and drew a blank in his first seven internationals, only scoring in his last two appearances. When Battlefield collapsed in 1888, he devoted himself to Queen's Park and won two Scottish Cups in 1890 and 1893. He retired a year later and was immediately elected President of Queen's Park and sat on the SFA Council, while he was also President of the Scottish Amateur Athletic Association for 1899-1900. A Glasgow lawyer, he fell seriously ill in 1902 and a testimonial fund was set up to help him, including a match between Rangers and Queen's Park. His health never really recovered and he died in 1914 on a visit to Millport, just short of his fiftieth birthday.

Willie SEMPLE (1/0, 1886)
William Semple
Born 22 July 1861 Causeystane, Blantyre, Lanarkshire
Died 11 February 1940 Union Street, Motherwell, Lanarkshire
Scotland v Wales 1886c.
Cambuslang 1882-90.

Born in Blantyre, son of a builder, Semple moved to Cambuslang as a young man and became one of the stars of the local club when it was at the peak of its powers. An excellent left back, he played for them in four Lanarkshire Cup finals, winning the trophy twice, in 1884 and 1885. Meanwhile he represented Lanarkshire several times and was capped once for Scotland, against Wales in 1886, when his leadership qualities were recognised with the captaincy in a 4-1 victory. When Cambuslang joined the Glasgow FA they won the first Glasgow Cup in 1888, defeating Rangers in the final, but it all went wrong a week later when they made their only appearance in a Scottish Cup final, losing 6-1 to Renton. After Semple retired in 1890 he continued to serve Cambuslang as its secretary, representing Lanarkshire at the Scottish FA. He worked for his entire adult life in Motherwell as a clerk for Colville & Sons at Dalzell Steelworks, retiring in 1927, and was an elder of Dalziel High Church, where he was a member of the choir for over 50 years.

Bill SHANKLY (5/0, 1938-39)
William Shankly OBE
Born 2 September 1913 Manse Place, Glenbuck, Ayrshire
Died 29 September 1981 Broadgreen Hospital, Liverpool
Scotland v England 1938, 1939; Ireland 1938; Wales 1938; Hungary 1938.
Cronberry Eglinton; Carlisle United 1932-33; Preston North End 1933-49 (FA Cup 1938) [guest during WW2 for King's Park Nov 1939, Northampton Town 1940-41, St Mirren Jan 1941, Liverpool May 1942, East Fife Aug-Nov 1942, Cardiff City Oct 1942, Arsenal 1942-43, Bolton Wanderers 1943-44, Luton Town 1943-44, Partick Thistle Jun 1944-Oct 1945].

Best remembered as an outstanding manager, it should not be forgotten that Bill Shankly also had a fine playing career that was curtailed by the Second World War. One of five brothers to play professionally, he was raised in Glenbuck but did not play for the famous Cherrypickers as they had just folded, and spent a season with nearby Cronberry Eglinton while working in a coal mine. His performances were enough to attract the attention of Carlisle United and he signed a professional contract in the summer of 1932. He spent half the season in the reserves and won his first senior medal in the North Eastern League Cup, then played regularly in the Third Division North where his gritty performances at right half persuaded Preston North End to bid £500 for his signature. He moved to the Second Division side in 1933 and had to wait until December for his first team debut, but after that there was no looking back as Preston won promotion and developed into a top side. They lost the FA Cup final in 1937, then Shankly won a winner's medal a year later with Preston's 1-0 victory over Huddersfield at Wembley. Earlier the same month he was overjoyed to make his debut for Scotland, also a 1-0 win at Wembley. He retained his place in the national team and only tasted defeat in his fifth and final cap, at home to England in 1939, before his career was interrupted by the Second World War, just as he was reaching his peak. His best years were effectively lost and although he won the League War Cup with Preston in 1941 he had to be content with turning out for a succession of clubs while serving with the RAF. Among them was a single appearance for his future employers Liverpool in May 1942, and he won the Scottish Summer Cup with Partick Thistle in 1945. He added to his international tally with seven wartime caps for Scotland, including a memorable 5-4 victory over England in April 1942, when he captained the team and scored a rare goal with a speculative shot from about 50 yards out. Returning to Preston after being demobbed, he was appointed player-coach of the reserves in the summer of 1947 and continued in that role, with occasional first team appearances, until his managerial appointment at Carlisle in March 1949. It was the first step in a glorious career as a manager that culminated in legendary status at Anfield during a 15-year reign. After two years at Brunton Park he was in charge at

Grimsby Town 1951-54, Workington 1954-55, Huddersfield Town 1955-59 and of course from 1959-74 when he established Liverpool as a major power, winning three league titles, two FA Cups and the UEFA Cup. He was made an OBE in 1974, and died seven years later after suffering a heart attack. Widely remembered as Bill, he was known as Willie to his family. There are numerous books about him, including his autobiography *My Story*.

Jimmy SHARP (5/0, 1904-09)
James Sharp
Born 11 October 1880 Jordanstone, Alyth, Perthshire
Died 18 November 1949 Keir Hardie House, Fulham Palace Road, London
Scotland v Wales 1904c, 1907, 1909; England 1907, 1908.
East Craigie; Dundee 1899-1904; Fulham 1904-05; Woolwich Arsenal 1905-08; Rangers 1908-09; Fulham Jan 1909-12; Chelsea 1912-15 [guest for Dundee Hibs 1915-16, Feb 1919]; Fulham Apr 1920.

Sharp joined Dundee from local junior side East Craigie as an 18-year-old, and went straight into the first team, spending five years at Dens Park. In 1902 he formed a full-back partnership with Johnnie Darroch and many years later, by an extraordinary coincidence, they died within 24 hours of each other. He was made captain of Scotland against Wales on his debut in 1904, played at his home ground of Dens Park, and went on to win four more caps later in the decade. He also made two appearances for the Scottish League and played cricket for Forfarshire. Three months after his international bow, he joined Fulham, and although there was no transfer fee as they were in the Southern League, when Fulham later entered the Football League they had to pay a sum to Dundee. The following year he joined Arsenal, and made over 100 league appearances in three years at Woolwich, then in 1908 he had half a season with Rangers before returning to London with Fulham. In summer 1910 he went to America to fulfil an ambition to visit the States, as he was not financially dependent on his income as a player, but when he returned in late October, Fulham officials were waiting for him at Liverpool docks to ensure he re-signed for them. They knew his worth, and shortly afterwards the *Scottish Referee* commented 'On his day Sharp is one of the most stylish backs in the game, getting through the maximum of work with the minimum of effort.' His final move was down the road to Chelsea, where he played until the outbreak of war. In 1915 he returned to Scotland to sign up for the Army and while training he played a season with Dundee Hibs; his last match for them was the Forfarshire Cup final in April 1916, although he did play in a friendly in 1919. He saw active service with the Black Watch and after being wounded in the thigh by a bullet he was taken prisoner at Cambrai in March 1918, spending eight months in a Munster camp. After he was released he returned to Fulham as coach, making a single first team appearance in an emergency in April 1920, aged 39. He was at Craven Cottage until 1926, then worked as a trainer for Walsall 1926-28 and Cliftonville in 1928-29. After leaving the game he worked in the building trade as a general labourer and lived in Fulham. He was hospitalised in September 1940 after being injured during an air raid but recovered and remained in the area until his death in 1949.

Frank SHAW (2/1, 1884)
Francis Watson Shaw
Born 13 May 1864 Paisley Road, Tradeston, Glasgow
Died 22 August 1920 Minehead, Somerset
Scotland v England 1884; Wales 1884 (1).
Pollokshields Athletic 1881-84 [guest for Queen's Park Apr 1884]; Battlefield Oct 1889.

Son of an ironmonger, Shaw packed a great deal into his brief association with Pollokshields Athletic. He played for Glasgow at 18 and was capped twice for Scotland aged 19, when he was described in the *Athletic News* as 'the best right wing forward in Scotland'. Shortly afterwards he made a single appearance for Queen's Park in the Charity Cup final of 1884, having gone along expecting to be a spectator but was asked to play in an emergency; sadly, there was no medal as the game against Third Lanark was drawn and he did not feature in the replay. His playing career was effectively over in November 1884 when, aged 20, he sailed for India where he went into business as a cotton merchant, setting up the firm Fleming Shaw and Co in Bombay and Karachi. Curiously he made a brief reappearance in Scottish football while on home leave in October 1889, turning out for Battlefield. After a successful business career in India he retired to Wokingham in Berkshire, where he served as a special constable during WW1. He was in poor health and died suddenly in Somerset while on holiday with his family, aged 56, leaving an estate worth almost £100k.

Don SILLARS (5/0, 1891-95)
Donald Currie Sillars
Born 30 October 1868 Argyle Cottage, Govan, Glasgow
Died 25 September 1905 Royal Infirmary, Glasgow
Scotland v Ireland 1891; England 1892, 1894; Wales 1893c, 1895c.
Battlefield 1885-87; Pollokshields Athletic 1887-88; Battlefield 1888-90; Rangers Nov-Dec 1890; Queen's Park Dec 1890-95 (Scottish Cup 1893).

Son of a wealthy master mariner, Sillars was educated at Glasgow Academy where he played rugby, but never took to the game and preferred to focus on football. He moved between Battlefield and Pollokshields Athletic, where he played in front of Wattie Arnott, until the two clubs merged late in 1888. Not a stylish player, he made up for it with hard work and energy and was a true sportsman who remained resolutely amateur. He was clearly destined for a better stage and played four matches with Rangers in the autumn of 1890, all of them Glasgow Cup ties against Third Lanark, then joined Queen's Park where he reached his peak. He played originally at full back, where he won his first Scotland cap in 1891, before moving to half back and went on to win five caps, two of them as captain. He also led Queen's Park to Scottish Cup success in 1893, although nobody knew then that this would be Queen's

Park's last victory in the competition. After he retired from the game in 1895 due to a knee injury, he remained on the Queen's Park committee, and worked in the city as a shipping store merchant. He was also a dedicated volunteer with the 5th Highland Light Infantry reserve for 16 years, and was made a Captain in 1894. He died as a result of a mysterious railway accident. On a Friday night after work he was seen off by a friend from St Enoch Station, heading for his home in Langbank, and was later discovered lying on the track just outside Glasgow, seriously injured. He was taken to the Royal Infirmary but never regained consciousness and died there three days later of a fractured skull, aged 36. How and why he fell from the train was never established. His gravestone is in Glasgow Necropolis.

Jamie SIMPSON (3/0, 1895)
James Simpson
Born 24 October 1870 Windmill Street, Saltcoats, Ayrshire
Died 26 March 1958 Rotherwood Avenue, Knightswood, Glasgow
Scotland v Wales 1895; Ireland 1895; England 1895.
Saltcoats Victoria 1890-94; Third Lanark 1894-1901.
Simpson played impressively at right half for Saltcoats Vics, at that time a senior club, and when he represented Ayrshire the *Scottish Referee* suggested he deserved an international cap. The first major club to recognise his potential was Third Lanark, who had already signed his team-mate Bob Barbour, and in 1894 Simpson was delighted to resume their half-back partnership at Cathkin Park. He did well in the pre-season practice games and went straight into the first team, where his progress was so swift that remarkably he won caps in all three Scotland internationals at the end of his first season as a professional. However, the last of those was a 3-0 defeat to England when Scotland were 'lucky to get nil' and he was never selected again. Not the quickest of players, he made up for it with dogged determination and robust tackling and remained with Third Lanark for the rest of his career, the Glasgow Charity Cup in 1898 being his only club honour. He retired in 1901 just before the club's golden era and was given a benefit match against Rangers in 1902. A plasterer to trade, he lived in Saltcoats where he helped to train a juvenile side after his playing days were over.

Jimmy SIMPSON (14/1, 1934-37)
James McMillan Simpson
Born 29 October 1908 Melville Road, Ladybank, Fife
Died 15 March 1972 Kingsacre Road, Kings Park, Glasgow
Scotland v Ireland 1934, 1935c, 1936c, 1937c; Wales 1934c, 1935c, 1936c, 1937c; England 1935c, 1936c, 1937c; Germany 1936c; Austria 1937c; Czechoslovakia May 1937c (1).
Newburgh West End; Dundee United 1925-27; Rangers 1927-40 (Scottish League 1933, 1934, 1935, 1937, 1939; Scottish Cup 1932, 1934, 1935, 1936); Dundee United 1941-42; St Mirren Jan-May 1942; Buckie Thistle 1946-47 player-coach.
Simpson's precocious talent was clear from an early age. He played for Dundee Schools while at Morgan Academy and was only briefly a junior with Newburgh West End before signing for Dundee United in 1925 as a 16-year-old. He spent two seasons at Tannadice, initially at centre forward before dropping to wing half, and when the team was relegated in 1927 he was transferred to Rangers for the sizeable fee of £1,000. He had already been selected for the SFA's summer tour of North America, despite being only 18, and on his return he played in the Glasgow Cup final against Celtic then made his Rangers league debut at centre half against Queen's Park on his 19th birthday. Curiously, both games were at Hampden and both were lost. He did not establish himself in the first team until 1931/32, but after that he didn't look back and became the engine room of the Rangers side which dominated Scottish football in the 1930s. A natural leader, he won five league titles and four Scottish Cups, and was the lynchpin of the national team, captaining Scotland in all except the first of his 14 internationals. He also made four appearances for the Scottish League. He was released by Rangers in 1940 and spent a year out of the game before Dundee United signed him, but after a few months he found the travel from Glasgow too much and he joined St Mirren for the remainder of the season. For the rest of the War he played for services teams, initially with the Home Guard and then the RAF. He took his first steps into management in 1946 as player-coach of Buckie Thistle for a season, which ended in a benefit match against Rangers. He then became Alloa manager late in 1947 until February 1949 and had little further involvement in the game. Having originally trained as an engineer he went into the licensed trade and managed a pub at Govan Cross. He was father of Ronnie Simpson, Celtic's European Cup-winning goalkeeper.

Geordie SINCLAIR (3/0, 1910-12)
George Leckie Sinclair
Born 12 December 1884 South St James Street, Edinburgh
Died 18 December 1959 Royal Infirmary, Edinburgh
Scotland v Ireland 1910, 1912; Wales 1912.
King's Park Juveniles; Newtongrange Star Apr 1906; Leith Athletic Apr 1906-08; Heart of Midlothian 1908-21; Dunfermline Athletic 1921-22; Cowdenbeath 1922-24.
A speedy outside right, Sinclair was a late starter in football as he had signed up with the Royal Artillery as a young man and did not enter the professional ranks until he was 21. From the Edinburgh juvenile side King's Park he played a couple of trials with Newtongrange Star before being signed by Leith Athletic in 1906. He transferred to Hearts in 1908, and curiously in his first match he scored against his old team in a Rosebery Cup tie. His consistency on the wing at Tynecastle earned him three Scotland caps, making his debut against Ireland in 1910, and he played twice for the

Scottish League in 1912 and 1919. In April 1914 Hearts held a benefit match for him with Everton providing the opposition, then his playing career came to a sudden halt when war broke out. As a reservist he was called up immediately and saw active service in France as a Driver with the Royal Field Artillery but after a year on the front line he was injured and discharged. The injury did not prevent him playing football and he returned to action with Hearts for several more years. When he was given a free transfer in 1921, together with teammate Bob Mercer he moved to Dunfermline Athletic for a year, before concluding his career with Cowdenbeath. In 1925 he went into the licensed trade in Edinburgh and ran Sinclair's Bar in Montrose Terrace for many years.

Leslie SKENE (1/0, 1904)

Dr Alexander Leslie Henderson Skene MB MC
Born 22 August 1882 Scottish National Institution, Larbert, Stirlingshire
Died 29 October 1959 Braddan, Isle of Man
Scotland v Wales 1904.
Larbert Broomage Albion; Stenhousemuir Aug-Sep 1900; Edinburgh University 1900-02 [guest for Stenhousemuir Aug 1901, Queen's Park Jan 1902, Sep 1902; Hibernian Mar 1902]; Stenhousemuir 1902-03; Queen's Park 1903-06; Stenhousemuir 1906-07; Fulham 1907-10; Glentoran 1910-12 (Irish League 1912).

Skene's unusual birthplace is explained by his father being superintendent at a psychiatric hospital, where he was brought up. Educated in Edinburgh at George Watson's College, he played rugby at school and developed a range of skills, perhaps best illustrated by his earliest mention in the *Falkirk Herald*, when he performed a violin solo at a Stenhousemuir Cricket Club social. Meanwhile, he started his goalkeeping career in Stirlingshire juvenile football, and made his debut for Stenhousemuir shortly before heading to Edinburgh University in 1900 to study medicine. It was soon clear he was too good for the varsity football team and he played for various senior sides as a guest then spent a season with Stenhousemuir, who reached the Scottish Cup semi-final and the Scottish Qualifying Cup final. Then he joined Queen's Park in 1903 and was in goal for their match which opened new Hampden Park in October that year, holding onto the match ball as a treasured souvenir. Lightly built and agile, he was selected for the Scotland team to face Wales in March 1904, two weeks after an appearance for the Scottish League, and was praised for his 'consistent and conspicuous ability' by the *Scottish Referee*. However, the paper also gave him this back-handed compliment: 'He fancies himself slightly, and wears blue stockings, this being to distinguish himself from Campbell, his partner, who wears red.' The 1-1 draw turned out to be his only cap. When his studies became too onerous, he left Queen's Park in 1906 and made sporadic appearances for Stenhousemuir before going to London the following summer to attend medical courses. He signed for Fulham as a professional as the club entered the Football League, expecting to be occasional cover but soon found himself first choice and played regularly until he suffered a broken collar bone late in 1909. He was a vocal and eloquent supporter of the Players' Union during his time in London. Unable to agree terms in 1910, he took a job in Belfast and joined Glentoran where he did so well that his side won the Irish League title and he played once for the Irish League in 1911. Meanwhile he continued to sit medical exams and finally qualified from Edinburgh University as a Bachelor in Medicine (MB) in 1911. He went on to specialise in mental disorders and his first appointment was at Hartwood Asylum in Shotts. He served in the Royal Army Medical Corps in WW1, was twice wounded at Gallipoli in 1915, and was awarded the Military Cross in 1918. After the War he was medical superintendent at the Murray Royal Hospital in Perth, then senior assistant physician at Tooting Bec Asylum in London, before moving to the Isle of Man Mental Hospital in 1922 as medical superintendent. He lived on the island for the rest of his life.

'Tod' SLOAN (1/0, 1904)

Thomas Parker Sloan
Born 4 October 1880 Main Street, Thornliebank, Renfrewshire
Died 18 May 1964 Crookston House, Glasgow
Scotland v Wales 1904.
North Park; Glasgow Perthshire 1899-00; Third Lanark 1900-11 (Scottish League 1904; Scottish Cup 1905) [guest for Gothenburg 1910].

Sloan started out with his local village team in Thornliebank before moving to Glasgow Perthshire for a year in junior football, then signed in 1900 for Third Lanark where he played the rest of his career. Initially an inside right, he later won his Scotland cap and major honours at centre half, and finally performed at right back, where his long limbs gave him height and considerable strength in the tackle. In his first season at Cathkin he won the Glasgow Charity Cup, but greater successes were to come with the Scottish League title and the Glasgow Cup in 1904, and the same year he won his single international cap against Wales, a 1-1 draw. Thirds lifted the Scottish Cup the following season, and he continued as a regular in the side for the rest of the decade, although in 1910 he took time out to study in Sweden and played for Gothenburg, touring with them in other Scandinavian countries and Russia. After he gave up playing in 1911 he remained involved for many with Third Lanark, becoming a director in 1919 and elected chairman in 1939. He was also a member of the Scottish League management committee and sat on SFA committees. He ran a restaurant in Rothesay for a while but was a carpenter to trade and later a manual studies teacher at Bernard Street school in Glasgow. His nickname Tod was after the famous American jockey Tod Sloan.

Bob SMELLIE (6/0, 1887-93)
Robert Smellie
Born 22 December 1867 Blantyre Park, Blantyre, Lanarkshire
Died 14 October 1951 Hairmyres Hospital, East Kilbride, Lanarkshire
Scotland v Ireland 1887, 1893; Wales 1888c; England 1889c, 1891, 1893.
Hamilton Academical 1884-85; Queen's Park 1885-96 (Scottish Cup 1890, 1893) [guest for Corinthian Jan 1890]; St Bernard's Jan 1896; Scottish Amateurs 1896-1901; Queen's Park Oct 1899.

A fine left back, Smellie was initially a Hamilton Accies player but will be remembered primarily for his influence at Queen's Park where he lifted the Scottish Cup twice. He made his international debut against Ireland in 1887 aged 19 and went on to win six Scotland caps, twice as captain, notably the memorable 3-2 win over England in 1889. He was also selected against England in 1890 and 1892 but each time had to decline due to illness. For Queen's Park he was the hero in 1890 as the team was on the point of losing the Scottish Cup final to Vale of Leven when Smellie's free kick led to a last-minute equaliser, and went on to win the replay. A bout of ill health forced him to miss the 1892 cup final and he went as far as announcing his retirement from football that autumn, but he recovered sufficiently to change his mind and returned to action with gusto, helping Queen's to win the cup in 1893 for the last time, defeating Celtic 2-1. He stopped playing seriously in 1896 although he turned out recreationally for the Scottish Amateurs for several years and to general astonishment he even made an appearance for Queen's Park in a friendly in 1899. He became a director of Queen's Park and spent over 50 years in the role, overseeing the construction and expansion of Hampden Park, and was club President in 1910-11. An auctioneer, he took over the family business LS Smellie & Sons Ltd in Hamilton, which is still going today, and was President of the Institute of Auctioneers and Appraisers. He was also President of Hamilton Golf Club from 1943-47. NB confusingly, there was another Bob Smellie playing in the 1890s, with Annbank, Sunderland and Walsall. In addition, R Smellie is listed in the Hamilton Accies team which won the Lanarkshire Cup in March 1881 and in a Scottish Cup tie the following year, which was probably his uncle of the same name.

Alec SMITH (20/3, 1898-1911)
Alexander Smith
Born 7 November 1875 East Main Street, Darvel, Ayrshire
Died 12 November 1954 Ardneuk, Darvel, Ayrshire
Scotland v England 1898, 1900, 1901, 1902, 1903, 1906, 1911; Wales 1900 (1), 1901, 1902 (1), 1903, 1905, 1907; Ireland 1900 (1), 1901, 1902, 1903, 1904, 1906, 1911.
Darvel; Rangers 1894-1915 (Scottish League 1899, 1900, 1901, 1902, 1911, 1912, 1913; Scottish Cup 1897, 1898, 1903).

Sunderland tried to sign Smith while he was at Darvel, but he rejected their offer and signed instead for Rangers in April 1894, having been invited for a trial by Nicol Smith, who was born in the same street. He spent an extraordinary 21 years at Ibrox, and curiously his first and last matches for the club were both friendlies against Notts County. His talents blossomed on the left wing, and helped to create the first great Rangers team through his ability to make chances for others, as well as scoring frequently himself. He endeared himself to the fans as part of the eleven which won the 'Three Cups' (Scottish, Glasgow and Charity) in 1896/97, a feat he repeated in 1900 and 1911, and was in the team which created the record of winning every league match in 1898/99. That was the first of his seven championship medals, and he scored in two of his three Scottish Cup final wins. It took him a while to come into the international reckoning and even after his first cap against England in 1898 there was a two-year gap, but once the new century dawned he was a fixture in the Scotland team until early 1907. There was then a lengthy interval before his final two selections against Ireland and England in 1911 aged 35, no less than thirteen years after his debut. He also played 14 times for the Scottish League. He spent his entire life in Darvel, where he was a partner in a successful lace-making business.

James SMITH (1/0, 1872)
James Smith
Born summer 1844 Aberdeen
Died 26 September 1876 East Lodge, Innes House, Urquhart, Moray
Scotland v England 1872.
Queen's Park 1867-70; South Norwood 1871-76; Crystal Palace Nov 1871, Mar 1872.

Born in Aberdeen, Smith was brought up in the north-east of Scotland, where he was educated at Fordyce Academy, then came to Glasgow to find work alongside his brother Bob (below). They were keen sportsmen and together they were founding members of Queen's Park in 1867, with James serving as club treasurer for two years before going to London in the footsteps of his brother. They joined the newly-founded South Norwood club, also playing a couple of times for Crystal Palace, then, having retained their membership of Queen's Park, were both selected for the first Scotland international in November 1872. Although Bob emigrated to USA the following year, James remained in London where he was a regular in the South Norwood team and sat on the FA committee as a representative of Queen's Park, in effect acting as a liaison for Scottish football. He worked as an artistic supplies salesman but in 1876, shortly after his last match for South Norwood, he fell ill and returned to the family home near Elgin, where his father was head gardener on an estate. He died there aged just 32 of a stroke and is buried in the local churchyard.

Jimmy SMITH (2/1, 1934-37)
James Smith
Born 24 September 1911 Bank Street, Slamannan, Stirlingshire

Died 4 December 2003 Ailsa Craig Nursing Home, Brand Street, Glasgow
Scotland v Ireland 1934, 1937 (1).
Argyll Rob Roy; East Stirlingshire Aug-Dec 1928; Rangers Dec 1928-47 (Scottish League 1931, 1933, 1934, 1935, 1937; Scottish Cup 1934, 1935, 1936); Dumbarton Aug-Oct 1947.

Smith was still a schoolboy at Airdrie Academy when he signed for Rangers, having impressed with over a goal a game in half a season at East Stirlingshire. He had to bide his time in the reserves for a couple of years at Ibrox before Sam English moved on and he was given his chance. Standing over six feet tall, he had the ideal physique for a striker and could strike the ball with head or feet, while he had excellent support from Bob McPhail and Alec Venters, among others. He remains Rangers' all-time record scorer (including wartime), and topped 30 league goals for five seasons in a row, from 1932 to 1937, his best tally being 41 in 1933/34. It was something of a golden age for Rangers, and Smith won five league titles as well as three Scottish Cups, the most memorable being the 1935 final when his double made the difference to defeat a plucky Hamilton side. Despite his superb scoring record, he was only capped twice by Scotland, both times against Ireland, and was never selected for the Scottish League. When war broke out in 1939 he was 28, and he was able to remain in Glasgow throughout the conflict, selected three times for Scotland in wartime internationals against England, all of them in 1941. After that his appearances for Rangers became less frequent but he remained on the fringes of the team until 1946, and scored in the famous match that year with Moscow Dynamo. After retiring from Rangers in 1947 he was persuaded to turn out for Dumbarton in August, making several appearances before he was appointed as Rangers trainer in October that year. He was later appointed chief scout and remained at Ibrox until 1967.

John SMITH (10/10, 1877-84)
Dr John Smith MD
Born 12 August 1855 Mauchline, Ayrshire
Died 16 November 1934 Brycehall, Kirkcaldy, Fife
Scotland v England 1877, 1879 (1), 1880, 1881 (2), 1883 (3), 1884 (1); Wales 1877, 1879 (2), 1881, 1883c (1).
Mauchline 1874-79; Edinburgh University 1878-85; Queen's Park Jan 1880-85 (Scottish Cup 1881, 1884); Swifts 1885-87; Corinthians 1884-88; Liverpool Ramblers 1884-88; Casuals 1886-88.
Educated at Ayr Academy where he played rugby, Smith was introduced to association football in his home town of Mauchline and played both codes while he was a student at Edinburgh University. He was a fine full back for the University rugby team, selected for Edinburgh and named as reserve for Scotland in 1876, but the lure of the association game was too great. In 1877 he was the first man from an Ayrshire side to be capped for Scotland, playing against England and Wales. Meanwhile he won the Ayrshire Cup with Mauchline in 1878 and later that year founded the association football club at Edinburgh University together with another future internationalist doctor, John Macdonald. His reputation grew so much that in 1880 he was invited to join Queen's Park, where he had five outstanding years, sometimes using the pseudonym 'JC Miller' (from his mother's maiden name). In 1881 he scored a hat-trick in the Scottish Cup final replay against Dumbarton, and twice in the 6-1 defeat of England at Kennington Oval (a possible third is reported as an own goal by Edgar Field). He continued to carve out victories for Scotland against England, scoring all three in the 3-2 win of 1883, while in 1884 he scored the only goal in the 1-0 victory which turned out to be his last international. The same year he played for Queen's Park in their FA Cup final defeat to Blackburn Rovers, and was awarded a Scottish Cup medal although the final did not take place.

Meanwhile, his medical career was underway: he graduated MA in 1878, MB in 1881 and finally MD in 1886 having acted as resident surgeon in Edinburgh Royal Infirmary and in Edinburgh and Glasgow Maternity Hospitals. Because of his work commitments he only played once for Queen's Park in 1885, in the FA Cup semi-final, then in 1886 he took up a post as clinical assistant at the Royal Ophthalmic Hospital at Moorfields in London. This prompted him to join Swifts and he was also invited to tour with Corinthians, but his football career was given a jolt in December that year when he was suspended by the Scottish FA for playing with Corinthians against Bolton Wanderers, a professional side. He was rightly annoyed at the inference that this made him a professional but it made little practical difference as the ban only applied to Scottish football and by then he was living in London. He played for Swifts in their run to the FA Cup semi-final, as well as guesting for Corinthians, Casuals and Liverpool Ramblers. As a change of sport, he resumed playing rugby on a tour of Australia in the summer of 1888 with the Shaw-Shrewsbury British Lions team, although his primary role was as referee and while he played in nine games none of them were test matches. On his return he went back to association football for Swifts before going into general practice in Kirkcaldy where he persuaded both Queen's Park and Corinthians to visit the town for friendlies. He was respected enough to be referee of the Scotland versus England match in 1892, and when he was too old for football, he took up bowls, golf and curling, and was vice-president of the Scottish Bowling Association in 1924. He spent the rest of his life in Kirkcaldy where he was a well-known figure as he refused to drive a car and went on his rounds in a Victoria carriage, drawn by a white veteran war horse.

Jock SMITH (1/0, 1924)
John Smith
Born 17 August 1893 Drumbuie Farm, Beith, Ayrshire
Died 16 April 1973 Belfast Hospital, Northern Ireland

Scotland v England 1924.
Neilston Victoria; Ayr United 1919-26; Middlesbrough 1926-30 (Second Division 1927, 1929); Cardiff City 1930-32 (Welsh Cup 1930); Distillery 1932-35.

Known as 'Fermer Jock' due to his family farming background, Smith had a considerably delayed start to his professional football career because of WW1, and he was already 25 when he signed for Ayr United in 1919. Although his preferred position was right back, for a while Ayr insisted on playing him in the forward line to make the most of his speed, before he developed a superb full-back partnership with Phil McCloy. The Ayr United pair were selected together for Smith's only international in 1924, and they did well in a 1-1 draw with England at Wembley. He was 30 by the time he was capped, but he still had plenty of energy under his belt and even after Ayr were relegated in 1925 he made an appearance for the Scottish League, shortly before he signed for Middlesbrough. He won two Second Division titles with Boro, then moved on to Cardiff City where he won the Welsh Cup in 1930. He ended his career in Northern Ireland with three seasons at Distillery, playing past his 40th birthday, and he enjoyed life in Belfast so much that he went into business there and remained in the city after his football days were over. He is buried in Belfast's Roselawn Cemetery together with his wife Maggie.

Nic SMITH (12/0, 1897-1902)
Nicol Smith
Born 25 December 1873 East Main Street, Darvel, Ayrshire
Died 6 January 1905 Kilmarnock Infirmary, Ayrshire
Scotland v England 1897, 1899c, 1900, 1902; Wales 1898, 1899c, 1900, 1901; Ireland 1899, 1900, 1901, 1902.
Vale of Irvine; Royal Albert; Darvel; Rangers Mar 1893-1905 (Scottish League 1899, 1900, 1901, 1902; Scottish Cup 1894, 1897, 1898).

A right back in the great Rangers side at the turn of the century, Smith was born in the same street as his teammate Alec Smith (above), although they were not related. Captain of Scotland at junior level, the 'Darvel Marvel' signed for Rangers in the spring of 1893 and won the Scottish Cup in his first full season, scoring a rare goal in the semi-final, and went on to lift the trophy twice more in 1897 and 1898. Powerfully-built and strong in the tackle, he played a major role in the team that won the Scottish League four seasons in a row, from 1899 to 1902, not to mention the Glasgow Cup four times, three Charity Cups and the Glasgow Exhibition Trophy in 1902. On the international front he made his Scotland debut in an exhilarating 2-1 win against England in 1897, the first of a dozen caps that saw him on the losing side just once, which happened to be the one match under his captaincy. He also made nine appearances for the Scottish League. Tragically, he fell ill after he played for Rangers against Third Lanark in late November 1904 and a few weeks later he died of enteric fever aged 31, the same infection which killed his wife, leaving five orphaned children. Rangers set up and organised a substantial trust fund for their benefit.

Bob SMITH (2/0, 1872-73)
Robert Smith
Born 1 May 1848 Aberdeen
Died 3 June 1914 St Joseph's Hospital, Chicago, Illinois, USA
Scotland v England 1872, 1873.
Queen's Park 1867-69; South Norwood 1871-73; Crystal Palace Nov 1871, Mar 1872.

Younger brother of James (above), Smith learned to play football at Fordyce Academy and carried on playing the game when he came to Glasgow in 1864 to work for a publisher. With a group of others from the North of Scotland, he was a founding member of Queen's Park in 1867 and played a key role in helping to popularise football in the city. Two years later when his employer went out of business he moved to London where he maintained a close connection with the Glaswegian club and was nominated by them to play for the Scotland eleven in three of the unofficial international series. He also represented Queen's Park (and by extension all of Scottish football) at meetings of the Football Association. His brother James joined him in London and they played for South Norwood, as well as a couple of times for Crystal Palace, which led to both being selected for Scotland in the first international of November 1872. Bob was retained in the team for the return match at the Oval in the spring, although according to one observer 'while no man ever worked harder in the field, he was not what could be called a brilliant forward.' In the autumn of 1873, a few months after his second cap, he emigrated to Wyoming where, in time, he opened a grocery store in Green River, was elected a member of the Wyoming House of Representatives, and founded the *Sweetwater Gazette* newspaper. Then, frustrated by the lack of civic progress in the town, he relocated 15 miles east to Rock Springs, taking his printing press with him and renaming his newspaper the *Rock Springs Miner* (which is still going strong). He left Wyoming in 1903 when he was appointed to the Indian Service in Oklahoma, and set up his own business in Muskogee, dealing in oil concessions. He died in 1914 in a Chicago hospital after visiting his son, a doctor there, and failed to recover after undergoing an operation.

Tom SMITH (2/0, 1934-38)
Thomas McCall Smith
Born 4 October 1908 Low Fenwick, Ayrshire
Died 21 June 1998 Ashton, Preston, Lancashire
Scotland v England 1934, 1938.
Cumnock Juveniles; Townhead Thistle; Kilmarnock Dec 1928-36; Preston North End Dec 1936-45 (FA Cup 1938) [guest in WW2 for Rochdale Aug-Sep 1942, Derby County 1942-43, Manchester United Feb 1943, Burnley Aug-Sep 1943].

Smith was educated at Cumnock Academy and had embarked on his studies at Glasgow University when he signed for Kilmarnock, and although he soon made his debut he was just too late to feature in Killie's 1929 Scottish Cup triumph. However, he broke into the first team after impressing on the club's tour of USA in the summer of 1930 and developed into a fine centre half. He won his first Scotland cap against England in 1934, a disappointing 3-0 defeat, and while he went on the Scottish FA tour of North America in 1935 he had to wait a long time for his second chance with the national team. Meanwhile he played for the Scottish League in October 1936, shortly before he joined Preston, where two of his uncles had played. He was made club captain and in April 1938 he was one of four Scots (the others being Andy Beattie, Bill Shankly and George Mutch) who enjoyed two memorable victories at Wembley, with Scotland defeating England 1-0 and then Preston winning the FA Cup final by the same score against Huddersfield. Unfortunately, he broke his leg in Prague on the club's summer tour and made just one first team appearance the following season. When war broke out in the autumn of 1939 his top level career was effectively over but while working for Lancashire Constabulary in Civil Defence he continued playing when he could and won the War Cup with Preston in 1941. He also made a Scotland appearance in a 5-4 win over England in 1942. When Preston closed down for a couple of years he played as a guest for Derby County and briefly for Rochdale, Manchester United and Burnley. He finally retired in 1945 when he was appointed as Kilmarnock manager but was forced to resign through illness after a couple of years and returned to live and work in Lancashire. As a royal curiosity, he was presented with the FA Cup in 1938 by King George VI, and when he captained the Civil Defence team to victory in the Inter-Allied Services Cup in 1942 he was presented with the trophy by the King's wife, Queen Elizabeth.

Peter SOMERS (4/0, 1905-09)
Peter Somers
Born 3 June 1878 Green Street, Strathaven, Lanarkshire
Died 27 November 1914 St Andrew's Nursing Home, Milton, Glasgow
Scotland v Ireland 1905, 1907; England 1905; Wales 1909.

Cadzow Oak; Hamilton Academical Sep-Dec 1897; Celtic Dec 1897-1900 [loan to Clyde Oct-Dec 1899]; Blackburn Rovers Feb 1900-02; Celtic 1902-10 (Scottish Cup 1904, 1907, 1908; Scottish League 1905, 1906, 1907, 1908, 1909); Hamilton Academical Jan 1910-11.

Brought up in Motherwell, Somers played just a couple of league games for Hamilton Accies before joining Celtic late in 1897. He struggled to make a consistent impact, although he was good enough to be selected for the first of three appearances for the Scottish League in February 1899. Celtic allowed him to go to Blackburn early in 1900, and he helped to steer Rovers clear of relegation, forming a fine attacking partnership with Hugh Morgan. When his wife became homesick he came back to Scotland in 1902 and that was Celtic's gain as in his second spell at the club he and his fellow inside forward Jimmy McMenemy supplied plenty of ammunition to Jimmy Quinn, laying the foundations for the great Celtic side that won six league titles in a row. Somers also won three Scottish Cups, scoring twice against Hearts in the 1907 final and again in the 1908 victory. He played four times for Scotland without really making a major impact, and when he drifted out of the Celtic team in 1910 he ended his career where it began, at Hamilton, but was out of the Accies team which reached the Scottish Cup final of 1911 just before he retired. Renowned for his intelligent play he had talents in other fields and was in great demand at social gatherings as a piano player. As a young man he served an engineering apprenticeship in Motherwell but when he retired from football he set up in business running the Criterion Bar in Hamilton. He was appointed a director of Hamilton Accies, in whose service he died aged just 36 after he caught a chill watching a player at a Dykehead v Nithsdale Wanderers match. The infection spread so quickly that ten days later he was dead, having had a foot amputated to no avail. His son John played in Ireland for Dolphin in the 1920s.

Bill SOMERS (3/0, 1879-80)
William Scott Somers
Born 22 November 1853 Perth
Died 9 July 1891 Foryd Hotel, Rhyl, Wales
Scotland v England 1879; Wales 1879, 1880.
Eastern 1873-76 [guest for Partick Jan 1876]; Third Lanark 1876-79; Queen's Park 1879-81 (Scottish Cup 1880).
Born in Perth, where his unmarried mother seems to have gone to escape scandal, the birth year of 1853 appears on Somers' christening register although later records indicate it was probably 1854. He was brought up in St Andrews but when he was ten his mother married a Glasgow oil merchant called William Scott and he added his stepfather's surname as a middle name. He started out in football as a full-back for Eastern, taking part in the first Scottish Cup competition in 1873, and played as a guest for Partick in their cross-border friendly in Darwen at New Year 1876. Then he joined Third Lanark and was in the team which contested the first Glasgow Charity Cup final

and the 1878 Scottish Cup final, before moving to Queen's Park in 1879 where he finally won the Scottish Cup in 1880. That summer he travelled to New York to pursue negotiations for a transatlantic tour by a Scottish select (a venture which collapsed due to the death of the SFA secretary, William Dick) but his conversations were inadvertently reported in the press and he was ridiculed at home for his bombastic exaggeration of his own talents. That probably explains why he retired from football in 1881, although it could have been to focus on his business. He had worked for his stepfather's oil manufacturing company in Glasgow, but after he took it over the venture failed and he was declared bankrupt in 1884. By then he had married and moved to north Wales where his wife's family ran the Foryd Hotel in Rhyl. He persevered in his career and was described as an analytical chemist on his death certificate after he died suddenly from flu in 1891. Football was not his only sport, he was a member of Clyde Amateur Rowing Club and won the Clyde Challenge Cup for junior scullers in 1877.

George SOMMERVILLE (1/1, 1886)
George Sommerville
Born 11 June 1863 Forth, Lanarkshire
Died 7 February 1929 Brooklands Avenue, Uddingston, Lanarkshire
Scotland v England 1886 (1).
Hamilton Academical 1883-85; Rangers Jan-Oct 1885; Queen's Park Oct 1885-87 (Scottish Cup 1886) [guest for Hamilton Academical Apr 1886]; Uddingston Aug-Oct 1887; Queen's Park Oct 1887-88; Uddingston 1888-91.

When Sommerville was capped for Scotland against England in 1886, the *Scottish Referee* reported that his 'superior shooting power' was the decisive quality that secured his selection at centre forward, and he repaid that faith with the late goal which rescued a 1-1 draw. However, it seems the fame went to his head as the same newspaper wrote in 1888 that 'he was a good man until the laudation spoiled him'. An adept dribbler, he had started out at Hamilton Academical alongside Bob Smellie, another future internationalist, and then spent less than a calendar year at Rangers before Queen's Park invited him to join them. He made a scoring debut in unusual circumstances, an FA Cup tie against Partick Thistle in October 1885, and ended the season winning the Scottish Cup and being making his Scotland debut. He left Queen's Park in 1887 to join a new club in his home town of Uddingston but after a few months he was persuaded to give it another season at Hampden before returning to Uddingston in 1888 to play out his career. He helped to bring the club up to a reasonable standard, taking it to the Lanarkshire Cup final, but it was a far cry from the heady days of international glory and his rapid rise to fame was equalled by his speedy return to obscurity. Having initially trained as a tailor in his father's drapery business, he later worked as an advertising agent.

Finlay SPEEDIE (3/2, 1903)
Finlay Ballantyne Speedie MM
Born 18 August 1880 High Street, Dumbarton
Died 5 February 1953 Wallace Street, Dumbarton
Scotland v Wales 1903 (1); Ireland 1903; England 1903 (1).
Artizan Thistle; Strathclyde; Clydebank; Rangers Oct 1900-06 (Scottish League 1901, 1902; Scottish Cup 1903); Newcastle United 1906-08 (Football League 1907); Oldham Athletic 1908-09; Bradford Apr 1909; Dumbarton 1909-20 (Second Division 1911) [guest for Arbroath Jan-Mar 1916].

A creative inside forward who could play on the left or right, Speedie had an unusual arrangement in junior football to play for Clydebank in cup ties and Strathclyde in league matches. That stopped when he signed for Rangers in October 1900 and made an instant impact, winning his first medal within a few weeks in the Glasgow Cup, while at the end of the season he won the league title. Those successes were repeated the following season, with the Glasgow Exhibition Trophy thrown in, and he added a Scottish Cup medal in 1903. His consistent good form partnering Alec Smith earned him a selection for all three Scotland internationals in 1903, scoring against Wales on his debut and netting a fine equaliser against England. However, he was not capped again and his only other representative honour was for the Scottish League in 1905. His Ibrox career ended in 1906 after a series of disappointments: in the 1904 Scottish Cup final he scored twice early on to give his side a commanding lead which they then surrendered to Celtic, in the 1905 final they were overcome by Third Lanark, and due to injury he hardly played at all in 1905-06. He was given a benefit match and sold to Newcastle United where he found a new lease of life and slotted into the team immediately, scoring twice on his debut. Newcastle won the Football League title in his first season, but after their FA Cup final defeat in 1908 he was sold to Oldham. They allowed him to leave in the spring and after a handful of games for Bradford he returned to Dumbarton in 1909. Remarkably, he spent over a decade with his home town team, and captained them to win the Second Division in 1911, although with no automatic promotion they had to wait two years before securing enough votes to enter the First Division. In 1911 he scored a hat-trick of penalties in a Scottish Cup tie against Ayr United, despite having worked a full night shift as a marine engineer in Denny's Yard, Dumbarton. During WW1 he fought with distinction in the Argyll and Sutherland Highlanders, and was awarded the Military Medal in 1918 for conspicuous gallantry at the front line in France. Meanwhile he continued to play football whenever he could, for Arbroath during his training and for Dumbarton while on leave. He picked up again at Boghead when he was demobbed and did not hang up his boots until 1920. He continued to work in the shipyards and coached Dumbarton in the 1930s. His elder brother Willie played for Third Lanark, his nephew Bob for Dumbarton.

Jimmy SPEIRS (1/0, 1908)
James Hamilton Speirs MM
Born 22 March 1886 Aikenhead Road, Govan, Glasgow
Died 20 August 1917 Pommern Redoubt, Flanders, Belgium
Scotland v Wales 1908.
Annandale; Maryhill Apr-Jun 1905; Rangers 1905-08; Clyde 1908-09; Bradford City 1909-12 (FA Cup 1911); Leeds City Dec 1912-15.

Speirs came to Rangers in 1905 aged 19, after a short spell with Maryhill juniors, and made his debut in the autumn. He won a Glasgow Charity Cup medal in his first season, scoring twice in the final, but that was his only honour in three years at the club and he was often on the fringes of the Rangers team. However, he was called up to the Scotland team against Wales in March 1908, which proved to be his only cap. He moved on that summer to Clyde, where he did very well, helping them to third place in the league and a cup semi-final, and was signed by Bradford City in the summer of 1909. They made him team captain and he achieved legendary status by scoring City's only goal of their FA Cup final victory in 1911, heading home after 15 minutes of the replay to defeat Newcastle United. He dropped down a division when he joined Leeds City in December 1912 and maintained his scoring record there until professional football was wound up for the War. He enlisted in May 1915 with the Queen's Own Cameron Highlanders, and was awarded the Military Medal for his bravery in the Battle of Arras in April 1917. Promoted to Sergeant that summer, on 20 August he was on manoeuvres at the Pommern Redoubt during the Battle of Passchendaele when he was badly wounded, and although he managed to crawl into a shell hole he was never seen alive again. His grave is in Dochy Farm New British Cemetery in Flanders.

Jimmy STARK (2/0, 1909)
James Robertson Stark
Born 15 August 1877 Comedie Cottage, Ruchazie, Glasgow
Died 18 March 1969 Royal Alexandra Hospital, Paisley
Scotland v Ireland 1909c; England 1909c.
Mansewood; Pollokshaws Eastwood; Glasgow Perthshire 1898-1900; Rangers 1900-07 (Scottish League 1901, 1902; Scottish Cup 1903); Chelsea 1907-08; Rangers Oct 1908-10; Morton 1910-15.

Stark had several years in junior football, notably at Glasgow Perthshire where he won the North Eastern Cup twice, and played for the Glasgow junior select against Ireland. Another future internationalist, Tod Sloan, was in the same team. He had a trial for Rangers in April 1900 and soon signed up, playing his part in two league titles in his first two seasons, and the Scottish Cup in his third. He developed a reputation as a terrifically hard worker, a dogged centre half with the knack of popping up in the right place to foil opposition attacks. On occasion, he could also play on either wing. Although Rangers suffered a downturn and there were no further major honours that decade, Stark continued to pick up medals and could be well satisfied with winning the Glasgow Cup twice, three Charity Cups and the Glasgow Exhibition Cup of 1902. However, Rangers lost the Scottish Cup finals of 1904 and 1905, not to mention the league play-off in 1905. Sunderland tried to buy him, then David Calderhead tempted him to come to newly-promoted Chelsea in 1907. After a year in London, he refused to sign a new contract and after much speculation as to his next club, William Wilton persuaded him to return to Ibrox. He appeared rejuvenated and had a wonderful season, not just winning international recognition at the age of 31, but appointed Scotland captain for both of his caps. He found that responsibility had a downside when Scotland, 2-0 down to England with a few minutes left, were awarded a penalty by his namesake, the referee James Stark. Nobody wanted to take it so as captain he was forced to take the kick himself and his poor shot was saved. He never took a penalty again. In 1909 he captained the Scottish League to a 3-1 win over the English, and took part in the notorious undecided Scottish Cup final. A year later he moved on to Morton, was made club captain, and in October he found himself back at Ibrox for a league game against Rangers. A Greenock butcher had promised the Morton players a live lamb for each goal they scored, and to general astonishment they won 5-1. As two of the players scored twice Stark, as captain, was given one of the surplus lambs while the other was kept as a club mascot. He had five years at Morton and retired from football in 1915, after which he worked as a gardener and lived in Renfrew.

Davie STEELE (3/0, 1923)
David Morton Steele
Born 29 July 1894 Rankin Street, Carluke, Lanarkshire
Died 23 May 1964 Belton Street, Moldgreen, Huddersfield, Yorkshire
Scotland v Ireland 1923; Wales 1923; England 1923.
Corehouse Thistle; Cumnock; St Mirren Nov 1913-19; Douglas Water Thistle 1919; Bristol Rovers Nov 1919-22; Huddersfield Town 1922-29 (Football League 1924, 1925, 1926); Preston North End 1929-30.

Steele was brought up in Kirkfieldbank, just outside Lanark, where his family had a fruit farm and he played for the local juvenile team, Corehouse Thistle. He worked as a miner before his football career took off. After a few months with Cumnock juniors he was given a trial by St Mirren and they signed him in November 1913 but he had barely played for the club when they sent him on loan to Abercorn. When he did play a full season at Love Street, the War then intervened and he joined the Army in 1916, playing no football for three years. He was released by St Mirren and resumed in junior football with Douglas Water Thistle in 1919 before joining Bristol Rovers, at that time in the Southern League. They became founder members of the Third Division North, then in 1922 his career finally sparked into action when he joined Herbert Chapman's Huddersfield Town. Switching from left to right half, in his first season with Huddersfield he won international honours, playing in all three of Scotland's matches in the space of a few weeks in the spring of 1923. Perhaps he should have won more caps, but he was able to concentrate on Huddersfield's terrific achievement in winning the Football League three years in a row. He also played in the FA Cup final of 1928, lost to Blackburn Rovers. At the age of 35 he joined Preston North End for a season before hanging up his boots in 1930. After he retired he coached briefly with Bury and Ashton National before spending four years in Denmark with BK. He then returned to England for a coaching post at Sheffield United, and remained in Yorkshire for the rest of his life with managerial appointments at Bradford (1936-43), Huddersfield Town (1943-47) and Bradford City (1948-52), where he also ran a pub in Pudsey, just outside the town. His son of the same name was killed in action in a raid on St-Nazaire in 1942.

George STEVENSON (12/4, 1927-34)
George Stevenson
Born 4 April 1905 Nitshill Terrace, Kilbirnie, Ayrshire
Died 10 May 1990 Ravenscroft, Strathpeffer, Ross-shire
Scotland v Wales 1927, 1930, 1931 (1); Ireland 1928, 1930 (1), Sep 1931 (1), 1932, 1934; England 1930, 1931 (1), 1934; France 1930.
Kilbirnie Ladeside; Motherwell 1923-40 (Scottish League 1932).

Known by the fans as 'the prince of inside forwards', Stevenson epitomised Motherwell's golden era with over 500 appearances, rarely missing a match at his only senior club. Signed by 'Sailor' Hunter in 1923 from Ayrshire junior club Kilbirnie Ladeside, he was a hugely influential figure as Motherwell became one of Scotland's top sides for a decade, winning the league title in 1932 and finishing second or third on seven occasions. However, that was his only major honour, as all three Scottish Cup finals he played in were lost, in 1931, 1933 and 1939. His chief role was goal provider from inside left or right although he could be relied on to score regularly and he reached double figures in eleven of his seasons. Meanwhile, he had an impressive Scotland career, having made his debut in 1927 against Wales he held his place for the Ireland match but was dropped for the clash with England, which denied him the chance of being a Wembley Wizard. However, he was recalled in 1930 and over the next four years took his caps tally up to twelve, scoring in four of them, and also made ten appearances for the Scottish League between 1927 and 1934. After his final game for Motherwell in 1940, at the end of the first wartime season, he retired from playing but remained at the club and assisted John Hunter through the war years. In 1942 he donated all his Scotland jerseys to the SFA, who needed them for wartime internationals. He was appointed Motherwell manager in 1946 and had several cup successes, winning the Scottish League Cup in 1950 and the Scottish Cup in 1952. He survived relegation in 1953 to win the Second Division at the first attempt, but resigned in 1955 after another second-bottom finish in the league.

Allan STEWART (2/1, 1888-89)
Allan Stewart
Born 12 April 1865 North Hamilton Street, Kilmarnock, Ayrshire
Died 2 October 1907 Queen's Road, New Cross, London
Scotland v Ireland 1888 (1); Wales 1889.
Pilgrims 1885-86; Queen's Park 1886-90 (Scottish Cup 1890) [guest for Cowlairs Sep 1888, Corinthians Jan 1889].

Stewart was born in Kilmarnock but came as a boy to Glasgow, where he made his name as a centre half with Pilgrims, who played near his home in Paisley Road. He caught the eye of Queen's Park and was recruited in 1886 when the team changed to a three half-back system. He quickly settled in the side and unusually for a half back in an era of heavy pitches, he was famous for shooting from distance and could score from 30 yards out. He was made club captain in 1888, the year in which he scored on his Scotland debut against Ireland, and was picked again for the team to face Wales in 1889. He also played as a guest for Cowlairs in their Glasgow Exhibition Cup victory in 1888 and once for Corinthians against Celtic in January 1889. His final season for Queen's Park was perhaps his most successful, as he scored the winning goal in both the Glasgow Cup final and in the 1890 Scottish Cup final replay, after which he retired from top level action. He moved to London for his work as a financial clerk and died there suddenly aged 42, described in one obituary as 'a strenuous, virile yet most gentlemanly player', although the *Scottish Referee* was less kind, calling him a 'rare, plodding half-back'.

Andy STEWART (1/0, 1894)
Andrew Stewart
Born 26 September 1871 Crown Street, Gorbals, Glasgow
Died 23 August 1939 Sinclair Street, Helensburgh, Dunbartonshire
Scotland v Wales 1894.
Minerva; Third Lanark 1890-94; Partick Thistle Apr-May 1894; Queen's Park 1894-99 [guest for St Bernard's Mar-Sep 1896; Derby County Apr 1896; Scottish Amateurs 1896-97].

Outside right, an excellent dribbler, Stewart flitted in and out of the Third Lanark team in the early 1890s as his business career allowed and remained resolutely amateur. Although hardly of the top order, he was good enough to be capped in 1894 against Wales. He then joined his elder brother David (below) at Queen's Park and spent five years with the club, while using his amateur status to move around. In 1896 he played several matches for St Bernard's and also turned out for Derby County on their tour of Scotland when they were short of numbers. He was appointed as secretary of the Scottish Amateurs in 1896 but still turned out occasionally for Queen's Park when required and was last reported in the Strollers eleven in 1899. However, he appears to have stopped playing seriously to focus on his job as a timber merchant in the family business of Wylie, Stewart and Marshall, which ran the Western Sawmills at Port Dundas in north Glasgow.

Davie STEWART (3/0, 1893-97)
David McGregor Stewart
Born 13 December 1869 Camden Street, Gorbals, Glasgow
Died 3 August 1933 Murray's Royal Asylum, Perth
Scotland v Wales 1893; Ireland 1894, 1897.
Minerva; Queen's Park 1891-1901 (Scottish Cup 1893) [guest for St Bernard's May 1894]; London Caledonians 1900-03.

Stewart and his younger brother Andy (above) had a prosperous upbringing in Partick, sons of the proprietor of Western Sawmills, and David pursued his football while developing a professional career as a consulting engineer. He started out with Minerva in junior football and represented the Glasgow Junior League before joining Queen's Park in 1891. He played in their Scottish Cup final defeat in his first season then won the trophy in 1893 when Celtic were beaten 2-1. Described by the *Scottish Referee* as 'dour, determined and loyal to the backbone', he was a steady half back, occasionally tried in the forward line but with little success. He made his Scotland debut against Wales that year and was selected twice more in 1894 and 1897. In an era when Queen's Park stayed aloof from Scottish League membership, he had limited competitive opportunities at club level and towards the end of the decade made only sporadic appearances, with the added complication of poor health. However, he was able to contribute to the running of the club by sitting on its committee, and was still in good enough form to feature in the Scottish Cup final of 1900, lost 4-3 to Celtic. That autumn he left Glasgow for a new job in London, where he played for London Caledonians in the latter stages of his career. Later in life he suffered from mental illness which ultimately led to him being placed in an asylum in Perth, where he died in 1933 from 'suicidal strangulation'.

Dunkie STEWART (1/0, 1888)
Duncan Cameron Stewart
Born 8 May 1865 Chapel Lane, Port Glasgow, Renfrewshire
Died 26 January 1958 Clune Brae, Port Glasgow, Renfrewshire
Scotland v Ireland 1888c.
Port Glasgow Athletic 1882-87; Dumbarton 1887-92 [guest for Port Glasgow Athletic 1888-89]; Port Glasgow Athletic Aug 1893.

Stewart developed a reputation as a fine full-back with Port Glasgow, where he partnered a young Tom Brandon. He had won representative honours for Renfrewshire when he left the Port to take up a job in Belfast in the spring of 1887 and when he returned later that year, he crossed the River Clyde to join Dumbarton. His continued good form there earned him a Scotland cap, and he was team captain in his only international, a 10-2 win over Ireland. In 1888-89 he gravitated between Dumbarton and Port Glasgow, then increasingly his work as a ship's joiner curtailed his appearances. In 1890 he travelled to the far east, and in 1892 to Australia, but he did play football when he came home on leave, including for Dumbarton in April 1892 and for Port Glasgow in August 1893. He remained based in Port Glasgow, where he was an active member of Clune Park Church choir, until his death aged 92.

George STEWART (4/0, 1906-07)
George Lindsay Stewart
Born 11 December 1882 Hill Street, Wishaw, Lanarkshire
Died 10 November 1962 Park Hospital, Davyhulme, Lancashire
Scotland v Wales 1906, 1907; England 1906, 1907.
Wishaw Thistle; Wishaw; Strathclyde; Hibernian 1904-06; Manchester City 1906-11 (Second Division 1910); Partick Thistle 1911-12; Stalybridge 1912-13; Merthyr Town 1913-14.

An outside right, small in stature but powerfully built, Stewart could dribble and cross with the best of them, also packing a good shot. Having played for the Glasgow Junior League and coming close to the Scotland junior team, he joined Hibs from Strathclyde in 1904, replacing another right winger of the same surname (John Stewart, who went to QPR). He became part of the international set-up in 1906, playing twice for Scotland and once for the Scottish League in a five-week period; that was his second league cap, having played against the Irish in 1904. He was clearly a great talent and in the summer of 1906 Manchester City paid Hibs the substantial fee of £650 to take him south. He had an impressive start to his career in England and retained his place in the Scotland side for two more games in 1907. However, his five years in Manchester were topsy-turvy as City finished third in 1908 then were relegated on goal average in 1909, before bouncing straight back to the top league as Second Division champions. Stewart returned to Scotland with Partick Thistle in 1911 but could not settle and ended his playing career in the relative backwaters of Stalybridge and Merthyr. When he retired, he went to Stretford in Manchester where he married and spent the rest of his life working in heavy industries, as a blacksmith and chain maker, and latterly as a motor transport driver.

Willie STEWART (2/1, 1898-1900)
William Garven Stewart
Born 7 January 1875 Struan Terrace, Crosshill, Glasgow
Died 30 April 1951 Bootle General Hospital, Liverpool
Scotland v Ireland 1898 (1), 1900.
Queen's Park 1894-1900; Third Lanark Jan-Sep 1901; Newcastle United 1901-03.
Brought up in a middle class household (his father was manager of Glasgow Corporation Water Works), Stewart trained as an electrical engineer while making his way as a footballer with Queen's Park. A speedy outside right, he was capped in 1898, scoring against Ireland, and really came to the fore in 1900 when he made his second appearance for Scotland, then a few weeks later he scored for Queen's Park in the Scottish Cup final. His career as an amateur footballer was often dictated by his professional life as a maritime engineer, a conflict which caused him to fall out with Queen's Park early in 1901 due to his frequent unavailability. He joined Third Lanark, and later the same year when his work took him to Tyneside he played for Newcastle United for a couple of seasons. He subsequently went to Merseyside, where he lived in Bootle and worked for the White Star Line shipping company.

Dave STORRIER (3/0, 1899)
David Storrier
Born 25 October 1872 Fergus Street, Arbroath, Angus
Died 27 January 1910 Panmure Street, Arbroath, Angus
Scotland v Wales 1899; Ireland 1899c; England 1899.
Arbroath Dauntless; Arbroath 1891-93; Everton 1893-98; Celtic 1898-1901 (Scottish Cup 1899, 1900); Dundee Nov 1901-02; Millwall Athletic 1902-04.
A muscular left-back, Storrier won the first of several Forfarshire caps aged 19 while playing for Arbroath. After a couple of impressive seasons he joined Everton in 1893 and spent five years with the club, finishing consistently in the top half of the league and reaching the FA Cup final in 1897, which was lost to Aston Villa. He was allowed to leave Everton the following summer and was happy to join Celtic, where he had three excellent years. In his first season at Parkhead he was selected for all three of Scotland's matches in 1899, captaining the side against Ireland, and in fact he played international football on four consecutive Saturdays, as in the middle of the sequence he made an appearance for the Scottish League against the Football League. A fortnight later he captained Celtic to Scottish Cup victory over Rangers, and won the trophy for a second time in 1900. He made one more appearance for the Scottish League early in 1901 but curiously that summer he was suspended by Celtic on suspicion of malingering, when he may simply have been ill. He was offloaded to Dundee in November 1901 and they appointed him club captain until the end of the season. In the summer of 1902, he was hit on the head by a cricket ball while playing for Arbroath United, but he recovered sufficiently to sign for Millwall where he was again made captain, and remained in London for two years before retiring from the game. He came home to Arbroath to go into business as a grocer and continued to play cricket enthusiastically. However, at the end of the decade his health declined and he died of tuberculosis early in 1910, aged 37.

Willie SUMMERS (1/0, 1926)
William Summers
Born 14 July 1893 Whitehill Road, Burnbank, Lanarkshire
Died 23 February 1972 Hairmyres Hospital, East Kilbride, Lanarkshire
Scotland v England 1926.
Burnbank Athletic 1914-18; Airdrieonians 1918-20; St Bernard's 1920-21; St Mirren 1921-27 (Scottish Cup 1926); Bradford City Sep 1927-32 (Third Division North 1929); Newport County 1932-33.
A strapping centre half, over six feet tall, Summers had a lengthy period in junior football, captaining Burnbank Athletic while working as a coal miner in the war years, and did not turn senior until he was 25. He had two years at Airdrie and a season with St Bernard's, then in the Central League, before he joined St Mirren in 1921, where he had the best years of his career. Saints finished consistently in the top six of the league in the early twenties, and it all came together for Summers in one amazing week in April 1926. At the age of 32 he was outstanding as St Mirren won the Scottish Cup, beating Celtic 2-0, and seven days later he was capped by Scotland in a 1-0 win over England. Strangely enough there had been a strong rumour earlier in the season that he had been suspended by the club, which Saints and the player were forced to deny, and he successfully sued the *Sunday Post* for defamation, winning £100 in damages. There could have been a second cap as he was named in the Scotland side to face Wales that autumn, but an injury the week before the match kept him out for four months. He started the 1927-28 season in a buzz of transfer speculation which concluded with Bradford City signing him for a fee of £1,620, joining another Burnbank veteran Tommy Cairns in Yorkshire. It proved a good investment for City as he spent five years with the club and helped them to win the Third Division North title in his second season. He concluded with a year at Newport County before retiring from the game just before his 40th birthday. He ran the Barrack Tavern in Bradford for a few years then came back to Scotland to run another pub in Hamilton.

Scot SYMON (1/0, 1938)
James Scotland Symon
Born 9 May 1911 Viewbank, Errol, Perthshire
Died 29 April 1985 Dalkeith Avenue, Dumbreck, Glasgow
Scotland v Hungary 1938.
Errol Amateurs; Perth North End; Dundee Violet; Dundee 1930-35; Portsmouth 1935-38; Rangers 1938-47 (Scottish League 1939, 1947).
Educated at Perth Academy, which played rugby, Symon nevertheless preferred the round ball and worked his way up through junior football, playing for Scotland juniors in 1930 while at Dundee Violet. Later that year he signed for Dundee and developed into an influential half back, playing

either in the centre or on the flanks. After five years at Dens Park, he was sold to Portsmouth where he was elected club captain in 1936. However, his third season, in which he played alongside former Dundee team mate Jimmy Guthrie, ended in a narrow escape from relegation and in the summer of 1938 he returned to Scotland with Rangers. He spent the rest of his football career at Ibrox, although while waiting for the transfer to be negotiated he was in the news for an entirely different sporting achievement: he played cricket for Scotland against the touring Australians at Dundee, and took five wickets for 33 runs. It was September by the time he played for Rangers, and he showed such good form that he completed a unique international double by making his Scotland debut in December, against Hungary. His season ended with the league title, and he got married that summer, but then the Second World War intervened. He worked as a draughtsman in Linthouse shipyard, a reserved occupation which allowed him to continue playing for Rangers although by the end of the War he was only on the fringes of the team. He still contributed to another league title in the first post-war season before he retired in the summer of 1947. Immediately he embarked on an outstanding managerial career, starting at East Fife where he took the team to two League Cup victories, then at Preston North End where they reached an FA Cup final. That earned him the top job at Rangers from 1954-67, a period which brought 15 trophies and a European final, but he was unceremoniously dumped in 1967. His final position was as manager and then general manager of Partick Thistle, where he put together the team that beat Celtic 4-1 in the League Cup final of 1971. See his biography *Great Scot* by David Leggat.

T

Tommy TAIT (1/0, 1911)
Thomas Somerville Tait
Born 30 September 1879 Mountstewart Cottage, Carluke, Lanarkshire
Died 2 October 1942 Fraser Street, Cleland, Lanarkshire
Scotland v Wales 1911.

Wishaw Rovers; Petershill May 1899; Cambuslang Rangers Aug-Dec 1899; Airdrieonians Dec 1899-1903 (Second Division 1903); Bristol Rovers 1903-06 (Southern League 1905); Sunderland 1906-12; Dundee 1912-13; Armadale 1913-14; Jarrow Aug-Sep 1914; Armadale Oct 1914-15.

A right half, Tait was not the quickest of players but was very strong physically and had a knack for being in the right place at the right time to make a crucial tackle and win the ball. After bouncing around a few junior clubs, he joined Airdrie in December 1899 and by the time they won the Second Division title in 1903, several English clubs were angling for his signature. He chose to join Bristol Rovers that summer, and there he won another championship medal as they took the Southern League title in 1905. He was transferred to Sunderland the following year and made over 180 appearances in six seasons, although in 1909 he was one of 17 players suspended by the club for the 'crime' of joining the Players' Union. An amnesty was soon declared and he found his best form alongside the legendary Charlie Thomson in the half-back line. That led to his only Scotland cap in 1911 against Wales, aged 31, and he was a reserve against England the following month. As he approached the veteran stage he joined Dundee in 1912 and was unfortunate to break his wrist in only his second match which forced him to miss a couple of months. He moved on to Armadale and had a brief connection with Jarrow in 1914 before war broke out. He returned to Armadale and hung up his boots in 1915 but remained with the club on its board of management. He worked in the shipyards during WW1 and ran a Lanarkshire hotel in the 1920s. His son, also Tommy, played for Sunderland and Reading, among others.

Jack TAYLOR (4/2, 1892-95)
John Daniel Taylor
Born 27 January 1872 Clyde Street, Dumbarton
Died 21 February 1949 Grange Road, West Kirby, Cheshire
Scotland v Wales 1892, 1893; Ireland 1894 (1), 1895 (1).
Dumbarton 1889-94 (Scottish League 1891, 1892); St Mirren 1894-96; Everton 1896-1912 (FA Cup 1906); South Liverpool 1912-13; Wallasey Borough 1913-14.

Taylor joined Dumbarton as a 17-year-old and played a key role at outside right in the club's greatest-ever team, winning two league championships in 1891 and 1892. He was called into the Scotland team in 1892 and went on to win four caps, scoring the winning goal against Ireland in 1894, and also made six appearances for the Scottish League, including a goal in the first league international in 1892. He turned professional with St Mirren in 1894 and was in the prime of his career and an established internationalist when was signed by Everton two years later. It was to prove a perfect match as he made 400 league appearances for the Goodison Park side over 16 years, long enough to earn three benefit matches. Known as 'Honest Jack', he was captain of the Everton team which lifted the FA Cup in 1906 and played in the finals of 1897 and 1907. His top level career was effectively ended when he was struck in the throat by a ball during the FA Cup semi-final of 1910 and although he remained on the playing staff for another couple of years it was mainly in the reserves. Even when he was released aged 40, he wanted to carry on playing and spent a couple of seasons with local sides, ending up with Wallasey Borough in the Liverpool Combination. He worked as an insurance agent in the Liverpool area and died there in 1949 at his home named Alclutha, which was the ancient name for Dumbarton.

Joe TAYLOR (6/0, 1872-76)
Joseph Taylor
Born 16 December 1850 Wellington Street, Dunoon, Argyllshire
Died 4 October 1888 Victoria Terrace, Mount Florida, Glasgow
Scotland v England 1872, 1873, 1874, 1875c, 1876c; Wales 1876.
Queen's Park 1870-77 (Scottish Cup 1874, 1875, 1876).
Son of a hotel keeper in Dunoon, Taylor grew up in the town and was successful locally as a runner, winning numerous athletic contests at the Cowal Gathering in 1869 and 1870. When he came to Glasgow to work around that time, he joined Queen's Park and they soon made use of his athleticism, speed and leadership on the football field. He was selected at full back for the first Scotland international in 1872 and retained his place every year until 1876, captaining the side twice against England. He also won the first three Scottish Cups, the latter two as team captain. According to DD Bone: 'No man who captained the Queen's Park was so much respected both on the field and in private life. None hated unfair or rough play more.' After giving up playing in 1877, still only 26 years old, he continued his involvement with the club and was elected President for 1878-79, while he worked as a clerk for a drapery wholesaler. Sadly, he was struck down with pleurisy and tuberculosis and although he went to New Zealand in an attempt to clear his lungs, it was to no avail. He returned home to Mount Florida and died there in 1888, aged 37, leaving a wife and four children. Queen's Park met Third Lanark in a fund-raising match in aid of his family, and not only did 7,000 spectators turn out to pay their respects, Queen's Park added a further £50 to the fund. He is buried in Cathcart Cemetery.

'Cocky' TAYLOR (1/0, 1892)
William Kay Taylor
Born 30 November 1869 Grange Place, Causewayside, Edinburgh
Died 24 December 1948 Northern General Hospital, Edinburgh
Scotland v England 1892.
Dalry Primrose; Heart of Midlothian 1888-93 (Scottish Cup 1891) [guest for St Bernard's Apr & Aug 1890]; Blackburn Rovers Jan-May 1893; Heart of Midlothian 1893-1900 (Scottish League 1897); Leith Athletic 1900-01; Barholm Rovers 1902-03.
An effervescent character who was very popular among his fellow players, Taylor was a key player in a golden era for Hearts just before the turn of the century, although he had long periods in the reserves when his form dipped. Starting out with junior side Dalry Primrose, he was given a trial with Hearts reserves in the autumn of 1888 and by the following year had signed for the club. An outside right, he was mainly a creator of goals but could also net them and once scored four in a league match against St Bernard's. In his one international, his performance against England in 1892 was excellent, but the game ended in a heavy defeat and he was not selected for Scotland again. He was in the first Hearts side to lift the Scottish Cup in 1891 and his time at Tynecastle was only was interrupted in 1893 for an eventful half season at Blackburn, where the highlight was their 2-1 defeat of league champions Sunderland in the FA Cup. He was back in Edinburgh that summer but a run of poor form meant he missed out on Hearts' second Scottish Cup win in 1896, although he was back in the team the following season for a league title triumph. In his twilight years he spent a season with Leith Athletic before he retired in 1901. However, a year later he made a final appearance for Barholm Rovers in Creetown, who were drawn against Dundee in the Scottish Cup then scratched from the tie because of travel difficulties. Brought up in Causewayside on the southside of Edinburgh, he was a joiner to trade like his father, and never married.

Willie TELFER (2/0, 1932-33)
William Morton Telfer
Born 21 March 1909 Springhill Buildings, Stane, Lanarkshire
Died 15 May 1986 Law Hospital, Carluke, Lanarkshire
Scotland v Ireland 1932, 1933.
Blantyre Celtic 1927-29; Motherwell Oct 1929-41 (Scottish League 1932) [guest for Airdrieonians 1939-40, Dumbarton 1940-41].
Telfer was left half for Motherwell through their glory years of the 1930s, making over 280 league appearances. A stylish and creative player, he came to Fir Park from Blantyre Celtic in 1929 and slotted into the first team almost immediately. He remained a regular for the rest of the decade, missing just one game in their triumphant league-winning season of 1931/32. However, he was unlucky enough to miss long periods through illness and injury, suffering tonsillitis, a broken leg and a perforated ulcer at various times. He won two caps for Scotland against Ireland in 1932 and 1933, the latter of which was a poor home defeat which effectively ended his international chances. In addition, he made one appearance for the Scottish League against the Irish, in which he scored a rare goal. The league title was his only major club honour as he did not enjoy good fortune in the Scottish Cup: he played in the final of 1931, in which Motherwell threw away a two goal lead in the last ten minutes before losing the replay, missed the 1933 final through injury, and was in the side which was thrashed by Clyde in 1939. During the War he played as a guest for Airdrie and Dumbarton before retiring in 1941. He lived all his life in Shotts, where he was a taxi driver.

Bobby TEMPLETON (11/1, 1902-13)
Robert Bryson Templeton
Born 29 March 1880 Sandyknowe, Coylton, Ayrshire
Died 2 November 1919 Grange Knowe, Kilmarnock, Ayrshire
Scotland v England 1902 (1), 1903, 1904, 1910, 1912; Wales 1903, 1905, 1913; Ireland 1908, 1910, 1912.
Kilmarnock Roslin; Rugby XI 1897-98 [trials for St Mirren Mar 1898, Hibernian Apr 1898]; Aston Villa 1898-1903 (Football League 1900); Newcastle United Feb 1903-04;

Woolwich Arsenal Nov 1904-06; Celtic 1906-07 (Scottish League 1907; Scottish Cup 1907); Kilmarnock Oct 1907-13; Fulham 1913-15.

Templeton was a tremendously gifted left winger who was a delight to watch when he was in the mood and could equally be a frustrating failure, which resulted in him moving to some big clubs without settling at any of them. As a talented youth in Kilmarnock he was selected for the Scotland junior team and had trials for St Mirren and Hibs before signing for Aston Villa, who were then at the top of the English game. In his five years at Villa they won two consecutive league titles, although he played just once in the first of these, and a dozen times in the second as he could never establish himself as a regular. However, he was good enough to win his first cap, scoring after just three minutes of his Scotland debut against England in 1902, although strangely he failed to find the net again in ten more internationals. He was sold to Newcastle early in 1903, went to Arsenal the following year, then made a major impact at Celtic, where he won the league and cup double in 1907. Despite those triumphs they let him go to Kilmarnock, where he continued to be selected for Scotland and, for good measure, played three times for the Scottish League. He left in 1913 for a swansong at Fulham before he retired in 1915. One strange claim to fame is that Templeton once won a £10 bet to step into a lion's cage and twist its tail! He escaped unscathed at Bostock & Wombwell's menagerie in Kilmarnock on 22 August 1908, but he was not the first footballer to do so, as Andy Hannah had done the same trick in Liverpool in 1893. For about ten years he ran the Royal Hotel in Kilmarnock together with fellow internationalist Jim Young until he died of a heart attack aged just 39; Young then took over the tenancy but he too suffered an early death three years later.

Sandy THOMSON (1/1, 1909)
Alexander Thomson
Born 18 February 1877 Forsyth Street, Airdrie, Lanarkshire
Died 3 July 1959 Hartwood Hospital, Shotts, Lanarkshire
Scotland v Ireland 1909 (1).
Coatbridge Caledonia [trial for Albion Rovers Feb 1899]; Airdrieonians 1899-1916 (Second Division 1903).

An Airdrieonians legend who devoted his life to the club, Thomson was inside right for a generation at the start of the 20th century. Small in stature but a superb artiste on the ball, his first experience of football was with Albert School in the Airdrie Schools Cup, then he progressed to a local junior side and joined Airdrieonians in 1899. He played his first four years in the Second Division, then when the club won the title in 1903 they were elected to the First. Thomson only played three games in their first season upstairs, but after that he was almost ever-present until 1916, and in total played over 450 league matches. He helped to make Airdrie a team to be reckoned with, and four times they reached fourth place in the league. His only international recognition came against Ireland in 1909 aged 32, when he scored the third goal of a 5-0 win at Ibrox. Originally a coal miner, he later became an engineer in Airdrie and supported his local team all his life.

Alec THOMSON (3/0, 1926-32)
Alexander Thomson
Born 14 June 1902 Mitchell Street, Buckhaven, Fife
Died 12 November 1975 Low Pleasance, Larkhall, Lanarkshire
Scotland v England 1926; France 1932; Wales 1932.
Glencraig Celtic; Wellesley Juniors; Celtic Nov 1922-34 (Scottish League 1926; Scottish Cup 1925, 1927, 1931, 1933); Dunfermline Athletic 1934-37.

Signed from Wellesley Juniors, the same club as John Thomson (no relation), Thomson was a skilful inside right who barely missed a match for Celtic over a ten year period. Although it took him a year to settle into the club, once he was established in the team his creativity became indispensable for a side which was always in the top four during his time there. He could only celebrate one league title in 1926, which was also his best season for goals with 16, but he did win the Scottish Cup four times, and played in two other finals. In 1931 he was one of three Thomsons in Celtic's cup-winning eleven, alongside John and Bert. A provider rather than a scorer of goals, he had few opportunities on the international front and had to wait six years after his first cap, against England in 1926, before his next selection in 1932. However, he did make five appearances for the Scottish League between 1925 and 1930, three against the Irish then two against the Football League. As he drifted out of the picture with Celtic, they allowed him to move on to Dunfermline in 1934 but he found it a struggle with a team that was always battling relegation, and indeed they went down in his final season. A bricklayer to trade, he settled in Larkhall.

Andy THOMSON (2/0, 1886-89)
Andrew Thomson
Born 27 August 1865 Grahamston, Barrhead, Renfrewshire
Died 2 June 1936 Adamton Road, Prestwick, Ayrshire
Scotland v Ireland 1886; Wales 1889c.
Levern; Arthurlie 1882-88; Third Lanark 1888-94 (Scottish Cup 1889).

A calm and dependable full back, Thomson would surely have won further honours had his career not coincided with the peerless Wattie Arnott. Described by the *Scottish Referee* as 'one of the most respected and gentlemanly players that ever donned a jersey', he was brought up in Barrhead and joined local side Arthurlie as a young man. He was good enough to be selected for Renfrewshire in 1885 and was selected for Scotland the following year against Ireland, aged 20. He joined Third Lanark in 1888 and spent the best years of his career at Cathkin, with his first season being full of drama as he started 1889 with his arm in a sling after breaking his collar bone, then recovered in time to win the Scottish Cup final in February against Celtic. Two months later he was capped for the second time as captain of the Scotland side, one of six Third Lanark players in the team that faced Wales, likely in recognition of their cup victory. His only other representative honour was as captain of the Scottish League in 1893, but it ended in a surprising 3-0 victory for the Irish. He had a prosperous business as a coal merchant and as his commitments grew he gave up playing in 1894, apart from occasional friendlies. By then he had moved from Barrhead to Pollokshields, although his new home attracted attention of the wrong kind as his gold medals were stolen in a burglary. Thirds played a benefit match for him in 1898 against Preston North End. Eventually he retired to Prestwick, where he died in 1936. NB he is mistakenly listed in some books as two different players.

Charlie THOMSON (21/4, 1904-14)
Charles Bellany Thomson
Born 12 June 1878 Prestonpans, East Lothian
Died 6 February 1936 Drumsheugh Gardens, Edinburgh
Scotland v Ireland 1904, 1905 (2), 1906, 1907c (1), 1908c, 1911, 1914; Wales 1905, 1906c, 1907c, 1908c, 1909c, 1912c, 1913c; England 1905c, 1907c, 1908c, 1910c, 1912, 1913c, 1914 (1).
Prestonpans; Heart of Midlothian 1898-1908 (Scottish Cup 1901, 1906); Sunderland 1908-1919 (Football League 1913) [guest for St Bernard's 1915-16].

A giant of his era, Thomson barely missed a Scotland match for a decade and was a powerful centre half for just two clubs, Hearts and Sunderland. Brought up in a fishing community on the East Lothian coast, he played for his local team in Prestonpans before joining Hearts in 1898. Featuring mainly at centre half, although flexible enough to appear at full back or in the forward line, he won the Scottish Cup with them in 1901 and captained Hearts to another success in 1906. International recognition came relatively late and he was first capped by Scotland in 1904, aged 25, but his excellence made him a mainstay of the national team for the next decade. Instantly recognisable for his waxed moustache, immensely popular for his uncompromising approach, he was such a natural leader that he was named captain of Scotland against England in 1905 and in total was captain for 13 of his 21 internationals. Unusually for a defender he scored four goals for Scotland, the first three of them all penalties against Irish goalkeeper Billy Scott. He also made five appearances for the Scottish League, four of them against the Football League. To the despair of the Hearts support he was sold to Sunderland in 1908 for a £1,000 fee and despite having just turned 30 he went on to become a Roker Park legend. He was an integral part of the team considered the greatest Sunderland side of the century, making over 260 first team appearances. Their peak came in 1913, winning the Football League title and narrowly missing an FA Cup double by losing 1-0 to Aston Villa in the final. His career came to an end in the First World War and he played his last game for Sunderland in 1915. He returned to Scotland and played a season with St Bernard's in the Eastern League while running the Black Bull pub in his native Prestonpans, but in 1917 he was called up to the Army and served in Italy. He did not formally retire from playing until he was demobilised in 1919 and went back to his pub, remaining in charge until he died in a nursing home while undergoing treatment for a perforated ulcer, aged 57.

Charlie THOMSON (1/0, 1937)
Charles Morgan Thomson
Born 11 December 1910 Wodrow Street, Pollokshields, Glasgow
Died 8 May 1984 Liddle Avenue, Sherburn Hill, Co Durham
Scotland v Czechoslovakia May 1937.
Pollok; Sunderland 1931-46 (Football League 1936; FA Cup 1937) [guest for South Shields and Carlisle United 1939-40]; Spennymoor United 1946-47.

Thomson played all his senior football in England with just one club and, like his namesake above, he was a great servant to Sunderland. He made over 260 appearances for the club and was considered one of the best attacking right halves in the country when Sunderland won the League in 1936, then defeated Preston North End 3-1 in the FA Cup final the following season. However, he was regularly overlooked by the Scotland selectors and was awarded just one international cap. A few weeks after his cup success, he played against Czechoslovakia in Prague in May 1937 and although he was a reserve the following season he was not selected again by the time war broke out. As Sunderland closed down for the duration of the conflict, that effectively ended his top level career. He played as a guest for South Shields and Carlisle United before joining the Army in 1940, and as he saw active service for five years, some of it in the Middle East, his only football was in services teams. He did return to Sunderland when he was demobbed and played his last games for the reserves in 1946, then when he was released he signed for Spennymoor United in the North-Eastern League. A painter and decorator, he remained in the north-east for the rest of his life.

'Napper' THOMSON (1/0, 1920)
David Thomson
Born 4 September 1892 Hill Street, Dundee
Died 22 September 1955 Royal Infirmary, Dundee
Scotland v Wales 1920.
Fairfield; Dundee 1913-17; Dundee Hibernian 1917-18; Dundee Mar 1919-27.

Son of a blacksmith in Dundee's Hilltown, Thomson spent his entire life in the city and was a fabulous servant to Dundee FC. Known from an early age as 'Napper', his playing career started in midfield with junior side Fairfield, who won their league and three cups in his final season there, and it was no surprise that he stepped up in 1913. He was versatile enough to play anywhere but he soon settled into his preferred position at full back. When Dundee closed down in the War, he had a brief spell with Dundee Hibs while working in a local shipyard, and he was one of the first to be reinstated at Dens Park when the club got going again in 1919. The following year he made his Scotland debut in Wales, partnering Alec McNair in defence, but although he reportedly played well it turned out to be his only cap. However, he did make two appearances for the Scottish League in 1921, and the same year he earned a bumper benefit at Dens Park with Celtic providing the opposition. There were regular rumours of interest from English clubs but no offer came, and he spent the rest of his career in Dundee where the nearest he came to further honours was the Scottish Cup final of 1925, lost narrowly to Celtic. He was effectively forced to retire in 1927 when he wanted to leave Dundee and refused their financial offer, but as the club demanded a transfer fee and retained his registration he was frozen out. By the time he was released in 1930 there was no prospect of him playing again. Meanwhile, he took up cricket and played for Downfield in the Strathmore Union. For many years he ran a pub in Dundonald Street until the illness that led to his death in 1955. Over 250 mourners attended his funeral at Dundee Crematorium.

James THOMSON (3/0, 1872-74)
James John Thomson
Born 25 December 1851 Hilltop, Annan, Dumfriesshire
Died 21 July 1915 Broadlands Road, Highgate, London
Scotland v England 1872, 1873, 1874c.
Queen's Park 1871-74 (Scottish Cup 1874).

Thomson not only played in Scotland's first three internationals, he captained Queen's Park to victory in the first Scottish Cup final in 1874, and his achievements are recorded for posterity as his cap and medal are now in the Scottish Football Museum. Born near Annan, he came to Glasgow as a young man and took up football with Queen's Park just as the sport was developing. He played a major role in bringing the club to the fore and although he missed the 1872 FA Cup semi-final through injury he was usually at the heart of the team in the half-back role. He was also an all-round athlete, winning several events in Queen's Park's annual sports. Having made his contribution to the club's early successes, he left Glasgow for Liverpool in October 1874 to embark on a career in the meat trade and went on to become a highly successful businessman. He rose to be chairman and managing director of Eastmans Ltd, a major meat importer which had over 600 shops in the UK and substantial interests in Argentina. When he died in London in 1915 he left £46,000 in his will.

John THOMSON (4/0, 1930-31)
John Murie Galloway McCallum Thomson
Born 28 January 1909 Balfour Street, Kirkcaldy, Fife
Died 5 September 1931 Victoria Infirmary, Glasgow
Scotland v France 1930; Wales 1930; Ireland Feb 1931; England 1931.
Bowhill Rovers; Wellesley Juniors; Celtic Nov 1926-31 (Scottish Cup 1927, 1931) [loan to Ayr United Dec 1926].

In one of the greatest tragedies of Scottish football, Thomson was fatally injured at the age of just 22 while playing for Celtic just as he seemed destined to be one of the stars of the 1930s. Born in Kirkcaldy, he moved to a nearby mining village and went down the pits while developing his skills in Fife junior football. The 'Laddie frae Cardenden' was already recognised as an outstanding goalkeeper when Celtic signed him in November 1926, and although he was loaned to Ayr United for a couple of reserve matches, he was recalled in February and thrown into the Celtic first team when Peter Shevlin was dropped. He was such a success that he played in every match to the end of the season, winning the Scottish Cup in 1927 as an 18-year-old. From then until his death he barely missed a game, with just a few weeks out through injury in the spring of 1930. He made his Scotland debut in Paris that summer, keeping a clean sheet, and retained his place for all three home internationals the following season, conceding just one goal. He also made four appearances for the Scottish League. In the summer of 1931 he enjoyed a six-week tour of America with Celtic, having just won his second Scottish Cup, and was set for another glorious season. Then came that fateful September afternoon at Ibrox. Early in the second half he dived bravely at the feet of Rangers forward Sam English, whose knee crashed into Thomson's head. He was carried off the field and rushed to the Victoria Infirmary, but died five hours later of a depressed fracture of the skull. His death shocked the nation, and his funeral procession in Cardenden was watched by tens of thousands of mourners. His grave remains a place of pilgrimage to this day and there is a memorial display at Kirkcaldy Galleries including his last Scotland jersey.

Jock THOMSON (1/0, 1932)

John Ross Thomson
Born 6 July 1906 Balgonie Cottage, Thornton, Fife
Died 21 October 1979 Sunnyside Royal Hospital, Montrose, Angus
Scotland v Wales 1932.
Thornton Rangers; Dundee 1924-30; Everton Mar 1930-44 (Second Division 1931; Football League 1932, 1939; FA Cup 1933) [guest for Aldershot 1939, Aberdeen Jan-May 1940, Hearts Aug-Nov 1940, Fulham Oct 1940, Carnoustie Panmure 1941-44].

Thomson was a strapping left half who started out with his local junior side in Fife and joined Dundee in 1924, making his debut in unusual circumstances against Barcelona on the club's summer tour of Spain. He made his first competitive start in November that year but his next match was not until April 1926. However, once he was in the Dundee team he barely missed a game over the next four seasons. There were no trophies at Dens Park and his only recognition was one appearance for the Scottish League, against the Irish in 1929. That all changed after his move to Everton in the spring of 1930, which was the launchpad to a highly successful decade for the Merseyside club, although it began with a fruitless attempt to avoid relegation. His first three seasons brought an incredible run of success, with back-to-back titles in the Second and First Divisions, followed by the FA Cup in 1933. Less memorable was his one Scotland cap, a humiliating 5-2 home defeat to Wales in 1932 which was compounded by him scoring an own goal in the opening minutes. He lost his Everton place for a while to Joe Mercer, but eventually played nearly 300 games for the club and the decade ended with him captaining the side to another championship in 1939. Shortly after the outbreak of the Second World War he joined the Physical Training Corps as a Sergeant-Instructor and played for a variety of clubs and Army sides before settling with junior team Carnoustie Panmure while stationed on Tayside. He stopped playing in 1944 and returned to Everton as a coach after the War until he was appointed manager of Manchester City in November 1947. He gave up the job three years later when City were about to be relegated and left football to go into the hotel business, running the 19th Hole Hotel in Carnoustie. He retired in 1974 and lived in the town until his death five years later.

Bob THOMSON (1/0, 1927)

Robert Thomson
Born 23 September 1903 Woodlands Crescent, Falkirk, Stirlingshire
Died 28 December 1972 Stanhope Avenue, Finchley, London
Scotland v England 1927.
West End Amateurs; Laurieston Villa 1922-23; Falkirk 1923-27; Sunderland Apr 1927-28; Newcastle United Oct 1928-34; Hull City 1934-35; Racing Club de Paris 1935-36; Ipswich Town 1936-37 (Southern League 1937).

Thomson was a late developer, already 22 when he made his senior debut, which perhaps accounts for him knocking two years off his age and giving a false date of birth in later paperwork. A solid left back, not the tallest but tough and determined, he joined Falkirk in 1923 although he did not break into the first team until October 1926. He made a great impression and by the spring of 1927 was selected for the Scottish League against the Football League, then two weeks later for Scotland against England at Hampden. In the latter game he came up against the mercurial Dixie Dean, who pounced on Thomson's poor pass-back just before the end to clinch victory for the visitors. Despite this blunder, his performances had already attracted Sunderland who bought him the following week but he failed to settled at Roker Park and made just 22 appearances in a year and a half. In 1928 he was moved on to Newcastle United in an exchange for fellow Scotland internationalist Bobby McKay and he had a better time on Tyneside initially, then was dropped after a couple of seasons and spent three years mostly in the reserves. In 1934 he transferred to Hull City, although he wanted to leave after a season and the club, not unreasonably, demanded a fee so he went to France and coached Racing Club de Paris without appearing for their first team. A year later he wound up at Ipswich Town where he won the Southern League title in 1937 and was good enough to play for the Southern League representative team. He retired that summer and coached Ipswich until 1950, then managed Ajax in Amsterdam for two years to 1952. When he was dismissed, he returned to London and lived with his wife in Finchley until his death.

Bertie THOMSON (1/1, 1931)

Robert Austin Thomson
Born 12 July 1907 Buchanan Street, Johnstone, Renfrewshire
Died 17 September 1937 Argyle Street, Glasgow
Scotland v Wales 1931 (1).
Glasgow Perthshire; Celtic Oct 1929-33 (Scottish Cup 1931, 1933); Blackpool 1933-34; Motherwell Nov 1934-35.

Thomson joined Celtic from Glasgow Perthshire in the autumn of 1929, and made his debut shortly afterwards at outside right. He had ideal attributes as a winger with excellent ball control and a dogged determination to attack the opposition defence. He spent four years at Celtic Park, the highlights being two Scottish Cup victories, both against Motherwell. In 1931 his cross in the dying seconds of the final led to the own goal that gave Celtic a second chance, and he netted twice in the replay four days later. Two years on, his persistence led indirectly to the only goal of the 1933 final that won the cup for Celtic again.

Meanwhile he made his Scotland debut against Wales in October 1931, scoring once in a 3-2 win, and made two appearances for the Scottish League. However, his attitude to training got him into trouble at Celtic, and he was suspended by manager Willie Maley for two months in the autumn of 1932. Two games into the following campaign he was sold to Blackpool but made little impact there and came back to Scotland at Motherwell, again without fitting in and he was released at the end of the season. Now out of work, his domestic life took a downward turn and he was charged three times with assault, culminating in a conviction for stabbing his wife. To make matters worse, he suffered from heart trouble and at the age of just 30 he collapsed at home and died in his mother's arms. Fondly remembered by the Celtic support, thousands of them lined the streets to follow his funeral procession to Abbey Cemetery in Johnstone.

Sam THOMSON (2/0, 1884)
Samuel Thomson
Born 14 February 1862 Wellwood Row, Muirkirk, Ayrshire
Died 23 December 1943 Watling Street Road, East Ribbleton, Lancashire
Scotland v Ireland 1884, Wales 1884.
Lugar Boswell 1880-84; Rangers Feb-Mar 1884; Preston North End 1884-90 (Football League 1889, 1890; FA Cup 1889); Wolverhampton Wanderers 1890-91; Everton Aug-Oct 1891; Accrington Oct 1891-92.
Easily spotted due to his 'fair flowing locks', Thomson was a forward in the great Lugar Boswell side which won the Ayrshire Cup in 1881 and reached the final again two years later. He also played several times for Ayrshire, scoring a hat-trick on his debut against Edinburgh in 1881. While several of his team-mates were tempted away to bigger clubs, notably future internationalists John Auld, Jimmy McLaren, Jimmy McGhee and Jimmy Lundie, Thomson was the only one to be capped by Scotland while still with Lugar Boswell, selected against Ireland and Wales in 1884. Curiously in the two months between the internationals he played a few games for Rangers. That summer he went to Preston as a professional, playing mainly on the left wing but also at centre forward, and was a part of the 'Invincible' team that won the Football League and FA Cup double in 1889. He even scored the third goal in their 3-0 FA Cup final victory over Wolves. The next season Preston retained the league title but Thomson was lured away to join Wolves, for which the club was fined £50. By then he was starting to struggle due to ankle problems, the result of being kicked too often, and he only lasted a season at Wolves, then had short spells with Everton and Accrington before retiring in 1892. Having worked as a railway clerk before coming south, he settled in Preston and was landlord of the Bowling Green Inn, later called the Hotel Continental. In 1910 he was honoured for his bravery in rescuing two boys from drowning in the River Ribble.

Willie THOMSON (4/1, 1892-98)
William Thomson
Born 4 May 1868 Wester Ardoch, Cardross, Dunbartonshire
Died after 1911
Scotland v Wales 1892 (1), 1893, 1898; Ireland 1898.
Dumbarton 1888-93 (Scottish League 1892); Aston Villa Aug-Oct 1893; Newton Heath Oct 1893-94; Dumbarton 1894-98; Clyde 1898-1901.
Thomson started as an inside right with Dumbarton and took his time to progress from their second eleven, making just two appearances as they shared the Scottish League title in 1891. However, he was almost ever-present when they won the flag outright the following year, which was the springboard for a call-up to the national team and he scored for Scotland against Wales in the first minute of his debut in 1892. When he was selected again the following season this gave him the impetus to turn professional and he signed for Aston Villa in the summer of 1893. With no first team opportunities, he was transferred in October to Newton Heath, where he only managed three matches, all of them lost, and after just one disappointing season in England he came home to Dumbarton. Undaunted, he switched to centre half, an astute move which put him back in the international reckoning, and he made an appearance for the Scottish League against the Irish in 1895. Even after Dumbarton dropped out of the league in 1897, he won two more Scotland caps in 1898 when he filled in for Neil Gibson against Wales and Ireland. That summer he joined Clyde, where he spent the rest of his playing career before retiring in 1901. He was very much on the small side for a half back, so that the *Scottish Referee* rather cruelly remarked 'They say that little Thomson has been engaged by Barnum and Bailey as a companion to the dog-heading footballer.' He lived most of his life in Dumbarton High Street, never married, and worked as a gardener or labourer. His date of death is currently unknown.

Willie THOMSON (1/0, 1896)
William Thomson
Born 29 April 1874 Rosebank Road, Dundee
Died 12 December 1917 James Watt Dock, Greenock, Renfrewshire
Scotland v Wales 1896.
Clydemore; Our Boys 1892-93; Dundee 1893-96; Bolton Wanderers 1896-99; Victoria United Oct 1899; Bristol City Oct 1899-1900.
After a short time in juvenile football, Thomson stepped up to Our Boys, and then to Dundee following the merger between his old club and East End. He played at outside right in Dundee's first ever league match in August 1893, and remained with the club until he finished his apprenticeship as an electrical engineer in 1896. That year he won his Scotland cap, a 4-0 win over Wales at Carolina Port in his home city, and he took the opportunity to turn professional with Bolton Wanderers in the summer. After three years of First Division football the club was relegated in 1899, and he was released as his knee kept giving way. It was feared his career was over but he underwent an operation from one of the earliest sports specialists, HA Barker, and was able to return to action a few months later, playing briefly for Victoria United in Aberdeen before signing for Bristol City. However, he failed to make an impression and returned home the following summer. During WW1 he was an engineer in the port at Greenock and died of a fractured skull when he lost his balance and fell into the hold while working on the steamer Rio Preto in James Watt Dock.

Tom TOWNSLEY (1/0, 1925)
Thomas Townsley
Born 28 April 1898 King Street, Reddingmuirhead, Stirlingshire
Died 10 April 1976 Cottage Hospital, Peterhead, Aberdeenshire
Scotland v Wales Oct 1925c.
Laurieston Villa; Cowie Wanderers; Falkirk 1919-25; Leeds United Dec 1925-31; Falkirk Oct 1931-33; Bo'ness 1933-34; Peterhead 1934-38.

From a coal-mining family in Polmont, where his father was under-manager of Redding Colliery, Townsley worked at the pit himself until he was called up to serve with the Scots Guards in the final year of the War. He was fortunate enough to be too late to see active service, and on being demobbed in 1919 he joined Falkirk from Cowie Wanderers. He was an immense figure for Falkirk at centre half, made captain from 1922, and the following year he made the first of four appearances for the Scottish League, the last two as captain. Then in the autumn of 1925 he captained the full national team on his debut, but despite leading Scotland to an impressive 3-0 win over Wales in Cardiff he was not selected again. Transfer rumours had been rife for some time, with Falkirk rejecting interest from Newcastle, Sunderland and Blackpool, and a few weeks after winning his cap he was sold to struggling Leeds United for around £5,000. He made an immediate impact and helped them to escape relegation by a single point, but they did go down to the Second Division in 1927. Promoted at the first attempt, they reached fifth place two years later then were then relegated again in 1931, at which point he returned to Falkirk. The fans were delighted at his return, with the local paper saying 'Falkirk never possessed a more whole-hearted player or one who was more popular with the crowd'. He was released in 1933, spent a year with Bo'ness and was then recruited to join Peterhead in the Highland League, initially as player-coach then as manager from 1938 for many years. He liked it so much in the north-east that he spent the rest of his life in the town where he worked as a greenkeeper.

Alec TROUP (5/0, 1920-26)
Alexander Troup
Born 12 May 1895 Queen Street, Forfar, Angus
Died 2 January 1952 Brechin Road, Forfar, Angus
Scotland v England 1920, 1926; Wales 1921; Ireland 1921, 1922.
Forfar North End; Forfar Athletic Jan 1914-15; Dundee 1915-23 [guest for Ayr United Mar-Apr 1917]; Everton Jan 1923-30 (Football League 1928); Dundee Feb 1930-33.

The tenth and youngest child of a fish merchant in Forfar, Troup was enthralled by football from an early age and came up through the ranks of local juvenile and junior teams before making his debut for Forfar Athletic on New Year's Day 1914. After a season and a half of impressive performances in the Central League, Athletic closed for the War and he signed for Dundee, but as a plasterer to trade there was no escape from military service and he joined the Royal Engineers late in 1916. He played as a guest for Ayr United while training, then Sapper Troup saw active service in France and was not able to return to regular football until he was demobbed in 1919. When Dundee started up again that summer, he was able to embark properly on his football career and was such a great success on the left wing that he was called into the national team for the 1920 showpiece against England, when Scotland raced into a 4-2 lead then contrived to lose the match. A year later he won two more caps, against Wales and Ireland, and played twice for the Scottish League. A fourth cap followed in 1922. All this persuaded Everton to pay around £4,000 to take him to Goodison Park early in 1923, and they certainly got their money's worth with the highlight being the Football League title in 1928. He only made the Scotland team once more, against England in 1926, but it must be pointed out that he would surely have won more caps were it not for Alan Morton on the left wing, not to mention Adam McLean. Troup remained at Everton until the end of the decade, then made a triumphal return home to Dundee early in 1930. He hung up his boots in 1933 at the age of 38, having set up in business as a shopkeeper in his native Forfar, where he also worked as a plasterer. Sadly, he contracted throat cancer and died in his sleep aged 56. See his biography *Wee Troupie: The Alec Troup Story* by David Potter.

Thomas TURNER (1/0, 1884)
Thomas Turner
Born 10 October 1858 Kelburne Street, Barrhead, Renfrewshire
Died 26 July 1944 Alameda, California, USA
Scotland v Wales 1884.
Arthurlie 1877-1889 [guest for Third Lanark Apr-May 1884].

Turner was a one-club man, a goalkeeper for his local team Arthurlie for over a decade. He was good enough to be selected regularly for Renfrewshire and the Scotch Counties from 1879 onwards, but only won one full cap, for Scotland against Wales in 1884. The following month he played in goal as a guest for Third Lanark in their Glasgow Charity Cup matches but had the embarrassment of conceding eight to Queen's Park in the final. Towards the end of his playing career he also refereed matches, including a Scottish Cup semi-final. The eldest son of a Barrhead auctioneer, he was a banker's clerk in the town before he emigrated with his wife Isabel to the California coast in 1889. He worked as an accountant for the railroad in Alameda, near San Francisco, and spent the rest of his life there.

Willie TURNER (2/1, 1885-86)
William Martin Muir Turner
Born 25 April 1864 South Portland Street, Gorbals, Glasgow
Died 8 June 1936 South Bar, Troon, Ayrshire
Scotland v Ireland 1885 (1), 1886.
Pollokshields Athletic 1882-86 [guest for Edinburgh University Apr 1886].

The son of a stockbroker, Turner was educated at Glasgow Academy, leaving when he was 14 to start his business career. Having played rugby at school, he switched to the association game and came to the fore at Pollokshields Athletic where he was in the forward line. He played the first of several matches for Glasgow against Sheffield in 1883 and was called into the Scotland team in 1885, scoring the second goal in an easy victory over Ireland. He was capped again the following year but then appears to have given up the game aged 22 to focus on his growing business as a wine merchant. He lived in Dumbreck and played tennis for Pollokshields, reaching the final of the West of Scotland championship in 1890, then later in life he moved to a large house on the outskirts of Troon where he and his wife played golf.

U

Duncan URQUHART (1/0, 1933)
Duncan Urquhart
Born 18 August 1908 Wardlaw Street, Gorgie, Edinburgh
Died 28 April 1956 Watson Crescent, Ardmillan, Edinburgh
Scotland v Wales 1933.
Newtongrange Star; Hibernian 1928-35 (Division Two 1933); Aberdeen Sep 1935-37; Barnsley Sep-Oct 1937; Barrow Oct 1937-38; Forfar Athletic Oct 1938; Clapton Orient Oct-Dec 1938.

A solid and dependable left back, Urquhart gave great service to Hibs but found he could not replicate his form elsewhere. Having joined them from Newtongrange Star, the early years of his senior career were a challenge as Hibs struggled near the foot of the First Division table and were relegated in 1931. It took them two years to return to the top flight and after they won the Second Division championship in 1933, Urquhart won his Scotland cap that autumn as a late replacement for Peter McGonagle, making up an all-Edinburgh defence alongside Harkness and Anderson of Hearts. He started out the 1935/36 season as Hibs captain, but with the team struggling in the league, he was unsettled by barracking from the crowd and the club agreed to give him a free transfer. He was snapped up by Aberdeen, but in two seasons played just six league games and he never regained the form which put him in international contention. In 1937, after Aberdeen had finished second in the league and reached the club's first Scottish Cup final, he was released to join Barnsley, and after a few reserve games he moved on again, this time to Barrow. They let him go the following summer, and although Forfar and Clapton Orient gave him trials, he ended his football career aged 30. He came home to Edinburgh where he worked as a labourer in a chemical works until his death, aged 47.

V

Tom VALLANCE (7/0, 1877-81)
Thomas Vallance
Born 27 May 1856 Succoth Farm, Cardross, Dunbartonshire
Died 16 February 1935 Pitt Street, Blythswood, Glasgow
Scotland v England 1877, 1878, 1879, 1881; Wales 1877, 1879, 1881c.
Rangers 1872-84.

One of the earliest stars of Rangers, Vallance was not only captain of the team, he was inextricably linked to the club's growth and early success. He grew up on the banks of the Gareloch before he came to Glasgow to pursue a career as a mechanical engineer in a shipyard. Standing over six feet tall, he joined Clyde Amateur Rowing Club and then met up with friends who had recently formed Rangers Football Club on Glasgow Green. He was soon hooked on the game, became an outstanding full back, and led the team to their first major final, the Scottish Cup of 1877. The same year he won his first two caps for Scotland and went on to play four times against England, including the crushing victories of 7-2 in 1878 and 6-1 in 1881, and in three wins over Wales. With Rangers, he was in the first side to win a trophy, the Glasgow Charity Cup in 1879, with his younger brother Alick also in the team. His stature in the game was clear in 1880 when he took over the management of the Scotch-Canadian team after the death of SFA secretary

William Dick. A talented all-round athlete, he even set a Scottish long jump record at the Queen's Park sports in 1881. The following year he went to Assam to manage a tea plantation but soon fell victim to fever and dysentery and was forced to return home. Although his playing days were essentially over, he rejoined Rangers and did make a few more first team appearances, but his chief worth was as club President from 1883-89. Rather than returning to his engineering career, he went into the drinks trade and for many years he ran the Club Restaurant in Glasgow with his wife Marion. Sadly, their son Harold was killed in WW1. A talented artist whose pictures were exhibited at the Royal Scottish Academy, Vallance died of a stroke at home in 1935.

Alex VENTERS (3/0, 1933-39)
Alexander Venters
Born 9 June 1913 Stenhouse Street, Cowdenbeath, Fife
Died 30 April 1959 West Park Street, Cowdenbeath, Fife
Scotland v Ireland 1933; England 1936, 1939.
South End Rovers; St Andrews United; Cowdenbeath Dec 1930-33; Rangers Nov 1933-46 (Scottish League 1934, 1935, 1937, 1939; Scottish Cup 1935, 1936); Third Lanark Feb 1946-47; Blackburn Rovers Feb 1947-48; Raith Rovers Jan-May 1948.
The son of a Cowdenbeath player, Venters first came to the fore with his home town team at inside forward, playing on the left or right. He had superb ball control and was still only 20 when he was capped against Ireland in September 1933. He joined Rangers for around £2,000 a few weeks later and by the end of the season was part of a title-winning side. That was followed by three more league titles and two Scottish Cups before the end of the decade. He developed a reputation for one of the hardest shots in football and although for most his career he supported the centre forward, he had a much more direct role in 1938-39 when he was Scottish football's top scorer with 35 league goals. Meanwhile he added to his international tally with two more caps, against England in 1936 and 1939, and made five appearances for the Scottish League. During the War he remained in Glasgow and won numerous trophies with Rangers, also playing in four unofficial Scotland matches. By 1945 he had drifted out of the team and he wound down his career at Third Lanark, Blackburn Rovers and Raith Rovers before retiring in 1948. He ran a pub for a while before returning to his original trade as a compositor in the newspaper industry, but died of a heart attack at home, aged just 45.

W

Tom WADDELL (6/2, 1891-95)
Thomas Smith Waddell
Born 9 September 1870 Hilton Terrace, Crosshill, Glasgow
Died 31 January 1956 Main Road, Elderslie, Renfrewshire
Scotland v Ireland 1891 (1), 1893, 1895; England 1892, 1893 (1), 1895.
Victoria; Queen's Park 1889-97 (Scottish Cup 1893) [guest for Corinthians Apr 1892, St Bernard's May 1893].

Son of a restauranteur, Waddell was educated at Glasgow High School along with two other future internationalists, Willie Gulliland and Willie Lambie, and they all went on to great success together at Queen's Park. Like his friends, Waddell started out with Victoria on the south side of Glasgow and stepped up to Queen's Park in 1889. He made his first team debut the following year and made such an impression in his first season that he was selected for Scotland, scoring in a 2-1 win against Ireland in 1891. His team also won the Glasgow Charity Cup. In 1892 his goal put Queen's Park ahead in the Scottish Cup final, only for Celtic to then score five, but he did win the cup the following year in a forward line that contained his old friends Gulliland and Lambie. He played once as a guest for Corinthians, scoring against Renton, and for St Bernard's in the Rosebery Charity Cup final of 1893. Meanwhile he continued his Scotland career, scoring against England in 1893 despite suffering from toothache, and won his last two caps in 1895. That summer he was laid low for several months by pleurisy, which ended his top level involvement although he did recover sufficiently to play friendlies and recreational matches until the turn of the century. He was voted onto the Queen's Park committee and followed a professional career as a partner in a machine tool engineering company, Clifton and Waddell, based in Johnstone, Renfrewshire.

Hughie WALES (1/0, 1932)
Hugh Morrison Wales
Born 6 May 1910 Garnock View, Kilwinning, Ayrshire
Died 12 April 1995 Foothills Hospital, Calgary, Alberta, Canada
Scotland v Wales 1932.
Kilwinning Rangers; Motherwell 1929-46 (Scottish League 1932) [guest during WW2 for Charlton Athletic 1943-45, Chelsea Sep 1943, Aldershot 43-44 (one game), Crystal Palace 44-45 (one game)]; Elgin City player-manager 1946-47; Winnipeg Scottish player-coach 1948-49.
An attack-minded half-back, Wales was much in demand as a junior at Kilwinning but as his father was a friend of Motherwell manager John Hunter, that is where he went as a 19-year-old in 1929. He spent almost all his career at Fir Park, playing over 300 league matches in their golden era and was usually good for two or three goals a season as he could shoot with power and accuracy from distance. He was part of the team that won the Scottish League title in 1932 but his only cap later that year was less memorable, as it was the astonishing 5-2 home defeat for Scotland against Wales. He also played in three Scottish Cup finals for Motherwell which were all lost. He spent the first year of the Second World War in a munitions factory then served as an anti-aircraft gunner with the Army, appearing mainly for services teams. However, he did play for his club when

he could, and when training in the London area he featured for Charlton Athletic and sporadically for other sides. For two years he was stationed in Egypt where he spotted Willie Redpath in a services team and recommended him to Motherwell, who promptly signed the future international. When he left Fir Park in 1946 he had a brief spell as player-coach at Elgin before emigrating to Canada with his family; it was something of a homecoming as he had met his wife Hazel in Canada in 1933 while visiting his brother there. They settled in Winnipeg where he coached and played for Winnipeg Scottish, and he was later head coach for Luxton High School. He moved in 1965 to Calgary where he was employed by Aquitaine Oil until his retirement, and spent his later years playing competitive curling.

Frank WALKER (1/0, 1922)
Francis Gemmell Fulton Walker
Born 11 April 1897 Meikle Cloak, Lochwinnoch, Renfrewshire
Died 10 June 1949 Civil Service Nursing Home, Drummond Place, Edinburgh
Scotland v Wales 1922.
Paisley Grammar School FP; Queen's Park 1916-19; Third Lanark Nov 1919-26.

A versatile forward who could play on either side although his preferred position was inside left, Walker played for his Former Pupils' club on leaving school, and was attracted to Hampden as his brothers were already at Queen's Park. However, he hardly played for the club as he was sent to Harrogate for a year's Civil Service training and did not come back to Glasgow until 1916. He soon made the first eleven, but not long afterwards he was called up and joined the Royal Field Artillery, being posted to the front in the autumn of 1917. He spent nearly two years in France and Germany, then when he came home was persuaded to turn professional with Third Lanark where his brother Jim was now settled. He had six good years at Cathkin without winning any club honours, but was recognised in representative teams. He played for Glasgow against Sheffield in 1920 and 1921, and was a travelling reserve for two internationals before finally winning a Scotland cap in 1922, as Wales won 2-1 in deep snow at Wrexham. When Third Lanark were relegated in 1925, after a disastrous collapse from fifth place in January, he tried to retire at that point but was persuaded to return in January 1926. He was unfit after nine months out of the game and shortly before the end of a match against Bathgate he broke his leg in a collision with Willie Cringan and his career was definitively over. He was one of the earliest players to write a volume of memoirs, and published *Some Football Reminiscences* in 1928 in conjunction with Third Lanark Supporters Club. An Inspector of Taxes with the Inland Revenue, he lived in Edinburgh's Fairmilehead until his death aged 52, of complications following a stomach operation.

George WALKER (4/0, 1930-31)
George Walker
Born 24 May 1909 Ship Inn, Musselburgh, Midlothian
Died 14 April 1986 Wharfedale Hospital, Otley, Yorkshire
Scotland v France 1930; Ireland Feb 1931; Austria 1931; Switzerland 1931.
Rosslyn Juniors; St Mirren Nov 1926-33; Notts County 1933-36; Crystal Palace 1936-39; Watford 1939-40.

Football certainly ran in the Walker family as he was a nephew of the great Bobby Walker, who was a partner with his father George in the Ship Inn, his birthplace. Signed by St Mirren in autumn 1926 as a raw 17-year-old junior, he soon found himself in the side as a replacement for centre half Willie Summers who had left for Bradford. Despite his youth he settled immediately and was such a success that he was almost ever-present for the next six years, making over 200 league appearances. His good form earned international recognition and he made his Scotland debut in Paris in 1930 in the week of his 21st birthday. All four of his caps were away from home, and while he could be pleased with his defensive efforts in the first two, with clean sheets against France and Ireland, the continental tour of 1931 started with a humiliating 5-0 defeat to Austria. He was dropped for the Italy game and returned to face Switzerland. He also made two appearances for the Scottish League against the Irish in 1931 and 1932. Financial troubles at St Mirren forced the club to sell him to Notts County in 1933, clearing their overdraft and giving the player his first taste of English football. He was made captain but had joined a struggling team, who were relegated in his second season and he spent the last five years of his career in the Third Division South, going from Notts County to Crystal Palace, again as captain, and had just gone to Watford when the Second World War broke out. He joined the RAF shortly afterwards and was involved in aircraft production until he was put on service duties from 1942. In 1945 he won a golf match for the RAF against Oxford University. As the son of a publican, he was well placed to go into the licensed trade and ran a pub in Otley, where he lived until his death. Curiously in 1935 both of his sisters married footballers on the same day in Glasgow: Jenny to Bobby Hogg of Celtic, and Mary to Tom Fenner of Bradford City.

John WALKER (5/1, 1895-1904)
John Walker
Born 24 August 1873 Fortissat, Salsburgh, Lanarkshire
Died 17 February 1937 Pilot Mound, Manitoba, Canada
Scotland v Ireland 1895 (1), 1898, 1904; Wales 1897, 1904.
Armadale; Heart of Midlothian 1893-98 (Scottish League 1895, 1897; Scottish Cup 1896); Liverpool 1898-1902 (Football League 1901); Rangers 1902-05; Morton 1905-06.

Walker was brought up in the mining communities of central Scotland, and worked as a pithead labourer in Torphichen before football took over. He played with nearby Armadale as a young man then signed for Hearts in 1893, going on to a highly successful five years with the club. Playing on the left of the forward line, usually in the inside position, he won two league titles and notably scored twice in the match in February 1895 when the first championship was secured with a 4-0 win over Celtic. He was in the Hearts side which won the Scottish Cup in 1896, defeating local rivals Hibs 3-1 in the final. Meanwhile he made his international debut in 1895, scoring twice against Ireland, and some reports credit him with another against Wales in 1897, but his shot was deflected in off the head of Welsh defender WR Jones for an own goal. After a third cap in 1898 Hearts sold him to Liverpool for £350, and he won another league title at Anfield in 1901. Coming back to Scotland a year later with Rangers, he was denied a final major honour as he scored in the drawn Scottish Cup final of 1903 and played in the replay, but was out injured when Rangers lifted the cup in the second replay. He was a losing finalist the following year. However, he could be consoled with two more Scotland caps in 1904, after a six year gap. He also played five times for the Scottish League, spread over eight years, and for Glasgow against Sheffield in 1904. His last club was Morton where his playing career was ended by a knee injury in 1906. He emigrated to Canada in 1910, and worked in Winnipeg for Manitoba Telephones, then during WW1 he returned home to serve with the Signal Corps of the Canadian Engineers, and was sent to France in the dying months of the conflict with the 1st Tramways Company. In 1925 he moved to Louise County in Manitoba where he took up farming with his elder brother Thomas and two sisters. Sadly, he died in 1937 after an accident with a motorised saw, when he was struck by a slipped pulley belt.

Jock WALKER (9/0, 1911-13)
John Walker
Born 17 November 1883 Wilson Street, Beith, Ayrshire
Died 16 December 1968 Manchester Road, Swindon, Wiltshire
Scotland v Wales 1911, 1912, 1913; Ireland 1911, 1912, 1913; England 1911, 1912, 1913.
Burnbank Athletic; Raith Rovers Nov 1903-04; Beith 1904-05; Rangers 1905-07 [loans to Beith Nov-Dec 1905; Ayr Parkhouse May 1906; Cowdenbeath 1906-07]; Swindon Town 1907-13 (Southern League 1911); Middlesbrough 1913-21 [guest for Swindon Town 1915-16]; Reading 1921-23.
A full back who was renowned for his uncompromising tackling and commitment, it took a while for Walker's career to get underway. He was 20 when he stepped up from Burnbank juniors to Raith Rovers, and although he had a couple of runs in the team the following summer he came home to Beith, then in the Scottish Combination. Raith had retained his league registration so they were able to demand a fee when Rangers signed him in 1905 but he was in and out of the side at Ibrox, and they allowed him to return to Beith for cup-ties, then farmed him out to Cowdenbeath. The Fife side immediately appointed him captain and finally he started to show his true potential, sufficient for Swindon Town to buy him from Rangers in the summer of 1907. His career took off at Swindon and he not only won the Southern League title in 1911, the club finished runners-up three times and twice reached the semi-final of the FA Cup. This kind of form could not be ignored and he played in nine consecutive Scotland matches from 1911 to 1913, and made four appearances for the Southern League. Middlesbrough paid £1,200 for him in the summer of 1913, then when the club stopped for the War in 1915 he was loaned back to Swindon until they, too, ceased operations. In October 1917 he was convicted at Wiltshire Assizes of sexual assault on a girl and sentenced to 12 months in prison with hard labour. Somewhat surprisingly from a modern perspective, on his release he was able to resume at Middlesbrough for their first post-war season in 1919 and two years later he moved to Reading, where he ended his playing career. After retiring he applied to become a director of Swindon Town but was turned down. He focussed instead on running his fish and chip shop on Swindon's Manchester Road, where he remained for the rest of his life, and was so well known the junction was called Walker's Corner.

Bobby WALKER (29/8, 1900-13)
Robert Staig Walker
Born 10 January 1879 Dalrymple Place, Dumbiedykes, Edinburgh
Died 28 August 1930 Royal Infirmary, Edinburgh
Scotland v Ireland 1900, 1902 (1), 1903, 1904, 1905 (1), 1906, 1907 (1), 1908, 1912 (1); England 1900, 1901, 1902, 1903 (1), 1904, 1905, 1908, 1909, 1912, 1913; Wales 1901, 1902 (1), 1903, 1904 (1), 1905, 1907, 1908, 1909 (1), 1912, 1913.
Dalry Primrose; Heart of Midlothian 1896-1913 (Scottish Cup 1901, 1906).

Walker was a junior internationalist when he joined Hearts in 1896, aged 17, and went on to become the outstanding player of his era. A superb playmaker at inside right, he set a record caps total that stood for two decades until it was beaten by Alan Morton, and he would have won even more had it not been for a three-year hiatus between 1909 and 1912. He made his debut for Hearts in a title-winning season although he did not establish himself in the team until the following year. However, honours soon followed and he captained Hearts to the Scottish Cup in 1901 and won another medal in 1906, also playing in the finals of 1903 and 1907. For Scotland he made his debut in 1900 and by the time of his last cap in 1913 he had played 29 times, scoring eight goals of which the most memorable was the winner against England in 1903. Surprisingly, despite his leadership qualities, he never captained the side. Among his many other honours he made 14 appearances for the Scottish League between 1899 and 1911. He retired in 1913 and appeared in charity matches after that. For many years with his brother George he ran the Ship Inn in Musselburgh, where he was an active supporter of local football and regularly loaned his international jerseys for matches. He was a director of Hearts from 1920 and wrote a column for the *Daily Express*, but sadly died in 1930 aged just 51. Huge crowds turned out for his funeral at North Merchiston Cemetery and his obituary in *The Scotsman* said 'Hearts never had a more brilliant forward than Walker. He was amazingly clever in manipulating the ball and it was on skill alone that he relied, for he was never favoured with physique.' His brother Alex played for Hearts and Motherwell, his nephew George was a Scotland cap, while his son Robert fought with the International Brigades in the Spanish Civil War.

Tommy WALKER (21/9, 1934-46)
Thomas Walker OBE
Born 26 May 1915 Main Street, Livingston Station, West Lothian
Died 11 January 1993 St Columba's Hospice, Edinburgh
Scotland v Wales 1934, 1935, 1936 (1), 1937, 1938 (2); England 1935, 1936 (1), 1937, 1938 (1), 1939; Ireland 1935 (1), 1936, 1937, 1938 (1); Germany 1936; Austria 1937; Czechoslovakia May 1937, Dec 1937; Netherlands 1938 (1); Hungary 1938 (1); Switzerland 1946.
Livingston Violet; Broxburn Rangers; Linlithgow Rose Feb-May 1932; Heart of Midlothian 1932-46 [guest for Chelsea 1944-45]; Chelsea 1946-48; Heart of Midlothian Dec 1948-49.

A Scottish Schools internationalist, Walker signed provisionally for Hearts aged 16 and was released to play junior football for Linlithgow Rose until his next birthday. He went to Tynecastle in 1932 and was a regular in the team from 1933 onwards, going on to become the club's greatest inside right since his namesake Bobby (no relation). Although he won no major honours with Hearts as a player, he was immense for Scotland and made his debut aged 19. He had taken his total up to 20 caps by the time the Second World War intervened, yet he was only 24 at the time. He scored nine times for Scotland, including a nerveless penalty against England in 1936, and found the net in five consecutive internationals in 1938, the most notable being the winner at Wembley, the first goal ever scored live on television. He also played five times for the Scottish League. During the War he joined the Signals Regiment, playing regularly for the Army and he took a Tommy Walker XI on tour to India to entertain the troops. He played for Scotland in ten wartime matches, making an unusual contribution as he donated a set of his old Scotland strips to the SFA when they were short of clothing coupons. After being demobbed he won one more Scotland cap against Switzerland in 1946. That summer he was transferred for £6,000 to Chelsea, whom he had played for as a guest in wartime, and made over 100 appearances before returning to Edinburgh in 1948. Back at Hearts he was appointed as assistant to manager Davie McLean and made just one more first team appearance, then after McLean's death in February 1951 he became manager. He led Hearts to an extraordinary period of success, presiding over two league titles, the Scottish Cup and four League Cups, and his work was recognised in 1960 when he was made an OBE. After he resigned in 1966 he was briefly manager of Dunfermline Athletic and Raith Rovers, then served as a director of Hearts in the 1970s.

Willie 'Shoogly' WALKER (2/0, 1909-10)
William Walker
Born 18 January 1884 Gladstone Place, Yoker, Dunbartonshire
Died 2 May 1945 Eastern District Hospital, Duke Street, Glasgow
Scotland v Ireland 1909, 1910.
Glasgow Perthshire; Rangers 1902-03; Clyde 1903-07; Reading 1907-08; Clyde 1908-17; Clydebank Oct 1917-21; Fraserburgh 1921-23 player-coach.

A solid right half, known as 'Shoogly' for his artistic football, Walker was a promising teenager when he signed for Rangers in 1902 but failed to make an impression and managed just two first team appearances. After a season at Ibrox he joined Clyde, then in the Second Division, where he prospered and spent most of his career. Clyde were elected to the First Division in 1906, and although he spent a year with Reading in the Southern League he was soon back at Shawfield where he had his most successful season. In 1909 the club finished third in the league, while he was selected for the Scottish League against the Football League, then a month later he made his full Scotland debut in a 5-0 defeat of Ireland. The following year he was capped a second time against the same opponents but lost 1-0, while Clyde nearly won the Scottish Cup, leading 2-0 late in the final before Dundee equalised and won the second replay. He returned to Hampden for the 1912 Scottish Cup final, which ended in another defeat, this time to Celtic. Still, there were consolations with the Glasgow Charity Cup in 1910, another Scottish League appearance in 1912 and a Glasgow Cup victory in 1915. He moved closer to his home in 1917 to play for Clydebank, and spent four years with them, including their highest-ever league finish, fifth place in 1920. He ended his career with a couple of years coaching at Fraserburgh, who reluctantly let him go in 1923 for financial reasons. He returned to Glasgow and was living in Whiteinch at the time of his death in 1945. His brother Isaac played for Third Lanark.

Andy WATSON (3/0, 1881-82)
Andrew Watson
Born 24 May 1856 Georgetown, Guyana
Died 8 March 1921 Forest Road, Kew, Surrey
Scotland v England 1881c, 1882; Wales 1882.
Maxwell; Parkgrove 1875-80; Queen's Park Apr 1880-87 (Scottish Cup 1881, 1882, 1886) [guest for Corinthians Jan, Mar & Dec 1883, Mar & Dec 1884, Jan 1885; Edinburgh University Apr 1883 & Apr 1886; Brentwood Nov 1883; Battlefield Jan & Apr 1887]; Pilgrims 1882-83; Swifts 1882-85; Bootle 1887-88.
Watson is a remarkable figure in Scottish football history, not just because he was the first black player to be capped by Scotland but for the way he excelled at the game. His

international debut was a case in point, as captain of the Scotland side which defeated England 6-1 in London, a record away victory over the English which stands to this day. Born in British Guiana (now Guyana) to a Scottish sugar plantation manager and a local woman, he came to Britain as a boy and never returned to the land of his birth. Educated at King's College School in London, where he played rugby, he first came to Scotland in 1874 and matriculated at Glasgow University, although he dropped out after a year to set up a wholesale business. By then he had taken up association football and made his mark in five years with Parkgrove, where he was club secretary and was selected to play for Glasgow against Sheffield. He became such a skilful full back that he was invited to join Queen's Park in April 1880 and within weeks won his first trophy, the Glasgow Charity Cup. That summer the Scottish Football Annual gushingly described him as 'One of the very best backs we have; since joining Queen's Park has made rapid strides to the front as a player; has great speed and tackles splendidly; powerful and sure kick; well worthy of a place in any representative team.' That last point was confirmed the following spring when he was appointed captain of Scotland for the astonishing defeat of England, and two days later he helped Scotland to beat Wales 5-1. He also won his first Scottish Cup in 1881 and repeated the feat the following year. In 1882 he was one of seven Queen's Park players in the national team which thrashed England 5-1 in Glasgow, but this would prove to be his final cap as he moved to London that summer. This provided him with the opportunity for a broader footballing experience, mainly with Swifts but also for a variety of other teams, notably the elite Corinthians. He often returned to Glasgow to play for Queen's Park in important matches, including their Scottish Cup final success of 1886, until he went to Liverpool to focus on his career as a maritime engineer. On Merseyside he spent a final season playing for Bootle, notionally as an amateur although there were accusations that he was paid. He travelled the world on merchant ships until he retired around 1910, settling with his second family (his first wife had died young) in Kew, on the outskirts of London, where he died in 1921. His grave in Richmond Cemetery has recently been refurbished. See his biography *Andrew Watson, A Straggling Life* by Llew Walker.

Jimmy WATSON (6/0, 1903-09)
James Watson
Born 4 October 1876 Gracies Road, Windmillhill, Lanarkshire
Died 12 June 1942 St Joseph's Hospital, Victoria, British Columbia, Canada
Scotland v Wales 1903; England 1903, 1904, 1905, 1909; Ireland 1909.

Burnbank Athletic; Clyde Dec 1897-99; Sunderland Jan 1900-07 (Football League 1902); Middlesbrough Apr 1907-10; Shildon 1910-11.

Born and brought up in Larkhall, Watson spent three years as a junior at Burnbank where he played for Lanarkshire, and was given trials with Hearts and Sheffield United, while there were reports about interest from Everton. However, he ended up signing for Clyde in December 1897 and proved himself an excellent investment, described by the *Scottish Referee* as 'a tall swanky back of desperate do-or-die order. Not too particular as to his methods'. Sunderland bought him in early 1900 and he celebrated their Football League title in 1902. The following year he was capped for Scotland at left back, doing well against Wales in his first match, then four weeks later he put in an excellent performance in the 2-1 win over England where he neutralised his opposing winger, Harry Davis. He was retained in the Scotland teams against England for the next two years but both were lost. After seven seasons in Sunderland he went down the road to Middlesbrough, where he continued his good form and was called up for two more Scotland appearances in 1909, facing England and Ireland. When Middlesbrough narrowly escaped relegation in 1910 he concluded his senior career and played for a season with Shildon, a move which was made attractive by a tenancy at the Mason's Arms pub. A year later he went back to Larkhall before emigrating to Canada with his family and they settled in 1920 in Powell River, north of Vancouver, where he lived until his death.

James WATSON (1/1, 1878)
James Andrew Kennedy Watson
Born 21 February 1855 Main Street, Bridgeton, Glasgow
Died 24 May 1915 Maxwellton, East Kilbride, Lanarkshire
Scotland v Wales 1878 (1).
Rangers 1874-78.

An early recruit to the fledgling Rangers club by 1874, Watson played regularly in their forward line for over four years. He was in the side which reached the Scottish Cup final in 1877 but had the misfortune to head an own goal in the deciding third match. He was capped the following year and scored one of Scotland's goals in a convincing 9-0 win over Wales in March 1878 but stopped appearing in Rangers teamlines in September that year and appears to have retired. A played called J Watson subsequently played for Third Lanark, and made a few appearances for Rangers in the autumn of 1882, but it is not clear if this is the same man. However, he clearly retained a close link to the club as he served on its committee and was elected President of Rangers in 1890-91. In his professional life he taught English at Kelvinside Academy in the 1890s and 1900s, and was later headmaster of Calder Street School in East Kilbride. He never married and died in 1915 of pneumonia which he contracted after a scratch on the hand by a cat. He is buried in Cathcart Cemetery.

Phil WATSON (1/0, 1933)
Philip Watson
Born 23 February 1907 Shottskirk Road, Shotts, Lanarkshire
Died 26 March 1990 Aylminton Walk, Lawrence Weston, Bristol
Scotland v Austria 1933.
Wishaw Juniors; Hamilton Academical 1927-32 [guest for Solway Star May 1928]; Blackpool Feb 1932-37; Barnsley Dec 1937-38; Queen of the South Mar 1938-46.
Watson was a dominant centre half who was occasionally fielded as a centre forward which reflected his tendency to go forward when the opportunity presented itself. He joined Hamilton Accies in the summer of 1927 from Wishaw Juniors, and made nearly 200 appearances in five years at Douglas Park. He was soon recognised as one of the top defenders in the country and in 1930 he was a reserve for the Scotland team that faced France and played for the Scottish League in the autumn. Blackpool paid around £3,000 to sign him in February 1932 and he helped them to avoid relegation from the First Division by a single point, although they went down the following year. He won his Scotland cap in a 2-2 draw with Austria in November 1933, but Second Division football was hardly a recommendation for further honours. When Blackpool returned to the top league in 1937 he refused to accept terms and had a brief interlude at Barnsley which saw him make just four appearances before he joined Queen of the South. He enjoyed something of a revival in Dumfries as club captain, including a memorable victory over Rangers at Ibrox on the last day of the season which saved Queens from relegation in 1938. He remained with the club through the War but his career was interrupted by several years in the services, and although he returned in 1945 he retired the following year. He moved south to work as an operative in a mill in Bristol and retired to the suburb of Lawrence Weston where he died in 1990. From a noted football family, he was the son of Celtic player Philip Ross Watson (1881-1953), and his grandfather, also Philip, played for Dykehead in the 1880s.

Willie WATSON (1/0, 1898)
William Watson
Born 19 April 1873 Reken Dyke Lane, Westoe, Northumberland
Died 29 September 1929 Bridgend, Shotts, Lanarkshire
Scotland v Wales 1898.
Dykehead 1893-95; East Stirlingshire 1895-97; Falkirk 1897-98.
A goalkeeper who was capped by Scotland despite being born in England, Watson kept his birthplace a secret from the Scottish FA. He spent his early years in South Shields before moving to Lanarkshire with his mother and brothers in the 1880s after the death of his father. He worked in the coal mines around Shotts and became a goalkeeper with local team Dykehead, then signed for East Stirlingshire in 1895, helping the team to the Scottish Qualifying Cup final. By this time he was living and working as a miner in Falkirk, where he got married and started a family. Having represented Stirlingshire, he joined the town's other team, Falkirk in 1897 and performed well enough that season to win his international honour against Wales. For Watson, however, this was almost his final football act as he gave up the game in the summer of 1898 and returned to Shotts, where he was employed as a coal hewer down the mine. It was heavy work which probably contributed to his death of chronic bronchitis in 1929, aged 56.

Frank WATT (4/3, 1889-91)
Francis Watt
Born 16 February 1866 Waterside Cottage, Kilbirnie, Ayrshire
Died 29 August 1951 Firbank, Kilbirnie, Ayrshire
Scotland v Ireland 1889 (2); Wales 1889, 1890; England 1891 (1).
Kilbirnie 1885-95 [guest for Third Lanark Dec 1887, May 1891, Mar 1893; Clydesdale Harriers Feb 1889; Queen's Park Aug-Oct 1891; Rangers Jan-May 1892].
A legend in Kilbirnie where he was the town's only internationalist, Watt was a dashing right-sided forward with speed, strength and a reputation for accurate crosses. His first football success came when he captained Kilbirnie to victory in the Ayrshire Cup in 1888, although he had already won a number of prizes in local athletic meetings. After several appearances for Ayrshire, he was called up to the Scotland team in 1889 and his debut was so impressive, scoring twice in the first ten minutes against Ireland, that he was retained for the team to face Wales five weeks later. The following year he was capped again for the Wales match then in 1891 he lined up against England and scored a few minutes from the end but it was too late to prevent a 2-1 defeat. He was much sought after by English clubs and was reported to have signed for Halliwell in the summer of 1889, and to have been offered £200 cash in hand from Everton. However, he refused all inducements as he was in business and wanted to remained amateur. As he was often in Glasgow on business, occasionally he turned out for Third Lanark, which earned him an appearance for Glasgow against Sheffield in 1888. Then in 1891 he started the season with Queen's Park where he partnered Willie Berry, played a few more games for Kilbirnie and appeared for Rangers in the second half of the season. After that he seems to have remained with Kilbirnie until he retired in 1895. One of seven brothers, he lived all his life in Kilbirnie where he was a coal merchant and was a prominent figure in the town. He was appointed honorary president of Kilbirnie Ladeside, the junior side which succeeded the old Kilbirnie team, and performed the opening ceremony of the town's golf course in 1925.

Willie WATT (1/1, 1887)
William Wallace Watt
Born 13 April 1864 Freeland Bank, Partick, Lanarkshire
Died 31 December 1943 Queens Drive, Crosshill, Glasgow
Scotland v Ireland 1887 (1).
Queen's Park 1881-88 (Scottish Cup 1884); Athenians 1887-88.
Watt was a forward for Queen's Park in the mid-1880s, although his top level career was short and he was rarely able to be sure of his place in the team. His style was too erratic as the *Scottish Referee* later recalled: 'Watt gave you the impression that he would outwit and outpace all opponents, and plunk the ball in the net, when, lo, like a child he stumbled over a blade of grass, fankled himself, and all his work was lost.' He was brought up on the

southside of Glasgow and joined Queen's Park as a young man, where he played mainly in the reserves for three years. He was due to make his competitive debut in the 1884 Scottish Cup final and strangely he ended up winning a medal despite not playing a match in that season's competition. Queen's Park were due to play Vale of Leven in the final on 23 February but when their opponents refused to turn up, the SFA awarded the cup to Queen's, who allocated the medals to the team selected for the day. Watt made his bow a week later, scoring the opening goal in the FA Cup semi-final win over Blackburn Olympic, and was retained for the final which was lost to Blackburn Rovers. The following year he partnered Willie Harrower in attack in most of the FA Cup ties but both were dropped for the final. Watt had to be content with winning the Glasgow Charity Cup in 1885, scoring the only goal of the final. His one international honour came towards the end of his career, against Ireland in 1887, a 4-1 victory in which he scored after five minutes. That autumn he played for an Edinburgh amateur side, the Athenians, then returned to Glasgow and turned out for Queen's Park Strollers. He appears to have given up football around 1888 and took up cricket instead, captaining Cathcart CC through most of the 1890s and acting as club secretary. The son of a ship owner, he followed his father into the industry and worked for J&A Allan, a major shipping company. He never married and died on the last day of 1943. NB he was mistakenly identified in Douglas Lamming's *Who's Who* as William Wilson Watt.

Willie WAUGH (1/0, 1937)
William Waugh
Born 2 February 1910 The Loan, Torphichen, West Lothian
Died 21 April 1974 Broomyknowe Drive, Livingston Station, West Lothian
Scotland v Czechoslovakia Dec 1937.
Durhamtown Rangers [trials for Bathgate Sep 1928]; Heart of Midlothian Dec 1928-42 [loans to Third Lanark 1929-32 (Second Division 1931); Hibernian Feb-May 1936]; Albion Rovers Jan-Apr 1943; East Stirlingshire 1945-46.
A safe goalkeeper, Waugh signed for Hearts at Christmas 1928 from Durhamtown Rangers, a juvenile team, having played a couple of league matches on trial for Bathgate. Rather than consign him to the reserves, Hearts sent him out on loan to Third Lanark for three seasons to gain experience, where he won a Second Division championship medal in 1931. However, even when he returned to Tynecastle in 1932 he rarely had a first team opportunity and made just four appearances in as many years before another loan spell at Hibs in the spring of 1936. The following season he was finally given a chance and was first choice at Hearts for three years, doing so well that he was called up to the Scotland team in December 1937 when Jerry Dawson was out injured, and kept a clean sheet against Czechoslovakia. There was speculation he might also play in the England match but the position went to Dave Cumming and Waugh was only named as reserve. He was still in the Hearts goal when war broke out, and although he continued to play when he could, he was allowed to leave in 1942. He played briefly for Albion Rovers, then two years later signed for East Stirlingshire for a final season, and was reported as being so keen to play that even a broken rib didn't stop him. He lived all his adult life in Livingston Station, and was a cousin of Tommy Walker (above).

Jamie WEIR (4/2, 1872-78)
James Biggar Weir
Born 23 November 1851 Thistle Street, Gorbals, Glasgow
Died 23 April 1889 Warrina Hospital, South Australia
Scotland v England 1872, 1874, 1875; Wales 1878 (2).
Queen's Park 1870-80 (Scottish Cup 1874, 1875, 1880).
Weir was a star forward for club and country throughout the 1870s, with a rare talent for ball control and dribbling, valued even in a passing team like Queen's Park. One frustrated opponent described how it was nearly impossible to tackle him as his bandy legs formed a 'crab-like circle' from which the ball could not escape, while the football writer DD Bone wrote: 'Who could dribble and keep possession of the ball like Weir? In all the contests Queen's Park engaged in for ten years, none was more popular among the spectators, and emulated by the young generation of players, than Weir.' He was one of the eleven Scots who faced England in the very first international in 1872 and went on to make four appearances for the national team, scoring twice against Wales on his last cap in 1878. He also won the Scottish Cup three times. Quite a character, he once entered a burning building on the way home from a night out and helped to rescue the occupants. The son of a housebuilder, he was a joiner for the family business but after his father's death in 1880 he emigrated to Australia, where he married. Towards the end of the decade he found work on the transcontinental railway being built from the south to the north coast, and early in 1889 he was based at Warrina, a remote construction camp about 620 miles north of Adelaide. Sadly, he contracted typhoid and died after a few weeks in the makeshift hospital.

John WEIR (1/0, 1887)
John Weir
Born 10 January 1865 Crossmyloof, Glasgow
Died 11 January 1946 Moorlands Infirmary, Rossendale, Lancashire
Scotland v Ireland 1887.
Wellpark; Third Lanark 1884-87; Liverpool Stanley Sep 1887; Bootle Sep-Oct 1887; Everton Oct 1887-90; High Park 1890-92; Rossendale 1892-95 player-coach; Rawtenstall 1895-96.
Weir worked as an apprentice blacksmith in Glasgow while playing football for Wellpark, and joined Third Lanark in 1884. A competent half back, he spent three years with the club and was selected for Scotland in the 4-1 win against Ireland in February 1887, also playing a week later for Glasgow against Edinburgh. After his marriage that summer he went to Merseyside, whether purely for work or because he was offered a football position is hard to say. He played briefly for Liverpool Stanley, then a few weeks at Bootle, before signing for Everton in October, much to the chagrin of his Bootle colleagues. They did not forget his disloyalty and he suffered a dislocated shoulder in a roughhouse of a match when the two sides next met. To make matters worse, he was then suspended for being a professional and had to sit out until the following autumn. However, he completed a full season for Everton in the opening year of the Football League, before suffering a

broken arm in September 1889 which forced him to miss several months. He came back to win the Liverpool Senior Cup in the spring of 1890 but was then released and this time he moved up the road to Southport where High Park, of the Lancashire Alliance, made him team captain. Two years later his next stop was Rossendale of the Lancashire League as player-coach, and his final club was Rawtenstall in the Lancashire Combination. Meanwhile he followed his trade as a blacksmith hammerman in Southport, before taking a less physically demanding job as a press operator with Lambert Howarth, a slipper manufacturer in Rawtenstall. He continued to live in Rossendale where he was club trainer for many years, and brought up a family of 13 children.

Jock WHITE (2/0, 1922-23)
John White
Born 27 August 1897 Deedes Street, Airdrie, Lanarkshire
Died 11 February 1986 Monklands District Hospital, Airdrie, Lanarkshire
Scotland v Wales 1922; Ireland 1923.
Ashfield; Bedlay Juniors 1919-20; Albion Rovers Jan 1920-22; Heart of Midlothian 1922-27; Leeds United Feb 1927-30; Heart of Midlothian 1930-34; Margate 1934-35; Leith Athletic Jan-Apr 1936.
The only Albion Rovers player ever to be capped, White had a delayed start to his senior career due to WW1 and served with the Royal Navy in the last year of the War. He was 22 when he joined Albion Rovers early in 1920 and, with his younger brother Jimmy alongside him in the forward line, immediately played a part in the club's run to the Scottish Cup final, which was lost 3-2 to Kilmarnock. Having proved himself as an outstanding centre forward or inside right, he made his Scotland debut against Wales in February 1922, and that summer Hearts signed him for £4,000 in the face of stiff competition from both sides of the border. It was a good investment as he was the Scottish League's top scorer in his first season with 30 goals and played for Scotland a second time, which turned out to be his last full international. However, he did make four appearances for the Scottish League, scoring five times. His strike rate for Hearts declined but in February 1926 he achieved the unusual feat of scoring four goals in each of three consecutive matches: cup ties against Dundee United and Alloa, then a league game against Hamilton. Early in 1927 Leeds United paid around £5,600 for him in a doomed attempt to save themselves from relegation, although they did bounce back the next year. By the time he left Elland Road in 1930, after over 100 league games, they were fifth in the First Division. He was welcomed back at Hearts and continued to bang in goals for another four seasons. In 1934 a lucrative offer took him to Margate for a year, then he played briefly for Leith Athletic before retiring. He worked as a blacksmith in Airdrie and spent his Saturdays as a scout for Hearts until the Second World War, in which he was a Police reservist. He spent the rest of his life in Airdrie and never married. As well as Jimmy, his other brothers Willie and Tom also played professionally.

Wattie WHITE (2/0, 1907-08)
Walter Logie White
Born 15 May 1882 Cowan's Row, Crookedholm, Ayrshire
Died 8 July 1950 Danehurst Street, Fulham, London
Scotland v England 1907, 1908.
Hurlford Thistle; Bolton Wanderers 1902-08; Everton Dec 1908-10; Fulham Oct 1910-23.

White was working in the Ayrshire coal mines when he was spotted playing junior football for Hurlford. He signed for Bolton Wanderers in 1902 and was soon featuring regularly at inside left and although his club was relegated in his first season, they reached the final of the FA Cup in 1904, lost 1-0 to Manchester City. That was followed by promotion the next season and his fine scoring record was good enough to earn a Scotland call-up in 1907. He was capped twice against England, both games ending as 1-1 draws, but later admitted that he was too nervous to enjoy the experience. After another relegation in 1908 he was transferred to Everton along with Bob Clifford for around £1,500, then went off the boil and in the autumn of 1910 moved to Fulham where he dropped to half-back. He spent over a decade with the London club, interrupted by active service in WW1 as a gunner with the Royal Garrison Artillery. He was wounded in 1918, spending three months in hospital, but recovered sufficiently to return to the game, and played until he was 40. He continued to be involved with Fulham as a handyman and lived locally until his death in 1950.

Andy WHITELAW (2/0, 1887-90)
Andrew Whitelaw
Born 19 May 1865 Levenbank Terrace, Jamestown, Dunbartonshire
Died 2 January 1938 Byron Street, Mansfield, Nottinghamshire
Scotland v Ireland 1887; Wales 1890.
Jamestown; Vale of Leven 1885-91; Notts County 1891-93; Heanor Town 1893-94; Leicester Fosse 1894-95; Heanor Town 1895-97; Ilkeston Town 1897-98.
A fast and hard-tackling right back, Whitelaw won two Scotland caps early in his career while at Vale of Leven, where his partnership with Johnny Forbes made the team a defensive powerhouse. He was captain of Vale for several years and reached the Scottish Cup final of 1890, only losing to Queen's Park in a replay. However, his time there ended in acrimony following a lengthy dispute and in the summer of 1891 he turned professional at Notts County, who needed a reserve because of their uncertainty about Thomas McLean's knee. It was a life-changing move for Whitelaw as he spent the rest of his life in the English Midlands. His two seasons at Notts County went well but he was allowed to leave in 1893 and embarked on a tour of clubs nearby. First, he spent a season with Heanor Town in the Derbyshire League, which they won along with the Derbyshire Senior Cup, but he was too good for this level and was recruited by Leicester Fosse. He was in and out of the team, so returned for a second spell at Heanor, by now in the Midland League and good enough to take Southampton to a replay in the FA Cup in 1897. The club

temporarily disbanded that summer which provoked another move to Ilkeston Town, where he played for a final season in the Midland League before retiring. He settled in Mansfield where he worked as an asphalter and married Elizabeth, daughter of the cricketer Fred Wyld.

Andy WILSON (6/2, 1907-14)
Andrew Wilson
Born 4 December 1878 Troax, Colmonnell, Ayrshire
Died 13 March 1945 Patterton Farm, Kilwinning, Ayrshire
Scotland v England 1907, 1908 (1), 1912 (1), 1913; Wales 1913; Ireland 1914.
Irvine Meadow XI 1897-99; Clyde 1899-1900; Sheffield Wednesday 1900-20 (Football League 1903, 1904; FA Cup 1907).

A strapping centre forward, Wilson spent two decades at Sheffield Wednesday where he made well over 500 appearances. Brought up on his father's farms in Colmonnell and Irvine, he was educated at Irvine Royal Academy but did not play football until he was in his late teens. Some friends encouraged him to join Irvine Meadow where as a left back he won the Ayrshire Cup and other local trophies. He changed position in the summer of 1899 when Clyde signed him as a makeshift centre forward and never looked back. He stood out in a disastrous season for Clyde which saw them relegated, so when a scout recommended Wilson to Sheffield Wednesday they paid £200 for his signature. It was a great investment, as although it took him a while to adjust to the speed of the English game, his goals helped Wednesday to consecutive league titles in 1903 and 1904 and the FA Cup of 1907. The same year he made his Scotland debut against England which ended 1-1, as did his second cap in 1908, in which he scored. He had to wait four years for his next call-up, yet another 1-1 draw with England in which he played alongside his brother David. By 1914 he had taken his caps total to six and strangely he was never on the winning side in an international as five of his games were draws and the other lost. During WW1 his appearances for Wednesday were restricted by work and injury, but he carried on playing until 1920, just before he turned 40, and still holds the club records for appearances and goals. He then embarked on a career in management, starting at Bristol Rovers where he recruited several of his former Wednesday team mates. He resigned in 1926 and had a year out before being appointed at Oldham Athletic for another five years, and concluded with a season at Stockport County. He then returned to the family farm in Ayrshire and died there of pneumonia in 1945. He related his life story in great detail in the *Star Green 'Un*, through the summer of 1915. As well as David (below), his brothers Jimmy and Alex were also footballers.

Andy WILSON (12/13, 1920-23)
Andrew Nisbet Wilson
Born 15 February 1896 Brown Street, Newmains, Lanarkshire
Died 13 October 1973 Hurlingham Mansions, New Kings Road, Fulham, London
Scotland v Wales 1920, 1921 (2), 1922, 1923 (2); Ireland 1920 (1), 1921c (1), 1922 (2), 1923 (1); England 1920 (1), 1921 (1), 1922 (1), 1923 (1).
Cambuslang Rangers; Middlesbrough Feb 1914-19 [guest during WW1 for Hamilton Academical Apr 1917, Dec 1917; Heart of Midlothian Jan 1918-19; Leeds City Apr 1918]; Dunfermline Athletic 1919-21; Middlesbrough 1921-23; Chelsea Nov 1923-31; Queen's Park Rangers Oct 1931-32; Nimes 1932-34 player-manager.

Wilson had a superb record as a Scotland centre forward, averaging over a goal a game, but his international career lasted just four years before he was eclipsed by Hughie Gallacher. The son of a policeman, he started out with Cambuslang Rangers where his scoring soon attracted attention, and he was once carried shoulder-high by his team mates after a Junior Cup hat-trick. He joined Middlesbrough for just £10 in 1914, in the face of stiff competition from numerous clubs although a few months later, having made little impact on Teesside, the War broke out and he signed up with the Highland Light Infantry. He was badly wounded by shrapnel at Arras and lost the use of his left hand and forearm but despite the handicap he returned to football, wearing a glove to hide his withered limb. He played for his regimental team and guested for Hamilton before joining Hearts, scoring over a goal a game for them in 1918-19 as they reached the Scottish Victory Cup final. He played in two of Scotland's Victory Internationals against Ireland and England in 1919, scoring four times, before making his full Scotland debut the following year. Meanwhile, in the summer of 1919, although he wanted to remain in Scotland, Middlesbrough refused to sell him, so he used a loophole to sign for Dunfermline, then in the Central League and therefore outside their jurisdiction. Nonetheless, he continued to be selected regularly for Scotland, scoring more often than not. Two years later in 1921, after he toured Canada and USA with a Scottish select, Dunfermline were admitted to the Scottish League and he was obliged to return to Middlesbrough. They sold him in 1923 to Chelsea for a record fee of around £6,500 and he made well over 200 first team appearances for the London side but did not earn any more caps. He ended his English career with a season at QPR and was then appointed player-manager of Nimes in France, before returning to manage Clacton Town, Walsall and later Gravesend & Northfleet. He also coached Chelsea and after retiring was elected President of Chelsea Supporters Club. A fine bowls player, he was capped by England in 1948.

Davie WILSON (1/2, 1900)
David Wilson
Born 21 February 1880 Pollok Street, Kingston, Glasgow
Died 20 June 1926 Bothwell Street, Blythswood, Glasgow
Scotland v Wales 1900 (2).
Langside Athletic; Queen's Park 1897-1906.

A sparkling inside forward, Wilson was just 17 when he joined Queen's Park from a local junior side and was thrown straight into the first team. He established himself as a regular and was good enough to represent Glasgow against Sheffield, then made his Scotland debut against Wales in February 1900. He was still only 19, a couple of weeks before his 20th birthday, and scored two first-half goals, but he was not selected again, although he later made two appearances for the Scottish League eleven. His season ended with a Scottish Cup final defeat to Celtic and that summer Queen's Park entered the Scottish League. He was one of their top scorers and almost ever-present for the first three years of league matches and also scored the only goal at the official opening of the new Hampden Park in 1903. However, that was virtually his last high-profile match as by then he was trying to focus on his legal career, following in the footsteps of his father as a solicitor in Glasgow. He played occasionally until 1906 then continued his involvement on the Queen's Park committee. He served with the Seaforth Highlanders in WW1 and died suddenly of a heart attack in 1926, aged just 46.

Dave WILSON (1/0, 1913)
David Wilson
Born 14 January 1885 Craig, Colmonell, Ayrshire
Died 9 April 1959 Finsbury Park Road, London
Scotland v England 1913.
St Mirren 1901-04; Hamilton Academical Aug-Nov 1904; Bradford City Nov 1904-06; Oldham Athletic 1906-21 [guest for Stockport County Nov 1918, Chesterfield May 1919]; Nelson 1921-24 player-manager (Third Division North 1923).

Just 16 when he joined St Mirren in 1901, Wilson had a brief association with Hamilton Accies as a centre forward and two years at Bradford City before settling at Oldham Athletic in 1906. He became a club legend and played 264 consecutive league matches, a record which stood for many years, and in total over 500 senior games at half-back for Oldham over 15 years. His only Scotland cap came against England in 1913, in the same match as his brother Andy (above), the last time two brothers played together for Scotland until Jock and Davie Shaw in 1946. During WW1 he was exempted from military service and ran a tobacconist shop in Oldham, playing for the side whenever he could. He was caught up in an attempted bribery case in 1917 and gave evidence in court, and at the same time he had domestic trouble as he divorced his wife for adultery. He thought about retiring in 1920, decided to commit himself for another season and left Oldham the following summer, only to be immediately snapped up by Nelson, newly admitted to the Third Division. They appointed Wilson as player-manager and he led the club to an unexpected triumph, winning the Third Division North title in his second season, but the club was out of its depth in the Second Division and came straight back down. He finally hung up his boots in 1924 on their return to the Third and continued managing Nelson for one more year, when he resigned as he felt the club directors were interfering too much. After working as a stockbroker in Blackpool he had a surprise appointment as manager of Exeter City in 1928 but was dismissed in February 1929. His next stop was as coach of Stuttgarter Kickers in Germany for a season, after which he left the game for good. He spent the rest of his life with his second wife in north London, where he worked in the grocery trade. In addition to Andy (see above), two other brothers were prominent players, Jimmy for St Mirren and Preston, Alex for Preston and Oldham.

Geordie WILSON (6/0, 1904-09)
George Williamson Wilson
Born 8 September 1883 Berry Street, Lochgelly, Fife
Died 31 May 1960 West 15th Avenue, Vancouver, British Columbia, Canada
Scotland v Wales 1904, 1906; Ireland 1905; England 1905, 1907, 1909.
Buckhaven; Cowdenbeath 1902-03; Heart of Midlothian 1903-06 (Scottish Cup 1906); Everton 1906-07; Distillery Aug-Nov 1907; Newcastle United Nov 1907-1915 (Football League 1909; FA Cup 1910); Raith Rovers 1915-20; East Fife 1920-21 (Scottish Qualifying Cup 1920); Vancouver St Andrew's 1923-24 player-manager.

Wilson was a tricky left winger, small in stature but strongly built and fast. After coming up through local sides in Fife, he was signed by Hearts from Cowdenbeath in 1903, and was such an immediate success that he made his Scotland debut against Wales later that season. Further caps followed in 1905 against Ireland and England, and shortly after his fourth cap in 1906 he achieved legendary status by scoring the winning goal for Hearts to defeat Third Lanark in the Scottish Cup final. He was transferred to Everton that summer, but despite a fine season and another Scotland cap, he was dropped from their FA Cup final team after a dispute with the directors. They sent him on loan to Distillery until they worked out what to do with him and it turned out to be a blessing for the player as he thrived in Ireland and was even picked to play for the Irish League. Soon Newcastle United came in with a record transfer fee of £1,600 which was the springboard for eight marvellous seasons on Tyneside in which he picked up League and Cup winner's medals, not to mention playing in two other FA Cup finals. When Newcastle closed down for the War in 1915, he returned to Fife and worked as a miner while playing for Raith Rovers, also running a hairdressing salon in Kirkcaldy. Having initially been given military exemption, he was called up in 1917 and served as a merchant seaman until the spring of 1919, which meant missing two full seasons. He made only sporadic appearances for Raith Rovers on his return, and signed for East Fife in 1920, winning another medal when his goal helped them to win the Scottish Qualifying Cup. He emigrated to Canada in 1922 and the following year was appointed player-manager of St Andrew's in Vancouver, winning the British Columbia Cup aged 40. By 1926 he was back in Scotland and took up the reins as manager of Raith Rovers, winning promotion for the side in his first season before resigning midway through the second due to ill health. He emigrated to Vancouver for a second time and remained there for the rest of his life. Ironically, he died while his old club Hearts were in Vancouver, as they played tour matches there on 28 May and 4 June.

Hugh WILSON (1/0, 1885)
Hugh Wilson
Born 5 August 1859 New Road, Mauchline, Ayrshire
Died 14 December 1946 Westonlee Terrace, Dumbarton
Scotland v Wales 1885.
Mauchline 1877-84; Dumbarton 1884-86.
Remarkably, Wilson has been missing from the Scotland record books since his playing days. He was brought into the Scotland team to face Wales in 1885 as a late replacement for Leitch Keir, and although his name was recorded initially in SFA records he then disappeared until his rediscovery during research for this book. He had a fine pedigree, winning the very first Ayrshire Cup competition with Mauchline in 1878, aged 18, and represented Ayrshire and Scotch Counties several times. He moved to Dumbarton in 1884 and played for a couple of years, while he worked as a wood turner. He spent the rest of his life in Dumbarton, marrying no less than four times.

Hughie WILSON (4/0, 1890-1904)
Hugh Wilson
Born 18 March 1869 Bilboa, Mauchline, Ayrshire
Died 5 April 1940 Kilmarnock Infirmary, Ayrshire
Scotland v Wales 1890, 1902; England 1897; Ireland 1904.
Mauchline; Newmilns; Sunderland 1890-99 (Football League 1892, 1893, 1895); Bedminster 1899-1900; Bristol City 1900-01; Third Lanark 1901-07 (Scottish League 1904; Scottish Cup 1905); Kilmarnock Apr 1907-08.

Wilson won four caps over a 14-year period, gaining his first honour in 1890 at left half while with Newmilns. Later that year he turned professional with Sunderland where he really showed his class and took part in their glory years with three league championships in 1892, 1893 and 1895. Known as 'Lalty' he was famous for his long one-handed throw-ins, which apparently were responsible for a revision of the laws in 1895 to insist that throws must be two-handed. He was capped for a second time in Scotland's impressive 2-1 win over England in 1897. He left Sunderland in 1899, aged 30, for the relative obscurity of the Southern League at Bedminster, which merged with Bristol City a year later. It might have indicated his career was winding down yet he was far from finished, and when he returned to Scotland in 1901 with Third Lanark he found a new lease of life. In six years at Cathkin, he was outstanding and won a Scottish League title, the Scottish Cup, two more Scotland caps and made an appearance for the Scottish League. His career finally ended in 1908 after a season at Kilmarnock, shortly before he turned 40. His son John was a noted left back with Hearts, Dunfermline and Hamilton.

Jim WILSON (4/0, 1888-91)
James Wilson
Born 6 July 1865 Main Street, Bonhill, Dunbartonshire
Died 28 February 1900 Arthur Street, Alexandria, Dunbartonshire
Scotland v Wales 1888; England 1889, 1890, 1891.
Vale of Leven Wanderers; Vale of Leven 1884-93.
A fine goalkeeper, Wilson's three successive caps against England give a clear indication of his standing in the game. He played for Vale of Leven over a ten year period, having started out as a forward with Vale of Leven Wanderers, but was tried in goal as an experiment. He was so adept that by the end of his first season with Vale of Leven he was their goalkeeper in the 1885 Scottish Cup final. That final and his other showpiece in 1890 were both lost, as were two Glasgow Charity Cup finals in 1886 and 1887. However, he did record two victories from six Dunbartonshire Cup finals. He stopped playing serious football in 1893 but continued as a referee and after he took charge of the Aberdeenshire Cup final of 1897 he was even reported playing for Vale of Leven in a friendly later that year. A crack marksman with the Dunbartonshire Volunteers, he shot in the Queen's Hundred at Bisley. He worked as a press printer in Alexandria, and died in 1900 of pneumonia aged 34.

Peter WILSON (4/0, 1926-33)
Peter Wilson
Born 25 November 1904 Bogfauld, Beith, Ayrshire
Died 13 February 1983 St Inan's Drive, Beith, Ayrshire
Scotland v Ireland 1926, Feb 1931; France 1930; England 1933.
Beith; Celtic 1923-34 (Scottish League 1926; Scottish Cup 1925, 1927, 1931, 1933) [loan to Ayr United Sep & Nov 1923]; Hibernian 1934-38; Dunfermline Athletic 1938-39 player-manager.
A cultured left half who played a major role in a string of Celtic successes in the inter-war years, Wilson was calm and calculating on the ball. He was recruited from Beith in 1923 and spent over a decade at Celtic Park, winning the league title just once in 1926 and the Scottish Cup four times. Along the way he won four Scotland caps but they were spread over several years and he never managed to establish himself in the national team, although he was

considered good enough to face England in 1933. He also made four appearances for the Scottish League. When he could not agree terms with Celtic in 1934 they placed him on the transfer list and he found a new lease of life at Hibs who made good use of his experience, and he was dedicated enough to commute from his home in Beith to Edinburgh for training. After four years he was released in 1938 to become player-manager of Dunfermline but left on the outbreak of war and joined the Royal Navy. Later he scouted for Derby County and did some coaching for Kilmarnock but did not have a full-time role in football again. Having originally trained as a cabinet maker he worked as a stores superintendent in a chemical factory. NB he was born to a single mother as Peter Williamson and was then adopted by Thomas and Janet Wilson, whose surname he took.

Willie WISEMAN (2/0, 1926-30)
William Wiseman
Born 11 October 1896 Meikle Wartle, Rayne, Aberdeenshire
Died 2 January 1981 Chalmers Hospital, Edinburgh
Scotland v Wales 1926; Ireland 1930.
Aberdeen University 1920-22; Queen's Park 1922-30 (Second Division 1923).
Wiseman was an efficient and powerful left back with Queen's Park in the 1920s at a time when the club was going through a purple patch and reached as high as fifth place in the First Division. He grew up in the fishing village of Portsoy, where his father was a tailor, and was educated at Fordyce Academy, the same school as some of the Queen's Park founders in the 1860s. When the First World War broke out he signed up for the Gordon Highlanders, rising to the rank of Captain, and saw active service on the Western front where he was wounded, later spending time with the Army in India. On his return, he studied engineering at Aberdeen University where he not only played football but also represented the university at golf and tennis. He was still a student when he joined Queen's Park in 1922, while qualifying as a chartered engineer at Glasgow Technical College. After winning promotion in his first season he eventually racked up over 260 appearances for the Hampden side and built an impressive international pedigree. He was capped twice by Scotland in 1926 and 1930, and played once for the Scottish League and six times for the Scotland amateur team. He worked in Dumbarton until he gave up playing in 1930 to take up a post with the roads department of Banff County Council. He coached Deveronvale when the club was founded in 1938 and in later years was convenor of their selection committee. In the Second World War he was a Major in the Royal Engineers, finding and training recruits for large scale engineering projects, then he returned to Banff where he was county surveyor from 1951 until his retirement in 1962. He spent his later years in Edinburgh and died there in 1981.

David WOTHERSPOON (2/0, 1872-73)
David Wotherspoon
Born 9 April 1849 Townhead Street, Hamilton, Lanarkshire
Died 28 February 1906 Leven Street, Pollokshields, Glasgow
Scotland v England 1872, 1873.
Queen's Park 1867-74; Clydesdale Feb 1874-77.
Wotherspoon was an enthusiastic founding member of Queen's Park in 1867, and served on the club committee from 1869 to 1874, some of that time as club secretary. Although usually a half-back, he played as a forward for Scotland in the first two internationals and was reserve for the third. He was selected for Glasgow against Sheffield in 1874, by which time he had moved over to join Clydesdale along with Robert Gardner, and they both played for their new side in the first Scottish Cup final in 1874, losing to Queen's Park. He appears to have stopped playing football around 1877. Brought up in Hamilton, Wotherspoon worked in the metal trade in Glasgow, initially as a clerk at an iron merchant and by the 1880s was employing two men in his own business. At the time of his death from tuberculosis in 1906, leaving a wife and five daughters, he was described as a lime quarry shareholder. His younger brothers Thomas and John also played for Queen's Park while his elder sister Marion has a unique place in Scottish football history as she sewed the red lion crests on the early international shirts.

Tom WYLLIE (1/1, 1890)
Thomas Wyllie
Born 5 April 1870 Welltrees Street, Maybole, Ayrshire
Died 28 July 1943 Maxwell Road, Pollokshields, Glasgow
Scotland v Ireland 1890 (1).
Maybole; Rangers 1888-90; Everton Dec 1890-92; Liverpool 1892-93; Bury 1893-97 (Second Division 1895); Bristol City 1897-98.
Wyllie came to Glasgow from Maybole and spent two and a half seasons at Rangers, making his debut in a friendly against the touring Canadians in September 1888 and scoring a hat-trick in his first competitive match, a Glasgow Cup tie against United Abstainers. An excellent right winger, his consistent form led to international recognition and he scored on his Scotland debut in a defeat of Ireland, a few days before his 20th birthday, shortly after playing for Glasgow against Sheffield. The following season he played in Rangers' first ever league match in August 1890, then in December that year he went south to Everton as a professional. Unusually both his teams that season won their leagues, although he only made four appearances for each so did not do enough to earn a medal. He established himself as a regular for Everton then in 1892 was one of the first signings for the newly-formed Liverpool side. He spent a year playing for them in the Lancashire League and starred in an important local triumph as he scored the only goal of the Liverpool Senior Cup final against his old club Everton. However, rather than stay with Liverpool as they entered the Football League, he signed for Bury in the Lancashire League, and stuck with them for four years as they were elected to the Second Division, winning it at the

first attempt. That set up a promotion 'test match' against the team which finished bottom of the First, which just happened to be Liverpool. Bury won 1-0 and Wyllie enjoyed two seasons in the top division. In 1897 he moved on again to Bristol City, who had just turned professional in the Western League, retiring after a year although he remained involved in the game as a referee. He opened a newsagent shop in Bristol and worked as an insurance agent, but later in life he returned to Glasgow where he was an agent for a clothing manufacturer.

Y

Benny YORSTON (1/0, 1931)
Benjamin Collard Yorston
Born 14 October 1905 Walker Road, Torry, Kincardineshire
Died 19 November 1977 King's Road, Chelsea, London
Scotland v Ireland Feb 1931.
Mugiemoss [trial for Alloa Oct 1924]; Aberdeen Richmond 1925-26; Montrose Sep 1926-27; Aberdeen Mar 1927-32; Sunderland Jan 1932-34; Middlesbrough Mar 1934-1945 [guest during WW2 for St Mirren 1939-40; Brentford Mar-Apr 1940, Aldershot Apr 1940, Reading Apr 1940, Hibernian Dec 1940-41, East Fife Oct-Nov 1942, Lincoln City Jan 1943, Hamilton Academical Feb 1943]; Dundee United Nov 1945.

Capped as a junior against Ireland in 1925 while at Mugiemoss, Yorston had trials for several clubs including a scoring debut for Alloa and for Hibs and Aberdeen reserve teams. However, his lack of inches, at 5 feet 5, counted against him and he remained in junior football until he started his senior career at Montrose, in the Scottish Alliance. He soon showed he could be a prolific scorer, netting 40 times for Montrose in half a season and was snapped up by Aberdeen for just £30 in March 1927. He was given a chance to shine on the club's tour of South Africa that summer, responded with a barrowload of goals, and went on to score over 100 in the league for Aberdeen in less than five years, including a record 38 in 1929/30. He only won a single Scotland cap, against Ireland early in 1931. Later that year he was one of five first-team players who were sensationally transfer-listed by Aberdeen, for reasons which have never been made clear but were probably linked to betting, and Yorston was sold to Sunderland for £2,000. He found it hard to settle and was plagued by illness, and a couple of years later he joined Middlesbrough where he spent the rest of his career. During the War he served in the Army as a Sergeant-Instructor in Physical Training, which gave him the opportunity to guest for a number of clubs, mainly in Scotland but also a few in the south during his training. After being demobbed he was released by Middlesbrough in the autumn of 1945 and played a single match for Dundee United before retiring. He was a scout for Bury then moved to London, where he went into the flat-letting business in South Kensington until his death in 1977. He was an uncle of Harry Yorston, who played for Scotland in 1955.

Sandy YOUNG (2/0, 1905-07)
Alexander Simpson Young
Born 23 June 1880 Lochside, Slamannan, Stirlingshire
Died 17 September 1959 Abercorn Terrace, Portobello, Midlothian
Scotland v England 1905; Wales 1907.
Slamannan Juniors; St Mirren 1899-1900; Falkirk 1900-01; Everton 1901-11 (FA Cup 1906); Tottenham Hotspur Aug-Nov 1911; Manchester City Nov 1911-12; South Liverpool 1912-14.

From junior football in his village team, Young went to St Mirren in 1899 and scored regularly in his debut season, then returned closer to home with Falkirk, who were at that time in the Central Combination. A natural scorer, he was clearly destined for better things and his 1901 move to Everton for a £100 fee inaugurated a decade with the club which saw him make his Scotland debut against England in 1905. However, he is more fondly remembered as the man who scored the only goal of the FA Cup final to beat Newcastle in 1906, which took the cup to Merseyside for the first time. The following season he was top scorer in the First Division and made his second appearance for Scotland, against Wales. When the goals started to dry up, he left Everton in 1911 and his career dwindled with short spells at Spurs and Manchester City before he wound up his football days at South Liverpool in the second division of the Lancashire Combination. They did at least win their league in 1913. He retired the following year and emigrated to Australia to go into farming with his brother John, which might have been the last anyone heard of him but tragedy intervened. In December 1915 he was charged with John's murder and all sorts of stories emerged about his character in the press, notably the *Liverpool Echo* hinting at mental health problems, describing him as 'a very sombre man', 'highly strung' with 'peculiar habits'. This was confirmed by the directors of Everton, who wrote to the mayor of Tongala, near Melbourne, offering to submit medical testimony 'to prove the fact that Young is and has been mentally unsound'. The charge was reduced to manslaughter, and he was sentenced to three years in prison and an asylum. When released in 1920, he sailed back to Britain where he spent the rest of his life. He died aged 79 in a home near Edinburgh and although he was buried in an unmarked plot in Seafield Cemetery, the Everton Heritage Society funded a headstone for him which was dedicated in 2014.

'Sunny Jim' YOUNG (1/0, 1906)
James Young
Born 10 January 1882 Kirktonholm Street, Kilmarnock, Ayrshire
Died 4 September 1922 Kilmarnock Infirmary, Ayrshire
Scotland v Ireland 1906.
Dean Park; Kilmarnock Rugby XI [trial for Kilmarnock Aug 1901]; Stewarton; Shawbank; Barrow Feb-Jun 1902; Bristol Rovers 1902-03; Celtic 1903-17 (Scottish League 1905, 1906, 1907, 1908, 1909, 1910, 1914, 1915, 1916; Scottish Cup 1904, 1907, 1908, 1911, 1912, 1914).

For a man who won so many honours at Celtic, it is astonishing that Jim Young won only one cap for Scotland. A hard-working and dependable right half, his career got off to a stuttering start with an unsuccessful trial at Kilmarnock, a couple of junior teams, then professional contracts in the relative backwaters of Barrow and Bristol. His arrival at Celtic was almost an accident as he was at Bristol Rovers in the spring of 1903 when a Celtic scout signed his team mate Bob Muir. When Young remarked that he would also like to come back to Scotland, as he was homesick, the club took him at his word. He won his first medal almost immediately as he played in the Charity Cup semi-finals and final, and that launched him on a magnificent career that would see him at Celtic Park until he retired. The fans gave him his nickname Sunny Jim, apparently from a character in an advert for Force breakfast cereal. In his first full season Celtic won the Scottish Cup, defeating Rangers 3-2, then embarked on their famous six-in-a-row title wins. During this run he played in Scotland's 1-0 defeat of Ireland in Dublin in 1906 which proved to be his only international, although he did make six appearances for the Scottish League. The medals continued to flow at Celtic with five more Scottish Cups and he took his league-winning total up to nine with a further three consecutive titles. A knee injury concluded his long career in 1916 and the following year he took over the tenancy of the Royal Hotel in Kilmarnock along with former internationalist Bobby Templeton. Sadly, they both died suddenly as Templeton had a heart attack in 1919, and three years later Young was riding pillion on a motorbike with sidecar that collided with a tram just outside Kilmarnock. He died of his injuries in hospital, just 40 years old, and left a widow and three children. Many of his former colleagues and thousands of fans turned out for his funeral procession to Kilmarnock New Cemetery.

A FEW RECORDS

All statistics relate to 1872-1939 unless stated.

Youngest international debuts

Two players were selected at 17 years old but were unable to play, although they were capped subsequently:
John Lambie, born 18 December 1868; Ireland 20 March 1886 – 17y 92d
Woodville Gray, born 10 June 1866; Ireland 26 January 1884 – 17y 230d

18 years old:
John Lambie born 18 December 1868; v Ireland 19 February 1887 – 18y 63d.
Lambie was not just Scotland's youngest ever player, he was also the youngest captain.
Fred Anderson, born 17 November 1855; v England 7 March 1874 – 18y 110d
Bob Christie, born 15 November 1865; v England 15 March 1884 – 18y 121d
Bill Sellar, born 21 October 1864; v England 21 March 1885 – 18y 151d
Sandy McLaren, born 25 December 1910; v Norway 26 May 1929 – 18y 152d
'Dyke' Berry, born 27 May 1875; v Wales 24 March 1894 – 18y 301d
John R Gow, born 17 April 1869; v Ireland 24 March 1888 – 18y 342d
Archie Ritchie, born 12 April 1872; v Wales 21 March 1891 – 18y 343d
James Richmond, born 22 March 1858; v England 3 March 1877 – 18y 346d

19 years old:
Willie Anderson, Jack Baird, David Black, George Bowman, Robert Neilson Brown, James Duncan, James 'Daddy' Dunlop, Woodie Gray, Willie Groves, Thomas 'Kiltie' Hamilton, Jack Harkness, Jack Hunter, Alex Jackson, Bob Kelso, Willie Lambie, Tommy Law, Dan Liddle, James McAdam, Neil McCallum, Bob McColl, Tommy McInnes, David McPherson, John 'Kitey' McPherson, Neil Munro, Peter Pursell, Frank Shaw, Bob Smellie, Tommy Walker, Davie Wilson, Tom Wyllie.

For comparison, these are the 18-year-old debutants in the modern era:
Denis Law born 24 February 1940; v N Ireland 18 October 1958 – 18y 236d
Willie Henderson born 24 January 1944; v Wales 20 October 1962 – 18y 269d
Willie Johnston born 19 December 1946; v Denmark 13 October 1965 – 18y 298d
Kieran Tierney born 5 June 1997; v Wales 29 March 2016 – 18y 298d
Danny Wilson born 27 December 1991; v Wales 16 November 2010 – 18y 324d
Paul McStay born 22 October 1964; v Uruguay 21 September 1983 – 18y 334d
Garry O'Connor born 7 May 1983; v Nigeria 17 April 2002 – 18y 345d
Oliver Burke born 7 April 1997; v Denmark 29 March 2016 – 18y 357d

Oldest international debuts

Jock Buchanan, born 25 February 1894; v England 13 April 1929 – 35y 47d
Stewart Davidson, born 1 June 1886; v England 9 April 1921 – 34y 313d
32 years old: Donald Colman, Alec Herd, Peter Kerr, Jimmy Lawrence, Willie Summers, Sandy Thomson.
31 years old: James Blair, James Bowie, Tully Craig, William Dunlop, Alex Graham, Andy Herd, Tom Kelso, Willie Muir, Jimmy Stark, Tommy Tait.
30 years old: Alex Bell, Joe Donnachie, Jock Ewart, Jack Fraser, Jock Gilmour, Tom Hamilton, Sailor Hunter, Willie King, Willie Loney, Will McColl, Don McKinlay, Frank O'Rourke, Bob Parlane, Willie Robb, Jock Smith, William Wiseman.

Youngest goalscorers

18 years old:
Fred Anderson, born 17 November 1855; v England 7 March 1874 – 18y 110d
'Dyke' Berry, born 27 May 1875; v Wales 24 March 1894 – 18y 301d
James Richmond, born 22 March 1858; v England 3 March 1877 – 18y 346d

19 years old:
David Black, Neil Munro, Willie Groves, Neil McCallum, Davie Wilson (2), Tommy McInnes, Bob McColl (2), Tom Wyllie, James McAdam.

Debut goalscorers (two or more goals)

4 goals:
Sandy Higgins v Ireland 1885 (only cap)
Charlie Heggie v Ireland 1886 (only cap)
Billy Dickson v Ireland 1888 (only cap)
Johnny Madden v Wales 1893

3 goals:
Gilbert Rankin v Ireland 1890
John Barker v Wales 1893
Jimmy Gillespie v Wales 1898 (only cap)

2 goals:
Peter Campbell v Wales 1878
Jimmy Gossland v Ireland 1884 (only cap)
Alec Latta v Wales 1888
Frank Watt v Ireland 1889
Thomas Chambers v Wales 1894 (only cap)
John Walker v Ireland 1895
Bobby Neill v Wales 1896
Jimmy McKee v Wales 1898 (only cap)
Johnny Campbell v Wales 1899
Davie Wilson v Wales 1900 (only cap)
Wattie Aitkenhead v Ireland 1912 (only cap)
Tom Miller v England 1920
Jimmy Nisbet v Norway 1929

Captain on debut

Bob Gardner v England 1872
Andy Watson v England 1881
Willie Semple v Wales 1886 (only cap)
John Lambie v Ireland 1887
Donald Gow v England 1888 (only cap)
Dunkie Stewart v Ireland 1888 (only cap)
Tom Robertson v Ireland 1889
Jock Gillespie v Wales 1896 (only cap)
John Ritchie v Wales 1897 (only cap)
Matt Scott v Wales 1898 (only cap)
Albert Buick v Ireland 1902
Jimmy Sharp v Wales 1904
Jimmy Stark v Ireland 1909
Willie Cringan v Wales 1920
Tom Townsley v Wales 1925 (only cap)

15 or more caps

Alan Morton, 31 caps
Bobby Walker, 29
Charles Thomson, 21
Tommy Walker, 21*
Hugh Gallacher, 20
Alec Smith, 20
Andy Anderson, 23
George Brown, 19
Bob McPhail, 17
Jamie Brownlie, 16
Jimmy McMullan, 16
Jacky Robertson, 16
Jimmy Delaney, 15*
Alec McNair, 15
* Including caps after WW2

At the other end of the scale, 270 of the 615 internationalists in this book were capped just once.

Deaths aged under 30

James 'Daddy' Dunlop, 21*
John Thomson, 22*
Jimmy Main, 23*
Peter Dowds, 24
George Allan, 24
Peter Scarff, 24
Kenny Anderson, 25
Jimmy Logan, 25*
Bob Downie, 26
Jack Hunter, 27
Angus Douglas, 29
Angus McKinnon, 29
* Died as a direct result of playing football

Killed on military service

Thomas Jackson, 9 October 1916 on the Somme, aged 39
Jimmy Speirs, 20 August 1917 in Flanders, aged 31
Donald McLeod, 6 October 1917 in Flanders, aged 35
Bob Christie, 15 May 1918 in Rouen, aged 52
Alex Jackson, 15 November 1946 in Egypt, aged 41

Military decorations

Military Cross: Leslie Skene
Distinguished Conduct Medal: Jock Buchanan
Military Medal: George Brewster, Joe Cassidy, George Key, Sandy Higgins, Finlay Speedie, Jimmy Speirs.

Births outside Scotland

England: Arthur Kinnaird, Willie Watson
Ireland: Willie Maley, Jimmy McKee
Canada: Eadie Fraser, Joe Kennaway
India: Henry Renny-Tailyour
South Africa: Alex Bell

Close relatives

Father and son:
Sandy Higgins (1885) and son Sandy (1910-11)
Neil Gibson (1895-1905) and son Jimmy (1926-30)
Barney Battles (1901) and son Barney (1930)
Jimmy McMenemy (1905-20) and son John (1933)
Jimmy Blair (1920-24) and son Jimmy (1946)
Jimmy Simpson (1934-38) and son Ronnie (1967-68)

Brothers:
3: Alick, James and Gladstone Hamilton
2: Willie and Dyke Berry, Bob and Alec Christie, John and Donald Gow, William and Geordie Ker, George and Willie Key, Johnny and Willie Lambie, Baldy and Jimmy McCall (half-brothers), Jack and Jimmy McDougall, Hugh and Tuck McIntyre, Harry and Moses McNeil, David and John McPherson, Matt and Bob Scott, James and Robert Smith, Andy and David Wilson.

Brothers in same game:
James and Robert Smith (1872 v England), Harry and Moses McNeil (1876 v Wales), Andy and David Wilson (1913 v England).

In the modern era, the only brothers to have played together for Scotland are Jock and David Shaw (1946 v Belgium) and Steven and Gary Caldwell (five matches 2004-09). Other brothers to be capped are Eddie and Frank Gray, John and Alan Hansen, John and Willie Hughes, Alex and Jimmy Scott.

Played for another national team

USA: Barney Battles junior (1925), Jack Marshall (1926).
Canada: Joe Kennaway (1926).
Great Britain: Jim Crawford (1936 Olympic Games).
Football League: Tom Brandon, David Calderhead, George Dewar, Tom McInnes, Nick Ross, Hugh Wilson (all 1891); Donald Gow, Willie Groves, Tom McInnes (all 1892).
Irish League: George Wilson (1907), Leslie Skene (1911), Joe Cassidy (1930).
Canadian/American Select: Neil Munro (1891).
England (wartime): Jimmy McMullan (1918).

Success in other sports

Cricket: John Macdonald (Scotland 1880), Scot Symon (Scotland 1938), Willie Maxwell (Belgium 1913 and Staffordshire), William Gibb (Gentlemen of Scotland), Henry Renny-Tailyour (Kent), Hugh McIntyre (Lancashire), Archie Rowan (Glasgow), Jock Hepburn (Clackmannanshire), Jimmy Sharp (Forfarshire).

Rugby: Henry Renny-Tailyour (Scotland 1872), John Smith (Edinburgh 1876, British Lions 1888), Alexander McGeoch (Glasgow 1875), Willie Robertson (Glasgow 1886).

Athletics: Scottish title holders – Jim Crawford (75, 100 and 220 yards), Willie Beveridge (100 yards and quarter mile), Willie Maley (100 yards), John R Gow (120 yards hurdles).

Bowls: Jack Clelland (Scotland 1911), Willie Agnew (Scotland 1928), Andrew Wilson (England 1948).

Curling: Bob Christie (Scotland 1908 and 1914).

SCOTLAND INTERNATIONALS 1872-1939

This is a complete record of all 188 international matches played by Scotland up to 1939. As ever with football statistics, there are a few uncertainties as the Scottish FA did not keep an official record.

In particular, there are conflicting reports in newspapers about goalscorers, and for several matches in the Victorian era it is impossible to know for sure who scored. I have taken a view based on the balance of probabilities, after checking numerous newspaper reports, but I am sure that other historians will disagree with some of my conclusions. Similarly, the timing of goals is often approximate or a 'best guess', as few reports bothered to state precise timings, and these are given primarily to indicate the sequence of goals. The identity of the Scotland captain against Ireland in 1886 has not been ascertained, and the referee of the match against Ireland in 1887 was not recorded in any newspaper. Crowd figures are mainly approximate. The numbers against each player indicate their caps total to date, with a full stop after their final cap.

It is also worth mentioning that the status of some matches is open to question. The Ibrox Disaster match against England on 5 April 1902 is not included even though it started as an official international, as when the accident happened the match was declared void by both associations, even though it was played to a finish. Scotland's games v Norway and Netherlands in 1929 are not recognised as full internationals by our opponents. On the other hand, Denmark give full international status to a match against a Scotland amateur eleven in 1932.

1.
30 November 1872
Scotland - England 0-0 (0-0)
Referee: William Keay (Glasgow, Scotland).
Crowd: 2,500 (West of Scotland Ground, Partick)
Team: Robert Gardner (1/Queen's Park), captain
Joseph Taylor (1/Queen's Park)
William Ker (1/Queen's Park)
James John Thomson (1/Queen's Park)
James Smith (1./Queen's Park)
William Muir Mackinnon (1/Queen's Park)
James Biggar Weir (1/Queen's Park)
Robert Leckie (1./Queen's Park)
David Wotherspoon (1/Queen's Park)
Robert Smith (1/Queen's Park)
Alexander Rhind (1./Queen's Park).

2.
8 March 1873
England - Scotland 4-2 (no half-time)
Referee: Theodore Lloyd (London, England)
Crowd: 3,000 (Kennington Oval, London)
Goals: 1-0 Kenyon-Slaney 1, 2-0 Bonsor 10,
2-1 Renny-Tailyour 15, 2-2 Gibb 20,
3-2 Kenyon-Slaney 75, 4-2 Chenery 85.
Team: Robert Gardner (2/Queen's Park), captain
Joseph Taylor (2/Queen's Park)
William Ker (2./Queen's Park)
James John Thomson (2/Queen's Park)
Robert Smith (2./Queen's Park)
William Muir Mackinnon (2/Queen's Park)
Henry Waugh Renny-Tailyour (1./Royal Engineers)
Arthur Fitzgerald Kinnaird (1./Wanderers)
John Edward Blackburn (1./Royal Engineers)
William Gibb (1./Clydesdale)
David Wotherspoon (2./Queen's Park).

3.
7 March 1874
Scotland - England 2-1 (2-1)
Referee: Archibald Rae (Glasgow, Scotland)
Crowd: 7,000 (West of Scotland Ground, Partick)
Goals: 0-1 Kingsford 22, 1-1 Anderson 40,
2-1 A McKinnon 44.
Team: Robert Gardner (3/Queen's Park)
John Hunter (1/Third Lanark)
Joseph Taylor (3/Queen's Park)
Charles Campbell (1/Queen's Park)
James John Thomson (3./Queen's Park), captain
James Biggar Weir (2/Queen's Park)
John Ferguson (1/Vale of Leven)
Henry McNeil (1/Queen's Park)
William Muir Mackinnon (3/Queen's Park)
Angus McKinnon (1./Queen's Park)
Frederick Anderson (1./Queen's Park).

4.
6 March 1875
England - Scotland 2-2 (1-1)
Referee: Alfred Stair (London, England)
Crowd: 2,000 (Kennington Oval, London)
Goals: 1-0 Wollaston 24, 1-1 McNeil 34,
2-1 Alcock 70, 2-2 Andrews 75.
Team: Robert Gardner (4/Clydesdale)
John Hunter (2/Eastern)
Joseph Taylor (4/Queen's Park), captain
Alexander Kennedy (1/Eastern)
Alexander McLintock (1/Vale of Leven)
James Biggar Weir (3/Queen's Park)
William Muir Mackinnon (4/Queen's Park)
Henry McNeil (2/Queen's Park)
Thomas Cochrane Highet (1/Queen's Park)
Peter Andrews (1./Eastern)
John Douglas McPherson (1./Clydesdale).

5.
4 March 1876
Scotland - England 3-0 (3-0)
Referee: William Campbell Mitchell (Glasgow, Scotland)
Crowd: 15,000 (West of Scotland Ground, Partick)
Goals: 1-0 Mackinnon 8, 2-0 McNeil 12,
3-0 Highet 35.
Team: Alexander McGeoch (1/Dumbreck)
Joseph Taylor (5/Queen's Park), captain
John Hunter (3/Third Lanark)
Alexander McLintock (2/Vale of Leven)
Alexander Kennedy (2/Eastern)
Henry McNeil (3/Queen's Park)
William Muir Mackinnon (5/Queen's Park)
Thomas Cochrane Highet (2/Queen's Park)
William Miller (1./Third Lanark)
John Ferguson (2/Vale of Leven)
John Campbell Baird (1/Vale of Leven).

6.
25 March 1876
Scotland - Wales 4-0 (1-0)
Referee: Robert Gardner (Glasgow, Scotland)
Crowd: 17,000 (West of Scotland Ground, Partick)
Goals: 1-0 Ferguson 40, 2-0 Mackinnon 54,
3-0 Lang 59, 4-0 H McNeil 80.
Team: Alexander McGeoch (2/Dumbreck)
Joseph Taylor (6./Queen's Park)
Robert Walker Neill (1/Queen's Park)
Alexander Kennedy (3/Eastern)
Charles Campbell (2/Queen's Park), captain
Thomas Cochrane Highet (3/Queen's Park)
John Ferguson (3/Vale of Leven)
James Joseph Lang (1/Clydesdale)
William Muir Mackinnon (6/Queen's Park)
Moses McLay McNeil (1/Rangers)
Henry McNeil (4/Queen's Park).

7.
3 March 1877
England - Scotland 1-3 (0-1)
Referee: Robert Ogilvie (Clapham Rovers, England)
Crowd: 2,000 (Kennington Oval, London)
Goals: 0-1 Ferguson 25, 0-2 Richmond 48,
1-2 Lyttelton 55, 1-3 Ferguson 69.
Team: Alexander McGeoch (3/Dumbreck)
Robert Walker Neill (2/Queen's Park)
Thomas Vallance (1/Rangers)
Charles Campbell (3/Queen's Park), captain
James Phillips (1/Queen's Park)
James Tassie Richmond (1/Clydesdale)
William Muir Mackinnon (7/Queen's Park)
John Cunningham McGregor (1/Vale of Leven)
John Smith McDougall (1/Vale of Leven)
John Smith (1/Mauchline)
John Ferguson (4/Vale of Leven).

8.
5 March 1877
Wales - Scotland 0-2 (0-0)
Referee: William Dick (Secretary, Scottish FA)
Crowd: 4,000 (Racecourse, Wrexham)
Goals: 0-1 Campbell 55, 0-2 Burnett og 70.
Team: Alexander McGeoch (4./Dumbreck)
Robert Walker Neill (3/Queen's Park)
Thomas Vallance (2/Rangers)
Charles Campbell (4/Queen's Park), captain
James Phillips (2/Queen's Park)
John Smith (2/Mauchline)
John Cunningham McGregor (2/Vale of Leven)
John Ferguson (5/Vale of Leven)
John Smith McDougall (2/Vale of Leven)
Henry McNeil (5/Queen's Park)
John Hunter (4./Third Lanark).

9.
2 March 1878
Scotland - England 7-2 (4-0)
Referee: William Dick (Secretary, Scottish FA)
Crowd: 10,000 (Hampden Park, Glasgow)
Goals: 1-0 McDougall 7, 2-0 McGregor 32, 3-0 McNeil 39, 4-0 McDougall 41, 5-0 McDougall 46,
6-0 Mackinnon 62, 6-1 Wylie 65, 7-1 McNeil 70,
7-2 Cursham 75.
Team: Robert Gardner (5./Clydesdale)
Andrew McIntyre (1/Vale of Leven)
Thomas Vallance (3/Rangers)
Charles Campbell (5/Queen's Park), captain
Alexander Kennedy (4/Third Lanark)
James Tassie Richmond (2/Queen's Park)
John Cunningham McGregor (3/Vale of Leven)
John Smith McDougall (3/Vale of Leven)
Thomas Cochrane Highet (4./Queen's Park)
William Muir Mackinnon (8/Queen's Park)
Henry McNeil (6/Queen's Park).

10.
23 March 1878
Scotland - Wales 9-0 (6-0)
Referee: Robert Gardner (Glasgow, Scotland)
Crowd: 6,000 (Hampden Park, Glasgow)
Goals: 1-0 Campbell 4, 2-0 Weir 15, 3-0 Campbell 18, 4-0 Baird 37, 5-0 Ferguson 38, 6-0 Weir 42,
7-0 Ferguson 50, 8-0 Watson 60, 9-0 Lang 70.
Team: Robert Parlane (1/Vale of Leven)
James Sibbald Robertson Duncan (1/Alexandra Ath)
Robert Walker Neill (4/Queen's Park), captain
James Phillips (3./Queen's Park)
David Davidson (1/Queen's Park)
John Ferguson (6./Vale of Leven)
John Campbell Baird (2/Vale of Leven)
James Joseph Lang (2./Third Lanark)
James Biggar Weir (4./Queen's Park)
James Andrew Kennedy Watson (1./Rangers)
Peter McGregor Campbell (1/Rangers).

11.
5 April 1879
England - Scotland 5-4 (1-4)
Referee: Charles Wollaston (London, England)
Crowd: 4,500 (Kennington Oval, London)
Goals: 1-0 Mosforth 5, 1-1 Mackinnon 15, 1-2 McDougall 23, 1-3 Smith 26, 1-4 Mackinnon 41, 2-4 Bambridge 48, 3-4 Goodyer 60, 4-4 Bailey 75, 5-4 Bambridge 83.
Team: Robert Parlane (2/Vale of Leven)
William Scott Somers (1/Third Lanark)
Thomas Vallance (4/Rangers)
Charles Campbell (6/Queen's Park), captain
John Campbell McL McPherson (1/Vale of Leven)
Robert Paton (1/Vale of Leven)
William Wightman Beveridge (1/Ayr Academy)
William Muir Mackinnon (9./Queen's Park)
John Smith (3/Mauchline)
Henry McNeil (7/Queen's Park)
John Smith McDougall (4/Vale of Leven).

12.
7 April 1879
Wales - Scotland 0-3 (0-1)
Referee: James William Archibald Cooper (Secretary, Wales FA)
Crowd: 2,000 (Racecourse, Wrexham)
Goals: 0-1 Campbell 34, 0-2 Smith 65, 0-3 Smith 85.
Team: Robert Parlane (3./Vale of Leven)
William Scott Somers (2/Third Lanark)
Thomas Vallance (5/Rangers)
David Davidson (2/Queen's Park)
John Campbell McL McPherson (2/Vale of Leven)
Henry McNeil (8/Queen's Park)
John Smith McDougall (5./Vale of Leven), captain
Peter McGregor Campbell (2./Rangers)
John Smith (4/Mauchline)
Robert Paton (2./Vale of Leven)
William Wightman Beveridge (2./Ayr Academy).

13.
13 March 1880
Scotland - England 5-4 (3-2)
Referee: Donald Hamilton (Parkgrove, Scotland)
Crowd: 12,000 (Hampden Park, Glasgow)
Goals: 1-0 Ker 5, 1-1 Mosforth 6, 2-1 Baird 40, 2-2 Bambridge 41, 3-2 Ker 43, 4-2 Ker 50, 5-2 Kay 70, 5-3 Sparks 80, 5-4 Bambridge 85.
Team: Archibald Rowan (1/Caledonian)
Alexander McLintock (3./Vale of Leven)
Robert Walker Neill (5./Queen's Park), captain
Charles Campbell (7/Queen's Park)
John Campbell McL McPherson (3/Vale of Leven)
John Smith (5/Edinburgh University)
Moses McLay McNeil (2./Rangers)
George Ker (1/Queen's Park)
John Cunningham McGregor (4./Vale of Leven)
John Campbell Baird (3./Vale of Leven)
John Leck Kay (1/Queen's Park).

14.
27 March 1880
Scotland - Wales 5-1 (2-0)
Referee: Donald Hamilton (Parkgrove, Scotland)
Crowd: 2,000 (Hampden Park, Glasgow)
Goals: 1-0 Davidson 40, 2-0 Beveridge 42, 3-0 Campbell 60, 4-0 McAdam 65, 5-0 Lindsay 70, 5-1 Roberts 88.
Team: George Gillespie (1/Rangers)
William Scott Somers (3./Queen's Park)
Archibald Lang (1./Dumbarton)
David Davidson (3/Queen's Park), captain
Hugh McIntyre (1./Rangers)
James Douglas (1./Renfrew)
James McAdam (1./Third Lanark)
Malcolm John Eadie Fraser (1/Queen's Park)
Joseph Lindsay (1/Dumbarton)
John Campbell (1./South Western)
William Wightman Beveridge (3./Edinburgh Univ.)

15.
12 March 1881
England - Scotland 1-6 (0-1)
Referee: Francis Arthur Marindin (London, England)
Crowd: 8,500 (Kennington Oval, London)
Goals: 0-1 Smith 10, 0-2 Hill 52, 1-2 Bambridge 64, 1-3 Ker 69, 1-4 Field og 70, 1-5 Smith 74, 1-6 Ker 89.
Team: George Gillespie (2/Rangers)
Andrew Watson (1/Queen's Park), captain
Thomas Vallance (6/Rangers)
Charles Campbell (8/Queen's Park)
David Davidson (4/Queen's Park)
David Hill (1/Rangers)
William McGuire (1/Beith)
George Ker (2/Queen's Park)
Joseph Lindsay (2/Dumbarton)
Henry McNeil (9/Queen's Park)
John Smith (6/Edinburgh University).

16.
14 March 1881
Wales - Scotland 1-5 (1-4)
Referee: Llewelyn Kenrick (Oswestry, Wales)
Crowd: 1,500 (Racecourse, Wrexham)
Goals: 1-0 Crosse 4, 1-1 Ker 7, 1-2 McNeil 8, 1-3 Bell og 10, 1-4 Ker 44, 1-5 Morgan og 52.
Team: George Gillespie (3/Rangers)
Andrew Watson (2/Queen's Park)
Thomas Vallance (7./Rangers), captain
John Campbell McL McPherson (4/Vale of Leven)
David Davidson (5./Queen's Park)
William McGuire (2./Beith)
David Hill (2/Rangers)
George Ker (3/Queen's Park)
Joseph Lindsay (3/Dumbarton)
Henry McNeil (10./Queen's Park)
John Smith (7/Edinburgh University).

17.
11 March 1882
Scotland - England 5-1 (2-1)
Referee: John Wallace (Beith, Scotland)
Crowd: 10,000 (Hampden Park, Glasgow)
Goals: 1-0 Harrower 10, 1-1 Vaughton 35, 2-1 Ker 44, 3-1 McPherson 46, 4-1 Ker 70, 5-1 Kay 85.
Team: George Gillespie (4/Rangers)
Andrew Watson (3./Queen's Park)
Andrew McIntyre (2./Vale of Leven)
Charles Campbell (9/Queen's Park), captain
Peter Miller (1/Dumbarton)
Malcolm John Eadie Fraser (2/Queen's Park)
William Anderson (1/Queen's Park)
George Ker (4/Queen's Park)
William Harrower (1/Queen's Park)
John Leck Kay (2/Queen's Park)
Robert McPherson (1./Arthurlie).

18.
25 March 1882
Scotland - Wales 5-0 (1-0)
Referee: Donald Hamilton (Glasgow, Scotland)
Crowd: 5,000 (Hampden Park, Glasgow)
Goals: 1-0 Kay 25, 2-0 Ker 70, 3-0 Fraser 72, 4-0 Fraser 80, 5-0 McAulay 89.
Team: Archibald Rowan (2./Queen's Park), captain
Andrew Hair Holm (1/Queen's Park)
James Sibbald Robertson Duncan (2./Alexandra Ath)
Charles Campbell (10/Queen's Park)
Alexander Kennedy (5/Third Lanark)
Malcolm John Eadie Fraser (3/Queen's Park)
David Hill (3./Rangers)
George Ker (5./Queen's Park)
James McAulay (1/Dumbarton)
John Leck Kay (3/Queen's Park)
James Tassie Richmond (3./Queen's Park).

19.
10 March 1883
England - Scotland 2-3 (2-2)
Referee: John Sinclair (Belfast, Ireland)
Crowd: 7,000 (Bramall Lane, Sheffield)
Goals: 0-1 Smith 20, 1-1 Mitchell 22, 1-2 Smith 30, 2-2 Cobbold 44, 2-3 Smith 52.
Team: James McAulay (2/Dumbarton)
Andrew Hair Holm (2/Queen's Park), captain
Michael Paton (1/Dumbarton)
Peter Miller (2/Dumbarton)
John Campbell McL McPherson (5/Vale of Leven)
Malcolm John Eadie Fraser (4/Queen's Park)
William Anderson (2/Queen's Park)
John Smith (8/Edinburgh University)
John Inglis (1/Rangers)
John Leck Kay (4/Queen's Park)
William Neilson McKinnon (1/Dumbarton).

20.
12 March 1883
Wales - Scotland 0-3 (0-2)
Referee: Robert Lythgoe (Birkenhead, England)
Crowd: 2,000 (Racecourse, Wrexham)
Goals: 0-1 Fraser 35, 0-2 Anderson 38, 0-3 Smith 60.
Team: James McAulay (3/Dumbarton)
Andrew Hair Holm (3/Queen's Park)
Walter Arnott (1/Queen's Park)
Peter Miller (3/Dumbarton)
John Smith (9/Edinburgh University), captain
John Campbell McL McPherson (6/Vale of Leven)
Malcolm John Eadie Fraser (5./Queen's Park)
William Anderson (3/Queen's Park)
John Inglis (2./Rangers)
John Leck Kay (5/Queen's Park)
William Neilson McKinnon (2/Dumbarton).

21.
26 January 1884 (British Championship)
Ireland - Scotland 0-5 (0-2)
Referee: Thomas Hindle (Darwen, England)
Crowd: 3,000 (Ballynafeigh, Belfast)
Goals: 0-1 Harrower 12, 0-2 Gossland 30,
 0-3 Goudie 60, 0-4 Gossland 70, 0-5 Harrower 85.
Team: John Inglis (1./Kilmarnock Athletic)
John Forbes (1/Vale of Leven)
Walter Arnott (2/Queen's Park), captain
John Graham (1./Annbank)
William Fulton (1./Abercorn)
Robert Brown (1/Dumbarton)
Samuel Thomson (1/Lugar Boswell)
James Gossland (1./Rangers)
John Wilson Goudie (1./Abercorn)
William Harrower (2/Queen's Park)
John Macaulay (1./Arthurlie).

22.
15 March 1884 (British Championship)
Scotland - England 1-0 (1-0)
Referee: John Sinclair (Belfast, Ireland)
Crowd: 10,000 (Cathkin Park, Glasgow)
Goal: 1-0 Smith 7.
Team: James McAulay (4/Dumbarton)
Walter Arnott (3/Queen's Park)
John Forbes (2/Vale of Leven)
Charles Campbell (11/Queen's Park), captain
John Campbell McL McPherson (7/Vale of Leven)
Francis Watson Shaw (1/Pollokshields Athletic)
William Anderson (4/Queen's Park)
John Smith (10./Queen's Park)
Joseph Lindsay (4/Dumbarton)
Robert Main Christie (1./Queen's Park)
William Neilson McKinnon (3/Dumbarton).

23.
29 March 1884 (British Championship)
Scotland - Wales 4-1 (1-1)
Referee: Robert Muir Sloan (Liverpool, England)
Crowd: 5,000 (Cathkin Park, Glasgow)
Goals: 0-1 W Roberts 15, 1-1 Lindsay 22,
2-1 Shaw 49, 3-1 Kay 65, 4-1 Kay 87.
Team: Thomas Turner (1./Arthurlie)
Michael Paton (2/Dumbarton), captain
John Forbes (3/Vale of Leven)
Alexander Kennedy (6./Third Lanark)
James McIntyre (1./Rangers)
Robert Brown (2./Dumbarton)
Francis Watson Shaw (2./Pollokshields Athletic)
Samuel Thomson (2./Lugar Boswell)
Joseph Lindsay (5/Dumbarton)
John Leck Kay (6./Third Lanark)
William Neilson McKinnon (4./Dumbarton).

24.
14 March 1885 (British Championship)
Scotland - Ireland 8-2 (4-0)
Referee: John Rodgers Harvey (Sheffield, England)
Crowd: 4,000 (Hampden Park, Glasgow)
Goals: 1-0 Barbour 11, 2-0 Turner 12, 3-0 Higgins 15,
4-0 McPherson 35, 5-0 Calderwood 51,
6-0 Higgins 53, 7-0 Higgins 80, 8-0 Higgins 82,
8-1 Gibb 84, 8-2 Gibb 89.
Team: William Crawford Chalmers (1./Rangers)
Hugh McHardy (1./Rangers)
James Bryden Niven (1./Moffat)
Robert Robison Kelso (1/Renton)
John Campbell McL McPherson (8./Vale of Leven), captain
Alexander Barbour (1./Renton)
John Marshall (1/Third Lanark)
William Martin Muir Turner (1/Pollokshields Ath)
Alexander Higgins (1./Kilmarnock)
Robert Calderwood (1/Cartvale)
William Lamont (1./Pilgrims).

25.
21 March 1885 (British Championship)
England - Scotland 1-1 (0-1)
Referee: John Sinclair (Belfast, Ireland)
Crowd: 8,000 (Kennington Oval, London)
Goals: 0-1 Lindsay 20, 1-1 Bambridge 57.
Team: James McAulay (5/Dumbarton)
Walter Arnott (4/Queen's Park)
Michael Paton (3/Dumbarton), captain
Charles Campbell (12/Queen's Park)
John James Gow (1./Queen's Park)
William Anderson (5/Queen's Park)
Alexander Hamilton (1/Queen's Park)
William Sellar (1/Battlefield)
Joseph Lindsay (6/Dumbarton)
David Steele Allan (1/Queen's Park)
Robert Calderwood (2/Cartvale).

26.
23 March 1885 (British Championship)
Wales - Scotland 1-8 (0-3)
Referee: Robert Muir Sloan (Liverpool, England)
Crowd: 2,000 (Racecourse, Wrexham)
Goals: 0-1 Lindsay 8, 0-2 Anderson 20, 0-3 Allan 30,
1-3 RA Jones 50, 1-4 Lindsay 56, 1-5 Lindsay 76, 1-6
Anderson 80, 1-7 Anderson 84, 1-8 Calderwood 88.
Team: James McAulay (6/Dumbarton)
Walter Arnott (5/Queen's Park)
Michael Paton (4/Dumbarton), captain
Robert Robison Kelso (2/Renton)
Hugh Wilson (1./Dumbarton)
Alexander Hamilton (2/Queen's Park)
William Anderson (6./Queen's Park)
Joseph Lindsay (7/Dumbarton)
Robert Calderwood (3./Cartvale)
Robert Brown (1./Dumbarton)
David Steele Allan (2/Queen's Park).

27.
20 March 1886 (British Championship)
Ireland - Scotland 2-7 (2-5)
Referee: John Wolstenholme (Darwen, England)
Crowd: 3,000 (Ballynafeigh, Belfast)
Goals: 0-1 Heggie 15, 0-2 Heggie 17, 1-2 Condy 19,
1-3 Heggie 22, 1-4 Kelly 32, 1-5 Dunbar 40,
2-5 Johnson 44, 2-6 Heggie 60, 2-7 Gourlay 75.
Team: James Connor (1./Airdrieonians)
Andrew Thomson (1/Arthurlie)
William McLeod (1./Queen's Park)
John Cameron (1./Rangers)
Leitch Keir (1/Dumbarton)
Robert Fleming (1./Morton)
James Kelly (1/Renton)
Charles Winton Heggie (1./Rangers)
William Martin Muir Turner (2./Pollokshields Ath)
James Gourlay (1./Cambuslang)
Michael Dunbar (1./Cartvale).
Captain: not known

28.
27 March 1886 (British Championship)
Scotland - England 1-1 (0-1)
Referee: Alexander H Hunter (Secretary, Wales FA)
Crowd: 11,000 (Hampden Park, Glasgow)
Goals: 0-1 Lindley 35, 1-1 Sommerville 80.
Team: James McAulay (7/Dumbarton)
Walter Arnott (6/Queen's Park), captain
Michael Paton (5./Dumbarton)
Charles Campbell (13./Queen's Park)
John Macdonald (1./Edinburgh University)
Alexander Hamilton (3/Queen's Park)
William Sellar (2/Battlefield)
George Sommerville (1./Queen's Park)
Joseph Lindsay (8./Dumbarton)
Woodville Gray (1./Pollokshields Athletic)
Ralph Allan Aitken (1/Dumbarton).

29.
10 April 1886 (British Championship)
Scotland - Wales 4-1 (1-0)
Referee: John Sinclair (Belfast, Ireland)
Crowd: 3,500 (Hampden Park, Glasgow)
Goals: 1-0 McCormick 30, 2-0 Harrower 47,
3-0 Allan 58, 4-0 Allan 60, 4-1 Lundie og 88.
Team: George Gillespie (5/Queen's Park)
James Lundie (1./Hibernian)
William Semple (1./Cambuslang), captain
Robert Robison Kelso (3/Renton)
Andrew Jackson (1/Cambuslang)
John Marshall (2/Third Lanark)
Robert McCormick (1./Abercorn)
James McGhee (1./Hibernian)
William Harrower (3./Queen's Park)
David Steele Allan (3./Queen's Park)
James McCall (1/Renton).

30.
19 February 1887 (British Championship)
Scotland - Ireland 4-1 (2-1)
Referee: not known
Crowd: 1,000 (Hampden Park, Glasgow)
Goals: 1-0 Watt 5, 1-1 Browne 40, 2-1 Jenkinson 42,
3-1 Lowe 55, 4-1 Johnston 75.
Team: John Edward Doig (1/Arbroath)
Andrew Whitelaw (1/Vale of Leven)
Robert Smellie (1/Queen's Park)
John Weir (1./Third Lanark)
Thomas MacMillan (1./Dumbarton)
James Hutton (1./St Bernard's)
Thomas James Jenkinson (1./Hearts)
John Alexander Lambie (1/Queen's Park), captain
William Wallace Watt (1./Queen's Park)
James Lowe (1./St Bernard's)
William Johnston (1/Third Lanark).

31.
19 March 1887 (British Championship)
England - Scotland 2-3 (1-1)
Referee: John Sinclair (Belfast, Ireland)
Crowd: 12,000 (Ewood Park, Blackburn)
Goals: 0-1 McCall 30, 1-1 Lindley 32, 1-2 Keir 52,
2-2 Dewhurst 53, 2-3 Allan 54.
Team: James McAulay (8/Dumbarton), captain
Walter Arnott (7/Queen's Park)
John Forbes (4/Vale of Leven)
Robert Robison Kelso (4/Renton)
John Robertson Auld (1/Third Lanark)
Leitch Keir (2/Dumbarton)
John Marshall (3/Third Lanark)
William Robertson (1/Dumbarton)
William Sellar (3/Battlefield)
James McCall (2/Renton)
John Allan (1/Queen's Park).

32.
21 March 1887 (British Championship)
Wales - Scotland 0-2 (0-1)
Referee: Aaron Boulan Hall (Liverpool, England)
Crowd: 2,000 (Racecourse, Wrexham)
Goals: 0-1 Robertson 40, 0-2 Allan 80.
Team: James McAulay (9./Dumbarton), captain
Walter Arnott (8/Queen's Park)
John Forbes (5./Vale of Leven)
Robert Robison Kelso (5/Renton)
John Robertson Auld (1/Third Lanark)
Leitch Keir (3/Dumbarton)
John Marshall (4./Third Lanark)
William Robertson (2./Dumbarton)
William Sellar (4/Battlefield)
James McCall (3/Renton)
John Allan (2./Queen's Park).

33.
10 March 1888 (British Championship)
Scotland - Wales 5-1 (3-1)
Referee: John Charles Clegg (Sheffield, England)
Crowd: 8,000 (Easter Road Park, Edinburgh)
Goals: 1-0 Paul 6, 2-0 Munro 30, 3-0 Latta 35,
3-1 Doughty 42, 4-1 Groves 65, 5-1 Latta 75.
Team: James Wilson (1/Vale of Leven)
Andrew Hannah (1./Renton)
Robert Smellie (2/Queen's Park), captain
James Johnston (1./Abercorn)
James McCrorie Gourlay (1./Cambuslang)
James McLaren (1/Hibernian)
Alexander Latta (1/Dumbarton Athletic)
William Groves (1/Hibernian)
William Paul (1/Partick Thistle)
John McPherson (1/Kilmarnock)
Neil Munro (1/Abercorn).

34.
17 March 1888 (British Championship)
Scotland - England 0-5 (0-4)
Referee: John Sinclair (Belfast, Ireland)
Crowd: 10,000 (Hampden Park, Glasgow)
Goals: 0-1 Haworth 30, 0-2 Hodgetts 33,
0-3 Dewhurst 36, 0-4 Goodall 44, 0-5 Dewhurst 49.
Team: John Lindsay (1/Renton)
Walter Arnott (9/Queen's Park)
Donald Robertson Gow (1./Rangers), captain
James Kelly (2/Renton)
Leitch Keir (4./Dumbarton)
Robert Robison Kelso (6/Renton)
Alexander Hamilton (4./Queen's Park)
William Hall Berry (1/Queen's Park)
William Sellar (5/Battlefield)
James McCall (4/Renton)
John Alexander Lambie (2./Queen's Park).

35.
24 March 1888 (British Championship)
Ireland - Scotland 2-10 (2-7)
Referee: Robert Parlane (Belfast, ex Vale of Leven)
Crowd: 5,000 (Solitude, Belfast)
Goals: 0-1 Dewar 5, 0-2 Dickson 7, 0-3 Breckenridge 15, 1-3 Lemon 18, 1-4 Aitken 24, 2-4 Dalton 30, 2-5 Dickson 33, 2-6 Dickson 40, 2-7 Dickson 44, 2-8 McCallum 53, 2-9 Wilson og 77, 2-10 A Stewart 83.
Team: John McLeod (1/Dumbarton)
Duncan Cameron Stewart (1./Dumbarton), captain
Archibald McCall (1./Renton)
Allan Stewart (1/Queen's Park)
George Dewar (1/Dumbarton)
Andrew Jackson (2./Cambuslang)
Neil McCallum (1./Renton)
John Robertson Gow (1./Rangers)
William Anderson Dickson (1./Strathmore)
Thomas Breckenridge (1./Hearts)
Ralph Allan Aitken (2./Dumbarton).

36.
9 March 1889 (British Championship)
Scotland - Ireland 7-0 (4-0)
Referee: William Heaton Stacey (Sheffield, England)
Crowd: 6,000 (Ibrox Park, Glasgow)
Goals: 1-0 Watt 7, 2-0 Watt 10, 3-0 Black 25, 4-0 Groves 32, 5-0 Groves 50, 6-0 Groves 70, 7-0 McInnes 88.
Team: John Edward Doig (2/Arbroath)
James Adams (1/Hearts)
Michael McKeown (1/Celtic)
Thomas Robertson (1/Queen's Park), captain
David Calderhead (1./Queen of the South Wanderers)
John Buchanan (1./Cambuslang)
Francis Watt (1/Kilbirnie)
Thomas McInnes (1./Cowlairs)
William Groves (2/Celtic)
Robert Boyd (1/Mossend Swifts)
David Gibson Black (1./Hurlford).

37.
13 April 1889 (British Championship)
England - Scotland 2-3 (2-0)
Referee: John Sinclair (Belfast, Ireland)
Crowd: 10,000 (Kennington Oval, London)
Goals: 1-0 Bassett 15, 2-0 Bassett 17, 2-1 Munro 55, 2-2 Oswald 60, 2-3 McLaren 65.
Team: James Wilson (2/Vale of Leven)
Robert Smellie (3/Queen's Park), captain
Walter Arnott (10/Queen's Park)
James Kelly (3/Celtic)
George Dewar (2./Dumbarton)
James McLaren (2/Celtic)
James Oswald (1/Third Lanark)
William Hall Berry (2/Queen's Park)
Alexander Latta (2./Dumbarton Athletic)
John McPherson (2/Cowlairs)
Neil Munro (2./Abercorn).

38.
15 April 1889 (British Championship)
Wales - Scotland 0-0 (0-0)
Referee: William Henry Jope (Wednesbury, England)
Crowd: 6,000 (Racecourse, Wrexham)
Team: John McLeod (2/Dumbarton)
Andrew Thomson (2./Third Lanark), captain
John Rae (1/Third Lanark)
Allan Stewart (2./Queen's Park)
Alexander Lochhead (1./Third Lanark)
John Robertson Auld (3./Third Lanark)
Francis Watt (2/Kilbirnie)
Henry Campbell (1./Renton)
William Paul (2/Partick Thistle)
William Johnston (2/Third Lanark)
James Hannah (1./Third Lanark).

39.
22 March 1890 (British Championship)
Scotland - Wales 5-0 (3-0)
Referee; William Finlay (Belfast, Ireland)
Crowd: 7,500 (Underwood Park, Paisley)
Goals: 1-0 Wilson 10, 2-0 Paul 35, 3-0 Paul 44, 4-0 Paul 60, 5-0 Paul 70.
Team: George Gillespie (6/Rangers), captain
Andrew Whitelaw (2./Vale of Leven)
John Winning Murray (1./Vale of Leven)
Matthew McQueen (1/Leith Athletic)
Andrew Campbell Brown (1/St Mirren)
Hugh Wilson (1/Newmilns)
Robert Neilson Brown (1./Cambuslang)
Francis Watt (3/Kilbirnie)
William Paul (3./Partick Thistle)
James Dunlop (1./St Mirren)
Daniel Rodger Bruce (1./Vale of Leven).

40.
29 March 1890 (British Championship)
Ireland - Scotland 1-4 (1-1)
Referee: William Heaton Stacey (Sheffield, England)
Crowd: 5,000 (Ballynafeigh, Belfast)
Goals: 0-1 Rankin 15, 1-1 Peden 25, 1-2 Rankin 50, 1-3 Rankin 85, 1-4 Wyllie 86.
Team: John McLeod (3/Dumbarton), captain
Richard Dunn Hunter (1./St Mirren)
John Rae (2./Third Lanark)
John Russell (1./Cambuslang)
Isaac Begbie (1/Hearts)
David Mitchell (1/Rangers)
Thomas Wyllie (1./Rangers)
Gilbert Rankin (1/Vale of Leven)
John McPherson (3/Cowlairs)
John Watson Bell (1/Dumbarton)
David Baird (1/Hearts).

41.
5 April 1890 (British Championship)
Scotland - England 1-1 (1-1)
Referee: John Reid (Ireland)
Crowd: 26,379 (Hampden Park, Glasgow)
Goals: 0-1 Wood 17, 1-1 McPherson 37.
Team: James Wilson (3/Vale of Leven)
Walter Arnott (11/Queen's Park)
Michael McKeown (2./Celtic)
Thomas Robertson (2/Queen's Park)
James Kelly (4/Celtic)
James McLaren (3./Celtic), captain
William Groves (3./Celtic)
William Hall Berry (3/Queen's Park)
William Johnston (3./Third Lanark)
John McPherson (4/Cowlairs)
James McCall (5./Renton).

42.
21 March 1891 (British Championship)
Wales - Scotland 3-4 (2-1)
Referee: Charles Crump (Birmingham, England)
Crowd: 4,000 (Racecourse, Wrexham)
Goals: 0-1 Logan 5, 1-1 Bowdler 12, 2-1 Owen 45,
2-2 Buchanan 51, 2-3 Boyd 59, 3-3 Owen,
3-4 Boyd 80.
Team: John McCorkindale (1./Partick Thistle)
Archibald Ritchie (1./East Stirlingshire)
James Hepburn (1./Alloa Athletic)
Matthew McQueen (2./Leith Athletic)
Andrew Campbell Brown (2./St Mirren)
Thomas Robertson (3/Queen's Park), captain
William Gulliland (1./Queen's Park)
Robert Blackburn Buchanan (1./Abercorn)
James Logan (1./Ayr)
Robert Boyd (2./Mossend Swifts)
Alexander Keiller (1/Montrose).

43.
28 March 1891 (British Championship)
Scotland - Ireland 2-1 (1-0)
Referee: William Heaton Stacey (Sheffield, England)
Crowd: 8,000 (Celtic Park, Glasgow)
Goals: 1-0 Waddell 7, 2-0 Low 60, 2-1 Crawford 85.
Team: George Gillespie (7./Queen's Park), captain
Donald Currie Sillars (1/Queen's Park)
William Paul (1./Dykebar)
Thomas Hamilton (1./Hurlford)
John White Clelland (1./Royal Albert)
James Paterson Campbell (1/Kilmarnock)
James Low (1./Cambuslang)
Robert Clements (1./Leith Athletic)
William Bowie (1./Linthouse)
Thomas Smith Waddell (1./Queen's Park)
James Fraser (1./Moffat).

44.
6 April 1891 (British Championship)
England - Scotland 2-1 (2-0)
Referee: William Morrow (Moyola Park, Ireland)
Crowd: 10,000 (Ewood Park, Blackburn)
Goals: 1-0 Goodall 20, 2-0 Chadwick 30, 2-1 Watt 85.
Team: James Wilson (4./Vale of Leven)
Walter Arnott (12/Queen's Park), captain
Robert Smellie (4/Queen's Park)
Isaac Begbie (2/Hearts)
John McPherson (1./Hearts)
John Jack Hill (1/Hearts)
Gilbert Rankin (2./Vale of Leven)
Francis Watt (4./Kilbirnie)
William Sellar (6/Queen's Park)
William Hall Berry (4./Queen's Park)
David Baird (2/Hearts).

45.
19 March 1892 (British Championship)
Ireland - Scotland 2-3 (1-2)
Referee: John Taylor (Secretary, Wales FA)
Crowd: 10,000 (Solitude, Belfast)
Goals: 0-1 Keiller 17, 0-2 Lambie 28,
1-2 Williamson 42, 1-3 Ellis 70, 2-3 Gaffikin 86.
Team: Andrew Baird (1/Queen's Park)
George Alexander Bowman (1./Montrose)
John Drummond (1/Falkirk)
Robert William Marshall (1/Rangers)
Thomas Robertson (4./Queen's Park), captain
Peter Dowds (1./Celtic)
William Gulliland (2/Queen's Park)
David Murray McPherson (1./Kilmarnock)
David Thomson Ellis (1./Mossend Swifts)
William Allan Lambie (1/Queen's Park)
Alexander Keiller (2/Montrose).

46.
26 March 1892 (British Championship)
Scotland - Wales 6-1 (4-0)
Referee: John Reid (Ireland)
Crowd: 600 (Tynecastle Park, Edinburgh)
Goals: 1-0 Thomson 2, 2-0 Hamilton 8,
3-0 McPherson 15, 4-0 McPherson 44, 5-0 Baird 55,
6-0 Hamilton 65, 6-1 B Lewis 87.
Team: Robert Downie (1./Third Lanark)
James Adams (2/Hearts)
James Orr (1./Kilmarnock)
Isaac Begbie (3/Hearts)
James Paterson Campbell (2./Kilmarnock)
John Jack Hill (2./Hearts), captain
John Daniel Taylor (1/Dumbarton)
William Thomson (1/Dumbarton)
James Hamilton (1/Queen's Park)
John McPherson (5/Rangers)
David Baird (3./Hearts).

47.
2 April 1892 (British Championship)
Scotland - England 1-4 (0-4)
Referee: Dr John Smith (Kirkcaldy, Scotland)
Crowd: 20,000 (Ibrox Park, Glasgow)
Goals: 0-1 Chadwick 1, 0-2 Goodall 14,
0-3 Southworth 16, 0-4 Goodall 25, 1-4 Bell 80.
Team: John McLeod (4/Dumbarton)
Daniel Doyle (1/Celtic)
Walter Arnott (13/Queen's Park)
James Kelly (5/Celtic)
William Sellar (7/Queen's Park), captain
David Mitchell (2/Rangers)
Donald Currie Sillars (2/Queen's Park)
William Kay Taylor (1./Hearts)
Thomas Smith Waddell (2/Queen's Park)
Alexander McMahon (1/Celtic)
John Watson Bell (2/Dumbarton).

48.
18 March 1893 (British Championship)
Wales - Scotland 0-8 (0-5)
Referee: William Heaton Stacey (Sheffield, England)
Crowd: 4,500 (Racecourse, Wrexham)
Goals: 0-1 Madden 4, 0-2 Madden 14, 0-3 Barker 19,
0-4 Barker 35, 0-5 Barker 40, 0-6 Madden 47,
0-7 Lambie 62, 0-8 Madden 89.
Team: John McLeod (5./Dumbarton)
Daniel Doyle (2/Celtic)
Robert Foyer (1/St Bernard's)
Donald Currie Sillars (3/Queen's Park), captain
Andrew McCreadie (1/Rangers)
David McGregor Stewart (1/Queen's Park)
John Daniel Taylor (2/Dumbarton)
William Thomson (2/Dumbarton)
John Madden (1/Celtic)
John Bell Barker (1/Rangers)
William Allan Lambie (2/Queen's Park).

49.
25 March 1893 (British Championship)
Scotland - Ircland 6-1 (4-1)
Referee: John Taylor (Secretary, Wales FA)
Crowd: 12,000 (Celtic Park, Glasgow)
Goals: 1-0 Sellar 7, 2-0 S Torrans og 15,
3-0 Sellar 18, 4-0 McMahon 28, 4-1 Gaffikin 44,
5-1 Kelly 60, 6-1 Hamilton 70.
Team: John Lindsay (2/Renton)
James Adams (3./Hearts)
Robert Smellie (5/Queen's Park)
William Patrick Maley (1/Celtic)
James Kelly (6/Celtic), captain
David Mitchell (3/Rangers)
William Sellar (8/Queen's Park)
Thomas Smith Waddell (3/Queen's Park)
James Hamilton (2/Queen's Park)
Alexander McMahon (2/Celtic)
John Campbell (1/Celtic).

50.
1 April 1893 (British Championship)
England - Scotland 5-2 (1-1)
Referee: John Charles Clegg (Sheffield, England)
Crowd: 16,000 (Richmond Athletic Ground, London)
Goals: 1-0 Gosling 10, 1-1 Waddell 25, 1-2 Sellar 47,
2-2 Cotterill 64, 3-2 Spiksley 69, 4-2 Spiksley 72,
5-2 Reynolds 75.
Team: John Lindsay (3./Renton)
Walter Arnott (14./Queen's Park)
Robert Smellie (6./Queen's Park)
William Patrick Maley (2./Celtic)
James Kelly (7/Celtic), captain
David Mitchell (4/Rangers)
William Sellar (9./Queen's Park)
Thomas Smith Waddell (4/Queen's Park)
James Hamilton (3./Queen's Park)
Alexander McMahon (3/Celtic)
John Campbell (2/Celtic).

51.
24 March 1894 (British Championship)
Scotland - Wales 5-2 (2-2)
Referee: Joseph McBride (Ireland)
Crowd: 10,000 (Rugby Park, Kilmarnock)
Goals: 0-1 Morris 21, 0-2 Morris 34, 1-2 Berry 40,
2-2 Barker 44, 3-2 Chambers 70, 4-2 Chambers 75,
5-2 Barker 85.
Team: Andrew Baird (2./Queen's Park)
David Crawford (1/St Mirren)
Robert Foyer (2./St Bernard's)
Edward McBain (1./St Mirren)
James Kelly (8/Celtic), captain
John Johnstone (1./Kilmarnock)
Andrew Stewart (1./Third Lanark)
Thomas Chambers (1./Hearts)
David Alexander (1/East Stirlingshire)
Davidson Berry (1/Queen's Park)
John Bell Barker (2./Rangers).

52.
31 March 1894 (British Championship)
Ireland - Scotland 1-2 (0-2)
Referee: Edward Phennah (Wrexham, Wales)
Crowd: 6,000 (Solitude, Belfast)
Goals: 0-1 Torrans og 25, 0-2 Taylor 32,
1-2 Stanfield 65.
Team: Francis Barrett (1/Dundee)
David Crawford (2/St Mirren)
John Drummond (2/Rangers)
Robert William Marshall (2./Rangers), captain
William Longair (1./Dundee)
David McGregor Stewart (2/Queen's Park)
John Daniel Taylor (3/Dumbarton)
James Blessington (1/Celtic)
David Alexander (2./East Stirlingshire)
Robert Scott (1./Airdrie)
Alexander Keiller (3/Dundee).

53.
7 April 1894 (British Championship)
Scotland - England 2-2 (1-1)
Referee: Jack Reid (Ireland)
Crowd: 45,107 (Celtic Park, Glasgow)
Goals: 1-0 Lambie 7, 1-1 Goodall 12,
2-1 McPherson 75, 2-2 Reynolds 85.
Team: David Haddow (1./Rangers)
Donald Currie Sillars (4/Queen's Park)
Daniel Doyle (3/Celtic), captain
Isaac Begbie (4./Hearts)
Andrew McCreadie (2./Rangers)
David Mitchell (5./Rangers)
William Gulliland (3/Queen's Park)
James Blessington (2/Celtic)
Alexander McMahon (4/Celtic)
John McPherson (6/Rangers)
William Allan Lambie (3/Queen's Park).

54.
23 March 1895 (British Championship)
Wales - Scotland 2-2 (1-2)
Referee: William Henry Jope (Wednesbury, England)
Crowd: 4,000 (Racecourse, Wrexham)
Goals: 1-0 W Lewis 10, 1-1 Madden 30,
1-2 Divers 39, 2-2 Chapman 60.
Team: Francis Barrett (2./Dundee)
Donald Currie Sillars (5./Queen's Park), captain
Robert Glen (1/Renton)
James Simpson (1/Third Lanark)
William McColl (1./Renton)
Alexander Keiller (4/Dundee)
John Herbert Fyfe (1./Third Lanark)
John Murray (1./Renton)
John Madden (2./Celtic)
William Sawers (1./Dundee)
John Divers (1./Celtic).

55.
30 March 1895 (British Championship)
Scotland - Ireland 3-1 (1-1)
Referee: Richard P Gregson (Blackburn, England)
Crowd: 15,000 (Celtic Park, Glasgow)
Goals: 1-0 Lambie 1, 1-1 Morrison 25, 2-1 Taylor 65,
3-1 Walker 75.
Team: Daniel McArthur (1/Celtic)
John Drummond (3/Rangers), captain
Daniel Doyle (4/Celtic)
James Simpson (2/Third Lanark)
David Russell (1/Hearts)
Neil Gibson (1/Rangers)
John Daniel Taylor (4./St Mirren)
Thomas Smith Waddell (5/Queen's Park)
John McPherson (7/Rangers)
John Walker (1/Hearts)
William Allan Lambie (4/Queen's Park).

56.
6 April 1895 (British Championship)
England - Scotland 3-0 (3-0)
Referee: John Reid (Ireland)
Crowd: 42,500 (Goodison Park, Liverpool)
Goals: 1-0 Bloomer 30, 2-0 Gibson og 35,
3-0 Smith 44.
Team: Daniel McArthur (2/Celtic)
John Drummond (4/Rangers)
Daniel Doyle (5/Celtic)
David Russell (2/Hearts)
James Simpson (3./Third Lanark)
Neil Gibson (2/Rangers)
William Allan Lambie (5/Queen's Park)
John McPherson (8/Rangers)
James Oswald (2/St Bernard's), captain
Thomas Smith Waddell (6./Queen's Park)
William Gulliland (4./Queen's Park).

57.
21 March 1896 (British Championship)
Scotland - Wales 4-0 (2-0)
Referee: Joseph McBride (Ireland)
Crowd: 11,700 (Carolina Port, Dundee)
Goals: 1-0 Neill 17, 2-0 Keiller 30, 3-0 Paton 59,
4-0 Neill 88.
Team: Robert Macfarlane (1./Morton)
Duncan McLean (1/St Bernard's)
Robert Glen (2/Renton)
John Gillespie (1./Queen's Park), captain
Robert Scott Gibson Neill (1/Hibernian)
William Blair (1./Third Lanark)
William Thomson (1./Dundee)
Daniel John Ferguson Paton (1./St Bernard's)
Robert Smyth McColl (1/Queen's Park)
Alexander King (1/Hearts)
Alexander Keiller (5/Dundee).

58.
28 March 1896 (British Championship)
Ireland - Scotland 3-3 (3-2)
Referee: James Cooper (Blackburn, England)
Crowd: 8,000 (Solitude, Belfast)
Goals: 0-1 McColl 7, 1-1 Barron 20, 1-2 McColl 25,
2-2 Milne pen 32, 3-2 Barron 43, 3-3 Blessington 80.
Team: Kenneth Anderson (1/Queen's Park)
John Drummond (5/Rangers)
Peter Meehan (1./Celtic)
Neil Gibson (3/Rangers)
James Kelly (9./Celtic), captain
George Hogg (1/Hearts)
Patrick Murray (1/Hibernian)
James Blessington (3/Celtic)
Robert Smyth McColl (2/Queen's Park)
John Cameron (1./Queen's Park)
William Allan Lambie (6/Queen's Park).

59.
4 April 1896 (British Championship)
Scotland - England 2-1 (2-0)
Referee: Humphrey Jones (Bangor, Wales)
Crowd: 56,500 (Celtic Park, Glasgow)
Goals: 1-0 Lambie 29, 2-0 Bell 34, 2-1 Bassett 80.
Team: John Edward Doig (3/Sunderland)
John Drummond (6/Rangers), captain
Thomas Brandon (1./Blackburn Rovers)
George Hogg (2./Hearts)
James Cowan (1/Aston Villa)
Neil Gibson (4/Rangers)
Alexander King (2/Hearts)
William Allan Lambie (7/Queen's Park)
Thomas Hyslop (1/Stoke City)
James Blessington (4./Celtic)
John Watson Bell (3/Everton).

60.
20 March 1897 (British Championship)
Wales - Scotland 2-2 (1-1)
Referee: Thomas Armitt (Leek, England)
Crowd: 5,000 (Racecourse, Wrexham)
Goals: 0-1 Ritchie pen 11, 1-1 Morgan-Owen 40,
1-2 WR Jones og 60, 2-2 Pugh 75.
Team: John Patrick (1/St Mirren)
John Lindsay Ritchie (1./Queen's Park), captain
David Richmond Gardner (1./Third Lanark)
Bernard Breslin (1./Hibernian)
David Russell (3/Celtic)
Alexander Keiller (6./Dundee)
John Kennedy (1./Hibernian)
Patrick Murray (2./Hibernian)
James Oswald (3./Rangers)
James Andrew McMillan (1./St Bernard's)
John Walker (2/Hearts).

61.
27 March 1897 (British Championship)
Scotland - Ireland 5-1 (4-0)
Referee: James Cooper (Blackburn, England)
Crowd: 15,000 (Ibrox Park, Glasgow)
Goals: 1-0 McPherson 5, 2-0 Gibson 25,
3-0 McColl 35, 4-0 King 44, 4-1 James Pyper 62,
5-1 McPherson 70.
Team: Matthew Dickie (1/Rangers)
Duncan McLean (2./St Bernard's)
John Drummond (7/Rangers), captain
Neil Gibson (5/Rangers)
William Urquhart Baird (1./St Bernard's)
David McGregor Stewart (3./Queen's Park)
Thomas Pollock Low (1./Rangers)
John McPherson (9./Rangers)
Robert Smyth McColl (3./Queen's Park)
Alexander King (3./Celtic)
William Allan Lambie (8./Queen's Park).

62.
3 April 1897 (British Championship)
England - Scotland 1-2 (1-1)
Referee: R Thomas Gough (Oswestry, Wales)
Crowd: 35,000 (Crystal Palace, London)
Goals: 1-0 Bloomer 22, 1-1 Hyslop 27, 1-2 Miller 83.
Team: John Patrick (2./St Mirren)
Nicol Smith (1/Rangers)
Daniel Doyle (6/Celtic)
Neil Gibson (6/Rangers)
James Cowan (2/Aston Villa)
Hugh Wilson (2/Sunderland)
John Watson Bell (4/Everton)
James Miller (1/Rangers)
George Horsburgh Allan (1./Liverpool)
Thomas Hyslop (2./Rangers)
William Allan Lambie (9./Queen's Park), captain.

63.
19 March 1898 (British Championship)
Scotland - Wales 5-2 (4-1)
Referee: William Heaton Stacey (Sheffield, England)
Crowd: 3,500 (Fir Park, Motherwell)
Goals: 1-0 Gillespie 12, 2-0 Gillespie 20, 3-0 McKee
29, 4-0 McKee 40, 4-1 Thomas 44, 5-1 Gillespie 61,
5-2 Morgan-Owen 89.
Team: William Watson (1./Falkirk)
Nicol Smith (2/Rangers)
Matthew McLintock Scott (1./Airdrie), captain
William Thomson (3/Dumbarton)
Alexander Jack Christie (1/Queen's Park)
Peter Campbell (1./Morton)
James Gillespie (1./Third Lanark)
James Miller (2/Rangers)
James McKee (1./East Stirlingshire)
Hugh Morgan (1/St Mirren)
Robert Findlay (1./Kilmarnock).

64.
26 March 1898 (British Championship)
Ireland - Scotland 0-3 (0-2)
Referee: John Lewis (Blackburn, England)
Crowd: 5,000 (Solitude, Belfast)
Goals: 0-1 Robertson 30, 0-2 McColl 42,
0-3 Stewart 70.
Team: Kenneth Anderson (2/Queen's Park)
Robert Robison Kelso (7./Dundee), captain
Daniel Doyle (7/Celtic)
William Thomson (4./Dumbarton)
David Russell (4/Celtic)
Alexander King (4/Celtic)
William Garven Stewart (1/Queen's Park)
John Campbell (3/Celtic)
Robert Smyth McColl (4/Queen's Park)
John Walker (3/Hearts)
Thomas Robertson (1./Hearts).

65.
2 April 1898 (British Championship)
Scotland - England 1-3 (0-2)
Referee: Thomas Robertson (Glasgow, Scotland)
Crowd: 40,000 (Celtic Park, Glasgow)
Goals: 0-1 Wheldon 3, 0-2 Bloomer 21, 1-2 Miller 50, 1-3 Bloomer 85.
Team: Kenneth Anderson (3./Queen's Park)
John Drummond (8/Rangers)
Daniel Doyle (8./Celtic)
Neil Gibson (7/Rangers)
James Cowan (3./Aston Villa), captain
John Tait Robertson (1/Everton)
John Watson Bell (5/Everton)
John Campbell (4/Celtic)
William Sturrock Maxwell (1./Stoke City)
James Miller (3./Rangers)
Alexander Smith (1/Rangers).

66.
18 March 1899 (British Championship)
Wales - Scotland 0-6 (0-1)
Referee: Charles E Sutcliffe (Burnley, England)
Crowd: 12,000 (Racecourse, Wrexham)
Goals: 0-1 Campbell 22, 0-2 McColl 50,
0-3 Campbell 53, 0-4 Marshall 70, 0-5 McColl 75,
0-6 McColl 85.
Team: Daniel McArthur (3./Celtic)
Nicol Smith (3/Rangers), captain
David Storrier (1/Celtic)
Neil Gibson (8/Rangers)
Henry James Hall Marshall (1/Celtic)
Alexander King (5/Celtic)
John William Campbell (1/Rangers)
Robert Cumming Hamilton (1/Rangers)
Robert Smyth McColl (5/Queen's Park)
John Watson Bell (6/Celtic)
Davidson Berry (2/Queen's Park).

67.
25 March 1899 (British Championship)
Scotland - Ireland 9-1 (5-0)
Referee: Charles E Sutcliffe (Burnley, England)
Crowd: 12,000 (Celtic Park, Glasgow)
Goals: 1-0 McColl 5, 2-0 Christie 6, 3-0 Hamilton 20,
4-0 McColl 21, 5-0 Bell 35, 6-0 McColl 47,
6-1 Goodall 52, 7-1 Hamilton 65, 8-1 Berry 70,
9-1 Campbell 80.
Team: Matthew Dickie (2/Rangers)
Nicol Smith (4/Rangers)
David Storrier (2/Celtic), captain
Neil Gibson (9/Rangers)
Alexander Jack Christie (2/Queen's Park)
Alexander King (6./Celtic)
John William Campbell (2/Rangers)
Robert Cumming Hamilton (2/Rangers)
Robert Smyth McColl (6/Queen's Park)
Davidson Berry (3./Queen's Park)
John Watson Bell (7/Celtic).

68.
8 April 1899 (British Championship)
England - Scotland 2-1 (2-0)
Referee: James Torrans (Belfast, Ireland)
Crowd: 37,000 (Villa Park, Birmingham)
Goals: 1-0 Smith 25, 2-0 Athersmith 40,
2-1 Hamilton 52.
Team: John Edward Doig (4/Sunderland)
Nicol Smith (5/Rangers), captain
David Storrier (3./Celtic)
Neil Gibson (10/Rangers)
Alexander Jack Christie (3./Queen's Park)
John Tait Robertson (2/Southampton)
John William Campbell (3/Rangers)
Robert Cumming Hamilton (3/Rangers)
Robert Smyth McColl (7/Queen's Park)
Hugh Morgan (2./Liverpool)
John Watson Bell (8/Celtic).

69.
3 February 1900 (British Championship)
Scotland - Wales 5-2 (4-1)
Referee: Charles E Sutcliffe (Burnley, England)
Crowd: 12,500 (Pittodrie Park, Aberdeen)
Goals: 1-0 Bell 2, 2-0 Wilson 7, 3-0 Wilson 35,
4-0 Hamilton 37, 4-1 Parry 45, 4-2 Butler 60,
5-2 A Smith 61.
Team: Matthew Dickie (3./Rangers)
Nicol Smith (6/Rangers)
David Crawford (3./Rangers)
James Hay Irons (1./Queen's Park)
Robert Scott Gibson Neill (2./Rangers)
John Tait Robertson (3/Rangers)
John Watson Bell (9/Celtic)
David Wilson (1./Queen's Park)
Robert Smyth McColl (8/Queen's Park)
Robert Cumming Hamilton (4/Rangers), captain
Alexander Smith (2/Rangers).

70.
3 March 1900 (British Championship)
Ireland - Scotland 0-3
Referee: Charles E Sutcliffe (Burnley, England)
Crowd: 6,000 (Solitude, Belfast)
Goals: 0-1 Campbell 8, 0-2 A Smith 23,
0-3 Campbell 83.
Team: Henry George Rennie (1/Hearts)
Nicol Smith (7/Rangers)
Robert Glen (3./Hibernian)
Neil Gibson (11/Rangers)
Henry James Hall Marshall (2./Celtic), captain
William Orr (1/Celtic)
William Garven Stewart (2./Queen's Park)
Robert Staig Walker (1/Hearts)
John Campbell (5/Celtic)
Patrick Callaghan (1./Hibernian)
Alexander Smith (3/Rangers).

71.
7 April 1900 (British Championship)
Scotland - England 4-1 (4-1)
Referee: James Torrans (Belfast, Ireland)
Crowd: 63,000 (Celtic Park, Glasgow)
Goals: 1-0 McColl 1, 2-0 Bell 6, 3-0 McColl 25,
3-1 Bloomer 28, 4-1 McColl 44.
Team: Henry George Rennie (2/Hearts)
Nicol Smith (8/Rangers)
John Drummond (9/Rangers)
Neil Gibson (12/Rangers)
Alexander Galloway Raisbeck (1/Liverpool)
John Tait Robertson (4/Rangers), captain
John Watson Bell (10./Celtic)
Robert Staig Walker (2/Hearts)
Robert Smyth McColl (9/Queen's Park)
John Campbell (6/Celtic)
Alexander Smith (4/Rangers).

72.
23 February 1901 (British Championship)
Scotland - Ireland 11-0 (5-0)
Referee: R Thomas Gough (Oswestry, Wales)
Crowd: 15,000 (Celtic Park, Glasgow)
Goals: 1-0 Campbell (R), 2-0 Campbell (R),
3-0 Russell, 4-0 Campbell (C) 5-0 McMahon,
6-0 Hamilton, 7-0 McMahon, 8-0 Hamilton,
9-0 McMahon, 10-0 Hamilton, 11-0 Hamilton.
Team: George Chappell McWattie (1/Queen's Park)
Nicol Smith (9/Rangers)
Bernard Battles (1/Celtic)
David Russell (5/Celtic)
George Anderson (1./Kilmarnock)
John Tait Robertson (5/Rangers)
John William Campbell (4./Rangers)
John Campbell (7/Celtic)
Robert Cumming Hamilton (5/Rangers), captain
Alexander McMahon (5/Celtic)
Alexander Smith (5/Rangers).

73.
2 March 1901 (British Championship)
Wales - Scotland 1-1 (0-0)
Referee: Charles E Sutcliffe (Burnley, England)
Crowd: 1,000 (Racecourse, Wrexham)
Goals: 0-1 Robertson 74, 1-1 Parry 80.
Team: George Chappell McWattie (2./Queen's Park)
Nicol Smith (10/Rangers)
Bernard Battles (2/Celtic)
Neil Gibson (13/Rangers)
David Russell (6./Celtic)
John Tait Robertson (6/Rangers), captain
Mark Dickson Bell (1./Hearts)
Robert Staig Walker (3/Hearts)
Robert Smyth McColl (10/Queen's Park)
John Campbell (8/Celtic)
Alexander Smith (6/Rangers).

74.
30 March 1901 (British Championship)
England - Scotland 2-2 (1-0)
Referee: James Torrans (Belfast, Ireland)
Crowd: 35,000 (Crystal Palace, London)
Goals: 1-0 Blackburn 35, 1-1 Campbell 53,
1-2 Hamilton 70, 2-2 Bloomer 75.
Team: Henry George Rennie (3/Hibernian)
Bernard Battles (3./Celtic)
John Drummond (10/Rangers)
Andrew Aitken (1/Newcastle United)
Alexander Galloway Raisbeck (2/Liverpool)
John Tait Robertson (7/Rangers), captain
Robert Staig Walker (4/Hearts)
John Campbell (9/Celtic)
Robert Smyth McColl (11/Queen's Park)
Robert Cumming Hamilton (6/Rangers)
Alexander Smith (7/Rangers).

75.
1 March 1902 (British Championship)
Ireland - Scotland 1-5 (0-1)
Referee: Frederick Bye (Sheffield, England)
Crowd: 12,000 (Grosvenor Park, Belfast)
Goals: 0-1 Hamilton 43, 0-2 Walker 49, 0-3 Hamilton 70, 0-4 Hamilton 74, 0-5 Buick 76, 1-5 Campbell 85.
Team: Henry George Rennie (4/Hibernian)
Nicol Smith (11/Rangers)
John Drummond (11/Rangers)
George Key (1./Hearts)
Albert Thoroughgood Buick (1/Hearts), captain
John Tait Robertson (8/Rangers)
William McCartney (1./Hibernian)
Robert Staig Walker (5/Hearts)
Robert Cumming Hamilton (7/Rangers)
John Campbell (10/Celtic)
Alexander Smith (8/Rangers).

76.
15 March 1902 (British Championship)
Scotland - Wales 5-1 (1-0)
Referee: Joseph McBride (Ireland)
Crowd: 12,000 (Cappielow Park, Greenock)
Goals: 1-0 Robertson 38, 2-0 Buick 47, 3-0 Smith 50,
4-0 Walker 55, 4-1 Morgan-Owen 70,
5-1 Campbell 89.
Team: Henry George Rennie (5/Hibernian)
Henry Hogg Allan (1./Hearts)
John Drummond (12/Rangers)
Hugh Wilson (3/Third Lanark)
Albert Thoroughgood Buick (2./Hearts)
John Tait Robertson (9/Rangers)
John Campbell (11/ Celtic), captain
Robert Staig Walker (6/Hearts)
Robert Cumming Hamilton (8/Rangers)
Alexander McMahon (6./Celtic)
Alexander Smith (9/Rangers).

77.
3 May 1902 (British Championship)
England - Scotland 2-2 (0-2)
Referee: James Torrans (Belfast, Ireland)
Crowd: 15,000 (Villa Park, Birmingham)
Goals: 0-1 Templeton 3, 0-2 Orr 30, 1-2 Settle 70, 2-2 Wilkes 71.
Team: Henry George Rennie (6/Hibernian)
Nicol Smith (12./Rangers)
John Drummond (13/Rangers)
Andrew Aitken (2/Newcastle United), captain
Alexander Galloway Raisbeck (3/Liverpool)
John Tait Robertson (10/Rangers)
Robert Bryson Templeton (1/Aston Villa)
Robert Staig Walker (7/Hearts)
Robert Smyth McColl (12/Newcastle United)
Ronald Orr (1/Newcastle United)
Alexander Smith (10/Rangers).

78.
9 March 1903 (British Championship)
Wales - Scotland 0-1 (0-1)
Referee: Frederick Kirkham (Preston, England)
Crowd: 11,000 (Cardiff Arms Park, Cardiff)
Goal: 0-1 Speedie 25.
Team: Henry George Rennie (7/Hibernian)
Andrew McCombie (1/Sunderland)
James Watson (1/Sunderland)
Andrew Aitken (3/Newcastle United)
Alexander Galloway Raisbeck (4/Liverpool), captain
John Tait Robertson (11/Rangers)
Robert Bryson Templeton (2/Newcastle United)
Robert Staig Walker (8/Hearts)
John Campbell (12./Celtic)
Finlay Ballantyne Speedie (1/Rangers)
Alexander Smith (11/Rangers).

79.
21 March 1903 (British Championship)
Scotland - Ireland 0-2 (0-1)
Referee: Thomas Kirkham (Hanley, England)
Crowd: 17,000 (Celtic Park, Glasgow)
Goals: 0-1 Connor 9, 0-2 Kirwan 87.
Team: Henry George Rennie (8/Hibernian)
Archibald Gray (1./Hibernian)
John Drummond (14./Rangers), captain
John Halliday Cross (1./Third Lanark)
Peter Neilson Robertson (1./Dundee)
William Orr (2/Celtic)
David Lindsay (1./St Mirren)
Robert Staig Walker (9/Hearts)
William Porteous (1./Hearts)
Finlay Ballantyne Speedie (2/Rangers)
Alexander Smith (12/Rangers).

80.
4 April 1903 (British Championship)
England - Scotland 1-2 (1-0)
Referee: William Nunnerley (Wrexham, Wales)
Crowd: 36,000 (Bramall Lane, Sheffield)
Goals: 1-0 Woodward 10, 1-1 Speedie 57, 1-2 Walker 59.
Team: John Edward Doig (5./Sunderland)
Andrew McCombie (2/Sunderland)
James Watson (2/Sunderland)
Andrew Aitken (4/Newcastle United)
Alexander Galloway Raisbeck (5/Liverpool), captain
John Tait Robertson (12/Rangers)
Robert Bryson Templeton (3/Newcastle United)
Robert Staig Walker (10/Hearts)
Robert Cumming Hamilton (9/Rangers)
Finlay Ballantyne Speedie (3./Rangers)
Alexander Smith (13/Rangers).

81.
12 March 1904 (British Championship)
Scotland - Wales 1-1 (1-0)
Referee: Thomas Kirkham (Hanley, England)
Crowd: 12,000 (Dens Park, Dundee)
Goals: 1-0 R Walker 5, 1-1 Atherton 50.
Team: Alexander Leslie Henderson Skene (1./Queen's Park)
Thomas Alexander Jackson (1/St Mirren)
James Sharp (1/Dundee), captain
William Orr (3./Celtic)
Thomas Parker Sloan (1./Third Lanark)
John Tait Robertson (13/Rangers)
John Walker (4/Rangers)
Robert Staig Walker (11/Hearts)
Alexander Bennett (1/Celtic)
Alexander Macfarlane (1/Dundee)
George Williamson Wilson (1/Hearts).

82.
26 March 1904 (British Championship)
Ireland - Scotland 1-1 (0-1)
Referee: Frederick Kirkham (Preston, England)
Crowd: 1,000 (Dalymount Park, Dublin)
Goals: 0-1 Hamilton 22, 1-1 Sheridan 70.
Team: Henry George Rennie (9/Hibernian)
Thomas Alexander Jackson (2/St Mirren)
John Bell Cameron (1/St Mirren)
George Turnbull Henderson (1./Rangers)
Charles Bellany Thomson (1/Hearts)
John Tait Robertson (14/Rangers), captain
John Walker (5./Rangers)
Robert Staig Walker (12/Hearts)
Robert Cumming Hamilton (10/Rangers)
Hugh Wilson (4./Third Lanark)
Alexander Smith (14/Rangers)

83.
9 April 1904 (British Championship)
Scotland - England 0-1 (0-0)
Referee: William Nunnerley (Wrexham, Wales)
Crowd: 45,000 (Celtic Park, Glasgow)
Goal: 0-1 Bloomer 58.
Team: Peter McBride (1/Preston North End)
Thomas Alexander Jackson (3/St Mirren)
James Watson (3/Sunderland)
Andrew Aitken (5/Newcastle United)
Alexander Galloway Raisbeck (6/Liverpool)
John Tait Robertson (15/Rangers), captain
Thomas Bruce Niblo (1./Aston Villa)
Robert Staig Walker (13/Hearts)
Alexander Brown (1./Middlesbrough)
Ronald Orr (2./Newcastle United)
Robert Bryson Templeton (4/Newcastle United).

84.
6 March 1905 (British Championship)
Wales - Scotland 3-1 (1-0)
Referee: Frederick Kirkham (Preston, England)
Crowd: 6,000 (Racecourse Ground, Wrexham)
Goals: 1-0 Watkins 30, 2-0 AG Morris 47,
3-0 Meredith 50, 3-1 Robertson 86.
Team: Henry George Rennie (10/Hibernian)
Andrew McCombie (3/Newcastle)
Thomas Alexander Jackson (4/St Mirren), captain
Andrew Aitken (6/Newcastle United)
Charles Bellany Thomson (2/Hearts)
John Tait Robertson (16./Rangers)
Robert Bryson Templeton (5/Woolwich Arsenal)
Robert Staig Walker (14/Hearts)
Samuel Watson Kennedy (1./Partick Thistle)
Thomas Tindal Fitchie (1/Woolwich Arsenal)
Alexander Smith (15/Rangers).

85.
18 March 1905 (British Championship)
Scotland - Ireland 4-0 (2-0)
Referee: Thomas Kirkham (Hanley, England)
Crowd: 35,000 (Celtic Park, Glasgow)
Goals: 1-0 Thomson pen 14, 2-0 Walker 35,
3-0 Quinn 50, 4-0 Thomson pen 61.
Team: William Howden (1./Partick Thistle)
Donald McLeod (1/Celtic)
William Forbes McIntosh (1./Third Lanark)
Neil Gibson (14./Partick Thistle), captain
Charles Bellany Thomson (3/Hearts)
James Hay (1/Celtic)
James McMenemy (1/Celtic)
Robert Staig Walker (15/Hearts)
James Quinn (1/Celtic)
Peter Somers (1/Celtic)
George Williamson Wilson (2/Hearts).

86.
1 April 1905 (British Championship)
England - Scotland 1-0 (0-0)
Referee: William Nunnerley (Wrexham, Wales)
Crowd: 40,000 (Crystal Palace, London)
Goal: 1-0 Bache 80.
Team: John Lyall (1./Sheffield Wednesday)
Andrew McCombie (4./Newcastle United)
James Watson (4/Sunderland)
Andrew Aitken (7/Newcastle United)
Charles Bellany Thomson (4/Hearts), captain
Peter McWilliam (1/Newcastle United)
Robert Staig Walker (16/Hearts)
James Howie (1/Newcastle United)
Alexander Simpson Young (1/Everton)
Peter Somers (2/Celtic)
George Williamson Wilson (3/Hearts).

87.
3 March 1906 (British Championship)
Scotland - Wales 0-2
Referee: John Lewis (Blackburn, England)
Crowd: 25,000 (Tynecastle Park, Edinburgh)
Goals: 0-1 WL Jones 50, 0-2 JL Jones 65.
Team: James Smith Raeside (1./Third Lanark)
Donald McLeod (2/Celtic)
Andrew Richmond (1./Queen's Park)
Alexander McNair (1/Celtic)
Charles Bellany Thomson (5/Hearts), captain
John May (1/Rangers)
George Lindsay Stewart (1/Hibernian)
Alexander Macfarlane (2/Dundee)
James Quinn (2/Celtic)
Thomas Fitchie (2/Woolwich Arsenal)
George Williamson Wilson (4/Hearts).

88.
17 March 1906 (British Championship)
Ireland - Scotland 0-1 (0-0)
Referee: Frederick Bye (Sheffield, England)
Crowd: 8,000 (Dalymount Park, Dublin)
Goal: 0-1 Fitchie 52.
Team: Henry George Rennie (11/Hibernian)
Donald McLeod (3/Celtic)
David Alexander Hill (1./Third Lanark)
James Young (1./Celtic)
Charles Bellany Thomson (6/Hearts)
John May (2/Rangers), captain
Gladstone Hamilton (1./Port Glasgow Athletic)
Robert Staig Walker (17/Hearts)
James Quinn (3/Celtic)
Thomas Fitchie (3/Woolwich Arsenal)
Alexander Smith (16/Rangers).

89.
7 April 1906 (British Championship)
Scotland - England 2-1 (1-0)
Referee: William Nunnerley (Wrexham, Wales)
Crowd: 102,741 (Hampden Park, Glasgow)
Goals: 1-0 Howie 40, 2-0 Howie 55, 2-1 Shepherd 82.
Team: Peter McBride (2/Preston North End)
Donald McLeod (4./Celtic)
William Peden Dunlop (1./Liverpool)
Andrew Aitken (8/Newcastle United)
Alexander Galloway Raisbeck (7/Liverpool), captain
Peter McWilliam (2/Newcastle United)
George Lindsay Stewart (2/Hibernian)
James Howie (2/Newcastle United)
Alexander William Menzies (1./Hearts)
George Turner Livingston (1/Manchester City)
Alexander Smith (17/Rangers).

90.
4 March 1907 (British Championship)
Wales - Scotland 1-0 (0-0)
Referee: James Mason (Burslem, England)
Crowd: 7,715 (Racecourse Ground, Wrexham)
Goal: 1-0 AG Morris 88.
Team: Peter McBride (3/Preston North End)
Thomas Alexander Jackson (5/St Mirren)
James Sharp (2/Arsenal)
Andrew Aitken (9/Middlesbrough)
Charles Bellany Thomson (7/Hearts), captain
Peter McWilliam (3/Newcastle United)
George Lindsay Stewart (3/Manchester City)
George Turner Livingston (2./Rangers)
Alexander Simpson Young (2./Everton)
Thomas Fitchie (4./Queen's Park)
Alexander Smith (18/Rangers).

91.
16 March 1907 (British Championship
Scotland - Ireland 3-0
Referee: John Lewis (Blackburn, England)
Crowd: 26,000 (Celtic Park, Glasgow)
Goals: 1-0 O'Rourke 40, 2-0 Walker 48,
3-0 Thomson pen 82.
Team: William Muir (1./Dundee)
Thomas Alexander Jackson (6./St Mirren)
William Barbour Agnew (1/Kilmarnock)
William Key (1./Queen's Park)
Charles Bellany Thomson (8/Hearts), captain
Alexander McNair (2/Celtic)
Alexander Bennett (2/Celtic)
Robert Staig Walker (18/Hearts)
Francis O'Rourke (1./Airdrie)
Peter Somers (3/Celtic)
John Fraser (1./Dundee).

92.
6 April 1907 (British Championship)
England - Scotland 1-1 (1-1)
Referee: Thomas Robertson (Glasgow, Scotland)
Crowd: 38,000 (St James' Park, Newcastle)
Goals: 0-1 Crompton og 2, 1-1 Bloomer 40.
Team: Peter McBride (4/Preston North End)
Charles Bellany Thomson (9/Hearts), captain
James Sharp (3/Arsenal)
Andrew Aitken (10/Middlesbrough)
Alexander Galloway Raisbeck (8./Liverpool)
Peter McWilliam (4/Newcastle United)
George Lindsay Stewart (4./Manchester City)
Robert Staig Walker (19/Hearts)
Andrew Wilson (1/Sheffield Wednesday)
Walter Logie White (1/Bolton Wanderers)
George Williamson Wilson (5/Everton).

93.
7 March 1908 (British Championship)
Scotland - Wales 2-1 (0-1)
Referee: James Mason (Burslem, England)
Crowd: 18,000 (Dens Park, Dundee)
Goals: 0-1 Jones 30, 1-1 Bennett 60, 2-1 Lennie 87.
Team: Henry George Rennie (12/Hibernian)
William Barbour Agnew (2/Kilmarnock)
George Duncan Chaplin (1./Dundee)
Alexander McNair (3/Celtic)
Charles Bellany Thomson (10/Hearts), captain
James Hill Galt (1/Rangers)
Alexander Bennett (3/Celtic)
Robert Staig Walker (20/Hearts)
James Hamilton Speirs (1./Rangers)
Alexander Macfarlane (3/Dundee)
William Lennie (1/Aberdeen).

94.
14 March 1908 (British Championship)
Ireland - Scotland 0-5 (0-2)
Referee: John T Ibbotson (Derby, England)
Crowd: 10,000 (Dalymount Park, Dublin)
Goals: 0-1 Quinn 3, 0-2 Galt 25, 0-3 Quinn 55,
0-4 Quinn 70, 0-5 Quinn 75.
Team: Henry George Rennie (13./Hibernian)
James Mitchell (1/Kilmarnock)
William Barbour Agnew (3./Kilmarnock)
John May (3/Rangers)
Charles Bellany Thomson (11/Hearts), captain
James Hill Galt (2./Rangers)
Robert Bryson Templeton (6/Kilmarnock)
Robert Staig Walker (21/Hearts)
James Quinn (4/Celtic)
Robert Smyth McColl (13./Newcastle United)
William Lennie (2./Aberdeen).

95.
4 April 1908 (British Championship)
Scotland - England 1-1 (1-0)
Referee: James Mason (Burslem, England)
Crowd: 121,452 (Hampden Park, Glasgow)
Goals: 1-0 Wilson 27, 1-1 Windridge 75.
Team: Peter McBride (5/Preston North End)
Alexander McNair (4/Celtic)
James Sharp (4/Arsenal)
Andrew Aitken (11/Middlesbrough)
Charles Bellany Thomson (12/Hearts), captain
John May (4/Rangers)
James Howie (3./Newcastle United)
Robert Staig Walker (22/Hearts)
Andrew Wilson (2/Sheffield Wednesday)
Walter Logie White (2./Bolton Wanderers)
James Quinn (5/Celtic).

96.
1 March 1909 (British Championship)
Wales - Scotland 3-2 (3-0)
Referee: Thomas Campbell (Blackburn, England)
Crowd: 6,000 (Racecourse Ground, Wrexham)
Goals: 1-0 Davies 23, 2-0 Jones 26, 3-0 Davies 39,
3-1 Walker 70, 3-2 Paul 73.
Team: Peter McBride (6./Preston North End)
Thomas Collins (1./Hearts)
James Sharp (5./Fulham)
John May (5./Rangers)
Charles Bellany Thomson (13/Sunderland), captain
Peter McWilliam (5/Newcastle United)
Alexander Bennett (4/Rangers)
John Hunter (1./Dundee)
Robert Staig Walker (23/Hearts)
Peter Somers (4./Celtic)
Harold McDonald Paul (1./Queen's Park).

97.
15 March 1909 (British Championship)
Scotland - Ireland 5-0 (2-0)
Referee: James Mason (Burslem, England)
Crowd: 24,000 (Ibrox Stadium, Glasgow)
Goals: 1-0 McMenemy 14, 2-0 Macfarlane 20,
3-0 Thomson 48, 4-0 McMenemy 77, 5-0 Paul 84.
Team: James Brownlie (1/Third Lanark)
James Main (1./Hibernian)
James Watson (5/Middlesbrough)
William Walker (1/Clyde)
James Stark (1/Rangers), captain
James Hay (2/Celtic)
Alexander Bennett (5/Rangers)
James McMenemy (2/Celtic)
Alexander Thomson (1./Airdrie)
Alexander Macfarlane (4/Dundee)
Harold McDonald Paul (2/Queen's Park).

98.
3 April 1909 (British Championship)
England - Scotland 2-0 (2-0)
Referee: James Stark (Airdrie, Scotland)
Crowd: 27,000 (Crystal Palace, London)
Goals: 1-0 Wall 3, 2-0 Wall 15.
Team: James Brownlie (2/Third Lanark)
John Bell Cameron (2./Chelsea)
James Watson (6./Middlesbrough)
Alexander McNair (5/Celtic)
James Stark (2./Rangers), captain
Peter McWilliam (6/Newcastle United)
Alexander Bennett (6/Rangers)
Robert Staig Walker (24/Hearts)
James Quinn (6/Celtic)
George Williamson Wilson (6./Newcastle United)
Harold McDonald Paul (3./Queen's Park).

99.
5 March 1910 (British Championship)
Scotland - Wales 1-0 (0-0)
Referee: Herbert Bamlett (Gateshead, England)
Crowd: 22,000 (Rugby Park, Kilmarnock)
Goal: 1-0 Devine 75.
Team: James Brownlie (3/Third Lanark)
George Law (1/Rangers)
James Mitchell (2/Kilmarnock)
Alexander McNair (6/Celtic)
William Loney (1/Celtic)
James Hay (3/Celtic), captain
Alexander Bennett (7/Rangers)
James McMenemy (3/Celtic)
James Quinn (7/Celtic)
Archibald Forbes Devine (1./Falkirk)
George Clarke Robertson (1/Motherwell).

100.
19 March 1910 (British Championship)
Ireland - Scotland 1-0 (0-0)
Referee: John Howcroft (Bolton, England)
Crowd: 17,000 (Windsor Park, Belfast)
Goal: 1-0 Thompson 54.
Team: James Brownlie (4/Third Lanark)
George Law (2/Rangers)
James Mitchell (3./Kilmarnock)
William Walker (2./Clyde)
William Loney (2./Celtic)
James Hay (4/Celtic), captain
George Leckie Sinclair (1/Hearts)
John Kay McTavish (1./Falkirk)
James Quinn (8/Celtic)
Alexander Higgins (1/Newcastle)
Robert Bryson Templeton (7/Kilmarnock).

101.
2 April 1910 (British Championship)
Scotland - England 2-0 (2-0)
Referee: James Mason (Burslem, England)
Crowd: 106,205 (Hampden Park, Glasgow)
Goals: 1-0 McMenemy 20, 2-0 Quinn 32.
Team: James Brownlie (5/Third Lanark)
George Law (3./Rangers)
James Hay (5/Celtic)
Andrew Aitken (12/Leicester Fosse)
Charles Bellany Thomson (14/Sunderland), captain
Peter McWilliam (7/Newcastle United)
Alexander Bennett (8/Rangers)
James McMenemy (4/Celtic)
James Quinn (9/Celtic)
Alexander Higgins (2/Newcastle United)
Robert Bryson Templeton (8/Kilmarnock).

102.
6 March 1911 (British Championship)
Wales - Scotland 2-2 (1-1)
Referee: James Mason (Burslem, England)
Crowd: 14,000 (Ninian Park, Cardiff)
Goals: 1-0 AG Morris 20, 1-1 Hamilton 35,
2-1 AG Morris 65, 2-2 Hamilton 89.
Team: James Brownlie (6/Third Lanark)
Donald Colman (1/Aberdeen)
John Walker (1/Swindon Town)
Thomas Somerville Tait (1./Sunderland)
Wilfrid Lawson Low (1/Newcastle United)
Peter McWilliam (8./Newcastle United), captain
Alexander Bennett (9/Rangers)
James McMenemy (5/Celtic)
William Reid (1/Rangers)
Alexander Macfarlane (5./Dundee)
Robert Cumming Hamilton (11./Dundee).

103.
18 March 1911 (British Championship)
Scotland - Ireland 2-0 (1-0)
Referee: Herbert Bamlett (Gateshead, England)
Crowd: 32,000 (Celtic Park, Glasgow)
Goals: 1-0 Reid 23, 2-0 McMenemy 53.
Team: James Brownlie (7/Third Lanark)
Donald Colman (2/Aberdeen)
John Walker (2/Swindon Town)
Andrew Aitken (13/Leicester Fosse), captain
Charles Bellany Thomson (15/Sunderland)
James Hay (6/Celtic)
Angus Douglas (1./Chelsea)
James McMenemy (6/Celtic)
William Reid (2/Rangers)
Alexander Higgins (3/Newcastle United)
Alexander Smith (19/Rangers).

104.
1 April 1911 (British Championship)
England - Scotland 1-1 (1-0)
Referee: William Nunnerley (Wrexham, Wales)
Crowd: 38,000 (Goodison Park, Liverpool)
Goals: 1-0 Stewart 20, 1-1 Higgins 88.
Team: James Lawrence (1./Newcastle United)
Donald Colman (3/Aberdeen)
John Walker (3/Swindon Town)
Andrew Aitken (14./Leicester Fosse)
Wilfrid Lawson Low (2/Newcastle United)
James Hay (7/Celtic), captain
Alexander Bennett (10/Rangers)
James McMenemy (7/Celtic)
William Reid (3/Rangers)
Alexander Higgins (4./Newcastle United)
Alexander Smith (20./Rangers).

105.
2 March 1912 (British Championship)
Scotland - Wales 1-0 (0-0)
Referee: James Mason (Burslem, England)
Crowd: 32,000 (Tynecastle Park, Edinburgh)
Goal: 1-0 Quinn 88.
Team: James Brownlie (8/Third Lanark)
Alexander McNair (7/Celtic)
John Walker (4/Swindon Town)
Robert Mercer (1/Hearts)
Charles Bellany Thomson (16/Sunderland), captain
James Hay (8/Newcastle United)
George Leckie Sinclair (2/Hearts)
James McMenemy (8/Celtic)
James Quinn (10/Celtic)
Robert Staig Walker (25/Hearts)
George Clarke Robertson (2/Sheffield Wednesday).

106.
16 March 1912 (British Championship)
Ireland - Scotland 1-4 (1-2)
Referee: Herbert Bamlett (Gateshead, England)
Crowd: 12,000 (Windsor Park, Belfast)
Goals: 0-1 Aitkenhead 8, 0-2 Aitkenhead 23,
1-2 McKnight pen 44, 1-3 Reid 60, 1-4 R Walker 70.
Team: James Brownlie (9/Third Lanark)
Alexander McNair (8/Celtic), captain
John Walker (5/Swindon Town)
James Eadie Gordon (1/Rangers)
Wilfrid Lawson Low (3/Newcastle United)
Alexander Bell (1./Manchester United)
George Leckie Sinclair (3./Hearts)
Robert Staig Walker (26/Hearts)
William Reid (4/Rangers)
Walter Allison Campbell Aitkenhead (1./Blackburn Rovers)
Robert Bryson Templeton (9/Kilmarnock).

107.
23 March 1912 (British Championship)
Scotland - England 1-1 (1-1)
Referee: James Mason (Burslem, England)
Crowd: 127,307 (Hampden Park, Glasgow)
Goal: 1-0 Wilson 7, 1-1 Holley 13.
Team: James Brownlie (10/Third Lanark)
Alexander McNair (9/Celtic), captain
John Walker (6/Swindon Town)
James Eadie Gordon (2/Rangers)
Charles Bellany Thomson (17/Sunderland)
James Hay (9/Newcastle United)
Robert Bryson Templeton (10/Kilmarnock)
Robert Staig Walker (27/Hearts)
David Prophet McLean (1./Sheffield Wednesday)
Andrew Wilson (3/Sheffield Wednesday)
James Quinn (11./Celtic).

108.
3 March 1913 (British Championship)
Wales - Scotland 0-0 (0-0)
Referee: Isaac Baker (Crewe, England)
Crowd: 4,500 (Racecourse, Wrexham)
Team: James Brownlie (11/Third Lanark)
Robert Abbie Orrock (1./Falkirk)
John Walker (7/Swindon Town)
James Eadie Gordon (3/Rangers)
Charles Bellany Thomson (18/Sunderland), captain
James Campbell (1./Sheffield Wednesday)
Andrew McAtee (1./Celtic)
Robert Staig Walker (28/Hearts)
William Reid (5/Rangers)
Andrew Wilson (4/Sheffield Wednesday)
Robert Bryson Templeton (11./Kilmarnock).

109.
15 March 1913 (British Championship)
Ireland - Scotland 1-2 (1-2)
Referee: John Adams (Birmingham, England)
Crowd: 12,000 (Dalymount Park, Dublin)
Goals: 0-1 Reid 16, 0-2 Bennett 32, 1-2 McKnight 42.
Team: James Brownlie (12/Third Lanark)
Donald Colman (4./Aberdeen), captain
John Walker (8/Swindon Town)
Robert Mercer (2./Hearts)
Thomas Logan (1./Falkirk)
Peter Nellies (1/Hearts)
Alexander Bennett (11./Rangers)
James Eadie Gordon (4/Rangers)
William Reid (6/Rangers)
James Anderson Croal (1/Falkirk)
George Clarke Robertson (3/Sheffield Wednesday).

110.
5 April 1913 (British Championship)
England - Scotland 1-0 (1-0)
Referee: Alexander Jackson (Glasgow, Scotland)
Crowd: 52,000 (Stamford Bridge, London)
Goal: 1-0 Hampton 37.
Team: James Brownlie (13/Third Lanark)
Alexander McNair (10/Celtic)
John Walker (9./Swindon Town)
James Eadie Gordon (5/Rangers)
Charles Bellany Thomson (19/Sunderland), captain
David Wilson (1./Oldham Athletic)
Joseph Donnachie (1/Oldham Athletic)
Robert Staig Walker (29./Hearts)
William Reid (7/Rangers)
Andrew Wilson (5/Sheffield Wednesday)
George Clarke Robertson (4./Sheffield Wednesday).

111.
28 February 1914 (British Championship)
Scotland - Wales 0-0 (0-0)
Referee: Harold Taylor (Altrincham, England)
Crowd: 10,000 (Celtic Park, Glasgow)
Team: James Brownlie (14/Third Lanark)
Thomas Kelso (1./Dundee)
Joseph Dodds (1/Celtic)
Peter Nellies (2./Hearts), captain
Peter Pursell (1./Queen's Park)
Harry Alexander Anderson (1./Raith Rovers)
Alexander Pollock Donaldson (1/Bolton Wanderers)
James McMenemy (9/Celtic)
James Greig Reid (1/Airdrie)
James Anderson Croal (2/Falkirk)
John Browning (1./Celtic).

112.
14 March 1914 (British Championship)
Ireland - Scotland 1-1 (0-0)
Referee: Herbert Bamlett (Gateshead, England)
Crowd: 31,000 (Windsor Park, Belfast)
Goals: 0-1 Donnachie 70, 1-1 Young 89.
Team: James Brownlie (15/Third Lanark)
Joseph Dodds (2/Celtic)
Alexander McNair (11/Celtic), captain
James Eadie Gordon (6/Rangers)
Charles Bellany Thomson (20/Sunderland)
James Hay (10/Newcastle United)
Alexander Pollock Donaldson (2/Bolton Wanderers)
James McMenemy (10/Celtic)
William Reid (8/Rangers)
Andrew Wilson (6./Sheffield Wednesday)
Joseph Donnachie (2/Oldham Athletic).

113.
4 April 1914 (British Championship)
Scotland - England 3-1 (1-1)
Referee: Herbert Bamlett (Gateshead, England)
Crowd: 105,000 (Hampden Park, Glasgow)
Goals: 1-0 Thomson 4, 1-1 Fleming 18,
2-1 McMenemy 51, 3-1 Reid 67.
Team: James Brownlie (16./Third Lanark)
Alexander McNair (12/Celtic)
Joseph Dodds (3./Celtic)
James Eadie Gordon (7/Rangers), captain
Charles Bellany Thomson (21./Sunderland)
James Hay (11./Newcastle United)
Alexander Pollock Donaldson (3/Bolton Wanderers)
James McMenemy (11/Celtic)
William Reid (9./Rangers)
James Anderson Croal (3./Falkirk)
Joseph Donnachie (3./Oldham Athletic).

114.
26 February 1920 (British Championship)
Wales - Scotland 1-1 (1-0)
Referee: James Mason (Burslem, England)
Crowd: 15,000 (Ninian Park, Cardiff)
Goals: 1-0 Evans 5, 1-1 Cairns 78.
Team: Kenneth Campbell (1/Liverpool)
Alexander McNair (13/Celtic)
David Thomson (1./Dundee)
James Eadie Gordon (8/Rangers)
William Cringan (1/Celtic), captain
James McMullan (1/Partick Thistle)
James Greig Reid (2/Airdrie)
John Crosbie (1/Ayr United)
Andrew Nisbet Wilson (1/Dunfermline)
Thomas Cairns (1/Rangers)
Alan Lauder Morton (1/Queen's Park).

115.
13 March 1920 (British Championship)
Scotland - Ireland 3-0 (2-0)
Referee: James Mason (Burslem, England)
Crowd: 39,757 (Celtic Park, Glasgow)
Goals: 1-0 Wilson 8, 2-0 Morton 42,
3-0 Cunningham 55.
Team: Kenneth Campbell (2/Liverpool)
Alexander McNair (14/Celtic), captain
James Blair (1/Sheffield Wednesday)
James Bowie (1/Rangers)
Wilfrid Lawson Low (4/Newcastle United)
James Eadie Gordon (9/Rangers)
Alexander Pollock Donaldson (4/Bolton Wanderers)
James McMenemy (12./Celtic)
Andrew Nisbet Wilson (2/Dunfermline)
Andrew Cunningham (1/Rangers)
Alan Lauder Morton (2/Queen's Park).

116.
10 April 1920 (British Championship)
England - Scotland 5-4 (2-4)
Referee: Thomas Dougray (Bellshill, Scotland)
Crowd: 35,000 (Hillsborough, Sheffield)
Goals: 1-0 Cock 10, 1-1 Miller 13, 2-1 Quantrill 15,
2-2 Wilson 21, 2-3 Donaldson 31, 2-4 Miller 40,
3-4 Kelly 57, 4-4 Morris 67, 5-4 Kelly 74.
Team: Kenneth Campbell (3/Partick Thistle)
Alexander McNair (15./Celtic), captain
James Blair (2/Sheffield Wednesday)
James Bowie (2./Rangers)
Wilfrid Lawson Low (5./Newcastle United)
James Eadie Gordon (10./Rangers)
Alexander Pollock Donaldson (5/Bolton Wanderers)
Thomas Miller (1/Liverpool)
Andrew Nisbet Wilson (3/Dunfermline)
John Paterson (1./Leicester City)
Alexander Troup (1/Dundee).

117.
12 February 1921 (British Championship)
Scotland - Wales 2-1 (1-1)
Referee: James Mason (Burslem, England)
Crowd: 20,824 (Pittodrie, Aberdeen)
Goals: 1-0 Wilson 11, 1-1 Collier 30, 2-1 Wilson 46.
Team: Kenneth Campbell (4/Partick Thistle), captain
John Marshall (1/Middlesbrough)
William McStay (1/Celtic)
Joseph Harris (1/Partick Thistle)
Charles Ross Pringle (1./St Mirren)
James McMullan (2/Partick Thistle)
Alexander Archibald (1/Rangers)
Andrew Cunningham (2/Rangers)
Andrew Nisbet Wilson (4/Dunfermline)
Joseph Cassidy (1/Celtic)
Alexander Troup (2/Dundee).

118.
26 February 1921 (British Championship)
Ireland - Scotland 0-2 (0-1)
Referee: Arthur Ward (Kirkham, England)
Crowd: 35,000 (Windsor Park, Belfast)
Goals: 0-1 Wilson pen 10, 0-2 Cassidy 87.
Team: Kenneth Campbell (5/Partick Thistle)
John Marshall (2/Middlesbrough)
William McStay (2/Celtic)
Joseph Harris (2./Partick Thistle)
Alexander Graham (1./Arsenal)
James McMullan (3/Partick Thistle)
Alexander McNab (1/Morton)
Thomas Miller (2/Manchester United)
Andrew Nisbet Wilson (5/Dunfermline), captain
Joseph Cassidy (2/Celtic)
Alexander Troup (3/Dundee).

119.
9 April 1921 (British Championship)
Scotland - England 3-0 (1-0)
Referee: Arthur Ward (Kirkham, England)
Crowd: 100,000 (Hampden Park, Glasgow)
Goals: 1-0 Wilson 20, 2-0 Morton 47,
3-0 Cunningham 57.
John Ewart (1./Bradford City)
John Marshall (3/Middlesbrough), captain
James Blair (3/Cardiff City)
Stewart Davidson (1./Middlesbrough)
George Brewster (1./Everton)
James McMullan (4/Partick Thistle)
Alexander McNab (2./Morton)
Thomas Miller (3./Manchester United)
Andrew Nisbet Wilson (6/Dunfermline)
Andrew Cunningham (3/Rangers)
Alan Lauder Morton (3/Rangers).

120.
4 February 1922 (British Championship)
Wales - Scotland 2-1 (2-0)
Referee: Arthur Ward (Kirkham, England)
Crowd: 10,000 (Racecourse, Wrexham)
Goals: 1-0 L Davies 7, 2-0 S Davies 25,
2-1 Archibald 66.
Team: Kenneth Campbell (6/Partick Thistle)
John Marshall (4/Middlesbrough), captain
Donald McKinlay (1/Liverpool)
David Ditchburn Meiklejohn (1/Rangers)
Michael Gilhooley (1./Hull City)
William Collier (1./Raith Rovers)
Alexander Archibald (2/Rangers)
John White (1/Albion Rovers)
Andrew Nisbet Wilson (7/Middlesbrough)
Francis Gemmell Fulton Walker (1./Third Lanark)
Alan Lauder Morton (4/Rangers).

121.
4 March 1922 (British Championship)
Scotland - Ireland 2-1 (0-1)
Referee: Arthur Ward (Kirkham, England)
Crowd: 40,000 (Celtic Park, Glasgow)
Goals: 0-1 Gillespie 43, 1-1 Wilson 70,
2-1 Wilson 83.
Team: Kenneth Campbell (7/Partick Thistle)
John Marshall (5/Middlesbrough)
Donald McKinlay (2./Liverpool)
James Hogg (1./Ayr United)
William Cringan (2/Celtic)
Thomas Allan Muirhead (1/Rangers)
Alexander Pollock Donaldson (6./Bolton Wanderers)
James Kinloch (1./Partick Thistle)
Andrew Nisbet Wilson (8/Middlesbrough)
Andrew Cunningham (4/Rangers), captain
Alexander Troup (4/Dundee).

122.
8 April 1922 (British Championship)
England - Scotland 0-1 (0-0)
Referee: Thomas Dougray (Bellshill, Scotland)
Crowd: 33,700 (Villa Park, Birmingham)
Goal: 0-1 Wilson 62.
Team: Kenneth Campbell (8./Partick Thistle)
John Marshall (6/Middlesbrough)
James Blair (4/Cardiff City), captain
John Gilchrist (1./Celtic)
William Cringan (3/Celtic)
Neil McBain (1/Manchester United)
Alexander Archibald (3/Rangers)
John Crosbie (2./Birmingham)
Andrew Nisbet Wilson (9/Middlesbrough)
Thomas Cairns (2/Rangers)
Alan Lauder Morton (5/Rangers).

123.
3 March 1923 (British Championship)
Ireland - Scotland 0-1 (0-0)
Referee: Arthur Ward (Kirkham, England)
Crowd: 30,000 (Windsor Park, Belfast)
Goal: 0-1 Wilson 70.
Team: William Harper (1/Hibernian)
John Hutton (1/Aberdeen)
James Blair (5/Cardiff City), captain
David Morton Steele (1/Huddersfield Town)
David Main Liston Morris (1/Raith Rovers)
Neil McBain (2/Everton)
Alexander Archibald (4/Rangers)
John White (2./Hearts)
Andrew Nisbet Wilson (10/Middlesbrough)
Joseph Cassidy (3/Celtic)
Alan Lauder Morton (6/Rangers).

124.
17 March 1923 (British Championship, postponed
from 3 February)
Scotland - Wales 2-0 (1-0)
Referee: Isaac Baker (Crewe, England)
Crowd: 25,000 (St Mirren Park, Paisley)
Goals: 1-0 Wilson 6, 2-0 Wilson 55.
Team: William Harper (2/Hibernian)
John Hutton (2/Aberdeen)
James Blair (6/Cardiff City)
John McNab (1./Liverpool)
William Cringan (4/Celtic), captain
David Morton Steele (2/Huddersfield Town)
Henry Ritchie (1/Hibernian)
Andrew Cunningham (5/Rangers)
Andrew Nisbet Wilson (11/Middlesbrough)
Thomas Cairns (3/Rangers)
Alan Lauder Morton (7/Rangers).

125.
14 April 1923 (British Championship)
Scotland - England 2-2 (1-2)
Referee: Arthur Ward (Kirkham, England)
Crowd: 71,000 (Hampden Park, Glasgow)
Goals: 0-1 Kelly 31, 1-1 Cunningham 35,
1-2 Watson 43, 2-2 Wilson 55.
Team: William Harper (3/Hibernian)
John Hutton (3/Aberdeen)
James Blair (7/Cardiff City)
David Morton Steele (3./Huddersfield Town)
William Cringan (5./Celtic), captain
Thomas Allan Muirhead (2/Rangers)
Denis Lawson (1./St Mirren)
Andrew Cunningham (6/Rangers)
Andrew Nisbet Wilson (12./Middlesbrough)
Thomas Cairns (4/Rangers)
Alan Lauder Morton (8/Rangers).

126.
16 February 1924 (British Championship)
Wales - Scotland 2-0 (0-0)
Referee: Herbert W Andrews (Prestwich, England)
Crowd: 26,000 (Ninian Park, Cardiff)
Goals: 1-0 W Davies 60, 2-0 L Davies 72.
Team: William Harper (4/Hibernian)
John Marshall (7./Llanelly)
James Blair (8./Cardiff City), captain
David Ditchburn Meiklejohn (2/Rangers)
Neil McBain (3./Everton)
Thomas Allan Muirhead (3/Rangers)
Alexander Archibald (5/Rangers)
William Fraser Russell (1/Airdrie)
Joseph Cassidy (4./Celtic)
John Reid McKay (1./Blackburn Rovers)
Alan Lauder Morton (9/Rangers).

127.
1 March 1924 (British Championship)
Scotland - Ireland 2-0 (0-0)
Referee: G Noel Watson (Nottingham, England).
Crowd: 30,000 (Celtic Park, Glasgow).
Goals: 1-0 Cunningham 85, 2-0 Morris 89.
Team: William Harper (5/Hibernian)
John Hutton (4/Aberdeen), captain
James Hamilton (1./St Mirren)
Peter Simpson Dennitts Kerr (1./Hibernian)
David Main Liston Morris (2/Raith Rovers)
James McMullan (5/Partick Thistle)
James Greig Reid (3./Airdrie)
Andrew Cunningham (7/Rangers)
Hugh Kilpatrick Gallacher (1/Airdrie)
Thomas Cairns (5/Rangers)
Alan Lauder Morton (10/Rangers).

128.
12 April 1924 (British Championship)
England - Scotland 1-1 (0-1)
Referee: Thomas Dougray (Bellshill, Scotland)
Crowd: 65,000 (Wembley Stadium, London).
Goals: 0-1 Cowan 41, 1-1 Walker 60.
Team: William Harper (6/Hibernian)
John Smith (1./Ayr United)
Philip McCloy (1/Ayr United)
William Clunas (1/Sunderland)
David Main Liston Morris (3/Raith Rovers)
James McMullan (6/Partick Thistle), captain
Alexander Archibald (6/Rangers)
William Duncan Cowan (1./Newcastle United)
Neil Harris (1./Newcastle United)
Andrew Cunningham (8/Rangers)
Alan Lauder Morton (11/Morton).

129.
14 February 1925 (British Championship)
Scotland - Wales 3-1 (2-1)
Referee: Arthur Ward (Kirkham, England)
Crowd: 25,000 (Tynecastle, Edinburgh)
Goals: 1-0 Meiklejohn 9, 2-0 Gallacher 19,
2-1 Williams 45, 3-1 Gallacher 62.
Team: William Harper (7/Hibernian)
James Nelson (1/Cardiff City)
William McStay (3/Celtic)
David Ditchburn Meiklejohn (3/Rangers)
David Main Liston Morris (4/Raith Rovers), captain
Robert Hunter Brown Bennie (1/Airdrie)
Alexander Skinner Jackson (1/Aberdeen)
James Dunn (1/Hibernian)
Hugh Kilpatrick Gallacher (2/Airdrie)
Thomas Cairns (6/Rangers)
Alan Lauder Morton (12/Rangers).

130.
28 February 1925 (British Championship)
Ireland - Scotland 0-3 (0-3)
Referee: G Noel Watson (Nottingham, England)
Crowd: 41,000 (Windsor Park, Belfast)
Goals: 0-1 Meiklejohn 4, 0-2 Gallacher 20,
0-3 Dunn 35.
Team: William Harper (8/Hibernian)
James Nelson (2/Cardiff City)
William McStay (4/Celtic)
David Ditchburn Meiklejohn (4/Rangers)
David Main Liston Morris (5/Raith Rovers), captain
Robert Hunter Brown Bennie (2/Airdrie)
Alexander Skinner Jackson (2/Aberdeen)
James Dunn (2/Hibernian)
Hugh Kilpatrick Gallacher (3/Airdrie)
Thomas Cairns (7/Rangers)
Alan Lauder Morton (13/Rangers).

131.
4 April 1925 (British Championship)
Scotland - England 2-0 (1-0)
Referee: Arthur Ward (Kirkham, England)
Crowd: 92,000 (Hampden Park, Glasgow)
Goals: 1-0 Gallacher 36, 2-0 Gallacher 85.
Team: William Harper (9/Hibernian)
William McStay (5/Celtic)
Philip McCloy (2./Ayr United)
David Ditchburn Meiklejohn (5/Rangers)
David Main Liston Morris (6./Raith Rovers), captain
James McMullan (7/Partick Thistle)
Alexander Skinner Jackson (3/Aberdeen)
William Fraser Russell (2./Airdrie)
Hugh Kilpatrick Gallacher (4/Airdrie)
Thomas Cairns (8./Rangers)
Alan Lauder Morton (14/Rangers).

132.
31 October 1925 (British Championship)
Wales - Scotland 0-3 (0-0)
Referee: Ernest Pinckston (Birmingham, England)
Crowd: 25,000 (Ninian Park, Cardiff)
Goals: 0-1 Duncan 75, 0-2 McLean 85, 0-3 Clunas 88.
Team: William Robb (1/Rangers)
John Hutton (5/Aberdeen)
William McStay (6/Celtic)
William Clunas (2./Sunderland)
Thomas Townsley (1./Falkirk), captain
James McMullan (8/Partick Thistle)
Alexander Skinner Jackson (4/Huddersfield Town)
John Duncan (1./Leicester City)
Hugh Kilpatrick Gallacher (5/Airdrie)
Alexander Wilson James (1/Preston North End)
Adam McLean (1/Celtic).

133.
27 February 1926 (British Championship)
Scotland - Ireland 4-0 (2-0)
Referee: G Noel Watson (Nottingham, England)
Crowd: 30,000 (Ibrox, Glasgow)
Goals: 1-0 Gallacher 13, 2-0 Cunningham 42,
3-0 Gallacher 60, 4-0 Gallacher 65.
Team: William Harper (10/Arsenal)
John Hutton (6/Aberdeen)
William McStay (7/Celtic), captain
Peter Wilson (1/Celtic)
John McDougall (1./Airdrie)
Robert Hunter Brown Bennie (3./Airdrie)
Alexander Skinner Jackson (5/Huddersfield Town)
Andrew Cunningham (9/Rangers)
Hugh Kilpatrick Gallacher (6/Newcastle United)
Thomas McInally (1/Celtic)
Adam McLean (2/Celtic).

134.
17 April 1926 (British Championship)
England - Scotland 0-1 (0-1)
Referee: Thomas Dougray (Bellshill, Scotland)
Crowd: 49,000 (Old Trafford, Manchester)
Goal: 0-1 Jackson 36.
Team: William Harper (11./Arsenal)
John Hutton (7/Aberdeen)
William McStay (8/Celtic), captain
James Davidson Gibson (1/Partick Thistle)
William Summers (1./St Mirren)
James McMullan (9/Manchester City)
Alexander Skinner Jackson (6/Huddersfield Town)
Alexander Thomson (1/Celtic)
Hugh Kilpatrick Gallacher (7/Newcastle United)
Andrew Cunningham (10/Rangers)
Alexander Troup (5./Everton).

135.
30 October 1926 (British Championship)
Scotland - Wales 3-0 (2-0)
Referee: William E Forshaw (Liverpool, England)
Crowd: 41,000 (Ibrox, Glasgow)
Goals: 1-0 Gallacher 20, 2-0 Jackson 35,
3-0 Jackson 73.
Team: Allan McClory (1/Motherwell)
William McStay (9/Celtic), captain
William Wiseman (1/Queen's Park)
James Davidson Gibson (2/Partick Thistle)
Robert Gillespie (1/Queen's Park)
James McMullan (10/Manchester City)
Alexander Skinner Jackson (7/Huddersfield Town)
Andrew Cunningham (11/Rangers)
Hugh Kilpatrick Gallacher (8/Newcastle United)
Thomas McInally (2./Celtic)
Adam McLean (3/Celtic).

136.
26 February 1927 (British Championship)
Ireland - Scotland 0-2 (0-1)
Referee: G Noel Watson (Nottingham, England)
Crowd: 40,000 (Windsor Park, Belfast)
Goals: 0-1 Morton 44, 0-2 Morton 89.
Team: John Diamond Harkness (1/Queen's Park)
John Hutton (8/Blackburn Rovers)
William McStay (10/Celtic), captain
Thomas Allan Muirhead (4/Rangers)
James Davidson Gibson (3/Partick Thistle)
Thomas Craig (1/Rangers)
Alexander Skinner Jackson (8/Huddersfield Town)
James Dunn (3/Hibernian)
Hugh Kilpatrick Gallacher (9/Newcastle United)
James Howieson (1./St Mirren)
Alan Lauder Morton (15/ Rangers).

137.
2 April 1927 (British Championship)
Scotland - England 1-2 (0-0)
Referee: Arthur Ward (Kirkham, England)
Crowd: 111,214 (Hampden Park, Glasgow)
Goals: 1-0 Morton 48, 1-1 Dean 55, 1-2 Dean 85.
Team: John Diamond Harkness (2/Queen's Park)
William McStay (11/Celtic), captain
Robert Thomson (1./Falkirk)
Thomas Kelly Morrison (1./St Mirren)
James Davidson Gibson (4/Partick Thistle)
James McMullan (11/Manchester City)
Adam McLean (4./Celtic)
Andrew Cunningham (12./Rangers)
Hugh Kilpatrick Gallacher (10/Newcastle United)
Robert Lowe McPhail (1/Airdrie)
Alan Lauder Morton (16/Rangers).

138.
29 October 1927 (British Championship)
Wales - Scotland 2-2 (1-2)
Referee: Arthur Kingscott (Long Eaton, England)
Crowd: 16,000 (Racecourse Ground, Wrexham)
Goals: 0-1 Gallacher 13, 0-2 Hutton pen 15,
1-2 Curtis 43, 2-2 Gibson og 75.
Team: William Robb (2./Hibernian)
John Hutton (9/Blackburn Rovers)
William McStay (12/Celtic)
David Ditchburn Meiklejohn (6/Rangers)
James Davidson Gibson (5/Aston Villa)
James McMullan (12/Manchester City), captain
Alexander Skinner Jackson (9/Huddersfield Town)
Robert McInnes McKay (1./Newcastle United)
Hugh Kilpatrick Gallacher (11/Newcastle United)
George Stevenson (1/Motherwell)
Alan Lauder Morton (17/Rangers).

139.
25 February 1928 (British Championship)
Scotland - Ireland 0-1 (0-1)
Referee: Arthur Ward (Kirkham, England)
Crowd: 55,000 (Firhill, Glasgow)
Goal: 0-1 Chambers 10.
Team: Allan McClory (2/Motherwell)
John Hutton (10./Blackburn Rovers)
William McStay (13./Celtic)
Thomas Allan Muirhead (5/Rangers), captain
David Ditchburn Meiklejohn (7/Rangers)
Thomas Craig (2/Rangers)
Henry Ritchie (2./Hibernian)
James Dunn (4/Hibernian)
James Edward McGrory (1/Celtic)
George Stevenson (2/Motherwell)
Alan Lauder Morton (18/Rangers).

140.
31 March 1928 (British Championship)
England - Scotland 1-5 (0-2)
Referee: William Bell (Motherwell, Scotland)
Crowd: 80,868 (Wembley, London)
Goals: 0-1 Jackson 2, 0-2 James 44, 0-3 Jackson 65,
0-4 James 67, 0-5 Jackson 85, 1-5 Kelly 89.
Team: John Diamond Harkness (3/Queen's Park)
James Nelson (3/Cardiff City)
Thomas Law (1/Chelsea)
James Davidson Gibson (6/Aston Villa)
Thomas Bradshaw (1./Bury)
James McMullan (13/Manchester City), captain
Alexander Skinner Jackson (10/Huddersfield Town)
James Dunn (5/Hibernian)
Hugh Kilpatrick Gallacher (12/Newcastle United)
Alexander Wilson James (2/Preston North End)
Alan Lauder Morton (19/Rangers).

141.
27 October 1928
Scotland - Wales 4-2 (3-1)
Referee: Arthur Kingscott (Long Eaton, England)
Crowd: 55,000 (Ibrox, Glasgow)
Goals: 0-1 W Davies 12, 1-1 Gallacher 25,
2-1 Gallacher 42, 3-1 Gallacher 49, 4-1 Dunn 56,
4-2 W Davies 75.
Team: John Diamond Harkness (4/Queen's Park)
Douglas Herbert Gray (1/Rangers)
Daniel Blair (1/Clyde)
Thomas Allan Muirhead (6/Rangers)
William Walter Stewart King (1/Queen's Park)
James McMullan (14/Manchester City), captain
Alexander Skinner Jackson (11/Huddersfield Town)
James Dunn (6./Everton)
Hugh Kilpatrick Gallacher (13/Newcastle United)
Robert Lowe McPhail (2/Rangers)
Alan Lauder Morton (20/Rangers).

142.
23 February 1929 (British Championship)
Ireland - Scotland 3-7 (2-4)
Referee: Albert Fogg (Bolton, England)
Crowd: 35,000 (Windsor Park, Belfast)
Goals: 0-1 Gallacher 3, 0-2 Gallacher 9, 0-3 Gallacher
14, 1-3 Rowley 16, 1-4 Jackson 36, 2-4 Rowley 42,
2-5 Gallacher 51, 3-5 Bambrick 58, 3-6 Gallacher 76,
3-7 Jackson 82.
Team: John Diamond Harkness (5/Hearts)
Douglas Herbert Gray (2/Rangers)
Daniel Blair (2/Clyde)
Thomas Allan Muirhead (7/Rangers)
David Ditchburn Meiklejohn (8/Rangers)
James McMullan (15/Manchester City), captain
Alexander Skinner Jackson (12/Huddersfield Town)
William Stewart Chalmers (1./Queen's Park)
Hugh Kilpatrick Gallacher (14/Newcastle United)
Alexander Wilson James (3/Preston North End)
Alan Lauder Morton (21/Rangers).

143.
13 April 1929 (British Championship)
Scotland - England 1-0 (0-0)
Referee: Arnold Josephs (South Shields, England)
Crowd: 110,512 (Hampden Park, Glasgow)
Goal: 1-0 Cheyne 89.
Team: John Diamond Harkness (6/Hearts)
James Scrymagour Crapnell (1/Airdrieonians)
Joseph Nibloe (1/Kilmarnock)
John Buchanan (1/Rangers)
David Ditchburn Meiklejohn (9/Rangers)
James McMullan (16./Manchester City), captain
Alexander Skinner Jackson (13/Huddersfield Town)
Alexander George Cheyne (1/Aberdeen)
Hugh Kilpatrick Gallacher (15/Newcastle United)
Alexander Wilson James (4/Preston North End)
Alan Lauder Morton (22/Rangers).

144.
26 May 1929
Norway - Scotland 3-7 (2-3)
Referee: Fredrik Schieldrop (Bergen, Norway)
Crowd: 4,000 (Brann Stadium, Bergen)
Goals: 1-0 Kongsvik 4, 1-1 Rankin 6, 1-2 T Craig 27,
1-3 Cheyne 30, 2-3 Berg-Johannesen 37,
2-4 Nisbet 47, 2-5 Nisbet 52, 2-6 Cheyne 64,
2-7 Cheyne 68, 3-7 Kongsvik 76.
Team: Alexander McLaren (1/St Johnstone)
James Scrymagour Crapnell (2/Airdrieonians)
Joseph Nibloe (2/Kilmarnock)
William Noble Imrie (1/St Johnstone)
Allan Craig (1/Motherwell)
Thomas Craig (3/Rangers), captain
James Nisbet (1/Ayr United)
Alexander George Cheyne (2/Aberdeen)
David McCrae (1/St Mirren)
Robert Rankin (1/St Mirren)
Robert Howe (1/Hamilton Academical).

145.
1 June 1929
Germany - Scotland 1-1 (0-1)
Referee: Otto Olsson (Eskilstuna, Sweden)
Crowd: 42,000 (Grunewald Stadium, Berlin)
Goals: 1-0 Ruch 50, 1-1 Imrie 87.
Team: Alexander McLaren (2/St Johnstone)
Douglas Herbert Gray (3/Rangers)
James Scrymagour Crapnell (3/Airdrieonians)
Hugh Auld Morton (1/Kilmarnock)
William Noble Imrie (2/St Johnstone)
Thomas Craig (4/Rangers), captain
James Nisbet (2/Ayr United)
Alexander George Cheyne (3/Aberdeen)
David McCrae (2./St Mirren)
Robert Rankin (2/St Mirren)
James Nicholson Fleming (1/Rangers).

146.
4 June 1929
Netherlands - Scotland 0-2 (0-2)
Referee: Otto Olsson (Eskilstuna, Sweden)
Crowd: 25,000 (Olympic Stadium, Amsterdam)
Goals: 0-1 Fleming 30, 0-2 Rankin 44 pen.
Team: Alexander McLaren (3/St Johnstone)
Douglas Herbert Gray (4/Rangers)
Joseph Nibloe (3/Kilmarnock)
Hugh Auld Morton (2./Kilmarnock)
Allan Craig (2/Motherwell)
Thomas Craig (5/Rangers), captain
James Nisbet (3./Ayr United)
Alexander George Cheyne (4/Aberdeen)
James Nicholson Fleming (2/Rangers)
Robert Rankin (3./St Mirren)
Robert Howe (2/Hamilton Academical).

147.
26 October 1929 (British Championship)
Wales - Scotland 2-4 (0-2)
Referee: William McLean (Belfast, N Ireland)
Crowd: 25,000 (Ninian Park, Cardiff)
Goals: 0-1 Gallacher 7, 0-2 Gallacher 20, 1-2
O'Callaghan 55, 2-2 L Davies 63, 2-3 James 82,
2-4 Gibson 88.
Team: John Diamond Harkness (7/Hearts)
Douglas Herbert Gray (5/Rangers)
Joseph Nibloe (4/Kilmarnock)
James Davidson Gibson (7/Aston Villa)
John Ainslie Johnston (1/Hearts)
Thomas Craig (6/Rangers)
Alexander Skinner Jackson (14/Huddersfield Town)
Thomas Allan Muirhead (8./Rangers), captain
Hugh Kilpatrick Gallacher (16/Newcastle United)
Alexander Wilson James (5/Arsenal)
Alan Lauder Morton (23/Rangers).

148.
22 February 1930 (British Championship)
Scotland - Ireland 3-1 (1-1)
Referee: Arnold Josephs (South Shields, England)
Crowd: 30,000 (Celtic Park, Glasgow)
Goals: 1-0 Gallacher 31, 1-1 McCaw 39,
2-1 Gallacher 61, 3-1 Stevenson 72.
Team: Robert Connon Middleton (1./Cowdenbeath)
Douglas Herbert Gray (6/Rangers)
William Wiseman (2./Queen's Park)
James Davidson Gibson (8./Aston Villa)
David Ditchburn Meiklejohn (10/Rangers), captain
Thomas Craig (7/Rangers)
Alexander Skinner Jackson (15/Huddersfield Town)
George Stevenson (3/Motherwell)
Hugh Kilpatrick Gallacher (17/Newcastle United)
Alexander Wilson James (6/Arsenal)
Alan Lauder Morton (24/Rangers).

149.
5 April 1930 (British Championship)
England - Scotland 5-2 (4-0)
Referee: William McLean (Belfast, N Ireland)
Crowd: 87,375 (Wembley Stadium, London)
Goals: 1-0 Watson 11, 2-0 Watson 28,
3-0 Rimmer 30, 4-0 Jack 33, 4-1 Fleming 49,
5-1 Rimmer 55, 5-2 Fleming 62.
Team: John Diamond Harkness (8/Hearts)
Douglas Herbert Gray (7/Rangers)
Thomas Law (2./Chelsea)
John Buchanan (2./Rangers)
David Ditchburn Meiklejohn (11/Rangers), captain
Thomas Craig (8./Rangers)
Alexander Skinner Jackson (16/Huddersfield Town)
Alexander Wilson James (7/Arsenal)
James Nicholson Fleming (3./Rangers)
George Stevenson (4/Motherwell)
Alan Lauder Morton (25/Rangers).

150.
18 May 1930
France - Scotland 0-2 (0-1)
Referee: Raphael Van Praag (Belgium)
Crowd: 25,000 (Stade de Colombes, Paris)
Goals: 0-1 Gallacher 42, 0-2 Gallacher 85.
Team: John Murie G M Thomson (1/Celtic)
James Nelson (4./Cardiff City)
James Scrymagour Crapnell (4/Airdrieonians), capt.
Peter Wilson (2/Celtic)
George Walker (1/St Mirren)
Frank Robert Hill (1/Aberdeen)
Alexander Skinner Jackson (17./Huddersfield Town)
Alexander George Cheyne (5./Aberdeen)
Hugh Kilpatrick Gallacher (18/Newcastle United)
George Stevenson (5/Motherwell)
James Connor (1/Sunderland).

151.
25 October 1930 (British Championship)
Scotland - Wales 1-1 (1-1)
Referee: Charles Ernest Lines (Birmingham, England)
Crowd: 15,000 (Ibrox Park, Glasgow)
Goals: 0-1 Bamford 6, 1-1 Battles 42.
Team: John Murie G M Thomson (2/Celtic)
Douglas Herbert Gray (8/Rangers)
John Rooney Gilmour (1/Dundee)
Colin Duncan McNab (1/Dundee)
Robert Gillespie (2/Queen's Park), captain
Frank Robert Hill (2/Aberdeen)
Daniel McRorie (1./Morton)
George Clark Phillips Brown (1/Rangers)
Bernard Battles (1./Hearts)
George Stevenson (6/Motherwell)
Alan Lauder Morton (26/Rangers).

152.
21 February 1931 (British Championship)
Ireland - Scotland 0-0
Referee: Herbert Edward Hull (Burnley, England)
Crowd: 20,000 (Windsor Park, Belfast)
Team: John Murie G M Thomson (3/Celtic)
James Scrymagour Crapnell (5/Airdrieonians)
Joseph Nibloe (5/Kilmarnock)
Peter Wilson (3/Celtic)
George Walker (2/St Mirren)
Frank Robert Hill (3./Aberdeen)
John Livingstone Murdoch (1./Motherwell)
Peter Scarff (1./Celtic)
Benjamin Yorston (1./Aberdeen)
Robert Lowe McPhail (3/Rangers)
Alan Lauder Morton (27/Rangers), captain.

153.
28 March 1931 (British Championship)
Scotland - England 2-0 (0-0)
Referee: Alfred James Atwood (Newport, Wales)
Crowd: 129,810 (Hampden Park, Glasgow)
Goals: 1-0 Stevenson 60, 2-0 McGrory 62.
Team: John Murie G M Thomson (4./Celtic)
Daniel Blair (3/Clyde)
Joseph Nibloe (6/Kilmarnock)
Colin Duncan McNab (2/Dundee)
David Ditchburn Meiklejohn (12/Rangers), captain
John Miller (1/St Mirren)
Alexander Archibald (7/Rangers)
George Stevenson (7/Motherwell)
James Edward McGrory (2/Celtic)
Robert Lowe McPhail (4/Rangers)
Alan Lauder Morton (28/Rangers).

154.
16 May 1931
Austria - Scotland 5-0 (2-0)
Referee: Paul Ruoff (Bern, Switzerland)
Crowd: 45,000 (Hohe Warte Stadion, Vienna)
Goals: 1-0 Schall 8, 2-0 Zischek 13, 3-0 Vogel 49,
4-0 Zischek 69, 5-0 Sindelar 77.
Team: John Jackson (1/Partick Thistle)
Daniel Blair (4/Clyde), captain
Joseph Nibloe (7/Kilmarnock)
Colin Duncan McNab (3/Dundee)
James McDougall (1/Liverpool)
George Walker (3/St Mirren)
Andrew Robb Love (1/Aberdeen)
James Paterson (1/Cowdenbeath)
James Ferrier Easson (1/Portsmouth)
James Robertson (1/Dundee)
Daniel Snedden Hamilton Liddle (1/East Fife).

155.
20 May 1931
Italy - Scotland 3-0 (2-0)
Referee: Peter 'Peco' J Bauwens (Cologne, Germany)
Crowd: 25,000 (Stadio Nazionale del PNF, Rome)
Goals: 1-0 Constantino 6, 2-0 Meazza 42, 3-0 Orsi 87.
Team: John Jackson (2/Partick Thistle)
Daniel Blair (5/Clyde)
Joseph Nibloe (8/Kilmarnock)
Colin Duncan McNab (4/Dundee)
James McDougall (2./Liverpool), captain
John Miller (2/St Mirren)
Andrew Robb Love (2/Aberdeen)
James Paterson (2/Cowdenbeath)
William Gillespie Boyd (1/Clyde)
James Robertson (2./Dundee)
Daniel Snedden Hamilton Liddle (2/East Fife).

156.
24 May 1931
Switzerland - Scotland 2-3 (1-2)
Referee: Albino Carraro (Padova, Italy)
Crowd: 10,000 (Parc des Charmilles, Geneva)
Goals: 0-1 Easson 22, 0-2 Boyd 24, 1-2 Buche 31, 2-2 Fauguel 66, 2-3 Love 89.
Team: John Jackson (3/Partick Thistle)
James Scrymagour Crapnell (6/Airdrieonians), capt.
Joseph Nibloe (9/Kilmarnock)
Colin Duncan McNab (5/Dundee)
George Walker (4./St Mirren)
John Miller (3/St Mirren)
Andrew Robb Love (3./Aberdeen)
James Paterson (3./Cowdenbeath)
William Gillespie Boyd (2./Clyde)
James Ferrier Easson (2/Portsmouth)
Daniel Snedden Hamilton Liddle (3./East Fife).

157.
19 September 1931 (British Championship)
Scotland - Ireland 3-1 (2-1)
Referee: Isaac Caswell (Blackburn, England)
Crowd: 40,000 (Ibrox Park, Glasgow)
Goals: 1-0 Stevenson 5, 1-1 Dunne 21, 2-1 McGrory 34, 3-1 McPhail 75.
Team: Robert White Hepburn (1./Ayr United)
Daniel Blair (6/Clyde)
Robert MacAulay (1/Rangers)
Alexander Massie (1/Hearts)
David Ditchburn Meiklejohn (13/Rangers), captain
George Clark Phillips Brown (2/Rangers)
James Crawford (1/Queen's Park)
George Stevenson (8/Motherwell)
James Edward McGrory (3/Celtic)
Robert Lowe McPhail (5/Rangers)
James Connor (2/Sunderland).

158.
31 October 1931 (British Championship)
Wales - Scotland 2-3 (1-2)
Referee: Isaac Caswell (Blackburn, England)
Crowd: 10,860 (Racecourse Ground, Wrexham)
Goals: 1-0 Curtis 12 pen, 1-1 Stevenson 25, 1-2 Thomson 31, 1-3 McGrory 54, 2-3 Curtis 78.
Team: John Diamond Harkness (9/Hearts)
Daniel Blair (7/Clyde)
Robert MacAulay (2./Rangers)
Alexander Massie (2/Hearts)
David Ditchburn Meiklejohn (14/ Rangers), captain
George Clark Phillips Brown (3/Rangers)
Robert Austin Thomson (1./Celtic)
George Stevenson (9/Motherwell)
James Edward McGrory (4/Celtic)
Robert Lowe McPhail (6/Rangers)
Alan Lauder Morton (29/Rangers).

159.
9 April 1932 (British Championship)
England - Scotland 3-0 (1-0)
Referee: Samuel Thompson (Belfast, N Ireland)
Crowd: 92,180 (Wembley Stadium, London)
Goals: 1-0 Waring 36, 2-0 Barclay 79, 3-0 Crooks 88.
Team: Thomas Hamilton (1./Rangers)
James Scrymagour Crapnell (7/Airdrieonians), capt.
Joseph Nibloe (10/Kilmarnock)
Colin Duncan McNab (6./Dundee)
Allan Craig (3./Motherwell)
George Clark Phillips Brown (4/Rangers)
Alexander Archibald (8./Rangers)
James Marshall (1/Rangers)
Neil Dewar (1/Third Lanark)
Charles Edward Napier (1/Celtic)
Alan Lauder Morton (30/Rangers).

160.
8 May 1932
France - Scotland 1-3 (1-3)
Referee: Albino Carraro (Padova, Italy)
Crowd: 8,000 (Stade Olympique de Colombes, Paris)
Goals: 0-1 Dewar 14, 0-2 Dewar 27, 0-3 Dewar 40, 1-3 Langiller 43 pen.
Team: John Diamond Harkness (10/Hearts)
James Scrymagour Crapnell (8/Airdrieonians)
Joseph Nibloe (11./Kilmarnock)
Alexander Massie (3/Hearts)
Robert Gillespie (3/Queen's Park), captain
John Miller (4/St Mirren)
James Crawford (2/Queen's Park)
Alexander Thomson (2/Celtic)
Neil Dewar (2/Third Lanark)
Robert Lowe McPhail (7/Rangers)
Alan Lauder Morton (31/Rangers).

161.
17 September 1932 (British Championship)
Ireland - Scotland 0-4 (0-2)
Referee: William P Harper (Stourbridge, England)
Crowd: 40,000 (Windsor Park, Belfast)
Goals: 0-1 King 3, 0-2 McPhail 35, 0-3 McPhail 67,
0-4 McGrory 75.
Team: Alexander McLaren (4/St Johnstone)
Douglas Herbert Gray (9/Rangers)
James Scrymagour Crapnell (9./Airdrieonians), capt.
Alexander Massie (4/Hearts)
John Ainslie Johnston (2/Hearts)
William Morton Telfer (1/Motherwell)
James Crawford (3/Queen's Park)
George Stevenson (10/Motherwell)
James Edward McGrory (5/Celtic)
Robert Lowe McPhail (8/Rangers)
James King (1/Hamilton Academical).

162.
26 October 1932 (British Championship)
Scotland - Wales 2-5 (0-4)
Referee: William P Harper (Stourbridge, England)
Crowd: 31,000 (Tynecastle Park, Edinburgh)
Goals: 0-1 JR Thomson og 9, 0-2 Griffiths 20,
0-3 O'Callaghan 25, 0-4 Astley 43,
0-5 O'Callaghan 46, 1-5 Dewar 63, 2-5 Duncan 70.
Team: Alexander McLaren (5./St Johnstone)
Douglas Herbert Gray (10./Rangers)
Daniel Blair (8./Aston Villa)
Hugh Morrison Wales (1./Motherwell)
John Ainslie Johnston (3./Hearts), captain
John Ross Thomson (1./Everton)
James Crawford (4/Queen's Park)
Alexander Thomson (3./Celtic)
Neil Dewar (3./Third Lanark)
Alexander Wilson James (8/Arsenal)
Douglas Duncan (1/Derby County).

163.
1 April 1933 (British Championship)
Scotland - England 2-1 (1-1)
Referee: Samuel Thompson (Belfast, N Ireland)
Crowd: 134,170 (Hampden Park, Glasgow)
Goals: 1-0 McGrory 4, 1-1 Hunt 30, 2-1 McGrory 81.
Team: John Jackson (4/Partick Thistle)
Andrew Smellie Anderson (1/Hearts)
Peter William McGonagle (1/Celtic)
Peter Wilson (4./Celtic)
Robert Gillespie (4./Queen's Park), captain
George Clark Phillips Brown (5/Rangers)
James Crawford (5./Queen's Park)
James Marshall (2/Rangers)
James Edward McGrory (6/Celtic)
Robert Lowe McPhail (9/Rangers)
Douglas Duncan (2/Derby County).

164.
16 September 1933 (British Championship)
Scotland - Ireland 1-2 (0-2)
Referee: Edward Wood (Sheffield, England)
Crowd: 27,131 (Celtic Park, Glasgow)
Goals: 0-1 Martin 8, 0-2 Martin 13, 1-2 McPhail 60.
Team: John Diamond Harkness (11/Hearts)
Andrew Smellie Anderson (2/Hearts)
Peter William McGonagle (2/Celtic), captain
Alexander Massie (5/Hearts)
Alexander Innes Low (1./Falkirk)
William Morton Telfer (2./Motherwell)
James Murray Boyd (1./Newcastle United)
Alexander Venters (1/Cowdenbeath)
James Edward McGrory (7./Celtic)
Robert Lowe McPhail (10/Rangers)
James King (2./Hamilton Academical).

165.
29 November 1933 (British Championship)
Wales - Scotland 3-2 (2-0)
Referee: Edward Wood (Sheffield, England)
Crowd: 40,000 (Ninian Park, Cardiff)
Goals: 1-0 Evans 25, 2-0 Robbins 35, 3-0 Astley 56,
3-1 Macfadyen 76, 3-2 Duncan 81.
Team: John Diamond Harkness (12./Hearts)
Andrew Smellie Anderson (3./Hearts), captain
Duncan Urquhart (1./Hibernian)
Matthew Busby (1./Manchester City)
John Blair (1./Motherwell)
James Sime McLuckie (1./Manchester City)
Francis Reynolds McGurk (1./Birmingham City)
John McMenemy (1./Motherwell)
William Macfadyen (1/Motherwell)
James Ferrier Easson (3./Portsmouth)
Douglas Duncan (3/Derby County).

166.
29 November 1933
Scotland - Austria 2-2 (1-1)
Referee: Joannes Langenus (Antwerp, Belgium)
Crowd: 62,000 (Hampden Park, Glasgow)
Goals: 1-0 Meiklejohn 7, 1-1 Zischek 41,
2-1 Macfadyen 49, 2-2 Schall 53.
Team: James Kennaway (1./Celtic)
Andrew Smellie Anderson (4/Hearts)
Peter William McGonagle (3/Celtic)
David Ditchburn Meiklejohn (15./Rangers), captain
Philip Watson (1./Blackpool)
George Clark Phillips Brown (6/Rangers)
Duncan Henderson Ogilvie (1./Motherwell)
Robert Bruce (1./Middlesbrough)
William Macfadyen (2./Motherwell)
Robert Lowe McPhail (11/Rangers)
Douglas Duncan (4/Derby County).

167.
14 April 1934 (British Championship)
England - Scotland 3-0 (1-0)
Referee: Samuel Thompson (Belfast, N Ireland)
Crowd: 92,363 (Wembley Stadium, London)
Goals: 1-0 Bastin 43, 2-0 Brook 80, 3-0 Bowers 88.
Team: John Jackson (5/Chelsea)
Andrew Smellie Anderson (5/Hearts)
Peter William McGonagle (4/Celtic)
Alexander Massie (6/Hearts), captain
Thomas McCall Smith (1/Kilmarnock)
John Miller (5./St Mirren)
William Lindsay Cook (1/Bolton Wanderers)
James Marshall (3./Rangers)
Hugh Kilpatrick Gallacher (19/Chelsea)
George Stevenson (11/Motherwell)
James Connor (3/Sunderland).

168.
20 October 1934 (British Championship)
Ireland - Scotland 2-1 (0-1)
Referee: Henry Norman Mee (Mansfield, England)
Crowd: 39,752 (Windsor Park, Belfast)
Goals: 0-1 Gallacher 43, 1-1 Martin 76,
2-1 Coulter 89.
Team: James Dawson (1/Rangers)
Andrew Smellie Anderson (6/Hearts)
Peter William McGonagle (5/Celtic)
Alexander Massie (7/Hearts), captain
James Simpson (1/Rangers)
Andrew Clark Herd (1./Hearts)
William Lindsay Cook (2/Bolton Wanderers)
George Stevenson (12./Motherwell)
James Smith (1/Rangers)
Patrick Gallacher (1/Sunderland)
James Connor (4./Sunderland).

169.
21 November 1934 (British Championship)
Scotland - Wales 3-2 (1-0)
Referee: Samuel Thompson (Belfast, N Ireland)
Crowd: 26,334 (Pittodrie Stadium, Aberdeen)
Goals: 1-0 Duncan 23, 2-0 Napier 46, 2-1 Phillips 73,
3-1 Napier 85, 3-2 Astley 88.
Team: Allan McClory (3./Motherwell)
Andrew Smellie Anderson (7/Hearts)
Peter William McGonagle (6./Celtic)
Alexander Massie (8/Hearts)
James Simpson (2/Rangers), captain
George Clark Phillips Brown (7/Rangers)
William Lindsay Cook (3./Bolton Wanderers)
Thomas Walker (1/Hearts)
David McCulloch (1/Hearts)
Charles Edward Napier (2/Celtic)
Douglas Duncan (5/Derby County).

170.
6 April 1935 (British Championship)
Scotland - England 2-0 (1-0)
Referee: Samuel Thompson (Belfast, N Ireland)
Crowd: 129,693 (Hampden Park, Glasgow)
Goals: 1-0 Duncan 43, 2-0 Duncan 50.
Team: John Jackson (6/Chelsea)
Andrew Smellie Anderson (8/Hearts)
George Cummings (1/Partick Thistle)
Alexander Massie (9/Hearts)
James Simpson (3/Rangers), captain
George Clark Phillips Brown (8/Rangers)
Charles Edward Napier (3/Celtic)
Thomas Walker (2/Hearts)
Hugh Kilpatrick Gallacher (20/Derby County)
Robert Lowe McPhail (12/Rangers)
Douglas Duncan (6/Derby County).

171.
5 October 1935 (British Championship)
Wales - Scotland 1-1 (1-1)
Referee: Isaac Caswell (Blackburn, England)
Crowd: 35,004 (Ninian Park, Cardiff)
Goals: 0-1 Duncan 35, 1-1 Phillips 42.
Team: John Jackson (7/Chelsea)
Andrew Smellie Anderson (9/Hearts)
George Cummings (2/Partick Thistle)
Alexander Massie (10/Hearts)
James Simpson (4/Rangers), captain
George Clark Phillips Brown (9/Rangers)
James Delaney (1/Celtic)
Thomas Walker (3/Hearts)
Matthew Armstrong (1/Aberdeen)
William Mills (1/Aberdeen)
Douglas Duncan (7/Derby County).

172.
13 November 1935 (British Championship)
Scotland - Ireland 2-1 (0-0)
Referee: Henderson Nattrass (Durham, England)
Crowd: 30,000 (Tynecastle Park, Edinburgh)
Goals: 0-1 Kelly 49, 1-1 Walker 58, 2-1 Duncan 89.
Team: John Jackson (8./Chelsea)
Andrew Smellie Anderson (10/Hearts)
George Cummings (3/Partick Thistle)
Alexander Massie (11/Hearts)
James Simpson (5/Rangers), captain
Alexander Cockburn Hastings (1/Sunderland)
James Delaney (2/Celtic)
Thomas Walker (4/Hearts)
Matthew Armstrong (2/Aberdeen)
William Mills (2/Aberdeen)
Douglas Duncan (8/Derby County).

173.
4 April 1936 (British Championship)
England - Scotland 1-1 (1-0)
Referee: William R Hamilton (Belfast, N Ireland)
Crowd: 93,267 (Wembley Stadium, London)
Goals: 1-0 Camsell 30, 1-1 Walker 77 pen.
Team: James Dawson (2/Rangers)
Andrew Smellie Anderson (11/Hearts)
George Cummings (4/Aston Villa)
Alexander Massie (12/Aston Villa)
James Simpson (6/Rangers), captain
George Clark Phillips Brown (10/Rangers)
John Crum (1/Celtic)
Thomas Walker (5/Hearts)
David McCulloch (2/Brentford)
Alexander Venters (2/Rangers)
Douglas Duncan (9/Derby County).

174.
14 October 1936
Scotland - Germany 2-0 (0-0)
Referee: Henderson Nattrass (Durham, England)
Crowd: 50,000 (Ibrox Stadium, Glasgow)
Goals: 1-0 Delaney 67, 2-0 Delaney 83.
Team: James Dawson (3/Rangers)
Andrew Smellie Anderson (12/Hearts)
George Cummings (5/Aston Villa)
Alexander Massie (13/Aston Villa)
James Simpson (7/Rangers), captain
George Clark Phillips Brown (11/Rangers)
James Delaney (3/Celtic)
Thomas Walker (6/Hearts)
Matthew Armstrong (3./Aberdeen)
Robert Lowe McPhail (13/Rangers)
Douglas Duncan (10/Derby County).

175.
31 October 1936 (British Championship)
Ireland - Scotland 1-3 (1-1)
Referee: Thomas Thompson (Newcastle, England)
Crowd: 45,000 (Windsor Park, Belfast)
Goals: 1-0 Kernaghan 25, 1-1 Napier 27,
1-2 Munro 47, 1-3 McCulloch 63.
Team: James Dawson (4/Rangers)
Andrew Smellie Anderson (13/Hearts)
Robert Francis Dudgeon Ancell (1/Newcastle United)
Alexander Massie (14/Aston Villa)
James Simpson (8/Rangers), captain
George Clark Phillips Brown (12/Rangers)
Alexander Dewar Munro (1/Hearts)
Thomas Walker (7/Hearts)
David McCulloch (3/Brentford)
Charles Edward Napier (4/Celtic)
Douglas Duncan (11/Derby County).

176.
2 December 1936 (British Championship)
Scotland - Wales 1-2 (0-1)
Referee: Arthur W Barton (Repton, England)
Crowd: 23,858 (Dens Park, Dundee)
Goals: 0-1 Glover 22, 1-1 Walker 59, 1-2 Glover 77.
Team: James Dawson (5/Rangers)
Andrew Smellie Anderson (14/Hearts)
Robert Francis Dudgeon Ancell (2./Newcastle United)
Alexander Massie (15/Aston Villa)
James Simpson (9/Rangers), captain
George Clark Phillips Brown (13/Rangers)
Alexander Dewar Munro (2/Hearts)
Thomas Walker (8/Hearts)
David McCulloch (4/Brentford)
William Mills (3./Aberdeen)
Douglas Duncan (12/Derby County).

177.
17 April 1937 (British Championship)
Scotland - England 3-1 (0-1)
Referee: William McLean (Belfast, N Ireland)
Crowd: 149,547 (Hampden Park, Glasgow)
Goals: 0-1 Steele 40, 1-1 O'Donnell 47,
2-1 McPhail 80, 3-1 McPhail 88.
Team: James Dawson (6/Rangers)
Andrew Smellie Anderson (15/Hearts)
Andrew Beattie (1/Preston North End)
Alexander Massie (16/Aston Villa)
James Simpson (10/Rangers), captain
George Clark Phillips Brown (14/Rangers)
James Delaney (4/Celtic)
Thomas Walker (9/Hearts)
Francis O'Donnell (1/Preston North End)
Robert Lowe McPhail (14/Rangers)
Douglas Duncan (13/Derby County).

178.
9 May 1937
Austria - Scotland 1-1 (0-0)
Referee: Joannes Langenus (Antwerp, Belgium)
Crowd: 63,000 (Prater Stadium, Vienna)
Goals: 1-0 Jerusalem 78, 1-1 O'Donnell 80.
Team: James Dawson (7/Rangers)
Andrew Smellie Anderson (16/Hearts)
Andrew Beattie (2/Preston North End)
Alexander Massie (17/Aston Villa)
James Simpson (11/Rangers), captain
Alexander McNab (1/Sunderland)
James Delaney (5/Celtic)
Thomas Walker (10/Hearts)
Francis O'Donnell (2/Preston North End)
Charles Edward Napier (5./Celtic)
Torrance Gillick (1/Everton).

179.
15 May 1937
Czechoslovakia - Scotland 1-3 (1-2)
Referee: Peter 'Peco' J Bauwens (Cologne, Germany)
Crowd: 35,000 (Sparta Stadium, Prague)
Goals: 0-1 Simpson 14, 1-1 Puc 31, 1-2 McPhail 32, 1-3 Gillick 69.
Team: James Dawson (8/Rangers)
Robert Brown Hogg (1./Celtic)
Andrew Beattie (3/Preston North End)
Charles Morgan Thomson (1/Sunderland)
James Simpson (12/Rangers), captain
George Clark Phillips Brown (15/Rangers)
James Delaney (6/Celtic)
Thomas Walker (11/Hearts)
Francis O'Donnell (3/Preston North End)
Robert Lowe McPhail (15/Rangers)
Torrance Gillick (2/Everton).

180.
30 October 1937 (British Championship)
Wales - Scotland 2-1 (1-0)
Referee: Charles E Argent (St Albans, England)
Crowd: 41,800 (Ninian Park, Cardiff)
Goals: 1-0 B Jones 26, 2-0 Morris 51, 2-1 Massie 72.
Team: James Dawson (9/Rangers)
Andrew Smellie Anderson (17/Hearts)
George Cummings (6/Aston Villa)
Alexander Massie (18./Aston Villa)
James Simpson (13/Rangers), captain
George Clark Phillips Brown (16/Rangers)
Robert Frame Main (1./Rangers)
Thomas Walker (12/Hearts)
Francis O'Donnell (4/Preston North End)
Robert Lowe McPhail (16/Rangers)
Douglas Duncan (14./Derby County).

181.
10 November 1937 (British Championship)
Scotland - Ireland 1-1 (0-1)
Referee: Arthur James Jewell (London, England)
Crowd: 21,878 (Pittodrie Park, Aberdeen)
Goals: 0-1 P Doherty 14, 1-1 Smith 49.
Team: James Dawson (10/Rangers)
Andrew Smellie Anderson (18/Hearts)
George Cummings (7/Aston Villa)
Duncan MacKenzie (1./Brentford)
James Simpson (14./Rangers), captain
Alexander Cockburn Hastings (2./Sunderland)
James Delaney (7/Celtic)
Thomas Walker (13/Hearts)
James Smith (2./Rangers)
Robert Lowe McPhail (17./Rangers)
Robert Reid (1/Brentford).

182.
8 December 1937
Scotland - Czechoslovakia 5-0 (3-0)
Referee: Thomas Thompson (Newcastle, England)
Crowd: 41,000 (Ibrox Stadium, Glasgow)
Goals: 1-0 Black 1, 2-0 McCulloch 30, 3-0 Buchanan 38, 4-0 McCulloch 62, 5-0 Kinnear 70.
Team: William Waugh (1./Hearts)
Andrew Smellie Anderson (19/Hearts), captain
George Cummings (8./Aston Villa)
George Robertson (1./Kilmarnock)
Robert Johnston (1./Sunderland)
George Clark Phillips Brown (17/Rangers)
Peter Symington Buchanan (1./Chelsea)
Thomas Walker (14/Hearts)
David McCulloch (5/Brentford)
Andrew Black (1/Hearts)
David Kinnear (1./Rangers).

183.
9 April 1938 (British Championship)
England - Scotland 0-1 (0-1)
Referee: William R Hamilton (Belfast, N Ireland)
Crowd: 93,267 (Wembley Stadium, London)
Goals: 0-1 Walker 6.
Team: David Scott Cumming (1./Middlesbrough)
Andrew Smellie Anderson (20/Hearts)
Andrew Beattie (4/Preston North End)
William Shankly (1/Preston North End)
Thomas McCall Smith (2./Preston North End)
George Clark Phillips Brown (18/Rangers), captain
John Vance Milne (1/Middlesbrough)
Thomas Walker (15/Hearts)
Francis O'Donnell (5/Blackpool)
George Mutch (1./Preston North End)
Robert Reid (2./Brentford).

184.
21 May 1938
Netherlands - Scotland 1-3 (0-0)
Referee: Charles E Argent (St Albans, England)
Crowd: 50,000 (Olympic Stadium, Amsterdam)
Goals: 0-1 Black 52, 0-2 Murphy 56, 0-3 Walker 70, 1-3 Vente 85.
Team: James Dawson (11/Rangers)
Andrew Smellie Anderson (21/Hearts)
James Carabine (1/Third Lanark)
Thomas McKillop (1./Rangers)
James Dykes (1/Hearts)
George Clark Phillips Brown (19./Rangers), captain
Alexander Dewar Munro (3./Blackpool)
Thomas Walker (16/Hearts)
Francis O'Donnell (6./Blackpool)
Andrew Black (2/Hearts)
Francis Murphy (1./Celtic).

185.
8 October 1938 (British Championship)
Ireland - Scotland 0-2 (0-1)
Referee: Reginald A Mortimer (Huddersfield, England)
Crowd: 40,000 (Windsor Park, Belfast)
Goals: 0-1 Delaney 33, 0-2 Walker 48.
Team: James Dawson (12/Rangers)
James Carabine (2./Third Lanark), captain
Andrew Beattie (5/Preston North End)
William Shankly (2/Preston North End)
James Dykes (2./Hearts)
George Paterson (1/Celtic)
James Delaney (8/Celtic)
Thomas Walker (17/Hearts)
John Crum (2./Celtic)
John Divers (1./Celtic)
Torrance Gillick (3/Everton).

186.
9 November 1938 (British Championship)
Scotland - Wales 3-2 (1-1)
Referee: Thomas Thompson (Newcastle, England)
Crowd: 34,810 (Tynecastle Park, Edinburgh)
Goals: 0-1 Astley 20, 1-1 Gillick 38, 2-1 Walker 83, 3-1 Walker 84, 3-2 L Jones 86.
Team: John Bell Brown (1./Clyde)
Andrew Smellie Anderson (22/Hearts), captain
Andrew Beattie (6/Preston North End)
William Shankly (3/Preston North End)
Robert Denholm Baxter (1/Middlesbrough)
Archibald Miller (1./Hearts)
James Delaney (9/Celtic)
Thomas Walker (18/Hearts)
David McCulloch (6/Derby County)
Robert Beattie (1./Preston North End)
Torrance Gillick (4/Everton).

187.
7 December 1938
Scotland - Hungary 3-1 (3-0)
Referee: Henderson Nattrass (Durham, England)
Crowd: 23,000 (Ibrox Stadium, Glasgow)
Goals: 1-0 Walker pen 19, 2-0 Black 27, 3-0 Gillick 28, 3-1 Sarosi pen 72.
Team: James Dawson (13/Rangers)
Andrew Smellie Anderson (23./Hearts), captain
Andrew Beattie (7./Preston North End)
William Shankly (4./Preston North End)
Robert Denholm Baxter (2/Middlesbrough)
James Scotland Symon (1./Rangers)
Alexander McLuckie McSpadyen (1/Partick Thistle)
Thomas Walker (19/Hearts)
David McCulloch (7./Derby County)
Andrew Black (3./Hearts)
Torrance Gillick (5./Everton).

188.
15 April 1939 (British Championship)
Scotland - England 1-2 (1-0)
Referee: William R Hamilton (Belfast, N Ireland)
Crowd: 149,269 (Hampden Park, Glasgow)
Goals: 1-0 Dougal 20, 1-1 Beasley 67, 1-2 Lawton 88.
Team: James Dawson (14./Rangers)
James Carabine (3./Third Lanark)
George Cummings (9./Aston Villa)
William Shankly (5./Preston North End)
Robert Denholm Baxter (3./Middlesbrough), captain
Alexander McNab (2./West Bromwich Albion)
Alexander McLuckie McSpadyen (2./Partick Thistle)
Thomas Walker (20/Hearts)
James Dougal (1./Preston North End)
Alexander Venters (3./Rangers)
John Vance Milne (2./Middlesbrough).

Printed in Great Britain
by Amazon